HISTORY OF THE
CATHOLIC CHURCH

JAMES HITCHCOCK

HISTORY OF THE CATHOLIC CHURCH

From the Apostolic Age to the Third Millenium

IGNATIUS PRESS   SAN FRANCISCO

Imprimatur: † The Most Reverend Edward Rice
Auxiliary Bishop, Archdiocese of St. Louis
October 26, 2012

In accordance with CIC 827, permission to publish has been granted on October 26, 2012, by the Most Reverend Edward Rice, Auxiliary Bishop, Archdiocese of St. Louis. Permission to publish is an indication that nothing contrary to Church teaching is contained in this work. It does not imply any endorsement of the opinions expressed in the publication; nor is any liability assumed by this permission.

Cover art: *Christ the King*
Mosaic, circ A.D. 800, Lateran Palace, Rome
Photograph by Fr. Lawrence Lew, O.P.

Cover design by John Herreid

For the Kassings:
Don, Alexandra,
Francesca, Anna, Amelia, Dominic

Contents

Acknowledgments

My interest in church history was fostered by, among others, my under-graduate professors, the late Thomas P. Neill and the Rev. Joseph A. McCallin, S.J., of St. Louis University, and my graduate professors, the late E. Harris Harbison and Joseph R. Strayer of Princeton University. I have especially profited from discussions about church history with my colleagues at St. Louis University—Thomas Madden, Damian Smith, and Warren Treadgold.

Introduction

The Catholic Church is the longest-enduring institution in the world, and her historical character is integral to her identity.

The earliest Christians claimed to be witnesses to the life, death, and Resurrection of Jesus, thereby making Christianity a historical religion, emanating from a Judaism that was itself a historical religion. Christianity staked its claim to truth on certain events, notably that at a precise moment in history the Son of God came to earth. The Gospels have a ring of historical authenticity partly because of the numerous concrete details they contain, the care with which they record the times and places of Jesus' life.

While there is no purely historical argument that could convince skeptics that Jesus rose from the dead and appeared to His disciples, His Resurrection can scarcely be excluded from any historical account. Marc Bloch, the great medievalist who was a secular-minded Jew (he perished in a German prison camp), observed that the real question concerning the history of Christianity is why so many people fervently believed that Jesus rose from the dead, a belief of such power and duration as to be hardly explicable in purely human terms.[1]

But an awareness of the historical character of the Church carries with it the danger that she will be seen as only a product of history, without a transcendent divine character. While Christians can never be indifferent to the reliability of historical claims, since to discredit the historical basis of the Gospel would be to discredit the entire faith, they must be aware of their limits.

The modern "historical-critical method" has provided valuable help in understanding Scripture—explicating the precise meaning of words, recovering the social and cultural milieu in which Jesus lived, situating particular passages in the context of the entire Bible. But it understands the Bible primarily in terms of the times in which it was written and can affirm no transcendent meaning.

Also, modern scholarship itself is bound by its own times, and the historical-critical method has a history of its own that can also be

---

[1] Marc Bloch, *The Historian's Craft* (New York: Vintage Books, 1954), 32.

relativized. Some scholars cultivate a spirit of skepticism about almost everything in Scripture, including its antiquity and the accuracy of its accounts. A major fallacy of this skepticism is the assumption that, while religious believers are fatally biased, skeptics are objective and disinterested. Some practitioners of the historical-critical method take a far more suspicious view of Christian origins than most historians take toward other aspects of ancient history. (Far more is known about Jesus than about many of the Roman emperors.)

Then there are the attempts of some historians to make Jesus a modern man—the claim that He "liberated" women in the feminist sense or that He was the leader of a political movement. Such claims necessarily assume that from the very beginning the leaders of the Church systematically falsified the record, concealing the fact that women were among the Twelve, for example.

The distinction between "the Jesus of history" and "the Christ of faith" was formulated by certain modern theologians as part of the effort to "demythologize" Jesus as the Son of God and Redeemer of the universe, dismissing that belief as a theological construct only loosely connected, if at all, to the actual, historical Jesus.

A fundamental flaw of the historical-critical method is that, while at various times it has called virtually all traditional beliefs into question, it offers no sure replacement, merely many competing theories. If the babel of scholarly voices is taken at face value, it forces the conclusion that there is no reliable knowledge of Jesus. But Christians can scarcely think that God gave the Bible to man as a revelation of Himself but did so in such a way as to render it endlessly problematical, or that for many centuries its true meaning was obscured and only came to light in modern times.

Thus, while making use of scholarship, Christians must ultimately read Scripture with the eyes of faith. Its central message—salvation through Jesus Christ—is incomprehensible to those who treat it as a merely human document.

The most influential recent attempt to discredit the historicity of the New Testament is the rediscovery of certain "Gnostic gospels" (all written later than the New Testament itself) upon which popular works such as *The Da Vinci Code* are based. These "gospels" are accounts of Jesus' life and teachings allegedly written by Mary Magdalen, Judas Iscariot, and the Apostles Philip and Thomas.

Gnosticism (see Chapter Two below, pp. 36–39) was the only heretical movement in the history of the Church that considered it unimportant whether the Gospel narratives were historically true. The Gnostics rejected the historical accounts in the New Testament not in order to propose a different history but in order to turn the faith into a myth that stood outside time. For them, the historicity of the New Testament was an embarrassment, since the wholly spiritual God could not have entered into the world of matter and time.

The most lasting division in the history of Christianity was the Protestant Reformation of the sixteenth century, but even then, both Catholics and Protestants agreed on the ultimate authority of the New Testament and the early creeds, a core of faith that was normative. Now, however, proponents of the Gnostic gospels, including even some professed Christians, seek to reopen questions that had been settled since at least the fourth century.

By excluding in principle the very possibility of divine revelation, they imprison Christianity entirely within the movement of history, essentially reducing questions of faith to factional struggles within the Church. If orthodox Christianity does not represent revealed truth, it must be seen as merely the triumph of one party over another, making it possible to cancel seventeen centuries of history in order to redefine the very foundations of the Church.

Modern feminism has much to do with this effort, because the Gnostic "gospels" can be used to claim that the New Testament was actually a kind of masculine conspiracy to conceal the role of women in the early Church, despite the fact that Gnosticism by no means respected women in the sense that feminists understand respect. Gnosticism also has a certain modern appeal because it offers "spirituality" divorced from dogma, its "gospels" treated as interesting and possibly inspiring myths to be read in the same way the myths of other religions can be read, embodying no final and binding truth.

The historical character of the Church is embodied above all in her affirmation of Tradition—the handing on of the faith from generation to generation, guided by the Holy Spirit. The attempt to appeal to the Scripture against Tradition is a denial of that historicity.

The question of the historical character of the Church does not cease with her biblical roots but has relevance to her entire history. A great deal turns on one of the most basic (and most disputed) questions of the Church's history—the development of doctrine. As with the truth of the Bible, it is a question that ultimately cannot be settled by history itself but only by faith.

Quite early, Christians realized that the Gospel did not provide a detailed exposition of every aspect of their faith. Rather, it was an embryo or seed, containing the whole of divine revelation but awaiting a gradual unfolding. Thus fidelity to Tradition is a paradox that has been at the heart of virtually all theological issues over the centuries—the faith must be handed on intact, but the Church's understanding of that faith develops in ways that could not have been anticipated in earlier times. The development of doctrine is a progressive widening and deepening of the meaning of the original truth, and heresy can be either false innovation or a rigid adherence to older teachings. (Some heretics rejected the decrees of the Council of Nicaea as innovations.) Dogma is seldom officially defined unless it has first been questioned, and heresy perhaps serves the divine purpose of forcing the Church to reflect more deeply on her beliefs, to understand them in ever more comprehensive and precise ways.

As in the Reformation of the sixteenth century, there have been repeated moves to "purify" the faith by removing its "accretions". But such a process violates the historical nature of the Church, which does not allow for the nullification of teachings that have become part of the core of belief. The movement of history is irreversible.

Unlike classical Protestantism, modern attempts to find "authentic" Christianity is driven less by the desire to recover the original Gospel than by the desire to be free of dogma of any kind. But those who think that doctrinal orthodoxy is unimportant, even a distortion of the Gospel, must recognize that this "error" was perpetrated very early in the history of the Church, again raising the insoluble conundrum of how God could have given men the Gospel, then allowed it to be distorted almost immediately, only to be recovered many centuries later.

After the Second Vatican Council, many Catholics, in the name of "objectivity", in effect surrendered their right to have their own history. But at precisely that moment, the legitimacy, even indeed the inevitability, of "committed" scholarship was being urged with respect to racial or ethnic history, women's history, and numerous other subjects, all of which demand a sympathetic, even apologetic, approach to their subjects.

Rather than historical "objectivity", which implies personal detachment on the part of the scholar, the historian's ideal ought to be honesty—an approach that is committed but strives to use evidence with scrupulous fairness. A temptation for all committed scholars (by no means only Christians) is that of deducing historical reality from dogmatic principles instead of studying the evidence. Believing historians must avoid the trap of nostalgia, whereby the Middle Ages, for example, are presented as the highpoint of history, from which everything since has been a decline—an approach that proves embarrassing when neglected inconvenient information surfaces. (Modern social history requires a more complex understanding of the "ages of faith", for example, by showing that there was often a wide gap between official Church teaching and popular practice.)

To idealize a past age is actually heretical from a Christian perspective, implying as it does that the age was without sin, that the redemption of mankind was completed at some point. On the contrary, with their knowledge of the subtleties of the sinful heart, Christians should be especially sensitive to the ways in which good is often perverted even by righteous men.

One of the Catholic elements that throughout history has been a stumbling block to some are the sacred rituals that have always been integral to the life of the Church. A recurring heresy is an excessively "spiritual" concept of the faith. The Church is sacramental, in that, invisible grace is ordinarily transmitted through visible means—something that is fitting, even necessary, because of the Incarnation itself: the eternal God took flesh, even becoming subject to death, and the Church must therefore also be incarnate in the world.

The divine and human realities of the Church came together, for example, in some of the general councils, which were marked not only by often ruthless maneuvering but even sometimes by violence. The *odium theologicum* ("theological hatred") wells up over and over again, precisely because theological questions are the most important of all—not only of life and death but of eternal salvation and the very order of the universe. Passion is appropriate but always in need of being tempered by charity. The Church believes that, despite such human frailties, the Holy Spirit protects her from fundamental error and that good is brought out of evil.

While in every age the Church demonstrates her power to transform the world, the moral weaknesses of both her leaders and her members are at the same time both a scandal and an ironic witness to her divine character—mere men could never have accomplished the good that the Church has achieved over two millennia. Left entirely to men, the Church ought to have perished at many points in her long history.

Some modern Catholics, under the influence of the prevailing cultural relativism, are preoccupied with "inculturation"—the ways in which the Gospel is incarnated in particular cultures. But although the term itself is new, the entire history of the Church is really the history of inculturation, which occurs continuously, whether or not consciously. This must occur in order to make the Gospel meaningful, even though it carries the risk of betraying the Gospel. Modern skepticism (including that of some professed Catholics) treats all change as self-validating, all forms of inculturation as legitimate. But inculturation has perhaps occurred most authentically whenever the faith has been young and vigorous, confident of its ability to absorb elements of a pagan culture and transform them for its own purposes. When the Church is in a spiritually weakened condition, the reverse often happens—the Gospel is used for alien purposes.

Beginning with the Judaism of Jesus' day, the Gospel has always had a disruptive effect on cultures. If it did not, it would not be the Gospel, which requires fundamental conversion on the part of its hearers, does not allow them to remain part of their culture unchanged, and ultimately requires the transformation of the culture itself.

The Christian understanding of history is intimately bound up with one of the most perplexing of all doctrines—divine providence. Blessed John Henry Newman said that human experience seems to force the conclusion that mankind was implicated in some "primordial catastrophe". History offers believers no knowledge of the exact nature of that catastrophe, but faith informs them that it occurred. Even on a purely human level, history cannot be understood apart from the reality of sin, especially of universal selfishness. Rooted in universal human nature, sin is a constant in man's affairs, although its character and intensity vary with time and place. Those who deny that a tendency toward evil is basic to human nature cannot make sense of history, which becomes merely endless, incomprehensible tragedy.

Divine revelation reveals little about the inner nature of God but much about His actions in history. The Incarnation itself validates history, as the eternal descends into the temporal, and men have no way of working out their salvation except in this life.

But one of the greatest temptations for Christians is to deduce the specific manifestations in history from a general belief in divine providence. Whole theologies of history have been based on this, but each has finally failed as a comprehensive explanation of historical events. In particular, the belief that specific catastrophes are direct divine punishment for sin dies hard, and for obvious reasons—the laudable desire to make sense of events and the less laudable desire to see one's enemies punished.

Edifying stories of devout people saved from danger by divine intervention (a city spared the plague, an angelic visitor steering a child away from a precipice) leave unanswered the question why countless other people, even more pious and innocent, have been allowed to perish. Christians can readily understand this on the individual level—suffering is redemptive, and God takes His servants when He wants them. But it is far more difficult to explain the fate of whole societies, the mystery with which Israel was forced to wrestle obsessively.

Christianity played a crucial role in the development of man's understanding of history itself, vanquishing the cyclical view of endless repetition that expressed a kind of despair, the sense that men were trapped in a process they could not control. Christianity gave history an *eschaton*, a goal toward which it relentlessly moves and which for the first time allowed that movement to have meaning. But the Christian approach to history is also not completely linear; it revolves around a particular moment—the coming of Christ—from which time is reckoned both forward and backward.

The Hebrews' sense of history was driven by their urgent need to find a comprehensible purpose in the repeated catastrophes that they suffered, even as their faithless enemies repeatedly triumphed over God's chosen people. Making moral sense of history has preoccupied men ever since, since the story of mankind is to a great extent the story of good betrayed and turned into evil. If history were solely the story of the saints, it would already be infinitely valuable, but its value lies also in the story of sinners, of the entire great drama of human life. The dichotomy of time and eternity is nowhere more evident than in the fact that justice often does not triumph in this world. The study of history confirms that evil men often flourish and the good are often defeated, with no reversal or vindication in this life.

But how then can men be held to account for their wickedness? It is a question that often leads to the use of history for moral judgment. Contemporary secular historiography is awash with this kind of moralism, as the past is continuously ransacked for examples of alleged injustices to select peoples (by no means everyone), and appropriate condemnation is pronounced.

Such moralism is perhaps inevitable to Secular Liberalism, which is almost required to assume man's goodness, is sympathetic with everything it deems to be "progressive", and can only salvage meaning from the wreckage of man's dreams by pronouncing condemnations on those who appear responsible. But a basic flaw in such moralism is that it can no longer have any effect—the perpetrators have passed into God's hands.

The Christian recognition of man's freedom is the only resolution of the mystery of evil—since men can and do make responsible decisions, to understand all is not to forgive all. Jesus' parable of the wheat and the tares teaches that good and evil exist together in the world, and the reality of human freedom provides the only satisfactory explanation of moral evil—God's mysterious willingness to grant that freedom and permit its full exercise, even when it is used to thwart His divine plan. Brutus was free not to assassinate Caesar, but then in what sense did God will the death of Caesar? His death was not a preordained script that had to be played out as written.

The Protestant historian Herbert Butterfield saw the action of God in history as like a composer masterfully revising his music to overcome the inadequacies of the orchestra that plays it.[2] There is a constant double movement, both upward and downward, and the work of redemption proceeds only slowly, against the inertia of human resistance. Men are surprised by each new turn of the pages of the book of history.

---

[2] Herbert Butterfield, *History and Human Relations* (New York: MacMillan, 1952), pp. 13–14.

I Beginning at Jerusalem

Within ten days of Jesus' return to the Father,[1] His disciples (a Greek term for those who had "submitted" to His teachings)[2]—despite having encountered Him several times after His death—were huddled in an upper room in Jerusalem, frightened and confused. But Jesus had promised that He would send the Spirit upon them, and on that day, they experienced an unseen power in the midst of a great wind, with tongues of fire hovering over each of their heads. Their fear vanished, and they were suddenly filled with zeal and courage.

It was the day of a major Jewish feast—Pentecost ("fifty days" after the Passover Sabbath)—and the city was crowded with visitors, devout Jews from all over the Near East, North Africa, and other regions. Led by Peter, the Eleven whom Jesus had specially chosen as His Apostles (those who were "sent"), stood up in public and began to preach. Simple and unlearned men, they knew no language except their sacred Hebrew and their vernacular Aramaic. But the crowd marveled that everyone seemed to hear the message in his own tongue. Skeptics claimed that the preachers were merely drunk, but three thousand people, according to the Acts of the Apostles, received the message and were baptized ("bathed").

During His time on earth, Jesus spoke of His "Church" (*ecclesia*—"assembly" or "gathering"). He did not prescribe a detailed structure but gathered His disciples into a unified community with Peter and the other Apostles in positions of authority. The events of Pentecost showed that this Church would not remain merely a congregation of like-minded people but would be held together by divine power.[3] On Pentecost, the Spirit molded a collection of deeply flawed men into a force that would transform the world.

The Birth of the Church

The First Pentecost

The Church of the Apostles

---

[1] The question of the exact years in which Jesus lived is meaningless, since the designation "A.D." ("*Anno Domini*"—the year of the Lord) was established several centuries later, based on an estimate of when He was born. Thus the life of Jesus determined the dates of the calendar rather than the other way around.

[2] Unless otherwise indicated, all such New Testament terms are from the Greek.

[3] There is no warrant in the New Testament for individual discipleship outside a community of believers.

Christianity and Judaism

The Jewish Legacy

Christianity emerged from the culture of the Jews, a culture different from all others in being based on a covenant between God and His people according to which God is active in history, transforming the world and associating man with the divine mission. Judaism, alone among the great spiritual movements of history, did not build on a great civilization. The Jews were a nomadic warrior people, their God the god of battles, and contact with more advanced civilizations tended to weaken and contaminate them.

God's people were poor while His enemies were kings, and the prophets resolved this baffling and frustrating paradox by revealing that those enemies were in reality God's chosen instruments of punishment—the Jews' defeats were signs of the truth of their religion. The prophets foretold the destruction of Israel, which happened not because God was weak but because the people were sinful. The promise made to Israel was liberation not from political bondage but from sin itself, from a power greater than man.

Thus, out of suffering, Judaism as a world religion was born. All of history was moving toward the reign of justice, the ultimate coming of the power and glory of God, and Israel's misfortunes strengthened this belief, allowing national hopes to be transferred to the supernatural plane.

Christ: The Fulfillment of Jewish Hopes

The more the great pagan empires spread, the more the Jews clung to their own faith, their very political weakness forcing them to conceive of the Kingdom in spiritual terms, based on the Word of the God of righteousness and truth. In contrast to all other ancient religions, history had ultimate meaning for the Jews, moving toward the end of time. The Kingdom would be restored when the Jews finally received the Messiah, the Promised One, the Anointed One, the Christ.

The Jews did not, however, all agree in their understanding of the Messiah—or other aspects of their faith. Rome was a more formidable enemy than any other, and the Roman occupation of Palestine again raised hopes among some Jews that the Messiah would be a political savior. The Sadducees, who did not believe in personal resurrection, cooperated with the Romans; the Zealots actively opposed the conquerors; the Pharisees believed in resurrection and in strict ritual observance; while the Essenes of Qumran, who possessed a military character, expected two messiahs—one military, one priestly.[4] Jesus summoned the Twelve from the midst of these factions, including even Simon the Zealot, and their divergent, even contradictory, views of Judaism often hampered the Apostles from truly understanding what Jesus was saying.

---

[4] The Qumran community is known primarily through the Dead Sea Scrolls, which, contrary to what was once thought, have little to do with early Christianity, although St. John the Baptist may have had connections to the community.

Jesus was profoundly Jewish, but He did not merely seek to make people better Jews. His relations with the Pharisees were especially crucial, because of the subtle, easily misunderstood ways in which He both affirmed the Jewish faith and enjoined His followers to go beyond it—the central issue of "the Law" that would eventually be resolved by St. Paul.

Jesus the Christ

Jesus and Judaism

The first three Gospels (*evangelion*—"good news") are primarily "synoptics" of Jesus' life, in that each follows a similar narrative outline. The Gospels give historical accounts of the life of Jesus, including His ancestry and the circumstances of His birth, in order to disclose the reality of the Incarnation—that Jesus the Christ is none other than the eternal God, who took flesh and entered human history. Like Judaism, but unlike most other religions, Christianity is not mythical, in that it is based on events that took place not in a timeless realm but within human history itself. Thus the writers of the Gospels situate the life of Jesus very precisely in a particular time and place—by listing those who held public office at the time; by recording that "in the fifteenth year of the reign of Tiberius Caesar [which began in A.D. 14], . . . the word of God came to John, . . . in the wilderness" (Lk 3:1,2); and by carefully noting the location of each of Jesus' sermons or miracles. But the Evangelists did not think it necessary to provide a comprehensive account of Jesus' life (notably, they omitted almost everything between His birth and the beginning of His public ministry) but recorded only those facts that had significance for His mission in the world. But at the same time, the biblical narratives were considered to be historical, not merely symbolic or literary. The historical and theological purposes of the Gospels complemented one another.

The Good News

The Gospel of John, the last of the four to be written, is both a narrative and an extended theological meditation on the meaning of Jesus' life, particularly on the nature of divine love. It is also in John's Gospel that Jesus' identity—as the Incarnation of the Eternal Word, the Word that was God—is fully disclosed, something that perhaps did not become clear to His followers until they had meditated on His life and teachings for some years.

At first, Jesus was probably regarded by His disciples as the greatest of the prophets, but gradually they began to recognize Him as the promised Messiah who preached the coming of the Kingdom. His life and teachings unfolded on several levels simultaneously, none of which could be taken in isolation. Most accessible to human understanding in every age has been His role as a moral teacher who preached the highest and most sublime ideal of self-sacrificing love. But such a view cannot explain why He was treated so ferociously by the authorities.

The Promised One

Jesus was an ascetic who, with an occasional respite, such as the marriage feast at Cana, enjoined His disciples to live lives of prayer and fasting, of the renunciation of worldly goods, of intense self-discipline. He cast out devils and faced down the Evil One, curing both spiritual and physical illness. Above all, He warned His hearers to repent their sins and accept forgiveness from His loving Father, in order to escape eternal fire and to receive eternal life. His numerous miracles confirmed His credibility, and some of His sayings ("Before Abraham was, I am"), along with His transfiguration before three of His Apostles, provided intimations of His divinity.

Up to a point, Jesus acted in the traditional role of a prophet, commanding people to observe the Law—the traditional practices of prayer, fasting, and almsgiving—but castigating them for their hypocritical legalism, their failure to comprehend the spiritual and moral nature of religion. But, as the more astute among the Jews recognized, in many of His sermons and parables, Jesus implicitly claimed for Himself the obedience that a good Jew was supposed to give to the Law. He claimed lordship over the Sabbath and the Temple, and the Jewish authorities eventually understood the claims He was making, as when He drove the money changers out of the Temple and announced that He could destroy that sacred place and rebuild it within three days. His triumphal entry into Jerusalem precipitated His arrest, as the Jewish leaders at last saw Him as a blasphemer, one who made Himself "equal to God".

Christ the King

The Roman occupation of Palestine followed the pattern generally prevalent throughout the Empire. A rather small coterie of officials and soldiers looked after imperial interests and kept order, but as far as possible the institutions of self-government remained in place. The religious leaders had broad discretion in dealing with internal Jewish problems, so that Jesus was arrested by the soldiers of the high priest; then, while the priests tried to enlist the cooperation of the cautious and somewhat skeptical Roman officials, there followed a kind of bureaucratic dance in which Jesus was sent back and forth between the puppet king Herod Antipas (d. 39) and the Roman procurator Pontius Pilate (d. ca. 36).

The Romans did not see Jesus as a political threat, except insofar as He stirred up discord among the Jews. The Jewish leaders urged His prosecution primarily for offenses that were religious in nature but which necessarily seemed to involve a political agenda—the coming of "the Kingdom", however that was understood. Significantly, when Jesus was given the opportunity by Pilate to deny that He was a king, He merely parried the question ("You say so") and, whatever doubts he may have had, Pilate finally concluded that it was prudent to cooperate with the high priest, who warned him that Jesus was a subversive who might inspire a rebellion. Thus Pilate condemned Jesus to death by crucifixion, a form of punishment reserved for the worst criminals.

On the morning of the third day after Jesus' death, some of His disciples found His tomb empty and an angel announcing that He had risen. In that event, the ultimate mystery of the Christian faith was finally revealed—that, by Jesus' sacrifice, life overcame death, good overcame evil, victory overcame defeat, and hope overcame despair, all in a complete and final way. By His conquest of death, Jesus redeemed not only mankind but the entire universe, which since Adam's time had been groaning under the burden of sin.

Victory over Death

Part of the genius of Christianity was that it did not shrink from the horrible way in which Jesus' public life ended but actually placed it at the very center of the faith. The symbol of the cross did not become ubiquitous for several centuries, but St. Paul already boasted that, even though the cross was an obstacle to nonbelievers, "We preach Christ, and Him crucified."

As Jews, the early Christians believed in angels ("messengers"), who heralded Jesus' birth, Resurrection, and Ascension; ministered to Him while He was on earth; and sing the praises of God through all eternity. From Scripture, three angels are known by name—Michael ("like God"), Gabriel ("the struggle of God"), and Raphael ("God heals"). Protecting angels—assigned to each nation and even to each individual—would herald the Second Coming, lead the saints into Paradise, and cast the damned into Hell, which, Jesus warned, was "prepared for the devil and his angels".

Early Christian Doctrine

Angels and Devils

Satan ("the adversary") appeared in the Old Testament, as someone permitted by God to accuse men of sin and to test their fidelity, even to the point of tempting Jesus just before He began His public ministry.

Christians thought Satan was the serpent who tempted Eve, and they also thought that the Old Testament name Lucifer ("light bearer") referred to him. (Somewhat unaccountably, Lucifer remained an honorable Christian name for two centuries.) From the Book of Revelation, Satan was recognized as a fallen angel who had originally been given responsibility for the earth but who rebelled out of resentment of the incarnate Christ, who he foresaw would supplant him.

There are legions of devils under Satan's command (many of whom Jesus cast out), and in a sense, the world does belong to Satan. Both angels and devils struggle for the souls of men, but men remain free and ultimately cannot be coerced. In the end, Satan will be vanquished by God, the Creator and ruler of all. Quite early, the Christian rite of baptism included the exorcism of evil spirits.

The God of the Jews was the Lord of history, governing human events through His providence, a belief that was greatly expanded by Christianity, which taught that the ultimate meaning of history is the unfolding of the Kingdom and that, since nothing is independent of God's rule, good must ultimately triumph over evil, Jesus' own apparent defeat

The Kingdom

being the culmination of this—His persecutors unwittingly served the Father's purposes.

The Jews rebelled against Rome three times in the first and second centuries after Christ, but Christianity preached the coming of a nonpolitical Kingdom, one that is in some ways already present, based no longer on ancestry but on purity of heart, although open even to sinners. The ways of the Kingdom are in many respects the reverse of those of human society—triumph emerges only from defeat, suffering is the necessary prerequisite to glory, he who would save his life must lose it, the humble will be exalted, to give is better than to receive.

Christianity appealed to the prophetic and apocalyptic elements in Judaism rather than to its rituals and proclaimed even more emphatically the presence of God in history, looking forward to the end of time. Before returning to His Father, Jesus promised that He would come again, at which time He would pronounce final and definitive judgment on mankind, separating sheep from goats, casting the unrepentant into everlasting fire, and inviting the faithful into His Kingdom.

Savior and Redeemer

The Letters of Paul are the oldest records of Jesus' life and work, and they present a developed theology of Jesus as nothing less than a divine being whose life and death transformed the universe. Jesus offered Himself to the Father on behalf of the sins of mankind, and He is the only means by which men can be saved.

Continuity with Judaism

The Christians saw fundamental continuity between their own faith and that of the Jews, because Jesus revealed the one true God—the God of the Jews—to the entire world. Beginning on Pentecost, the followers of Jesus proclaimed that He alone fulfilled the promises of the Jewish prophets. Thus the sacred books of the two religions fit together harmoniously. Christians insisted that the Old Testament could be ultimately understood only in the light of the New, although most Jews did not recognize that unity.

Paul and the Law

Observance of the Law of Moses was the essence of Judaism, but Paul made a radical break with that tradition, dismissing "the Law" as a barrier that Christ had broken down, thereby giving man a new spiritual freedom. Paul's polemic was not anarchical antinomianism ("against the law"). Rather he was one of the most astute of psychologists, as in his exasperated cry, "I do not do what I want, but I do the very thing I hate" (Rom 7:15). He made a subtle and profound analysis of human nature as enslaved to the inherited sin of Adam, a slavery which the Law exposes but which in itself it is powerless to overcome. Christ conferred freedom, but it is a paradoxical freedom—not self-will but the conquest of self-will, which is the very instrument of bondage.

Jesus was the New Adam who destroyed the sinful inheritance of the Old. When they accepted baptism, therefore, Christians did not merely join a community but through that mystical action were "baptized into Christ's death" and thereby enabled to participate in His Resurrection, overcoming the slavery of sin. Men had to crucify their own natures and die to sin in order to become the adopted children of God.

The New Adam

Paul expounded the ultimate understanding of the Church—that she is nothing less than Christ's own Body, of which all believers are members, organically linked to one another and to Christ as their Head.

The Mystical Body

Paul boldly asserted that, "If Christ has not been raised, then our preaching is in vain and your faith is in vain" (1 Cor 15:14), and from the beginning, Jesus' followers believed that His tomb was empty and that He had risen bodily. As with everything else having to do with Him, it was crucial to Jesus' followers that His Resurrection was an actual historical event, one that was dated to the day and almost to the hour. The Apostles made many converts, claiming to be actual witnesses to the Resurrection and sealing their testimony by working miracles, especially of healing, solely in the name, and by the power, of Jesus, a power so impressive that one Simon the Magician tried to buy it from them.

Christian Life

The Eucharist

The Christians met regularly on their new Sabbath—the first day of the week, the day of the Resurrection—for prayers and "the breaking of the bread", which soon came to be called the Eucharist ("thanksgiving"). In the Eucharist, the worshippers offered themselves to God and participated in the sacrifice of Jesus, the Lamb of God, sharing in both His death and His Resurrection, their earthly gifts transformed into heavenly ones.

There was no open invitation to partake of the Eucharist. In fact, Paul issued the awful warning that those who received the Body of Christ unworthily received it "unto their damnation" (1 Cor 11:29). It was not primarily a community meal. Christians did celebrate an *agape* ("love feast")—but Paul rebuked the Corinthians for conflating the two and turning the Eucharist into an occasion of worldly merriment, asking sarcastically if they did not have homes where they could enjoy human fellowship, and asking rhetorically, "The bread that we eat, is it not the body of the Lord?" (1 Cor 10:16). Gradually, the *agape* was separated from the Eucharist, then abandoned.

The worshippers did not gather around a table facing one another but, as later artists portrayed accurately, followed the ancient banquet custom of all sitting (or reclining) on the same side of the table. As the *agape* meal was separated from the Eucharist, worshippers stood throughout the latter, sometimes raising their arms to Heaven in supplication.

The eucharistic sacrifice was seen as the fulfillment of the Old Testament sacrifices of Abel, Abraham, and Melchizedek, and Christians continued using a number of Jewish customs in their worship: Scripture readings, recitation of the Psalms (now understood to refer primarily to Christ), intercessory prayers, congregational responses (especially *Amen*—"so be it"), prayers at regular hours during the day. Quite early, they adopted the Jewish custom of fasting, observing Wednesdays and Fridays for that purpose.

Almost all the words of the Eucharist were directed to God, with the worshippers never addressing one another and the celebrant addressing them only rarely. His occasional "The Lord be with you" was in a sense his brief acknowledgment of their presence amidst his continuing speaking to God on their behalf, and their reply—"And with your spirit"—a recognition of the celebrant's special mediating role.

The Sacraments

The embryo of the Catholic sacramental system was present from the beginning. Jesus decreed the necessity to be born again of water and the Spirit to enter the Kingdom of Heaven. On the night before His death, He commanded that the Eucharist be celebrated as He Himself was doing, and the repentance of sins was central to His message (and He gave His apostles power to forgive sins in John 20:23). Peter and John journeyed to Samaria to lay hands on newly baptized converts, in order that the Spirit would come upon them, and the Letter of James[5] urged the flock to summon their leaders to the bedsides of the sick to pray over them and anoint them with oil. Deacons were ordained by the Apostles also by the laying on of hands.

Although immersion was the usual mode of baptism, in imitation of Jesus' baptism in the Jordan River, the practice of simply pouring water on the convert's head also appeared quite early. Baptism was always administered in the name of Father, Son, and Spirit, not merely as a symbolic action but as an event that causes the recipient to be "signed with the sign of faith", a kind of spiritual seal impressed on the soul.

Deposit of Faith

In the years before the Gospels were written, during the generation following the Resurrection (until roughly the year 60), the word *Scripture* meant what Christians would later call the Old Testament—there was no authoritative book from which they could learn about their own faith. The Gospel message was kept alive by traditions, most of them probably oral, within the living community of the Church. Paul rebuked the Galatians for departing from those traditions (the "deposit of faith") and following false teachings and warned them not to give up those traditions even if told to do so by "an angel from heaven".

---

[5] There were two Apostles named James, who were later called James the Greater and James the Less, supposedly because of their ages. The New Testament calls one "the brother of the Lord" (Gal 1:19), but it is not clear if that refers to the author of the Letter. According to tradition, James the Greater went to Spain but later returned to Jerusalem to be martyred.

After Pentecost, Jesus' followers retained the dominant sense of being guided by the Spirit. Paul warned that no one could make the basic affirmation of faith—"Jesus is Lord"—except through the power of the Spirit, which is manifested in various ways, as when Paul and his traveling companion Timothy were told by the Spirit not to preach in Asia (roughly modern Turkey). The Apostles relied on this continuing inspiration, and Paul identified a range of gifts granted by the Spirit to individuals: to teach, to heal, to work miracles, to prophesy, to discern spirits, to speak in tongues.

The Spirit

The infant Church could therefore be considered *charismatic* (from the word for "gift"), in that it was guided by direct divine inspiration, manifested through inspired individuals. But that was not enough. *Kerygma* ("kernel") is the heart of the faith as found in Scripture, but it is impossible to separate such a kernel from the ways in which the Church understands it.

It was sinful to reject the inspiration of the Spirit, but, while extolling the charisms, Paul ceaselessly warned against leaders (including, potentially, himself) who made their own teachings the substance of the faith. Particularly in the dispute over the Law, his powerful personality and his absolute conviction of being right were not in themselves sufficient. Formal deliberation by the Apostles as a group was required, with Peter acting as their head, the responsibility that had been entrusted to him by Jesus.

After the New Testament had been written, Christians read it as a coherent whole, not as representing divergent viewpoints. They had a strong sense of belonging to a unified Church, not to particular local communities each with its own theology. In the second century, adherence to false teachings came to be called *heresy*, a Greek word meaning "choice", because heretics were not unbelievers but professed Christians who emphasized some teachings at the expense of others.

One Gospel

From the beginning, the Church had both an invisible and a visible character, spirit and flesh, inner life and external discipline, simultaneously both an institution and a spiritual community. The ecclesial offices were not administrative only but possessed spiritual power and authority, with office-holders not simply chosen by the community, for the sake of good order, but by the action of the Spirit, in order to represent Christ.

Ecclesial Offices

Jesus personally called the Twelve, corresponding to the twelve tribes of Israel, and He later designated seventy-two disciples, thereby establishing inner and outer circles among His immediate followers, with the Twelve possessing ultimate authority.

The Twelve

Despite its name, the Acts of the Apostles recounts the activities of only a few of the Twelve, probably because the rest had departed on long missionary journeys from which they never returned. Some of that group presided over a local church (James at Jerusalem, Peter for a time at Antioch). Paul was called an apostle because he had encountered the risen Christ in person and, apart from the Twelve, he alone had apostolic authority, making periodic visits to the communities over which he exercised authority and attempting to guide those communities through letters.

Pauline Offices

Paul identified apostles, prophets, evangelists, pastors, and teachers as those who had been given special authority in the Church, although it is not clear precisely how those offices related to one another or whether they were entirely separate.

Bishops

In his First Letter to Timothy, Paul referred to the office of bishop (*episcopos*: "overseer") and laid down the requirements for that office, showing that, as new communities of believers were formed, they were under the direct supervision of an Apostle or of someone who succeeded to apostolic authority. Perhaps as a counterweight to the authority of the spiritual charisms, in describing the bishop, Paul emphasized the virtues and practical prudence of the head of a household. St. Clement, bishop of Rome (ca. 91–100), said that the Apostles appointed bishops in the communities which they oversaw.

Priests

Full consciousness of a distinctively Christian priesthood probably did not emerge until the Church had broken decisively with Judaism, since until then many Christians regarded the Jewish priests as still having authority and continued going to the Temple for sacrifice.

Acts identified *presbyteroi* as local church officials, an office that already existed among Greek-speaking Jews and that meant "elders". At first, the bishop alone probably presided at the Eucharist, and it is not clear if the presbyters were ordained for any sacramental role. But as the Church grew, the term was used for lower clergy who were authorized by the bishop to preside at the Eucharist, and the word thereby came to mean "priest" in the Catholic sense.

Deacons

At one point, the Apostles chose seven deacons ("servants"), thereby establishing a new office, an action that, along with the various decisions about the binding nature of the Law, illustrated the authority structure of the early Church—on matters of importance the Apostles deliberated, then announced their decision to the rest of the disciples.

Women

Several women were the first to discover that Jesus' tomb was empty, and Paul had two female associates—Phoebe and Prisca—about whom little is known. But Paul also enjoined women to "keep silence in the churches" (1 Cor 14:34), and no woman held formal office, although some—Mary above all—undoubtedly had the kind of unofficial, charismatic authority that has been exercised in every age by holy individuals.

Widows had a special status and special duties in the Church, especially in ministering to other women. They were discouraged from remarrying (sometimes forbidden to, as Paul forbade bishops to do), so as to witness to the Kingdom, where, as Jesus said, "They [men] neither marry nor are given in marriage" (Mt 22:30). Virgins—unmarried women—also became a recognized category of Christians, and there was an official order of deaconesses, although it did not involve formal ordination and disappeared quite early.

The Moral Life

Marriage and Celibacy

When Paul warned that "the desires of flesh are against the Spirit" (Gal 5:17), he did not equate sin only with physical acts but used the word *flesh* to refer to man's entire lower nature, particularly his self-will. But sexual lust is one of the strongest and most immediate expressions of self-will, which makes its conquest a necessary step toward a truly spiritual life. Thus he listed adulterers, fornicators, and sodomites as among those who could not enter the Kingdom of Heaven.

Peter was married (Jesus cured his mother-in-law), as probably were the other Apostles and, indeed, most people in the early Church. But nothing is known of the Apostles' married lives—the writers of the Gospel apparently saw no particular relevance in it. Significantly, no one claimed that Jesus was married, and the weight of the New Testament is against it.

Paul was celibate for the sake of the Kingdom, something he extolled as a higher state for those who could follow it, a teaching that does not seem to have been controversial among his married contemporaries. He enjoined bishops to be the husbands of only one wife, an injunction that was obviously not directed at the sin of bigamy but was rather to urge that they remain unmarried if widowed.

Paradoxically, with celibacy as the ideal, marriage was also exalted. Contrary to most prevailing ancient customs (but not those of the Jews), only in marriage could there be legitimate sexual activity. Paul's theology of marriage was far more exalted than anything known to the pagan world—an intimate union of man and wife like that of Christ and His Church.

Paul's famous injunctions "Wives, be subject to your husbands" and "Husbands, love your wives" (Eph 5:22, 25) were understood in that context, which was a major moral advance over the prevalent Roman custom of the "double standard" of sexual behavior for men and women and the virtually absolute authority that Roman husbands and fathers had over their families.

Marriage was also honored in the high value the Church placed on children, against a pagan society in which unwanted babies were put out to die of exposure. The begetting of children was always considered the principal purpose of Christian marriage, so that abortion and contraception were condemned from the earliest times.

Thus celibacy was extolled not because marriage is evil but because it is highly meritorious to give up something good for a still higher good. (Among the Jews, celibacy and other kinds of asceticism were mainly practiced by the somewhat marginal sect of the Essenes.)

Property

Little is known about the finances of the early Church. Paul plied the trade of a tent-maker but reminded his hearers that, if he chose to ask for it, he was entitled to their material support, in order to enable him to devote himself entirely to the work of the Gospel. It is likely that other early leaders were supported in their work by the community.

The Sermon on the Mount was the heart of Jesus' social teaching, but He laid down no plan for a just social order and thereby deprived all social orders of divine authority, something that, paradoxically, made social change possible. His preaching was directed primarily at persons. Living as Jesus urged would necessarily bring about profound changes in the world, since it demanded a radical inversion of ordinary human relationships (e.g., "Love your enemies"). The heart of the Gospel was the promise of the Kingdom of Heaven, so that no earthly evil could be ultimate and Christians were urged to endure gladly every kind of suffering for the sake of Christ.

Acts records that the early Christians shared their goods but, although Jesus repeatedly warned against an attachment to possessions, the Church did not condemn private property as such. A married couple, Ananias and Sapphira, were struck dead after selling some land and giving only part of the proceeds to the Church, while claiming that it was the full amount. But their sin was lying, not clinging to what was rightfully theirs. Paul ruled that, if people would not work, they also should not eat.

Private property would not exist in the Kingdom. While a few people would renounce it completely as a living reminder of the nature of that Kingdom, wealth was given to some in order that they could aid those in need. Property was intimately linked with stewardship; it could not be used merely for personal satisfaction.

Charity

The establishment of the diaconate, following complaints of inequities in the distribution of food to the needy, was justified by the Apostles on the grounds that "it is not right that we should give up preaching the word of God to serve tables" (Acts 6:2), a pointed reminder of the Church's true purpose. The hungry in body were to be fed, but spiritual hunger was far worse, requiring that the Church's spiritual mission always take precedence over her humanitarian service.

Paul identified the three basic virtues as faith, hope, and love and pronounced that "the greatest of these is love" (1 Cor 13:13), which "binds everything together in perfect harmony" (Col 3:14). Jesus' threefold injunction to pray, fast, and give *alms* (Latin for "mercy") was considered the practical basis of the Christian life, and some Church leaders urged giving alms even to nonbelievers.

Although some early Christians rejoiced that such love was characteristic of their community ("By this all men will know that you are my disciples, if you have love for one another" [Jn 13:35]), from the beginning there were also divisions. The deaths of Ananias and Sapphira—believed to be the direct work of the Spirit—shows that discipline could be stern indeed. Paul sometimes rebuked his hearers for their quarrelsomeness, and the establishment of the diaconate resulted from the first ethnic squabble in the history of the Church, when hellenized (Greek-speaking) Christians complained that their widows were not being treated equally in the distribution of food.

The early Christians had no developed system of "social ethics" as such and were not reformers or revolutionaries in the modern sense. They did not advocate the overthrow of the existing social order, nor even its radical transformation in political terms.

Spiritual Equality

Christianity proclaimed a radical idea of equality but in an essentially negative way—all men are equal in sin and in need of redemption; none can be saved by their own merits, least of all by their social standing. The Church accepted social hierarchy as justified in worldly terms but reminded people that it had no significance in the Kingdom.

In his First Letter to Timothy, Paul included slave-traders among those who could not enter the Kingdom. But, famously, he also urged, "Slaves, be obedient to those who are your earthly masters" (Eph 6:5). Slavery was considered a result of Adam's fall and as such was not condemned. Slaves had to be respected as human beings and as adopted children of God, but it was not considered imperative that their transitory earthly status be changed. *The Shepherd*, perhaps the earliest Christian documents after the Bible itself, was purportedly written by an ex-slave, and some ex-slaves even became bishops, including Pope St. Calixtus I (217–222).

Slavery

Paul set forth a concept of slavery far higher than any prior to that time, an ideal in which slaves are spiritually equal to their masters, since all Christians are slaves of Christ. In the context of the Kingdom, slavery has no significance ("There is ... neither slave nor free ... for you are all one in Christ Jesus" [Gal 3:28]). Paul wrote a letter to a Christian slave-owner, Philemon, urging him to receive back a runaway slave, Onesimus, who was also a Christian, urging Philemon to treat Onesimus as he would treat Paul himself and wishing that he could keep Onesimus with him as a helper in his labors.

Jesus' only directly political teaching was His famous injunction, "Render to Caesar the things that are Caesar's and to God the things that are God's" (Lk 20:25), which meant that His followers should pay their taxes, since the coin in question was already Caesar's property—it had his image on it. Some Jews criticized Jesus for associating with tax

The State

collectors, who were considered agents of an oppressive government. Jesus forbade His followers to resist His unjust arrest, and when summoned before Pilate He did not deny the procurator's authority. Paul told his hearers to be obedient to the state, and in even the most severe persecutions, the early Christians never denied the state's temporal authority.

Radical Conversion

Because Jesus condemned the values on which "the world" is based, His followers were revolutionaries in a far deeper sense than the merely political, preaching a fundamental change in human nature itself, the inward adoption of a way of life that would radically transform the world. This way of life was possible not by human effort alone, but by the grace Christ won for man and offered through His Church, which He commanded His Apostles to spread throughout the world.

Peace

The early Church was not pacifist but pacific, meaning that she incessantly preached the imperative of living peacefully but did not condemn war in principle. The courage and dedication of soldiers were extolled as virtues all believers should cultivate. Christians served in the Roman army, a practice that was sometimes criticized not because war was sinful in itself but because the army constituted a spiritual environment that was dangerous to the whole Christian way of life.

The Spread of the Gospel

The Fulfillment of the Promise

The apostolic message was at first primarily directed to the Jews, announcing that the old faith was not abolished but actually fulfilled in Jesus and marshaling the sayings of the prophets in order to show that their words foretold the coming of Jesus. The synagogues were places for teaching as well as worship, and the first Christians went there to find receptive audiences, inviting Jews not to deny their faith but to fulfill it. Christians claimed that they understood the Scripture better than the Jews did, because the prophets foretold the Christ.

Persecution

But this inevitably provoked strong reaction from the religious authorities. Several of the Apostles were at various times arrested and kept in prison, and James was put to death by Herod Antipas, possibly as a gesture of piety toward the Jewish religion of which Herod was a notoriously poor representative. One of the early converts, a young man named Stephen, preached with such vehemence, denouncing the "hardheartedness" of his hearers, that he became the first Christian martyr, stoned to death in the manner prescribed for blasphemers.

Conversion of Saul

Among those who joined in this stoning was Saul, a Pharisee who had studied under a leading rabbi and who took his faith with intense seriousness. But after being thrown to the ground on the road to Damascus (Syria) and hearing a voice ask, "Saul, Saul, why do you persecute me?" (Acts 9:4) he became the model of all converts. Saul came from a hellenized Jewish background at Tarsus in Syria, and "Paul" was the hellenized form of his name, by which he now became known. Suddenly, he was a fervent and passionate exponent of the religion he had once hated. He considered himself the least of the Apostles, because he had persecuted the Church. Paradoxically, it was precisely his intense Jewish piety that led Paul to see Israel as unfaithful to God's promises, so that he proclaimed that in the new dispensation there would be neither Jew nor Greek, an announcement for which some of the original Twelve were not prepared.

Paul saw that the Christian faith is cosmopolitan by its very nature, not only because Jesus commanded His followers to "make disciples of all nations" but because His Resurrection promises the transformation of the whole world. That expectation was progressively modified as it became clear that His Second Coming (*parousia*) would not occur soon, thereby making the whole world a field for continued efforts to spread of the Gospel.

"All Nations"

With Paul in the lead, the Church moved out into the larger hellenistic world. In the ensuing centuries, none of her leaders were of Jewish background, and many of the early theologians wrote treatises to show that the Gospel had supplanted the Jewish faith.

The word *Gentiles* meant simply "the nations"—all those who did not belong to the chosen people—and even those who insisted that Christians had to observe the Jewish Law never excluded Gentiles from the Church. Jesus praised the faith of a Roman centurion, and Acts records both the admission of several Gentiles to baptism and the existence of Christian communities at Antioch and Damascus, although they were probably composed mainly of converted Jews.

Christianity penetrated the wider world primarily through the Jews of the Diaspora ("dispersion"), who had settled all over the Empire. Probably for a time, most of the early converts were hellenized Jews rather than Gentiles as such, as was Paul's missionary companion Timothy, the son of a Greek father and a Jewish mother who had accepted the Gospel. The hellenization of the Diaspora Jews opened for the Apostles a door into the Gentile world.

Jewish Diaspora

Paul made three missionary journeys around the eastern Mediterranean, thereby greatly expanding the geographical scope of the Church, his letters serving as a way of remaining in communication with the local communities and of reminding them of his teachings.

Paul the Missionary

The first great crisis in the history of the Church erupted when Paul began to teach that the Law was no longer binding, specifically that male Christians had no need to be circumcised and that no Christian had to observe the Jewish dietary regulations. The issue was resolved

The Law

only with difficulty. James, the head of the church at Jerusalem, for a time upheld the old ways, while Peter, the chief of the Apostles, had a vision in which he was instructed that no foods are to be considered unclean, since all have been created by God. (Christianity is unusual among great religions in not forbidding any particular food to its adherents.)

Although the exact sequence of events is unclear, Peter seems to have first affirmed the binding nature of the Law, until persuaded otherwise by Paul. Acts records a relatively easy resolution of the issue, in which some of the requirements of the Law were abrogated and others retained, but in his Letter to the Galatians Paul reported a somewhat tenser meeting in which "I opposed him [Peter] to his face" (Gal 2:11). In various of his Letters, Paul warned against "false teachers" who were imposing circumcision but also urged converts to be patient with the "weaker brethren" who might be scandalized by those who were emancipated from the Law. This dispute gives insight into the nature of authority in the early Church, with Peter's authority needed to confirm Paul's authority, but the two ultimately considered complementary. (Historically, the Church has often venerated Peter and Paul together.)

The Greek New Testament

Christians seem to have relied mainly on the Greek translation of the Old Testament called the Septuagint (so-called because it was believed to have been compiled by seventy rabbis), and after the first century, few Christian writers seem even to have understood Hebrew. Significantly, the New Testament was composed in Greek, which made it accessible to the largest number of people throughout the Empire.

Jewish Christians

As various of the Apostles left on their missionary journeys, the church in Palestine itself probably continued for the most part to observe Jewish Law, although there was also a good deal of anti-Christian polemic from Jewish sources. Some communities of "Jewish Christians" survived in the Holy Land for several centuries but were increasingly isolated from the larger Church and fell into heresy, rejecting Paul's authority, venerating gospels that were not accepted elsewhere, propounding an elaborate mythology of angels and demons, and possessing a strong sense that the last days were near. Some Jewish Christians were called Ebionites (from a Hebrew word for "poor") and others Nazarenes. Their exact theology is uncertain, but they sometimes referred to Jesus as an angel or a prophet. At the other extreme, a heretical sect founded by a man named Marcion (d. ca. 150) demanded a complete break with Judaism, rejecting the Old Testament as pertaining to another God.

The destruction of the Temple by the Romans after the Jewish rebellion of the year 70—a desecration completed by later building a temple to Jupiter on the site—confirmed for most Christians that God's action in history was now taking place on a much wider stage. For some, this destruction was a necessary act of divine providence, since Christ Himself is the new Temple. Thus worshippers no longer faced Jerusalem when they prayed but turned toward the East, to greet the rising sun, the symbol of the risen Christ.

The Gospel to the Gentiles

Although the total number of Christians remained fairly small, the movement spread even beyond the farthest eastern boundaries of the Empire. Early traditions traced the founding of various far-flung local churches to the evangelical efforts of particular Apostles—James the Greater in Spain, for example, the disciple St. Joseph of Arimathea in Britain, St. Bartholomew in Persia, St. Jude Thaddeus in Mesopotamia (modern Iraq), St. Thomas in India, St. Mark in Egypt.

The Greeks

Paul sought to spread the Good News in more than just a geographical sense, bringing it into unfamiliar cultures. He first took Christianity to Europe through Macedonia, immediately to the north of Greece, his first missionary stop being Philippi, the place where the assassins of Julius Caesar had been vanquished a century before.

Bringing the Gospel to the Gentiles was in some ways far more difficult than bringing it to the Jews, because the missionaries had no obvious point of contact with polytheists. Paul's claim at Ephesus that the pagan gods were frauds provoked the wrath of craftsmen who made their living by fashioning silver images of the goddess Artemis (Diana). The silversmiths started a riot in which crowds shouted for hours, "Great is Artemis of the Ephesians", and threatened violence against the Christians, until a town official stopped them. In Athens, Paul noticed an altar dedicated to the "Unknown God" (the Athenians' way of hedging their religious bets) and tried to gain the pagans' attention by proclaiming that he had come to speak to them precisely of this unknown deity, who in reality is the only God. But his message about Christ crucified puzzled and repelled his hearers (a "folly to Gentiles" [1 Cor 1:23]), so that his initial success was meager.

But paradoxically, as the Gospel spread, its fate became increasingly entwined, in a variety of ways, with the fate of the very Empire whose minions had crucified the Christ.

2   The Seed of Christians

Pax Romana

Although the Roman Empire eventually attempted to exterminate the Church, the early Christians believed that God made use of all things for His own purposes and had given the Empire itself a providential role in the spread of the faith. As St. Paul explained, Jesus was sent "when the time had fully come" (Gal 4:4), when the necessary conditions had been met. The Empire formed a geographical and cultural unity, and the *Pax Romana* (Roman peace) allowed relatively safe and easy travel all over the Mediterranean, thereby facilitating missionary efforts. By preaching and making use of synagogues in cities and large towns, evangelizers were able to reach the largest number of people.

One of the paradoxes of the early Church was the fact that the capital city of her great persecutor became the center of her life, with the martyrdom of Peter and Paul at Rome—a reenactment of the martyrdom of the Lord Himself—serving as the foundation stone of the Church's lasting victory.

Gnosticism

But as persecution from without intensified in the late second century, the Church found herself threatened internally by something even more dangerous, because it seduced even sincere believers. Although Christianity's greatest appeal was its promise of eternal life, it now found it necessary to emphasize its incarnational character, proclaiming the goodness of creation and the reality of time in the face of a strong force that found the world so repugnant that it yearned for release.

Dualism

Gnosticism is the name given to a variety of movements, most of them pagan but some ostensibly Jewish or Christian. At stake was the most fundamental of all the teachings of the Judaeo-Christian faith—that one God created the universe and rules over it. Gnosticism, by contrast, was fundamentally dualist, positing two equal gods ruling two wholly separate realms of the universe—spiritual and material, light and dark, good and evil.

It promised redemption not from sin but from Fate—from history itself—teaching that men, composed of souls and bodies that are ultimately incompatible, are trapped between the two realms because of some primordial catastrophe. Salvation consists in freeing the soul from the prison of the body, achieved through the acquisition of secret knowledge (*gnosis*).

Gnosticism was Christianity's greatest threat because the Church claimed to possess the true *gnosis*—the Gospel—which Gnosticism sought to transform for its own purposes, offering what was to many people a credible explanation of the mystery of how evil could exist in a universe governed by an all-good God and a radical solution to the widespread sense of the meaninglessness of life. *True Gnosis*

Gnosticism required the rejection of the Old Testament, since the all-good God could not have created the material universe, which is the realm of a second, perhaps lesser, divinity. Gnostics also reinterpreted Jesus Himself, whom they could not accept as a real man who once lived on earth. Thus they tended to approach the New Testament in a wholly "spiritual" way, as composed mainly of allegories of the soul in its relationship to God. Their denial of history, including the New Testament accounts of Jesus' life (He could not really have died), allowed them to "transcend" particular beliefs and to soar into the realm of the mystical imagination. *Gnostic Gospels*

Various early books written under Gnostic auspices—the "gospels" of Judas, Thomas, and Philip as well as stories about Mary Magdalen—differed substantially from the four Gospels and sometimes contradicted them. All were written much later than the New Testament.

Morally, Gnosticism was paradoxical. It urged the rejection of the flesh in order to enter the realm of the spirit and therefore placed no positive value on marriage. But the renunciation of sexual relations was thought to be possible only for an elite, leaving the masses to live lives of unredeemed sensuality. *Flesh and Spirit*

Gnosticism was refuted chiefly by St. Irenaeus (d. ca. 195), bishop of Lyon in Gaul (France), in his *Treatise on Heresies*, one of the earliest Western theological works of any kind. Against the secret knowledge promised by the Gnostics, Irenaeus emphasized that the truths of Christianity are accessible to all. Christ is the true saving *gnosis*, and the events recounted in the Gospel really happened. Irenaeus stressed the limits not only of human reason but of divine revelation as well—God reveals only His dealings with man, not His own inner divine reality, which Gnosticism claimed to penetrate. The goodness of creation was affirmed by Irenaeus, including the goodness of the human body. *Irenaeus*

The Gnostic Marcionites were especially emphatic in their denial that the Creator of the Old Testament is the God of the New Testament, and they consequently rejected the entire Old Testament, as well as those parts *Marcionites* of the New Testament that stressed Jesus' continuity with Judaism. Irenaeus was the first theologian to speak of the New Testament as "Scripture" in the same sense as the Old.

Creation

Against the elaborate Gnostic cosmology, St. Clement of Alexandria (d. ca. 217) asserted that God created the universe from nothing, a doctrine that became a basic Christian teaching. It both affirmed God's absolute power—"all things were made through him" (Jn 1:3)—and maintained an absolute distinction between God and the universe: He did not create the universe out of Himself, hence the universe is not divine.

The Soul

The belief that the soul preexists its incarnation in the body was widespread in the ancient world; and, as employed by the Gnostics and others, it effectively denied human sinfulness, evil is not the result of human action but of the misfortune of the soul's entrapment in an alien environment. From Paul, Irenaeus developed a contrasting theory of redemption—Adam was created free but fell into Satan's clutches, a bondage inherited by all his descendants until righteousness was restored by Christ, who shed His blood to ransom men from the devil.

Some Christians saw the idea of the natural immortality of the soul as a pagan error, but St. Ambrose of Milan (d. 397) eventually formulated the accepted orthodox teaching: the soul is immortal by nature but God also brings about the resurrection of the body, a uniquely Christian belief that affirms the goodness of the flesh.

The World of Spirits

Belief in magic was almost universal in the ancient world, and all ancient religions believed in the existence of a whole panoply of supernatural beings with power in the world—some gods, some angels, some demons. Gnosticism accounted for evil by teaching that demons rule the material universe. Demons had to be fought against continually and could be vanquished only through divine power.

Belief in magic was shared by Christians, who usually treated it not as fraudulent or delusory but as a genuine and dangerous manifestation of evil power, not denying the existence of supernatural beings but understanding them in new ways. But it required some period of meditation to understand how precisely they fit into the divine economy (in some early Christian writings Jesus was Himself called an angel). Eventually, based on Scripture, the Church developed a complex theology of both angels and fallen angels—devils—who are completely under God's power but whom He allows to have power over the affairs of men.

The Victory of Orthodoxy

Gnosticism did not fade away as a result of the work of Irenaeus and others; the battle went on for several centuries. But the Church's eventual victory had a profound effect not only on her own life but on the entire Western world and the Christian Near East. Had it been victorious, Gnosticism might have penetrated the culture of the Roman Empire in such a way as to create a new world religion of deep pessimism and rejection of the world. Western culture would have lost that sense of the importance of human activity in history that distinguished it from the fatalism that at times affected much of the East.

The Locus of Truth

Canon of Scripture

The later principle of *sola scriptura* ("the Bible alone") could not have resolved the Gnostic issues, because the authority of the Church had first to determine which books were divinely inspired and what they meant. By excluding certain books as unsuitable to be read in the liturgy, the Church in effect declared the Gnostics' own writings to be apocryphal ("hidden") and unreliable.

Creeds

Paul denounced false teachings of a somewhat practical kind, such as the necessity of circumcision. The Gnostic threat, however, now led the Church to require assent to formal doctrines as set forth in creeds, one of the first instances of a pattern that would recur over and over again in the history of the Church: doctrines becoming fully conscious, and formally stated, only after being called into question.

Hierarchy

Gnosticism was vanquished in large part because of the Church's hierarchical nature, her ability to define the meaning of the faith in ways that were binding on the faithful, in contrast to movements, like Gnosticism itself, that were held together primarily by some theory of inspiration and were only loosely organized. One of the Church's legacies from the Romans was precisely her sense of order and discipline, including her sense of law. The problem of organization was particularly crucial after the generation of the Apostles had passed away.

After the New Testament itself, one of the earliest Christian records is *The Shepherd*, a dialogue in which a confused Christian named Hermas receives enlightenment from angels, one of whom is called "the Shepherd". The book describes the tripartite clerical division of bishop, priest, and deacon.

Pope St. Clement I wrote a letter of rebuke to the Christians of Corinth in Greece, wherein for the first time he spoke of the laity ("people of God") and exhorted them to obey their clergy, a defense of hierarchy ("rule by priests") that he based on the order of Israel, now transferred to the Church. For years afterward, Clement's letter was publicly read at Corinth as the voice of authority.

Ignatius of Antioch

A few years later, St. Ignatius (d. ca. 107), bishop of Antioch, was arrested and sent to Rome for trial, presumably because, like Paul, he was a Roman citizen. Along the way, he sent letters ahead to seven local churches through which he expected to pass, letters that are the earliest account, after the New Testament itself and *The Shepherd*, of the structure of the early Church. To all his hearers, he stressed the crucial importance of both the Eucharist and the office of bishop, around whom the faithful must gather and without whom there could be no legitimate Church.

Marks of the Church

Eventually, the true Church came to be identified by four signs— being one, holy, catholic, and apostolic. Her unity could be discerned by empirical evidence and her apostolic character by historical evidence, but her holiness transcended her human face and referred to her inner reality as the Body of Christ.

Catholicity

Ignatius called the Church "catholic"—universal—in the sense both of the whole Church, transcending local communities, and the universality of her truth, omitting nothing. For Ignatius, who was said to have known St. John the Evangelist personally and who was familiar with Paul's Letters, not only Scripture but Tradition ("handing on") was an important witness to truth.

Apostolic Succession and Tradition

Irenaeus particularly stressed "apostolic succession" as the ultimate guarantor of truth, meaning primarily the transmission of authentic apostolic teachings from generation to generation through a line of bishops. Divine revelation was believed to have ended with the last Apostle (St. John, in the late first century), so that the most damaging charge that could be leveled at a theologian was that he introduced novelty. All Christians, of whatever theological school, constantly appealed to the authority of both Scripture and the previous interpreters of Scripture, requiring that every seemingly new idea be found, at least implicitly, in truths already believed.

Ignatius, Irenaeus, and others identified the essential elements that defined Catholicism and would later come to define Eastern Orthodoxy: a divinely established "visible" Church, episcopal authority, apostolic succession, Tradition, and the centrality of the Eucharist. Irenaeus made the terms *orthodox* ("correct teaching"), *catholic* ("universal"), *apostolic*, and *traditional* virtually synonymous.

Tradition

At Alexandria (Egypt), one of the great intellectual centers of the new faith, St. Clement (d. ca. 217) and Origen (d. ca. 254) spoke of Tradition as being found not only in formal doctrinal statements but also in the liturgy, catechetical writings, and creeds recited at baptism. Divine truth was to be found in the Scripture, but not only there. Numerous beliefs commonly accepted by later Christians came down solely through Tradition—both matters of substantive belief, such as the Assumption of Mary into Heaven, and lesser things, such as Joachim and Anna being the names of Mary's parents and the Magi being named Caspar, Melchior, and Balthasar. The doctrine of the virgin birth of Jesus could not be proved or disproved from the

Bible alone, since the Hebrew word for "virgin" (*almah*) was also the word for "young woman", whom readers would assume to be a virgin. The reference to Jesus' "brothers" in the New Testament was also ambiguous, since the Greek word (*adelphoi*) could mean blood relatives in general.

The Church of Rome

Peter and Paul

There was a Christian community in Rome, probably made up of converted Jews, even before the arrival of Peter and Paul, and no one in the early centuries disputed the claim that they both lived in Rome and were martyred there. This intimate connection to Peter—the rock upon whom Jesus said He would build His Church—was the basis of the church of Rome's claim to rank above all other local churches. The latter part of Acts is an account of Paul's arrest by the Roman authorities and his demand to be taken to Rome for trial, although the account breaks off abruptly.

The Early Fathers

The writings of the early Church Fathers testify to Rome's unique status. Ignatius, for instance, extolled the church of Rome as especially worthy of respect,[1] recalling Peter's martyrdom at Rome, and from a very early time, the Church venerated the Apostle's tomb, which, according to a very ancient tradition and the evidence of modern excavations, lies under the great basilica of the Vatican, while Paul was killed and buried on the site of the basilica later named after him "Outside the Walls".

As a young priest, Irenaeus came to Rome to consult the bishop. He also thought it appropriate to record the names of all the bishops of Rome to his own day, the first three of whom—Sts. Linus (67–76), Cletus (76–91), and Clement (91–100)—are still commemorated in the Roman liturgy immediately following the Apostles themselves.

The Fathers also record how the early Christians relied on the pope to settle disputes. St. Polycarp (d. ca. 155), bishop of Smyrna (Asia Minor), traveled to Rome to discuss the disputed date of Easter with Pope St. Anicetus (ca. 155–166), although the two could not agree. Later Pope St. Victor I (ca. 189–199), after excommunicating several Eastern bishops for observing a day of Easter different from that of the West, acceded to Irenaeus' entreaty to rescind the sentence. Before they drifted into heterodoxy, the great African theologians Tertullian (d. ca. 220) and Origen (d. ca. 254) also exalted the see of Rome, and during a brief lull in the persecution, the Emperor Aurelian (270–275) referred a Church dispute at Antioch to Pope St. Felix I (269–274).

---

[1] The argument has sometimes been made that the office of bishop was an innovation of the post-apostolic period. However, Ignatius wrote within two generations of the Apostles, and the argument from silence—that, if something is not mentioned in a particular text, it did not occur—is one of the weakest of historical arguments. As John's Gospel says, much happened in the life of Jesus (and, by extension, in the life of the Church) that was not recorded in Scripture (see Jn 21:25).

A Cosmopolitan See

The international character of the see of Rome was reflected in the fact that, while the Roman Church continued to choose her bishops from among her own priests, some of those chosen were of African or Greek origin—priests who had migrated to serve in the capital of their faith.

Over time, the bishop of Rome employed several titles, of which "vicar of Christ" was by far the most important. The term *pope* was a colloquial name for "father" (*pappa*), often used for other bishops but in time considered an exclusive, semi-official title of the bishop of Rome.

Divisions

The see of Rome itself did not always rise above the troubled waters of the early centuries. One of the persistent tensions in the early Church was the degree of rigor demanded of Christians. By modern standards, that Church was rigorous indeed, but for people like Tertullian, she was too lax. The priest Hippolytus (d. 235), who took very rigorous positions on moral questions, attacked Pope St. Zephyrinus (199–217) as corrupt. Hippolytus was then himself proclaimed pope by a dissident group, thereby becoming the first "anti-pope". Eventually, however, he was reconciled with Pope St. Pontian (230–235), and the two were martyred together.

Ecclesiastical Structure

The Worthiness of Her Members

Hippolytus championed the not uncommon idea that the Church was the community of the righteous, in opposition to which Pope St. Calixtus I (217–222) compared her to Noah's ark, encompassing a representative part of the human race, and he pointed to Jesus' parable of the wheat and the tares, where the just and the unjust are to be separated only at the final harvest (see Mt 13:24–30).

Hippolytus, despite his rigor, supported the claim that ultimate authority resides in the duly ordained officers of the Church, independent of their personal worthiness, a doctrine that, as it came under periodic attack, became a bedrock of Catholic teaching. Novatian (d. 258), a wealthy man who became an anti-pope in opposition to Pope St. Cornelius (251–253), held that those who compromised the faith could never be reconciled. Novatian was driven out of Rome, but his schism spread to Gaul and Spain.

Bishops

Bishops in the early centuries were elected locally (there were over a hundred in Italy alone in the mid-third century), although the process by which this occurred varied—the Latin word *electio* did not mean "majority vote" but simply "choice", no matter how arrived at. Consensus was sought, and in some cases it was achieved through direct inspiration—articulated by one or more inspired members of the flock—that a particular individual was God's choice, a claim that then had to be ratified by the whole community as the will of the Spirit.

But election alone did not make a man a bishop. Also required was the laying on of hands by other bishops (usually three), part of the process that insured apostolic succession. Thus each local church had to keep an exact record of the spiritual lineage of its bishops.

By the mid-third century, the Church at Rome had grown to about sixteen thousand people, and seven clerical orders were recognized. There were fifty-two doorkeepers and exorcists, the former being more than mere ceremonial officers, since only the baptized were permitted to be present at the Eucharist, and the latter functioning as custodians of the holy water and oil and allowed to impart minor blessings. There were forty-two acolytes ("messengers"), who sometimes brought Communion to the sick or to prisoners; seven subdeacons; seven deacons; and forty-six priests. There was also an office of lector or reader, sometimes filled by boys, whose purity made them worthy to read aloud some of the biblical texts in the liturgy, although the Gospel had to be proclaimed by a deacon.

Minor Orders

Because of their experience in governing, deacons were not infrequently elected bishops, although some men remained in that order all their lives. Deacons were attached directly to the bishop as his aides, not permitted to celebrate the Eucharist but allowed to distribute Communion and to baptize. St. Tarcisius (d. ca. 200), who was probably a deacon, was killed by a mob at Rome because, while carrying the Eucharist—perhaps to those in prison—he refused a demand to give it up. The preaching of *homilies*—sermons that "broke open" the difficult scriptural texts—was considered integral to the Eucharist and was also one of the deacon's primary tasks.

Deacons

Deacons were important figures, since their care for the poor involved administering the property of the Church. At Rome, there were fifteen hundred widows and other needy people who were the responsibility of the Church, and during periods of peace she opened churches and cemeteries. From time to time, there were warnings against greedy or dishonest deacons.

Most early Christians probably believed in the speedy return of Jesus, and the disappointment of that expectation caused a crisis for some, while for others it confirmed the need for hierarchy, because the Church would have to endure for a long time. The development of the hierarchy provoked the heresy of Montanism in the late second century. Named for its leader, it rejected hierarchy as an obstacle to pure inspiration and located authority in prophets and prophetesses, dreams and visions, anticipating the immanent Second Coming of Christ.

The Montanist Heresy

Based on prophecies in the Book of Revelation, some early Christians embraced millenarianism (from the Latin word for "thousand"), according to which Jesus would one day return and rule over the earth for a thousand years. But Christ was also a continuing Real Presence in

Millenarianism

the Eucharist, and the two beliefs were brought together in the eucharistic acclamation "Christ will come again."

Liturgy

Liturgy was a pagan term signifying any kind of religious duty, and the rituals of the Church were called *mysterioi* ("sacred actions") in Greek and *sacramenta* in Latin, the latter meaning "an oath", since Christians took an oath of faithfulness to Christ.

From the beginning, the Eucharist was considered simultaneously a memory of Jesus' action at the Last Supper, a thanksgiving, and an oblation or offering in which He is Himself the sacrificial victim, the only offering worthy to be made to the Father. St. Justin Martyr (d. 165) described the liturgy of the Eucharist as consisting of prayers, a greeting of peace, the presentation of gifts, thanksgiving, and the reception of Communion. At the Offertory, the faithful brought to the deacon not only the bread and wine to be used in the sacrifice but other fruits of the field as well, as gifts for the poor and as a sign of the goodness of creation. The Lord's Prayer, with its petition for the forgiveness of sins, was part of the Eucharist from an early date, recited by the people.

The repentant anti-pope Hippolytus left a record of the Eucharist as celebrated at Rome in the early third century. Scriptural readings began the service, following which the bishop and the presbyters spread their hands over the gifts and said prayers, to which the people responded. During a long prayer of thanksgiving, the bishop pronounced the words by which Christ had instituted the Eucharist—"This is my body . . . this is my blood" (Mt 26:26, 28; Mk 14:22, 24; Lk 22:19, 20)—followed by the *epiklesis* ("invocation") calling down the Holy Spirit on the gifts.

The Real Presence

From the earliest days, the eucharistic elements were treated as the actual Body of Christ. The material character of the Eucharist—the reality of bread and wine, flesh and blood—was emphasized, with the transformation of bread and wine into Christ's Body and Blood paralleling the transformation of the individual Christian through divine grace. Like Paul before them, Ignatius, Irenaeus, Justin, and others referred to the Eucharist as "bread" but also proclaimed that in eating it Christians were fed with the very Body of Christ. No one in the early Church treated the eucharistic presence as merely a sign— their concept of symbol was of something that actually made present the thing symbolized.

At the end of the Eucharist, some of the consecrated hosts (a name for a sacrificial victim) were reserved for the sick, but some could also be given to the congregation, who took them to their homes and consumed them each day, before taking any other food or drink. Eucharistic elements that were left over might also be consumed by the clergy, buried, or even burned but were never simply discarded or eaten casually. At Rome, the unity of the Church was maintained in part by the bishop's offering the Eucharist in the morning, then sending deacons or others to bring the consecrated elements to people throughout the city, a gift that was also sometimes sent as a gesture of love and unity to the Church in other cities.

Sacrifice

The early theologians proclaimed the sacrificial nature of the Eucharist, particularly its efficacy when offered on behalf of the dead. Since Jesus Himself is the new Temple, the Church transformed the sacrificial worship of the Jews, with Jesus as the unbloody sacrifice who replaces the holocaust of animals, a sacrifice that is properly celebrated with solemn ceremonies, requiring meticulous attention to ritual practices.

For a long time, the Eucharist was celebrated only on Sunday, but by the later third century, it was being celebrated daily in Carthage (North Africa), a practice that gradually spread in the West but not in the East.

Daily Prayers

Even before the Divine Office was established as a public rite, prayers were enjoined to be said at the third, sixth, and ninth hours of the day, corresponding to the hours when Jesus hung on the Cross. Hippolytus urged washing the hands, breathing into them, and making the sign of the cross before praying.

Church Buildings

For a time, Christianity was distinguished from paganism partly by the fact that it did not require that worship be performed only at specially consecrated sites. The early Christians usually met in private homes, although occasionally a house was turned into a permanent place of worship, the oldest known such structure, at Dura-Europos (Syria), dating from the second century. But in time, church buildings came to be treated as sacred. By 300, at the height of persecution, there were forty churches at Rome, even though it was still permissible to worship wherever the faithful gathered. *Ecclesia* ("gathering"), the Greek equivalent of *church*, meant both the assembly of the faithful and the building where the assembly met.

Images

Some early Christians inherited the Jewish opposition to images, but in time the Church embraced them, recognizing beauty as a reflection of the Creator, art in the service of God being the natural corollary of the Incarnation. (The church at Dura-Europos had biblical scenes painted on its walls.) Christian images were not merely means of instruction but themselves possessed a sacred character worthy of veneration.

On tombs and elsewhere, Christians placed the symbol of the cross; the Greek letters *chi* and *ro* (the beginning of the word *Christ*); and the Greek letters *iota, eta, sigma* (*IHS*—the first letters of Jesus' name). Other symbols included the anchor for hope, because it saved those in peril of the sea; the ship as the bark of Peter that would bring Christians safely into the harbor of the Kingdom; the Good Shepherd; the sacrificial lamb; and the fish, whose Greek letters *iota, kappa, theta, upsilon, sigma—ikthus*—were a kind of code for "Jesus Christ Son of God Savior".

From Revelation came the symbols of the four Evangelists: the man for Matthew, who elaborated the human genealogy of Jesus; the ox for Luke, who began with Zechariah's sacrifice in the Temple; the lion for Mark, who began with John the Baptist in the wilderness; and the soaring eagle for John, whose writings elevated readers to the Eternal Word.

Before they developed their own styles, Christians used familiar Greek imagery, so that the earliest images of Jesus were of a beardless young man—the Good Shepherd—based on representations of the god Apollo and thus immediately recognizable as divine.

Theology

The Scriptures were universally accepted as divinely inspired, although there was some uncertainty as to the exact nature of that inspiration. Some people held that the Evangelists had been put into a kind of trance and that the Holy Spirit simply dictated through them, but this idea was eventually rejected in favor of the belief that the Spirit merely guided the authors and preserved them from error.

Levels of Exegesis

Theology ("the study of God") consisted primarily in the close reading of Scripture and the attempt to unlock its inner meaning. The literal truth was always affirmed, but it was considered less significant than other levels of meaning: *typological*, in which Old Testament events prefigure the coming of Christ; *allegorical*, in which biblical events are understood as referring to spiritual realities, such as the relation of the soul to God; and *anagogical*, which points toward the future.

Catechesis

The liturgy itself served as the chief means of educating the faithful, through lengthy readings from Scripture and even lengthier sermons (from the Latin *sermo*, meaning "word", in the sense of an authoritative verbal pronouncement).

Admission to the Church was by no means easy, in part because of a fear of spies who might betray the community to the authorities. The baptismal sponsor was originally a member of the Church who could vouch for the trustworthiness of the candidate or *catechumen* (one to be "instructed"). The catechumenate was ordinarily a three-year period of instruction and probation, with emphasis on Scripture and the ethical teachings of Christianity, in order to judge whether the candidates were worthy of baptism.

The Liturgy of the Catechumens was an adaptation of the worship of the synagogue, in which the earliest Christians continued to participate. The catechumens left before the reading of the Gospel, because they were not yet ready to hear the fullness of the Word. After their departure from the liturgy, they gathered to receive instruction that would prepare them to be baptized. The Lord's Prayer was said shortly before Communion, because it was not thought suitable that the catechumens should learn it until they had been properly instructed.

Baptism was conferred at Easter, when the new Christians participated in the death and Resurrection of Jesus, freeing them from sin and death and incorporating them into the life of Christ. Candidates for baptism were anointed with oil, a traditional Jewish rite. Given the extremely demanding preparation that catechumens had to undergo, most baptisms were of adults. There is evidence, however, of entire households being baptized, including children, and in the third century, Origen said this was an apostolic tradition, even though some theologians opposed it.

Baptism

Also during the third century, the rite of calling down the Holy Spirit on the baptized emerged as the separate rite of confirmation in the West, while in the East it remained part of the baptismal ceremony itself.

Confirmation

At first, there was little emphasis on the Church's power to reconcile sinners, since baptism itself took away sin and the primary emphasis was therefore on the faithful preservation of baptismal grace.

Penance

Celsus (d. ca. 200), who wrote the most sustained pagan polemic against Christianity, accused the Christians of promoting moral laxity through easy forgiveness, an issue that also troubled some Christians. In time, grave sins had to be confessed publicly, followed by a lengthy period of official penance during which the penitent could not participate in the Eucharist and his gifts and those of notorious sinners were refused.

Throughout the early centuries, there was debate over whether certain sins—murder, adultery, and apostasy—could be forgiven at all in this life, and some Christians denied that soldiers, civil servants, or teachers could even be baptized (the last because they instructed students in the pagan myths). But this was not the prevailing belief. Despite the Church's orientation toward peace, Christians did serve in the army, where the chief moral evil was thought to be the requirement of offering incense to the god-emperor, the refusal of which caused the soldier saints George, Alban, and Maximus to be martyred during the late third century.

Origen, whose father was a martyr, was an extreme ascetic, considered to be excessively rigorous in his moral teachings—according to legend he castrated himself because of Jesus' admonition "If your right eye causes you to sin, pluck it out" (Mt 5:29; see Mt 18:9). But paradoxically, he came to be regarded as a heretic in part because he believed that the eventual restoration of the fallen universe implied the possibility of universal salvation—even Satan might eventually repent.

Deadly Sins

Eight basic sins were commonly recognized, forerunners of the classic list of the seven "deadly sins" that kill grace in the soul—gluttony, luxury (love of pleasure), love of money (covetousness, envy), sadness, anger, *acedia*, vainglory, and pride. Sadness was perhaps akin to the modern phenomenon of depression and was considered sinful because it involved an element of despair, while *acedia* was a jaded world-weariness or boredom. Vainglory and pride were distinguished in that the former was mere egotistical boasting or desire for praise and recognition, while the latter was the far more serious sin of following one's own will rather than the will of God.

Church and Empire

The Church Grows

The Church was growing rapidly, even constituting a majority in some districts in the Near East and by 300 perhaps counting as many as forty thousand in Rome. Although she may have appealed primarily to the poor and outcast, there were also aristocratic converts, including some in the imperial household itself, possibly even the wife and daughter of the persecuting emperor Diocletian (284–305).

Pagan Hostility

The Jews, prior to their rebellion of 70, were treated by the Romans in a special way because they were so tenacious in their religious fidelity—not required to do anything that violated their faith, even to the point that Roman officials observed the prohibition against Gentiles entering the sacred precincts of the Temple. Christians were treated more harshly than Jews, especially after the destruction of the Temple and as the distinction between the old and new religions became apparent. (Jews sometimes encouraged and supported the persecution of Christians.)

Some pagan hostility to Christianity was mere popular gossip, stimulated by the fact that Christians were of necessity secretive, so that only garbled snatches of their beliefs were generally known. Thus they were accused of practicing secret vices, including cannibalism, presumably because of the Eucharist, although most educated Romans probably did not believe such stories.

The Conflict of Values

But in a sense persecution was almost inevitable. The Empire underwent a long crisis that was military and financial in nature but also moral—a loss of patriotism that made citizens unwilling to assume their traditional duties, a prosperity that rendered them indolent and hedonistic, and a series of despotic rulers who made citizenship meaningless. In the Greco-Roman world, citizenship—full participation in the life of society—was considered the highest duty.

Even though Christians obeyed the law, their otherworldliness was thought to hasten the decline. They formed their own society within the Empire, obedient to the state in a passive way (they prayed even for evil emperors) but detached from it. Jesus authorized the payment of taxes, and Christians pointed out that not only were criminals virtually unknown among them, but they also cared for their own poor rather than letting them become public charges.

The Christian teaching that sexual activity is permissible only within marriage, for the sake of procreation, was an implicit condemnation of the rampant hedonism of Roman life, something that Caesar Augustus (29 B.C.–A.D. 14) also tried unsuccessfully to curb. But Christianity went directly against law and custom in its complete prohibition of abortion, a prohibition found in the *Didache* ("teaching"), one of the earliest Christian writings. Not only did the Romans practice abortion, every father had the right to decide whether or not a newborn child should be allowed to live. The Church also departed from Roman law in certain other ways, as in allowing marriage between a free woman and a slave.

However, the Church came into her most serious and inevitable conflict with the state over the cult of emperor-worship, a practice that expanded over time and by the later third century was regarded by the Roman authorities as the necessary basis of imperial unity. Increasingly, the emperor was exalted as "Son of God", a title Christians considered appropriate only to Jesus.

Christ the King

To the degree that the Romans understood the Christian movement, they were alarmed by the implications of the exchange between Pilate and Jesus ("So you are a king?"; "You say that I am king" [Jn 18:37; see Lk 23:3]) and the unintended affirmation of the mocking inscription that Pilate placed above Jesus' head on the Cross: "INRI" (*Jesus Nazarenus Rex Judaeorum*—"Jesus the Nazarene, King of the Jews").

In no way did the Christians seek to establish a worldly kingdom, but in affirming that they were citizens of the Kingdom of Heaven ("Here we have no lasting city" [Heb 13:14]), and that ultimately they had no king but Jesus, they were withholding their ultimate loyalty from the Empire. In a number of ways, the Church proposed herself as a kind of substitute for the Empire. The word *evangelion* had been used for the emperors' public boasts of their achievements but was now appropriated for the Gospels, which were thereby proclaimed to be much better news than anything that emperors could announce.

From the Roman standpoint, the demands made on Christians were quite minimal—a little incense offered to the gods of the state. Christianity would have been readily accepted if Jesus had been regarded as simply one god among many, as the emperor Philip the Arab (244–249) was rumored to do in his private chapel. But to the Christians this was a violation of the First Commandment, in some ways the worst possible sin. As both Jews and Christians made clear, monotheism was "intolerant" by its very nature—in the Gloria, which was an ancient hymn, the repetition "you alone" was an explicit denial of all other pretended deities.

Civil Religion   The official religion of the Empire was still a civic religion in which the welfare of the state depended on the good will of the gods and failure to give them due honor might bring divine wrath. Military defeats, epidemics, and other misfortunes were thus sometimes blamed on the Christians' disrespect for the old gods, and, ironically, they were considered atheists because of that disrespect.

Martyrdom   *Martyr* is a Greek word for "witness", applied to those whose deaths were the ultimate witness to the truth they espoused. After the martyrs came the confessors—those who professed their faith openly but did not actually suffer death. Suffering and martyrdom became the highest Christian ideal, an integral part of Christian life from the beginning. To Ignatius, the Eucharist was intimately connected to martyrdom, planting in the believer the seeds of Christ's presence, which martyrdom brought to fulfillment, and in his letters to the seven churches, he forbade them to make any effort to spare him his fate, of which there is no direct record.

Martyrdom was another point of division between heretics and orthodox believers, in that many of the Gnostics rejected it and even ridiculed it, because of the significance it gave to the death of the body.

Local churches preserved detailed accounts of their martyrs in their liturgies, as the church at Rome did by invoking the early popes and the third-century martyrs Agatha, Lucy, Agnes, Cecilia, Anastasia, Lawrence, Cosmas and Damien, and others.

Martyrdom was even venerated to the point where some Christians had to be warned not to seek it, since the achievement of that ultimate crown was entirely a matter of God's will. When a group of Christians presented themselves to a Roman magistrate and demanded punishment, he remarked dryly that there were cliffs and rivers available to those who wished to commit suicide.

Martyrdom was inflicted in a variety of ways. Stephen was stoned to death, which was the Jewish penalty for blasphemy. Under Nero (54–68), Christians were coated with tar and set on fire in the amphitheatre to light the night games, and over the next two centuries, numerous Christians were sent into the arena to be torn apart by wild beasts, as Ignatius anticipated would happen to him.

Paul, as a Roman citizen, was honorably beheaded, while Peter was dishonorably crucified (upside down, according to tradition, because he did not consider himself worthy to die as his Lord had died). Some martyrs were mutilated, sent to the mines, and worked to death; others were buried alive, burned en masse, or strapped into iron chairs that were slowly heated until they roasted to death.

St. Perpetua was a North African woman put to death, along with her slave Felicity, around 200. Her unbelieving father begged her to recant for the sake of her infant son, but she insisted that she had a higher duty to God and lamented that her father, alone of her family, would not rejoice in her death. St. Lawrence (d. 258) was a Roman deacon who, when ordered to turn over the treasure of the Church to the authorities, showed them the poor instead and said, "This is our treasure." He reportedly joked, "Turn me over, I'm done on this side", as he was slowly roasted on a gridiron.

Those who did not die a martyr's death sought burial near those who had. Altars were erected over martyrs' tombs, and the Eucharist was sometimes celebrated in cemeteries or in underground catacombs, although those were not the regular sites of worship and were not ordinarily used as hiding places. Christians adapted the pagan custom of the *refrigerium* ("refreshment" or "coolness"), a ritual meal at the graves of the martyrs, not merely to commemorate the dead but to participate in the communion of saints—living and dead joined together in Christ. The custom of venerating relics began with the preservation of the bloody robes of the martyrs, which were treated with great reverence.

Persecution was not consistent. The first wave came under Nero in the year 67, when Peter and Paul were among those put to death at Rome, probably because the hated emperor needed scapegoats to blame for the great fire that destroyed a good part of the city and that rumor accused him of having started. Domitian (81–96), whom even pagans counted among the wicked, initiated a persecution that inspired the image of the "Great Beast" in Revelation—the Whore of Babylon that symbolized for Christians an empire that had become the sworn enemy of Christ.

Persecution

Trajan (98–117), one of the five "good emperors" of the era, laid down a common-sense policy: provincial administrators were not to seek Christians out nor pay attention to irresponsible accusations but were to act only on credible charges, examine the accused, and persuade them to recant their beliefs.

Some Christians hoped for sympathy from the philosopher-emperor Marcus Aurelius (161–180), but he despised them for not fully supporting the Empire and ordered a persecution that was particularly severe in Gaul (modern France). Paradoxically, his debauched and sadistic son Commodus (186–192) proved to be more tolerant. Alexander Severus (222–235) was somewhat friendly to the Christians, but his successor Maximin (235–236) was cruel. Decius (249–251) initiated the first general persecution.

By far the greatest persecution began in 303 under Diocletian, almost at the end of his reign, nothing less than an attempt to exterminate the Church altogether, a campaign that probably did not stem from personal hatred of Christianity but from his effort to rekindle the old religious loyalties. He was reported to have turned against the Christians after learning that several of them had made the sign of the cross during an official pagan ritual, thereby causing it to fail.

Diocletian

The Seed of Christians

Thousands were martyred under Diocletian, and, besides official persecution, Christians were also often assaulted by hostile mobs. But the persecutors found themselves up against a unique phenomenon: a people who were not intimidated by torture and death but actually seemed to grow stronger, thereby giving rise to the famous boast, "The blood of martyrs is the seed of Christians", a claim that could have both a supernatural explanation—divine grace is poured out on a faithful people—and a more natural one—many pagans were inspired by the courage and joyful fidelity of the martyrs and therefore began to take their claims seriously.

Apostasy

But Christians were not uniformly brave. Some public officials were simply following orders and suggested to the accused how they might evade punishment through a fairly minimal conformity that fell short of outright denial of the faith, such as refraining from formal Christian worship or turning the sacred books over to the authorities for inspection, in order to look for evidence of vice or treason.

This provoked a major crisis in the Church, because some priests acceded to this demand, considering it a less serious offense than actually conforming to the state religion. Many Christians apostatized completely, and among the clergy there were numerous instances of various kinds of surrender. According to legend, Pope St. Marcellinus (296–304) first made accommodations to Diocletian, then repented and was martyred.

The church at Carthage especially exalted martyrdom, and its rigor gave rise to deep and lasting divisions within the North African church. Tertullian, its greatest luminary, taught that apostates—those who abandoned the faith in time of persecution—could not be readmitted even if repentant. He ended by joining the Montanists, who condemned what they considered the laxness of Church discipline, which they blamed for the disappearance of the charisms.

But St. Cyprian (d. 258), bishop of Carthage and one of the most important Western theologians, went into hiding during a persecution, continuing to govern his flock through a kind of secret network, an action that he justified on the grounds that, like Paul at Ephesus, his continued activity was needed for the good of the Church, affirming that even heretics and apostates could be reconciled if they were repentant.

Rigorism

Some Christians held that those to whom God gave the charism of suffering possessed ultimate authority, but Cyprian upheld the office of the bishop. His own seeming evasion of martyrdom caused him to lose some authority, and he reminded his flock that, holy as the martyrs and confessors were, they did not replace the apostolic hierarchy. (Cyprian was eventually beheaded.)

Schism occurred in Egypt under a bishop named Meletius (d. ca. 324) and elsewhere in North Africa under a bishop named Donatus

(d. ca. 355), both of whom held that those who lapsed under persecution could never be received back into the Church. Both schisms endured for centuries.

While generally less rigorous than Carthage, the church at Rome also split over the issue, with Pope Cornelius taking a more lenient view and being opposed by the anti-pope Novatian. Pope St. Stephen I (254–257) quarreled with Cyprian over the question, with Cyprian denying that baptism could be validly administered by someone in schism. In his dispute with Cyprian, Stephen became the first pope known to have cited the text "Thou art Peter" to establish his authority, but Cyprian did not bend. However, after his death, the Donatists proved so divisive that the church at Carthage adopted the Roman position on baptism.

Diocletian's reign marked the last successful effort to maintain the Empire intact. Realistically, he divided the imperial power, setting up a "tetrarchy" of four men, each of whom had responsibility for part of the Empire. When he retired in 305—the first emperor in well over a century who did not die a violent death—civil war inevitably broke out among those appointed to share authority. The ultimate victor was a general named Constantine, who would soon effect the most far-reaching religious revolution in the history of the world.

3   The Triumph of the Cross

Pagan Culture

A Spiritual Crisis

The conversion of the emperor Constantine (305–337) was sudden and in some ways mysterious, but it did not occur entirely out of the blue. Perhaps unrecognized even by most Christians, for three centuries, certain elements in Roman culture were helping to prepare for the triumph of the new faith.

From at least the time of Augustus, the mood of the Roman world had been one of spiritual restlessness and searching, verging at times on despair. Augustus was partially successful in reviving the old religion, but the spiritual crisis persisted.

For Romans, fulfillment was to be achieved by being a good citizen, but citizenship had little meaning under even the best of authoritarian rulers, while under tyrants like Nero, and amidst the ubiquitous violence and instability of the military emperors of the third century, life could be a nightmare.

The citizen's basic religious duty—participating in the required rituals of sacrifice—was easily, even mechanically, discharged. This simple religion had nothing to say about the meaning of life except that men were under the power of inscrutable Fate, which left people free to seek for meaning in any way they could.

Pessimism

Some looked for it in philosophy or in what were called the mystery cults—Near Eastern religions that promised to unlock the hidden secrets of the universe but whose inner teachings and practices were revealed only to their devotees. These religions were profoundly pessimistic, often teaching that the world was ruled by demons and offering deliverance from the endless cycle of meaningless repetition.

Christianity, on the other hand, taught that time is not revolving but moves in a purposeful direction, so that what begins in time culminates in eternity. The coming of Christ, a unique and unrepeatable event, destroyed the ancient view of history as cyclical.

Philosophy

The weaknesses of Roman religion were the weaknesses of Greek religion as well, weaknesses that had helped stimulate philosophical speculation—a search for meaning through the use of human reason rather than in the myths. Philosophy was considered a search not merely for intellectual understanding but for a way of life, for true happiness. There was a rarified kind of monotheism found, for example, in the philosopher Epictetus (d. ca. 100) and the last of the "good emperors", Marcus Aurelius.

As they were with most aspects of high culture, the Romans were not highly creative philosophically, and they readily acknowledged their debts to the Greeks. Completing what Alexander the Great (356–323 B.C.) had begun, the Roman Empire spread Greek civilization wherever it conquered.

Stoicism (named for a kind of courtyard where philosophers walked and talked) was perhaps the most widely followed of the philosophies, a high-minded doctrine teaching that the soul is a breath of the transcendent *Logos* and that the key to happiness is freedom from desire and the calm acceptance of Fate (hence the popular concept of a Stoic as someone who endures pain uncomplainingly). Stoicism taught an elevated moral code, but it was cold and viewed history as a circular process that the individual could not overcome. Many Stoics, like Marcus Aurelius, emphasized a detached devotion to duty and despised Christians as overly passionate and fanatical.

Stoicism

Epicureanism (named after its founder) taught that the events of life are random, and it aimed to liberate people from the fear of death by celebrating the pleasures of life. While it could degenerate into the crude hedonism of "Eat, drink, and be merry", at its best it urged sensual moderation and extolled the higher pleasures like beauty and love.

Epicureanism

Some serious-minded pagans, after being disillusioned with every philosophical school, found their way into the Church. Justin Martyr was a philosopher who opened a school at Rome. To Justin, Jesus was the ultimate philosopher, and he believed that all truth is one, hence all truth is the truth of God. He was the first Christian apologist, and he aimed, if possible, to persuade Marcus Aurelius himself.

Christian Wisdom

Unlike the various philosophies, Christianity did not appeal only to intellectuals or to those who had the leisure to contemplate life's mysteries but, like all great religions, could be made intelligible and personally relevant to a wide variety of people. Its credibility lay partly in the fact that it appealed to a recent historical person, Jesus Christ, rather than to remote mythical beings. Also, the Christian Scriptures contained a rich and coherent account of its beliefs, in contrast to the diffuse myths of the pagans.

The Christian emphasis on human free will, albeit impaired by sin, was a liberating alternative to belief in Fate. Christianity recognized the ultimate emptiness of a purely earthly existence, offered hope of eternal life, and laid down an inspiring ethic based on love and the practical discipline necessary to achieve it. In contrast to the mystery religions, Christianity did not promise the deliverance of the soul from the body but the salvation of the whole man. Suffering was not abolished but sublimated to higher ends.

The Conversion of Constantine

Although their numbers were not large, a significant number of educated, aristocratic Romans had been attracted to Christianity well before the time of Constantine. Thus his sudden conversion may not have seemed bizarre to at least some cultured people.

In Hoc Signo Vinces

The exact circumstances of Constantine's conversion are uncertain. His mother, St. Helena (d. 330), was already a Christian, but an account written some years later reported that on the eve of the crucial battle of the Milvian Bridge in 311, Constantine saw a vision of the cross or of a *chi-ro*, with the words, "In this sign you shall conquer." As a result, he had the *chi-ro* put on the standards and armor of his soldiers, but along with the symbolism of *Sol Invictus*—the Unconquered Sun—which had become a dominant Roman cult. Victorious over his enemies, Constantine became the undisputed ruler of Rome and attributed his victory to the God of the Christians.

An Imperfect Conversion

Constantine underwent an equivocal kind of conversion, at first failing to understand the most elementary teaching of Christianity—that there is only one God—so that for a time Jesus continued to share official status with the Sun. His approach was entirely in keeping with the polytheism that prevailed throughout the ancient world, allowing the gods of other peoples to be incorporated into the Roman *pantheon* ("all the gods"), their power added to that of the Roman gods. Only gradually did Constantine grasp the true nature of the faith he had imperfectly embraced, and in some ways, he remained unconverted, baptized only on his deathbed and then by a bishop of heretical beliefs.

At its simplest, conversion to Christianity was the recognition of a new power in the world, far superior to the old. Through her sacraments and her symbolism, the Church made unseen spiritual beings visible. But the old powers remained real for some time, and, as on the shields of Constantine's soldiers, both Christian and pagan symbols appeared side by side in public places. Some people practiced both Christian and pagan rituals, praying to both the one God and the many.

Emperor under God

Ironically, Diocletian's fanatical efforts to wipe out the Christian movement may have contributed to its triumph, by demonstrating its profound strength, which made it suitable to serve as a new spiritual basis for the Empire. Christianity had proven to be one of the few living forces in Roman culture. With the conversion of Constantine, the authority of the emperor was affirmed as divinely ordained, a comprehensive order whose task was to maintain justice in the world.

Toleration and More

The stages of the religious revolution succeeded one another very rapidly. Complete toleration was granted to Christianity by the Edict of Milan of 313, and the emperor soon returned all confiscated Church property, exempted the Church from taxes and the clergy from military service, and appointed bishops to be civil judges in their local communities.

A Moral Revolution

By his decrees, Constantine also sought to bring about a kind of moral revolution: establishing Sunday as the day of rest, in commemoration of Christ's Resurrection; abolishing crucifixion; forbidding the branding of criminals on the face, since the face is the image of the soul; depriving slave-owners of the power of life and death over their slaves. Usury (excessive interest on loans) was condemned, there was a widespread freeing of slaves, and charitable works were extolled.

He expressed horror at the bloodiness of pagan sacrifices, in contrast to the unbloody sacrifice of Christ, but the bloody games in the circuses were not suppressed for another century, until a monk ran into the amphitheatre in protest and was torn to pieces by the beasts.

Christianity revitalized the Roman family as the basis of all social life by enjoining fidelity on both husband and wife—holding up Paul's ideal relationship between them as like that of Christ and His Church—and including even slaves as part of the family. Because sexual relationships were permitted only within marriage, slaves were now allowed to marry. Constantine enacted a series of severe laws concerning sexual conduct, including death by torture for any man who seduced a virgin. The new order curbed patriarchal authority in one important respect—no longer did fathers have power of life and death over their newborn children.

Divorce had been easy among the Romans, but in Constantine's decrees, it was allowed to women only if their husbands committed murder or practiced magic and to men only if their wives were unfaithful, sold their bodies, or induced abortions. For the most part, the Church recognized the legitimacy of a second marriage after divorce, if the couple did suitable lengthy penance. The "Pauline privilege" allowed a Christian to separate from a pagan spouse ("Do not be mismated with unbelievers" [2 Cor 6:14]), but often a Christian wife was the instrument of her husband's conversion.

The True Cross

Though a moral reformer, Constantine was also ruthless and cruel, even to the point of having his wife and his son murdered because of a suspicion that they were plotting against him. The murders so disturbed his mother, Helena that, as expiation of her son's sins, she set off on her famous quest for the true Cross, which led eventually to the unearthing of three crosses near Jerusalem that were venerated as the execution instruments of Jesus and the two thieves.

The Church Triumphant

Mass Conversion

The emperor's official endorsement of Christianity naturally stimulated many conversions to the Church, so that before long a majority of people were at least nominally Christian. Motives for conversion were undoubtedly mixed: there were those who had wanted to convert but had been afraid; those who took the imperial endorsement as a guarantee of truth; those who, sincerely if superficially, merely adopted the prevailing beliefs of their culture; and those who calculated that in worldly terms it was not a bad thing to profess the same religion as the emperor.

A New Rome

Just as Diocletian had realistically divided the governing power of an empire too large to be ruled effectively by one man, so Constantine realistically reached a hitherto unthinkable conclusion: the capital of the Empire of Rome did not have to be Rome. In every respect—density of population, wealth, social and cultural sophistication—the Near East was superior to the West, and, if the emperor could only adequately rule half the Empire, it was the Eastern half that merited his efforts. Thus in 330, Constantine transferred his capital to the old city of Byzantium, renamed as Constantinople (modern Istanbul), at the exact point where Asia and Europe come together.

It was a decision that would have momentous consequences for the Church. Although at certain periods there continued to be an emperor in the West, subject to the emperor at Constantinople, the transfer of the capital gave the popes an independence from imperial control not enjoyed by the Eastern patriarchs. Having ceased to be the political capital of the Empire, Rome's primary significance was now as the capital of the Church, the epithet "Eternal City" acquiring primarily a religious rather than a political meaning. Rome's center was now the Vatican hill, believed to be the site of Peter's martyrdom and burial.

Julian the Apostate

Paganism still survived. One of Constantine's successors, his nephew Julian (361–363), was called the Apostate because he renounced the Christian faith that he felt had been forced on him by some of the very people who had murdered members of his family during the interminable dynastic conflicts. During his brief reign, there was some localized persecution of Christians, although it was not official policy.

Julian tried to reinstate the old cults in their favored positions, requiring Christians to pay for the building of pagan temples. Showing a subtle understanding of Christian beliefs, he ordered the rebuilding of the Temple at Jerusalem to refute the claim that Judaism had been replaced by Christianity. But the builders kept encountering problems that stopped the project, something that Christians took as a divine sign. The Julian interlude cast light on the precarious nature of some conversions: the bishop of Troy in Asia Minor, for instance, once showed the emperor a collection of idols he had saved and said that he had become a Christian only in order to keep the old religion alive in secret.

Julian's efforts were reversed after his death in battle, when, according to a contemporary legend, he cried out, "O pale Galilean, you have conquered!" Pagan temples survived for a time, although they were sometimes destroyed by mobs who thought they were the haunts of devils. Most Christians probably considered paganism tolerable so long as they did not pollute themselves by contact with pagan rites.

The Western emperor Gratian (359–383) renounced the title of high priest, and in 391, the emperor Theodosius I (379–395) forbade all pagan worship and closed the temples, although pagans continued to hold public office until the time of Justinian I (527–565), who closed the school of philosophy at Athens, the final sign of Christianity's victory.

The End of Paganism

But pagan loyalties survived sufficiently for some people to charge that the misfortunes of the Empire were caused by its abandonment of the gods. St. Augustine (d. 430), bishop of Hippo (North Africa), wrote his seminal work *The City of God* primarily to refute the claim that the sack of Rome by barbarians had that cause. On the contrary, he asserted, the cause was Rome's own innumerable sins.

Some Church leaders, notably Ambrose, condemned forced conversions. But—momentous for the later history of the Church—Augustine, after first rejecting the practice, reluctantly accepted it in the case of the warlike Donatists, who were an acute pastoral problem in his own diocese. His justification was Jesus' parable of the man who gave a banquet and whose final command to his servants, with regard to those they would meet in the streets, was "compel [them] to come in" (Lk 14:23). Augustine pointed out that, even if the first generation of converts was coerced, their descendants might embrace the faith with sincerity.

Religious Coercion

After Constantine's conversion, it was sometimes the practice to baptize large numbers of people who had not undergone the earlier kind of rigorous catechumenate. This too had its justification in Augustine, whose *City of God* demonstrated that the Church was not an elite community of saints but a place where wheat and tares grow side by side until the final harvest. Beyond practical expediency, the practice of mass conversions was justified by belief in the objective power of the sacraments, independent of subjective dispositions, so that those who received baptism were cleansed of their sins and received an infusion of grace.

Wheat and Tares

From the Stoics, Christians got the concept of natural law, an idea that allowed a particularly fruitful interplay between pagan philosophy and divine revelation. Paul had spoken of the law of God written on

Natural Law

the hearts of men, and the philosophical idea of natural law seemed to be a recognition of that reality. Natural law transcended civil law and was the basis on which all human law was to be judged. Beyond natural virtues, there were "theological" virtues pertaining to God—faith, hope, and charity—that are not attainable by human effort and could only be achieved through divine grace.

The Christian State

Although the Gospel promised freedom, even in pagan times the Church never questioned the coercive authority of the state, something that was rendered necessary by the Fall. Because sinful men could not be relied upon to do good and avoid evil voluntarily, they needed the state to suppress bad behavior through the threat of punishment.

At the same time, Christianity also offered membership in a universal community that transcended the Empire itself. The Church was a universal state that would ensure peace and justice. She represented the common unity of mankind that was greater than the unity of the Empire.

In the East, attitudes to the state went much further than mere acceptance. Bishop Eusebius of Caesarea (d. 339), the first Christian historian, declared that the Empire itself was the Kingdom of Christ and Constantine the new David. But Constantine's conversion turned out to be a mixed blessing, in that he could not prescind from his imperial authority in dealing with religious matters of which he had an incomplete understanding. Thus, from the beginning, the power of the emperors threatened the Church's integrity.

Constantine approached the great theological controversies of his reign (see Chapter Four below) primarily as conflicts that threatened the peace of the Empire, a concern that was not unwarranted, since the great religious disputes provoked murders, riots, and other violent conflicts. Constantine regularly intervened to settle disputes in accord with the political situation at a given moment. Each ecclesiastical faction had its partisans at court, vying with each other for imperial support.

Whereas the East saw church and state as one, the West tended to see them as two distinct societies. In contrast to Eusebius and other Eastern bishops, St. Hilary of Poitiers (d. ca. 368) and St. Ambrose affirmed both loyalty to imperial authority and a vigorously independent Church.

The Episcopal Office

Ambrose was prefect of the City of Milan—the imperial representative—when the bishop died. Fearing strife between two rival factions, Ambrose presided over the election of a new bishop, and during the proceedings someone (reportedly a child) shouted out his name, and he was speedily acclaimed as bishop. As yet a catechumen, he first received baptism, then was ordained deacon, priest, and bishop on successive days.

Ambrose and his people saw his acclamation as a manifestation of the divine will, but, in worldly terms, it was also a sign of changing times. However important the prefect of the city might be, he was less important, in the eyes of eternity and perhaps in the eyes of history as well, than the bishop, who represented an institution that was increasingly important, even as the authority of the Empire waxed and waned in the West. A few years later, also in Milan, Augustine renounced the study of rhetoric, a skill that might have brought him political preferment, in order to become a monk and eventually, under circumstances similar to those of Ambrose, a bishop.

An increasing number of bishops were taken from the upper ranks of society, and when imperial authority collapsed in the West in the fifth century, it was they who emerged as the natural leaders of society, fulfilling the role of the old Roman senators. When necessary, they were the only force capable of withstanding the imperial bureaucracy. Conscientious bishops believed that their own souls were imperiled by the sins of their people, since at the Last Judgment they would be held accountable for their flocks.

Care of the Needy

Almsgiving (from the Latin word for "kindness") was a way of atoning for one's sins. The bishops functioned as spokesmen for the poor, and the Church became the organizer of charities and the principal agency for the distribution of poor relief, keeping stores for the needy and in times of emergency even selling liturgical vessels for that purpose (at Antioch the Church reportedly supported three thousand widows and orphans). Julian the Apostate goaded his fellow pagans to imitate the Christians in their generosity, while the great patriarch of Constantinople, St. John Chrysostom ("the Golden-Tongued", d. 407), excoriated the people of his city, especially the rich, for their injustices and their neglect of the needy. (He antagonized people by his bluntness and was soon deposed.)

The Ecumenical Councils

There had always been meetings of Church leaders to settle disputed questions, such as the "Council of Jerusalem" that addressed the issue of the necessity of Jewish practices for Christian converts. But beginning in the fourth century, there was a long series of councils by which definitive ecclesiastical judgments were rendered. The *ecumenical* council (from the Greek word for "the world") was a gathering of the bishops of the entire Church, while provincial councils or synods represented particular regions and were binding only on those regions, unless adopted elsewhere. The participants ("Fathers") of such councils were primarily the bishops as successors of the Apostles, who were believed to be guided by the Holy Spirit. Little distinction was made between bishops and theologians, because most of the great theologians of the age were bishops, who often engaged in theological speculation in order to address pressing questions that had arisen in their jurisdictions.

Dioceses   Diocletian divided his vast Empire into local administrative units called "dioceses", which also became the name of the territory ruled by a bishop. The authority of bishops in their dioceses was carefully defined. The Council of Sardica (modern Sofia) in 341 forbade bishops from being "translated" (changed to another place) from one see ("seat") to another, in keeping with the tradition whereby bishops were considered married to their sees. (After the great theologian St. Gregory Nazianzen [d. 389] had been made patriarch of Constantinople, he was forced to resign because of that rule.) Sardica also admonished bishops to respect the boundaries of other bishops' sees, forbade them to be absent from their sees for more than three successive Sundays, and set up a process for investigating bishops accused of misconduct, with final appeal to the see of Rome.

Also in the fourth century, episcopal sees were gathered into "provinces", each of which was under a "metropolitan" (later called an archbishop), who exercised general oversight over the sees of his province. The need for such a system was dictated mainly by the large number of sees—about five hundred in North Africa alone—required by the fact that the bishop was expected to have close contact with his people, who gathered around him for the Eucharist.

Parishes   The early Christians were an urban people, if for no other reason than that cities provided the best opportunity for evangelization. The *pagani* were literally the rural people—those who had not yet heard the Gospel and still worshipped the old gods. But with the end of persecution, and with sudden numerical growth, "stational churches"— what were later called parishes—were established in the larger cities. In Rome, the pope went each Sunday in solemn procession to one of these churches, where he celebrated the Eucharist surrounded by all his clergy. Gradually, each church was placed under the jurisdiction of a priest, which then made large sees possible. As the Church spread into the countryside, the bishop no longer presided solely over an urban church but gained responsibility for a wide geographical territory.

Church Finance   Beginning with Constantine, churches were often endowed by having the income from particular properties assigned to their use, income that was sometimes confiscated from pagan temples. Bishops essentially controlled that wealth, and gradually the clergy came to be paid regular salaries. The accumulation of property was considered yet another result of the Fall, something that God allowed so that the rich could help the needy.

The Jewish custom of tithing—giving a tenth of one's income to the Temple—was not generally practiced by Christians. Bishops reminded their flocks that all money given to the Church had to be voluntary. (Chrysostom uttered a modern-sounding complaint in one of his sermons, expressing exasperation that, as often as he reminded his hearers of the need to increase their donations, it did no good.)

The episcopal office now became desirable in worldly terms, something that had not been true under persecution, giving rise to complaints about luxury-loving prelates who flaunted their wealth and power. In the later fourth century, George of Cappadocia (d. 361), patriarch of Alexandria, who had been a dishonest merchant before being elected bishop, was murdered after he systematically exploited the episcopal office for financial gain.

Converts came from all social classes (there was even a professional wrestler called "The Creeper"), and care was taken to distinguish between social classes on earth, which were legitimate, and the Kingdom of Heaven, where they did not exist. Without condemning wealth or social status, the Church was egalitarian: in the Kingdom relationships between rich and poor were almost inverted, as saintly beggars could be superior to princes, and slaves might be more exalted than their masters. One bishop forbade his deacons to make room for aristocratic latecomers to the Eucharist but commanded them to find seats for the poor.

Social Classes

There was no Christian nuptial ceremony in the early centuries, so that in some ways marriage remained a matter of civil law, although by 400, couples who had been married according to civil law would subsequently go before a priest for a blessing. The essence of marriage was consent, something that in effect made the formal act of betrothal already a marriage.

Marriage and Celibacy

The importance of renunciation was upheld even at the cost of sacrificing lesser goods like marriage. Orthodox Christianity looked on marriage very favorably, but the Church judged that severe asceticism (a term derived from the training undergone by athletes) was also necessary, in order to overcome the hedonism of the pagan society.

Based on the example of Jesus and the words of Paul, the Church valued virginity more highly than marriage, while rejecting the Gnostic error of condemning human sexuality altogether. Virgins were a recognized category of Christians, and they had great prestige for having foregone marriage for the sake of the Kingdom. Jesus' exhortation to His followers to leave their families in order to follow Him was taken quite seriously—it was believed that the Apostles had done precisely that, leaving their wives and children to be cared for by their extended families. (Thus the Gospel mentions Peter's mother-in-law but not his wife.)

The procreation of children was considered the principal purpose of marriage, along with the Pauline concession of marriage as a remedy for lust (some theologians even held that sexual intercourse was at least a venial sin even for married couples, because it surrendered to lust). Widows were discouraged from remarrying, on the grounds that—past the childbearing age—they were motivated by the desire for sexual pleasure.

Clerical Celibacy

Cultus among the Romans designated the duties and rituals centered on the worship of a particular god, and Christians adapted cultic elements of worship from both the Romans and the Jews, including the idea of the priest as someone set aside to officiate at the rituals. There was a Jewish tradition that only a *celibate* (the Latin word for the "unmarried") could mediate between God and man, so that Jewish priests separated from their wives during the times when they were exercising their office. Although St. Paul extolled celibacy, most clergy in the early centuries were probably married. But virginity, which was considered total dedication of the individual to God, gave unmarried women a prestige that often exceeded that of priests, making it seem appropriate that priests too should be celibates.

Quite early, neither priests nor deacons were permitted to marry after ordination and may have been required to abstain from sexual relations with their wives. (Gregory Nazianzen succeeded his father as a bishop, but the younger Gregory may have been born before his father was ordained.) In the East, the requirement of perpetual marital continence was in time limited to bishops, who were eventually prohibited from marrying at all. Priests and deacons could still not marry after ordination and were required to be continent on days when they celebrated the Eucharist. (As with other moral imperatives, the law of celibacy was often violated, and contending factions in the Church accused each other of licentiousness.)

A monk named Jovinianus (d. 405) was condemned by the Church in both Rome and Milan for arguing against celibacy, fasting, and other kinds of asceticism. He provoked a characteristically fierce polemic from St. Jerome (d. 420),[1] who as a priest at Rome had served as secretary to a pope. But Jerome harmed his argument by appearing to condemn marriage altogether, and this and other instances of his extreme asceticism caused him to leave Rome to become a hermit in Bethlehem.

Women in the Church

Following Jewish custom, men and women were probably separated in orthodox Christian assemblies, and the only evidence that women may have exercised priestly responsibilities in the early Church are the occasional denunciations of Gnostic practice. A few tomb inscriptions commemorate a *presbytera* or an *episkopa*—feminine forms of the words for "priest" and "bishop"—but they probably honored the wives of

---

[1] Jerome is an intriguing conundrum in the attempt to understand sanctity, since he was given to extreme vituperativeness in his numerous quarrels, including quarrels with St. Augustine, an illustration of the maxim that it is possible to be damned through imitating the vices of saints.

male clergy, who were sometimes given titles indicating their husbands' ranks.

Constantine turned over some pagan temples to be used as churches and at his own expense built great new churches at Rome and Jerusalem, a large one at Rome that came to be dedicated to St. John the Baptist and was the official seat of the pope. (The name *Lateran* derived from the family that had once owned the site.) In Constantinople, he built two major churches dedicated to Christ—the Hagia Eirene ("Holy Peace") and the Hagia Sophia ("Holy Wisdom"), the second of which, rebuilt by Justinian, still survives as a museum.

Sometimes, with obvious symbolic intent, Christian houses of worship were constructed over old temples, such as San Clemente in Rome, which was built over a temple of the Persian god Mithra, and another Roman church called Santa Maria Sopra Minerva ("St. Mary above Minerva"). The great circular temple of the Pantheon became Santa Maria Rotonda ("round"). Like human converts, churches—both new and adapted—were solemnly anointed with oil as part of their consecration to God.

The pagan temples were primarily houses of the gods, not places of worship, so that the Christians, instead of adapting the temple style to their own use, most commonly used the style of the *basilica* (from the Greek word for "ruler")—halls where public business was transacted. Basilicas were symmetrical, oblong buildings with shallow peaked roofs, supported in the interior by double rows of columns. As churches, they were often elaborately decorated, usually with mosaics, especially of Christ reigning from on high in glory, presiding over the "business" of His people. In Roman basilicas, the official chair (*cathedra*) of the magistrate was placed at one end, in a semi-circular alcove called the apse, where clients approached him to ask for justice or mercy. Now the altar was placed in the apse, with the bishop's *cathedra* behind it. (Among the titles adopted by the bishop of Rome was "Supreme Pontiff", a name taken directly from the pagan Roman priesthood. Pontiffs were literally "bridge-builders", although the exact meaning of the title is uncertain.)

Churches often had separate baptistries, partly for privacy, because adult converts had to remove their clothes and descend naked into the pool before presenting themselves to the assembly in the white robes of purity. Baptistries and pools were often octagonal, since the risen Christ was Himself called the eighth day of Creation.

It was considered appropriate that every kind of riches be devoted to the worship of Christ, who had triumphed and who ruled over the universe. Chalices, candlesticks, and other liturgical vessels were fashioned of gold and precious gems, as was the cross itself, even though it had been a shameful instrument of death. Churches often had elaborate mosaic floors, their walls hung with rich tapestries. As the Eucharist came to be celebrated in permanent houses of worship, the communion table was replaced by a marble altar that was appropriate to the offering of sacrifice, an altar that also symbolized the sacrificial victim, Christ Himself, so that the priest kissed the altar during the Eucharist.

The Liturgy

The official worship of the Church came to be called the *liturgy*, the Greco-Roman name for a donation made to a temple to subsidize the official rites. The Christian liturgy was a coming together of the "horizontal" synagogue and the "vertical" Temple—both instruction and community and the expectation of the heavenly Kingdom. The Church's new freedom led to the increasingly solemn and elaborate celebrations—as always, more so in the East than in the West.

Entrance Rite

Liturgies began with processions in which all ranks of the clergy participated, accompanied by singing or chanting, and over time, some of those chants and litanies, such as the *Kyrie* ("Lord, have mercy"), were incorporated into the liturgy itself. Incense, which in ancient times was a sign of honor to important people, was used both to honor God and to symbolize prayers rising to Heaven, just as the incensing of the faithful by a deacon symbolized God's blessing descending on them. Candles were used not merely for material light but as symbols of the Light of Christ brought into the world. The ceremonial kiss, or greeting of peace, was a pagan custom that was enacted in the Christian liturgy when the procession reached the sanctuary, where the clergy greeted one another and kissed the altar and the Gospel book. The laying on of hands was the ancient symbol of blessing and continued to be used in the rite of ordination. However, the sign of the cross gradually replaced it as the distinctive Christian form of blessing.

Prayers

"In the name of the Father. . ." was an ancient Christian blessing that became the formal preliminary to all public prayers. The Latin word *oratio*, which was a formal address to the gods, to public officials, or to the citizens, was now used to mean a liturgical prayer that followed a stereotyped rhetorical form—a set formula of praise, followed by a succinct summary of the petitioners' needs, concluding with a dignified request to be heard in the name of Jesus. The song of the angels on Christmas was originally a part of Morning Prayer but also came to be chanted in processions and was in time expanded into the Gloria, the ultimate hymn of praise, an exuberant acknowledgment that the worship of God is the most fundamental human duty.

Readings

As in the synagogue, psalms were sung before each of the three scriptural readings, which consisted of one from the Old Testament, the second usually from Paul, the third from one of the Gospels. At one time, the readings each Sunday began at the point where they had ended the previous week, so that the entire Scripture would eventually be read. But gradually, particular passages came to be assigned for particular days. Because the Gospel was the Word of Christ Himself, its proclamation was accompanied by particularly solemn ceremonies: the presentation of the book by the deacon to the celebrant, the celebrant's blessing of the deacon, the procession to the place of proclamation, the incensing of the book, the kissing of the book by the deacon, and the solemn reminder, "This is the Gospel of the Lord." Priests eventually took over the primary responsibility for preaching, although deacons continued to have that authority.

Ordinarily, the celebrant did not face the congregation. Instead, both he and the congregation faced eastward, toward the rising sun, the symbol of the Resurrection and the Second Coming of Christ. (The dead too were often buried facing east, in preparation for their own resurrection.) Kneeling, which was often the posture of adoration in the Old Testament, was introduced at certain points in the liturgy, although standing probably remained the ordinary posture of the faithful. Liturgical dancing was found only in heretical sects and was explicitly disapproved by Ambrose, Augustine, and others.

Ad Orientem

The priest washed his hands at the Offertory not only because they were soiled by the gifts he handled but because the ritual washing of the hands was an ancient preparation for prayer. The *Sanctus*—"Holy, holy, holy", from the words of Isaiah (Is 6:3)—was also an early part of the liturgy, recognizing that it was celebrated in union with the heavenly hosts.

Offertory

Although Jesus had used unleavened bread at the Last Supper, as required for the Passover, both leavened and unleavened bread were used in the Eucharist in the early centuries. Leavened bread—brought by the laity from home—was sometimes baked into symbolic shapes like crowns or wreaths and stamped with sacred symbols. Leavened bread gave off crumbs, which priests and people were commanded to treat with the utmost reverence.

Bread

From the beginning, the priest's recitation of the words of Jesus— "This is my body ... this is my blood" (Mt 26:26, 28; Mk 14:22, 24; Lk 22:19, 20)—was the crucial moment of the Eucharist. In the earliest Eucharists, the complete account of the Last Supper was read, at the conclusion of which the transformed bread and wine were shown to the people as the Body and Blood of Christ. In the East, an *epiklesis*, in which the priest called upon the Holy Spirit to bring about this transformation, was considered essential to the sacrifice, but in the West, this was not a particular prayer but a general petition that the offering be found worthy.

Consecration

Communion   As congregations grew in size, it may have been customary for the laity to remain in their places as deacons brought Communion to them. Eventually, the laity began to approach the altar, although not too near—altar rails were introduced as early as the fourth century. Communion was probably received in cupped, newly washed hands, with the left hand made into a "throne" for the right hand that received the sacred host with the priest's solemn announcement, "The Body of Christ".

Dismissal   An element of imperial court ceremonial was incorporated into the liturgy in the command, "*Ite missa est*" (roughly, "go, you are sent"), the traditional words dismissing people from attendance at court. From this, by the year 400, the Eucharist in most Western countries was called by some variation of *missa*.

Vestments   For the first few centuries, the celebrant probably did not wear distinctive vestments, and when he began to do so they were seen as St. Paul's "armor of God", which the priest put on in order to signify that he was not acting in a purely human capacity. They were based on ordinary Roman garments: the alb ("white"), which was the basic male robe; the cincture ("binding"), which was the belt that held the alb closed and signified the wearer's readiness to face the world; the amice, which was a kind of hood; the maniple, which was a towel either carried or tied to the wrist and used to purify the sacred vessels; and the chasuble ("little house"), which was the cloak that covered all the rest. In particular, the scarf called the stole became the essential priestly garment, to be worn for all celebrations of the divine mysteries.

    The deacon wore a coat called a dalmatic, with his stole over one shoulder, both so arranged as to keep his right arm free for the various tasks he performed during the liturgy. Beginning in the fourth century, bishops carried shepherd's staffs or crooks as symbols of their office.

Baptism   Baptism could be administered by pouring as well as by immersion. The ceremony obviously signified washing, but immersion also symbolized death and resurrection—the convert descended into the depths, then rose out of them. The power of baptism to remit sins was so great that rigorists held that sins committed after baptism were possibly unforgivable, and this motivated some people—Constantine but also future saints such as Basil, Gregory Nazianzen, Ambrose, Augustine, and Chrysostom—to delay receiving it. On the other hand, the formulation of the doctrine of Original Sin in the later fourth century made baptism, especially of infants, imperative, lest the person die unshriven and damned. (Prior to Constantine, infant baptism also protected against infanticide, by making the child a member of the family, formally accepted by his father.)

Divine Office

The continuity between Judaism and Christianity was manifest in the incorporation of the Psalms—understood as referring in various ways to Christ—at the heart of Christian prayer, especially in the daily prayers that came to be called the Liturgy of the Hours or the Divine Office ("duty"). The Psalms were often chanted, and, as in the Old Testament, singing was considered an especially appropriate way of worshipping, so that various hymns were also composed and introduced into worship. As bishop of Milan, Ambrose was in a sense the founder of Christian hymnology. Musical instruments were sometimes used in pagan worship to ward off demons, so that at first they were forbidden in Christian rites. But they were gradually accepted, to the point where Augustine wrote a treatise on the theological significance of music in which he made the famous remark that "He who sings, prays twice."

Liturgical Languages

The major bishoprics—Rome, Antioch, Alexandria, Carthage—possessed liturgical authority that was followed by less prestigious sees. Greek, Latin, and Syro-Aramaic were the important liturgical languages, but various regional Rites developed, such as the Gallic, the Coptic in Egypt, the Chaldean in Mesopotamia, the Mozarabic in Spain, and the Syro-Malabar in India.

   The Church at Rome remained predominantly Greek into the third century, when Latin was adopted because it was the spoken language of the people, leaving the Kyrie as the last remnant of the old Greek liturgy. In contrast to some other Rites, Rome's liturgy was characterized by a kind of sober restraint, seldom employing poetry or imaginative imagery and reciting the prayers in a kind of monotone that eschewed dramatic effect.

Confession

Public confession was increasingly common, and grave sins required heavy penances, such as fasting, wearing rough garments, not bathing or shaving, and abstaining from marital relations. Some theologians thought that the gravest sins—murder, apostasy, adultery, abortion—could be forgiven only once in a lifetime. The period of probation after confession was long (a quarter of a century in extreme cases), during which the individual was excommunicated ("out of communion"), until finally readmitted in a special ritual that might be implemented in stages over several years: first standing outside the church during the Eucharist, then remaining in the vestibule, finally rejoining the worshipping community but still excluded from the sacrament. Penance was often accompanied by dramatic expressions of remorse, some of it spontaneous—spiritual teachers urged penitents to weep real tears—some of it ritualized.

Weddings

The first Christian wedding liturgies made their appearance during the fourth and fifth centuries, their relative lateness perhaps reflecting the belief that a true marriage was brought about not by the action of the priest but by the mutual vows of the couple.

Patron Saints

The Roman institution of the *patron*—a kind of father who bestowed favors on his loyal followers—was now applied to the saints, most of whom were invoked for special purposes: the Armenian bishop-martyr Blaise (d. ca. 315) against diseases of the throat, for example; the Roman virgin-martyr Cecilia (d. ca. 300) by musicians; the Italian bishop Erasmus (d. ca. 300), who had been disemboweled, for intestinal disorders. The saints were regarded as friends of God who served as intercessors for sinful mankind, images of Christ who served as new models of sanctity after the age of the martyrs had ended. Unsophisticated people might unwittingly treat the saints like a pantheon of pagan gods, each with a specific identity and power, but the learned also embraced their cults with the correct attitude.

Pilgrimage

The new freedom that the Church enjoyed in the fourth century made possible the practice that would be the summit of popular piety for many centuries—the pilgrimage. The sites of the martyrs' graves were carefully remembered, and with the end of persecution, increasingly elaborate shrines were built over them, establishing a close connection between the martyrs and the local community, with a special emphasis on the saint's healing powers. The pilgrimage meant coming into contact with the holy person's relics and asking for special blessings.

Originally, all Christians were seen as pilgrims, perpetual wanderers who were not at home in the world. The new pilgrimage (Helena's quest of the true Cross was an early example) was not a formality. It was very long (several years) and fraught with dangers of various kinds, including bandits and diseases, so that pilgrims often died on the way, something that was considered a kind of blessing, because the pilgrimage was a symbol of the soul's journey toward Paradise and a pilgrim who died on route was practically assured of Heaven.

The chief pilgrimage places in the early centuries were Jerusalem and Rome, the latter in order to visit the tombs of Peter and Paul. Although the new city of Constantinople claimed to have received the faith from St. Andrew the Apostle, Peter's brother, it had no martyrs, hence no relics, which required its bishops to make strenuous efforts to obtain some.

Church and Culture

Besides the political problems created by the sudden conversion of the Empire, there were even more profound cultural issues, in that Christians lived in the shadow of the very rich and ancient Hellenistic civilization that had achieved great things in every area of life—philosophy, poetry, art, science. Just as the hostile Empire provided the political and physical framework within which the Church could spread, the seemingly alien Hellenistic civilization provided the cultural framework. With their triumph, Christians in effect became the custodians of that civilization. Difficult though it would have been to achieve, they might have tried to destroy Hellenistic civilization as irredeemably pagan, and, had they done so, the later history of the world would have been unimaginably different.

Christian art developed beyond the simple copying of familiar images. *Art* Jesus was no longer portrayed as a youth but in a much more vigorous and commanding way, with the dark hair and beard that were an accurate representation of a Jew of the first century. Despite warnings about the dangers of idolatry, Christians began to make religious statues and other sculpted figures. The symbol of the cross had been used sparingly in the early centuries and was almost always shown empty, to announce Christ's triumph over death. The devotion was greatly stimulated by Helena's discovery in the Holy Land, and crosses with the image of the suffering Jesus became increasingly common. Certain images could be recognized as depicting saints because the subjects had around their heads the luminous circle called the *nimbus* ("cloud") or the halo (a circular platter).

If in a sense pagan philosophies like Stoicism were neutral, pagan art *Literature* and literature were not, because they were often based on the myths of the gods and they distracted people from the Gospel. St. Augustine lamented that he had shed more tears over Virgil's *Aeneid* than over his own sins, and, conversely, Julian forbade Christians to teach literature, because of its link to the old gods. The myths, though, could be ridiculed as fictions embodying absurd stories of all-too-human gods—a fact that could be seen as lessening their value, but that also lessened their danger. After some uncertainty, most educated Christians concluded that Christians could read poetry for its beauty and wisdom without compromising their faith. There developed also a substantial body of Christian poetry and hymnody.

The early Church sanctified space. The church building was the place *Architecture* where the heavens opened and were glimpsed by man, a sense that was even stronger in the East than in the West. (Chrysostom taught that "fear and shuddering" were the appropriate emotions during worship.) The building was centered, as the Temple had been, on the marble altar of sacrifice, which now signified Christ, often surmounted by an imposing canopy and surrounded by paintings on the walls. Burial took place both in the underground catacombs and in cemeteries. Since Christians had to be buried in consecrated ground, cemeteries were usually next to churches, plots of land from which the unbaptized, the excommunicated, and suicides were excluded.

The Church also sanctified time, adapting the Roman calendar but *The Calendar* abolishing all civil holidays, which to the Romans were also religious feasts. The entire calendar now became a cycle of feasts: beginning originally only the Sabbath, with later the addition of a few of the major feasts of Jesus, then commemorations of the martyrs, and finally feasts assigned to other saints as well. (The Church commemorated martyrs on the days of their deaths, which were considered to be the days of their births into Heaven.)

But despite some efforts to change their names, the Roman religion survived permanently in the West in the months of the year named after the gods Janus, Mars, Maia, and Juno; the feast of purification (Februarius); and Julius Caesar and Caesar Augustus; and in the days of the week dedicated to the sun, the moon, and the god Saturn, followed by the numbering of the seventh through tenth months.

Advent

The pre-Christmas season of Advent ("coming") was observed in Gaul as early as the fourth century, with the gathering darkness of December appropriately conveying the darkness of the world before the coming of the Savior. The feast of the Nativity of the Lord (later called "Christ's Mass" in England) coincided closely with the winter solstice (December 21) and the pagan feast of *Sol Invictus*.

Christmas

Whether or not the Christian feast was celebrated at that time for that reason, it was regarded as highly appropriate to displace *Sol Invictus* and to welcome Christ, the Light of the world, at the beginning of winter. Converts were told that in honoring the sun they had unwittingly been honoring their Savior.

Epiphany

In the East, the feast of the Epiphany (January 6)—the first manifestation of Jesus to the Gentiles—was equally as important as Christmas and was eventually introduced into the West.

Annunciation

If Jesus was born on December 25, He had to have been conceived on March 25, which in time became the feast of the Annunciation, the day of the Incarnation. Because the day on which Christ came into the world began the new dispensation, March 25 was officially observed as the start of the new year, although local customs varied in this regard.

Lent

The season of Lent (in northern Europe named after a pagan feast of returning spring) was first observed in the fourth century, its discipline permitting but one meal a day and no wine or meat at all. The church at Jerusalem began the customs of the Palm Sunday procession and the Good Friday veneration of the cross, both of which spread to the West.

Easter

The feast of Christ's Resurrection (later called "Easter" in the North, after a pagan feast) was, except for the Sabbath, the first Christian feast to be celebrated, earlier than the Nativity. The Easter Vigil was a ritual watch at Jesus' tomb, beginning in darkness, then relighting the lamps and recapitulating the history of salvation through lengthy Scripture readings. In the early centuries, there were sharp disputes over Easter's date, with some local churches using the spring equinox as their guide and others the Jewish Passover; either way it coincided with the earth's coming to life after the dead time of winter.

Christmas, Easter, and other feasts continued to have pagan under- *Popular Piety*
tones, in accordance with the Church's decision to adapt pagan civi-
lization rather than to suppress it. The summer solstice—the day on which the sun reached its zenith (June 21)—eventually became the feast of St. John the Baptist, because he had said of Jesus, "He must increase, but I must decrease" (Jn 3:30). To a degree, the pagan feasts survived underground, along with their familiar customs, such as the abundance of lights at the two solstices.

This strategy was not without its perils. Over the centuries, pagan and Christian elements often mingled indiscriminately in popular piety, so that unsophisticated people might fail to understand their true Christian meaning. But in the early centuries, the Church approached pagan civilization almost as though it were an estate sale—the soul had gone out of it, so that the newcomers were free to take from it whatever things they found useful and to incorporate them into an entirely different network of belief. The Church was confident that she could absorb pagan civilization rather than be absorbed by it.

When the Church emerged from persecution to become a favored **Monasticism**
institution, and believers no longer risked suffering and death, the standards of membership were inevitably lowered, which for some Christians meant that a more demanding faith was now required.

There were pagan hermits, but Greco-Roman civilization had little *Desert Hermits*
respect for them, because men were supposed to live primarily as cit-
izens. (The Greek word *idiot* meant someone who shirked the duties of public life.) Similarly, the Qumran community that separated itself from the world in a radical way was a dramatic departure from Jewish tradition.

Around the year 270, in the Egyptian desert, a man named Paul became the first known Christian hermit, and in the next century, St. Anthony of the Desert (d. 356) became the model Christian monk (from the Greek *monos*, meaning "one"), living first in a hut on the edge of a village, then gradually moving farther and farther away.

As Jesus Himself had done in the desert, the monk in his solitude tested *The Hermit's Life*
himself against devils, who possessed the power both to assault and torment him physically and to subject him to every kind of temptation.

Anthony devoted himself to prayer, fasting, and all-night vigils, to conquer not only the demands of the body but also the subtler temptations of the soul as well, to offer himself to God in a continuous, lifelong martyrdom. He first experienced a prolonged sense of abandonment in his retreat but finally received a vision of Christ, an alternation of dryness and illumination that became characteristic of much of later Catholic spirituality. After achieving peace, Anthony began to give spiritual counsel to others and even went to Alexandria to oppose heresy, dying there at age 105.

Flight from the World

At first, monasticism was not considered a special way of life but merely the renunciation of the world that all Christians were called upon to make. But as it did become a distinctive way of life, the terms *monk*, *hermit*, *anchorite* (originally someone who fled in order to avoid paying taxes), and *cenobite* (from the word for "cell") were used interchangeably. Most monks were male, but there were some women. They did not live in literal deserts but in marginal places—abandoned forts, even old tombs—where they had access to minimal food and water. Famously, St. Simeon Stylites (d. 459) lived for thirty-seven years on top of a pillar (*stylos*) in Syria, receiving life's necessities by letting down a basket on a long rope.

Monks had a number of motives for fleeing the world: imitation of Jesus' own forty days in the desert; the most extreme kind of ascetical self-discipline, with no regular shelter or supply of food; a life devoted entirely to prayer. Ultimately, the monk, alone in the desert, had to confront his own soul and in the process to confront Satan, as Jesus had confronted him. Monks were revered as men of great spiritual power, able to effect cures and, having wrestled with Satan and overcome him, able to protect others from his onslaughts. They were thought to possess extraordinary powers of exorcism. Monasticism spread rapidly, so that around the year 400 there were said to be seven thousand monks in the Near East.

Monks as Martyrs

Monasticism was considered a continuation of the tradition of martyrdom, the reaffirmation of the contradiction between Church and world, making the significance of the monks' lives both negative and positive—fleeing from the corruption of civilization in order to seek a greater treasure. (Some monks, however, manifested attitudes of misogyny and a hatred of marriage that bordered on the Gnostic condemnation of the flesh.)

A Higher Charity

While the desert monks had seemingly turned their backs on the human race, they justified themselves by what they regarded as the highest kind of charity—praying for their fellow men and serving as living reminders that Christians have no lasting city. Love of God and neighbor were not considered separate obligations. Because of sin, neither could be achieved except through divine grace, which a life of self-denial helped make possible.

Ambrose distinguished two acceptable ways of living the Christian life—the monastic calling and an ordinary life of virtue in the world, including especially fasting and almsgiving, that was sufficient for salvation. But the monastic writers tended to allow no such distinction and often implied that their manner of life was the only authentic one, to which every Christian must sooner or later come. While recognizing that few people would actually choose their lifestyle, they taught that the renunciation of all worldly satisfactions was the only road to Heaven, albeit it might be achieved in stages.

Those considered the wisest and holiest were called Desert Fathers or Mothers. The abbot or abbess (from the Aramaic word *abba*—"loving father"—by which Jesus addressed His own Father) was the novice monk's experienced guide. They left a body of writings that were avidly read by others, so that the monk's life served as a kind of benchmark by which Christians in the world measured the degree of their own discipleship of Christ. *Abbots*

There were, however, problems with the culture of the desert monks. Some were former criminals or had otherwise led wicked lives, and they retained certain rough, even violent, edges. Having rejected the world, monks were held in some suspicion by the authorities of both church and state, who saw them almost as anarchists but who could not ignore their great spiritual authority. *Disorders*

The paradox of monasticism manifested itself quite early, in that, as they became famous for their holiness, monks like Simeon Stylites attracted crowds of people to hear their teachings, to be healed, or to settle disputes. Sometimes monks left the desert and returned to the cities, where they acted like Old Testament prophets, castigating the people for their sins, taking sides in theological disputes, even participating in riots.

The monastic life was a charism, a lay vocation that was sometimes in tension with the sacramental Church. Monks were dependent for the sacraments on nearby village priests and sometimes went for years without partaking of the Eucharist. Some allowed their ascetical practices to degenerate into a kind of athletic competition over who could fast the longest or sleep on the hardest ground, adopting practices that seemed both ostentatious and pointlessly difficult. Some were driven insane by the solitary life.

The Egyptian monk Pachomius (d. 346) was the first to gather male hermits into communities. Basic to his rule were the two practices that were considered essential to all subsequent monastic life: common prayer at appropriate hours of the day and some kind of labor, following the examples of both Martha and Mary. *Pachomius*

Monks were to be cenobites, living near one another in separate cells but sharing prayer and daily tasks in common, eating two meals a day (never meat or cooked food), and fasting completely on Wednesday and Friday. Some of the early monasteries were in effect large towns, and Pachomius placed great emphasis on the necessity of labor and economic self-sufficiency, assigning tasks to monks according to their skills.

Pachomius' sister Mary drew female hermits into communities, and when Jerome went to Palestine, he was followed by a group of devout noble women whom he had guided in Rome, who formed monastic communities of their own, based partly on Pachomius' *Rule*, something that to a great extent superseded the traditional category of virgins.

Wandering Holy Men

Although Pachomius and others did much to regularize monastic life, in the East there continued to be a significant number of freewheeling "holy men" who had no official status but were greatly venerated by the people. The extremes of Eastern monasticism were repugnant to the West: Augustine scorned those he called "long-haired frauds" who exploited popular credulity.

Obedience

Crucial to the subsequent development of monasticism, the radical element in Pachomius' *Rule* was the obligation of complete obedience to the abbot, who became the superior of the community. Pachomius' *Rule* was of almost military strictness, according to which monks were to work out their salvation not by self-chosen practices but by submitting to a regimen, the disciplining of the will that was itself the most meritorious form of asceticism. The more extreme kinds of bodily asceticism were even forbidden or discouraged, as manifestations of self-will.

Thus, paradoxically, the word *monk* ceased to mean "one" or "alone" and began to designate someone who lived in a community, although hermits never completely disappeared from the Church, especially in the East.

Basil

St. Basil (d. 379) was a monk of Asia Minor—later a bishop—whose *Rule* became the basis for most Eastern monasticism. He condemned the hermit life as self-centered and extolled small monastic communities in which monks could live as brothers and where the Divine Office and manual work took up virtually the whole day.

As it developed, monasticism in both East and West demonstrated the ability to combine asceticism with engagement in social and cultural activity. Basil preferred that monasteries be near towns, so that the monks could serve the needs of the people and be associated with schools, orphanages, and guesthouses, a custom that would have a profound effect on later civilization.

Eastern monasteries also became centers of learning. Gregory Nazian- *Gregory Nazianzen*
zen called monasticism the "true philosophic life", because only there
did the individual achieve genuine *gnosis*. Developing an idea of Origen, both Gregory Nazianzen and St. Gregory of Nyssa (Basil's
brother, d. ca. 395) saw the soul's inner unity with Christ as the purpose of prayer and hence of the monastic life. The soul is made to
know God and desires to return to Him, but its way is impeded by sin
and the seductiveness of worldly images.

Nazianzen described interior spiritual states but warned that God is
found not in such experiences but in transcending all experiences.
The ultimate test of authentic spirituality is the love between the soul
and God, which overflows into love of mankind.

Monasticism broadened the concept of sainthood. Previously, only mar- *A New Sanctity*
tyrs were commemorated in the liturgy, and they alone were called
saints. But at the end of the fourth century, that title was conferred on
the Gallic monk and bishop Martin of Tours (d. 397), a former Roman
soldier, who had introduced monasticism into the West before serving
as a bishop. Thus began the tradition by which non-martyrs were venerated for their heroic virtue, classified as either confessors or virgins.

St. John Cassian (d. ca. 433), after living the monastic life in the East, *Cassian*
founded a monastery at Marseilles according to Pachomius' *Rule*. Ascetical practices were of no value unless they led to love of God and
neighbor, Cassian declared, and he warned against excess—extreme
fasting was as bad as gluttony. His *Rule*, which was followed by all
successful later Western monastic enterprises, was moderate and balanced, acknowledging the hermit's life as the highest monastic vocation but considering it suitable only for a few and only after years of
living as a cenobite.

A few years later, Augustine founded a monastery in North Africa *Augustine of Hippo*
and wrote a rule based not on the desert but on the primitive church,
providing that monks should also be priests. As happened to Augustine himself, monks were increasingly elected bishops, because of their
reputations for holiness, their celibacy, and other ascetic practices deemed
appropriate qualities for the episcopal office. Augustine himself wept
at having to leave his monastery, and some monks even fled to avoid
election as bishops.

4 Holy Wisdom

Ignatius of Antioch and Irenaeus of Lyon were among the first of a group of men who dominated the intellectual life of the Church for four centuries and who received a title that designated their entire era: the Fathers of the Church, so called because they lived in the formative age of Christianity, when seminal understandings were forged about many aspects of belief and practice. The Fathers' writings about the Christian faith would profoundly influence the entire subsequent history of the Church.

The Fathers were exceptional both in learning and in holiness and were close to the time of Christ, all of which were thought to give them a superior understanding of the faith. Many of the Fathers were also bishops, and their speculations arose directly out of their responsibility of guiding their flocks through treacherous waters. They wrote not in a spirit of abstract speculation but with the sense that the welfare of souls was at stake.

Orthodoxy

Theology, however, was itself fraught with the possibility of error, and Christianity, much more than any other religion in the history of the world, placed doctrinal orthodoxy close to the center of its life, a sometimes excessive concern for doctrinal clarity that was motivated by both the Greek passion for philosophical certitude and the religious passion to be faithful to the Gospel. Sins could be forgiven, but false doctrine could not be, because it poisoned the soul. In order to enter the Kingdom, it was necessary to do the Father's will, but no one could know the Father's will unless he understood the Church's teachings.

Thus the Church over time formulated a whole series of *dogmas*—things required to be believed—that were set forth in explicit creeds. The creeds were originally affirmations of faith by candidates for baptism, hence were cast in the singular "I believe" rather than the communal "We believe", and the singular form was retained after they came to be recited during the Eucharist. The creedal texts varied rather widely, although they always included an affirmation of faith in the Father, the Son, and the Holy Spirit and the life, death, and Resurrection of Jesus. What was called the Apostles' Creed developed over time out of other early affirmations. What was "believed" was found in the liturgy, what was "taught" was found in sermons and treatises, and what was "confessed" was found in creeds and official dogmas.

Already in the writings of Paul and in Acts there existed what would later be called the *Magisterium* ("master" or "teacher")—a locus of authority capable of pronouncing definitively on matters of faith. While such pronouncements were always based on theological arguments, the authority of the Magisterium ultimately did not depend on the persuasiveness of such arguments, since heretics by definition remain unpersuaded. Heresy could be either false innovation or a stubborn clinging to true but inadequate old formulas. Originally, heresy was not distinguished from schism ("cutting"), but eventually schism was defined as a division in the Church that did not involve doctrine (for example, two rival claimants for episcopal office).

Magisterium

Jerome, in his hermitage at Bethlehem, devoted himself to translating the whole Bible into Latin, a translation called the *Vulgate* ("people's book") because at the time Latin was the spoken language of most people in the West.

The Vulgate

Prior to Jerome, Christians outside Palestine mainly relied for their knowledge of the Old Testament on the Septuagint, which had been written in Greek. Jerome, however, translated directly from the Hebrew.

Use of the Bible was facilitated by the invention of the book—pages of manageable size bound together so as to allow them to be turned over one by one, replacing long unwieldy scrolls that had to be laboriously unrolled. Gradually, the Greek word for a book (*biblia*) came to have only one meaning, the Bible.

Some books (Esther, Maccabees) appeared in the Septuagint but not in other compilations, and among local churches there were even some differences as to the books of the New Testament. St. Athanasius, the patriarch of Alexandria (d. 373), was the first to list definitively the twenty-seven books of the New Testament, and a few years later, the Council of Rome officially established the canon ("rule") of the Scripture, decreeing precisely which books belonged there.

Judaism was to a great extent hostile to Hellenistic civilization, and, had Christianity remained entirely within the Hebrew cultural ambience, its theology would have developed in very different ways. In particular, it would probably have been content to affirm merely that "Jesus is Lord", without inquiring too closely into the meaning of that affirmation. But Christianity went beyond its Jewish roots and spread wherever Hellenistic civilization was influential.

Speculative Theology

Had the majority of Jews not rejected the Gospel, it might not have been taken to the Gentiles. As it was, Greek, not Hebrew or Aramaic, was the first common language of the Church, the language of the

New Testament. One of the Church's greatest achievements—one of the great creative achievements in the history of the world—was to bring about a synthesis between Christianity and classical civilization in the highly sophisticated theology of the second through fifth centuries.

Christians realized quite early that the Evangelists and Apostles did not provide a detailed exposition of every aspect of their faith. Rather, their writings were an embryo or seed, containing the whole of divine revelation but subject to gradual unfolding, analogous to human life from conception to old age. Insofar as they were able, believers were required not to accept the teachings of their faith passively but to explore them ever more deeply. Thus, with the tools of Greek philosophy, Christian theology became philosophical.

Philosophy

The Church's momentous decision to seek harmony with Hellenistic culture involved an almost passionate embrace of Greek philosophical ideas. This decision, which had deep and lasting results, was motivated by the recognition that Greek philosophy represented reason's highest achievement, requiring that every attempt to understand the world must begin there. Although Irenaeus, against the Gnostics, warned against improper speculation about the inner nature of God, the Church assumed that man is intended to know God, that questions that arise from the Gospel are meant to be answered insofar as humanly possible. The assumption was a validation of that thirst for knowledge that was characteristic of the Greek mind.

But the embrace of philosophy could not be uncritical. On the contrary, philosophical sophistication helped make Christians aware of its pitfalls. Pagan philosophy not only offered profound insights into Christian beliefs, but served as an antidote to itself, enabling theologians to avoid falsifications of those beliefs that might arise precisely from philosophy. Christianity employed reason to illuminate divine mysteries but controlled those speculations by recourse to the revealed word in Scripture, a way of theologizing that became endemic in the Church.

Philosophy provided the means to explore religious dogmas in sophisticated ways, but such sophistication required embarking on uncharted territory where the possibility of error was great, employing terms like *substance*, *being*, and *nature* that were not found in Scripture but were nonetheless thought to illuminate divine truth.

The Idea of God

Greek terminology helped Christian theologians describe the nature of God. The Old Testament spoke of God in ways that seemed to say that He was subject to emotion and capable of changing His mind. To the Greek philosophers, however, truth had to be immutable, so the Fathers insisted that God must be immutable and absolute, without limit or change, since change implies imperfection. The Fathers backed up the concept by also citing the voice that spoke to Moses from the burning bush—"I am Who am" (Ex 3:14, NAB) to show that God simply exists, without qualification, a rational conclusion confirmed by a biblical text whose full meaning might otherwise not be understood.

Justin also used Greek expressions to describe God. He declared that God must be everlasting, ineffable (His reality cannot be adequately expressed), nameless, changeless, impassible (He cannot be affected from outside Himself), and without origin—the Creator of all that is. Any other kind of being would be imperfect, hence could not be God. All of these Greek concepts corresponded with the Creator God of the Scriptures.

Justin

In the next century, Origen, also influenced by Neo-Platonism, asserted that God must be immaterial, because materiality too implies corruption and change. But the same Greek idea of perfection made it difficult for Origen to call God infinite, because that concept implies immobility, which would prevent Him from acting. Similarly, he found the concept of God's omnipotence perplexing, because it seemed to make Him responsible for evil. Origen upheld the orthodox belief that God created the world out of nothing, but he found that concept also difficult to understand and modified it by speculating that the universe is in an eternal process of always being created.

Origen

That the Church ultimately formulated the dogma that Jesus is both fully God and fully man should not obscure the difficulties the early Christians had in comprehending how this could be. The early heresies roughly divided between those that slighted His divinity and those that slighted His humanity. In the Scriptures, Jesus is a man, especially in that He suffers and dies, yet He also has divine power over demons, illness, and the forces of nature. He is at the center of the Gospel, where He both makes continued references to His Father and promises the Spirit who is to come. But what is the relationship between the three? To these most basic questions, the Gospel itself provided no explicit answer.

Christology

At the heart of the early theological controversies was John's designation of Jesus as the *Logos*. Christianity was made intellectually accessible to Neo-Platonists through the claim that the *Logos*—the order and reason behind the universe—is nothing less than Christ the Divine Word, who existed from all eternity, an idea also present in Paul.

The Logos

Ignatius of Antioch emphasized the unity of Christ in His twofold divine and human nature—spirit incarnated in flesh—and Irenaeus also affirmed the unity of the God-man, the *Logos* entering fully into human life in order to redeem mankind. God is not a remote being but makes Himself accessible to His creatures, even sharing their flesh.

Even though he was hostile to pagan thought in general, Tertullian also engaged in ambitious speculation. He argued that in Christ the divine and human substances remain distinct and, although the *Logos* was born of a human being, it was not incarnated as flesh. The antipope Novatian taught that Jesus' only element of humanity was the flesh itself, not a human soul or mind. Tertullian coined the Latin word *Trinity* ("three in one") and employed the nonphilosophical term *person* to designate each of the members of the Trinity. (At the time, *person* designated a mask of a type actors wore to present themselves to the public, but in applying it to the Trinity, Tertullian began a process by which it was eventually changed into its exact opposite— the individual's true inner self.)

Rival Christologies

Alexandria and Antioch were the respective centers of two rival Christologies. Following Origen, the Alexandrian school tended toward a highly spiritualized understanding of Scripture, while the Antiochians took a more literal and historical approach. The theology of Antioch tended also to dominate the patriarchal see of Constantinople, so that the conflict, although primarily theological, carried immense ecclesiastical implications. Constantinople had status as a patriarchate only because it was the capital of the Empire, and in the view of many, especially at Alexandria, it did not deserve to rank with the more ancient sees.

St. Clement, the patriarch of Alexandria (d. ca. 217), founded the theological tradition of his see city, holding that the *Logos* "entered into" or "attached itself" to the flesh as Christ's soul, making Christ free of all human passion.

Origen was a student of Clement and held that all souls exist from eternity, with one such soul destined for Jesus. Unlike other souls, Jesus' soul was completely subject to the *Logos*, so that His humanity was neither substantial nor permanent and after the Resurrection He ceased to be human. But Origen also seemed to subordinate the Son and the Holy Spirit to the Father, thereby making Christ less than fully God and setting in motion a series of controversies that would keep the Church in turmoil for two centuries. Pope St. Dionysius (259–268) condemned what he considered the excesses of Alexandrian theology, and Origen died in exile, amidst doubts concerning his orthodoxy.

Arianism

The christological controversy came to a head in the early fourth century through the teachings of Arius (d. 336), a priest of Alexandria and possibly a disciple of Origen, who gave his name to what became the most persistent and divisive heresy in the history of the Church. Arius wanted to preserve the idea of God as wholly transcendent, hence as indivisible, hence as unable to impart His substance to any other being. The *Logos* did not exist from eternity but was created by God out of nothing, before time began. The Son is a perfect creature, but a creature nonetheless, without direct knowledge of God and called "divine" only as a kind of courtesy. (Arians sometimes referred to

Jesus as an angel, at a time when the angelic nature had not yet been defined.) The *Logos* created the Holy Spirit, a formula that again made the three seem unequal.

Alexander, the patriarch of Alexandria (d. 328), condemned Arius as a heretic, but it was Alexander's successor, St. Athanasius, who pursued the issue to its farthest point, accusing Arius of polytheism and exiling him from Alexandria. For Athanasius, the *Logos* did not merely "enter into" a human person, as Arius held, but actually became man, continuing to exercise sovereign authority over the universe. Athanasius noted that the Church baptized in the name of Jesus and offered prayers to Him and that, if Jesus were not God, He could not have redeemed the human race.

In his exile, Arius won substantial support, including Eusebius of Nicomedia (d. 342), the patriarch of Constantinople (not the historian Eusebius), and when Constantine also endorsed Arius' ideas, there was an uproar that led the emperor in 325 to call the Council of Nicaea (Asia Minor) to settle the issue. After an intense struggle, the Council condemned Arius, declaring the Son to be "consubstantial" with the Father, that is, sharing the same substance. The issue finally turned on the Greek letter *iota*—the Son is *homoousios* ("the same" as the Father), not *homoiousios* ("like" the Father).[1]

Some time after Nicaea, a new creed was formulated to summarize orthodox beliefs. As against the Gnostics, the Nicene Creed affirmed that there is one God who is "Creator of heaven and earth and of all things visible and invisible". Against the Arians, the Creed stated that Jesus was "of one substance with the Father, by whom all things were made", and against the Docetists (below) that He actually "suffered, died, and was buried".

The Nicene Creed

But the decrees of Nicaea by no means ended the controversies, partly because of the actions of successive emperors. After the Council, the Arians appealed to Constantine, and over the next few decades, there followed a dizzying series of moves aimed at nullifying the results of Nicaea. Athanasius was exiled from his see five times, each time allowed to return, only to be exiled again as political alliances shifted.

When Constantine was dying in 336, he was baptized by the dubiously orthodox Eusebius of Nicomedia. Constantius II (337–361), Constantine's son and successor, remained favorable to the Arians, who repudiated the authority of the see of Rome and continued the fight. Ironically, Julian the Apostate tended to favor the orthodox party, because he judged the Arians to be dominant and wanted to weaken the Church as much as possible.

Imperial Intervention

[1] Although based on this episode, the maxim "It doesn't make an *iota*'s difference" reverses its significance. That one letter made all the difference.

At one point, Constantius summoned a council at Arles in Gaul that deposed Athanasius, a judgment in which the legates of Pope Liberius (352–366) acquiesced. Athanasius was driven out of Alexandria, and, when Liberius repudiated the judgment of Arles, the Pope was himself seized by the imperial troops and brought to the East, where he acquiesced in an ambiguous theological formula. But he once more repented his surrender, and the next emperor, Julian II, reversed the decision of Arles, although Arianism remained dominant in some places. (Liberius was the first pope not to be venerated as a saint.)

The emperor Valens (364–379) also supported the Arians, and the First Council of Constantinople (381), presided over by Meletius (d. 381), a bishop of Antioch whom Pope St. Damasus I (366–384) refused to recognize, seemed to uphold Arian ideas. But the condemnation of Arianism by the emperor Theodosius I in 388 was the final effective blow against a remarkably tenacious movement.

Docetism

But the slow vanquishing of Arianism only settled one side of the christological controversy—whether Jesus was fully divine. In part, precisely because of her strong affirmations of His divinity, the Church then found herself wracked with conflict over the question of His humanity. Antioch and Alexandria continued to represent alternative Christologies, now centering on the nature of Jesus, with the former positing both human and divine natures, united but distinct, the latter a total union of the two in which the human nature was absorbed by the divine.

Apollinarius (d. ca. 380), bishop of Laodicea (Asia Minor), was a disciple of Athanasius who was condemned by Pope Damasus and several councils and went into schism, claiming that Jesus has only one nature and that His flesh was already glorified during his earthly life. The term *Docetism* (from the Latin "to seem") was first used to describe the Gnostics and later applied to a Christology that in effect claimed that Jesus' human nature was an appearance only, even an illusion. (Some claimed that He was not actually crucified but slipped away, leaving Simon of Cyrene to suffer death on the cross.)

The Cappadocian Fathers

The mantle of theological orthodoxy now fell on Basil of Caesarea, his brother Gregory of Nyssa, and Gregory Nazianzen, who collectively became known as the Cappadocian Fathers, from the district of Asia Minor where they originated. (Basil and Gregory of Nyssa had been schoolmates of Julian the Apostate.) The Cappadocian Fathers held that there is a union of two natures (*hypostases*) in Christ—the "hypostatic union"—and that His human will did not sin, because the *Logos* controlled His human nature and rendered His flesh passive.

Hilary of Poitiers

St. Hilary of Poitiers, who helped transmit Eastern theology to the West, was one of the few Western theologians to write on the question, proposing that the *Logos* was solely divine before the Incarnation but "emptied" Himself (*kenosis*, in Paul's words)—in order to become human, because only then could He interact with men. The two natures, each complete in itself, were united in one Person. Ambrose held a similar position.

Theodore of Mopsuestia (d. ca. 428), anxious to counter any suggestion that God suffered or could in any way change, taught that in Jesus there were actually two "persons" united together—the divine dwelling in the human as if in a temple—of which only the human was incarnate, suffered, and died. Theodore denied that the prophecies of the Old Testament pertained to Jesus and spoke of a "loving accord" between Christ and His Father rather than of complete equality. Nestorius, patriarch of Constantinople (d. ca. 451), was an ascetic monk from Antioch who became a disciple of Theodore and gave his name to this heresy.

Nestorianism

St. Cyril of Alexandria opposed Nestorian theology, asserting that Christ was only one Person and must have been the incarnate *Logos*, which alone had the power to bring salvation to mankind. Among other things, Cyril appealed to the Eucharist, where Christ shares His Body with His people. But Cyril resisted the claim of two natures in Christ, holding that the human nature did not exist of itself but only in conjunction with the divine. Instead Cyril articulated a position that became known as Monophysitism—"one nature" (from the Greek *mono* and *phusis*).

Cyril of Alexandria

Theological passion was not confined to the learned. During the Arian controversy, it was noted that in their prayers the people reverenced Jesus as God, and a major issue in the Nestorian dispute was whether Mary is *Theotokos*—"Mother of God"—as she was popularly called, or only *Christokos*—"Mother of Christ". The divine motherhood of Mary was considered essential as a guarantee of the true humanity of Christ, but Nestorius denied the title *Theotokos* because Jesus did not derive His divinity from Mary. (Some heretics held that Jesus passed through Mary as water passes through a pipe.)

Theotokos

Cyril, however, insisted that, since Jesus was one Person, Mary was His Mother without equivocation and therefore must be called *Theotokos*. Cyril appealed to Rome against Nestorius, and Pope St. Celestine I (422–432) upheld the appeal. Suspecting that Nestorius was a kind of crypto-Arian, Cyril demanded that he affirm that "the Word of God suffered in the flesh", and at the First Council of Ephesus (431) the title *Theotokos* was affirmed and Nestorius and his followers were excommunicated. Nestorius retired to a monastery, claiming that he accepted all orthodox teaching. Cyril, however, did not win a complete victory and had to affirm that Christ had two natures.

The Robber Council Subsequently, a monk of Constantinople named Eutyches (d. 454) taught that Jesus was not fully human. Cyril's successor Dioscorus (d. 454) supported Eutyches, as did the Second Council of Ephesus (449), under strong pressure from the emperor Theodosius II (408–450). The emperor rebuffed the initiatives of Pope St. Leo I the Great (440–461), causing Leo to condemn Ephesus II as a "robber council". During the council, Monophysite monks beat the patriarch of Constantinople so badly that he died of his wounds, but elsewhere the Monophysites themselves were subjected to severe persecution.

Chalcedon The next emperor, Marcian (450–457), supported Leo, who sent his "Tome" ("book") to the Council of Chalcedon (451), in which he summarized the doctrine that Jesus was one Divine Person possessing two natures in perfect union with one another, making it proper even to say that the Son of God died. Not solely because of Leo's intervention, Chalcedon adopted that formulation; and, although not immediately accepted everywhere, its decrees would serve as the touchstone of all later orthodox belief.

The Trinity Just as the christological controversies struggled to do justice to both the divine and the human in Jesus, trinitarian controversies faced the challenge of remaining faithful to monotheism while treating Father, Son, and Holy Spirit as both one and three.

Modalism Modalism, also called Sabellianism after one of its leaders, was an early third-century attempt to understand the Trinity as "modes" of a single Person—the same Being manifesting itself in three different ways. It was sometimes called Patripassianism—"the Father suffered"—leading Tertullian to jibe that the modalists had crucified the Father.

Monarchianism A generation later, Paul of Samosata (d. 275), bishop of Antioch, was condemned for the heresy of Monarchianism, which sought to uphold the absolute sovereignty of the Father by denying that the Son and the Spirit are distinct divine Persons. One version of this was Adoptionism, which made Jesus a man who was adopted by the Father. Popes St. Zephyrinus (199–217) and St. Callistus I (217–222) showed some sympathy for Monarchianism, but Callistus eventually condemned the doctrine; and the Church at Rome accepted Tertullian's trinitarian theology.

Cappadocian Trinitarianism It was primarily the Cappadocian Fathers who developed the theology of the Trinity, according to which there are three *hypostases* (natures) in one *ousios* ("being"), none subordinated to the others. The Cappadocian Fathers laid the foundations of the theology of God, identifying Him as the First Cause of all that exists and the Unmoved Mover of the universe, setting forth both objective and subjective paths to knowing Him, and insisting on the necessity of "negative theology"—since God is ultimately beyond human understanding, whatever is affirmed of Him in human terms (for example, that He is just) must also be denied as inadequate.

Holy Spirit

In contrast to Christology, the theology of the Holy Spirit was underdeveloped in the early centuries. Some theologians denied the divinity of the Spirit, but the *Doxology* ("praise")—"Glory be to Father and to the Son and to the Holy Spirit"—affirmed it. Just as he championed the divinity of the Son, Athanasius did the same with respect to the Spirit.

The Council of Constantinople (381) declared that the Holy Spirit "proceeds from the Father and is no less adored and glorified", but the Council's authority was not fully accepted in the West, which eventually affirmed that the Holy Spirit "proceeds from both the Father and the Son" (*filioque*, in Latin).

Soteriology

Christ's death on the Cross was universally affirmed as important, but there was not complete unanimity as to its exact meaning. Soteriology (from the Greek for "savior") was not the subject of bitter dispute in the way that other questions were, but there was some uncertainty. Mankind was saved through the Incarnation, but salvation was variously understood as having been achieved by Jesus' example, by His teachings, or by the infusion of divine life into the human soul. (Justin Martyr, for example, primarily emphasized Jesus as the teacher of righteousness, to be emulated by His followers.)

In general, Western theology held that men inherit Adam's own sin, while Eastern theology taught that they merely inherit weak natures that make them prone to sin. In Eastern theology, men undergo "deification", becoming increasingly like God even as God condescends to become man.

Both Irenaeus and Clement of Alexandria taught that the divine image in man has been tarnished but not destroyed by Adam's sin and that Christ shed His Blood in order to ransom mankind from the devil. In accordance with his dominant allegorical understanding of Scripture, Origen made the Fall a cosmic myth about the rebellion of preexistent souls against their Creator, a rebellion of which the story of Adam and Eve is an allegory. Jesus' death began the process of the devil's defeat, and eventually—there being no Hell—all fallen souls will be gathered back to their Creator. The Cappadocian Fathers developed the idea that Jesus ransomed mankind from the devil, offering His life to His Father to appease the divine wrath toward sinful men and, in the ultimate act of love, taking mankind's punishment on Himself.

Mary

The tradition that Mary remained a virgin throughout her life was very ancient. In the West, Irenaeus formulated what became the common doctrine—just as Christ the New Adam atones for the sin of the first Adam, Mary was the New Eve who overcame the first Eve's infidelity. The Book of Revelation's vision of a woman crowned with stars (12:1) and the Book of Genesis' vision of a woman's heel crushing the head of a serpent (3:15) were understood to refer to Mary's role in redemption, and images from the Song of Songs ("Rose of Sharon"; "Ivory tower" (7:4) were also applied to her.

The East always led the way in Marian devotion. The first known Marian apparition in the history of the Church was to St. Gregory Thaumaturgus ("the Wonder-Worker", d. ca. 270), a bishop in Asia Minor. Eastern ideas were introduced into the West by Ambrose and others, and the Nestorian controversy led to the custom of dedicating churches in honor of Mary, notably St. Mary Major in Rome, and eventually to Marian feasts. Images of Mary appeared fairly early, first as holding the baby Jesus, later at the Annunciation and the Visitation.

Ecclesiology

Ecclesiology—the theology of the Church—was also not in much dispute in the early centuries, though the Montanists and the rigorists denied the possibility of the forgiveness of sin. Expanding on Paul, virtually all the Fathers defined the Church as the Body of Christ and understood baptism as infusing recipients with new life, incorporating them into that Body, permitting them to share in Christ's divinity, and giving them the gift of eternal life. As against the Donatists, the orthodox held that, while human agency is required, Christ is the true administrator of the sacraments, whose efficacy is due to the power of the Holy Spirit.

Marriage

The Gnostic and Manichaean heresies had the effect of strengthening the Church's teaching about the essential goodness of marriage, while at the same time guarding against disordered human appetites. The procreation of children was held to be the divinely ordained purpose of marriage, so that all forms of contraception, abortion, and sodomy were condemned in the strongest terms. Impotence rendered a marriage invalid, since in principle the man could not beget children, but sterility did not, and some theologians even disapproved of habitual continence, if its purpose was to prevent conception. For centuries, *coitus interruptus*—the sin of Onan (Gen 38:8–10), who spilled his seed upon the ground—was probably the common method of contraception, although there were also drugs and potions of dubious effectiveness. Some moralists thought that all forms of contraception amounted to abortion.

Drawing partly on the Stoics, the Fathers developed a theory of human sexuality according to which desire in itself was suspect, not because the flesh is evil but because passion might make the married couple forsake reason and become slaves to their emotions. Augustine, who experienced the power of sexual desire in his own life, proposed a teaching that never became official Catholic doctrine. He taught that the "loss of reason" that takes place in sexual intercourse is the means by which Original Sin is transmitted from parents to children and that even for married couples sexual desire is at least a venial sin.

"Spiritual marriage", in which husband and wife refrained from sexual intercourse for the sake of the Kingdom, was sometimes extolled, and, whatever that may have implied about the flesh, it had the effect of exalting an ideal of marriage based on friendship and mutual respect. To some extent, the ideal of spiritual marriage receded as monasticism developed, and "spiritual friendships" between men and women became a feature of monastic culture. One of the few reasons for which a marriage could be dissolved was to allow both parties to enter monastic life.

Women

In general, the society was patriarchal, giving men authority over women, but some theologians emphasized the complementarity of the sexes, implying some degree of equality, or understood human beings as primarily spiritual, which made sexual differences relatively unimportant, although Paul's proclamation that in Christ "there is neither male nor female" (Gal 3:28) was understood to refer to the Kingdom of Heaven.

Some theologians considered women less spiritual than men, hence as sources of carnal temptation, although recognized communities of virgins and nuns seemed to belie that.

Women could be learned. Basil and Gregory of Nyssa were educated by their grandmother, St. Macrina the Elder (d. ca. 340), and their sister, St. Macrina the Younger (d. 379), while the legend of St. Catherine of Alexandria (d. ca. 250) portrayed her as a philosopher so brilliant that she confounded the greatest pagan sages. St. Paula (d. 404), who followed Jerome to the Holy Land, and St. Marcella (d. 410), another of his disciples, who was martyred by the Visigoths, learned biblical languages at his behest.

Eschatology

There was some divergence of opinion among the Fathers concerning the fate of the soul after death. While its immortality was universally affirmed, some thought that it underwent a kind of sleep until the Last Judgment, when all will arise together. Belief in the resurrection of the body was universal, but there was disagreement as to the form the risen body would take.

The Theological Context

Odium Theologicum ("Theological Hatred")

Esoteric theological debates were by no means irrelevant to the mass of believers in the East, who often aligned themselves with particular factions. (When an Arian bishop entered the public baths of his city, for instance, everyone else withdrew, unwilling to share the water with a heretic.) While some of this was blind partisanship, the common people had keen religious sensibilities and were quick to detect things that went against their own piety, as many did in sensing that Arius was insufficiently respectful of Jesus' divinity or that some theologians denied the title "Mother of God".

Sometimes such partisanship manifested itself in rioting, and Basil and Gregory Nazianzen lamented that in some ways ecumenical councils brought out the worst in bishops. Cyril actively encouraged mob violence at Alexandria, and the debates at Nicaea and other councils sometimes erupted in strife, as when St. Nicholas of Myra (d. ca. 350) (the original of the Santa Claus legend) reportedly pulled the beard of an Arian bishop in vexation.

Lex Orandi Lex Credendi

During this period, the Church adopted the maxim *lex orandi est lex credendi* (literally, "The law of prayer is the law of belief"), meaning that the authentic teachings of the Church are found first of all in her liturgy, which is prior to dogma both temporally and in importance. The continued authority of the Old Testament, for example, was demonstrated by the fact that from the beginning the Church had used the Psalms in her prayers, and Augustine taught the existence of Purgatory (a place of purification or purging), based on the ancient custom of praying for the dead, justified by the Book of Maccabees (see 2 Macc 12:40–46). Arianism was refuted by pointing out that baptism was administered in the name of the Son as well as of the Father and, although liturgical prayers were ordinarily directed to the Father through the Son, the controversy gave rise to new prayers directed to Jesus. Chrysostom lamented a decline in the reception of Communion by the laity, apparently motivated by their heightened sense of Christ's divinity and their own unworthiness.

East and West

The Church in the East was a good deal more populous and sophisticated than that in the West, and it was primarily Easterners who were exercised by theological debate, while Westerners wondered whether the great controversies involved over-subtle questions of a kind that the Greek mind found fascinating. The West manifested the pragmatic Roman spirit, paying more attention to concrete issues and following the metaphysical disputes of the East with a certain detachment, although ultimately the popes issued final judgments on the great theological debates.

A rare exception was the case of the Spanish bishop Priscillian (d. 385), who was suspected by some of his fellow bishops of harboring Gnostic beliefs and whom they denounced as a sorcerer, which under Roman law was a capital offense. Priscillian was the first person in the history of the Church to suffer the death penalty at the behest of the ecclesiastical authorities, an action that was denounced by Ambrose, Martin of Tours, and others, so that Priscillian's accusers were forced to resign their sees.

Augustine of Hippo

North Africa was the exception to the West's relative lack of theological activity, and the greatest of the Latin Fathers was Augustine, who was born in North Africa to a pagan father and a Christian mother,

St. Monica (d. 387). After living a hedonistic and rather aimless life, Augustine began exploring a variety of spiritual movements, especially a type of Gnosticism called Manichaeism after its founder, all of which proved unsatisfying.

While teaching rhetoric at Milan, he met Ambrose and was converted after hearing a voice—an angel, he thought—commanding him to read a passage from Paul that condemned the life of the flesh. While still a recent convert, he felt his heart wrenched by Athanasius' account of Anthony of the Desert, and he returned to Africa to found a monastery. But on a visit to the town of Hippo, he was spontaneously acclaimed by the people as their new bishop and reluctantly left his monastery for an active life in which he both governed the local church and engaged in prodigious theological speculation that shaped the entire subsequent religious history of the West.

Conversion

Augustine wrote systematic treatises on many subjects, including biblical exegesis. He produced a large number of sermons, innumerable letters, and *On Christian Doctrine*, which was the first comprehensive guide to Catholic teaching. He was continually consulted by people from outside his own diocese, and he offered authoritative judgments on every kind of religious question.

He explored the relationship between God and the soul in a new literary genre that he invented—the autobiography—whose title, *Confessions*, meant not an admission of guilt (although it was that) but a profession of faith. The *Confessions* was not primarily a narrative of the events of the author's life but an account of his inner spiritual journey, especially the paradox whereby he sought truth yet kept turning away from it, until finally touched by divine grace. For Augustine, the crucial mystery of existence was the human will and its perverse attraction to evil. He was the first person in history able to recount his own subjective experiences while looking at them with ruthless objectivity, writing a psychologically acute account of his inner life that had no equivalent in the ancient world.

The Confessions

Neo-Platonism affirmed that the spiritual, transcendent, unseen world is real and the world of experience a pale copy that can give only hints of ultimate reality. Despite his experience of enslavement to the sins of the flesh, orthodoxy required Augustine to acknowledge matter as God's good creation. But in Neo-Platonic fashion, he defined it as the least of God's creatures.

Neo-Platonism

The soul is born with the seeds of all truth, which it receives from its Creator. But the body obscures those truths by deflecting the mind's attention to ephemeral material things, so that the less sensual a man is, the more likely he is to find truth, which is only gradually discovered through interior contemplation. Because of the insubstantiality of the world, meaning cannot ultimately be found in human experience. Knowledge is necessarily inward-looking, the recovery of lost memories, of the truth buried within the soul.

Time and Change

Like practically all thinkers of his time, Augustine was obsessed with the mystery of mutability—why things change and, since they do, how it is possible to know the truth. The chief theological problem for Augustine was how changing beings can relate to God, whose chief attributes are eternity and immutability, without which He would not be the ultimate reality. Augustine concluded that the mind's grasp of mere fragments of truth, the human sense of the incompleteness of life, and glimpses of unchanging eternity amidst the flux of time all affirm the existence of God, who alone is the absolute Being, the eternal truth.

The Human Will

Paradoxically, Augustine was preoccupied with the human will precisely because he saw human freedom as fragile and problematic. Man is not totally depraved, but his nature is badly scarred, so that he wars within himself, buffeted by the unlawful urges of concupiscence (desire). Direct divine intervention was necessary to make Augustine recognize his own derelictions.

In the most famous line of the *Confessions*, Augustine cried out, "Our hearts are restless, and they shall find no rest until they rest in Thee!" Happiness consists in partaking of the immutability of God, who created the universe out of love, in order to associate His creatures with Himself. But Augustine's anguished struggle to find the truth was continually thwarted by his own nature, his will enslaved to sin, leading him to define freedom as it would be understood throughout the whole subsequent history of Christianity—not the ability to do whatever he willed but the ability to obey the divine law. In order to achieve peace and happiness, it was necessary to subordinate the human will to the divine, to choose between spiritual and material goods, since the divine order is being continually deflected downward by a human nature oriented to its own selfish ends.

Left to themselves, all men are drawn to evil, hence all deserve damnation. Grace is literally a "gift", freely bestowed by God, without which men are powerless to do good. Augustine thought God predestined only a finite number of souls to Heaven, accommodating His grace to each individual in accordance with His foreknowledge of how each will respond to the gift and allowing wicked people to do evil in order to manifest the power of God's wrath.

Human Nature

Augustine's negative attitude toward sexuality to a great extent stemmed from his own early surrenders to unbridled lust. Whereas other vices (avarice, gluttony) could be controlled, his experience of lust was of complete loss of self-control, the very negation of true freedom and the obliteration of the image of God in the soul. Following Ambrose, he insisted that men inherit the sin of Adam—Original Sin—through the biological act of procreation itself, thereby making sin basic to human nature.

A necessary corollary of Augustine's position was that infants need to be baptized as soon as possible after birth and that unbaptized infants cannot enter Paradise but are instead sent to Limbo ("boundary"), which is technically Hell, in that those who live there are deprived of the presence of God, but they do not experience active torment.[2]

Augustine's position on the sinfulness of infants was based partly on his own experience and his deep insight into human psychology. One of the most famous passages in his *Confessions* is his story of stealing pears as a child, not because he was hungry but simply out of a perverse desire to do something forbidden. (By contrast, some of the Eastern Fathers held that newborn infants are innocent and only fall into sin when they became old enough to choose evil freely.)

Pelagianism

In keeping with his understanding of human nature, Augustine played a crucial role in combating the heresy that, after Gnosticism, posed the most serious threat in the West—Pelagianism, a heresy that, characteristic of the West, did not turn on abstruse metaphysical speculation but on practical implications. Pelagius (d. ca. 425) was a monk from Gaul who traveled widely, teaching that men do not inherit the sin of Adam but sin only in imitating him. Children are inherently sinless, and salvation can be attained by the vigilant protection of one's innocence, vigorous asceticism, and the cultivation of virtue.

Jerome condemned Pelagius' ideas with his usual ferocity, as did various popes and bishops, although Pelagius had popular support even at Rome and some episcopal support as well. Largely because of Augustine's efforts, the provincial Council of Carthage (418) condemned Pelagius and declared that Original Sin is inherited by every infant and that grace is indispensable.

For centuries, the uncertainties of travel and communication made it difficult for those in authority even to know the facts of a case, much less to make a competent judgment. Often the popes knew only what they were told by partisan representatives, who offered versions of events most favorable to their own causes. Thus Pelagius was condemned by Pope St. Innocent I (401–417), the condemnation was withdrawn by his successor St. Zosimus (417–418), but he was condemned again when the African Church appealed to Zosimus. The Council of Ephesus, a year after Augustine's death, made the condemnation definitive.

---

[2] A statement by the Holy See in 2007 noted that Limbo had never been an official doctrine of the Church and implied that it was no longer to be considered common teaching.

Semi-Pelagianism

But some orthodox people suspected Augustine of still holding Manichaean positions, making divine grace irresistible and human nature seem entirely evil, thereby ignoring Christ's call to universal salvation. In Gaul, some theologians formulated a position that came to be called "semi-Pelagianism", which, despite the name, in effect came to define Catholic orthodoxy.

Cassian affirmed that grace is resistible and compared the human heart to flint, which is capable of striking off sparks that God can set alight. God wills that all be saved but foresees that many will not be. The monk St. Vincent of Lerins (d. ca. 445) objected to Augustine's formulation as a novelty, asserting that the Church teaches only those things that have been believed "always, and everywhere, and by everyone", a maxim that was often later cited as the criterion of orthodoxy.

Pelagianism was again condemned at the Council of Orange (529), which affirmed that death and sin are inherited from Adam and that divine grace is necessary for any good human choice. But despite Augustine's enormous prestige, the Council stopped short of fully embracing his own statement of the question, and it condemned the doctrine of predestination.

The Nature of Evil

Augustine came as close to "solving" the mystery of evil as any theologian could, defining it, in Neo-Platonic terms, as nothing—the absence of good, a destructive negation—since otherwise the all-good God would be the author of evil.

Numerology

Plato had redeemed matter through mathematics, which transforms what is individual, concrete, and perishable into what is abstract, general, and eternal. (A physical ball is only a rough approximation of the geometric idea of the sphere, for example.) Partly based on this, Augustine formulated a theological discipline that had great influence for more than a thousand years but was eventually forgotten: numerology, the belief that hidden proportions exist between creatures and their Creator and can be understood through mathematical relationships. Certain numbers are fundamental—three because of the Trinity, four because of the Gospels—making their combinations, especially seven, equally significant. Seven also brings the Trinity together with the four basic physical substances—earth, air, fire, and water—thereby symbolizing creation. Practically all numbers in the Old Testament, such as the size of an army, had hidden mystical significance.

The Trinity

Augustine went further than any other theologian in attempting to understand the Trinity. The Word is the image of the Father and the prototype of all lesser beings, containing within Himself the divine Ideas, the patterns of everything that can possibly exist. The Holy Spirit is the love between the Father and the Son, a truth expressed in the *filioque* clause of the Creed. Whatever can be said of one Person of the Trinity must be said of all, Augustine insisted. The three share one will and act wholly in union with one another, cooperating fully in every divine action, so that, for example, the triune God, not the Father alone, created the universe, although it is permissible to "attribute" particular functions to each of the three Persons, as a help to human understanding.

Augustine found images of the Trinity everywhere in the universe, especially in the human soul, which measures time in a trinitarian way—the past as remembrance, the present as attention, the future as expectation—thereby making man not time's slave but its master and creator. The past does not die but is incorporated into the present and the future, partaking of the immutability of God Himself. Augustine was the first philosopher of history, the first man to discern an inner pattern in what to the ancients seemed like meaningless flux. In affirming the goodness of the flesh, Irenaeus and others remained faithful to the dogma of the Incarnation, and Augustine extended that fidelity to the redemption of time.

Augustine's great book *The City of God* was partly a work of history. Ultimately, history has no meaning and will pass away, its whole course, apart from divine grace, merely a series of towers of Babel. But for Augustine it had temporary meaning insofar as the Kingdom of Heaven is an extension of the earthly kingdom. "Two loves built a city", Augustine announced, with the story of Cain and Abel as the paradigm of human history—the continuing struggle between love of God and love of self, good and evil, divine grace and human selfishness, replaying itself in every generation.

The Two Cities

The Earthly City

The true significance of the world, according to Augustine, lies in the largely hidden birth processes of the City of God, a process for which the Church, conscious of her historical mission, serves as a dynamic force. The City of God is brought into being by divine love and is present wherever the power of that love is felt, thereby giving unity and significance to history. Because of human sinfulness, earthly kingdoms are inevitably founded on injustice and self-will, but God brings good out of evil, thereby giving even the earthly city its proper place in the moral order.

Wheat and Tares

Augustine forestalled any attempt to find the City of God on earth. The divine City is not identical with the Church, in that the City can never be fully realized on earth, even though City and Church are closely related. Augustine condemned Donatism and Pelagianism partly for what he saw as their elitism, their implicit rejection of the Church as the refuge of sinners—a mixed community of good and bad people. The parable of the wheat and the tares shows that mere membership in the Church is not a guarantee of salvation, since God's will is inscrutable and no one knows for certain who is among the elect.

The Heavenly City

The City of God is timeless and eternal, transcending all earthly kingdoms, superseding the old literal millenarianism that expected the Kingdom to be established on earth. Instead, Augustine equated the reign of Christ on earth with the struggling "Church Militant" that would eventually be gathered up into the "Church Triumphant", an idea that came to be the general understanding in the West, discouraging speculation about the end of the world.

Divine and Human Law

Augustine was a profoundly important political thinker because, following Ambrose, he deprived the state of its aura of divinity and subordinated it to the higher divine purpose, a subordination that made Western ideas of freedom and justice possible. In some ways, he was the antithesis of the historian Eusebius, in that he posited a dualism in which Empire and Church met but did not intermingle and Christians gave the state external loyalty only. Whereas Tertullian condemned the state as demonic and Eusebius surrounded the emperor with a divine aura, Augustine made the emperor himself subject to the Church.

Just War

Another of the innumerable ways in which Augustine had momentous influence was his understanding of war. The New Testament diverged from the Old, he judged, in that war has no place in the Kingdom of God. But war remains part of the Kingdom of Man, so that when the state acts in accordance with its true end—that of maintaining peace—it is in harmony with the divine purpose, but when it wages war unjustly, it becomes identified with evil. Augustine thereby laid the foundation for the theory of the "just war" that would guide most Christian thinking on the subject for the next fifteen hundred years, laying down certain conditions that have to be met before Christians could in good conscience participate in it: that it be declared by established authority, fought for a just cause (essentially to defend oneself or others) and for good motives, and used as a last resort when all else fails.

Coercion

Augustine reluctantly accepted coercion in matters of religion because the Donatists of North Africa had become a fanatical, often violent sect, with armed bands sometimes raiding the churches of the orthodox and killing people whom they despised as traitors to the faith. The civil authorities regarded the sect as criminals who required severe punishment, and, after agonized meditation, Augustine agreed, justifying such action not because the state has a right to intervene but because the Church has the right to make use of worldly power to achieve her spiritual ends.

By Augustine's day, the authority of the bishop of Rome was well established. None of them attended any of the great councils, although they sent legates, their absence dictated partly by the difficulties of travel but perhaps primarily by their understanding of their office as not that of one bishop among many but as supreme over all. In determining which councils were authentic and which were not, the judgment of the see of Rome was always crucial. Cyril of Alexandria presided at Ephesus in lieu of the pope, and Nestorius complained because the bishop of Rome was not present.

The distance between Rome and Constantinople perhaps also allowed the popes a certain detachment and, above all, an essential independence from imperial control, while the two Eastern patriarchs suffered because of the state's authority. Constantine and his successors wanted obedient bishops, and overall the Eastern hierarchy remained highly vulnerable to political pressure.

Paradoxically, the fact that the popes did not play a crucial role in the theological disputes was itself a kind of tribute to their authority: they were respected not because of their personal qualities or achievements but solely because of their office, including the perception that the see of Rome had never been the seedbed of heresy but had always retained the authentic faith.

Bishops in the East often asked for support from the bishop of Rome, gestures that confirmed the enormous prestige of the Roman see but did not necessarily imply complete acceptance of papal authority, since the often-chaotic conflicts of the Eastern church led bishops to look for allies wherever they could find them. When Basil of Caesarea asked for his support, Pope St. Damasus refused, because he mistrusted Basil, and when Gregory Nazianzen was translated to Constantinople, Damasus was among those condemning the move as irregular, forcing Gregory to resign.

Divisions

The see of Rome was itself not free of the troubles that affected so much of the East. Riots accompanied Damasus' election (see Chapter Four above, p. 84), partly because he had failed to support Liberius during the latter's exile and death. But Damasus, despite the controversial circumstances of his election, was one of the most assertive of the early popes, making the strongest claims to date concerning his authority as the heir of both Peter and Paul. The First Council of Constantinople (381), whose decrees were not fully accepted in the West, acknowledged the primacy of the see of Rome but called Constantinople "the New Rome", a claim Damasus ignored. (Constantinople was not originally an apostolic see, and its status was entirely due to secular politics.)

Chrysostom

Chrysostom, first a desert hermit, then a monk of Antioch, was made patriarch of Constantinople by the emperor Arcadius (395–408).

Chrysostom was an ardent reformer, who from his monastic days retained a certain attitude of misogyny and only gradually came to a positive view of marriage. His attempts to reform the clergy and to depose bishops for simony—the sin of attaining Church office by bribery, named for the character Simon the Magician in Acts—made him highly unpopular. When Chrysostom exercised his authority vigorously against a bishop accused of heresy and reportedly compared Arcadius' wife to the Old Testament harlot Jezebel, the emperor declared Chrysostom deposed and sent him into exile, where he died.

Innocent I nullified Chrysostom's deposition, and, at least in that instance, the church at Antioch, Chrysostom's original home, accepted the Pope's authority. Innocent's support was to no avail, although later, partly at Innocent's insistence, the church at Constantinople restored Chrysostom's name, as one of its greatest glories. The principal liturgy of the Eastern church is attributed to him and bears his name. Innocent, one of the most important of the early popes, asserted his authority wherever possible, as in establishing the canon of the Bible. His condemnation of Pelagius brought him praise from Augustine, who extolled "the Apostolic See".

Bishops and Emperors

The Council of Chalcedon protested imperial control of the Church, and the lives of Athanasius, Chrysostom, and Ambrose showed that a courageous bishop could withstand imperial wrath. Chalcedon hailed Pope Leo for his "Tome", with the Fathers crying out, "Peter has spoken through the mouth of Leo." But as the emperors shifted more and more authority to the see of Constantinople, Leo protested, to little avail.

In contrast, Ambrose, a contemporary of Chrysostom, showed a remarkable degree of independence from imperial control, on one occasion simply taking possession of a church that the authorities wanted to give to the Arians. After a riot destroyed a synagogue in Asia Minor, Emperor Theodosius I ordered local Christians to pay restitution, which led Ambrose to threaten him with excommunication, whereupon the emperor prostrated himself before the bishop and begged for absolution. (Ambrose's purpose was probably not to defend anti-Jewish violence but to assert the independence of the Church from state control.) A few years later, when Theodosius ordered a massacre of rioters who had killed an imperial official, Ambrose did excommunicate him. Theodosius repented of his actions as a result of Ambrose's strong protests and the emperor received pardon from Ambrose.

These incidents demonstrate a reality that would persist in the West for the next thousand years: although the Church lacked physical power, her spiritual authority was such that she could triumph even over the threat of military force.

Augustine wrote the *City of God* primarily to refute the pagan claim that the sack of Rome by the Visigoths in 410 was due to the wrath of the gods against the impious Christians; it was, he asserted, due to Rome's own sins. But as he lay dying in 430, Hippo itself was under siege by a people so terrible that their very name became a synonym for destructiveness—the Vandals. Justinian would later briefly reconquer North Africa, but the golden age of the Fathers, the most creative period in the entire history of the Church, was over. In the West, a long darkness was descending.

The Barbarian Onslaught

5 Light in Darkness

The Dark Ages

Falling Dominoes

The term *Dark Ages* applies chiefly in the West, in the period roughly 400 to 1000.[1] Although the Western Empire survived as an important entity for several centuries, and even experienced periodic recoveries, the darkness of the Dark Ages was the result of a series of falling dominoes. The ultimate doom of the Empire was ordained by its very habit of conquest, which eventually resulted in a territorial overexpansion that placed impossible strains on finances and manpower. In the West, the collapse of imperial authority that could guarantee order often reduced the struggle for power to murderous intrigues and rebellions. But that was not the only causes of moral disorder, which was equally prevalent in the sophisticated Byzantine Empire and extended even to the highest levels of the Church.

However oppressive it may have been, the Empire enforced a comprehensive social order that allowed ordinary life to go on. But as its armies gradually withdrew from its various provinces, and as invaders continued to break through even those narrower imperial boundaries, every aspect of life suffered. Trade and agriculture were severely disrupted by the collapse of the rule of law, by marauding armies who instilled in people a fear that inhibited planning for the future.

Disease

In the period roughly 540 to 750, both East and West were also ravaged by a pandemic—probably the bubonic plague—that was possibly even more devastating than the better-known outbreak of the fourteenth century. The struggle for survival was so all-consuming that there was little energy for other things, and cultural life therefore suffered on all levels, from philosophy to skilled crafts.

Barbarian Invasions

The barbarians were a people whose time had come and who showed more energy and determination than their exhausted enemies. The term *barbarian* had been coined by the Greeks, apparently in mockery of what to them was unintelligible gibberish ("*bar, bar*") spoken by

---

[1] The term is often used polemically to refer to all of Western history from the fall of Rome to the Renaissance and to imply that the triumphant Church deliberately plunged civilization into ignorance.

"uncivilized" people—those who were "outside the city", hence crude and backward. Along with political, economic, and cultural decline, the Dark Ages were a time of shocking moral evils—brutality and ruthlessness not necessarily worse than classical Roman behavior but often starker, especially since many of the perpetrators were professed Christians who were, in their own way, sincere in their faith. The Romans were scarcely a peaceful people, nor were the barbarians uniquely savage. All ancient peoples exalted courage in battle, but for the barbarians it was a way of life, almost the only way of achieving status.

Over a period of three centuries, the barbarian tribes, some of whom had lived settled lives as farmers before being forced off their lands by other tribes, migrated in a general pattern from northeast to southwest, pushed by enemies, by economic troubles, and by the attraction of treasure and a warmer climate. At first, the Romans sought to control the barbarian threat by allowing some tribes to settle in the Empire in return for military support against other tribes, an arrangement that in the long run proved suicidal. In the late fourth century, barbarians began to pour across the frontiers. The barbarians were restless nomads whose wealth consisted primarily of flocks of animals and whose spirit was profoundly warlike. Their migrations were wide-ranging and often unobstructed, with tribes repeatedly crossing one another's paths and doubling back on themselves, until they found some territory where they could settle permanently.

Migrations

The Visigoths (West Goths), coming from Asia Minor, stormed into Greece, looped around the Adriatic Sea, advanced almost to the southern tip of Italy, established a kingdom in central Italy, then looped back again, following the Mediterranean coast around into Spain, where they established a second kingdom.

Visigoths

Their enemies the Huns made an incursion into Italy under the fierce chieftain Attila (d. 453), advancing on Rome until persuaded to turn back by Pope Leo the Great, reportedly because the barbarian leader saw a vision of Peter and Paul above the Pope's head. Eventually, the Huns settled in the central European region that became Hungary.

Huns

The Ostrogoths (East Goths) were driven from the Black Sea region by the Huns and penetrated as far as Ravenna, the capital of imperial administration in the West, finally settling in the eastern European areas that were later called the Balkans.

Ostrogoths

The Vandals, beginning in the northeast, advanced across Germany into Gaul, southward into Spain, across the Mediterranean into Africa, then across again into Italy, sacking Rome in 455, and eventually establishing kingdoms in both North Africa and Spain.

Vandals

Franks and Lombards

The people whom the Romans called the Germans had lived north and east of the Rhine and Danube rivers for centuries, repeatedly threatening the Empire's borders. Now one German tribe, the Franks, crossed the Rhine and conquered Gaul, and another, the Lombards ("Long Beards"), first ventured into eastern Europe but eventually settled in northern Italy, giving their name to the region around Milan.

Angles and Saxons

The Angles, Saxons, and Jutes—all German tribes living beyond the Rhine—crossed to the island of Britain, renaming it England (Angleland). The pre-barbarian Celtic culture survived in Scotland; in Ireland; in the farthest western areas of Britain called Cornwall and Wales; in Brittany, which was westernmost Gaul; and in parts of Spain.

Rome Sacked

In 378, after being betrayed and oppressed by the Romans with whom they had made a pact, the Goths rebelled and at Adrianople (Asia Minor) inflicted a crushing blow on the Roman army, killing Emperor Valens. The Vandals sacked Rome in 410, as did the Visigoths in 455, although a nominal emperor survived until deposed by the Visigoths in 476. With the approval of the Byzantine emperor Zeno (475–491), the Ostrogoths conquered Italy in 488. Justinian I, the greatest of the Byzantine emperors, later reconquered it, but his achievement did not long survive his death.

Barbarian Society

Precarious New States

As the barbarian tribes settled down within the imperial boundaries, they established precarious states dependent on the personal qualities of their chieftains, who were now proclaimed by the title of "king" and whose kingdoms often disintegrated after the first kings passed from the scene.

Ambivalent Relations

The barbarians had a love-hate relationship with the remains of the Empire, on the one hand relishing robbery and sheer destruction for their own sakes but on the other, recognizing some of the achievements of Roman civilization and appropriating them for themselves. This relationship extended to religion. While eventually all the tribes became Christians, as pagans they attacked churches and monasteries with particular ferocity, because of the riches conspicuously available in those places but perhaps also because of a half-conscious resentment of an institution that possessed a mysterious authority so alien to the warrior code. The great Italian monastery of Monte Cassino was destroyed twice during the Dark Ages but refounded each time.

The Romanized Christians, including Italians, Spanish, Gauls, Africans, and some Britons, in turn had ambivalent attitudes toward the barbarians. They were terrified by wave upon wave of atrocities, yet they feared that the scourge had been sent by God to punish them for their own sins. Although to the Romans, barbarian life may have looked chaotic, the various peoples had detailed law codes that defined social hierarchies, protected the rights of the various classes, and embodied a rough concept of justice. The fragile power of the state gradually transferred the obligation of vengeance from the individual to an impersonal authority that was supposed to be guided by an ideal of justice, primarily through the custom of *wergild* (Old English for "man price"), which exacted monetary payment from transgressors, the amount being determined both by the nature of the offense and by the social statuses of the victim and the offended.

Society was organized around kinship and an ethic of personal loyalty, a society of free tribesmen in which each man had his place and lived in fidelity to strong leaders, who usually acted only in accord with the consensus of their warriors and whose power depended on the number of retainers they supported with war booty. Social status was to a great extent established by this booty and other gifts given and received. The Church was also expected to bestow gifts, although she tried to teach the barbarians that these were primarily spiritual in nature.
Tribal Society

Although sometimes polygamous, barbarian society valued marriage and punished adultery, because marriage was a means of establishing a dynasty and enhancing the family's wealth and power, while adultery undermined kinship ties. Although the Church tried to hold both sexes to the same code of sexual behavior, the barbarians, like the Romans, adhered to the "double standard" whereby the adultery of men was less serious than that of their wives. Men did not want to be responsible for children who were not their own.
Marriage

While high-minded pagan Romans could understand the ideal of chastity as the conquest of passion, it was, like the ideals of meekness and forgiveness, difficult for the barbarians to appreciate, a fact that probably made monasticism incomprehensible. The Irish monk St. Columban (or Columbanus, d. 615) was driven out of the Frankish kingdom because of his strict moral views, and another Irish monk, St. Kilian (d. ca. 689), was martyred in Germany by a newly converted barbarian chief whom he rebuked for retaining his mistresses and for marrying his cousin.
Chastity

Not all barbarians were pagans. The Goths had been converted to Arianism by the priest Ulfilas (d. 382), a former slave. There was an Arian Gothic church with a bishop at Constantinople and a Gothic translation of the Bible. The Ostrogoths and the Lombards were also converted to Arian Christianity during their wanderings, and the heresy was especially spread by the Vandals, who inflicted their savagery on orthodox Catholics with particular fury. For a time, there were Arian kingdoms in France, Italy, Spain, and North Africa, but by 600, most of their kings had been converted to orthodoxy and had commanded their subjects to do the same.
Arian Barbarians

The Church in the Barbarian World

A Higher Order

The barbarian invasions themselves caused many pagans to turn to Christianity for an ideal of universality that replaced the Empire. Since the Church transcended all earthly regimes, she was the only institution not dragged down by the Empire's fall, continuing to exist as an autonomous order. The monastic life was the dominant ideal of the Dark Ages, the principal source of hope in a bleak world. While relatively few people answered this "call to perfection", and while it was thought possible for those living in the world to be saved, monks and nuns served as models for the rest of mankind of how to live for the Kingdom.

Episcopal Cities

Cities survived in the Dark Ages primarily as centers of ecclesiastical life, with bishops having both religious and political authority. With the decline of the Roman Empire, towns survived primarily as the seats of episcopal authority, but in the later Dark Ages, merchants and other laymen formed themselves into self-governing "communes" that struggled with bishops for control.

Monasticism

As city life declined and most people came to live in rural villages, new means had to be found to serve their spiritual needs; and, since monasteries were usually built in remote areas, it was often monks who brought the faith to the pagans. Bishops, monasteries, and, to a lesser extent, lay lords carried out most of the charitable work of the age, as swarms of beggars regularly gathered outside their gates.

Patrick

Christianity probably came to Ireland sometime after the Roman conquest of Britain in the first century, since there were at least a few Christians on the Emerald Isle when St. Patrick arrived three hundred years later. Patrick (d. 493)[2] became the best known and most revered of all the saints of the Dark Ages. His origins are uncertain—though probably from Britain—but he was enslaved and taken to Ireland as a young man and, after regaining his freedom, returned there to convert the people, the first missionary known to have evangelized beyond the western frontiers of the Empire.

Irish Monasticism

Monasticism had become popular in Ireland by the sixth century, and it took a unique form in accord with the Irish customs whereby the island was divided not into territorial principalities but into semi-nomadic tribal units under chieftains. It was thus impractical to organize dioceses on the Continental model, and instead the monastery served as the basic unit of church life. Linked to particular clans and chieftains, some monasteries had as many as a thousand monks and

---

[2] There are few more disputed questions from this period than the dates of St. Patrick. The traditional date 493 requires that he lived to a very great age. Some historians doubt this and place his death thirty years earlier.

dependents, all of them regarded as the family of their patron saint. Abbots (sometimes abbesses) governed, with bishops serving only to administer the sacraments.

The Celtic monks observed very strict fasts, harnessed themselves to ploughs in the fields, prayed for long periods with their arms out-stretched like a cross, and even prayed while immersed in water up to their armpits—practices that served both to expiate sins and to bring the body under control.

For a time around 600, Ireland was the cultural leader of Europe, and—unusual in the ancient world—the movement of religious revival during the Dark Ages went from West to East, from Ireland and England to the Continent. While hermits had mostly been absorbed into monas-tic communities elsewhere in Europe, many monks continued to live that life in the British Isles. The Irishman St. Columba (or Col-umkille, d. 597) founded a monastery on the isle of Iona, off the west coast of Scotland, where the monks lived in cavelike cells on the bleak rocky shore, the spiritual center of Celtic Christianity. Iona and other Celtic monasteries, especially under Columban, founded daughter houses in Gaul, and when Columban was expelled from there, he went to northern Italy and helped to christianize the Lombards. St. Brendan (d. 578) was dubbed "The Navigator" because of his semi-legendary voyages over the northern oceans, including the establishment of monas-tic communities in Iceland.

St. Benedict of Nursia (or Norcia, d. ca. 550) was an Italian of noble birth who, like Ambrose, Augustine, and others, first studied rhetoric at Rome, then renounced the world and became a hermit. But, like Pachomius, he saw the perils of the solitary life and of lax discipline; Benedict's first community of monks tried to poison him because of his severity. After that, he founded a network of smaller monasteries at a place called Sub-iaco, then a larger community at Monte Cassino, while his sister St. Scho-lastica (d. ca. 543) founded communities of nuns.

Benedict

Benedict's *Rule* owed much to Cassian's, but it largely supplanted the latter, becoming the basis of almost all later Western monasticism. The vows of poverty, chastity, and obedience—renouncing property, mar-riage, and self-will respectively—were the heart of the monastic call-ing, the fulfillment of Jesus' summons to the rich young man (see Mk 10:17–22). Monks and nuns were cloistered ("closed"), formally sep-arated from the world outside the monastery. Benedict also bound his monks to stability—remaining in one monastery for a lifetime—because restless wandering was a sign of self-will and had been one of the chief abuses of earlier monastic life.

Benedict's *Rule* was characteristically Western in its practicality. Although there were strict dietary rules—never any meat and long seasonal fasts—he moderated hermetical asceticism, defined monastic

The Benedictine Rule

organization, regulated the details of daily life, and showed concern for the material needs of the community. The exhortation *ora et labora* ("Pray and work") became a kind of motto for the monastic life, with monks bound both to sing the daily Office in common and to support themselves through manual labor. Benedict and his followers did not extol manual labor for its own sake; they shared the general Christian belief of its necessity solely due to the Fall. But labor was an ascetic practice that had spiritual value, and the fact that it was integral to the lives of the monks gave it a dignity that it did not have in the classical world.

Nuns

Nuns followed a regimen similar to that of the monks, although with less strenuous physical labor. Their communities were also self-governing, under elected abbesses who had an authority unprecedented for women prior to that time. Just as brides had to bring dowries to their marriages, nuns were expected to bring dowries to their convents, which tended to create a division between richer and poorer houses, reflecting the social classes of the nuns. Many nuns were as learned as their male counterparts and wrote treatises or devotional works. The German nun Hrotsvitha (d. 1000) was widely known for her religious dramas (a rare genre at the time), poetry, and histories.

In both East and West, there were for a time double monasteries of both monks and nuns, sometimes under the authority of an abbess. Monks did the heavy manual labor, and the nuns made the monks' robes, but they were completely separate from one another in their daily lives. Abbots and abbesses were the parents of a family but above all the spiritual masters of a "school of divine service". The highest monastic virtue was humility, and obedience was the virtue that defined the monastic life. That life was considered distinct from the priestly calling, and the early Benedictines ordained only enough priests to celebrate the Eucharist for the community.

Monastic Life

A monastery was a self-sufficient village, comprising a church, a dormitory, a refectory (dining hall), a *scriptorium* ("writing place" or library), a chapter house (meeting room), a guesthouse, the necessary facilities for material needs—kitchen, store rooms, barns, and workshops for the various crafts—and surrounded by the fields that yielded food and other needs. The monasteries were models of efficiency, as monks were the first people to organize their days into precise, specialized units: times for prayer, times for work, times for eating and sleeping.

During the Dark Ages, the monasteries were living examples of civilized life, of exemplary order in an age of chaos, cities governed by laws based on Christian love, self-sufficient communities of hard-working men who lived at peace with one another. In a war-torn world, monasteries assumed roles foreign to their original cloistered ideal, notably schools where at least the rudiments of literacy and other skills were taught to aspiring monks and sometimes to the sons of lay lords as well. Boys and girls as young as seven (the accepted "age of reason") were sent to monasteries as oblates ("offerings") by their parents. Some interiorized the rule and were highly dedicated, but others remained misfits who were a source of trouble and disorder in monastic communities.

Besides the monks themselves, monasteries housed people who had been exiled in political struggles, penitents atoning for serious sins, ecclesiastical criminals, and networks of laborers integral to the monastic economy. One Frankish monastery comprised seven hundred people, of whom only three hundred were actually monks.

With the decline of towns, monasteries were among the densest population centers, which made them especially vulnerable both to military attack and to disease. During one visitation of such a disease, the flourishing English house of Jarrow was reduced to the abbot and a small boy.

Parents were thought to be the best judges of whom their children should marry, decisions that among the aristocracy were based largely on dynastic considerations and among the peasantry on economic advantage. But such arranged marriages complicated religious life. Female monasticism, for the first time in history, offered a way of life for women other than marriage, which sometimes created tensions between the woman's sense of her religious vocation and her family's determination that she marry, so that, paradoxically, her vow of obedience might at the same time be an exercise of her free will. St. Brigid of Kildare (Ireland, d. ca. 525) was a beautiful young woman who was said to have been miraculously made ugly when her parents tried to force her to marry, a transformation that allowed for, and was reversed upon, her entry to the convent.

Monasteries and Society

Monasteries too were infected by the world around them. Would-be reformers sometimes encountered armed resistance from corrupt monks who might, as in Benedict's case, attempt to poison their abbot. One seventh-century Frankish convent was split between two factions of nuns, each of whom accused the other of vile sins and each of whom enlisted thugs to intimidate the other.

Reform

At the beginning of the tenth century, the duke of Aquitaine in France established a new monastery at Cluny, endeavoring to protect if from undue influences by making it independent of both feudal and episcopal control, answerable only to the pope. Freed of such worldly ties, Cluny became the most vibrant center of monastic life in Europe, eventually presiding over a network of a thousand daughter houses.

Cluny

The Conversion of the Barbarians

Evangelization

The evangelization of Western Europe for the most part took place through the structure of the Empire, even as the Empire declined. At first, there was no effort to convert the barbarians beyond the imperial frontiers, although Augustine, because he did not sacralize the Empire, foresaw that the barbarians would one day be evangelized. Missionaries— those who were "sent"—were pilgrims who left their own lands to follow Christ, voluntary exiles, black-robed ascetics who were the embodiment of some mysterious spiritual power.

The Church and Classical Culture

To the barbarians, Christianity was Roman, so that the monks who converted Europe were the missionaries of classical culture as well as of the Church, representatives both of the Kingdom of Heaven and of a higher worldly civilization. To a great extent, the acceptance of Christianity involved the adaptation of Roman culture, which was institutionalized in the Latin liturgy and other things. But although the variety of spoken languages was thought to be the result of the Tower of Babel, and although Latin was considered a sacred language, the missionaries were also instrumental, as in England, in the development of the vernacular languages, by regularizing their grammar and putting them into writing. (Some missionaries feared that baptism administered in garbled Latin was invalid, but Pope St. Zachary [741–752] ruled that it was not.)

The Episcopal Office

The Church triumphed partly because she was a highly organized and disciplined institution, especially in her clergy, something for which the various kinds of paganism had no counterpart. Bishops impressed the barbarians by their spiritual authority but also because they represented the old Roman aristocracy, familiar figures from the Roman administrative system. The formation of a Christian legal system, adapted from Roman law, marked the first time in history that there existed, anywhere, an autonomous, self-governing body distinct from the state. The authority of the church courts extended even to what had previously been considered secular matters, like marriages and wills.

Worldliness

Because bishops and abbots were men of great importance, they tended to live rather luxurious lives, attended on their journeys by small armies of assistants and servants. The triumph of the Church meant that at every level, especially that of the papacy itself, ecclesiastical office was attractive to those who sought worldly prizes. There were complaints of simony among the Frankish clergy, and Martin of Tours, who was unusual in being a man of low birth (a former soldier), was not at home among polished prelates, some of whom he considered worldly and comfort-loving.

The Papacy

The papacy was both an independent spiritual power and the heir to the imperial tradition. The greatest of the popes during the Dark Ages,

St. Gregory I the Great (589–603), followed the precedent of Ambrose, Augustine, and others in abandoning his career as an imperial official to become a monk, later serving as papal ambassador to Constantinople. Up to 800, most popes were venerated as saints after their deaths, but there was much jockeying for office, sometimes accompanied by violence. Felix III (526–530), although himself venerated as a saint, named his own successor, Boniface II (530–532), and Boniface in turn named Vigilius, whom the priests of Rome would not accept. The imperial agent in Italy deposed Pope St. Silverius (536–538) and sent him into exile, where he died of starvation but, even before Silverius' fate was known, Vigilius, supported by the Empress Theodora (d. 548), was elected through simony and kept the papal office through an exceptionally long reign (537–555). Once he took office, however, Vigilius was no longer Theodora's puppet.

The Church was primarily governed by bishops individually and meeting in synods or regional councils. They administered their dioceses through officials called archdeacons, who did most of the work of oversight and who, despite their title, eventually came to be mainly priests. *Bishops*

The bishop's miter evolved from a simple cap and was not a sign of office until the eighth century, gradually evolving its unique triangular shape and becoming taller. By about 500, the authority of an archbishop required that he receive the pallium from the pope. Originally, a kind of scarf that designated a scholar or government official, the pallium evolved into a circular band worn over the shoulders. Made of purest wool in a Roman convent, it symbolized the Good Shepherd carrying the lost sheep across His shoulders.

In Italy, where there were two hundred and fifty dioceses, only bishops retained the authority to administer baptism. Elsewhere, however, the system of territorial parishes was extended and regularized, with the parish priest possessing full sacramental authority, although baptismal water had to be consecrated with holy oil and could only be blessed by a bishop. Most parish churches in rural areas were built by the local landlord, the parish being coterminous with his estate. He usually claimed the right to appoint the priest and, although it was legally forbidden, sometimes claimed the parish revenues as well. Rights over parishes were also held by bishops, cathedral chapters, and monasteries and could be sold or traded. *Priests*

Unlike in the East, there was no corps of educated lay bureaucrats in the West, so that much of the governing responsibility fell on the clergy, giving the Church influence over the state but also creating a potential source of corruption of the clergy.

The Church had grown up with the Empire as the natural political order, and Augustine's *City of God* contained a picture of the ideal *Sacral Kingship*

Christian emperor. Thus the fragmentation of the Empire into a multiplicity of barbarian kingdoms seemed less than ideal. But in the middle of the eighth century, Pepin the Short, the son of Charles Martel and the chief minister of the Frankish king Childeric III (743–752), deposed Childeric with the consent of the nobility, sent him to a monastery, and assumed the royal title for himself, thereby ending the Merovingian dynasty (named after a semi-legendary ancestor). Pepin appealed to the Pope for confirmation, and St. Zachary (741–752) approved the action on the grounds that Pepin could provide peace and order, as Childeric could not.

The subsequent solemn coronation of Pepin by St. Boniface in 751 marked the first revival of that Old Testament rite, the solemn affirmation of the idea of Christian monarchy that would dominate Catholic political thought for the next eleven centuries. The king now received a quasi-priestly character, symbolized by his being anointed at his coronation. Precedent for kingship was found in the Old Testament, whose kings possessed divine authority but who were also sinful men answerable to God's justice, with bishops serving in the role of the Old Testament prophets.

The Two Swords

The Church that anointed the king also restricted his authority under the classical theory of the Two Swords formulated by Pope St. Gelasius I (492–496)—God granted two swords of authority, one (temporal) to the state, the other (spiritual) to the Church, to be wielded separately but in harmony, with the spiritual having the higher authority.

Catechizing the Barbarians

Methods of Catechesis

The barbarians required simpler catechetical approaches from those used in the Hellenistic world. Although there were rudimentary efforts to teach doctrine to the neophytes, conversion was primarily measured by behavior—monogamy, observance of the Lenten fast, burial rather than cremation, and above all abandonment of the worship of the old gods.

Survival in the North

Christianity continued to exist in the remote northern part of Britain even after the withdrawal of the Romans in the third century, but it almost vanished elsewhere in the island. The invasion of the Angles, Saxons, and Jutes was resisted by a shadowy prince sometimes called Arthur, about whom virtually nothing is known but around whom many legends later collected.

Evangelization and Diplomacy

To an extent, evangelizing missions were like diplomatic missions, in that barbarians tended to regard missionaries as representatives of, and under the protection of, foreign monarchs, and receptivity to the Gospel to some extent depended on whether the barbarians welcomed a possible alliance. Conversion might also be hampered insofar as Christianity was seen as a foreign import, possibly as an entering wedge for foreign domination, so that kings and princes were careful about from whom they would accept the faith.

According to a contemporary story, in 597 Pope Gregory the Great saw a group of Angle slaves in the Roman market, punned that "they are not Angles but angels", and commissioned Augustine (d. 604), a Roman monk, to convert the island. England was a collection of small kingdoms, and St. Augustine landed in the southeastern kingdom of Kent, which was ruled by Ethelbert (ca. 590–616), whose wife was a Frankish Christian and who himself soon converted. Augustine was accompanied by forty monks and founded an episcopal see at Canterbury, making it the capital of English Christianity. But the older Celtic Christianity still survived in northern Britain, cut off from all contact with Rome.

Augustine of Canterbury

In Gaul, an old romanized aristocracy survived, most of whose members were Christian and from whose ranks many of the bishops were taken. The Frankish king Clovis (481–511) made an alliance with that aristocracy in becoming a Christian and was hailed as the new Constantine. But his kingdom fragmented after his death, mainly because of the barbarian custom of dividing the land among all the sons of the deceased.

Clovis

The English monk St. Willibrord (d. 739), with the support of the Frankish king, worked among the Germans and the Danes at the end of the seventh century and was succeeded by another English monk, Winfrid (or Wynfrith (d. 754), who was renamed Boniface ("well done") by the Pope and sent to the Germans, with the support of Pepin the Short. Like Martin of Tours, St. Boniface avoided associating with the Frankish bishops, who in turn regarded him as an overly stern interloper. (Boniface advised against women going on pilgrimages to the Holy Land, because "a great part of them perish and few keep their virtue").

Boniface

The conversion of the barbarians most often meant that the tribal leader accepted baptism, as Ethelbert did in Kent, whereupon his people followed. Noble Christian women who married barbarian princes were often instrumental in converting the societies into which they married, as happened with St. Clotilda (d. 545) among the Franks, Bertha (d. 612) among the Anglo-Saxons, St. Ludmila (d. 921) among the Bohemians, St. Olga (d. 969) among the Russians, and Leovigild (d. 589) among the Arian Spanish Visigoths.

Christian Queens

When a barbarian chief converted, he was expected by the Church to help christianize his people by supporting missionary efforts, building churches and monasteries, endowing bishoprics, and suppressing pagan

Mass Conversions

cults, an obligation that also extended to lesser lords. Unlike the Greeks and the Romans, the barbarians had little concept of individualism, so that no one opposed the king's conversion on the grounds of conscience. But to abandon the traditional religion of the tribe was dangerous, so that conversion to Christ disturbed some people because it angered the old gods. Zealous Christians who destroyed idols or desecrated pagan shrines were sometimes killed by mobs, and chieftains who converted did not always carry their nobles with them. Occasionally, a convert was driven out of his kingdom as a result.

The barbarians' strong sense of family caused some to be disturbed at the thought that their ancestors, having never heard the Gospel, were in Hell. One missionary to the Germans sought to overcome this by teaching that all pagans had been released from Hell by Jesus after His death, but Boniface considered that doctrine lax. Converts were taught the urgency of commemorating the dead and praying for their souls, customs that strengthened the sense of family solidarity, so that monasteries were sometimes founded explicitly for the purpose of having monks pray for the deceased of the founder's ancestors and for himself after his own death. In a world where sudden death was common, Christianity established a new dimension of family through the institution of the godparent, an office that was not a mere formality but created a new network of relationships for the child.

Pagan Survivals

As Constantine did for a time, many of the barbarians probably embraced Christianity as representing one god among many, albeit the greatest and most powerful. A Spanish king was known to keep two altars, one Christian, one pagan, and graves sometimes displayed both the cross and pagan symbols. If Christianity's principal appeal in the Hellenistic world was to truth, among the barbarians it was to a supernatural power that demonstrated that the Christian God was greater than the gods who were abandoned—the dramatic contrast between the saint and the warrior, this world and the world to come.

Rival Powers

Thus Patrick directly confronted the Celtic priests called *druids*, and Boniface won over a German tribe by boldly entering a forest and taking an axe to a large oak tree sacred to the god Odin. The Germans expected Boniface to be struck dead, and, when he was not, they concluded that the power of his God was greater than that of their own and used the wood of the tree to build a church. (After decades of highly effective work, Boniface was killed in the modern Netherlands, possibly not for religion but by robbers.)

Whatever its teachings, Christianity was often experienced by the barbarians not as pacific but as a powerful conqueror to whom it was entirely proper to submit. Violence was held in check only by the threat of God's even more powerful wrath. Dramatic manifestations of divine power were necessary because a religion was expected to bring tangible benefits, such as victory in battle, good crops, or salvation from illness. One missionary asked the Germans why their gods had given them the frozen and barren North as their land, while the true God reserved the warm and rich South for the Christians. (Such appeals could also backfire—during a visitation of the plague in the eighth century, one English king took his people back into paganism, because the new religion had failed to halt the disease.)

The promise of eternal life was the chief of the gifts the Church offered to people whose existence was bleak and precarious, with Jesus' triumph over death recognized as His greatest miracle. A missionary in England called attention to a bird flying in at one end of a banquet hall and out at the other, comparing its brief flight to human life on earth, surrounded by the vastness of eternity, a mystery to which only the Church held the answer.

Eternal Life

As with the Romans, barbarian society was in many ways based on a system of patronage, whereby individuals placed themselves under the protection of powerful men, a custom that supported the developing belief in the saints as mediators between God and man. Images of saints became common, and their relics were venerated with increasing fervor, the possession of relics demonstrating that the saint was present in the local community in a special way.

The Power of the Saints

Certain patterns of sanctity emerged in the Dark Ages that would continue to be venerated until early modern times: the boy who confounded his parents by recognizing his monastic vocation while still very young, the girl who vowed herself to chastity and refused all suitors, the rich man who renounced his wealth to live as a hermit, the rich widow who devoted herself entirely to the poor and sick, peasants who were the recipients of supernatural visions and messages, practitioners of severe penances. Saints manifested power while alive but even more after they were dead, dramatically vanquishing evil and bringing grace and divine favors to the communities with which they were associated. Lives of the saints (*hagiography*, from the Greek) were the most popular form of literature during the Dark Ages, emphasizing the miracles that confirmed that the saint represented a superior power. Martin of Tours was by far the most popular, the huge church built over his tomb becoming a major pilgrimage place.

Even though the lives of the saints included many stories of miraculous salvation from danger, they often ended in martyrdom, which was a delicate problem in that it seemed to imply defeat. But the martyrs could be understood by the barbarian as brave people slain in battle, manifesting a mysterious courage even higher than that of the warrior. The Anglo-Saxon poem *The Dream of the Rood* (cross) portrayed Jesus as a great chief who triumphed over Satan, the Apostles as His faithful warriors, and Heaven as their victorious banquet after victory, while a German paraphrase of the Gospel referred to Jesus as a "giver of mead" (war booty) and a model for warriors because He endured pain unflinchingly and ultimately overcame His enemies.

The Warlike Spirit

The barbarians' code of behavior probably made Jesus' teaching about forgiving one's enemies seem almost like an inversion of true righteousness, since the heart of the warlike spirit that dominated barbarian life was the corporate blood feud that was the major obstacle to inner conversion—the ethic of vengeance by which men were obliged to repay injuries done to themselves or their families. When a defiant warrior cut in two a golden cup that belonged to a church, Clovis, before his conversion, set matters right by cleaving the man's own skull in two.

The bishop St. Remi (or Remigius, d. ca. 533), in baptizing Clovis, abjured him to "burn what you have adored and adore what you have burned", and Clovis protected church property, acknowledged the special status of virgins, and respected the right of sanctuary, whereby a fugitive from the law could seek safety in a church for a limited period of time. But Clovis also sought to control the hierarchy, and his permission was required for a man to become a priest. Clovis' own family manifested the contradictions of the age. He was converted through the influence of his wife, St. Clotilda (d. 545), who despite her best efforts saw her sons develop into brutal and ruthless warrior chiefs. One of them, Clotaire I (558–561), murdered two of his young nephews to prevent their becoming his rivals, but a third nephew, St. Cloud (d. ca. 560), became a monk. Clotaire's wife St. Radegund (d. 587) left him to enter a convent.

However, the Church only partially stood aloof from barbarian culture, and in the process of christianizing the culture, the Church inevitably assimilated some barbarian elements to herself. Bishops were sometimes not men of peace but very much a part of the warrior culture: an eighth-century bishop of Mainz, for example, was deposed because he mounted a campaign of revenge against his father's slayer.

Magic

Church authorities constantly warned against the use of spells and of attempts to predict the future and forbade such things as the use of drinking horns as chalices at Mass. But innumerable pagan customs found a lasting home in popular Christian piety. Boniface set his face against almost all accommodations to pagan culture, but Gregory the Great urged the missionaries to adapt such customs wherever possible, turning pagan temples into churches and allowing the cults of the gods and the spirits to be transformed into the cults of the saints. Pagan shrines and magical practices became associated with Christian saints, as did wells or springs thought to be inhabited by a water spirit. In Sweden, the relatively small town of Uppsala was made the seat of an archbishopric in order to transform its character as a great pagan shrine. It was a strategy that eased the transition from paganism to Christianity but fostered an often intense piety in which pagan beliefs and practices survived under a thin Christian veneer, something that would endure even into the age of modern science.[3]

As the barbarians struggled to achieve political and social stability, new waves of conquest swept over the West. The Muslims destroyed what remained of the rich Christian culture of North Africa, conquered and occupied Spain in 711, and in 732 advanced across the Pyrenees into the Frankish kingdom as far as Poitiers, where they were turned back by Charles Martel ("the Hammer", d. 741), in a momentous battle that, had it gone the other way, would probably have resulted in all of Europe's becoming Muslim. (For a time, the Muslims continued to control parts of southern France.) Córdoba—a city of as many as ninety thousand people—became one of Europe's most important cultural and political centers. The Great Mosque (now a church), built around 800, was the grandest building constructed in the West during the Dark Ages, and there was also a university. At first, Islamic Spain was ruled from Damascus (Syria), but in 932 a caliphate (a Muslim institution that combined political and religious authority in one man) was also established at Córdoba.

In accordance with the Qur'an's instructions for dealing with "the people of the book" (the Bible), Christians under Muslim rule in Spain were not usually persecuted outright but had a distinctly inferior status and were vulnerable to periodic outbursts of violence. Occasional Christian rebellions produced martyrs who inspired yet further resistance. Conversions from Islam to Christianity were very few and were punished by death under Islamic law. Many Christians became Muslims, an act that was also punishable by death under Spanish Christian law.

During the eighth century, the Christian kingdom of Asturias was established in the mountains of northern Spain, to which a large number of Christians came as exiles from the South and which, under successive kings Alfonso I the Catholic, Alfonso II the Chaste, and Alfonso III the Great (739–910), was the precarious center of resistance to Muslim rule. (Alfonso IV became a monk.) The small kingdom of León became the center of Christian resistance. However, partly because of the internal strife endemic to the age, including sons against fathers and brothers against brothers, Spanish Christians were barely able to keep the limited territories they controlled. The discovery of what was believed to be the tomb of St. James the Greater at Compostela became Europe's most

New Invasions

Muslims in Spain

People of the Book

*The Christian
Counter-Offensive*

---

[3] Mild modern superstitions, such as carrying a rabbit's foot, can often be traced back to pre-Christian practices.

popular pilgrimage place and the rallying point for resistance to the Muslims. It was destroyed in 995 but was soon rebuilt.

The Carolingian Age

Pepin

Meanwhile, as the popes struggled against the Byzantine Empire, which still laid claim to Italy, the Lombards, even though having been christianized, constituted a more immediate threat to papal independence. Beginning in the eighth century, rival families, amidst murderous feuds, connived to place their own men on the papal throne and used the most brutal tactics to achieve their goal. Pepin responded to a papal appeal, and drove the Lombards from Rome.

The Donation of Constantine

Pepin also confirmed the pope's claim to certain Italian territories, based on a document from the papal archives called the *Donation of Constantine*, which purportedly showed that, when the first Christian emperor moved to the East, he ceded all political authority in the West to the pope. The papacy also relied on a collection of documents later called the *False Decretals*—purportedly compiled by St. Isidore, the scholarly bishop of Seville (d. 636) but actually compiled 250 years later—containing alleged papal decrees from the fourth century that also showed that the popes possessed temporal power.[4]

Ironically, the "donation of Pepin" had a negative effect on the Church, in that the pope's position as a secular lord plunged the papacy even more deeply into the morass of Italian politics and made the office extremely attractive in worldly terms, helping to corrupt papal politics for the next three centuries.

Charlemagne

Several times more the popes had to appeal to the Franks against the Lombards, and in 800 Pope St. Leo III (795–816), after being attacked and mutilated in the streets of Rome during a procession, fled across the Alps to ask for protection from Pepin's son Charles the Great (Charlemagne, 768–814), who answered the papal appeal by once again vanquishing the pope's enemies.

On Christmas Day, as Charlemagne was at Mass in St. Peter's Basilica, Leo placed a crown on his head and proclaimed him emperor. Although the imperial title has often been assumed to have been the reward Charlemagne demanded for his assistance to the Pope, the new emperor claimed that he had not anticipated it, and Leo may well have acted on his own, regarding a universal empire as the only fully legitimate kind of state and realizing that only a powerful monarch of great prestige could restore order to a chaotic world.

But the action was dubiously legal, in that the emperors at Constantinople still considered themselves the heirs of Rome. Thus the

---

[4] In premodern times, forgery was not considered as serious an offense as it later became. It was employed by people who thought that the forged document expressed a truth, even if it was not literal historical truth.

new state had no theoretical basis except that of the papacy itself. In bestowing the imperial title, the Pope appeared to make a dramatic assertion of his own authority, restoring the Roman Empire under the direct auspices of the Church. But the symbolism was ambiguous, in that Leo also prostrated himself before the new emperor as his legitimate secular lord and Charlemagne's proclamations announced that he had been "crowned by God".

At Aachen (Aix-la-Chapelle), Charlemagne built a palace that was the most ambitious Christian architectural undertaking in the West for centuries and where the unity of church and state was manifest by the imperial throne's being erected in the chapel itself, albeit in the west end, because the East was the throne of God. The chapel, which was of very modest size compared with those of the East, was nonetheless in the Eastern style, modeled after a Byzantine church at Ravenna, symbolizing the heavenly Jerusalem, with a dome from which Christ *Pantocrator* ("Ruler of All") presided.

The Imperial Court

Although Gregory the Great had condemned forced conversions, when Charlemagne brought eastern Germany under his control, he ordered the Saxons to become Christians, their acceptance of his religion being a necessary part of their submission to him. Conversion was to be signaled by refraining from assaults on priests and churches, observance of the Lenten fast, and burying rather than cremating the dead, and when Charlemagne learned that those demands were being disregarded, he slaughtered a reported 4,500 people, despite the objections of his monk-advisor, St. Alcuin of York (d. 804).

Forced Conversions

Charlemagne also ignored Church teaching when it seemed to undermine his dynastic interests. He married five times, divorced several of his wives, had six concubines, and, fearing that sons-in-law would become his rivals, forbade his daughters to marry and instead allowed them to have children by their paramours.

Marriage and Concubinage

Both a ruthless warrior and a man of ideals, Charlemagne made an ultimately unsuccessful attempt to establish a universal monarchy that was both Roman and Christian. He built up an effective centralized administrative system and traveled constantly in order to maintain his grip on so vast a territory. At its height, his empire included modern Germany, France, the Low Countries, Switzerland, northern Italy, and parts of Poland, Austria, and Hungary.

A Universal Monarchy

Charlemagne was able to conquer part of Spain, but it was later reclaimed by the Muslims, and he settled for a buffer state on the Spanish border. His Spanish invasion demonstrated the complexity of the Spanish situation. Some Muslim leaders, fearful of the powerful ruler of Córdoba, 'Abd ar-Rahmān I (756–788), encouraged Charlemagne, while the Catholic Basque people resisted him. (The legendary knight Roland [d. 778], who became the subject of an epic poem, was actually killed in the fight against the Basques, not the Muslims.)

Church and State

Like the Christian emperors before him, in trying to create an all-embracing sacred order, Charlemagne continually involved himself in Church matters, promulgating what became the universal Code of Canon Law and even successfully claiming authority over the liturgy. He intervened in the dispute over icons in the East (see Chapter Seven below, pp. 193–95), issuing a decree that sacred images were merely reminders of the person honored and were not to be venerated, a doctrine that went contrary to papal teaching.

The custom whereby bishops were elected by the people of a diocese had by Charlemagne's time evolved into election by chapters (Latin for "heads")—the cathedral clergy who aided the bishop in governing the diocese. But, in a pattern that was to be followed by many rulers over the centuries, Charlemagne often simply appointed bishops and required the chapters to acquiesce. He also sometimes left dioceses vacant in order to collect their revenues.

The End of the Empire

Charlemagne's experiments failed after his death. His son Louis the Pious (814–840), who was crowned by Pope Stephen IV (816–817) at Rheims, had the virtues indicated by his epithet, but he was a weak ruler. In 833, the Frankish bishops acquiesced in his deposition by his own sons, then reversed themselves two years later, after Louis managed to defeat his enemies. After his death, the Empire split first into three, then into two kingdoms—France and Germany—with the German ruler retaining the imperial title. The separate kingdoms were then also divided, their rulers often unable to maintain order in the face of constant warfare among powerful and independent-minded nobles. In the tenth century, episcopal support was crucial to the ascendancy of the Capetian dynasty in France (named for its first king), which would rule for almost four hundred years.

Alfred the Great

During the Dark Ages, the ideal of Christian kingship found its purest representative not in Charlemagne but in the Anglo-Saxon Alfred the Great (ca. 900), who held the marauding Vikings at bay, governed justly, encouraged piety and learning, and was venerated as a saint after his death. He was remarkable in being fully literate, even translating several Latin works.

Feudalism

Lord and Vassals

The society of the barbarians gradually evolved into the system later called feudalism, a precarious hierarchy with the king at the top, various grades of nobility below him, a small class of merchants, and the mass of people, mostly peasants, at the bottom. Booty increasingly took the form of land, a practice that tended to fragment both economic and political power among local lords only loosely subject to the king or emperor. Feudalism (from the Latin word for "contract") emerged as an attempt to maintain some degree of order in the absence of a strong central government. In this system, no one owned land outright. A *vassal* ("servant") was a free man who entered into a contract with a lord whereby he received land—a *fief* (*beneficium*, meaning "well done")—in return for loyalty and service, which were primarily military in nature. In practice, a lord's vassals were often in revolt against him.

Serfdom

The great majority of people were farmers, either as free peasants or, increasingly, as serfs, a term derived from the Latin word for slave but less absolute in its implications—lords did not have the power of life and death over their serfs, who were regarded less as personal property than as belonging to particular landed estates.

Ecclesiastical Benefices

The Church as an institution required economic resources, and from the time of Constantine, she too was given grants of land, to the point where she was eventually the largest possessor of that most valuable of earthly commodities. At every level, church offices were treated as "benefices", as though they were to be valued mainly in terms of their income, something that encouraged clerical greed and gave rise to the abuses called pluralism—holding more than one benefice at the same time—and absenteeism. However, beginning with Charles Martel, Frankish rulers appropriated a great deal of church land for their own purposes or granted it to laymen. As compensation, Charlemagne instituted a church tax based on the Old Testament tithe and ordered that a plot of land in each parish be reserved to the Church.

Prince Bishops

Since the possession of land included political authority, Emperor Otto I (962–973) solidified the new alliance of Church and Empire whereby bishops were territorial princes, an arrangement that gave them prestige and wealth but was another step in the process by which the spiritual and the temporal became so intertwined as to threaten the Church's integrity. The bishops were necessarily involved in complex feudal politics, including interminable small wars among rival lords and periodic revolts against the king.

Free Alms

Churchmen usually provided military service to their lords by subdividing their land still further, giving it to knights who fought in the priests' place. A minority of grants to the Church were gifts in "free alms", which only required the clerical recipient to pray for the donor. Priests were forbidden to shed blood, but even bishops occasionally fought in battles. (One of them evaded the letter of the law by assaulting his opponents with an iron ball on a chain, a weapon that could kill but did not cause much bleeding.)

Priestly Classes

Priests tended to be of the same social class as those whom they served, with the higher clergy having noble status, whatever their origins, and village priests living like the serfs to whom they ministered and sometimes themselves having servile status. Besides the spiritual value of celibacy, it was promoted to prevent clergy from establishing family dynasties, which were by no means unknown in the Dark Ages. Pope Silverius was the son of Pope St. Hormisdas (514–523)—fathered before Hormisdas was ordained—and Gregory the Great was the grandson of Pope Felix III. A serf could become a priest only with his lord's permission, but in an increasingly rigid hierarchical society the Church, partly because celibacy prevented the formation of clerical dynasties, rewarded merit. The highly learned Pope Sylvester II (999–1002), for example, was of peasant origins.

The Nadir of the Papacy

The ninth and tenth centuries were the nadir of the entire history of the papacy, when it again fell under the control of murderous factions. Some popes were notorious, and few could exercise even the least spiritual authority. Kings and emperors often treated the papacy as under their control, and popes in turn intrigued in secular politics. Ironically, although it was made subject to papal authority in order to protect its own purity, Cluny served as the spiritual center of the Church during an age of many unworthy popes. There were occasional saintly popes, such as Hadrian III (884–885), who was nonetheless murdered in one of the continuous intrigues that swirled around the papal office.

Papal Elections

One of Charlemagne's grandsons, Lothair (817–855), decreed that no papal election was valid unless given imperial approval, and he interfered with liberties of the Church in other ways. Another grandson, Louis II the German (843–876), confirmed the same decrees, but the clergy of Rome defied Louis in order to elect Benedict III (855–858). Imperial interference sometimes had unexpectedly good results, as a few years later Louis was able to bring about the election of St. Nicholas I (858–867), who proved to be strong and independent-minded. (When Nicholas refused to grant Louis' brother a divorce and deposed the Frankish bishops who sanctioned it, the emperor threatened the Pope with an army, a threat that was aborted only by Louis' sudden illness.)

"Bad Popes"

The unvirtuous John VIII (872–882), the subject of the entirely apocryphal story of "Pope Joan", was also murdered under uncertain circumstances, and Leo V (903) and the anti-pope Christopher both died in prison, probably on orders of Pope Sergius III (904–911). The low point in the history of the entire papacy was reached in 897, when the body of Pope Formosus (891–896) was exhumed by orders of Pope Stephen VI[5] (896–897), placed upon the papal throne in its vestments, formally "tried" for violations of Church law, found guilty, stripped of its vestments, and desecrated. Stephen himself was strangled in prison later that year, and Formosus' honor was restored.

Despite the existence of the Western Empire, Byzantine representatives remained influential at Rome, especially the Theophylactus family, which gave several popes to the Church. John XI (931–935) became pope through the machinations of his notorious mother, Marozia. John XII (955–964), Marozia's grandson, became pope at the age of sixteen and was accused of every kind of abuse. He was probably guilty of most of the accusations, and he was deposed by Emperor Otto I (962–973), who, dissatisfied with John's elected successor Benedict V (964), took Benedict to Germany and set up Leo VIII (964–965) in his place.

The Vikings

Besides the Muslims, the unending forces of disorder manifested themselves in the ninth century in the sudden explosion of the Northmen or Norsemen of Scandinavia—also called Danes or Vikings, from a word for an inlet of the sea. The Northmen were yet another in the long line of invaders for whom war was the principal activity of life. Ireland was their first target, but almost no part of Europe was safe, as they ravaged the British Isles, destroying the culture that had reached a peak under Alfred the Great; swept down the Atlantic along the Frankish coast, penetrating inland to sack Paris and Aachen; and continued around into the Mediterranean, inflicting havoc on both Muslim Spain and Catholic Italy. For a time, the Litany of the Saints included the plaintive cry, "From the peril of the Northmen, O Lord, deliver us!"

Brutality

The Northmen were brutal. A Saxon king, St. Edmund (d. 870), they dismembered while still alive, and an archbishop of Canterbury, St. Alphege (d. 1012), they beat to death with clubs and animal bones. Monasteries, because they were wealthy and often undefended, were their special targets, causing the great monasteries of Iona and Lindisfarne to be temporarily abandoned. For a time, monasticism survived by monks living in cave-like stone cells on barren islands off the coasts of Ireland and Scotland. The monks of Lindisfarne wandered for seven years with the body of their sainted abbot, Cuthbert (d. 687), until finding a new home.

New Settlements

At first mere raiders, in time, the Danes settled on lands they conquered, as in Ireland, where they founded the settlement that became

---

[5] There are some uncertainties about papal succession in this period, and Stephen VI is sometimes designated Stephen VII.

Dublin. In England, the Danelaw took up more than half the country, and a Dane, Oda (d. 926), even served as archbishop of Canterbury. The king of France bribed the Vikings with the extensive territory that came to be called Normandy, and a branch of the Vikings called the Rus gave their name to the territory that eventually became Russia. Danes colonized Iceland and Greenland and briefly (ca. 1000) what would later be called Newfoundland.

Viking Conversions

The Vikings often sought nothing less than the destruction of Christianity itself, and, although many became nominal Catholics during their travels, the missionaries sent to them had little effect. When they settled in Normandy, however, they became Christians as a condition of the grant. England was a source of Christian influence in Scandinavia, and the archbishopric of Bremen-Hamburg, on the Baltic coast of Germany, was also a center of missionary activity.

Two tenth-century Norwegian kings—Haakon the Good (946–961) and Olaf I Tryggvason (995–999)—were converted to Christianity in England, and Christianity became official in Denmark under King Canute (1016–1035), who also ruled much of England. St. Olaf II (1016–1030) made the new religion official in Denmark and, after being defeated and killed by Canute, was venerated as a saint even by his conqueror, a focal point of Viking popular religion. Olaf of Sweden (995–ca. 1022) became a Christian and imported English missionaries. Iceland was unique in the history of Christianity, becoming Christian by vote of the inhabitants in 1000, following established Icelandic custom. First, however, a pagan prophet went into a kind of trance, after which he announced that the island should be of one religion, so as to avoid division.

The Last Converts

In Central Europe, Bohemia became officially Christian under the duke St. Wenceslaus (d. 929),[6] who was murdered by his brother at the door of a church and venerated as a martyr. The Church first came to Poland from Bohemia, beginning with the marriage of a Polish prince to a Bohemian princess in 964. The missionary bishop St. Adalbert (d. 997) was sent to Poland from Bohemia and, after being killed by Germans who were contending for control of Polish territory, was venerated as the apostle of Poland. The Wends were Slavic people (so-called in the West because, as non-Christians, they could be made slaves) living on the borders between Germany and Poland. The Saxons made a partially successful effort to subdue and christianize the Wends in the tenth century, but the Wends later rebelled, returned to paganism, and slaughtered Christians. Around the same time as the Viking onslaughts, the Muslims invaded southern Italy, perpetrating yet another sack of Rome. At the same time,

---

[6] "Good King Wenceslaus" of the Christmas carol.

a new barbarian people—the Magyars—devastated central Europe before settling down in Hungary.

The Magyars, Poles, and Russians all became Christians around the same time as the Vikings, after which the recovery of Western civilization was rapid, based on a chain of Christian monarchies stretching from Ireland to Russia in the North and southward to Italy and Spain.

The Decline of Culture

Schools

The decline of the West could be measured by the closing of many schools in the midst of the struggle for survival. The most telling evidence was the gradual disappearance of the Greek language, something that cut off the Western Church not only from much of the richness of patristic theology but from the original text of the New Testament itself. Even before the barbarian onslaught, Augustine of Hippo did not read Greek, and Jerome learned it only after he moved to Palestine, although it survived for a while in some of the Irish monasteries.

Precarious Learning

Despite the overall decline of culture, learning was revered in the Dark Ages and knowledge limited only by the harsh conditions of life. Skill in Latin also declined, but Christians continued to respect classical learning, much of which was kept alive in various *encyclopediae*, such as those compiled by St. Isidore of Seville—elementary textbooks that minimally preserved the Western cultural heritage until such time as there might be a new intellectual flowering. The word *science* was simply the Latin term for "knowledge" and was not confined to the physical world. But knowledge of the physical world was preserved during the Dark Ages, as in the compilations of the German archbishop Rabanus Maurus (d. 856). There was measurable technological progress during the Dark Ages, especially in agriculture, building, and weaponry.

Magic

The people of the time were superstitious by modern standards, but they followed the Greek belief that such things as astrology and alchemy had a rational basis. Belief in witches and other forms of malignant magic survived from pagan times, but attitudes toward those beliefs varied. There were occasional prosecutions, but St. Caesarius of Arles (d. 543) used his episcopal authority to prevent the prosecution of accused witches, on the grounds that no man could interfere with God's power over nature; hence there was no such thing as sorcery. Boniface also warned that to believe in witches was un-Christian.

Monastic Learning

The early monks rejected classical civilization as pagan, thus the preservation of learning was not originally part of their task. But they had to teach Latin in order to prepare novices for the liturgy and the Bible, and this led to an interest in the whole spectrum of ancient learning. Many works by ancient writers are lost, but virtually all that survive come down in manuscripts industriously found, collected, and copied in monastic libraries during the Dark Ages.

The Bible   Jerome's Vulgate, which Alcuin was learned enough to correct in some places, was in universal use in the West, although the name that it bore no longer applied, because Latin was now the language only of the educated. Alcuin undertook to correlate its various manuscript versions and to have copies made for others, at a time when even some bishops did not have a complete Bible, which required the hides of over fifty calves. Numerous biblical commentaries were written, some for laymen. Besides hagiography, monks also compiled dictionaries and *encyclopediae* and wrote histories of their own times and earlier eras, a practice that continued to be a monastic specialty for the next thousand years.

Spain   Visigothic Spain was the intellectual center of Western Catholicism in the sixth and seventh centuries, and it preserved some knowledge of the ancient classics. Isidore of Seville was perhaps the most learned man of his age, and synods of Spanish bishops were the first to condemn Western Arianism. Spanish influence spread to Ireland and England and from there to France, which became the center of anti-Arian theology. In England, a vernacular Christian literature developed, especially at Lindisfarne. St. Bede the Venerable (d. 735), a monk of Jarrow, an offshoot of Lindisfarne, wrote a history of the Anglo-Saxons and had some knowledge of Greek, which allowed him to translate the Gospel of John into Anglo-Saxon and to transmit knowledge of the Eastern Fathers.

The Court of Charlemagne   Charlemagne's court was the center of a significant cultural renaissance, and, even though the Carolingian Empire was short-lived, its culture was enduring. Charlemagne's support of learning was part of his general program of religious revitalization. He enticed Alcuin, who was originally from Lindisfarne, to settle at his court, established a palace school where both clerics and laymen were educated, and encouraged the founding of monastic and cathedral schools throughout his empire. Charlemagne showed his respect for learning by himself struggling to read and write, at a time when most princes regarded those skills as best left to clerks. The court of Charlemagne revolutionized Western literacy, introducing punctuation and spaces between words, for example, and a kind of script that was so clear that it became the model for most later handwriting.

Alcuin   Alcuin loved the poetry of Virgil but found it so seductive that he forbade his pupils to read it. But, drawing on the theories of Cassiodorus and others, he laid the foundation of medieval learning by establishing a curriculum based on the "three ways" (*trivium*) of logic, grammar, and rhetoric and the "four ways" (*quadrivium*) of arithmetic, geometry, astronomy, and music. The first sought for truth in words and the second in mathematical relationships, with both together making up what came to be called the liberal arts, because they freed the student from ignorance.

There was some original theological and philosophical activity in the West during the Dark Ages, but virtually the entire body of Christian doctrine came down through the prism of Augustine, a man who, except for the Scriptures themselves, influenced the course of Catholicism more than any other person in history.

During the sixth century, certain writings from the East were attributed to St. Dionysius the Areopagite, whom Acts recorded as having been converted at Athens by St. Paul and who in the West was later identified with Dionysius (Denis), the first bishop of Paris. When this alleged authorship was eventually discredited, the writer became known as Pseudo-Dionysius, but his theology continued to have great influence for over a thousand years.

Mysticism
The Dionysian works were the first extensive exposition of Christian mysticism, the seeds of which lay in Paul's account of a man (presumably himself) who was taken out of himself and into Heaven. Dionysius described the mystical state as an exalted kind of prayer in which the soul utterly transcends the limits of human existence. The world of appearances conceals but also partly reveals the real world of the spirit, the transcendent realm.

The Divine Hierarchy
In Neo-Platonic terms, Pseudo-Dionysius' preferred name for God was "The One". Light is the ultimate metaphor for God but, paradoxically, precisely because of the brightness of that light, sinful men cannot see it. Light descends from God throughout the cosmos, fragmenting as it descends and thereby establishing a chain of being that stretches from the One to the lowest of creatures, all arranged in harmony according to the divine plan. Souls preexist with the angels but are plunged into bodies, where they can have only fleeting glimpses of truth but can discover the route by which reality descends and are thereby enabled to reascend to the heavenly realm.

Pseudo-Dionysius used the term *hierarchy* ("the rule of priests") for this cosmic order coming from on high, and he taught that the visible hierarchy of the Church mirrors the angelic hierarchy of eight distinct choirs (thrones, dominions, principalities, powers, angels, archangels, cherubim, seraphim) even as those angels' unceasing worship of God is mirrored in the liturgy. Thus the Neo-Platonic theory of the universe as a hierarchy of beings emanating downward from one ultimate source, and returning to that source by the same way, explained the hierarchical nature of society, where each person has an assigned place under the ultimate authority of pope and emperor.

Theology

The Augustinian Heritage

Pseudo-Dionysius

Negative Theology

Knowledge of God is innate in men, because the existence of imperfect beings implies the existence of a perfect Being from whom they derive their limited perfections. Pseudo-Dionysius' "negative theology" taught that, since God is absolutely One, no categories can ultimately be applied to Him. There is no time in God, and, although He foresees all things, He does not diminish human freedom, because He foresees human actions precisely as free.

Boethius

St. Severinus Boethius (d. ca. 524), an imperial official born into a prominent Roman family, was the last flowering of classical culture in the West and one of the most influential thinkers of the Dark Ages and the ensuing centuries. He knew Greek well, translated some of the writings of Plato and Aristotle, and made exploratory efforts at solving some of the questions that would engage later philosophers. As knowledge of Greek disappeared in the West, scholars took almost all their knowledge of ancient philosophy from Boethius, including especially Aristotle's system of logic.

Under Neo-Platonic influence, Boethius defined theology as the study of beings that exist outside matter and physics—beings that can be studied through the *trivium*—while the study of beings inseparable from matter was pursued through the mathematical *quadrivium*. Boethius affirmed the Greco-Roman idea of impersonal and inescapable destiny, but it could be overcome by submission to God's will. Human life is symbolized by the wheel of fortune, on which all men have a place but which rotates unpredictably, laying low the mighty and elevating the lowly.

Boethius taught that the cultivation of virtue is the practical purpose of philosophy, an idea that, in his highly influential book *The Consolations of Philosophy*, was tested in a way that philosophical theories seldom are—he wrote it in prison while awaiting execution because of a complex political-religious intrigue. Over the next thousand years, it remained one of the most widely read books in all of Christendom. Although based heavily on Stoicism and Neo-Platonism, with few overt Christian references, *Consolations* was suffused by a Christian spirit. It affirmed the purifying value of suffering and the transitoriness of the world and was the source of much of the medieval idea of the relationship between free will and divine providence.

Gregory the Great

Gregory the Great came to be designated as one of the four founding doctors (teachers) of the Western church, along with Jerome, Ambrose, and Augustine. In his practical theology, he struggled to shore up the moral and spiritual basis of civilization, besides being one of the most important of all the popes and the first to use the paradoxical title "servant of the servants of God". He incorporated some of the principles of the Penitentials in his book *Pastoral Care*, which emphasized conversion as the primary purpose of penance, analyzed the motives of particular sins, and treated subjective intention as relevant to the degree of guilt.

Purgatory

Although earlier theologians had speculated about the idea of a temporary period of punishment following death, Gregory was the first to give full expression to the doctrine of Purgatory, including the Mass as a sacrifice that could be offered on behalf of deceased souls. (The idea of a plenary [full] indulgence—the remission of all temporal punishment due to past sins—dates from the eighth century.)

The Contemplative Life

Gregory articulated the distinction between the active and contemplative life that became fundamental to Catholic spirituality, designating contemplation—a life devoted to prayer and meditation on the divine mysteries—as superior but insisting that a life of charity toward others, of fidelity to divinely ordained responsibilities, is a prerequisite. This was not simply a distinction between monks and others, since each person can live contemplatively in accordance with his state of life. Gregory, also influenced by Pseudo-Dionysius, described God as "boundless light", drawing the soul to itself to the point of causing it to forget even its own identity. Man longs for a vision of God, and occasional glimpses are possible, but for the most part man can only know God through images.

John Scotus ("the Scot") Eriugena (d. 877) was an Irishman who taught in France, bringing with him what little knowledge of Greek still survived in his native land. He too translated Greek philosophical works and considered philosophy, especially dialectic (logic), necessary for believers, because the divine commands can be obeyed only insofar as they are understood. The concept of *being*—that an idea in the mind represents something that really exists—was central to his thought, as it would be to later medieval philosophers. But influenced also by Pseudo-Dionysius' negative theology, Eriugena taught that, in a sense, nonbeing must also be attributed to God, because He can never be adequately understood in human terms.

Eriugena

The Neo-Platonic Hierarchy

Also as with Pseudo-Dionysius, the universe for Eriugena was a hierarchy of Neo-Platonic Ideas linking God and the world, Ideas that are eternal, in that God created them outside time. Because ultimate reality is One, multiplicity in the world is the result of sin. The Divine Word contains the seeds of all beings, a process of creation guided by the Holy Spirit in which each individual being is a symbol of an unseen spiritual Idea that is more real than itself, so that amidst the multiplicity of creation the mind can know the ultimate unity of God.

The world is not a prison for the soul but the place where the soul begins its return journey to God. Souls never completely forget God and come close to Him to the degree that they are not bodily, that they have knowledge of Him through direct divine illumination. Death marks the transition from division to unity, as the resurrected body is reabsorbed first by the soul, then by the Idea from which it originally emanated, and finally receives direct knowledge of Wisdom itself.

Influence of Eriugena

Eriugena's system was the most ambitious effort to date to forge a comprehensive synthesis of Greek philosophy and Christian doctrine—the ultimate reconciliation of faith and reason—and as such might have established itself as the dominant Catholic way of thought. But in the disordered days of the ninth century, Eriugena was little understood, and his influence remained limited.

Heresies

The late Dark Ages were a time of considerable theological ferment. The semi-Arian heresy of Adoptionism—that, while Christ was divine, the human Jesus was only the adopted son of the Father—reappeared in Spain in the eighth century, possibly influenced by the Islamic denial that God could become man. It was condemned by Pope Hadrian I (772–795). For the next three centuries, the most important theological work took place in Frankish or German monasteries.

The Virgin Birth

While the doctrine of Christ's virgin birth was always accepted, there was disagreement as to how it occurred. Ratramnus (d. ca. 868) held that His birth took place in the ordinary human way, while another monk, Paschasius Radbertus (d. 860), taught that Jesus had miraculously emerged from the womb through "closed doors".

The Real Presence

The Eucharist had always been regarded as the Body of Christ, but without much discussion of precisely how that was so. Ratramnus distinguished Christ's spiritual Body from His physical Body and held that He is present "figuratively" in the Eucharist, which is a memorial of His sacrifice on the Cross. (Eriugena held a similar belief.) In response, Radbertus set forth the first developed theory of the Real Presence, insisting that Christ's Body, as received by the faithful in the Eucharist, is the same Body that was borne by Mary and died on the Cross.

Liturgical Change

The defense of the Real Presence led to a number of new liturgical practices: heightened emphasis on the consecration as the moment when bread and wine became Christ's Body and Blood; the use of unleavened bread, to prevent crumbs; the practice of giving the laity unbroken hosts, for the same reason; allowing only clergy to touch the consecrated host and the sacred vessels; and the confession "Lord, I am not worthy" before Communion. Both consecrated elements were affirmed to be the Body of Christ wholly and entirely, and gradually the chalice ceased being offered to the laity. The heresy of Ratramnus led also to the practice of receiving Communion on the tongue while kneeling, a posture that in the Old Testament was the spontaneous action of those who found themselves in the presence of God. (The priest, acting for Christ, frequently genuflected ["knee bending"], but did not kneel.)

Infrequent Communion

Bede and others had advocated even daily Communion, but, as the sense of unworthiness grew, the reception of Communion by the laity became less and less frequent, to the point where it became necessary to require minimal reception—first at Christmas, Easter, and Pentecost, later reduced to Easter only. As only a few people approached the holy table on a given day, Communion was often distributed after Mass, when almost everyone had left, although it was considered meritorious merely to be in the presence of the eucharistic Christ, without receiving Him. Many people thought that it was necessary to go to confession before each Communion, and possibly to abstain from meat for a week, so that even nuns often received Communion only a few times a year, while the priest's sense of his own unworthiness was sometimes rendered acute by his regular celebration of Mass.

Marian Piety

Marian piety developed during the Carolingian period, much of it imported from the East but having a dynamic of its own. On the basis of ancient traditions, Mary's Assumption and her Immaculate Conception were widely but not universally believed, the Assumption regarded as necessary because Mary had been elevated above sinful mankind and therefore could not die.

Grace and Free Will

In the ninth century, a controversy again erupted over the relationship between grace and free will, a question Augustine had only partially resolved. Some of the disputants affirmed that men enjoy a natural freedom that allows them to respond to God's offer of faith, while others considered men free only to do evil, in accord with their sinful natures, thus making them totally dependent on grace. To the former, good works were meritorious, while to the latter they were not.

A basic issue was the mystery of God's sovereign power. Hincmar, archbishop of Rheims (d. 882), explained that God remains sovereign because from all eternity He foresees men's free decisions and incorporates them into His providence. But Ratramnus thought that belief in human merit took salvation out of God's hands and allowed men to determine their own fates and that, if God accepted good works as evidence of repentance, He would be changing His mind—first condemning, then justifying. Instead, therefore, He must decree men's fates from all eternity.

The German monk Gottschalk (d. 868), who was associated with Ratramnus, was imprisoned for holding that God hardens some people's hearts and withholds His grace from them, thereby making it impossible for them to choose good and predestining them to Hell. Gottschalk thought that Christ could not have died for all men, since He would then have wasted some of His precious Blood. Predestinarians like Gottschalk held that Christ died "for many", while Hincmar insisted that He died "for all", in the sense that His grace is available to all who accept it.

Liturgy

In a sense, the greatest cultural achievement of the Dark Ages was the liturgy, which was then given the basic form that it would retain for centuries.

The Power of Symbol

Barbarian culture was intensely communal and did not encourage interiority, so that the solemn and dramatic celebration of the sacred rites impressed the barbarians and taught them their faith more effectively than formal instruction. The Frankish clergy were especially sensitive to the dramatic power of ritual and symbol and added various genuflections, signs of the cross, and other gestures to the liturgy. In accordance with ancient rhetorical practice, repetitions, especially triple repetitions, were used to achieve emphasis.

Sacred Art

The barbarians lacked art in the traditional sense, some of their attempts at sacred pictures being quite crude. But their booty of gold and jewels led them to develop skills as jewelers, which they lavished on crucifixes and sacred vessels, as well as on the most elaborately illustrated manuscripts ever produced, a practice that was, paradoxically, perhaps linked to illiteracy: the book was a mysterious sacred object, venerated even by those who could not understand its contents.

Disputed Practices

The distinction between doctrine and discipline, a difference over "externals" were often treated as fundamental, because it was thought that there should be unity of practice. Thus when the two branches of English Christianity came together at the Synod of Whitby (664) the northerners accepted the Roman practice both for the date of Easter and for the clerical tonsure ("hair").

The tonsure was a prime example of how externals revealed the world of the spirit. Since hair is a principal focus of fashion and personal vanity, the desert monks let theirs grow wild and uncombed; the Roman tonsure cut most of it off, leaving only a narrow circle around a bald pate; and the Celtic tonsure shaved the front half of the head but let the back half grow long, a sign that the monk had relinquished his status as a warrior. Nuns' heads were symbolically shaved when they took their vows.

The Cross

The cross became the dominant Christian symbol during the Dark Ages, surpassing earlier themes such as the Good Shepherd and the *Pantocrator* image that was never common in the West. Originally, the cross was bare, to signify the Resurrection, but devotion to the image of the crucified Christ developed during the seventh century, as the faithful were reminded of their great sins that had crucified their Savior and were urged to share His sufferings. (The Reproaches ["O my people, how have I offended thee?"] became part of the Good Friday liturgy.)

Some people—monks in particular—objected to the number and variety of images, but the practice was defended partly on Old Testament grounds: the image of a serpent erected by Moses in the desert, which protected the Israelites from real serpents. *Images*

The liturgy had two overlapping temporal cycles. That of the seasons began with Advent and moved forward through Christmas, Epiphany, Lent, Holy Week, the Ascension, and Pentecost, while in the cycle of the saints practically every day of the year commemorated one or more saints, usually the days of their deaths, hence of their entries into Heaven. Feasts of the saints, including those of the Virgin Mary, steadily increased in number, the Assumption (also Dormition or "sleep"), the Annunciation, and the Purification being introduced into the West in the seventh century. In a sense, there was no such thing as secular time. A town, for example, would schedule a trade fair not on September 29 but on "Michaelmas". People lived primarily in sacred time, in accord with a calendar that commemorated the life of Christ and of His saints on particular days. *The Liturgical Cycle*

But the Church won only a partial victory over pagan time. The new year was March 25, the feast of the Annunciation, when the Son of God entered human history, but the Roman Kalends—January 1—was also observed. The custom of dating the years from the birth of Christ was not established until the sixth century, and even then the older system, based on the founding of Rome, continued in some places. Just as some Roman deities remained in the calendar, northern pagan deities were still commemorated, if gradually forgotten, in the days of the week named for the gods Tiw (Tuesday), Woden (Wednesday), Thor (Thursday), and Fridd (Friday). In England, the day of Christ's Resurrection adopted the name of the pagan feast of Easter and the period before Easter the name of a spring feast called Lent. Yule, a winter feast, became a name for Christmas. *Pagan Survivals*

Votive ("vow") masses—celebrations not in observance of Sunday or some great feast but offered for the special intentions of the faithful—dated from the late fifth century in the West. Their texts varied to some degree according to their purposes, masses for the dead being by far the most common. Since they were considered acts of private devotion, stipends (Latin for "wages") were offered to the officiating priest. *Votive Masses*

The Divine Office   The celebration of the complete liturgy—the *Opus Dei* ("work of God")—was the monks' principal task, taking up much of their day, so that they prayed in the name of the whole Church, fulfilling Christ's command to pray always, offering to God the unceasing praise owed Him by His creatures. The Psalms, understood as referring to Christ, were the substance of the Divine Office, which was chanted at fixed hours throughout the day: Matins ("Morning"), Lauds ("Praise"), Prime ("First"), Terce ("Third"), Sext ("Sixth"), None ("Ninth"), Vespers ("Evening"), and Compline ("Completion"). The hours of the Divine Office regulated the monastic day and, in the absence of clocks, that of the whole surrounding community, through the ringing of the church bells.

Chant   Liturgical chant came to be called Gregorian after the great pope, although it actually predated his reign. Boethius, drawing on Platonic Ideas, provided a theological justification for sacred music as an expression of the divine harmony of the universe itself. The see of Rome was conservative in this as in other ways, not adopting chant until the eighth century and for a long time forbidding hymns that were not directly biblical.

Prayer   Prayers directed to Christ were rare in the liturgy, with most prayers being formulated, "O God . . . through Jesus Christ Our Lord". But the Western church began to insist on the formula, "Glory be to the Father and *to* the Son . . ." in the Doxology rather than the Eastern "*through* the Son", which the West deemed open to Arian misunderstandings. Opposition to Arianism also led to a heightened devotion to the Trinity, now addressed in its unity as well as in the three Persons. The invocation of the Trinity was placed at the beginning of the Litany of the Saints, and private prayers commonly began with the sign of the cross and the declaration, "In the name of the Father . . .". Images of the Trinity became common, with the Father for the first time portrayed in human form, as an elderly patriarch with a white beard.

The Sacrifice of the Mass   Above all the Mass was understood as the continuation of the sacrifice of Calvary as the means of redemption, of which the repeated sign of the cross throughout the liturgy served as a reminder, as did associating the priest's act with the sacrifices of Abel, Abraham, and Melchizedek.

In contrast to the Eastern sense of the liturgy as an entry into eternity, the Western liturgy increasingly celebrated the historical events of Christ's life. The ritual of the Mass was sometimes interpreted in that way, with the priest's moving from one side of the altar to the other, for example, as symbolizing Jesus' being taken back and forth between Herod and Pilate.

The Mass itself was divided into the Ordinary (those prayers that never changed, especially the Canon, which included the Consecration) and the Proper ("belonging" to a particular feast), which included the entrance hymn, petitionary prayers, Scripture readings, Offertory prayers, Secret, Preface, Communion, and post-Communion prayers appropriate to the feast.

The Ordinary and the Proper

As early as the fifth century, the Gallic liturgy had absorbed certain Eastern influences, such as elaborate processions, the Kyrie, the Creed, Marian feasts, and a penchant for lengthy prayers. In the West, liturgical leadership passed to the Franks by default, because of the disordered conditions that prevailed at Rome. Alcuin made an adaptation of the Roman liturgy that retained certain of the Eastern innovations, was mandated for use throughout Charlemagne's empire, and was later readopted by Rome. For the first time, there was a universal liturgy, although a few relatively slight local variations survived, mainly in certain religious orders.

The Frankish Liturgy

Over time, the processional chants that expressed the participants' sense of unworthiness, their need to be purified, went from being personal prayers recited quietly by the priest to formal prayers said by him inaudibly at the foot of the altar ("Judge me, O God"), including the Confiteor ("I confess"), with the ancient custom of striking one's breast as an acknowledgment of sin. With the introduction of these preliminary prayers, the Introit ("entrance") no longer served as the processional hymn but became simply the first prayer said by the priest after reaching the altar.

Contrition

The Frankish liturgy offered prayers for the pope and various other categories of people, including those for whom a particular Mass was being offered. For a time, the petitions offered during the Canon were quite specific—a wedding anniversary, illness, prayers to become pregnant—but around 600 they were restricted to general terms. Except in Masses explicitly for that purpose, the dead were for a long time not commemorated in the liturgy, since such commemoration was considered to be the private concern of the mourners. In the early centuries, the prayers of petition were composed by the celebrant, but in the sixth century, a limited number were gathered together ("collects") and made official. Certain occasional hymns, such as the "Veni Creator" (Come, Creator Spirit) on Pentecost, became an integral part of particular liturgies, sung in response to the readings.

Special Prayers

Over time, the three lessons, one of them from the Old Testament, were reduced to two, except on major feasts. The first reading usually came from one of Paul's Letters and was thus called "The Epistle" even when it was not actually from a letter. The second was always

Readings

from the Gospels and was proclaimed with great solemnity, with the priest praying to be made worthy and the worshippers signing the cross on their foreheads, lips, and hearts to signify their resolution to understand the Gospel, take it to heart, and proclaim it. Gospel books were often elaborately decorated and kept in jeweled caskets when not in use.

Nicene Creed

The Creed was part of the liturgy in the East as early as the fifth century, adopted in the West in the sixth, and mandated for general use by Charlemagne. In the eleventh century, the Church at Rome acceded to the request of the emperor St. Henry II (1002–1024) to adopt this Frankish custom, thereby making it universal. The Creed was followed by intercessory prayers for the Church, chanted by the deacon. Since by now almost everyone was baptized as an infant, the Liturgy of the Catechumens was no longer considered distinct from the rest of the Mass, and no one was excluded.

Offertory

The laity continued to bring their offerings to church on Sunday, but their gifts were now often received and stored before Mass and eventually were supplanted by monetary collections and the tithe, so that the clergy alone brought forward the bread and wine at the Offertory. A drop of water was poured into the wine of the chalice to symbolize mankind's role in the work of salvation, a role that was real but that was overwhelmed by the power of Christ's Blood.

The Canon

The injunction, "Pray, brethren", originally addressed to the clergy, became the priest's call to the laity to assist him in offering the holy sacrifice, followed by the Preface (not a preliminary but something sung "in front of" the people), in which the duties of worship and thanksgiving were acknowledged, and concluding with the Sanctus, which proclaimed that the sacrifice was offered in union with the saints and angels.

The priest then began praying the Canon ("rule" or prescribed rite) of the Mass, which in the Frankish lands was said inaudibly, a practice that was later made universal. It was a silence that constituted a kind of inner chamber where the priest, acting alone but supported by the prayers of the faithful, undertook the awesome task laid on him by his ordination, beseeching God to accept their offering and, because he and the people were unworthy, calling upon the angels to transport it to the altar of Heaven.

Consecration

At all other times, the priest acted in the name of the people, but at the Consecration, as he dared to utter the words of Jesus at the Last Supper, he acted as Christ Himself. In the Frankish liturgy, the elevation of the sacred elements at the end of the Canon was the first view of them granted to the faithful. Accompanied by the chanted proclamation, "Through Him, with Him, and in Him", the priest announced that his consecratory task had been completed and that he was once again turning his attention to the congregation.

Whereas for centuries both priests and laity received Communion from a single loaf of bread, broken according to Christ's command, by the later ninth century, the laity were being given small individual hosts, and the priest's host alone was ritually broken, using only unleavened bread that was baked in monasteries. Beginning around 700, the hymn "Lamb of God", calling on Jesus as the sacrificial victim, was sung by the congregation at the point of the breaking of the host, the adoption of another Eastern practice.

Communion

The "kiss of peace" was a stylized embrace between two people, beginning with the celebrant, a gesture in which the higher ranking of the two placed his head briefly on each shoulder of the recipient, who then took the greeting to the next person in the hierarchy. For a time, the laity participated—men and women separately—but eventually the ritual was limited to the clergy. In most places, the kiss was exchanged at the beginning of the Eucharist, but at Rome and in North Africa it occurred before Communion.

Greeting of Peace

People often drank a little wine or water after receiving Communion, in order to prevent the sacred species in their mouths from being unintentionally dribbled out. After Communion, the priest carefully purified both the sacred vessels and his own fingers, and each church had a *piscina* ("pool"), an underground depository into which the water from the various purifications was drained, to prevent its being mingled with waste.

Post-Communion

For a long time, the unity of each local community had to be fulfilled in a communal Mass in which everyone participated. But "low masses", without procession or music and sometimes with only a priest and an acolyte, were eventually permitted, since the Mass was not only a communal act of worship but a divine action that bestowed grace on the faithful even when they were not present. This in turn led to the erection of side altars in larger churches (almost fifty in one German church), so that eventually more than one Mass might be celebrated at the same time. The Mass was not only a communal act of worship but a divine action that bestowed grace on the faithful even if they were not present.

Private Masses

Conventionally, the high altar was situated at the point where the long east-west nave ("ship") met the shorter north-south transept ("crossing"), so that the congregation might be gathered on three sides of the altar, albeit some distance away. In time, however, a greatly enlarged

The Altar

altar was more frequently placed in the apse—the semi-circular chapel at the rear of the sanctuary—thereby removing it even farther from the congregation. Increasingly, an altar screen—a practice taken from both the Jewish Temple and the Byzantine *ikonostasis* ("image screen")— separated the sanctuary from the congregation in many churches, although the West did not go as far as the Eastern practice of con- cealing the altar from the sight of the people. Often a small altar was erected in front of the screen for the faithful to assist at daily Mass.

Piety in Practice

Pilgrimages

Pilgrimages and the veneration of relics continued to be popular, but the Muslim conquest of the Near East all but ended trips to the Holy Land, and the perilous conditions of travel everywhere caused the faith- ful to turn increasingly to the shrines of local saints. Beginning in the fifth century, the remains of the martyrs were often taken from their graves and re-interred within the altars of churches, until eventually it was thought necessary that every altar contain a relic.

Penitentials

The Irish monks drew up books called Penitentials ("penance books"), elaborating a severe discipline that was also applied to the laity— identifying particular sins, offering guidance for dealing with them, and prescribing appropriate penances. Even though these monks were considered overly severe in their penances (half a year of fasting on bread and water, for example, or lifelong chastity for a married cou- ple), their manuals came to be widely used on the Continent, partly because of their precise delineation of the types and seriousness of sins and appropriate penances. The manuals helped to establish a unified moral teaching throughout the Western church and were used in parts of the East as well.

Private Confession

In time, this led to the practice of private confession by lay people, a custom that had previously been observed only at the time of death. At first, church officials were wary of the practice, but eventually they began to express misgivings about public confession instead and urged the practice of frequent confession on the laity, with an emphasis on the interior spiritual state, with the confessor acting as a physician of souls who prescribed painful but salutary remedies.

By the ninth century, private confession for lay people was required at least once a year, along with a whole new penitential discipline, including the silence of the confessor (the "seal of confession") so absolute that if, for example, he learned from a penitent of a plot on his own life, he could do nothing to thwart it. (St. John Nepomucen [d. 1393], confessor to the queen of Bohemia, was drowned by order of the king, for refusing to divulge the contents of her confession.)

Blessings

Over time, the Church sanctioned numerous blessings for specific purposes—for healing, for going on a journey, following childbirth, for a good harvest, for various worldly crafts—some of which, especially those related to physical nature, lay on the borderline between Christian prayer and lurking old superstitions. Often people made bargains with God, promising certain things—to build a church, to go on pilgrimage—if God would grant their requests.

Marriage

Both the Romans and the barbarians regarded consent as necessary for marriage, but it was the consent of the two families. The Church, on the other hand, required the consent of the marital couple themselves, and sexual consummation was considered necessary to ratify a marriage. By the ninth century, marriage ceremonies under church auspices were becoming common, although often conducted only at the church door or in the vestibule, which was constructed primarily for that purpose. The couple joined their right hands, crowns were placed on their heads, and they received a blessing. Following the example of Tobias in the Old Testament, the newlyweds were then urged to refrain from sexual relations for a certain period following the ceremony.

The Church's prohibition of marriage between close relatives, including in-laws, encountered strong resistance for centuries, because marriage was a way of cementing and enhancing family status, and powerful men thought they should be free to do whatever was advantageous.

Death

The Christian understanding of death came to express itself in ways that would endure for well over a thousand years. The hour of death was crucial, when angels and devils competed for the soul of the dying person, who, attended by a priest, was called upon to repent his sinful life. Important people, especially ecclesiastics, were buried in churches, in increasingly large and elaborate tombs. But most people were buried in unmarked graves in cemeteries attached to churches, and, as a burial ground became full, their decayed bodies were exhumed and the bones piled up in a "charnel [flesh] house", also near the church, to make room for others.

A Seedtime

The Dark Ages was a time of great destruction, profound pessimism, and almost inconceivable catastrophes, when the prospect of eternity was very real and the Church alone provided hope. But, although few people could see it at the time, it was also the seedtime of a new civilization. With the disappearance of the Roman Empire, the West was thrown back upon itself, forced by circumstances to develop its own distinctive civilization, a new synthesis forged out of Christianity, the political tradition of Rome, and Greek culture. The tension between Christianity and the barbarian cultures was the principal source of a new dynamic energy, the breakdown of the old being necessary for the creation of something new, which was primarily a spiritual unity forged by the Church.

The Year 1000   The year 1000 seemed to many people to be the appropriately symbolic date for the end of the world or the Second Coming of Christ. But when, allowing for the variant calendars in use in different places, the year 1000 was safely passed, Christians understood that the duration of human history might be long indeed.

Sylvester II   Pope Gregory VI died in 999, amid rumors of poison. Emperor Otto III (983–1002) then arranged the election of his former tutor Gerbert, the French archbishop of Ravenna, as Sylvester II (999–1003). Gerbert was the most learned man of the age, having studied in Spain and imbibed advanced Muslim science and mathematics as well as the conventional liberal arts, introduced Arabic numerals into Christian Europe, and reportedly invented the abacus and the pendulum clock. Whatever Otto may have intended, Sylvester's election seemed to promise that the second Christian millennium would be a time of genuine rebirth.

6 Christendom

The year 1000 does serve conveniently to mark the beginning of the end of the Dark Ages. The history of medieval[1] society is to a great extent the history of endless small wars and rebellions fought for limited goals. Massacres, assassinations, and the torture of enemies were still not uncommon, but overall it was a less disordered and violent time than the Dark Ages.

Just as the previous decline had been a series of falling dominoes set in motion by the collapse of the Roman state, so the recovery was due mainly to the growth of centralized states under strong kings, who, although they by no means put an end to random violence and frequent wars, nonetheless were able to achieve a level of stability and security unknown since Roman times. The revival of the state in turn made possible an economic revival, major signs of which were the systematic opening up of new lands, indicating significant population growth, and the revival of urban life, indicating a revival of trade. This in turn made possible the revival of cultural and intellectual life.

Recovery

Despite continuous internal conflict, medieval people believed in the idea of a unified Christendom based on Augustine's idea of the two cities, an exalted view of a universal society that came closest to realization during the thirteenth century, not because the faith was then perfectly lived but because all aspects of life were consciously oriented toward Christian beliefs. It was an age of contradictions—cruelty and charity, beauty and squalor—but in no other age did Christianity achieve such complete expression.

The Ideal of Society

Men of all ranks were part of a larger community, a hierarchical organism that transcended the boundaries of individual kingdoms. Every person and institution had a divinely ordained place in a graduated series of communities, each with its own sphere and authority, all of them intended to work harmoniously together. A twelfth-century monk

The Social Hierarchy

---

[1] *Medieval* is the adjective referring to the Middle Ages, a modern term that, dismissively, saw the period circa 500 to 1500 as having little significance of its own but as merely coming between ancient and modern times.

divided society into three groups: those who prayed (the clergy), those who fought (the nobility), and those who worked (everyone else, especially the peasants, who were perhaps eighty percent of the population).

Inequalities   This structure was seen as decreed by God; although changes could and did occur, there was no concept of sweeping social reform except among extreme millenarians, and even they expected radical change to occur entirely through God's action, not man's. Inequality, suffering, and injustice were regarded as natural effects of the Fall, to be alleviated as far as possible by individual acts of charity and by wise rulers. Social classes were fixed but not rigid, especially in the Church, where the majority of the higher clergy were probably of high birth but men of humble origins could rise in an institution that rewarded merit and did not recognize family dynasties.

Serfdom   Most bishoprics and monasteries owned serfs. The freeing of serfs was not a religious requirement but was regarded as meritorious. The insistence that serfs had souls and could be saved made their condition vastly better than that of slaves in ancient times. They were allowed to join Crusades (and received their freedom if they did so) and could become priests with their lord's permission. Marriages of serfs were valid even without such permission, and the child of one free parent was himself born free.

Jews   Jews had a unique position in medieval society. Because they had never been Christians, they were not considered heretics, but their situation was extremely precarious. The medieval view was that because they had willfully rejected Christ (the "perfidious Jew" of the Good Friday liturgy), they had earned the wrath of God and hence deserved to be under the rule of Christians. They were forbidden to own land, belong to guilds, or hold any kind of office—all of which would give them authority over Christians. Often they had to wear distinctive clothes and live in their own "ghettoes", and periodically their property was confiscated by kings or lords. During the Middle Ages, they were expelled from most of the countries of Europe at one time or another, the Papal States being the principal exception, although they were sometimes later readmitted.

Augustine and other theologians argued against the killing of Jews, since it was God's purpose that they should eventually be converted. Sometimes Jews were made to listen to sermons to persuade them of the truth of Christianity, and attempts were made to suppress the Talmud—the rabbinical commentary on Scripture—in the expectation that without those commentaries the Jews would see that the Bible foretold the coming of Christ. Beginning with Gregory the Great, a number of popes also officially condemned violence against the Jews. But they were subject to various kinds of harassment, mob violence, and false accusations of crime, often abetted by civil or ecclesiastical authorities, made scapegoats for such things as plagues and fires, and envied for their real or imagined wealth. Even into modern times, there was recurrent popular hysteria over the rumored kidnapping, torture, and murder of Christian children as part of Jewish ritual ("blood libel"), a hysteria that was always followed by the killing of Jews. Various popes denounced such stories as a fanciful misunderstanding of the Jewish religion.

A Pervasive Faith

The salvation of souls was the supreme good that outweighed all others, so that the Catholic faith was to suffuse every dimension of existence: morality, family life, social customs, art, economics, law, and government. The entire culture was organized in such a way that at every turn people were reminded of divine realities and drawn toward them. Thus church spires were the tallest structures in every town, and churches and outdoor shrines were everywhere. The hours of the day, announced by church bells, were organized according to the Divine Office, and the year was organized according to the liturgical feasts that reenacted the cycle of Christ's life and that of His saints.

The Common Good

In theory, the ruler had authority only for the purpose of ensuring the good of all, which made that authority patriarchal. Positions of authority were based on social rank but ideally motivated by a desire to promote the common good. There was no separation of church and state in the modern sense, but there was a distinction between the two such that, paradoxically, the very idea of Christendom, because of its intimate unity of spiritual and temporal authority, made Church-state conflict inevitable.

Divine and Human Law

The law of God that governed the universe was assumed to be visible in His creation and accessible to human reason. But because of the Fall, "positive" laws of church and state (those "posited" or "put in place" by authority) were also necessary. Just laws were not so much made as discovered, since they were based on the law of God. But positive laws did not simply apply divine law directly. Not everything that was immoral was illegal; prudence had to be employed in making human law reflect the divine. The state had its own sphere as the temporal organ of Christendom, possessing its own authority in those things that did not pertain to salvation.[2] The Church, however, had the ultimate authority to determine what did and did not pertain to salvation.

The Two Swords

John of Salisbury (d. 1180), an influential exponent of political theory, held that both the spiritual and the temporal swords belonged to the

[2] This was a major difference between Christendom and Islam, which saw government as simply the enforcement of the teachings of the Qur'an.

Church, which then granted temporal power to the state. Following ancient precedent, John even justified tyrannicide—the killing of a wicked and unjust ruler—and civil rebellion when it was sanctioned by the Church.

St. Thomas Aquinas (d. 1274), the most influential medieval thinker, affirmed monarchy as the best political system but insisted that the monarch had to act in accordance with natural law. In some medieval coronation rites, the king bound himself by an oath to obey the law, thereby seeming to recognize the conditional character of royal authority. But the meaning of Charlemagne's coronation remained ambiguous: Had the Pope conferred the imperial office on him or merely recognized it? Emperor Frederick I Barbarossa ("red-bearded", 1152–1190) was the first to call himself Holy Roman Emperor, thereby asserting that his authority came directly from God, but emperors still wanted to be crowned by the pope.

Sacral Monarchy

In being solemnly crowned by the Church, monarchs partook of some kind of divine character. The emperor actually became a canon of St. Peter's in Rome, in which capacity he could wear deacon's vestments and chant the Gospel at Mass. In France and England, the ritual of coronation included anointing with oils, which in France were said to have been brought from Heaven by angels. Kings had miraculous powers by which they could heal "the king's evil" (scrofula) with a touch.

Roman Law

The revival of Roman law supported imperial claims, with theoreticians of the Holy Roman Empire holding that the power of the state is derived directly from God and that the monarch is therefore answerable to no one but God. Some papalists claimed that the ruler ultimately has to be answerable to his subjects, but some imperialists adapted that argument to make the pope answerable to the members of the Church.

The Empire

The idea of Christendom seemed to require that, just as there was only one flock and one shepherd, so also there ought to be only one state, so that the existence of a number of independent kingdoms was merely accepted, not considered ideal. The great poet Dante Alighieri (d. 1321), who was also a political theorist, longed for the unification of his beloved Italy and saw the emperor as the only agency capable of bringing this about. The emperor, like God, functioned as the universal lawgiver, unifying mankind into one world state based on natural law. Although deeply devout, Dante held that the Church should enjoy no temporal authority.

Reform

Imperial Initiative

Sylvester II's pontificate was too brief to implement a sustained reform program. Both he and Otto III were driven out of Rome, and after Sylvester's death, the Italian nobility once again gained control of the papal elections. But the spirit of reform was in the air, and for a century, movements

for change struggled against entrenched interests, as reform gradually triumphed. A majority of the popes of the eleventh and twelfth centuries
were either monks or canons, which meant that to some extent they had
risen in the Church independent of the hierarchy of politically appointed
bishops. But in order to overcome the influence of the rapacious Italian
families, reform popes could only be put on the throne through the influence of the emperor, and when that failed, the results were disastrous—
Benedict IX (1032–1048), for example, was elected pope while in his
twenties and later resigned on condition that he be given back the money
he had used to bribe his election.

Emperor Henry III (1039–1056) deposed one pope and forced the election of three others in short succession, including his kinsman St. Leo IX
(1049–1054), who brought a coterie of reformers with him from Germany and became the real founder of the reform movement. Leo restored
the freedom of papal elections, forbade the clergy to be involved in violence, and castigated them for oppressing the poor. On one occasion,
he demanded that a council of bishops confess publicly whether they were
guilty of simony, and on the spot, he deposed those who were.

Leo IX

But at the end of his pontificate, Leo was taken prisoner by yet
another rising secular power—the Normans, who were making territorial claims on Sicily and southern Italy—and papal independence
remained precarious. Henry III appointed the next pope, Victor II
(1055–1057), in the last papal election under imperial control, but the
regents for the boy-emperor Henry IV (1056–1106) tried to depose
the reformer Alexander II (1061–1073). Imperial armies marched on
Rome and were thwarted only by a rebellion in Germany that required
their immediate return.

In order to diminish princely influence, Nicholas II (1059–1061) gave
the College of Cardinals sole authority to elect the pope, and Alexander III (1159–1181) required a two-thirds majority. The cardinals
("hinges") were originally the leading Roman clergy but by now were
primarily the members of the papal Curia. There were three ranks—
bishops, priests, and deacons—but membership in the Sacred College
was extremely small by modern standards, as low as six on occasion.
Conclaves ("with keys", because the cardinals were locked in) tended
to drag on, because of factionalism, causing various popes to require
the electors to live under straitened circumstances: one small cell, one
servant, and a meager diet. Medieval popes were usually Italians, although
at various times French, German, English, and Portuguese prelates were
chosen. By no means were all cardinals at the time of their elections,
and a few were not even bishops.

*The College of
Cardinals*

St. Gregory VII (Hildebrand, 1073–1085) was an Italian who had accompanied Leo IX from Germany and became himself one of the greatest

Gregory VII

of the popes, so that the crucial changes of the eleventh century came to be called the Gregorian or Hildebrandian Reform.

The Reform Program
The reformers identified two closely intertwined problems—the worldliness and corruption of the clergy and the control of lay lords over the Church, the second of which made the first almost impossible to correct. But the reform program was implemented only in fits and starts over a long time and was never completely achieved. By virtue of their offices, bishops were often intensely ambitious and powerful in both spiritual and secular terms, controlled great wealth, held high office in the state, and were continually involved in feudal alliances and plots.

Prince Bishops
The great theologian and monastic reformer St. Bernard of Clairvaux (d. 1153) excoriated worldly prelates as successors of Constantine rather than of Peter. The notorious bishop Odo of Bayeux (d. 1097), the brother of William I the Conqueror of England (1066–1087) and Normandy, led his own armies in battle and, following the death of Gregory VII, prepared to march on Rome to seize the papacy for himself, a plan that his brother thwarted.

Celibacy
During the Dark Ages, many parish priests were married, but in the eleventh century, celibacy was made a universal discipline in the Western church, even to the point of decreeing that priests must send away their wives and children, although many continued to keep mistresses. Celibacy had been held in the highest esteem from the beginning of the Church, since the celibate, by his very life, reminded people of the Kingdom of God, where all worldly attachments, including families, would be transcended. But celibacy was imposed on the clergy also to prevent them from establishing family dynasties.

Benefices
As "benefices", church offices were attractive investments that subordinated the welfare of the people to the interests of the patron. Technically, the bishop alone could appoint a pastor to a parish, but he often had to choose from nominees presented by a patron, who might be a layman, a monastery, or a cathedral chapter and who also claimed the tithes due to the priest. The reform popes kept a close watch on bishops, sometimes nullifying elections by cathedral chapters and appointing their own nominees instead. Chapters were often worldly, and to counteract that many were brought under a kind of monastic discipline.

Reforming Councils
The Second Lateran Council (1139), which took its name from the pope's cathedral in Rome, affirmed the reform program, including the election of bishops by cathedral chapters, and the Third Lateran Council (1179) added prohibitions against holding a plurality of benefices

and against laymen disposing of church property. The Second Council of Lyons (1274) decreed that bishops must be confirmed by the Holy See and that chapters were entitled to share in the governance of the diocese, which led to frequent disputes with bishops. Restrictions were placed on priests holding more than one benefice.

Because of the subservience of many bishops to lay control, the popes exempted many monasteries from episcopal authority, thereby making them centers of reform. But in some cases, lay patrons also had the power to appoint abbots, some of whom were not even monks and who merely collected the income of the abbey.

Monastic Exemptions

As vassals within the feudal system, bishops and abbots made a ceremonial submission to their lords on the occasion of receiving their lands. But it was also customary for the lords to "invest" (clothe) the prelates with the staffs and rings that were the symbols of their episcopal office. Gregory VII sought to suppress both the ritual and the reality of submission that lay behind it.

Clerical Vassals

Having often liberated the popes from the Italians, the emperors themselves now became the principal threats to papal freedom, leading to three centuries of conflict over the proper understanding of the two swords. If popes could excommunicate kings, monarchs could recruit docile bishops to declare the reigning pope illegitimate, thereby allowing the ruler to proclaim an anti-pope in his place. There was no legal or moral justification for this, and from 1000 until almost 1400, no anti-pope ever enjoyed more than brief and local authority.

Church and State

Emperor Henry IV defied Pope Gregory VII, bolstered by the support of many of the German bishops, one of whom denigrated Gregory's office by addressing him merely as "Brother Hildebrand". But Henry did not have the support of many of his lay vassals. In 1076, Gregory excommunicated and deposed him, and, faced with rebellion, Henry was forced to seek out the Pope, who was on his way to Germany to ratify the deposition. Henry found him at Canossa in Italy, where for three days the emperor stood in the snow as a penitent begging for absolution, an incident that made "going to Canossa" a metaphor for a humiliating surrender. Gregory granted him absolution, and Henry, once shriven, hurried back to Germany to reassert his authority against the rebellious nobles who had elected a new emperor. A synod of imperial bishops declared Gregory deposed and allowed Henry to name an anti-pope, and Gregory died in exile from Rome, no longer supported even by many of his own cardinals.

Emperor vs. Pope

Henry also kept Pope Bl. Urban II (1088–1099) out of the papal city for several years, and the emperor died unreconciled to the Church, in the midst of a rebellion by his son Henry V (1106–1125), who then drove Pope Paschal II (1099–1118) from Rome. Paschal first gave in to the emperor but then repented, and eventually Henry surrendered the right to invest bishops with their episcopal insignia. Papal-imperial tensions continued for a long time. In 1159, for example, Frederick Barbarossa set up an anti-pope and twice drove Pope Alexander III from Rome, although the emperor finally submitted.

The Power of the Keys

Conflicts were sometimes merely over immediate territorial or financial advantages, although popes and princes always invoked high moral and religious principles to justify their actions, and such principles were indeed at stake. Pope Gregory VII claimed sole authority to summon councils, appoint bishops, canonize saints, and depose emperors, the last not by temporal authority but by the spiritual authority that required the pope to make ultimate judgments concerning right and wrong—the "power of the keys", the authority to bind and loose that Jesus gave to the Church. (Gregory also claimed that popes became saints solely by virtue of their offices, a claim that later popes did not repeat.)

Excommunication

The pope had little actual temporal power, but excommunication, with the presumption (but not the certainty) of damnation, was taken very seriously. Interdict ("to pronounce among") was a prohibition on the administration of the sacraments in an entire territory, thereby placing additional pressure on a recalcitrant ruler. But these sanctions were ineffective unless a ruler's vassals seized on them as justification for asserting their independence. Even then, the leverage of the pope could be diminished by temporal rulers shrewdly taking advantage of his priestly duty. As a priest, Gregory could not refuse the emperor when he arrived at Canossa as a penitent, even though absolution deprived Henry's vassals of their grounds for rebellion and restored Henry to a position from which he could again threaten the papacy.

The Precariousness of Reform

The fight against lay investiture had limited results: it was officially forbidden but survived in some places. Monarchs and nobles continued to be involved in church affairs, especially in nominating bishops and collecting the revenues of vacant dioceses, a practice that motivated them to leave dioceses vacant as long as possible.

Although successful in its major goals, the Gregorian Reform by no means put an end to all problems, and the investiture issue was also by no means confined to the Empire. Pope Innocent II (1130–1143) had to struggle against an anti-pope who had Norman support and at one point was taken prisoner until he acknowledged Norman rule in southern Italy. King Philip I of France (1060–1108) was excommunicated three times during his long reign. In England, William the Conqueror supported reform, but his son, William II Rufus (1087–1100), whom the monastic chroniclers considered an enemy of the Church, exiled the archbishop of Canterbury, St. Anselm (d. 1109), for opposing investiture, although Rufus' brother Henry I (1100–1135) later submitted.

Ireland

Ireland, which had been the spiritual leader of the Church in the Dark Ages, was by now remote and isolated, wracked by continuous wars among territorial princes, each of whom was called a king. Two bishops—St. Malachy (d. 1148) and St. Laurence O'Toole (d. 1180)—tried with limited success to bring the island under the Gregorian reform. Momentously in terms of the history of the next nine centuries, the English Pope Hadrian IV (1154–1159), partly to implement reform, gave Ireland as a fief to Henry II of England (1154–1189), and a Norman aristocracy established itself there.

England

The most dramatic of the Church-state conflicts—even more than Canossa—occurred under King Henry II of England (1154–1189), who in consolidating his power forbade what he considered the improper use of excommunication, the consecration of bishops before they had rendered feudal homage to their lords, appeals from the royal courts to the papal court, and the ordination of serfs to the priesthood without their lords' permission. He especially rejected the Church's demand that those who had been ordained (including those in minor orders) be subject only to church courts when accused of a crime, a demand based partly on the principle that no one in England was exempt from royal authority and partly on the pragmatic consideration that the church courts could not inflict the death penalty. (Fugitives from the secular law could also take sanctuary in a church for a month.)

Becket

St. Thomas Becket (d. 1170) had been Henry's friend and advisor, but after becoming archbishop of Canterbury, he showed himself a champion of the rights of the Church. The conflict between them was prolonged and complex, with Becket twice going into exile, until Henry reportedly muttered, "Will no one rid me of this low-born priest?" Taking this as a command, four of Henry's knights traveled from Normandy to Canterbury and hacked Becket to death as he sought sanctuary in his cathedral. The incident aroused horror all over Europe, forcing Henry as a penitent to walk barefoot to the slain archbishop's tomb, there to be ritually scourged, and to concede some of the disputed issues to the papacy. The actual murderers also repented and went on to the Crusades (see Chapter Seven below, pp. 200–204), and Becket's tomb became the most important pilgrimage place in England (the destination of the characters in Geoffrey Chaucer's *Canterbury Tales*).

An International Order

The conflict between Becket and Henry II was over two ultimately irreconcilable dimensions of Christendom: the temporal power charged with the administration of justice in a particular kingdom and the spiritual power that defined a universal concept of justice. Were the clergy the subjects of their kings or the citizens of an international order?

Canon Law

An independent and dynamic Church possessed a complex machinery of government. Justinian's Code had become the basis of the law codes of most kingdoms, and in the mid-twelfth century the monk-lawyer Gratian of Bologna (d. ca. 1150) used Justinian to systematize the Church's canon law. As the church courts developed, they came to have jurisdiction not only over obvious spiritual issues—heresy, blasphemy, sorcery, simony—but also over marriage, wills, and usury, thereby inevitably becoming points of contention with kings.

So sophisticated was canon law that legal processes were often interminably complex and difficult, dragging on for years and comprehensible only to trained lawyers. John of Salisbury, one of the leading bishops and scholars of the age and a man who actually witnessed Becket's martyrdom, had severe misgivings about the cold rigor of law and urged greater dependence on the spirit of the Gospel. The papal courts at Rome also received a continuous stream of appeals from local ecclesiastical courts, and the papacy built up a sophisticated bureaucracy that served as a model for secular rulers, including a network of papal legates to the various princely courts and a financial system able to collect taxes from all over Europe.

The Papal States

Besides theoretical issues of authority, there was continuous conflict between popes and emperors over the control of Italy, as the emperors claimed their traditional sovereignty there and the popes struggled to maintain the security of their own domain. Italian politics was for centuries divided into two rival groups that existed in almost every state—the Guelfs (probably named for a German princely house), who looked to the papacy for leadership, and the Ghibellines (probably named for an imperial castle), who were loyal to the emperor.

Innocent III

Popes often successfully intervened in international conflicts. Papal authority reached its zenith with Innocent III (1198–1216), the most powerful of all the popes, who combined the roles of spiritual and temporal ruler. Kingship was a divine office, and Innocent conceived it his duty to ensure that kings acted accordingly, whereas no earthly authority could check the actions of the pope. Innocent first secured his rule over Rome itself and subsequently intervened in numerous conflicts: determining who was the rightful emperor, bringing the several Spanish kingdoms together in the war against the Muslims, and intervening in disputes between France and England and in internal disputes in both kingdoms.

Magna Carta

Innocent excommunicated King John of England (1199–1216), partly because the king refused to accept the papal nominee, Stephen Langton

(d. 1228), as archbishop of Canterbury. The English nobles, led by Langton, were then able to extort the Magna Carta ("Great Charter") of liberties from John, although, as Henry IV had done, the king hastily submitted to the Pope, even making himself a papal vassal, thereby causing Innocent to question the legitimacy of Magna Carta.

Emperor Frederick II (1215–1250) was the son of Henry VI, and after his father's death became Innocent's ward. After he came of age, Frederick invaded Germany, defeated a rival claimant, and was proclaimed emperor, so that the subsequent history of the Empire was one of almost continuous civil war, in which the leading bishops were deeply involved. Frederick was called the "marvel of the world", both because of his aggressive pursuit of his goals and because he seemed to live outside the mainstream of Christian culture. He vigorously persecuted heresy, but he was also rumored to have murdered three wives, and he outraged people by using Muslim soldiers in his Italian wars.

Frederick II

Frederick constituted a serious threat to papal independence because of his designs on Sicily, and he was excommunicated several times, both for failing to go on a crusade as he promised and for his territorial designs. The conclave that began in 1241 lasted a year and a half, during which the Roman civic authorities pressured, and even physically abused, the cardinals to force an election.

Innocent IV (1243–1254) was finally chosen and, after having been driven from Rome by Frederick's armies, summoned a council to judge the emperor. Frederick, however, captured a hundred bishops on their way to the meeting and held them prisoner. Innocent then fled to Lyons in France and transferred the council there, and this First Council of Lyons declared the emperor deposed, announced a crusade against him, and placed Germany under interdict. This was the first time a "crusade" was proclaimed against a Christian monarch. Frederick died unabsolved.

If Frederick II epitomized the popes' view of a bad ruler, St. Louis IX of France (1226–1270) embodied the Christian ideal. His mother, Blanche of Castile (d. 1252) ruled for him until he came of age and impressed on him the obligations of piety, going so far as to admonish him to regard the sins of his people as reflections on himself. Louis attended Mass daily, prayed with almost mystical intensity, affiliated himself with the Franciscans, supported the rights of the Church, and personally fed the poor from his table. He espoused a concept of justice based on divine law, discouraged trial by battle, made himself available to hear appeals from his subjects, and set up a system for the manumission ("sending from the hand") of serfs. He went on a crusade, was captured and ransomed, brought back relics from the Holy Land that he enshrined in the exquisite Sainte Chapelle in Paris, and died in North Africa while on another crusade.

Louis IX

Papal Politics

Pope Urban IV (1261–1264) supported the claims of Louis' brother, Charles of Anjou (d. 1285), to Sicily, thereby beginning a tangled conflict that would continue into the next century. Charles pressured the cardinals into electing the Frenchman Martin IV (1281–1285), and Martin blindly supported Charles' ambitions, including his claim to the Byzantine Empire, based on the Crusade of 1204 (see Chapter Seven below, p. 203). When Charles was driven out of Sicily in a rebellion in 1282, Martin excommunicated and deposed King Peter III of Aragon (1276–1285), who had accepted the Sicilians' invitation to become their ruler.

The Transformation of Society

Chivalry

The Church attempted to transform the feudal knight, the descendant of the barbarian warrior, into the Christian knight through the ideal of chivalry (from the French word for "horse"), which was a fusion of Christianity with the barbarian traditions. The knight was urged to dedicate his prowess to the protection of the weak and the defense of the faith, with his initiation into knighthood preceded by an all-night vigil before the altar and the blessing of his weapons and armor.

The *chansons de geste* ("songs of great deeds") glorified war in a good cause—legends of King Arthur, Charlemagne (the *Song of Roland*), and the Crusades. Some of these tales were amalgamated with the even more legendary search for the lost Holy Grail used by Jesus at the Last Supper, something that only a blameless knight could recover.

Restraints on Bloodshed

The Church sought to curtail feudal violence through the Peace of God, which forbade attacks on women, clergy, and other noncombatants, and the Truce of God, which allowed warfare only Monday through Wednesday of each week and forbade it completely during holy seasons and on an increasing number of holy days. The Peace of God and Truce of God, along with the new military religious orders and the Crusades, sought to redirect warlike impulses.

The Fourth Lateran Council (1215) made absolute the prohibition on clergy shedding blood. It forbade them to practice surgery and to participate in the traditional barbarian judicial process called the "ordeal", in which an accused person was "tried" either by being made to handle a hot iron or by being thrown into a pond. (If the hand failed to show burns, or the person failed to sink, this unnatural occurrence was taken as a supernatural sign of guilt.) Disputes between nobles were often settled through trial by battle, in which the antagonists fought one-on-one (the *duel*, meaning "two"). The outcome of the duel was believed to demonstrate which side had divine favor. The abolition of the ordeal, which left trial by jury as the principal judicial process, was a sign of the developing respect for reason in the West. The growing reliance upon rational proof culminated in philosophy and theology, although it grew alongside a great deal of credulity, even among the learned.

The commune movement often brought the citizens of towns into conflict with the bishops, who traditionally exercised governance of those towns. The most extreme case was at Rome itself, where a deposed abbot named Arnold of Brescia (d. 1155), an austere man who was nonetheless a revolutionary, accused Pope Hadrian IV of corruption, led a revolt that drove Hadrian out of Rome, seized church property, and proclaimed a commune that was meant to restore the ancient Roman Republic. The Pope returned, with Barbarossa's help, and Arnold was burned as a heretic.

Communes

The guilds, which usually controlled the town governments, were organizations of merchants and craftsmen. Although made up of commoners, they embodied the notion of social hierarchy in their division into masters, journeymen, and apprentices. In principle, guilds were at least as much religious and social as economic. They provided for the burial of dead members and aid to their survivors (a kind of insurance program), and each guild had its patron saint, patronal church, and patronal feast. There were also various kinds of confraternities ("brotherhoods") established for charitable purposes.

Guilds

The history of the Church in the Middle Ages is to a great extent the history of both new and reformed religious communities. Monasticism's success was in a sense also its failure, in that houses with reputations for austerity and holiness attracted generous donations that threatened to undermine those same virtues. Wealth was universally recognized as corruptive of monastic life, but there was no obvious solution. Monasticism was sometimes reformed by patrons or abbots who simply expelled lax monks and replaced them with more dedicated men. An early twelfth-century experiment placed temporal power in the hands of lay brothers, thereby allowing the clerics to devote themselves entirely to spiritual exercises, but the system proved to be merely a corrupting temptation to the brothers.

Religious Life

Reform

Cluny established a monastic system somewhat like feudalism—a pyramid with itself at the top, presiding over numerous dependent monasteries. By 1100, it had 1,450 daughter houses, some of which it had established, some of which had voluntarily placed themselves under its authority. Cluny was guided by a series of abbots who were elected when young and proved to be extraordinarily long-lived—only three between 954 and 1109. In order to ensure strict adherence to the Benedictine *Rule*, most of Cluny's dependent houses did not have elected abbots but were governed by priors ("firsts") appointed from Cluny, while the novices from all the monasteries received their formation at the motherhouse.

    While Cluny never became corrupt in a gross sense, and even gave the Church two reform popes—Urban II and Paschal II—its enormous wealth and the sheer size and complexity of its activities weakened the

Cluny

monastic spirit to some extent. The abbot resided in his own house, and much time was taken up with administration and with elaborate celebrations of the liturgy in a lavish church with rich mosaic floors, huge wall hangings, and accouterments such as eighteen-foot candlesticks. At the abbey of St. Denis near Paris, the altar cross was twenty-four feet high, and the church was hung with rich tapestries and gloried in its gold and jeweled sacred vessels.

Camaldolese

Perhaps partly because of dissatisfaction with the high degree of organization among the Benedictines, beginning in the late ninth century, there was a revival of the hermetical life, this time with formal structures based on the Benedictine *Rule*. St. Romuald (d. 1027) was an Italian abbot who was forced out of his monastery because of his severity and then formed a group of hermits into a new order called the Camaldolese, from their location, a group that practiced severe penances.

Carthusians

St. Bruno (d. 1101), a German, founded a new order of monks called the Carthusians, from the location of their first monastery near Chartreuse in the French Alps. They lived primarily as hermits and came together only for the liturgy and for occasional common activities.

Cistercians

In 1098, three Benedictines—St. Alberic (d. 1109), St. Robert (d. 1110), and St. Stephen Harding (d. 1134)—founded a new community dedicated to the strict observance of the Benedictine *Rule*. They were called Cistercians from the site of their monastery at Citeaux, also in France. The Cistercians embraced a life of meticulous celebration of the Divine Office, rigorous fasting, perpetual silence, and manual labor. They did not emphasize learning, as Cluny did. Perhaps precisely because of this severity, Citeaux gave birth to almost seventy daughter houses.

Avoiding all hint of luxury, Cistercians could not accept gifts or collect the tithes due to parishes under their patronage, and each monastery could possess only enough land to support itself. Through hard work and austerity, Cistercian monasteries gained a reputation for economic efficiency, both in agriculture and the production of wool for the market, and to achieve their desired solitude, they often pioneered the opening of new lands.

Contemplation

The new monasticism required discipline not only as penance for sin but as a means to undistracted contemplation, enabling the monk to know God in deeper ways, to move beyond limited human concepts to a mystical knowledge of the divine. The writings of the monastic theologians gave the Church a new spirit of interiority.

Bernard of Clairvaux

St. Bernard, who entered Citeaux with thirty of his relatives and companions and was soon made prior of its daughter house of Clairvaux, was in some ways the most important religious leader of the Middle

Ages, not only as a reformer of monastic life but as a theologian and preacher, even as an advisor to princes. One of his monks became pope as Bl. Eugene III (1145–1153).

Only somewhat less important than Bernard as a religious leader was Suger (d. 1151), a man of low birth who became abbot of St. Denis. Primarily because of the elaborateness of the Benedictine liturgy, Suger and Peter the Venerable, abbot of Cluny (d. 1156), sometimes found themselves at cross purposes with Bernard, who once rebuked Suger for St. Denis' relative laxness. Suger took the rebuke to heart, but he remained a man of affairs in ways rather different from that of the austere Bernard but equally representative of the spirit of the times.

Suger

The Norman Benedictine abbey of Bec, founded in 1039, was not affiliated with Cluny and emphasized study over elaborate liturgies. It became a center of intellectual life, with Bl. Lanfranc (d. 1089) and St. Anselm, two successive archbishops of Canterbury, among its abbots.

Abbey of Bec

Except for an occasional queen, abbesses were the most important women in the Middle Ages, far more powerful than most women before World War II could hope to be. They had a great deal of spiritual authority and presided over large, complex, and wealthy institutions, although, unlike abbots, they seldom became involved in secular politics. St. Hildegard of Bingen (d. 1179) was an educated German abbess who had mystical visions and wrote complex musical compositions to express them. With the approval of Bernard and Pope Eugene III, she advised bishops and sometimes spoke in public on pressing issues.

Abbesses

Canons were groups of clergy living in communities, as in cathedral chapters, and "canons regular" were secular clergy devoted to parish work or to education but living under a quasi-monastic rule. To bring the benefits of monasticism to parish life, St. Norbert of Xanten (d. 1134) founded the Premonstratensians, so called from the location of their monastery near the French town of Prémontré. Norbert, who was himself German, became the reforming archbishop of Magdeburg in Germany, from which he sent Premonstratensians as missionaries to central and eastern Europe.

Canons

Norbert of Xanten and the Englishman St. Gilbert of Sempringham (d. 1189) both founded double monasteries in which separate communities of men and women, under a common rule, shared the same church and participated in the same liturgies, in some cases with both under the authority of an abbess. But after a time the arrangement was forbidden.

Double Monasteries

St. Francis of Assisi (d. 1226) was perhaps the greatest figure of medieval Christianity and, after Jesus and the Virgin Mary, the most admired

"The Frenchman"

Christian in all of history. He was born Giovanni Bernadone in the commercial northern Italian city with which he is identified. His father was a wealthy cloth merchant, and the son made regular business trips across the Alps into southern France, where he picked up the fashionable French ways that earned him the nickname Francis ("the Frenchman").

"Il Poverello"

Unpredictably, Francis underwent a sudden conversion in which he repudiated his worldly ways, gave away all his possessions, and ritually stripped himself naked in front of the bishop, after this father disowned him, to symbolize his renunciation of all worldly goods and to show his dependence on the bishop, becoming known as *il poverello* ("the little poor man"). Like other medieval saints, he made a special point of ministering to lepers, precisely because they were social outcasts and their sores repelled him.

Like many converts of earlier centuries, he lived for a time as a hermit, until he felt called upon to return to society to preach a radically simple message, urging people to give up everything and to live with complete faith in God's benevolent providence. Adapting the courtly love poetry popular in southern France, he proclaimed his devotion to "Lady Poverty".

The Lesser Brothers

At first, Francis understood a divine message, "Build up My Church", to refer to ruined buildings, but in time he came to understand that his mission was to bring about a spiritual renewal. He did not intend to found a new religious order and at first merely attracted followers who wanted to live as he did. But eventually he consented to subject his group to a rule, in order to remain fully in communion with the Church, naming his new community the Order of Friars Minor (*Ordo Fratrum Minorum*—"Lesser Brothers"). But unlike most monastic pioneers, Francis had little regard for organization.

Holy Joy

He was not a social reformer, in that, far from wanting to eliminate poverty, he tried to persuade everyone to embrace it. Himself the product of an increasingly luxurious and acquisitive commercial society, he identified love of wealth as the principal root of sin. But despite his rigor, Francis manifested a kind of playful joy. In response to the recurrent heretical dualism that opposed spirit to matter, he had a sense of empathy with nature rare for his time, inspiring him to speak of "Brother Sun and Sister Moon" and even to preach sermons to animals.[3] Francis, who accompanied one of the

---

[3] Partly because of disputes among his followers as to his true intentions, many legends grew up around him, as in the *Little Flowers of St. Francis*, but their historical authenticity is almost impossible to determine. The "Prayer of St. Francis" ("Lord, make me an instrument of Thy peace..."), for instance, was unknown until the twentieth century.

Crusades, made the conversion of the Muslims the highest mission of his order, but for the most part that turned out to be an unrealistic goal.

Mendicants

Traditionally, monks could own nothing, but monasteries might be rich. Francis decreed that even the monasteries of his order should own nothing and that his followers should live as beggars ("mendicants"), but he reluctantly accepted an arrangement whereby they possessed their convents in fact but legally the buildings were held by "protectors" or "guardians". Eventually, Francis resigned as general of the order he founded, and after his death his followers erected a magnificent church at Assisi, something of which he probably would not have approved.

St. Dominic Guzmàn (d. 1221) was a Castilian priest who traveled to southern France around 1200 both to preach against heresy and to combat it through the example of a life of poverty. (Dominican mendicancy was intended to demonstrate that the orthodox too could be ascetic.) Like Francis, he quickly attracted followers. The Order of Preachers (*Ordo Predicatorum*), as Dominic called his community, followed the rule of the Augustinian canons. Their dedication to combating heresy drew them to the intellectual life, and their zeal, symbolized in the stark contrast of their black and white habits, inspired a pun on their name—"*Domini canes*" ("dogs of the Lord").

Dominic

Both new communities were called friars rather than monks because, although living in monasteries under monastic discipline, they devoted themselves primarily to pastoral work instead of ascetic and liturgical practices, combining the active and contemplative ways of life and bringing the fruits of monastic piety to the laity, especially in the growing towns and cities. The worldliness of many of the hierarchy was recognized as one of the chief evils in the Church, and for that reason both Francis and Dominic decreed that their friars should not become bishops. In time, however, both were forced to accede to the demands of popes to provide the Church with good prelates.

Action and Contemplation

Pope Innocent III was briefly repelled by Francis' slovenliness but soon changed his mind. Although preoccupied with international politics, Innocent recognized the authenticity of the new groups and, despite a ruling by the Fourth Lateran Council that there should be no new religious orders, quickly gave them papal approval. Francis and Dominic were both revered as saints even in their own lifetimes and were formally canonized only a few years after their deaths.

The Carmelites, the third of the mendicant orders, were founded in the Holy Land in 1209 by the Englishman St. Simon Stock (d. 1265).

Carmelites

It was first made up of hermits living on Mount Carmel and came to Europe a generation later.

Servites

The Order of the Servants of Mary was founded around 1300 in the highly prosperous city of Florence, by a small group of noblemen who were dissatisfied with their city's worldliness.

Nuns and Tertiaries

Both the older and newer religious orders had female branches. A disciple of Francis named Clare (d. 1253) founded a community of "Poor Ladies", who at first did charitable work in the world. But shortly thereafter, all officially recognized communities of women were required to be cloistered, a rule the "Poor Clares" were obliged to follow.

Both Franciscans and Dominicans established "third orders" ("tertiaries") for lay people who lived in the world but to some extent shared in the life of vowed religious.

The Age of the Friars

In some ways, the High Middle Ages were the age of the friars in the same way that earlier centuries had been the age of the monks. The Franciscans' unique combination of austerity and joy made them the most popular of religious communities, attracting thirty thousand members in their first century.

The Intellectual Life

Francis intended for his friars to preach a simple, heartfelt message and to eschew the intellectual life. But the prestige and importance of the universities was such that, almost immediately, both Franciscans and Dominicans began pursuing advanced studies. A University of Paris professor, William of St. Amour, spoke for many secular clergy in waging a fierce rhetorical war against the friars, even denying the importance of poverty, until he was himself ousted from the university at the behest of Pope Gregory IX (1227–1241). However, anti-mendicant hostility was so strong that a few years later the Dominican Aquinas had to be protected by royal archers as he lectured.

Fraticelli

The Franciscan movement also became the focus of prolonged and often bitter controversy, resented by many of the secular clergy as intruders into pastoral life but consistently supported by the papacy. A faction of friars called the *Fraticelli* ("Little Brothers"), or Spirituals, demanded that poverty be practiced very rigorously and were severe critics of clergy who did not do so. In retaliation, some secular clergy denied that Jesus had practiced absolute poverty or required it of His disciples. Some of the Spirituals adopted the Joachite prophecy concerning the third age of the Church and claimed that they would be the means of bringing it into being (see Chapter Eight below, pp. 158–59). Their leader, Peter John Olivi (d. 1298), appeared to teach that the papacy itself was the Antichrist. As general of the Franciscans and a cardinal, St. Bonaventure (d. 1274) opposed the *Fraticelli*, who were condemned but continued to be a vital movement.

The Snare of Wealth

Medieval people were repeatedly warned against the corrupting effects of riches, and complete renunciation of worldly goods was highly praised. But this presented a dilemma, because those who held high social positions, including the clergy, were expected to live in a style commensurate with their rank, so that those who did renounce their wealth virtually had to become monks. Privileged people were therefore supposed to practice inner detachment, and after death some bishops were discovered to have been wearing hair shirts beneath their splendid robes. Innocent III, the medieval pope most involved in worldly matters, wrote a standard treatise on the familiar theme of "contempt for the world" and recognized the importance of poverty.

Charity

Above all, the rich were expected to be generous in their charities, which was the reason God had given them wealth. There were few charities organized by the government as such, so that the needy depended on monasteries and on lay and clerical lords who distributed alms and endowed schools, hospitals, orphanages, leprosaria, and other institutions.

Usury

Somewhat unfairly, greed or avarice—one of the seven deadly sins— was often represented by a pinch-faced merchant or banker hoarding his money, much less often by a feudal lord whose wealth was in his land. Usury—the lending of money at interest for its "use"—was forbidden to Christians, thereby making money-lending the exclusive province of Jews. But despite the prohibition, the northern Italian cities gradually took over more and more of the trade, as the papacy itself began to work closely with the Italian banking houses. The prohibition on usury was based on the assumption that money is sterile and cannot reproduce itself and on the belief that it is wrong to profit from the misfortunes of those in need. But in the thirteenth century, canonists began to devise ways by which interest could be collected on loans made not because of need but for purposes of investment.

The Ideal of Justice

For the sake of the common good, the Church attempted to balance the interests of producers and consumers by condemning the vice of greed and encouraging "just wages" and "just prices", which, along with the regulation of the quality of goods, was undertaken by guilds and town governments. Especially in the financial and industrial cities of northern Italy, rising prosperity, with which the Christian conscience was not wholly at ease, was often seen as both the cause and the result of greed and as something that distracted people from their heavenly goal.

Heterodox Reform

"Reform" has been a constant theme in the history of the Church, meaning primarily a return to the "apostolic life" of simplicity and poverty. The program of reform led to demands for a "pure" Christianity that had allegedly been subverted over time. Such movements became heretical when they went beyond the condemnation of clerical abuses and denied the authority of the clerical office itself and of the sacramental system. Many adherents of dissident sects pursued a life of perfection on the margins of society, rejecting the idea of Christendom as a compromise of the Gospel and regarding the true Church as a small elite. Charismatic leaders—sometimes hermits—arose periodically. Bernard noted that their followers always included women and scoffed that sexual license was at the root of the phenomenon.

Tanchelm

In the Low Countries around 1100, a layman named Tanchelm (d. 1157) first put on monk's robes and preached in the fields, calling the Church a brothel and the sacraments a pollution, then put on regal garments and declared himself betrothed to the Virgin Mary. He was killed in an armed skirmish. Tanchelm's movement may have given rise to the Brethren of the Free Spirit, a loosely organized network of people who repudiated the Church and exalted semi-ecstatic mystical experiences, a movement that survived for several centuries.

Waldo

Peter Waldo was a merchant who—unheard of for a layman—translated the Bible into French and on that basis concluded that the Church was corrupt. He sold all his goods, abandoned his wife, and began preaching, attracting followers who were called the Poor Men of Lyons, the city where Waldo resided. He was expelled from Lyons in 1185, and his fate is unknown, although his movement, while never large, spread fairly widely.[4] After Waldo's death the Poor Men constituted a direct attack on the "institutional" character of the Church—hierarchy, priesthood, the sacraments, Purgatory. Each believer was thought to be inspired directly by the Holy Spirit, and the renunciation of property was the principal sign of authentic faith.

Humiliati

The *Humiliati* ("humble") were a lay group founded in Italy in the late twelfth century and composed of both men and women, single and married, who tried to live the simple life. They did not attack the Church and were approved by Innocent III, who allowed them to preach about morality but not about doctrine, based on the pope's judgment that they led good Christian lives but were not learned in theology.

Joachim of Flora

Millenarianism was often a feature of sectarian beliefs. Joachim of Flora (d. 1202) was a worldly Italian nobleman who underwent a conversion

---

[4] Although little known, Waldensianism still exists and is the oldest non-Catholic Christian body in the Western world.

of heart while on the Crusades. He became a Cistercian and was elected abbot but abandoned that office to devote himself to expounding what he claimed were the hidden meanings of Scripture. History, he taught, was divided into three ages, each guided by one of the Persons of the Trinity. The age of the Father was before the coming of Christ. The age of the Son—the age of the Incarnation, hence of the visible Church—was coming to an end, and the age of the Holy Spirit, beginning about 1260, would be characterized by a wholly spiritual faith based on divine inspiration and the achievement of human perfection. Joachitism stayed alive for centuries, often anticipating the imminent end of the world and opposing most institutional forms of religion.

Beguines and Beghards

The reform movement deeply influenced lay piety. Beguines and Beghards (the origin of whose names is uncertain) were respectively female and male groups that began in the Low Countries in the twelfth century. These groups were made up of lay people who were self-supporting and engaged in works of charity but who also took vows of chastity and lived in communities, which they were free to leave. (See Chapter Eight, p. 221 regarding the orthodoxy of the Beguines and Beghards.)

Cathars and the Albigensian Crusade

The major deviant religious movement of the Middle Ages was led by the Cathars ("Pure"), who began in the Near East with a species of Gnosticism or Manichaeism, made their way westward through the Balkans, and found a home in southern France, where they came to be called Albigensians, from the town of Albi. They were organized as a church, with its own clergy and dioceses. Catharism was scarcely a Christian heresy at all but a rival religion based on an extreme dualism of matter and spirit, postulating a universe divided between two opposed deities, of whom the biblical God was the god of evil and the Church was the invention of Satan. The Cathars preached perfection for the few "Perfect" and antinomianism for the many "Believers" and condemned marriage because human sexuality is inherently evil and the procreation of children traps souls in bodies. The Perfect refrained from all sexual activity, while the Believers were allowed free sex but were not supposed to procreate.

By the late twelfth century, the movement had the support of some French nobles, especially Count Raymond VI of Toulouse (d. 1222), as well as a popular base. The southern French bishops were despised as worldly, and a series of preaching missions mostly failed. When a papal legate was murdered in 1208, Innocent III proclaimed a crusade that captured several Cathar strongholds, committing atrocities in the process. Notoriously, a papal legate at one siege was reported to have shouted, "Kill them all! God will know His own!"

Complex political intrigues followed, in which Raymond, who had ostensibly repented, regained his lands, then again began protecting the Cathars. A second crusade followed in 1226, mounted by Louis VIII

(1223–1226) and Louis IX. Raymond submitted yet again, and about two hundred Cathars were burned as heretics. The movement gradually died out.

The Nature of Heresy

Heresy was considered a spiritual disease or infection that, if allowed to spread, would poison the entire community. Since God had revealed the truth to His Church, heretics were considered obstinately blind for having departed from that truth, motivated by pride and self-will rather than simple ignorance. (Some were admitted to be very ascetic, which was taken as further manifestation of their pride and as a snare to trap the simple.)

The Inquisition

The judicial processes later institutionalized in the Inquisition were first employed in 1022, when twelve canons of Orléans were burned at the stake, accused of denying the most fundamental doctrines of the faith, such as the creation of the world by God. The Inquisition, established in 1184, was directly under papal authority. Every diocese was ordered to have an office charged with ferreting out heresy, but in time the entire responsibility was given to the Franciscans and Dominicans.

Inquisition simply meant an inquiry that followed the procedures of Roman law, whereby an accusation in itself established some presumption of guilt. The accused, although not permitted to confront their accusers, could submit a list of their enemies, whose testimony was then inadmissible. The accused were allowed to answer the charges and were sometimes allowed to have counsel. Torture was permitted in order to obtain a confession, but it was used sparingly in heresy cases, since an individual who denied being a heretic was considered to have recanted. Defendants were often acquitted, convictions could be appealed to the pope and were sometimes overturned, and occasionally an overzealous inquisitor was removed and punished by the Holy See.

The chief purpose of the Inquisition was to persuade the accused heretic to recant, in which case he was made to do public penance. Inquisitors continued to look for signs of repentance and occasionally snatched a repentant heretic from the flames at the last moment. But since the time of the Donatists of North Africa, civil governments had sometimes put heretics to death, because heresy was regarded as destructive of the social order. The Justinian Code provided for the death penalty, although some churchmen, notably Bernard, protested the practice.

After the executions at Orléans, there were almost no executions for two centuries. Innocent III defined heresy as treason against God but did not authorize the death penalty, and the Fourth Lateran Council merely imposed banishment. But the Crusades—the war against the infidel overseas—seemed to dictate war also against domestic infidels. Condemned heretics were imprisoned, and, although the Inquisition was founded in part to keep the prosecution of heresy out of the hands of the state, recalcitrants were turned over to the civil government, which church officials now commanded to carry out the execution.

The Crusades in Europe

The material and spiritual recovery of the West was dramatically demonstrated when Urban II proclaimed the First Crusade ("war of the Cross") in 1095, an action that served several purposes: retaking the Holy Land from the Muslims, making pilgrimages once again possible, demonstrating concretely the unity of Christendom, and providing the European nobility with a cause worthy of their warlike spirit. Crusaders were invested with a cloak bearing the sign of the cross, and their property was placed under the protection of the Church during their absence.

Indulgences

The Crusaders took pilgrims' vows and received the indulgences traditionally attached to pilgrimages: grants by the Church that offered remission from the punishments deserved for one's sins both in this life and in Purgatory, a remission that could be applied to the souls of the deceased as well. (Sometimes those who impulsively took the vow later asked to be dispensed and were allowed to redeem it by a monetary payment in support of the Crusade, a practice that elided into the "sale" of indulgences.)

The Warlike Spirit

The Crusaders' cry was "God wills it", and they exemplified both the highest and lowest aspects of medieval civilization. The Crusades could not have been mounted without an overriding religious passion that turned warlike impulses outward, and the original motives of those who volunteered were almost always pious, since the expense was huge and the chance of never returning was equally great. Inevitably, however, there were opportunities for gratuitous brutality and greed.

The Jews

The Crusades aroused popular millenarian beliefs that were never far beneath the surface, with the recapture of the Holy Land seen as the immediate preliminary for the Second Coming. Although local bishops made some effort to protect them, the Jews were sometimes robbed and massacred by crusading armies marching through Europe, apparently in the belief that the Jews were as great an obstacle to a Christian claim to the Holy Land, as were the Muslims. (Some crusade preachers openly advocated anti-Jewish violence, although Bernard, who preached the Second Crusade, condemned it.)

Popular Enthusiasm

The Crusades awakened powerful and unpredictable emotions in people. Secular and ecclesiastical authorities opposed this hysteria but could not stem the emotions that made the Crusades into a genuinely popular movement. Many noncombatants accompanied the armies—clergy, including bishops, but also prostitutes.

During the First Crusade, a charismatic preacher called Peter the Hermit (d. 1115) attracted twenty thousand volunteers to Cologne, many of them peasants and other noncombatants who marched to the East in what was called the People's Crusade. In 1212, the Children's Crusade lured away thousands, not all of whom were children, many of whom never returned, and some of whom were sold into slavery in North Africa by unscrupulous sea captains. In 1251, hordes of poor people called *pastoraux* ("shepherds") rampaged through France under the direction of a mysterious figure called the Master of Hungary, demanding the liberation of the Holy Places and assaulting and even killing clergy. The movement was put down by Louis IX.

Conversions in Europe

Further sign of the medieval revival was the conversion of the few remaining pagan areas of Europe. The Magyars of Hungary were converted in the early eleventh century through their king, St. Stephen I (1000–1038), who married the sister of the sainted Henry II of Germany.

The Poles conquered the Wends of northeastern Europe in 1121 and began to rechristianize them. Pope Eugene III authorized a crusade against the Wends by Emperor Conrad III (1138–1152), specifying that the war should be fought to completion, without truce or compromise, and Bernard justified a policy of forced conversions. Christianity was thus extended along the Baltic coast (modern Estonia, Latvia, and Lithuania), partly by force and partly by missionary effort.

But progress was precarious: as late as 1261 a Lithuanian king apostatized, destroyed his cathedral, and built a pagan temple in its place, although a royal marriage to a Polish princess in 1385 permanently restored Catholicism. The Church gained a foothold in Finland around 1200, but the Lapps of the far North remained pagan, the last European people to do so.

The Reconquista

The Muslims were forced back in Western Europe during the eleventh century, entirely expelled from Sicily by the Normans, and slowly pushed back by the Spanish. In 1035, Catholic Spain was divided into the kingdoms of Navarre, Castile, and Aragon, with Castile gradually assuming leadership in the age of the legendary hero El Cid ("The Lord", d. 1099), and by 1100 Muslim Spain had been reduced to a collection of small principalities. The Reconquest led to the crusade ideal being applied to Europe as well as the Holy Land. When the Second Crusade was proclaimed in 1146, Pope Eugene III granted Crusader status to those fighting the Muslims in Spain, and volunteers came from all over.

However, a new Muslim invasion from Africa, as well as dissension among the Christians themselves, impeded the Reconquest that was the dominant reality of medieval Spain. In an extreme case, Alfonso VI of Castile (1065–1109) designated his son by his Muslim mistress to be his heir, provoking a rebellion by his legitimate sons in which the heir was killed. In 1212, an expedition of all the Spanish Catholic states inflicted a major defeat on the Muslims, and in 1239, the king of Castile, St. Ferdinand III (1217–1252), took Córdoba and forced the Muslims to reestablish their caliphate yet further south, at Granada, the last remaining Muslim state in the peninsula.

Asceticism—disciplining oneself to submit to God's will—was the dominant moral ideal of the Middle Ages, manifest most perfectly by monks and nuns but enjoined to one degree or another on everyone by fasting, the patient acceptance of suffering, lengthy devotions, self-imposed penances like scourging, and difficult and dangerous pilgrimages.

Prayer books for the laity, enabling the literate minority to perform their private devotions during Mass and at other times, became common, and "books of hours" (the Divine Office) were especially treasured, many of them elaborately illustrated. The books were in Latin, since those who were literate could read that sacred language.

Preaching was greatly valued, and priests deemed unqualified to compose their own sermons might read a homily from one of the Fathers of the Church. While homilies were expositions of the Scripture of the day's Mass, sermons could be on a variety of subjects and were increasingly preached outside Mass. In large churches, they were no longer delivered from the sanctuary ("holy place") but from pulpits ("platforms") erected halfway along the nave, to enable everyone to hear.

Pilgrimages remained the highest aspiration of popular devotion. A few people were able to travel to the Holy Land (some never able to return), while in Europe itself the most revered destinations were Rome and the shrine of St. James at Santiago de Compostela in Spain.

In terms of piety, the greatest achievement of the Middle Ages was devotion to the human Jesus, an intimacy begun by Bernard, in contrast to the earlier Western emphasis on Jesus as Judge of the living and the dead and the Byzantine sense of His remoteness.

Whereas in earlier centuries, the Passion of Christ was overshadowed by His Resurrection, devotion to His Passion, including intense personal sorrow, now became a hallmark of piety. Whereas in earlier centuries, the crucifix had been a grim reminder of the judgment awaiting all people, it now became an object of compassion, stirring the faithful to share in Christ's sufferings, just as He shared theirs, an emotion Bernard urged believers to accept as wholly appropriate. Devout people often engaged in self-scourging as a way of both expiating their sins and sharing in the Passion.

Devotion to Jesus in His Sacred Heart grew, promoted especially by two nuns: the Fleming St. Lutgardis of Aywières (d. 1246) and the

Devotional Life

Asceticism

Prayer Books

Preaching

Pilgrimages

The Human Jesus

German St. Gertrude the Great (d. 1302), both of whom experienced mystical union with the heart of Christ.

Crèche and Stigmata

Francis of Assisi was the first person known to have manifested the *stigmata* (originally, a term for a brand put on slaves)—the wounds of Christ imprinted on his hands and feet, the ultimate sharing in the sufferings of Christ. But Francis brought devotion to the human Jesus to another kind of fruition by introducing the *crèche*, or Nativity scene, into popular devotion. Daringly, later medieval art sometimes even portrayed the Christ Child at play.

Novenas

Although the liturgy itself seldom addressed Christ directly, people were increasingly encouraged to pray to Him in their private devotions. Novenas, which had become very popular by the High Middle Ages, were a series of prayers or devotions spread out over nine days or nine weeks, possibly because of the nine days Jesus' Apostles and disciples spent in the upper room after His Ascension.

Marian Piety

Marian piety also became intensely popular, offering the faithful a loving Mother who interceded for them with her Son, mitigating the demands of strict justice by mercy, another step in the process by which the harshness of the warrior culture was softened by other emotions. The principal Marian feasts were the Purification, the Annunciation, the Assumption, and her Nativity, and in time a special Office of the Blessed Virgin was introduced. The rule of Cluny required that every monastery have a "Lady chapel" and that it dedicate Saturday to Mary. The Marian shrine at Walsingham in England became one of the major pilgrimage places, and numerous churches and cathedrals were dedicated to Mary.

"Hail Mary"

The Annunciation—the moment when Mary was given her divine commission, her free acceptance of which became the model for all her Son's disciples—was the most popular of Marian themes, depicted already in the Roman catacombs. By 1100, the recitation of the Ave Maria, based on the angel's greeting, "Hail, full of grace", had become popular, partly as a way of affirming the goodness of childbearing. The rosary, with its continued repetition of that prayer, was first promoted by the early Dominicans, although not invented by them, and the public recitation of the Angelus ("The angel of the Lord declared unto Mary")—punctuating the day at three equal intervals—was introduced in the fourteenth century.

Marian Titles

The Song of Songs, which had traditionally been understood as expressing the love of Christ for His Church or the relationship of Christ and the soul, was now increasingly understood as referring to Mary.

From it, new Marian titles were taken, such as "Star of the Sea", who guides voyagers across the treacherous waters of life.

Sorrowful Mother
As devotion to Christ's Passion grew, so did devotion to the Sorrowful Mother, as in the hymn "Stabat Mater" ("At the cross her station keeping . . ."). The faithful were urged to experience Mary's sorrows in their own lives, sorrows eventually identified as seven: the prophecy of Simeon ("a sword shall pierce your soul"), the flight into Egypt, the temporary loss of the boy Jesus in the Temple, His carrying His Cross, His Crucifixion, taking down His body from the Cross, and His burial.

Assumption
Devotion to the Sorrowful Mother grew alongside devotion to the triumphant Mary, Queen of Heaven, who was portrayed as seated on a throne alongside her Son. Her Assumption into Heaven, which was almost universally believed in the East, was also widely accepted in the West, although it was not an official dogma until 1950. Although the Scriptures are silent about Mary's death, most theologians thought it inappropriate that the body that had given flesh to Christ should have been allowed to decay in the grave.

Immaculate Conception
Anselm, the greatest theologian of the eleventh century, taught the doctrine of the Immaculate Conception. Bernard had a particularly strong devotion to Mary and taught that, as the Mother of Jesus, her face was the most like His and was therefore a foretaste of the Beatific Vision. But neither Bernard nor Aquinas accepted the Immaculate Conception. (Bernard said he would defer to the judgment of the Holy See on the question, but no formal proclamation was forthcoming until 1854.)

Loreto
Perhaps the most startling belief about Mary, which was shared by many of the learned, was that the house where Jesus grew up in Nazareth had been miraculously transported to Loreto in Italy, where it became a major pilgrimage place.

Prayers for the Dead

There was a widely held belief that only a saintly minority would be saved and that most people were damned, which gave the practice of praying for the dead a special urgency. The Italian Dominican archbishop Jacobus de Voragine (d. 1298) compiled the *Golden Legend*, the greatest collection of saints' lives up to that time and the source of many later stories. (The word *legend* in the Middle Ages did not imply untruth but meant literally "something to be read".)

Saintly Royalty   Most canonized saints were clergy and religious, and the most conspicuous class of lay saints were royalty, who were honored less for their political achievements than for their piety and devotion to the Church. These included Henry II of Germany (1002–1024), Olaf II of Norway (1015–1030), Alfred (871–899) and Edward the Confessor (1042–1066) of England, Stephen I (1000–1038) and Ladislas I of Hungary (1077–1095), Canute IV of Denmark (1080–1086), Louis IX of France (1226–1270), Margaret of Scotland (1046–1093), Elizabeth of Hungary (1207–1231), and Elizabeth of Portugal (1271–1336). Piety did not always fit closely with politics. Henry II of Germany at one point allied himself with pagan tribes against the Catholic king of Poland, but on the other hand, one of his successors, Henry III, proclaimed a Day of Indulgence on which he solemnly forgave his enemies and asked that they forgive his transgressions.

Relics   There was a great deal of credulity about relics, and churches that claimed notable collections became pilgrimage places that were also sources of considerable revenue to the local community. Relics were solemnly enthroned, kept in rich and elaborate containers, carried in processions through the street, sometimes stolen, and avidly bought and sold, even though such commerce constituted simony. When Louis IX died in North Africa, there was competition between his son and his brother for possession of his body, which was divided between them, and when Aquinas died at a Cistercian monastery, the monks retained certain parts of his body before sending the remains to his Dominican confreres.

Marriage   The Church took increasing responsibility for matrimony, defining the degrees of blood relationship within which a valid marriage could
Validity   occur, requiring the free consent of the spouses, allowing an unconsummated marriage to be annulled ("made nothing"), and requiring a liturgical ceremony, although a marriage was considered valid so long as it could be shown that the couple had made a verbal commitment to each other. Divorce (literally, a "split" or "cutting") did not exist in the sense of the dissolution of a valid marriage, but church courts decided numerous appeals for separation, based on the serious misconduct of one of the spouses, and even more cases claiming the invalidity of the marriage, mainly because of lack of consent.

Besides the church ceremony, the marriage bed was also solemnly blessed before being occupied, and after childbirth, the new mother underwent the ceremony of "churching", the significance of which seems to have been understood in various ways—in some cases, as a kind of ritual purification, in others as a kind of ritual honor to motherhood.

Theologians took an increasingly positive view of marriage, as not merely a remedy for concupiscence, as Paul implied in one place, but as a divinely ordained sacrament, modeled on the relationship between Christ and His Church, as Paul said in another.

The culture of courtly love (see below) required the avoidance of pregnancy, which caused the Church to reiterate strongly that the purpose of marriage is procreation. Some theologians also justified marital sex on the Pauline grounds that it forestalled adultery, therefore the desire for children did not have to be a conscious motive. Aquinas considered sexual pleasure to be an inducement to the act of procreation and not necessarily sinful. To refuse to pay the "marital debt"—intercourse with one's spouse—was sinful, in that it might tempt the spouse to adultery, and moralists hesitated over approving the long absence from home of men who went on Crusades.

Procreation

Monastic life in itself was considered superior to life in the world, to the point where married couples were allowed to separate in order to enter religious life. But monastic life had its own temptations, so that a good layman might have a higher place in Heaven than an indifferent monk. Pope Alexander III stated that virginity was not necessary for a life of perfection and, paradoxically, certain monastic writers especially extolled the love between husband and wife.

The Lay Vocation

However, monarchs in particular, for pragmatic reasons, were often at odds with the Christian ideal of marriage, because they married and divorced in order to cement diplomatic alliances or promote their dynasties. Philip I of France was excommunicated for divorcing his wife and marrying his cousin, thereby committing a double sin. Eleanor of Aquitaine (d. 1204), the most celebrated woman of the twelfth century, was divorced by Philip's grandson, Louis VII (1137–1180), after allegedly carrying on an adulterous affair while on crusade with her husband. Pope Eugene III allowed the split because Louis and Eleanor were related by blood, and she then married Henry II of England, with whom she had an equally stormy relationship.[5]

Divorce

Almost all aristocratic marriages were arranged for dynastic or economic purposes; and, while prevailing customs did not make love a prerequisite for marriage, it was hoped that love would grow throughout the life of the married couple. Perhaps inevitably, therefore, alongside the Christian ideal of marriage there thus developed the culture of "courtly love", so-called because it was popular at the courts of the nobility.

Arranged Marriages

The medieval "romances" (so-called because, as vernacular French, they were derived from the language of Rome) revived the sense of

Courtly Love

---

[5] The film *The Lion in Winter* is a fictionalized account of their relationship.

love as a sexual passion deeply rooted in the soul, something celebrated among the ancients but largely ignored in early Christianity. Courtly love usually celebrated an attraction between a man and a woman who were not married to each other, an attraction that sometimes culminated in adultery, as in the story of the legendary King Arthur of Britain, whose queen, Guinevere, and his best knight, Lancelot, had an affair that destroyed the mythical kingdom of Camelot.

Troubadors

The courtly-love movement originated in southern France and probably owed much to Arabic sources, as well as to the Cathars. It was spread by traveling singers called *troubadours*—both male and female—the origin of whose name is uncertain. Courtly love celebrated an openly hedonistic way of life. Duke William IX of Aquitaine (d. 1127) had been a Crusader in Spain but, disillusioned by what he considered Christian hypocrisies, came to scoff openly at Christianity, as did an anonymous French work titled *Aucassin and Nicolette*. The German poet Walter von der Vogelweide (d. ca. 1236), although a monk, seemed ambivalent about Christian sexual morality.

Knight and Lady

But as it spread north, courtly love was modified in accord with attempts to christianize the warrior spirit through the code of chivalry, in which the lady was idealized and unattainable, while the knight served her unselfishly. The titles of "Our Lord" and "Our Lady", which became the most familiar ways of speaking of Jesus and Mary, were an outgrowth of this, transferring to them absolutely the conditional fidelity owed to one's feudal superiors. Pious knights vowed themselves to Mary's service.

Liturgy

Western Rites

The basic form of the Mass had been set during the Carolingian period and, after being adopted at Rome, became known as the Roman Rite, with a few alternative Rites with minor variations: the Ambrosian in Milan, the Gallican in parts of France, the Mozarabic in Spain, and the Sarum in England.

Ex Opere Operato

A recurring heresy, dating at least as far back as the Donatists, held that the validity of the sacraments depended upon the personal worthiness of the priest. Medieval theologians countered this with the doctrine that, if celebrated according to proper form, the sacraments were valid *ex opere operato* (literally, "from the work having worked"), that is, through the power of the ordained priesthood, independent of the priest's moral character.

Additions

There were further significant liturgical developments during the High Middle Ages. The Confiteor ("I confess") became a regular part of the Mass after 1200, and the Gloria in the eleventh century, although for a time, except on Easter, it was sung only by the bishop. The Creed too was introduced during that century.

By the thirteenth century, the congregation commonly knelt from the Sanctus until Communion and, amidst the silence of the Canon, were alerted to the impending consecration by the ringing of a bell. Whereas formerly the sacred elements had been shown to the people only at the end of the Canon ("Through Him, with Him, and in Him . . ."), the major elevation following the Consecration was now added. (The elevation of the chalice was not required until the sixteenth century, on the grounds that, when it was elevated, the faithful did not actually see the Blood of Christ.) Often the church bells were rung at the Consecration to signal to those outside the church that the miracle had occurred. At the end of the Canon, it was customary to bless various things connected with the people's work—fruit, lambs, bread, milk, honey.

Certain devotions that were originally private, such as the prayers before Communion—"Lord, I am not worthy" and a second Confiteor— gradually came to be officially prescribed. The "Last Gospel" (the first chapter of John) was a medieval innovation in the Mass, recited by the priest, who, paradoxically, returned to the altar after the people had been formally dismissed. Originally, the recitation of John 1 was itself considered a blessing that could overcome illness or bring other favors, and this private devotion was incorporated into the liturgy because of its great popularity. (The "last blessing" by the priest also came after the dismissal, since it too was originally a private devotion.)

During the thirteenth century, chasubles came to be made in various colors, to symbolize the liturgical seasons, and eventually the colors were standardized: white for the feasts of Christ and for virgins and confessors, red for martyrs, purple for the penitential seasons of Lent and Advent, green for the long period after Pentecost, black for the dead.

In larger churches, permanent rood screens, surmounted by crucifixes and other sacred images, were often erected to separate the nave from the sanctuary. The sheer size of some worshipping communities led to other significant changes, such as no longer administering the chalice to the laity. (But it was only in larger towns and monasteries that size presented a problem, since most people lived in villages, where Mass was celebrated in a rather small space, with the whole community present.)

Music was also integral to divine worship in larger churches, an expression of the divine harmony of the universe itself, closely linked to the mathematics of the *quadrivium*; in Platonic terms, a means whereby the soul could rise above mundane things and enter the heavenly realm. Anselm, however, warned that music existed not for itself but in order to lure the listener into paying attention to the divine words, and Bernard, who was suspicious of all aesthetic pleasure, warned against music that obscured the scriptural texts it was meant to support.

Chanting was both in praise of God and to allow the spirit of the liturgy to penetrate deeply into the soul through repetition. Cluny pioneered the practice of placing its monks in choir stalls, two groups facing each other and chanting antiphonally ("against the sound"). Besides plain chant, increasingly elaborate polyphonic Masses were being composed in the thirteenth century, now often sung by professional lay choirs located in high lofts above the entrance of the church.

Sacred Drama

Drama grew directly out of the liturgy, originally with clerics in vestments enacting scenes from the Gospels in the body of the church. In time, plays were written on Gospel subjects and performed with increasing elaborateness by professional actors, spilling out of the church and into the town square.

Eucharistic Piety

Eucharistic piety grew increasingly fervent, as in the eucharistic hymn of St. Thomas Aquinas, "O Salutaris Hostia" ("O saving host"). The new feast of Corpus Christi ("Body of Christ"), with processions winding through the streets, was established in the thirteenth century, and the practice of exposing the Blessed Sacrament in the monstrance ("showing") a little later. But paradoxically, this piety accompanied a decline in the reception of Communion. Gazing prayerfully at the sacred elements became a kind of substitute, culminating in "spiritual communion" with Jesus in one's heart.

Festivals

The liturgy was fundamentally joyous—the enactment of the redemption itself—and this joy spilled over into communal celebrations that took on a worldly, even profane, character. Mardi Gras ("Fat Tuesday") was a day on which people consumed whatever meat and lard they still had before the Lenten fast began, and in Latin lands it became *carnival* ("farewell to the flesh"), an excuse for riotous behavior.

Seven Sacraments

The word *sacrament* had always been used rather loosely, to refer to virtually any sacred thing. But the Fourth Lateran Council defined seven sacraments as the "visible forms of invisible reality" and the principal channels of divine grace, six of which were established by Jesus directly, while matrimony had been decreed by God in the Garden of Eden. Somewhat later, the term *sacramental* came to be used for objects, such as holy water and crucifixes, related to sacraments. The *cope*, which was originally a cape worn against the cold, and a shortened alb called the *surplice* (something "worn above") were vestments worn by the priest at ceremonies other than the Mass itself.

In the eleventh century, the people might confess their sins openly at Mass and receive absolution. But for mortal sins, private confession was still required, and absolution was not ordinarily granted at the time of confession but only after the penitent had completed a very demanding penance.

Penance

The use of revised Penitentials spread, partly on the assumption that many priests were not skilled in the care of souls and needed to follow a guidebook that delineated the various sins and indicated how they were to be treated. For the same reason, the friars were given faculties to hear confessions, because they were often better educated than the diocesan clergy and were perhaps thought to be more devout, a policy that seemed to undercut the parish system and became a principal cause of animosity toward the friars. Absolute secrecy was enjoined on confessors, who were told not even to look at the penitent, and one of the gravest of all sins—reserved to the Holy See itself for absolution—was a confessor's soliciting of sexual favors from a penitent.

In the midst of growing prosperity, people remained highly conscious of death, continually exposed to the symbolism that showed the virtues contributing to salvation and the corresponding vices leading to Hell. Good and bad acts were both thought of as being kept meticulously in a book that was opened at the gates of Paradise, where angels weighed souls in a balance. The "hour of our death" was crucial, because it was at that final moment, as angels and devils fought over the soul of the dying man, that salvation or damnation was determined, the deathbed conversion of the sinner being one of the most dramatic and often-told stories.

Last Things

The Hour of Death

People were judged immediately after death, a judgment that was ratified in the General Judgment at the end of the world. In keeping with Jesus' warnings, the end times were dreaded, so that the poem *Dies Irae* ("Day of Wrath") was eventually incorporated into the Mass for the dead. Cluny was the first community to celebrate the feast of All Souls, around 1050, and it was eventually extended to the entire Church, for a time the only feast on which a priest might celebrate more than one Mass.

Funerals were as elaborate as a family could afford, and men sometimes provided in their wills for clergy or other people, such as orphans, to accompany the body, wrapped in a shroud and carried on an open bier, to the grave while praying or chanting psalms. Confraternities ("brothers together") were societies established to ensure proper burial and prayers for their deceased members. The dismemberment of Aquinas' body was not a unique occurrence. Important people sometimes made provision for different parts of their bodies to be interred at different locations with which they had been associated in life.

Funerals

Prayers for the Dead

Funeral monuments commonly represented the deceased robed in the garments of his social rank, eyes closed and hands folded in peaceful eternal rest. But increasingly the monuments also displayed the image of a skeleton or a decaying body, reminders of the inevitability of death and judgment, something for which monks and others kept skulls close at hand. Tombs bore the names of the deceased and, most important, pleas to passersby to pray for their souls. Legacies were left to churches for the celebration of Masses, and the very rich set up endowments to support "Mass priests" (those without a regular benefice) whose sole duty was to pray for the soul of the donor. Special altars, and even whole chapels, were built onto churches for that purpose.

Last Will

The "last will and testament" was under the jurisdiction of the church courts because it was a witness (testament) to the will or wishes of the deceased, of the state of his soul at the time of death, hence an indication of his fate. The legacy was a crucial opportunity for manifesting one's faith and doing penance for one's sins, by leaving money for worthy purposes.

Sacred Architecture

The greatest manifestations of Christendom's recovery after 1000 were in the realm of high culture, particularly architecture. With a few exceptions, such as Charlemagne's chapel at Aachen, church-building declined during the Dark Ages but, soon after the symbolic date 1000 had been passed, a monk noted that the landscape was now dotted with the white stone of new churches. In some ways, the building of those Catholic megaliths was the most telling sign of the recovery of civilization.

The building of churches was a pious act in which people participated not only with their donations but by actually hauling stone and doing other manual labor, something in which even aristocratic ladies were said to participate. Church-building reflected the complex unity of the Christian society, in that, besides piety, it required wealth, technical skill, and civic pride. The great church, intended to last for centuries, was an act of faith not only in God but in the future of the city as well. (The names of some of the architects and artists are known, although in general their work was regarded as being done for God alone, not for public recognition.)

Byzantine

Eastern architectural styles survived in Italy, especially at Ravenna, which was the Byzantine capital in the West, and at Venice (St. Mark's Basilica), because of its close commercial ties with the East. But the recovery of the West primarily manifested itself in new architectural styles.

Romanesque

Romanesque architecture began in the eleventh century, developing from the Roman basilica style but with much larger structures, some rising more than a hundred feet and holding several thousand worshippers. Great churches crowned with domes continued to be built in the East, but the West expressed its aspiration for God by building higher and higher, with towers and steeples pointing to Heaven. Besides great cathedrals and abbeys (Cluny in France, Winchester and Durham in England), Romanesque churches were built especially in southern France, along pilgrimage routes to the shrine of Santiago de Compostela. To sustain their height, Romanesque churches had massive walls, huge pillars, and rounded ceilings. The interior walls were often painted with biblical scenes, and the columns were rich in sculpture, all of which had religious significance but also expressed the vivid imaginations of the artists: signs of the zodiac, exotic plants and animals, mythical monsters.

The "Gothic" style of architecture, as it was later disrespectfully dubbed (see Chapter Eight below, p. 242), began at Suger's Abbey of St. Denis in the earlier twelfth century. It was made possible by certain innovations in building techniques, especially the high vaulted arch of the roof and the "flying buttresses"—masonry structures that supported the walls from the outside, thereby alleviating the need for massive pillars on the inside. Like the Romanesque, the initial impression of the Gothic was of a building reaching up to Heaven. (The tower of Ulm in Germany was for centuries the tallest stone structure in the world.)

Gothic

Divine Light

But the greater significance of the Gothic, in contrast to the Romanesque, was the lightness of its structure: slender soaring pillars and relatively thin walls, allowing those walls to be opened by several levels of windows, thereby infusing the interior with a richness of light not possible in Romanesque buildings, a natural light transformed as it passed through rows of stained-glass windows.

Chartres

The cathedral of Chartres, begun in 1194, is the most famous and best-preserved example of the Gothic, the circumstances of its construction perfectly expressing the spirit of medieval piety. After the old cathedral burned down, the townspeople at first considered it a divine judgment and decided not to rebuild. But when the town's most celebrated relic, the cloak of the Virgin Mary, was found in the ruins, this was taken as a sign that they should erect an even greater structure.

Over the portals of many of the great churches was the triumphant scene of Christ reigning in glory and sitting in judgment over the souls of men, decreeing who would share in His heavenly glory and who would be cast into Hell. As worshippers entered the church, their minds were turned to the purpose of their existence on earth and the need to make themselves worthy to pass through the heavenly portals.

Christ in Glory

The Church as Book   The entire church building served as a course of instructions on the mystery of salvation, with both sculptured figures and painted glass representing characters from the Old Testament prefiguring the New, facing one another from opposite sides of the church: scenes from the life of Christ by which He redeemed the human race; the Evangelists who recorded the Good News; the contrasting wise and foolish virgins; saints who exemplified the true following of Christ; the choirs of angels; and both realistic and symbolic representations of the vices Christians had to eschew and the virtues they had to cultivate.

Expressing the sense of the unity of Christendom, the cathedrals included what might be considered secular scenes: banquets, hunts, events from history. Medieval sculptors occasionally produced male nudes and female figures (Eve), who, if not nude, were portrayed in sensuous poses. Apparently secular objects might have religious significance: the nut symbolizing Christ, whose divine nature is hidden under His human nature, just as the meat is hidden under the shell; the two wings of a dove symbolizing the contemplative and active dimensions of the spiritual life; the pelican as the Eucharist, because it was believed to feed its young with its own blood. Instruction took place on several levels simultaneously—picture stories for the unlearned, symbolism for the more sophisticated, and for everyone a perhaps largely subconscious imbibing of the underlying order of creation.

Cistercian Austerity   Cistercian churches, while they adopted Gothic verticality and lightness of structure, had plain glass windows, unadorned walls, and a minimum of statues, as Bernard railed against decorative religious art for distracting monks from the Scripture. He urged that money spent on decoration be given to the poor, although even he acknowledged that people in the world needed visible support for their faith.

Divine Proportion   Although less so than in the East, the interior of the church was intended to be itself an experience of Heaven, based on the metaphysics of light expounded by Pseudo-Dionysius, whom Suger and others thought was the same person as the patron of the great abbey. Gothic churches were built in accord with complex and precise geometrical relationships that were not merely aids to efficient construction but were thought to embody the underlying pattern of the universe itself, placed there by God and disclosed in the measurements of Solomon's Temple. As Plato had taught, mathematical relationships allowed the mind to move beyond chaotic physical reality to the eternal order underlying it.

The *quadrivium* of mathematical sciences was especially important at the cathedral school of Chartres and directly influenced the development of the Gothic. The geometer's tools —the compass and the ruler— were often depicted, and the number symbolism that came down from Augustine was embodied in all aspects of the church. Baptismal fonts, for example, were often octagonal, both because Christ was the "eighth day" of creation and because mankind was allotted seven ages from birth to death, and eight therefore symbolized new life. Sculptures of Christ and the saints were majestic and stylized, themselves ordered according to mathematical proportions, as befit the inhabitants of Heaven.

The monasteries remained the centers of intellectual life until the eleventh century, when, among other things, the increasingly complex requirements of the monastic liturgy left less time for study, and leadership passed to the cathedral schools located in towns. Anselm was still part of the monastic culture, but his work helped move theology away from that culture. He felt guilty about pondering philosophical problems while chanting the Divine Office and therefore avoided Cluniac houses. The one aspect of intellectual life where monks remained important was writing histories or chronicles, some of which, although composed for partisan purposes, are the only surviving detailed accounts of the events of their day.

The "Renaissance of the Twelfth Century" has been called the greatest of all such revivals, in that it marked the greatest progress within the shortest period of time. It was centered especially in the school of Chartres, under the direction of John of Salisbury, a Platonist who loved classical literature. But before long, intellectual life moved in a different direction from the Humanism of Salisbury, who warned that the emphasis on logic would bring about a decline in the study of the liberal arts, by making them seem insufficiently rigorous.

Fragmentary knowledge of Greek thought had survived through Boethius and Eriugena, especially the science of logic or dialectic. These parts of the *trivium* underlay the intellectual revival of the Middle Ages, creating a new way of thinking—abstract, technical, systematic—that came to be called Scholasticism, after the schools where it found its home.

In all aspects of life, there was a new urge for ordered systems. Scholasticism was the chief expression of this larger movement of increased rationality and self-consciousness, which also included the codification of canon law, the necessity of free consent to marriage, the outlawing of the ordeal in favor of the judgment of juries, and a formal process for canonizing saints according to some objective criteria rather than simply by popular enthusiasm.

Scholastics sought to deepen and clarify doctrines by defining them more precisely, something that often involved unfamiliar subtleties of technical language as applied to the divine mysteries.

The monk Berengar of Tours (d. 1088), making use of Aristotelian terminology, was condemned for holding that, since the appearances

The Intellectual Renaissance

Monastic and Cathedral Schools

School of Chartres

The Urge for Order

Scholastic Theology

Transubstantiation

("accidents") of bread and wine remain in the Eucharist after the Consecration, the underlying reality ("substances") of bread and wine must also remain. He taught that the Body and Blood of Christ are present in that the "sign" changes —a symbol that is not merely a reminder but that makes present that which it signifies. Berengar's formula prompted his opponents to insist that communicants actually tear the flesh of Christ with their teeth. (Berengar recanted, recanted his recantation, then recanted again.)

Lateran IV defined the doctrine of Transubstantiation ("substance crossing over" or changing), which was later developed by Aquinas' teaching that the Eucharist is unique in being—miraculously—the sole case in which the unseen substance changes but the visible accidents remain the same. (In every other case, the reverse happens: the size or color of an apple may change, for example, but it remains the same apple.) Transubstantiation thus became the accepted Western way of understanding the Real Presence.

Faith Seeking Understanding

The Scholastic movement essentially began with Anselm, who pushed the method of logical analysis further than anyone had, up to his time. He defined theology as "faith seeking understanding", in that the truths of faith can be neither proved nor disproved by human reason, but men are obliged to use reason to understand them as far as possible. Without minimizing the importance of Scripture, reason can venture where Scripture is either silent or unclear. Anselm especially used rational inquiry in his treatise *Why God Became Man*, where he tried to understand as far as possible the revealed truth of the Incarnation. Anselm's argument for the existence of God was based on the idea of a perfect Being, no greater than which can be conceived by the mind. Such a being must exist, he argued, because perfection implies existence. Finite beings have perfections, but they must derive those perfections from an all-perfect Being, without whom the very idea of perfection would be unintelligible. The biblical claim, "The fool has said in his heart 'there is no God'", showed that atheism was a failure not of belief but of reason. According to Anselm, men do not "believe" in God; they know that He exists.

Essence and Existence

Anselm was the first philosopher to employ the Aristotelian distinction between *essence* and *existence* to understand God, essence being that which a thing is (a man), existence the fact that it is (a particular man). In God alone, existence and essence are the same, in that His essence is simply to exist, without limit, whereas creatures exist only in limited ways. Their essences are restricted by their existence, and limitations define each unique person in contrast to others.

Soteriology

In many ways, the Passion of Christ dominated Catholic piety in the two centuries prior to Anselm, including a deep sense of guilt over the human sinfulness that had crucified the Savior. Severe penances, such as those advocated by the monk-cardinal St. Peter Damian (d. 1072), were in part an attempt to repay the debt that sinners owed to God and to avert as far as possible God's condemnatory judgment.

But to Anselm, no human recompense was possible. Based on Paul and Augustine, he proposed that mankind owed God an infinite, unpayable debt that only a man who was also divine could repay and which the second Person of the Trinity—freely and with infinite love—took upon Himself, suffering and dying to ransom mankind. Anselm also sought to resolve the issue of predestination, proposing that, since God exists in an eternal present rather than in time, His will and His foreknowledge are the same—nothing that He decrees is in the future; all is in the present.

The Limits of Reason

Scholasticism did not immediately sweep all before it, since in many ways it was revolutionary. Theology continued to be primarily the study and exposition of Scripture, but it was now done in new ways. (Stephen Langton, while a professor in Paris, was the first to divide the Bible into chapters and verses.) Peter Damian opposed the growing dominance of logic on the grounds that it placed limits on God, who has the power even to undo what has already occurred and to make two contradictory things both true.

"The Last of the Fathers"

Bernard was the most severe critic of the new mode of theology, fearing that it substituted sterile intellectualism for the living teachings of the Fathers of the Church. Himself called the last of the Fathers, Bernard was also one of the last of the monastic theologians, for whom the dominant concern was the salvation of souls rather than the pursuit of knowledge. Bernard's idea of knowledge was as much personal and affective as intellectual—humility (recognition of one's lowliness) leads to charity (sympathy for other people), which leads to compassion (true sorrow), which prepares the way for heavenly contemplation.

Mystical Theology

The tradition of mystical theology persisted among the Cistercians throughout most of the Middle Ages. Bernard was familiar with the Eastern idea of the progressive deification of the believer, and he saw the mystical experience—the soul's being taken out of itself and into God—as the culmination of the Christian life.

The monastery of St. Victor near Paris remained a center of a more traditional kind of theology. Richard of St. Victor (d. 1183) to some extent translated Augustinian ideas into Scholastic terms but deemphasized the power of reason by emphasizing the "cloud of darkness" that surrounds God. His colleague Walter of St. Victor (d. ca. 1180) actually cursed logicians: "May your dialectic be your damnation!"

Universities The cathedral schools were also being superseded, because they functioned somewhat like modern secondary schools, primarily imparting basic knowledge, whereas the intellectual revival of the eleventh and twelfth centuries required a new institution in which original thinking could take place. Thus the university was born.

Italy Probably stimulated by contact with Greek and Arabic culture, Bologna and Salerno in Italy, followed by Naples and Padua, were the first universities, a term from Roman law that designated a corporate body—a legal person—with its own autonomy. Bologna was the center for canon law, but the other Italian universities were primarily lay institutions, chartered by city governments and organized as student communes for the study of the primarily lay subjects of law and medicine. These medieval institutions already contained the basic features of the modern university: specialized knowledge, three degrees (bachelor, master, doctor) denoting levels of competence, and a commitment to intellectual inquiry.

The Sorbonne The University of Paris, called the Sorbonne after the bishop who first chartered it, grew out of the cathedral school of Notre Dame and was a university by 1200. Although it had a faculty of medicine, its curriculum was primarily church-related: liberal arts, theology, and canon law, the last probably being the most popular, because it led to employment in church bureaucracies. Oxford and Cambridge in England broke off from Paris in the earlier thirteenth century, and the new institution soon spread widely, with over eighty universities all over Europe by the end of the Middle Ages. The northern universities remained at least formally under the jurisdiction of the Church. (Gregory IX rebuked a bishop of Paris for not exercising sufficient oversight over the Sorbonne.)

The Profession of Theology In the patristic period, a theologian was simply someone deemed wise and learned in the things of God; many were bishops who theologized as part of their pastoral responsibilities. But now a theologian was understood as one who had attained the proper academic credentials, and the dwindling number of bishop-theologians were men who had gained the latter status before achieving episcopal office. Theologians in effect became a kind of guild, their primary constituency being in the universities themselves.

The Demand for Rigor The adaptation of Aristotelian logic to theology generated debates that were often even more subtle and difficult than those of the Fathers and that to some people seemed far removed from the spirit of the Gospel. But the stakes were very high—whether or not believing Christians could make use of their rational capacities to the fullest.

Following Aristotle, the Scholastics demanded not merely "opinion" or "probability" but "demonstration"—logical argument that was irrefutable. They adopted the method of disputation as their characteristic way of proceeding, sometimes in face-to-face debate between adversaries, sometimes in aggressive questioning of a master by his students, above all by the requirement that a thinker accurately state other positions and rebut them. The opinions of earlier thinkers were freely cited, but only as supporting evidence—appeals to authority could not defeat rational argument. (The *Sentences* of Peter Lombard [d. 1169] was one of the most influential books of the Middle Ages, a gathering together of the opinions by earlier philosophers and theologians, not for the purpose of settling those questions definitively but to serve as a basis for further exploration.)

Scientia was the Latin word for "knowledge", meaning certitude, and was roughly the equivalent of philosophy and by no means limited to the physical world. There was no clear separation between philosophy and theology. Philosophical ideas were explored as part of the study of theology, and theology was the "queen of the sciences", because it involved the highest and most certain truths.

The Queen of the Sciences

Since God gave man reason as the highest human power, no authentic discovery of reason was thought capable of denying a dogma of faith. However, since faith dealt with truths far above the human capacity to understand, it was reasonable to rely on faith for knowledge of supernatural mysteries. The dogmas of faith might then reveal ways in which reason had erred and might suggest answers to philosophical conundrums.

Faith and Reason

Scholasticism's inquisitive spirit was first exercised over the question of the "universals": how a general concept ("tree") could be applied to myriad particular beings (trees). What may have seemed like a mere technical quibble proved to have deep implications. "Realists" held that the mind perceives in individual things a nature that really exists and that is common to all things of the same species, hence that the mind perceives "universals", while "nominalists" held that the universals are merely names that the mind gives to things that resemble one another, without knowing their underlying reality.

Universals

Peter Abelard (d. 1142) confirmed the misgivings that some people had about the new philosophy. At least by his own account, when he appeared as a student at Paris he drove his professor from the lecture hall by relentless questioning. A brilliant logician, Abelard was in love with his subject and determined to push it as far as he could, which was beyond the point that many people thought valid. He questioned the reality of universals, on the grounds that there are so many differences among the various beings of a particular species that they share no common nature, that "nature" is merely the mind's attempt to impose order on endless variety. Based on Lombard, he wrote a

Abelard

book called *Yes and No*, in which he pointed out what he considered to be unresolved contradictions among the opinions of previous thinkers.

Contrary to the prevailing theory of Anselm, Abelard seemed to deny the doctrine of the atonement and instead understood Christ's death simply as a revelation of His infinite love, a position that was rejected as inadequate by Bernard and others. Struggling with the logical paradoxes of the doctrine of the Trinity, Abelard was accused of positing three gods and ultimately his work was condemned. (The iconoclastic theologian was protected to a degree by Bernard's own sometime opponent Peter the Venerable.)

Abelard was also undone by a seemingly unrelated matter—his love affair with the niece of a prominent priest, a young woman named Heloise (d. 1164), whom Abelard made pregnant. He and Heloise were both banished to monasteries, where they spent most of the rest of their lives and later exchanged letters about the sublimation of human love into the divine. Ironically, Abelard became a reforming abbot, whose recalcitrant monks once put poison in his chalice at Mass.

The Rediscovery of Aristotle

A much greater crisis than that provoked by Abelard was the West's rediscovery, in the later twelfth century, of not merely Aristotle's logic but his whole philosophy, which had been preserved in libraries in the Near East and translated into Arabic by Muslim scholars. Ironically, since the West had lost almost all knowledge of Greek, it was from those Arabic translations that Christians in Spain first learned of the immensity of Aristotelian thought.

Serious thinkers therefore had to become Aristotelians, because Aristotle, whom Dante called simply "the master of those who know", seemed to have offered the most complete and unified account of reality ever attempted, integrating its diverse aspects into a comprehensive system that included physics, psychology, ethics, politics, aesthetics, and finally metaphysics ("beyond physics")—the study of the ultimate nature of reality.

Athens and Jerusalem—Again

The Christian West was suddenly confronted with a comprehensive understanding of reality that was based entirely on reason and completely independent of religious faith, something that seemed to force them to choose between compromising their faith and abandoning their commitment to rational inquiry, a crisis comparable to that of the early Christians confronting classical paganism, when Tertullian asked, "What has Athens to do with Jerusalem?"

Averroës and the Two Truths

The Muslim scholars who developed Aristotle's thought—mainly the North African Avicenna (Ibn Sīnā, d. 1037) and the Spaniard Averroës (Ibn Rushd, d. 1198)—laid out a complete system that at key points was directly at odds with Christianity, Judaism, and Islam itself.

Averroës held that the Qur'an could be understood on several levels, depending on the intellectual sophistication of the reader. The various levels should not be confused, and no one should aspire to a level of understanding above his ability. This led to what was later called the "theory of the two truths": what is true on one level of understanding might not be true at another, although each remains true in its own way. Averroës never explained how faith and reason could be reconciled, and his failure marked the beginning of a wide divergence between Muslim and Christian thought, to the point where Muslim thinkers, who in 1100 had been far in advance of Christians in the study of the physical sciences, increasingly abandoned speculation completely, in order to protect the integrity of their religion.[6]

"Latin Averroism" referred to Christians who continued to take Aristotle completely on his own terms and reached conclusions similar to Averroës'. It survived in the lay-governed Italian universities. But the mainstream of Christian philosophers held that faith and reason were both avenues to truth and, if followed correctly, could not contradict one another, so that any apparent contradiction showed that one side or the other had failed to follow its own method correctly. Thus the Scholastics, beginning in the late twelfth century, began revising Aristotle's thought to bring it into harmony with divine revelation.

Latin Averroism

St. Albert the Great (d. 1280), a Dominican who taught at Paris and became archbishop of Cologne, was the first medieval thinker to accept philosophy as a self-contained discipline distinct from theology, a distinction that led him to teach that Aristotle's "natural" human virtues precede supernatural virtues, thereby enabling pagans to lead good lives and possibly to be saved.

Albert

The principal achievement in reconciling Christianity and Aristotle belonged to Albert's pupil Aquinas, an Italian Dominican who spent most of his professional life at Paris. For Aquinas, "grace builds on nature", and the reconciliation of the two—the material with the spiritual, the temporal with the eternal—was his great achievement. Aquinas wrote the *Summa contra Gentiles* (The Highest Summary against the Gentiles [nonbelievers]) to prove the reasonableness of faith and the *Summa Theologica* (The Highest Summary of Theological Truth) to understand the faith more deeply.

Aquinas

God intended all men to be saved, assumed Aquinas, therefore truth must be knowable through reason. Human nature was damaged by sin, so that men see, in St. Paul's words, only "through a glass, darkly" (1 Cor 13:12, KJV), but they do retain the light of reason. Faith and

---

[6] It was to this divergence that Pope Benedict XVI referred in his controversial remarks about Islam at Regensburg, Germany, in 2007.

reason cannot contradict one another, but the truths of God far transcend finite reason.

Unmoved Mover

Aquinas found the argument for the existence of God in Aristotle's idea that the universe is a chain of causes, each dependent on the previous cause, all of them dependent ultimately on the Prime or Unmoved Mover or First Cause, an impersonal Being far removed from a personal God. The universe is eternal, because the Unmoved Mover is eternal and cannot change, thus its creative action must also be eternal.

Sense Knowledge

But Aristotle was also a materialist, as shown in his principle, "Nothing is in the mind unless it was first in the senses", a claim that appeared to exclude even the possibility of knowing nonmaterial beings and in particular excluded the Platonic-Augustinian idea that the mind has innate knowledge of spiritual reality. Whereas earlier Christian theologians, following Plato, warned against immersion in the world of the senses, Aristotle seemed to say that such immersion was inescapable, which placed believers in a seemingly irresolvable dilemma, since, as the Bible asked rhetorically, "No one has ever seen God?" (Jn 1:18).

The abstruse concept of the "agent intellect"—the faculty by which the mind understands the nature of individual beings—proved to be an especially controversial issue. Avicenna believed that there is only one agent intellect and that it is shared by all men, a doctrine that implied the denial of the individual soul, which is merely part of a larger soul.

Daringly, Aquinas affirmed Aristotle's principle that all knowledge begins with sense knowledge, without which the mind is a blank slate. Aquinas was a firm realist for whom each person's agent intellect, through sense perception, perceives the true nature of things, the biblical doctrine of personal immortality implying that each person has a distinct agent intellect. So also, while the idea of an eternal universe might seem logical, Genesis showed that it was in error.

Whereas Augustinians believed that the soul is by nature oriented toward God, Aquinas followed Aristotle in seeing the mind as primarily oriented outward, toward the world. And whereas previous thinkers had treated the soul as an independent entity joined to a body, Aquinas saw the union of soul and body as fundamental, with the soul dependent on the body for knowledge.

But it was possible to get beyond sense knowledge, Aquinas affirmed, because in meditating on such knowledge the mind realizes that, as Aristotle also taught, there must be a chain of causes that brought sensible beings into existence. God is known through His effects in the world, and Aquinas proposed five "ways" by which to know His existence, each based on a particular kind of causality as defined by

Aristotle, leading to an ultimate Uncaused Cause, which, Aquinas concluded, "we call God". Aristotle had proven the existence of God without knowing that the Prime Mover was God. His Prime Mover—the First Cause—was revealed to be a personal, loving God who acts freely rather than out of necessity.

The Being of God

Following Anselm's definition of God as uniting essence and existence, Aquinas took the words of God to Moses in the burning bush, "I Am Who Am" (Ex 3:14, NAB), as revealing that, in Aristotelian terms, God is "pure being": that which exists fully and without limitation. Central to Aquinas' thought was the "analogy of being". Since God is the ultimate cause of all things, some of His perfections can be found in His creation, which reflects the perfection of God Himself, although in an imperfect way. This makes possible rational knowledge not only of God's existence but of His nature, since He is the infinite and unlimited form of every good thing—all-just, all-knowing, all-loving, all-good. Like his predecessors, Aquinas espoused negative theology, whereby what is affirmed of God must also be denied of Him, since all human concepts are ultimately inadequate. Men know God through analogy, in that He is like His creation yet also unlike it, and He can be defined negatively—as without spatial or temporal limitations, as doing no evil.

The Primacy of the Intellect

Aquinas' ethical theory departed from that of Augustine in holding that the will always desires good and that evil is less a perversion of the will than an error in understanding: the choice of an apparent good over a real one. The will naturally desires what is good, and the mind can know good, because good is that which accords with the divine order of creation. Thus according to natural law, reason understands moral right and wrong on the basis of the inherent purpose of human actions: fornication is wrong because the purpose of sex is the procreation of children; lying is wrong because the purpose of speech is to communicate truth.

The Thomistic Ascendancy

Along with Augustine, Aquinas was the most influential thinker in the history of the Catholic Church, the importance of whose achievement can hardly be exaggerated. He would in many ways dominate Catholic thought ever afterward, but his ideas remained to some extent controversial, especially his denial of the Augustinian idea of the direct divine illumination of the soul. Certain Scholastic positions were condemned by Church authorities shortly after Aquinas' death, although for the most part those condemnations remained dead letters. Thomism survived and flourished, becoming the official Dominican system. But no school was completely dominant, and there was considerable debate among scholars, including some who remained Platonists in the face of the triumph of Aristotle.

Bonaventure

Bonaventure was the founder of a Franciscan theological tradition that was primarily Augustinian and that diverged from Aquinas in certain important ways. According to Bonaventure, the mind does see images of God in the world but understands them only by looking within itself, where it receives direct divine illumination and is impelled by a love that draws the soul inexorably toward God in mystical contemplation. Since this requires the free response of the individual, Bonaventure's theology was also Augustinian in giving primacy to the will over the intellect in the discovery of truth.

Physics

Physics was a recognized branch of Greek philosophy and was studied even in the Dark Ages. The School of Chartres took considerable interest in the subject, mainly in Platonic terms, and Euclid's geometry was rediscovered at the same time as Aristotle's philosophy, both giving new impetus to the study of nature. Medieval philosophy created the intellectual environment which made the scientific study of nature possible, in that nature had been created by the all-powerful God who stood above His creation, meaning that nature itself did not partake of divinity and thus could be studied objectively. While understanding the universe as part of the ultimate divine order, medieval thinkers sought to explain it as far as possible in natural ways, minimizing direct divine intervention.

Monotheism assumed an underlying order to the universe, which men were endowed by the Creator with the ability to discover. Medieval science anticipated modern science in some ways. Albert the Great was an observant botanist, for example. Some philosophers speculated that the universe was composed of atoms, and others struggled toward a concept of gravity.

The Universe

Most educated people in the Middle Ages believed that the earth was round and the universe made up a series of concentric spheres, that of the earth being the lowest, surrounded by other spheres that were increasingly rarified as they rose closer to the heavens. Matter was understood in terms of its various substances, primarily earth, air, fire, and water. Supernatural magic was from the devil and hence condemned, but "natural" magic was the discovery, by reason and experiment, of the hidden secrets of nature, a study (alchemy) that was in some ways a forerunner of modern experimental science.

Mathematics

Aristotle thought it possible to understand the world through the nature of each being, trying to understand the motion of the arrow, for example, by speculating about something within the arrow. It was an approach that ultimately proved unfruitful, and its chief defect was its neglect of mathematics, which was a characteristically Platonic rather than Aristotelian pursuit. Plato thought that concrete beings, as mere shadows of transcendent "forms", did not possess a nature of their own and could therefore be studied only by the mathematical measurement of their behavior.

The Franciscans were more mathematically inclined, perhaps because their philosophical approach was more Augustinian, hence more Platonist, than the Dominicans. The English Franciscan bishop and philosopher Robert Grosseteste (d. 1253) accepted the Pseudo-Dionysian belief that the universe was constituted by the emanation of light from a divine source, but he also approached light in a scientific way and saw the importance of empirical observation.

Grosseteste

His pupil Roger Bacon (d. 1292), also a Franciscan, also engaged in empirical observation, invented a kind of telescope, and urged that technology be used to improve the conditions of human living. He was imprisoned for a time, possibly for practicing astrology, but he was not a religious skeptic—to the contrary, he urged the Church to use science in the struggle against infidels.

Bacon

In Bacon's day, China was probably the most technologically advanced society in the world, but the West was in the process of surpassing it through practical innovations in building, navigation, weaponry, and agriculture, as well as miscellaneous inventions like eyeglasses. The Church herself made extensive use of technology, especially in building, and only condemned the occasional invention, such as the catapult or the crossbow, which were deemed too destructive. (The condemned weapons continued to be used anyway, even on the Crusades.)

Medieval Technology

Like the Fathers of the Church who embraced classical learning, the Scholastics had a profound effect on Western civilization, in developing and handing on the Greek tradition of critical thinking. Scholasticism, a comprehensive system that sought to understand every aspect of reality in relation to the whole, expressed the idea of Christendom itself, the organization of the entire universe according to an overriding spiritual principle.

The Scholastic Achievement

This sense of unity was carried to its highest point by Dante, whose *Divine Comedy*, written in the early fourteenth century, was the most vivid expression of that ideal, bringing together abstract doctrine and concrete humanity in a great imaginative unity, an epic drama that revealed the divine plan and the way in which divine justice governed the universe.

The Divine Comedy

In the *Comedy*, Dante, lost and spiritually imperiled by his illicit and unrequited love for the memory of a deceased married woman named Beatrice, received from God—at Beatrice's entreaty—the guidance of the Roman poet Virgil, who took him on a tour of Hell and Purgatory to show him the reality of sin. (Heaven and Hell are described only vaguely in the Bible, and the Catholic image of those places derives in great part from the *Divine Comedy*.)

Hell

Dante's tour of Hell revealed that punishment for sin was not an arbitrary divine decree but rather the patterns of human behavior carried into eternity, with the sinner suffering in ways that were the natural and inevitable results of his earthly behavior: the lustful blown helplessly about like dry leaves, because they allowed their passions to dominate them; the gluttonous force-fed to the point of continuously regurgitating their food; the hypocrites weighed down by heavy leaden robes that appeared beautiful on the outside. The men and women in Hell were shown to be not so much damned by God as having damned themselves, by refusing to repent of their choices and accept the grace that would have enabled them to overcome their vices either during their lives on earth or in Purgatory.

The Hierarchy of Sins

Dante delineated a hierarchy of sins that, as a Thomist, he based on human reason. Thus the worst sins were lying, deceit, and treachery—the use of the intellect to subvert the truth rather than to disclose it. Those guilty of such sins, especially Judas, were trapped in ice in the lowest depths of Hell, because of their calculating and unloving acts of betrayal.

Purgatory

An equivalent array of sinners were in Purgatory, where, however, they had the joy of the certainty of eventual salvation, their crucial difference from the souls in Hell being the fact that they had repented and accepted divine mercy. The sufferings of Purgatory were not so much punitive as therapeutic, purifying the soul and making it worthy of Paradise.

Heaven

Virgil could show Dante the nature of evil because, as a good pagan, the Roman poet understood the natural law. But also as a pagan, he could not enter Heaven, at whose gates Beatrice herself became Dante's guide, since by her prayers Dante's disordered human love had been transformed into an understanding of divine love.

Beatrice guided Dante through the levels of Paradise on an upward spiritual journey that was the reverse of his journeys through Hell and Purgatory. The experience of Paradise was overwhelmingly that of a light so bright that it obscured much of what Dante encountered, of which he was not as yet worthy. In his spiritual ascent, he encountered the great saints, who by their words and deeds illustrated the hierarchy of virtues. His final guide in Paradise was St. Bernard (Dante as author giving him the honor of that role because Bernard had reached the heights of contemplation and because of his deep devotion to the Virgin Mary). Dante was finally drawn upward to the ultimate union of love with truth: "Like a wheel that as a whole rotates, my yearning and my will were borne along by the love that moves the Sun and all the stars."

Dante revealed the ordered unity of the cosmos itself, the linkage between Heaven and earth. But his great poetic synthesis was created at the very point when Christendom was on the verge of unraveling.

7   East and West

The Eastern Empire

Justinian

The emperors at Constantinople continued to call themselves emperors of Rome, and only gradually did the name *Byzantine* attach itself to their state. Justinian I (ca. 482–565) was the greatest of these emperors. Although of Balkan peasant origins, he was an educated man with an exalted sense of the authority of his office and the ability to extend his empire and to win back lost territories even in the West. Justinian set out to make Constantinople the most magnificent city in the world, especially in the rebuilding of the great church of Hagia Sophia, but the success of his reign was marred by a plague pandemic so severe that the authorities were scarcely able to dispose of all the corpses and from which he himself almost perished.

The Persian Threat

As the West increasingly fell under the control of the barbarians, the Eastern Empire remained relatively, albeit precariously, strong, mainly because of its sophisticated administrative structure and its vast wealth. The Persians conquered much of the Near East early in the seventh century, devastating the Christians of Jerusalem, moving on to conquer Egypt, and besieging Constantinople itself. But Emperor Heraclius (610–641) drove them off and in turn invaded Persia, recovering what was believed to be the true Cross and personally carrying it on his shoulders back to Jerusalem.

Court Intrigues

However powerful, emperors sometimes fell victim to plots. Phocas (602–610) seized the throne from Maurice (582–602) and had Maurice and his five sons killed, only to be killed himself eight years later. Constantine VI (780–797) was blinded and left to die at the instigation of his mother, Irene, who was herself subsequently forced into a convent.

State over Church

Justinian saw the Church as a branch of the state, and the relationship between the two was a complex one. Beginning in the mid-fifth century, the emperors were crowned by the patriarch, but it was the emperors who were responsible for preserving the integrity of the faith and who often regulated church life by their decrees. They had the authority to summon councils, as Constantine had done at Nicaea, but doctrinal issues had to be decided by the assembled bishops.

Emperors bluntly rejected any claim that they were subject to episcopal authority and in practice controlled much of the episcopacy. Although bishops nominated other bishops, including the patriarch, the emperor was not required to accept their nominees, which led to occasional flagrant abuses, as when the emperor Romanus I (920–944) named his sixteen-year-old son, Theophylact, patriarch. Like emperors, patriarchs and bishops were deposed with some frequency amidst the tangle of civil and religious factions.

Religious orders never developed in the East as they did in the West. *Monasticism*
Each monastery was essentially independent, although great houses exerted strong spiritual influence over lesser ones. The hermetical, cenobitic, and communal modes of life all flourished. Although monastic life was found all over the East, from the tenth century onward, the peninsula of Mount Athos, in a remote part of Greece, was considered the spiritual powerhouse of the Empire, as monks from a variety of places went there to establish monasteries of such rigor that not even female animals were allowed on the peninsula.

The monasteries were to some extent resistant to imperial authority, with the monks upholding what was considered the full purity of orthodox faith and therefore willing to confront even the emperor, although they were not immune from imperial censure. Some emperors resented the monasteries for attracting lavish donations that could have been used for other purposes.

Although Justinian's Code recognized the primacy of the see of Rome, *Emperors and Popes*
the popes were for a time treated as imperial administrators. The popes continued to be elected at Rome, but the emperors ratified their election, and during the sixth and seventh centuries, most of the popes were Greeks who had either been attracted to Rome as the capital of the Church or had come as refugees from imperial conflicts. As with everything else, the issue of ecclesiastical authority was closely intertwined with secular politics. The Empire continued to claim territory in Sicily and southern Italy, where there was a significant Eastern presence, including monasteries of Eastern monks.

In every Eastern quarrel, such as disputed elections of bishops, an appeal *Appeals to Rome*
was likely to be made to the pope, whose primacy of honor was universally acknowledged. During the fifth century, popes twice rebuked emperors for supporting heresy and reminded them of the necessity of being in communion with the see of the Apostles at Rome.

However, the same Council of Chalcedon that condemned Monophysitism definitively and hailed Leo the Great's "Tome" (see Chapter Four above, pp. 86 and 98) also issued an ambiguous decree that seemed to make the see of Constantinople equal to Rome, although the pope's name continued to come first among bishops for whom prayers were offered in the liturgy. It remained ambiguous whether the East acknowledged Rome as having actual ruling authority, and there was growing estrangement—for example, Hadrian I (772–795) was the first pope to omit reference to the reigning emperor in his own proclamations.

"The Second Rome"

The spiritual authority of Constantinople was precarious, in that, unlike Jerusalem, Antioch, Alexandria, and Rome, it was not an apostolic see but had been founded late and owed its prestige entirely to its being the capital of the Empire. It was claimed, however, that the church at Byzantium had been founded by the Apostle St. Andrew, Peter's brother; that Rome also derived its status primarily from having been the imperial capital; and that Constantinople was the New Rome.

Patriarchates

Some Easterners proposed that the see of Antioch should have primacy, since Peter had presided there before going to Rome. Alexandria traced its lineage to St. Mark the Evangelist. In the ninth century, when the city was under Muslim control, Venetian adventurers took the Apostle's body to Venice, where the magnificent Byzantine-style St. Mark's Basilica was built to house it. (Based on this, the archbishops of Venice have ever since been called patriarchs.)

Complex Relations

Theodoric, the Arian Ostrogothic king of Italy (475–526), sent Pope St. John I (523–526) to Constantinople to ask the emperor Justin I to tolerate the Arians, but upon John's return Theodoric threw him into prison, where he died. Theodoric's successor Theodahad sent Pope Agapetus I (535–536) to Constantinople to plead (he was unsuccessful) against an imperial invasion of Italy. Both popes were treated with the greatest honors in the imperial capital, and Agapetus, who died there, was bold enough to depose a patriarch of Constantinople whom he deemed heretical and to consecrate a successor.

But both popes also found themselves in a delicate position midway between the emperor who sought to reconquer Italy and the heretical Italian king who also threatened the independence of the papacy. Beginning in 556, the popes no longer sought confirmation of their elections from the emperors, and when the emperor Justinian II (685–695) attempted to impose various Eastern disciplinary practices on the West, Pope St. Sergius I (687–701) rejected his authority.

The Photian Schism

In 858, Emperor Michael III the Drunkard (842–867) deposed Patriarch Ignatius of Constantinople (d. 877) and appointed the layman Photius (d. 897) in his place, an act that Pope Nicholas I denounced after Ignatius appealed to him. Photius soon claimed authority in southern Italy, and Nicholas excommunicated him, whereupon Photius accused the Western church of heresy, because of the doctrine of Purgatory and the word *filioque* in the Creed. Then a Byzantine council declared Nicholas deposed. However, after an imperial coup, the new emperor, Basil I the Macedonian (867–886), sent Photius to a monastery and restored Ignatius. (Nevertheless Photius would be restored and removed yet one more time before his death.) The Fourth Council of Constantinople (869–870) affirmed the authority of the see of Rome, although the Council was later repudiated in the East.

The extent of papal authority remained uncertain in the East. In 903, Emperor Leo VI, having been widowed three times, married a fourth wife, for which he was excommunicated by the Eastern bishops. He then obtained a dispensation from Rome, which the Eastern clergy refused to recognize.

Part of Rome's prestige was its boast, which the East acknowledged, that it had never countenanced heresy and that in the great early debates it had been the ultimate arbiter of orthodoxy, as Leo the Great had been during the Nestorian dispute. But Rome's orthodoxy was in some ways passive, in that there was a good deal less theological activity in the West. Easterners might condescend to Westerners as theologically backward, but Westerners could point out that the East was the hatching ground of almost all heresies. (When an emperor patronizingly told a Western visitor that Westerners manifested a naïve, childlike faith, the visitor admitted the claim but replied that the faith of the East was like an old worn-out garment.)

The Orthodoxy of the Roman See

Monophysitism survived in Egypt, Ethiopia, and Syria, especially among hyper-ascetic monks who in their zeal actually killed the patriarchs of Alexandria and Antioch at various times. Monophysitism was closely linked with the doctrine of "deification", whereby, through grace, men can become progressively more like God, an idea largely unknown in the West, which would probably have resisted it because of the danger of Pelagianism. Though the church in Egypt and Ethiopia quite early made a translation of the Bible into the Coptic language, over time it went into schism.

Monophysitism

Monophysitism was closely intertwined with the twists and turns of court politics, enjoying some imperial support. Justinian accepted the decrees of Chalcedon, but his wife, the famous Empress Theodora (d. 548), continued to support the Monophysites. The daughter of a lowly animal trainer and, according to some accounts, at one time a prostitute, Theodora was a woman of extraordinary ability. Pope St. Agapetus I (535–536) went to Constantinople to counteract Theodora's influence and to plead with Justinian not to invade Italy, but he died while in Constantinople.

Theodora

Justinian's armies retook Rome shortly thereafter, and Theodora was then able to secure the election of the anti-pope Vigilius, in rivalry to the newly elected St. Silverius (536–538), whom the imperial agent in Italy deposed and sent into exile, where he died of starvation. The church at Rome then accepted Vigilius as the rightful pope, but when he too resisted Theodora's agenda, he was taken by force to Constantinople, where he eventually signed an ambiguous formulary that was condemned in the West. After Theodora's death, the Second Council of Constantinople (553) definitively reaffirmed the decrees of Chalcedon.

The Life of the Eastern Church

Odium Theologicum

Theological disputes in the East extended even to the level of the common people and not infrequently erupted in violence, fueled by obscure and illogical links that existed between theological opinions and loyalty to particular teams of professional charioteers. Early in his reign, Justinian was almost driven from Constantinople in the *Nike* ("win") riots, which may have been partly caused by Theodora's support of the Monophysites. He reportedly had thirty thousand people put to death as punishment.

Monothelitism

Patriarch Sergius of Constantinople (d. 638) at one point proposed that Christ had only one will, a theory (Monothelitism) that sought to preserve His unity but that seemed to its critics to overlook such things as His prayer in the garden to be spared the cup of suffering. Monothelitism was accepted by Pope Honorius I (625–638), but Pope Theodore I (642–649) deposed the Monothelite patriarch Paul of Constantinople, a judgment that was confirmed by Pope St. Martin I (649–655).

As a result, Martin was brought to Constantinople, where he was brutally treated and sent into exile, dying in Russia. But the Third Council of Constantinople (680), by affirming that Christ had both a human and a divine will—that He experienced all human emotions except sinful ones—vindicated Martin and implicitly condemned Honorius, a condemnation made explicit by Pope St. Agatho (678–681). Honorius' apparent espousal of Monothelitism was the sole blot on Rome's record of orthodoxy, and Pope St. Leo II (682–683) explained that Honorius had been merely negligent, not actively heretical.

Maximus the Confessor

St. Maximus the Confessor (d. 662), the last of the great Greek Fathers, had been secretary to Emperor Heraclius (610–641). He became a monk and was savagely mutilated for his opposition to the Monothelitism of Emperor Constans II Pogonatus (641–668). Maximus was also instrumental in the final condemnation of Monophysitism, proposing that the mystical union of two natures in Christ affirmed the goodness of creation and the inherent dignity of human nature. Maximus was the most prestigious of the various Easterners who acknowledged the primacy of Rome.

Liturgy

The Eastern church had three distinct liturgies, attributed to St. James the Less, St. Basil, and St. John Chrysostom, respectively, their differences from the West including the use of languages other than Greek, leavened bread, unwatered wine, and the *epiklesis* of the Holy Spirit to descend upon the Communion elements in order to make Christ present. The Eucharist was not celebrated daily in the East. At a time when the administration of confirmation was gradually being separated from that of baptism in the West, confirmation in the East was administered by *chrismating* ("anointing") the newly baptized baby, and the infant was then given Communion.

Even more than in the West, the experience of worship in the East was intended to offer a foretaste of Heaven. The liturgy included long chants without instrumental accompaniment and was celebrated amidst almost unimaginable solemnity and splendor. The walls of Eastern churches were covered with mosaics or paintings of biblical scenes or of saints, hence the liturgy was celebrated in the presence of the saints. The *iconostasis*—a gated wall adorned with holy images—separated the altar from the body of the church, so that worshippers had only occasional glimpses of the sacred eucharistic act.

The use of the dome was distinctive to the East, although it had also *The Dome* been used at Rome itself. It perhaps derived from the Platonic idea of the circle as the perfect form, since it has no beginning and no end, hence symbolizes eternity. Whereas in the West the eye was carried upward until vision was no longer possible in the great heights of the building, in Byzantine churches the worshippers saw Heaven in the mosaics of the dome, looking up to the image of the *Pantocrator*.

Icons ("images") were gradually introduced as a way of making Heaven *Icons* concretely imaginable, through the images of its inhabitants. But unlike the West, the East for the most part forbade the use of three-dimensional images, as constituting idols, the cross alone excepted. (There were some bas-relief sculptures, especially on the exterior of churches.) Two-dimensional pictures were permitted, and even exalted, not as mere representations of Christ and the saints but as a means by which holy persons were actually made present.

Iconoclasm

But the greatest crisis in the history of the Eastern church was precisely over such images. Beginning in 730, Emperor Leo III the Isaurian (717–741) condemned their use, possibly as a way of moving closer to the Jews and the Muslims. The Church became bitterly divided over the issue. Pope St. Gregory II (715–731) upheld the use of icons, and Leo sent a fleet to arrest him, which was, however, wrecked en route.

The *iconoclasts* ("image-breakers") insisted that icons of Jesus separated His divine and human natures, since the divine nature was incapable of visualization, and that the veneration of icons thus amounted almost to polytheism as well as to idolatry. The true image of the saint was the replication of his virtues in the life of the believer. The icono-clasts insisted that the cross was the only legitimate image. Although in general they still venerated the relics of the saints, they were sus-pected of not believing in saintly intercession, and Constantine V Copro-nymus (741–775) in 766 confirmed those fears by forbidding prayers to the saints.

Iconophilia

In the minds of many, the condemnation of images amounted to a kind of Gnosticism and the attendant denial of the Incarnation itself and of the sacraments, both of which presuppose the belief that God could come to man through material means. There was much popular resistance to iconoclasm, with the monks in particular opposing the emperor on the issue.

The *iconophiles* ("image-lovers") or *iconodules* ("image-worshippers") characterized the iconoclasts as Judaizers still attached to the Old Law and defended an ancient practice that had deep theological meaning. It was thought possible to ascend the ladder of being to God through a series of steps, of which visible images were one stage—Paul's char-acterization of earthly knowledge of the divine as "through a glass darkly" or the Platonic idea of images as "archetypes" of transcen-dental realities.

John of Damascus

St. John of Damascus (or Damascene, d. 749), the most important theologian of the age, was an iconophile who pointed out that the Jews in fact had images, notably the Ark of the Covenant, and that icons represented the history of Christ in the same way as the Gospels did. He formulated what became the standard teaching concerning the veneration of saints even in the West, distinguishing among dif-ferent Greek terms: *latreia* ("worship") for God alone, *hyper-duleia* ("high honor") for Mary, and *duleia* ("honor") for the saints.

The Icons Restored

Empress Irene (780–803) restored the icons in 787, when the Second Council of Nicaea reversed Emperor Leo III's ruling. But the contro-versy was by no means over, as the influence of the two parties see-sawed back and forth. The issue remained alive until Empress Theodora II at last restored the icons permanently in 843.

As it did with all its important decisions, the church at Constan-tinople sent the Pope at Rome formal notification of its restoration of the icons, and Hadrian I (772–795) approved the action. Later, both the iconoclast emperor Leo V (813–820) and some leading icono-phile monks appealed to Pope Paschal I (817–824), who sided with the latter. Emperor Leo V once again mandated iconoclasm; after he was murdered at the instigation of his successor, the brutal Michael II

(820–829), Paschal intervened again, although on both occasions his emissaries were maltreated by the emperors.

Connected to the veneration of icons was the cult of wandering holy men, who were believed to have great spiritual power and who often attracted large popular followings. Both emperors and bishops looked on them with mistrust, as embodying a charismatic authority at odds with hierarchy, and in the eighth and ninth centuries there was an organized campaign against them, during which some were put to death.

Holy Men

The suspicion that iconoclasm was at heart Gnostic was given plausibility by the survival of various forms of heretical dualism in the Empire, called by a variety of names, such as Bogomils and Paulicians. These movements forced Christian apologists once more to affirm the goodness of all creation.

The Survival of Dualism

The East remained theologically creative even beyond the patristic age, but among the important differences between East and West was the fact that the East did not develop a rigorous abstract theology like Scholasticism.

Theological Creativity

Pseudo-Dionysius (ca. 500) was perhaps Syrian. His principal works were *Mystical Theology*, *On the Divine Names*, and *On the Celestial Hierarchy*, which reflected Neo-Platonic philosophy in their account of the soul's ascent to God by stages, culminating in a final leap in the dark, thereby making negative theology an integral part of Eastern thought. Maximus the Confessor expounded a distinctive Eastern theology of deification—God became man so that man can become God, ascending through the series of stages described by Pseudo-Dionysius. Man has free will that is prone to sin but is transformed by divine grace.

Pseudo-Dionysius

Augustine of Hippo had brought Western theology to a level equal to that of the East; but just as Augustine knew no Greek, the East was losing knowledge of Latin; hence Maximus and other Eastern theologians were apparently unaware of Augustine's work. Augustine held that Original Sin was transmitted from parent to child through the very act of conception, whereas for Maximus, mankind shared in Adam's sin only in the sense of having a propensity for evil, not as something basic to human nature.

The Nature of Sin

Marian devotion was especially strong in the East because Mary was the human being who had advanced farthest along the road toward deification. By the eighth century, she was being referred to as "Mediatrix of All Graces", because salvation had come through her Son and therefore through her. In the West, the strong Augustinian doctrine of

Marian Devotion

Original Sin strengthened the belief that Mary was conceived without sin ("Immaculate Conception"), because otherwise she would have transmitted that inherited sin to her Son, a belief that seemed to be confirmed by the angel's greeting, "Hail, full of grace" (Lk 1:28).[1] Probably because the doctrine of Original Sin was given less prominence in the East, there was much less belief in the Immaculate Conception there.

Simeon the New Theologian

The most important Eastern theologian of the Middle Ages was St. Simeon the New Theologian, who lived late in the eleventh century. While the adjective *new* was usually a negative term in Eastern theology, Simeon received it as an encomium—he was a true theologian and therefore had to be distinguished from "The Theologian", Gregory Nazianzen. Simeon's approach was mystical, based primarily on the liturgy and the experience of monastic life, the lived faith as distinct from abstract speculation.

Prayers for the Dead

The Western belief in Purgatory was based on the fact that many people died without having completed the penances assigned to them and in the hope that a merciful God would allow them to discharge their obligation after death. But the Eastern church did not necessarily impose such penances in confession and prayed for the dead without explaining precisely why. Thus to the East, the doctrine of Purgatory looked suspiciously like the heresy of Origen—that the damned will eventually be released from Hell.

Adiaphora

Everyone acknowledged that there were *adiaphora*—things that were indifferent in terms of doctrinal orthodoxy but were nonetheless points of difference between East and West—leavened or unleavened bread, the style of tonsures, a drop of water in the wine of the Eucharist. These were not easily resolved, because they were customs so deeply imbedded in the entire way of life on both sides.

The West required unleavened bread on the grounds that it was the bread used by Jesus in the Passover Last Supper, while the East insisted that leavened bread was necessary in order for the Eucharist to be real food. The West's inclusion of a drop of water in the chalice was meant to symbolize a degree of human participation in the act of redemption.

Clerical Marriage

Somewhat paradoxically, although the East was on the whole considered more rigorous and "otherworldly" than the West, as the West moved toward universal clerical celibacy, the Eastern church still allowed clerical marriage, although bishops were drawn exclusively from the ranks of the celibate.

---

[1] The disagreement turned in part on the Greek words of the angel, which could mean "grace" in the supernatural sense but also "favor" as bestowed by a superior, supernatural grace being precisely such favor bestowed by God.

The disagreement over the *filioque* clause—that the Holy Spirit proceeds from both the Father and the Son—was the most substantive. The word had first been inserted into the Creed under Charlemagne, perhaps in order to guard against subordinating the Son to the Father, but Pope Leo III, while affirming the truth of the doctrine, declined to make it universal. No one denied it, and some Easterners affirmed it; but overall the East viewed it as an improper innovation.

Beginning with Justinian's uncle and predecessor Justin I (518–527), the church at Constantinople sent missionaries to the parts of the Near East that remained pagan—Ethiopia and Arabia, the Black Sea region, and southeastern Europe. (In the second century, Armenia actually had a Christian king, Tredatus II, about whom little is known.) Christians existed in the Persian Empire during the fourth century and were persecuted by adherents of the dominant religion, Zoroastrianism. Nestorianism survived there and in Syria, India, and even remote parts of China, which was missionized from Persia.

The conversion of a whole people meant, among other things, that a particular society that had lain outside the boundaries of Christendom had now been incorporated into that spiritual whole, into civilization itself.

The Bulgars of southeastern Europe were converted in 864, the Bohemians of central Europe in 929, the Poles in 966, and the Kievan Russians in 988. As in the West, conversions in eastern and central Europe were often accomplished through a king or prince—St. Wenceslaus of Bohemia (922–929), St. Vladimir of Kiev (972–1015), Boris of the Bulgarians (852–889), St. Stephen of Hungary (997–1038).

Cyril and Methodius

The saintly brothers Constantine (d. 869) and Methodius (d. 885) in a sense founded Eastern European Christianity. They were men of importance in Constantinople and friends of Photius, but Methodius became a monk while his brother remained an imperial official.

Although Rome and Constantinople were not as yet in schism from one another, there was rivalry in Eastern Europe over patriarchal oversight and the liturgy. Because they spoke the Slavic language, the brothers were sent to the kingdom of Greater Moravia, which encompassed much of central Europe and part of Poland and was a cultural battleground between Germanic and Byzantine influences.

The brothers developed a written Slavic language and composed a vernacular liturgy in that language, whose liturgical use came to be called Old Church Slavonic. In 867, the brothers visited Rome, where Pope Hadrian II (867–872) approved their vernacular liturgy. Constantine then entered a monastery, taking the name Cyril. He died soon afterward and was later commemorated in the Slavic alphabet that came to be called Cyrillic.

Methodius returned to Greater Moravia as its bishop, but for a time he was imprisoned by rival German bishops. After Methodius died, Pope Stephen VI (896–897) forbade the Slavonic liturgy, and Germanic influence obliterated much of Methodius' work, which survived only farther to the East. The Magyar invasion of 906–907 destroyed much of Moravian Christianity.

The Kievan Rus

Vladimir of Kiev sent emissaries to the leading centers of Christianity, including Rome, but affiliated his principality with the patriarchate of Constantinople because of his ambassadors' description of the heavenly liturgy as celebrated there. Boris of Bulgaria similarly vacillated between Rome and Constantinople, finally choosing the latter. Russian and Bulgarian churches were then built in the Byzantine style, even as Poland's orientation toward Rome was manifest in its Romanesque and Gothic churches.

The Great Schism

Michael Cerularius (Kerullarios, d. 1059), a patriarch of Constantinople, showed such independence that he clashed even with the emperor. He opposed Western religious practices—the *filioque*, priestly celibacy, unleavened bread in Communion—so aggressively that he closed the Latin churches in his see city.

Partly in response, Pope Leo IX in 1054 sent a delegation to Constantinople under Cardinal Humbert of Silva Candida (Humbert de Moyenmoutier, d. 1061). The delegates received a friendly welcome from Emperor Constantine IX (1042–1055), but Cerularius' intransigence was matched by Humbert, who pronounced an excommunication on the patriarch and placed the decree on the altar of Hagia Sophia. Although this incident has traditionally been treated as marking the final split between Catholicism and Eastern Orthodoxy, it was not seen as such at the time. Among other things, the force of Humbert's decree was doubtful, because Leo IX died during the episode.

Islam

While the Eastern Empire, like the West, still faced barbarian attacks, Islam was now by far its gravest danger. For the next more than two centuries, relations between East and West were dominated by the Crusades, which the East both welcomed, insofar as they reopened the Holy Land and pushed back the Muslims, and resisted, insofar as they involved the intrusion of the Western powers into a steadily shrinking Empire.

Muhammad

Islam ("submission") began in the Arabian peninsula with a wealthy merchant, Muhammad (d. 632), who was probably familiar with pockets of Jews who lived there. Muhammad claimed to be a prophet who had received from the angel Gabriel the revelation that there is only one God—Allah—and that all should completely submit to Allah by following Muhammad. The new faith dated itself from Muhammad's *hijirah* ("flight") in 622, when, in the face of fierce opposition, he left his native city of Mecca for Medina, from which he then mounted a triumphant military return to Mecca.

The new religion did not develop a complex theology, in the way Christianity did. Its sacred text—the Qur'an—is a collection of the sayings of Muhammad, who claimed his statements were revealed by God through the angel Gabriel. The Qur'an was compiled after Muhammad's death and deals primarily with matters of behavior: laws concerning worship, ascetical practices, and personal conduct. | *Qur'an*

No religion in history came to dominate so much territory in so brief a time. In the period from 638 to 643, three of the four Eastern patriarchates—Jerusalem, Antioch, and Alexandria—fell to those whom the Byzantines called "Arabian wolves". Persia was conquered in 652, and all of North Africa by 707. But Muslim conquest was restrained somewhat by a bitter and permanent split that occurred shortly after Muhammad's death, between Shiites, who held that the movement had to be led by a blood relative of the Prophet, and Sunnites, who elected their own caliphs. | *Conquest*

As Islam splintered, its principal capitals became Baghdad in Mesopotamia, Damascus in Syria, and Córdoba in Spain. The crescent became its symbol, and, coincidentally, the Islamic empires roughly came to describe a crescent on the map, stretching from Mesopotamia in the East, across North Africa, and curving northward to the Pyrenees. | *Schism*

Its conquests were principally at the expense of the Byzantine Empire. The Muslims reached Constantinople itself in the years 674 to 678 and again in 717 to 718 and were repulsed only with difficulty. There were occasional imperial victories, as when Monophysite Armenia was freed from Muslim rule in the 920s, and the victors found what was believed to be a burial cloth of Jesus. | *A Rising Threat*

Islam was a religion of radical monotheism, implacably hostile to anything that appeared to compromise that truth. While Christians were in disagreement for centuries over the use of force in spreading their faith, Muhammad had no such doubts, so that the new faith used the sword wherever it encountered resistance. | *Radical Monotheism*

But partial tolerance was allowed for "the people of the Book"—the Bible—because both Old and New Testaments were viewed by Muslims as divinely inspired and some biblical figures, from Abraham to Jesus, were considered great prophets. The error of Christianity, according to Muhammad, was its divinizing of Jesus, a heresy that he claimed | *"People of the Book"* to be empowered to correct. Like some Jews, Muslims regarded Christians as polytheists, because of the doctrine of the Trinity.

Muslim policy varied from time to time and place to place. The restricted theoretical toleration of Christians and Jews was often violated, and Christians subjected to harassment or persecution. But Christians also sometimes served as bureaucrats or soldiers of Muslim rulers—e.g., John Damascene was an official of the caliphate of Damascus.

Converts

In imperial territories conquered by Islam, such as Syria, equal tolerance was extended to both orthodox Christians and Monophysites and other heretics. Few Muslims seem to have converted to Christianity under the Empire, but a good number of Christians made the reverse journey. Because as heretics they did not enjoy the patronage of the Byzantine emperor, many Nestorians and Monophysites in particular became Muslims.

Enslavement

Christians who were captured either in battle or by Muslim-raiding parties that got as far north as England were often enslaved, and the religious order of the Mercedarians ("buyers") was founded especially to ransom them. Bl. Serapion (d. 1240) was a soldier in the Spanish wars who became a member of the order, went to Algiers to free captives, and was crucified for preaching Christianity. (Slavery of non-Christians existed to a limited degree in Europe, but the number of Muslim slaves was infinitesimal in comparison with the number of Christian slaves in Muslim lands.)

The Holy Land

Muslims controlled the Holy Land beginning in the seventh century, and Christians were allowed to visit the Holy Places but not to build shrines, although in 1009 a sultan who was possibly insane had the church of the Holy Sepulchre destroyed. An attempt was made in 1033 to organize a major pilgrimage to the Holy Land, since Christ had not returned a thousand years after His death, but would-be pilgrims soon found that the obstacles to such a project were formidable indeed.

Mutual Understanding

The emperors sometimes sponsored formal disputations between Christian and Muslim or Jewish scholars, primarily with the aim of converting the non-Christians but also having the effect of familiarizing Christians with Muslim and Jewish doctrines. In the West, Peter the Venerable arranged to have the Qur'an translated into Latin, so as to be able to refute it, and Aquinas' *Summa contra Gentiles* was in part aimed at converting Muslims.

The Crusades

The First Crusade

The timing of the First Crusade (1095) was fortuitous, in that the Muslims themselves were divided at the time. The leading Western European monarchs all happened to be excommunicated in 1095, and Urban II appointed a French bishop as the Crusade's official leader, while military leadership devolved on high-ranking members of the nobility. As many as 150,000 Christians answered the call, but the difficulties were enormous, and only about forty thousand finally arrived. Several crusading armies traveled by different routes and met at Constantinople, where they took oaths of fealty to the emperor, whose armies also participated in the war.

"The Franks"

The Byzantines viewed "the Franks" with misgivings or worse, the chronicler Anna Comnena (d. ca. 1148), daughter of the Emperor Alexius I Comnenus (1081–1118), seeing them as repulsive barbarians. The Crusaders often ignored their oaths to the emperor, and over the next two centuries, the emperors were not above negotiating secretly with the Muslims against the Crusaders.

Nobility and Brutality

The contradictions inherent in the crusade phenomenon were manifest from the beginning, as fierce warriors, enlisted in a noble cause, nonetheless sometimes terrorized other Christians before even catching sight of a Muslim and sometimes massacred Muslim towns that fell into their hands. (A Cistercian abbot, Gilbert of Nogent [d. ca. 1112], wrote a history of the First Crusade that was quite candid in its recounting of Crusader misbehavior.) The Muslims were equally brutal and had been so long before the Crusaders arrived.

The Latin Kingdoms

The First Crusade made steady progress. Jerusalem fell in 1099, and a kingdom was set up under French noblemen: first Godfrey of Bouillon (d. 1100), then his brother Baldwin (d. 1118). (Godfrey, but not Baldwin, rejected the title of king, because Jesus alone ruled in the Holy Land.) Muslims were at first treated tolerantly. The Western rulers attempted as far as possible to replicate the institutions they knew at home, particularly the feudal system, building Western-style castles to maintain security. As always with feudalism, there was constant intrigue and rivalry among the ruling houses and the military orders, not infrequently including minor wars.

The Church

There was a great influx of Westerners into the Near East, and a number of Latin churches were established; but Eastern Christians retained their own liturgies. The patriarchates of Jerusalem and Antioch were brought under papal authority and Western bishops appointed— usually by the king of Jerusalem, confirmed by the pope—to replace the Eastern prelates. Pope Paschal II (1099–1118) demanded that the Eastern churches recognize the Roman primacy, but a formal East-West dialogue two decades later failed to resolve the issue.

Knights Templar

In 1118, the Knights Templar were founded at Jerusalem on the site of Solomon's original Temple as a community of lay warriors. They eventually came to observe a monastic rule written for them by Bernard of

Clairvaux, which included life in community, vows, and the Divine Office. (The Templars may have possessed the Shroud of Turin, an ancient cloth that bears the image of a crucified man and is believed by many people to be the burial cloth of Jesus. The Shroud was probably taken from Constantinople in 1204 and was held by the Templars for the next century, first placed on public display in France in 1357.)

Knights of St. John

The Knights of St. John of Jerusalem (Knights Hospitalers) were founded around the same time as the Templars, to care for the sick and wounded. They operated a two thousand–bed hospital in Jerusalem, but they also evolved into a military order, known first as the Knights of Rhodes and later as the Knights of Malta. The Knights of Malta still exist as a fraternal order that cares for the sick, but the group long ago gave up its military character.

Both orders of knights built castles throughout the Christian territories and were the Christians' principal lines of defense. Unpredictably, they also became involved in banking, setting up a system by which money could be deposited with Knights in Europe and drawn out in the Holy Land, a system that facilitated pilgrimage and also made the Knights themselves wealthy.

"Prester John"

In 1122, Western Christians were given another motive for undertaking expeditions to the East, when a mysterious individual appeared in Rome claiming to be a powerful Christian king of a great unknown kingdom in the East. Later in the century, Pope Alexander III received a letter purportedly from the same ruler, and the quest for the illusory Prester ("Priest") John became an occasional minor obsession for the next four centuries.

The Second Crusade

The Christian states in the Near East struggled to survive during the first half of the twelfth century, and in 1145, the Second Crusade was preached by Bernard. Louis VII (1131–1180) of France became the first Western monarch to take the cross, followed by German Emperor Conrad III (1138–1152). The Crusade gained little, and Christians in the Near East remained divided by suspicions and conflicting ambitions. The cities of the Holy Land fell to the Muslims one by one, often accompanied by the slaughter of their inhabitants, and in 1187, the great Muslim ruler Saladin (d. 1193) retook Jerusalem, allowing the Christians limited toleration.

The Third Crusade

The Third Crusade followed, the largest military effort of the entire Middle Ages, financed by a "Saladin tithe" to be collected throughout Christendom. It seemed to fulfill the original papal dream of a united Christendom, although the Byzantine emperor Isaac II Angelus (1185–1195) did not welcome the Crusaders and secretly negotiated with the Muslims.

Frederick Barbarossa, Philip II Augustus of France (1180–1223), and Henry II of England agreed to lead the attack. But Henry died before he could set out and was replaced by his son Richard I the Lion-Hearted (1189–1199). Barbarossa died in the Holy Land in a freak accident, falling from his horse in full armor and drowning in a shallow stream. The two remaining leaders, Philip and Richard, quarreled, and the campaign that began with great expectations unraveled.[2] The Crusade failed to retake Jerusalem but did save other Christian holdings.

Notoriously, the Fourth Crusade (1204) was subverted by intrigues among the Crusaders themselves, mainly the Normans, who were the first warriors to arrive and who placed one of their own on the imperial throne; the Venetians, who provided transportation to the Near East; and the Byzantines. The Crusaders were first diverted to conquer a city in the Balkans that had rebelled against Venetian dominance, then the exiled Byzantine emperor Alexius IV Angelus (1203–1204) asked for their help.

The Fourth Crusade

The Crusaders took Constantinople, which was then perhaps the largest and richest city in the world, and—partly perhaps in retaliation for a massacre of Latin Christians some years before—brutally sacked it, desecrating churches and contemptuously placing a prostitute on the throne of the patriarch in Hagia Sophia.

Pope Innocent III, for whom the retaking of Jerusalem was the highest priority, at first condemned this perversion of the Crusade but then allowed it to stand, thereby creating an enduring grievance of the Eastern church against the West. A Latin bishop was named patriarch, whereupon most Eastern bishops left their sees and went into exile. The Crusaders deposed two Greek claimants for the imperial throne and installed a Western dynasty that lasted until 1261.

Until well into the fourteenth century, Venice kept control of the islands of Crete and Cyprus in the Eastern Mediterranean, where they allowed the Eastern Christians to retain their own observances. In some cases, Easterners and Westerners shared the same churches, each celebrating their own liturgy.

Shared Churches

The Fifth Crusade was proclaimed by Innocent III in 1213, but it did not begin for four years and like its predecessors had little effect. The Crusaders had concluded that it was strategically necessary to conquer Egypt in order to reconquer the Holy Land, but they failed in that goal. The most notable aspect of the Fifth Crusade was the presence

The Fifth Crusade

---

[2] While returning home, Richard was taken prisoner in Austria by a prince he had offended and was held for ransom, an incident that helped give rise to the Robin Hood legends, in which Richard's brother John is responsible for Richard's captivity.

of Francis of Assisi, who met with Sultan al-Kāmil (1218–1238) and boldly attempted to convert him to Christianity. (The sultan seemed impressed by the humble friar but showed no interest in converting.)

Frederick II

Emperor Frederick II was among those taking the cross, but he was excommunicated after several delays in setting out for the Holy Land. He then married the daughter of King John I of Jerusalem (1210–1237) and on that basis claimed the kingdom for himself. In 1229, he obtained Jerusalem through negotiations with a weakened al-Kāmil, but most Christians regarded this as a betrayal, because they held the city only at the sultan's pleasure, and Frederick promised that there was to be no crusade for at least ten years. Frederick soon returned to Germany, and in 1244, Jerusalem fell to the Muslims for the final time.

The Sixth Crusade

Louis IX mounted the Sixth Crusade in 1248, again pursuing the Egyptian strategy. He had some success, but at one point he was captured and had to be ransomed. In 1270, he invaded Tunis in North Africa, as a gateway to Egypt, but soon died of fever.

Later Efforts

Periodically thereafter, various Christian princes arrived in the Holy Land, with no lasting result. The last Christian outposts—Acre, Beirut, Haifa, and the biblical cities of Tyre and Sidon—fell in 1291, their survivors ruthlessly persecuted. There were occasional forays by European princes after that, and the Seventh Crusade (1365) attacked Egypt and sacked Alexandria before retreating.

Although the idea remained alive for another two centuries, in practice the crusade tradition came to an end when Pope Pius II (1458–1464) rallied support that melted away when he died suddenly.

Limited Pilgrimages

Franciscans made some converts from Islam during the ascendancy of the Latin Kingdoms in the Near East, and after the fall of those Christian outposts, they enjoyed a precarious tolerance in the Holy Land. They were permitted to care for the Christian shrines and to receive occasional pilgrims, a task they still perform. (Franciscan missionaries sent to North Africa were killed.)

Efforts at Reunion

Mughals

The Mughals (Mongols) were yet another wave of barbarians to invade Europe. They established an empire that stretched from China into eastern Europe. A Mughal army got as far west as the Adriatic Sea in 1265 but turned back voluntarily. It appeared for a time that Mughals and Christians in the Near East might ally against Islam.

Catholic Conversions

Because of Norman incursions in Byzantine Sicily, Emperor Michael VIII Palaeologus (1259–1282) sought Western allies, and in 1274, an Eastern delegation attended the Second Council of Lyons, when both

Emperor Palaeologus and Patriarch John Veccos (d. 1282) submitted to papal authority. But Pope Martin IV (1281–1285) antagonized Michael by supporting the claims of a French candidate to the imperial throne, and after Michael's death, Veccos was deposed and sent to a monastery.

In the face of the increasing threat of the Ottoman Empire (modern Turkey), Emperor John V Palaeologus (1341–1376, also 1379–1391) came to Rome in 1369 and actually became Catholic.

Relations between East and West became intertwined with the conciliar movement in the West (see Chapter Eight below, p. 216). A Greek delegation, desperate to solicit Western help against the Turks, attended the conciliarist Council of Basle in 1431. But when Pope Eugene IV (1431–1447) summoned his own council at Ferrara in 1439, a delegation of seven hundred, including Emperor John VIII Palaeologus (1425–1448), attended. Eugene announced a crusade, but with little effect.

At neither Ferrara nor Florence was there was much opportunity for a sophisticated exchange between East and West over the perennial issues that separated them. Florence eventually proclaimed that only those in communion with the Roman Church could be saved. On paper, it was a great success, as a number of Eastern prelates, perhaps hopeful of another crusade, subscribed to its decrees, but in practice it achieved little.

Councils of Florence and Ferrara

While the urgent hope for a crusade to turn back the Turks was the principal driving force behind Byzantine ecumenism, there was some genuine desire for reunion, and in 1452, reunion was actually proclaimed in Hagia Sophia. Despite bitter criticism of his actions, Emperor John VIII remained a Catholic, as did his son and successor Constantine XI (1449–1453), the last Byzantine emperor. The final rupture between Catholicism and Orthodoxy occurred in 1472, when the Orthodox formally repudiated the formulae agreed to by John VIII. Cyril Kontaris, patriarch of Constantinople (d. 1640), entered into communion with Rome but was deposed and murdered by the Turks.

Reunion Proclaimed

The final fall of the Empire to the Turks in 1453 brought an end to most Latin influence in the Near East, to the point where one Eastern bishop was reported to have said, with reference to the respective headdresses of Muslims and Catholic bishops, "Better a turban than a miter." But the fall of Constantinople by no means brought an end to the Christian-Islamic conflict. St. John of Capistrano (d. 1456), a Franciscan who had been the general of the order and a papal diplomat, personally led a successful crusade against the Turks in Serbia.

The Fall of Constantinople

At least for the popes of the sixteenth century, the crusading ideal was still not dead. Leo X (1513–1521) pressed hard to get the European monarchs to respond to the alarming expansion of the power of the

The Ottoman Threat

Ottomans, but over the next century, as successive popes tried vainly to mount new crusades, the Ottomans advanced further into eastern Europe. They were opposed by an occasional Balkan prince and by the Catholic Holy Roman Emperor Charles V (1519–1555). But for a time the Ottomans were in alliance with the Catholic king Francis I of France (1515–1547), an alliance dictated by the intense rivalry between France and the Holy Roman Empire.

Lepanto

During the 1520s, the Ottomans subdued Serbia, the isle of Rhodes, and Hungary. They advanced to the gates of Vienna and subsequently terrorized the coasts of Italy and Spain, enslaving innumerable Christians whom they took captive. But the Knights of Malta, on their tiny Mediterranean island, withstood the Turkish advance, and in 1571, the Spanish commander Don John of Austria (d. 1578), illegitimate son of Charles V and half-brother of Philip II of Spain (1555–1598), won a great naval victory over the Turks at Lepanto, off the coast of Greece, thereby liberating fifteen thousand Christian galley slaves and freeing the Western Mediterranean from the Muslim threat. Pope St. Pius V urged Catholics everywhere to pray the rosary for the cause of victory, and the Turkish ships were devastated by high winds. (Afterwards, Pius V established the feast of Our Lady of the Rosary on October 6, the date of the battle.)

The Battle of Vienna

In the later seventeenth century, the Catholic Louis XIV of France (1643–1715) encouraged the Turks to attack his arch-rival, Catholic Austria. But although they reached the gates of Vienna in 1683, they were turned back by an army under John III Sobieski, king of Poland (1674–1696). From that date, the Ottoman Empire began a long decline. Hungary gained its freedom a few years later.

The Uniates

After the Catholic-Orthodox split of the Middle Ages, the Holy See showed an increasing willingness to make accommodations with those Eastern Christians (sometimes called Uniates) who were in communion with Rome. The history is a complex one, but overall the official policy followed by the Holy See was enunciated by Pope Benedict XIV (1740–1758), who declared unequivocally that the Easterners had a right to retain their own customs. Pope Leo XIII (1878–1903) was particularly solicitous of the welfare of the Eastern churches.

Over the centuries, several Eastern-Rite seminaries were established in Rome. The Congregation for the Oriental Church was set up in 1917, and the Eastern churches have their own Code of Canon Law. Jesuits, who operate the Pontifical Oriental Institute in Rome, have a particular interest in the Eastern churches.

Liturgy

The liturgy—in both the Rites themselves and the languages in which they are celebrated—primarily defines these various churches. Although in modern times there have been many accommodations to Western practice, in general most Eastern Rites follow ancient Eastern customs: married priests, but not bishops; leavened bread in the Eucharist (which is not ordinarily referred to by the Latin word *Mass*); Communion in both kinds; an *ikonostasis* separating the sanctuary from the body of the church; baptism by immersion, immediately followed by chrismation; the Blessed Sacrament reserved mainly for the sick, not for veneration; standing during most of the Eucharist; and icons rather than statues as objects of devotion.

Monasticism is integral to the Eastern churches, their monks often called Basilians (distinct from the Latin-Rite order of the same name) because they follow the monastic rule of St. Basil the Great. Following the oldest pattern of monastic life, only a few monks in each monastery are ordained to the priesthood, since the monastic vocation is considered distinct.

Monasticism

The Uniates follow the Eastern custom of allowing priests to marry prior to ordination but choosing only celibates—often monks—as bishops. (At the behest of the Latin-Rite bishops, Eastern-Rite clergy in the United States are not allowed to be married, although the rule has not always been enforced.)

Celibacy

Each of the Eastern churches is headed by a prelate, some of whom bear the ancient title of "patriarch", who appoints bishops who in turn elect the patriarch, both subject to the confirmation of the Holy See. Since the nineteenth century, some patriarchs have been made cardinals, but others have declined the honor because they regard the cardinalate as an office of the Latin Rite. (Until 2000, one of the official papal titles was "patriarch of the West".)

Patriarchs

The history of most of the Eastern Rites is extremely complex, mainly because of changing political and ethnic conditions that strongly influence religious loyalties. The Easterners have often been victims of persecution, and immigration has dispersed them far beyond their original homelands. Virtually all have a presence in the United States and Canada.

Eastern Rites

The Byzantine Rite, which is the largest, uses Old Church Slavonic, the language originally introduced into the liturgy by Cyril and Methodius. The oldest continuous Byzantine-Rite communities are in Italy, where some of the monasteries of the South continued to use the Greek language after Rome adopted Latin and remained in communion with Rome after the schism of 1054, their number strengthened by refugees from Constantinople after 1453.

For a period in early modern times, these Byzantines were under Latin-Rite bishops, but their hierarchy was eventually restored, and it

Byzantine

was their integrity that Benedict XIV sought to protect. Italian Byzantine communities still survive in small numbers, an unbroken chain from the earliest centuries, and there are a relatively small number of Greek Catholics scattered around the Eastern Mediterranean, as well as Byzantine Catholic outposts in Albania, Estonia, Latvia, and Finland.

Ruthenian

The Ruthenians, who are closely related to the Russians ethnically, are a branch of the Byzantine Rite found mainly in the Ukraine, Poland, Slovakia, Serbia, and Hungary. Many call themselves Ukrainians, the name *Ruthenian* being primarily an ecclesiastical title.

In a sense, the Ruthenian Rite began when the metropolitan (archbishop) Isidore of Kiev (d. 1463) aroused the wrath of the czar by accepting the decrees of the Council of Florence and was forced to flee to Rome, where he was made a cardinal. As a result of his actions, there were some Russian converts. The Ruthenians under Polish rule continued in communion with Rome for a while, after which many fell away, but a formal reunion occurred in 1595, as a result of intense proselytization by Jesuits, who had a special mission to convert the Orthodox.

Andrew Bobola

Bitter strife between Orthodox and Uniates continued for another century after the reunion of 1595. St. Andrew Bobola (d. 1657) was a Polish Jesuit of noble birth who worked in Lithuania to convert the Orthodox. He was flayed alive by Cossack warriors, but there were some Russian converts after Catholic Poland came under Russian rule. In the eighteenth century, many of the leading Polish Ruthenians joined the Latin Rite, primarily for nationalistic reasons, as Poland was partitioned among Catholic Austria, Protestant Prussia, and Orthodox Russia.

The Russian government severely harassed the Ruthenians, culminating in their forced reunion with Orthodoxy. Some resisted in secret, and a number eventually returned to Rome when Russia officially granted religious freedom in 1905. The Ruthenian Rite was tolerated by the Austrians, but Russia conquered some of this Austrian territory during World War I and once again tried to return the Ruthenians to Orthodoxy.

Andreas Szeptycki

When Poland once again achieved independence after the war, there were sometimes violent clashes between Latin-Rite Catholics and Ruthenians, and the heroic St. Andreas Szeptycki, metropolitan of Lvov, was put under house arrest by the Polish government. But over the next generation, due mainly to his leadership, the Ruthenian church recovered. Later he was deported to Russia, where he died in 1944, at a time when he and his flock were being persecuted by both the Germans and the Soviets.

Josyf Slipyj

Szeptycki's successor, Josyf Slipyj (d. 1984), was also imprisoned by the Soviets for many years, and after World War II, the Soviet government again decreed the reunion of the Ruthenians with Orthodoxy, although few Ruthenians submitted. After the fall of the Soviet Union in the late 1980s, Catholic life began to revive, much of it stimulated by foreign clergy.

In predominantly Orthodox Transylvania (part of today's Rumania), a Byzantine Rite was recognized by the Holy See in 1697, after Jesuits had reconciled some of the Orthodox to the Catholic Church. A Bulgarian Uniate church was recognized in 1861, but its first bishop was, for political reasons, kidnapped and imprisoned by the Russians, and most of the laity returned to Orthodoxy.

The Near East

Anomalously, until 1922, the French government, no matter how anticlerical, was the official protector of Near Eastern Catholics and occasionally intervened militarily for that purpose, a responsibility undertaken because it helped protect French political interests in the region.

Melkites

The Melkites of Egypt and Syria derive their name from the Syrian word for "king", since after the Council of Chalcedon they remained loyal to the emperor, in contrast to the Monophysites. The Melkites came to be completely under the authority of Constantinople, in time adopted the Byzantine liturgy, and were part of the schism of 1054. But some became Catholics during the Crusades, and the reigning patriarchs of Antioch accepted the decrees of union promulgated by the Second Council of Lyons and the Council of Florence. The later history of the Melkite Rite was closely bound up with the rise and decline of Islam, and in the early seventeenth century a mission of Jesuits and Capuchins brought about a reconciliation with Rome. Melkites are numerous in Syria and Palestine but have suffered greatly during the various Near Eastern wars of recent times. They are under the patriarch of Antioch, who lives at Beirut (Lebanon), and use the ancient Antiochian liturgy in Syriac and Arabic.

Maronites

The Maronites derive their name from a Syrian monastery that strongly opposed the Monophysites after Chalcedon. However, in the seventh century, under imperial pressure, the Maronites accepted Monophysite doctrines. Under Muslim persecution, they later fled to Lebanon, where there was considerable strife with the Melkites. The Maronites were reconciled with Rome as a result of the Third Crusade. The reunion endured, although the later history of the Maronites was a complex and troubled one, including brutal persecution at the hands of both the Turks and other Lebanese. (Six thousand Maronites were slaughtered by Lebanese Muslims in 1860, until French intervention brought the persecution to an end.) Like the Melkites, the Maronites are headed by a prelate called the patriarch of Antioch. Their liturgy is in Syriac and Arabic, with a number of Western modifications that were added over the centuries.

Armenia

The church in Armenia also embraced Monophysitism in the early centuries, although there was a fragile reunion with Rome during the Crusades and a nominal acceptance of the decrees of Florence. Later missionary activity, especially by the Dominicans, had some success. Catholics as well as Orthodox were victims of the anti-Armenian genocide perpetrated by the Turks during World War I, and afterward, the persecution continued as parts of Armenia fell under the control of the Soviet Union. The Armenian patriarch also resides at Beirut. The church uses a modified version of the liturgy of St. Basil in the Armenian language.

Chaldeans

The church in Persia and Mesopotamia (modern Iran and Iraq) supported Nestorianism after its condemnation at Ephesus, and for the next thousand years, the Nestorian church was the greatest missionary force in the world, establishing Christian outposts as far away as China, until this great spiritual empire was essentially destroyed by the Mughals in the fourteenth century. In the sixteenth century, a split in the Nestorian church led some to be reconciled with Rome, and their later history is a tangled story of schisms, reconciliations, and yet further schisms.

The Iran-Iraq Catholics are called Chaldeans, after the ancient homeland of the patriarch Abraham, and use the Syriac language. Their patriarch resides at Baghdad. The existence of the Chaldean church was always precarious, because of the Muslims, and it too suffered greatly under the Turks during World War I. Following the American invasion of 2003, the majority of the 1.4 million Christian Iraqis were reported to have fled in the face of bitter civil war and a revived militant Islam.

Copts

The majority of Egyptian Christians also refused to accept the decrees of Chalcedon and became the separate Coptic ("Egyptian") church that retained Monophysite beliefs. Coptic legates accepted the decrees of Florence, but they had no effect. A small number of converts were made during the nineteenth century. The Coptic liturgy derives from the ancient liturgy of Alexandria, which was an adaptation of the Byzantine. It is celebrated either in Coptic or Arabic.

Ethiopia

Ethiopia, despite occasional missionary efforts over the centuries, remained firmly Monophysite. Formal reconciliation with Rome, for complex political reasons, was announced early in the seventeenth century, but attempts to impose the Latin Rite led to a reaction in which priests were martyred and all Catholics were expelled from the country. Later attempts at conversions led to still more martyrdoms, although some small progress was achieved. The few Ethiopian Catholics also follow the Coptic liturgy.

St. Thomas Christians

During the Middle Ages, the Holy See periodically sent legates to Christians in India, who traced their spiritual ancestry to St. Thomas the Apostle and who recognized the authority of a pope about whom they knew very little. At some point in the early Middle Ages, they seem also to have been evangelized by Nestorian missionaries from Babylon and, without necessarily becoming Nestorians, adopted the Chaldean liturgy.

When the Portuguese began arriving in India around 1500, the St. Thomas Christians recognized them as fellow Catholics. Temporarily without a bishop, apparently because of Muslim persecution, the Indian Christians were placed by the Holy See under the Chaldean patriarch of Baghdad. But the Portuguese in India were suspicious of the St. Thomas Christians, whom they considered Nestorians, and after the Portuguese clergy attempted to force a latinized liturgy on the native church, many of the St. Thomas Christians went into schism in 1653. Many subsequently returned to communion with Rome, but they were governed mainly by European bishops until the twentieth century, when the Syro-Malabar hierarchy was restored. In 1930, the remaining Indian schismatics reconciled with Rome as the Syro-Malankara Rite, which uses the ancient Antiochian liturgy.

Syro-Malabar Rite

The Syro-Malabar Rite is the largest Eastern church after the Ukrainians, and three of the ten largest orders of women in the Church—the Franciscan Clarist Congregation, the Congregation of the Mother of God of Carmel, and the Sisters of the Adoration of the Blessed Sacrament—are part of that Rite. It uses the Chaldean liturgy, including the Syriac language.

8 Decline and Rebirth

A Troubled Time

Like the year 1000, the year 1300 conveniently marked a new era in the history of the Church, albeit in an entirely different way, as one of the Church's most troubled periods.

A Fateful Conclave

In 1294, after a deadlocked, two-year conclave, the cardinals received a letter of rebuke from a saintly hermit, Peter di Morone, and in a sudden burst of emotion proceeded to elect its eighty-year-old author as pope. St. Celestine V (1294) was a seemingly inspired solution, but he had lived in his cell for forty years and proved incapable of governing the Church amidst serpentine intrigues and abdicated after a few months, the last pope to do so.[1]

Boniface VIII

He was succeeded by Boniface VIII, one of the key intriguers of the conclave, who sent Celestine to prison, where he soon died. (Dante placed both popes in Hell, although not by name, Celestine because he was guilty of "the great refusal" that brought Boniface to the papal throne.)

Unam Sanctam
Boniface had perhaps the most exalted concept of the papal office of any pope, but changing circumstances made that concept untenable. In 1302, he issued *Unam Sanctam* (One, Holy), asserting that the pope had supreme authority in both religious and secular affairs and that "it is necessary that every human creature be subject to the Roman pontiff", which was not a novel assertion. In the earlier Middle Ages, the popes had been the first bishops to wear miters. Now Boniface began wearing a double crown, representing his authority over both the spiritual and the temporal realms. A few years later, he added a third crown, the three together symbolizing his rule in Heaven, on earth, and in Purgatory.

Quarrels with Princes
Boniface VIII forbade secular rulers to tax the clergy and quarreled with Philip IV the Fair of France (1285–1314) and Edward I of England

---

[1] The incident is a caution against the attractive assumption that holiness alone is sufficient for a good shepherd.

over the issue. He first supported, then abandoned, the kingdom of Scotland, which Edward was attempting to subdue, and he first rejected, then accepted, Emperor Albert I (1298–1308). He proclaimed a crusade against the family of Colonna, one of whom had been his chief rival for the papal office.

Philip the Fair

Philip IV was a devout man, very conscious of being the grandson of St. Louis, but he was committed to strengthening royal power by any means necessary. Pretending that Celestine was still alive and still pope, he called for a council to depose Boniface and arrested the papal legate. Boniface issued a bull, *Clericis Laicos* (Clergy and Laity), in which he made the sweeping claim that the laity had always been enemies of the clergy, and he excommunicated not only Philip but his yet-unborn descendants, to the fourth generation.

Philip sent troops to arrest Boniface, who cried, "I will to suffer martyrdom", when they burst in on him at his palace at Anagni. The elderly pope was struck in the face and briefly kept prisoner until set free by the townspeople, but he died a month later.

The incident at Anagni was able to occur simply because Philip did not fear the Pope. The effects of excommunication had diminished greatly over time, perhaps mostly because of its use on behalf of the narrow political interests of the papacy. A century previously, the death of Boniface might have forced Philip to do penance. But while the murder of Thomas Becket at the hands of Henry II's knights provoked a backlash and made Becket a saint, the mistreatment of Boniface had almost the opposite effect.

National States

Significantly, it was the king of France, not the emperor, who defeated the pope, since the emergence of the national state was the key political development of the late Middle Ages. Philip's defeat of the papacy also marked the defeat of the larger ideal of a universal spiritual society. For three centuries, the movement of Christendom had been toward unity; now it began to reverse itself.

Denying the Authority of the Church

Philip the Fair had a group of "laicists" as his advisors, lawyers who claimed that worldly kingdoms were exempt from the authority of the Church and might therefore legitimately take the Church's property.

Marsilius of Padua (d. 1343), a kind of Averroist, wrote *Defender of Peace*, in which he denied virtually all papal authority and proposed what amounted almost to a theory of ecclesiastical democracy. He based his theory on the Aristotelian idea of the state as a natural organism with no power above it, so that of necessity the Church had to be subject to the state, her authority limited to teaching only, with transgressions of divine law to be punished only in the next life. For Marsilius and some others, the Church was only an invisible community of believers, not an incarnate body. He denied priestly hierarchy.

The Move to Avignon

Boniface VIII's successor, Bl. Benedict XI (1303–1304), denounced Philip's actions but did nothing to punish him. In 1305, to placate Philip, the cardinals elected a friend of the king, the Frenchman Clement V (1305–1314), who never set foot in Rome and made his headquarters at Avignon, a city that was culturally French but technically belonged to the king of Naples and which the Pope now purchased.

The Suppression of the Templars

Clement absolved Philip of all guilt, denounced Boniface, and annulled his bulls, although he resisted Philip's demand that Boniface be tried posthumously for heresy. Clement also reluctantly acquiesced in Philip's move against the Knights Templar. Philip had borrowed heavily from these banker-knights and sought to get possession of their great wealth. He accused them of blasphemy, heresy, sorcery, and sodomy, and a number were burned at the stake, including Grand Master Jacques de Molay.[2] Clement officially suppressed the order but assigned their treasure to other religious groups rather than to the king.

Papal Administration

The popes remained at Avignon for most of the rest of the century. Most of them were not scandalous in their personal lives, and some (Benedict XII [1334–1342] and Innocent VI [1352–1362]) were even reform-minded. Most—notably Clement VI (1342–1352)—were able administrators who centralized the administration of the Church and were particularly adept at finances, instituting the regular collection of papal fees from the various nations.

Papal Provisions

Because of the endemic factional strife in cathedral chapters, the Avignon popes succeeded in getting the authority to appoint all bishops and even to fill many lower church offices, although in practice they often merely ratified the nominations of princes. What came to be a serious abuse were papal "provisions"—promising a benefice to a man at the first vacancy, a favor that was often obtained by large payments to the Holy See and which sometimes resulted in several people in line for the same benefice. Like secular monarchs, the popes sold administrative offices to ambitious men, a practice that led to a swollen papal bureaucracy of sinecures who hoped to recoup their investments from fees.

Pluralism

Pluralism—holding more than one benefice at a time—and the necessary absenteeism that accompanied it, were also increasingly tolerated for payment of a fee. (One prelate—the future Julius II [1503–1513]—held seven bishoprics as well as other offices.) Nepotism (from the word for "nephew")—the favoring of relatives for benefices—was rife. Notably,

---

[2] Present-day legends of the Templars, as in the book and film *The Da Vinci Code*, are completely fanciful. The Masonic Order, claiming direct descent from the Templars, calls its youth branch the Order of DeMolay.

the Spaniard Calixtus III (1455–1458), although in general a conscientious pope, promoted his Borgia nephews, to the detriment of the Church.

Rome Abandoned

One of the Avignon popes' greatest expenses was for armies of mercenaries who fought to preserve the Papal States in Italy during the popes' absence. Their absence impoverished Rome and reduced it to near-chaos, so that at one point an official named Cola di Rienzo (d. 1354) seized control of the city and proclaimed the restoration of the ancient republic, until he was eventually defeated and murdered by a mob.

The prestige of the papacy now fell to its lowest point in over three hundred years, since, even if the Avignon popes were not dominated by the kings of France, they often appeared to be. By their abandonment of Rome, they seemed to have abandoned the claim to rule the universal Church and to have become merely competitors in international politics, unable to offer spiritual leadership but seeking only temporal security.

Pope and Emperor

Pope John XXII (1316–1334), one of the leading architects of papal administration, engaged in a prolonged struggle with Emperor Louis III (Louis of Bavaria) and several nations, notably England, passed laws restricting papal authority within their borders.

John XXII inadvertently raised the issue of papal infallibility when he preached "soul sleep"—the belief that at death the soul falls into a slumber from which it awakens only at the Last Judgment, a theory that seemed to deny the reality of Purgatory. Following protests, he recanted this view.[3]

Return to Rome

St. Bridget of Sweden (d. 1373) persuaded the reform-minded Urban V (1362–1370) to return to Rome, but he found conditions intolerable and did not remain. Pope Gregory XI (1370–1378), partly because of rebellion in the Papal States, returned to Rome in 1377 at the request of St. Catherine of Siena (d. 1380), a Dominican tertiary who exhorted him to do his duty.

After Gregory's death, the cardinals met in one of the most momentous conclaves in the history of the Church. In the face of frenzied popular demands that the papacy remain in Rome, the cardinals elected Urban VI (1378–1389), an Italian who had been at the court of Avignon.

The Great Western Schism

Although Catherine counseled moderation, Urban strongly denounced misconduct on the part of some of the cardinals, perhaps to justify his plan to appoint mainly Italians to the Sacred College. He even had some cardinals tortured. The majority of the older cardinals were French,

---

[3] This remains the clearest case in the history of the Church of a possibly heretical pope. However, John expounded his error only in a sermon, not in a formal dogmatic statement.

and they declared that Urban's election had been coerced. They elected another pope, a Swiss, who was named Clement VII, thereby beginning the Great Western Schism that would last for forty years.

Clement returned to Avignon, and the rival popes spent most of their efforts bidding for princely recognition. France naturally supported Avignon, and the Empire recognized Rome. In some dioceses, there were actually two bishops, each loyal to a different pope.

A Third Pope

Attempts to negotiate a settlement failed, and in 1408, the supporters of the Avignon pope, including the king of France, abandoned him. The Avignon cardinals then met at the Italian city of Pisa, declared both popes deposed, and elected yet another—John XXII.[4] The result, however, was that there were now three papal claimants instead of two.

Conciliarism

The conciliar movement had its origins earlier in the Middle Ages, among canonists and theologians who argued that ultimate authority in the Church lay with the general council, of which the pope was merely the agent. An evil pope, therefore, could be deposed by the cardinals who had elected him, and papal decrees could be appealed to a council. The theory gained a great deal of support during the Great Western Schism, when no pope was able to govern the Church, and it retained vitality for over a century.

The issue had practical implications—some conciliarists wanted to curtail papal revenues and the right of the pope to appoint bishops—and it had implications for later democratic theory, in presuming that authority resided in the entire community and must be accepted by that community in order to be binding.

Pierre d'Ailly (d. 1420)—chancellor of the Sorbonne, a cardinal, and one of the most influential figures of the age—was a leading conciliarist, as was his pupil, the canonist Jean Gerson (d. 1429), who was also chancellor of the Sorbonne. Gerson proposed a theory by which the pope functioned as a kind of constitutional monarch under the authority of the general council but was able to function on his own authority if necessary. The German bishop Nicholas of Cusa (d. 1464), one of the most original thinkers of the entire Middle Ages, also espoused a moderate conciliar position, although he became disillusioned by the movement and entered the papal service, ending his life as a cardinal in Rome.

Council of Constance

In 1413, Emperor Sigismund (1410–1437) forced the Pisan pope, John XXII, to summon a council to resolve the crisis. John soon resigned; the Roman pope, Gregory XII (1406–1415), approved the council and

---

[4] That the Avignon and Pisan popes after 1378 were considered invalid by the Church is indicated by the fact that some of their names and numbers were later used by other popes, notably by John XXIII (1958–1963).

abdicated; and the Avignon pope was deposed.[5] The Council of Constance, meeting in Switzerland, which was part of the Empire, elected Pope Martin V (1417–1431), who within a few years was able to reenter Rome and regain control of the Papal States.

At his election, Martin was required to agree that a general council was to be summoned at least every five years and, if the pope failed to do so, could meet on its own authority. After his election, Martin repudiated those decrees as illegitimate interference with papal authority, but he reluctantly summoned a council to meet at Basle (Switzerland). Pope Eugene IV (1431–1447) was also required to agree to conciliar demands at his election, but he dissolved the Council of Basle before it could meet.

Conciliarism Repudiated

A few years later Charles VII of France (1422–1461) issued the Pragmatic Sanction of Bourges, the classic statement of what came to be called Gallicanism—the quasi-independence of the French church from the papacy. The general council was declared superior to the pope, and the king claimed the authority to nominate bishops.

Gallicanism

As always, the politics of Italy was exceptionally complex and unruly, with popes and emperors vying for control and quasi-independent city-states (Milan, Venice, Florence) struggling against popes, emperors, and each other. Guelf and Ghibelline factions existed in most of the major cities, and papal armies strove to drive out the former and establish the latter, as well as to increase the boundaries of the Papal States.

Italian Politics

Amidst these intrigues, Pope Eugene was driven out of Rome and took refuge in Florence. Unauthorized, a council met at Basle, summoned Eugene to answer charges of misuse of office, declared him deposed for heresy when he failed to appear, and elected an anti-pope, the last in the long history of that phenomenon. Eugene himself then summoned a council that met at both Florence and at Ferrara, where he scored a triumph in seeming to obtain the submission to Rome of the representatives of Eastern Orthodoxy (see Chapter Seven above, p. 205). The Council of Florence-Ferrara also declared that papal authority was directly from God.

Basle and Florence

The Basle anti-pope had little support, and the conciliar movement began a slow decline, remaining alive mainly on paper. (One of the original adherents of the Basle anti-pope, Cardinal Aeneas Sylvius Piccolomini, himself later became pope as Pius II [1458–1464] and condemned Conciliarism.) Conciliarism was an impractical theory, since

Decline of Conciliarism

---

[5] Since Gregory XII appears on the official list of popes, his approval was necessary to make Constance a valid council.

it was difficult for anyone other than the pope to summon a council. It was not even certain who had voting rights—doctors of theology and canon law did so at Constance—and bishops were reluctant to travel to meetings that might last several years.

"The Bad Popes"

Sixtus IV

Pope Sixtus IV (1471–1484), a Franciscan who was notoriously immoral in his private life, set out to make the papacy a feared military force, placed his nephews in important principalities, and arranged their marriages with an eye to effecting strategic alliances. He supported a plot to assassinate the Medicis, the ruling Florentine family, who were to be killed at Mass by two priests. (An archbishop was hanged for his role in the affair.)

Alexander VI

Pope Alexander VI (1492–1503) was a Spanish cardinal, a member of the Borgia family, and a papal diplomat and curial official. After defeating Sixtus' nephew in a fierce election, he became one of the most notorious of all the popes, the worst since the tenth century. Alexander pursued Sixtus' goal of a militarily powerful papacy, but he also used his office to favor his children (eight altogether), marrying his daughter Lucrezia (d. 1519) to important princes (her multiple marriages gave her an unjustified reputation as a poisoner) and promoting the career of his son Cesare.

In 1494, Charles VIII of France conquered much of northern Italy and drove Alexander out of Rome, precipitating a decades-long series of wars in which the papacy was deeply entangled. Alexander subsequently made peace with Louis XII of France (1498–1515), granting him an annulment of his marriage on grounds of nonconsummation, in return for Louis' effecting the marriage of Cesare to a French duchess. With French support, Cesare then embarked on a campaign to conquer all of northern Italy, an effort that failed only at his father's death. In an ironic way, Alexander testified to the continuing power of faith in a worldly time, in that he was apparently not a cynic but a believer whose conscience was troubled by his sins.

Julius II

After a very brief interim papacy, Sixtus IV's nephew was elected as Julius II. He had no sons of his own and did not favor his family, but he exiled Cesare Borgia to Spain and plunged into Italian politics, regaining lost territories and sometimes himself donning armor and joining the papal armies in the field.

Disorder and Discontent

Demands for religious reform echoed continuously through the later Middle Ages, but there were only limited efforts to implement it. Anticlericalism was common: lay people often denigrated the clergy for greed, lust, laziness, dishonesty, and other real or imagined sins. Usually people did not lose their faith in the sacramental power of the priest, but sometimes this dissatisfaction led to doubts about Catholic doctrines.

The English poet William Langland (d. ca. 1400), in *The Vision of William concerning Piers* [Peter] *the Ploughman*, lamented the decline of Christendom and the defeat of true Christianity by the spirit of hardened selfishness. Like Dante, he was a deeply devout Catholic who was dissatisfied with the ways of the Church. A believer in the papacy, he deplored the failure of papal leadership and mourned the breakdown of the universal order of Christendom.

Langland

The higher clergy remained princes as well as prelates, living lives of luxury and often devoting themselves as much to secular politics as to religion. At the other extreme, the priest John Ball was a leader of the great English Peasants' Revolt of 1381, in which the archbishop of Canterbury, Simon Sudbury, was murdered while at prayer. (Ball was hanged.)

The English Peasants' Revolt

There was a prevalent impression that religious life had become quite corrupt, with monks and nuns violating their vows, living in quasi-luxury, taking lovers, or remaining away from their monasteries for long periods. The Camaldolese hermits were one of the strictest orders, but one Italian abbot attempted to murder his mistress' husband. An English Carmelite bishop, Thomas de Lisle (d. 1361), eventually had to flee the kingdom, after presiding for years over an organized gang of thieves and murderers. St. Catherine of Genoa (d. 1510), although herself a Franciscan tertiary, sharply rebuked a friar who claimed that his religious habit showed the superiority of his way of life, and Gerson advised his pious blood sisters to remain in the lay state.

Clerical Corruption

In his *Canterbury Tales*, Geoffrey Chaucer (d. 1400) satirized abuses through some of his characters, especially the Pardoner and the Summoner, two minor ecclesiastical officials who boasted that they could remit any offense for a suitable fee. Against them, Chaucer posed the character of the Parson, or parish priest, whose "tale" was a straightforward sermon on the seven deadly sins, fervently setting forth the Gospel teaching about true repentance.

Chaucer

The Black Death of 1347–1349 was the greatest natural disaster in Western history, a pandemic that first showed itself in a Mediterranean port and spread rapidly northward. It was probably a combination of bubonic plague spread by fleas dwelling on rats and pneumonic plague spread by direct human contact. The pattern was irregular and unpredictable. During the initial outbreak, some cities escaped almost entirely, while elsewhere whole towns were wiped out. The overall mortality rate was

The Black Death

probably about a third of the entire European population within a two-year period, but the disease then subsided, only to reappear as an occasional local phenomenon for the next four centuries. The Black Death increased the use of morbid images on funeral monuments, such as the Dance of Death—a skeleton with a scythe "harvesting" souls by pulling them along in a frenzied line.

Clergy and religious were particularly vulnerable to the plague, both because they usually lived in close communities and because they were expected to minister to the dying. Their response, predictably, ranged from cowardly flight to heroic self-sacrifice. The Black Death caused a great shortage of priests, mitigated only by the drastic reduction in the number of laity requiring their ministry, so that to some extent bishops were forced to ordain dubiously qualified men to fill the void.

A Surfeit of Priests

But after Europe had recovered, the sheer number of the ordained (236 priests for two churches in one German town, for example) contributed to what seemed like clerical rapaciousness. Many priests had to scramble to obtain whatever marginal benefices they could get, performing parochial duties at minimal pay for absentee pastors or, as "Mass priests", living on stipends that required them to do little but pray for the souls of deceased donors.

Heterodox Movements

In a pervasive atmosphere of spiritual anxiety and uncertainty, the difference between authentic searching and heresy often seemed unclear, with philosophical and theological movements, political ideas, reform movements, and conventional dynastic politics in complex relationships with one another.

Flagellation

The practice of flagellation—scourging oneself in order to share in Christ's sufferings, as a penance for sin and as a weapon against temptation—began with the early monks and nuns and continued throughout the Middle Ages and into modern times. In monasteries and convents, as in secular life, it was also inflicted as punishment. Although the practice was highly ritualized, it was intended to be painful and in some cases was carried to extremes (St. Clare's body, after years of scourging, was said to be covered with scars).

In the mid-thirteenth century, ritualized public flagellation began to be practiced by organized groups of lay people in reparation for sin and to ward off divine punishment. The participants wore distinctive garments and went in procession from town to town, on a journey of thirty-three days (for the years of Jesus' life on earth), each person whipping the person in front of him and loudly calling for repentance. Flagellants placed themselves completely under the authority of a lay master and sometimes repudiated clerical authority, and priests in turn were often hostile, especially when it seemed that flagellation was a substitute for sacramental confession.

Ritual flagellation threatened to go out of control during the Black Death, and Clement VI forbade the practice, partly because it was often accompanied by violent attacks on Jews. But it continued underground in some places, treated by the Inquisition as a heresy.

Although the more moderate Beguines and Beghards were tolerated, a number of people were burned at the stake for what was sometimes called the Beguine heresy, that is, the rejection of the sacramental priesthood. In 1310, the Flemish Beguine Margaret Porete was burned for teaching that the soul was entirely "free", not in any way bound by the strictures of intellect or will. The movement was ordered suppressed but was later given tentative approval.

Beguines and Beghards

The Spiritual Franciscans, who were sometimes identified with the Beguines, continued to flourish, splitting the Franciscan order into two factions, the Spirituals and the Conventuals (from "convent").

Fraticelli

In 1317, the Spirituals were condemned by John XXII for teaching that prelates who did not practice poverty had no authority. John declared that Christ and the Apostles owned property and that it was heresy to make absolute poverty the mark of a true Christian. The general of the Franciscans, Michael of Cesena (d. 1342), favored the Spirituals and was deposed by John, whereupon Michael took refuge at the court of Emperor Louis the Bavarian (1314–1347), who supported the Spirituals as part of his own continuing quarrel with the Pope.

The Franciscan William of Ockham (d. ca. 1349), the most important philosopher of the age, was a friend of Marsilius of Padua and also favored the Spirituals. He fled with Marsilius to Louis' court and supported the emperor in his quarrel with Pope John, whom Ockham condemned as a heretic. (Ockham probably died excommunicated.)[6]

John Wycliffe (d. 1384) was a priest and Oxford professor whose excoriation of clerical misconduct and privilege escalated into an attack on the priesthood itself, including the claim—recurring throughout the history of the Church—that a sinful priest cannot validly administer the sacraments. Like Marsilius, he wanted the Church to be stripped of all wealth and temporal power. He eventually denied Transubstantiation, confession to a priest, indulgences, clerical celibacy, and the veneration of images and relics, accusing the Church of having departed from biblical teachings. The true church, he held, was invisible, made up of those whom God predestined to salvation.

Wycliffe

Wycliffe was condemned as a heretic, but powerful nobles not only protected him (he was never arrested) but actually pressed for changes

---

[6] The fact that the circumstances of Ockham's death are unknown is unusual for a man of his prominence. Probably he perished in the Black Death and was quickly buried.

in the Church in keeping with his program. Eventually, however, his movement lost most of its aristocratic support, especially after the Peasants' Revolt of 1381, which some people blamed on Wycliffe's attacks on authority but which in fact he condemned.

Lollardy

Although some of Wycliffe's associates made a partial translation of the Bible into English, his movement survived primarily among unlearned people who came to be called Lollards, which was apparently a colloquialism for "psalm-singer". The Inquisition never existed in England, but after Wycliffe's death, Parliament passed a law against heresy, and a number of Lollards were burned at the stake, some of them after an armed rebellion. Lollardy survived as a small underground movement until the Protestant Reformation.

Hus

Jan Hus (d. 1415) was a Bohemian priest and professor who held ideas similar to Wycliffe's and may have been influenced by him. The Bible had been translated into the Czech language by his time, and he cited it as an authority against that of the Church. Hus survived for a time amidst the labyrinthine politics of the Great Western Schism, but its end left him vulnerable. He went to the Council of Constance with a promise of safety by Emperor Sigismund, but the Council condemned him nonetheless; he was burned at the stake, his close lay associate Jerome of Prague following shortly thereafter.

Utraquists

The Husite movement flourished in Bohemia, as the kingdom divided along religious lines, with Hus' followers demanding Communion in both kinds for the laity, uncensored preaching, and the abolition of church property, although they remained in formal union with the Church. The first of these demands led to their being called Utraquists (from the Latin word for "both"), their heresy being their insistence that the Eucharist was invalid unless Communion was administered in both kinds.

Taborites

A more radical strain of Husites were millenarians who called themselves Taborites, after the biblical mountain. They broke openly with the Church and took up arms against the king of Bohemia but were eventually crushed. Kings tolerated the Utraquists to some extent, and in 1485, the kingdom was divided into Catholic and Husite zones, each of which enjoyed religious freedom.[7]

Millenarianism

Other kinds of millenarianism continued to appear from time to time, some of it orthodox. The Spanish Dominican St. Vincent Ferrer

---

[7] Husites still exist as a non-Catholic body a century older than Lutheranism. Their principal modern embodiment is called the Moravian Brethren.

(d. 1419) saw the Great Western Schism as a sign of the end times and, after having supported the Avignon pope, helped bring the schism to an end. On the heterodox side, Hans Bohm, the "drummer of Niklashausen", attracted crowds to his obscure German town in 1476 by predicting the imminent Second Coming and urging radical social equality. He was put to death.

Witchcraft

Belief in witchcraft existed from time immemorial in almost every culture of the world; in the High Middle Ages, it attracted relatively little attention. But a systematic attack began in the late fifteenth century, possibly because of the pervasive spiritual anxiety of the age. Two German Dominican inquisitors, Henry Kramer (d. 1484) and Jacob Sprenger (d. 1495), were commissioned by Innocent VIII to study the phenomenon, and in 1486 they published a highly influential book, *The Hammer of Evildoers.*

Previous witch beliefs had been made up of scraps of folklore, but the *Hammer* now delineated a complex system of practices, such as intercourse with the devil, allegedly engaged in by those (mostly women) who sold themselves to Satan. As a printed work rather than oral tradition, the *Hammer* had wide influence in providing a theoretical account of popular beliefs and in standardizing procedures of prosecution.

Over the next almost two centuries, accusations of witchcraft were pursued very aggressively almost everywhere in Europe, as accused witches were closely interrogated and often tortured into confessing satanic practices.[8] Witchcraft was under the authority of the Inquisition because it was considered a species of heresy. Although some bishops and civil authorities resisted the Inquisition's authority, and the inquisitors themselves sometimes showed skepticism about popular superstitions, those who were convicted of witchcraft were burned at the stake.[9]

Spiritual Searching

There was deep dissatisfaction with what seemed like the oppressive complexity of church life. Abstract theology was an academic specialty that seemed remote from people's spiritual needs; the hierarchy was immersed in worldly concerns; greed was institutionalized; canon law was a bewildering system of legalisms that seemed to exist primarily for the purpose of granting exemptions; the liturgy was celebrated in such a way that the laity stayed at a distance; and the elaborate network of piety involved innumerable kinds of devotions to innumerable saints, seeming almost to exclude the possibility of direct access to God.

[8] Some of those condemned may have actually believed themselves to have magical powers. However, the claim of present-day "wiccans" to be continuing an ancient cult is wholly fanciful.

[9] In England, which had no Inquisition, witchcraft was a crime in civil law, and witches were hanged rather than burned.

God Near and Far

Paradoxically, late medieval Catholicism on the one hand seemed to make God inaccessible—by requiring the believer to navigate a complex system of doctrines, laws, and practices—and on the other, seemed to make him overly accessible, as necessarily responsive to successful navigators. But in the midst of all the spiritual confusion, the later Middle Ages was also a deeply religious time.

Traditional Piety

Traditional piety still had great power, and the invention of printing around 1450, probably by Johannes Gutenberg of Mainz, Germany (d. 1468), allowed Mass books, books of hours, and manuals of simple instruction to be produced for the laity. The *Golden Legend* was immensely popular, and devotion to the saints continued at the heart of popular piety. Particular saints were invoked for particular causes, and there was a great deal of credulity about miracles and supernatural experiences of all kinds. Shrines were visited by large numbers of pilgrims: the English laywoman Margery Kempe (d. ca. 1433), for example, was married with fourteen children but nonetheless made pilgrimages as far away as Jerusalem and kept a spiritual journal that was widely read.

The Passion

Devotion to Christ in His Passion was pervasive, with increasingly graphic representations of His sufferings, culminating in the great Issenheim Altarpiece of the German artist Matthias Grünewald (d. 1528). The Passion was often reenacted in processions out of doors and eventually brought inside churches in the form of the stations of the cross. The veneration of extremely graphic representations of the Passion was intense particularly in Spain, in part perhaps to manifest the difference of Catholicism from Judaism and Islam, both of which forbade the use of images.

Mary and Joseph

Belief in the Immaculate Conception and the Assumption of Mary, while not official dogma, was common, advocated particularly by Franciscans. Paralleling her Son, Mary was the object of devotion both in her sufferings and in her triumphs. Devotion to St. Joseph, which had been neglected in earlier centuries, grew in popularity after 1400, although in the West it was still rare for either men or churches to be named for him.

Women Saints

Unique among saints, Bl. Margaret of Città-di-Castello (d. 1320) was a young noblewoman who was physically deformed and was abandoned by her parents after an expected miraculous cure failed to occur. Taken in by others, she became a Dominican tertiary and spent her life mainly caring for children.

   Also as a Dominican tertiary, St. Catherine of Siena lived as an ascetic in her family's home, had mystical experiences, and offered her sufferings for the good of the Church, denouncing corruption and urging reform, especially of the hierarchy. She was greatly troubled by visions of large numbers of souls falling into Hell.

St. Bridget of Sweden was a widowed noblewoman, the mother of eight, who founded a religious order (named after her) that continued the otherwise obsolete practice of double monasteries of both men and women under an abbess. (Bridget justified the arrangement on the grounds that Mary had presided over the Apostles after the Ascension.) Like Catherine, Bridget was a mystic who enjoined the pope to return to Rome.

St. Frances of Rome (d. 1440), who was widowed after forty years, gathered a group of women who worked among the poor without vows or a formal community.

St. Catherine of Genoa (d. 1510) was forced into marriage, separated from her husband, then reunited with him. He supported her charities, and she attracted a number of followers.

The most extraordinary saint of the age (indeed, of any age) was Joan of Arc (d. 1431). As a woman and a visionary, she was not unusual on the roll of the saints, but as a peasant, the story of her life went completely contrary to the society of her time.

Joan of Arc

Leader of Men

Throughout most of the fourteenth and fifteenth centuries, England and France were engaged in the Hundred Years' War, which was essentially an English invasion of France. By Joan's time, the king of England successfully claimed to be king of France, and the yet-uncrowned French claimant, Charles VII (1422–1461), was sunk in lethargic inactivity. Joan appeared at his court claiming to have heard voices of saints commanding her to instruct Charles to mount resistance against the invaders. After much skepticism and numerous delays, he sent armies into the field, with Joan accompanying them in armor and rallying their spirit. The armies had sufficient success for Charles finally to be crowned.

"A Witch"

But the complexities of feudal politics were such that Charles' greatest vassal, the duke of Burgundy, was allied with the English. Joan was captured by the Burgundians; turned over to the English, with Charles doing nothing to rescue her; and tried by an ecclesiastical court made up of Frenchmen in league with England. From the English standpoint, her claims of supernatural revelations could only be evidence of sorcery. She was therefore tried as a witch. She confessed under pressure to being an imposter but then repudiated her confession and was burned at the stake.[10]

---

[10] She was canonized in 1920. Her sanctity is problematical insofar as she acted merely as a French patriot, but her canonization was based on her heroic virtue.

Henry VI   As always, religion and politics fit together in unpredictable ways. The English king under whom Joan was executed—Henry VI (1422–1461)—was a weak but pious monarch who was deposed and killed during the civil conflict called the Wars of the Roses. He himself came to be popularly venerated as a saint.

John of Capistrano   St. John of Capistrano (d. 1456) also had an unusual history. An administrator in the Papal States, he separated from his wife and entered the Franciscans, of which he eventually became minister general, reforming his order and scathingly criticizing the corruption of the clergy. He was sent to Bohemia to help suppress the Husite movement and while there also instigated measures against the Jews. A few years before his death, he personally led a battlefield charge that routed the Turks at Belgrade.

The Eucharist   Devotion to the Eucharist flourished even though sometimes independent of the reception of Communion, especially by adoring the sacred host in a monstrance. But Nicholas of Cusa, one of the greatest bishops and theologians of the age, found it necessary to remind his people that the Eucharist was intended as food, not primarily for adoration. Every church of any size had auxiliary altars, many of which were erected and maintained by guilds or confraternities and reserved for the use of the donors. *Chantry* ("singing") chapels or altars were endowed by pious people to ensure prayers for their souls after their deaths.

Sermons   Preaching was highly valued, to the point where in large churches the pulpit was often erected midway down the nave, so that the whole congregation could hear the preacher, something that also had the effect of separating the sermon from the Mass. Sermons were sometimes preached outside the context of the Mass altogether, and many churches had outdoor pulpits for that purpose.

Music   Except in monasteries, there was a movement away from the simplicity of Gregorian chant. Organs were introduced in churches, and patrons commissioned elaborate polyphonic Masses by composers such as Guillaume de Machaut (d. 1377), a development that tended to place church music in the hands of professionals rather than congregations.

Penance   There were serious efforts to implement the proper reception of the sacrament of penance. To effect this, guides were produced for the clergy, such as the English priest John Mirk's (d. ca. 1415) *Instruction for Parish Priests*. Jean Gerson provided detailed instructions on how to prepare people for death, identifying the deathbed as the crucial moment when the soul is suspended between salvation and damnation. Extreme unction ("last anointing") was usually administered only when the recipient was thought to be near death, and it was crucial that he make a final confession.

In life, prudent people endeavored to gain indulgences that would alleviate their sufferings in Purgatory, and such indulgences could be applied to the souls of those already dead. The last will and testament was also crucial, in that it was the legator's final effort to set his affairs in order, especially by proclaiming his faith, making gifts to charity, and providing for prayers for his soul. To die intestate was thought to show that the deceased had been unprepared.

Indulgences

In 1300, Boniface VIII announced the first Holy Year: a year of jubilee, pilgrimage, and the forgiveness of debts and offenses, and two hundred thousand pilgrims visited Rome. A century and a half later, the jubilee was still so popular that a limit had to be imposed on the time pilgrims could remain in the city.

The Holy Year

One crucial element of classical sanctity was no longer attainable: those who were orthodox in their beliefs had little prospect of martyrdom, although some devout souls admitted that they longed for the opportunity. It was now mainly heretics who suffered for their faith.

Martyrdom

Much of the religious spirit of the age expressed itself outside formal Church structures, although not necessarily in opposition to them. In the face of those dauntingly complex structures, personal religious experience more and more seemed to be the most reliable path to God. The spirit of reform was often toward a more spiritual and interior kind of piety, a liberation from burdensome traditions in order to return to a purer, earlier form of Christian practice.

Reform

The Heart of the Gospel

The Netherlander Gerhard Groote (d. 1384) declined to become a priest and accepted ordination as a deacon only so that he could preach, something that he was, however, eventually forbidden to do. He attracted followers and, although he was not in favor of monastic life, eventually formed a community called the Brethren of the Common Life, with houses for both men and women. Some members followed the rule of the Augustinian canons, but all were free to leave the community at any time. They took no vows but lived a life of poverty, supported by their own labors.

Brethren of the Common Life

A disciple of the mystic Bl. John Ruysbroeck (d. 1381), Groote formulated what came to be called the New Devotion, in which there was in fact little that was new. Its novelty lay entirely in its simplicity, in contrast to the complexities of Scholastic theology and elaborate forms of piety.

Kempis

Its greatest expression was *The Imitation of Christ* by Thomas à Kempis (d. 1471), which, next to the Bible, is the most widely read book in the history of Christianity and, along with the Bible, the only book continuously in print almost since the invention of printing. Kempis urged his readers simply to follow the teaching and example of Jesus in the Gospel: the spirit of humility, charity, and submission to God's will.

While not denigrating practices like the rosary or pilgrimages (he had great devotion to Mary), Kempis urged inner transformation of the soul, identifying stages in the soul's rise, of which a love of suffering for Jesus' sake was the highest. Men were to live always in expectation of imminent death. The last part of the book was an extended meditation on the Eucharist, in which Kempis urged the frequent reception of Communion.

Although widely read by lay people, the book in many ways seems to have been intended for monks and nuns. There was little of value in the world that could not be found in a monastic cell, Kempis warned, and each time a monk left his monastery he returned spiritually diminished.

Anti-Intellectualism

There is a distinct note of anti-intellectualism in the work, as Kempis repeatedly warned that, of itself, knowledge might be sterile, whereas a heartfelt effort to do God's will was salutary. Whereas for Aquinas and other Scholastics, a virtuous act was any act motivated by the intellect's assent to truth and the will's decision to act accordingly, for Kempis actual emotion was a necessary sign of authenticity. The penitent should shed real tears and experience desolation.

The Brethren taught in schools that stretched across northern Europe, their chief purpose being not so much learning as the inculcation of piety and moral character in their students. Great emphasis was placed on reading the Bible.

Mysticism

The highest expressions of late medieval piety were mystical, a phenomenon in which the soul transcended all objective manifestations of God, such as sacred images or even conscious thoughts, and encountered Him directly, amidst overwhelming light. Mysticism owed much to the Neo-Platonism of Pseudo-Dionysius, according to which the soul first emanated from God through stages of descent into this world, then returned to God through a series of ascents. *The German Theology* was an anonymous mystical work which taught that, since God was wholly transcendent, the divine could not enter the soul unless the human personality was suppressed.

Despite it being an indescribable experience, mysticism was not incompatible with rigorous Scholastic intellectualism—three of the leading mystics were German Dominicans.

Eckhart

Johannes Eckhart of Hochheim, usually called Meister Eckhart (d. 1327), was a kind of Thomist who nonetheless taught the Platonic doctrine that at its core the soul possesses a spark that unites it with its divine source. He was posthumously condemned for the heresy of pantheism ("everything is God")—absorbing all of creation into God's infinity— but the intended meaning of his work remained ambiguous and obscure. Johannes Tauler (d. 1361) also taught the existence of a divine "ground" of the human soul.

Suso

Bl. Henry Suso (d. 1365) made daring use of the language of courtly love, which he applied to the love between God and the soul in order to describe the stages of ecstasy through which the soul passed, cul- minating in its being "ravished" by God and becoming one with Christ. In Pseudo-Dionysian terms, he referred to God as "eternal nothing- ness". (The use of courtly love imagery by mystical writers derived in part from the Song of Songs, understood as an allegory of the rela- tionship of the soul and God.)

Ruysbroeck

Ruysbroeck, a Flemish canon regular, described the mystical state but warned against false signs and insisted that pride and uncharity were incompatible with its attainment.

English Mystics

There was also a school of English mystics. In contrast to Ruysbroeck, Bl. Richard Rolle (d. 1349), who became a hermit, taught that even works of charity might interfere with pure contemplation. The *Cloud of Unknowing* was an anonymous work whose title referred to God's dwelling in an impenetrable obscurity that could only be pierced by emptying the mind of all content. Walter Hilton (d. 1396), a canon regular, wrote *The Ladder of Perfection*, describing the stages by which the soul moved beyond reason to a direct knowledge of God, a pro- cess in which the will was absorbed into perfect divine love.

"Julian" of Norwich

The most prominent female mystic of the age, who wrote a long account of her ecstatic experiences, was called Bl. Julian of Norwich (d. ca. 1415), because she lived as an anchorite at a church dedicated to St. Julian. (Her actual name is unknown.) Like some other medieval writers, she sometimes referred to God as "mother" as well as Father, probably because every perfection, including that of motherhood, is necessarily present in God.

Anti-Mysticism

Mystics were sometimes suspected of tending toward antinomianism (believing that they could rely on inspiration rather than the moral law) and quietism (placing themselves so completely in the hands of God as to cease all striving for perfection).

D'Ailly was suspicious of mysticism and favored instead a simple and practical kind of spirituality, and Gerson also wrote a treatise on mysticism that emphasized common sense, humility, charity, the natural human virtues, and submission to the hierarchy. (But despite his suspicions of religious enthusiasm, Gerson championed the sanctity of Joan of Arc.)

Theology

The later Middle Ages was also a time of considerable intellectual ferment. Aquinas had constructed a grand synthesis of faith and reason, but not all who came after him were persuaded. The philosophers of the fourteenth century contented themselves with answers that they considered probable rather than certain.

Scotus

John Duns Scotus (d. 1308) was a Scottish Franciscan who taught at Oxford and Paris, carrying forward the intellectual tradition of Bonaventure and Grosseteste. For Scotus, the mind could not know being in itself, only individual beings, so that where Aquinas spoke of universals, Scotus emphasized *haecceity* ("this-ness"). The significance of this seemingly abstruse point was to render Aquinas' great synthesis of knowledge—his proof that the entire universe constitutes an intelligible whole—less credible, requiring men to accept their ignorance.

It was not possible to prove the existence of God by beginning with sensible objects, Scotus thought, because the natural order of nature could not rise to the supernatural. Thus Aquinas' First Cause was not God but something that was part of the universe itself.

Scotus was in the Augustinian tradition in giving the will primacy over the intellect: the mind informed the will, but the will first determined the perceptions of the mind. The best "proof" of the existence of God was the tendency of the human will toward absolute good, which must exist, since the will could not incline toward nonexistence. Whereas Aquinas emphasized that God decreed good and evil in accordance with the objective order of the universe, Scotus held that good was whatever God chose, although He could not will contradictions. To love God was the only thing that was good in itself; all other goods were merely decreed by God.

Nominalism

Following Scotus' idea of *haecceity*, later thinkers doubted the existence of universals and instead saw them in Abelard's terms, as mere names conveniently given to things that resembled one another. From that doctrine, the principal movement of late medieval philosophy came to be called Nominalism.

Ockham

William of Ockham was the most influential of the nominalists, holding that, since the mind could "perceive" things that did not actually exist (dreams, illusions), it did not know real things but only its own ideas, to which it gave names. Thus the scope of human reason was quite limited, and a great synthetic understanding of the universe was not possible. ("Ockham's Razor" was the principle that the simplest explanation of a phenomenon was to be preferred.)

Ockham undercut Aquinas' arguments for the existence of God by holding that, although the mind could follow the sequence of cause and effect as it encountered it in experience, it could not infer the existence of a cause from its effects. Thus God was unknowable on the basis of His creatures.

Fideism

This skepticism marked a crossroads in Western thought, allowing later philosophers to conclude that there is no rational basis for religious belief. However, instead of denying the validity of such belief, nominalists fell back on a kind of fideism (from the Latin word for "faith")— belief without a rational basis. In a sense, Ockham repudiated Anselm's principle that faith seeks understanding. Ockham saw no conflict between faith and reason but thought that man necessarily believed without understanding.

Voluntarism

Nominalism required a voluntaristic morality: the belief that right and wrong were simply decreed by God's inscrutable will and were not open to human understanding in the way that Thomistic realists thought they were. Nominalists considered the divine will so absolute that some (although not Ockham himself) speculated that God could lie, reverse the definitions of good and evil, will sin, and undo events that had already happened.

The Divine Absolute

After Scotus' time the battle between the "Old Way" (Realism) and the "New Way" (Nominalism) was a feature of university life. Nominalism, like mysticism, had an acute sense of the absoluteness of God, far beyond all human categories of understanding, and was partly a sense that both Thomistic theology and formal religious practices had made God too accessible. Gerson, for example, welcomed Nominalism because it discouraged speculation, which he thought inhibited God's freedom by making divine actions subject to the laws of human reason.

Predestination

Nominalists tended to reject Anselm's explanation of the Incarnation, holding that God simply willed to become man and that it was presumptuous to inquire further. Mankind could have been redeemed by a simple act of the divine will, so that Christ's death was in no way necessary. Some late-medieval theologians held a theory of predestination— that God decrees who is saved and who is damned—since otherwise it seemed to them that men, by their actions, would have the power to force God to grant them salvation.

Logic

In abandoning metaphysics as unknowable, nominalists became acute logicians, concerning themselves with technical problems that could be solved. No philosopher actually speculated on how many angels could dance on the head of a pin, but it would have been a legitimate nominalist subject, not in order to seek a numerical answer but in order to clarify the ideas of space and of spiritual beings.

Science

In transferring attention from the unknowable realm of metaphysics to the realm of empirical experience, Nominalism also contributed to the eventual development of modern science. During the fourteenth century, some philosophers—Giles of Rome (d. 1316), Jean Buridan (d. 1358), Nicole d'Oresme (d. 1382)—discarded the Aristotelian model of the universe and speculated that it was the earth that moved, not the sun.

Cusa

Nicholas of Cusa, perhaps the most original mind of the age, attempted to transcend Scholastic debates partly through Pseudo-Dionysius' negative theology ("learned ignorance", as Cusa called it) and by returning to Plotinus' idea of the One from which all things emanated and to which they returned. Cusa deemphasized rational speculation, positing the Infinite as the ultimate reality, knowable only by semi-mystical intuition. All religions contained some truth (he urged the study of the Qur'an, which he thought would prove the truth of Christ), but Christ alone embodied the full truth, resolving all contrarieties. Cusa was little understood, however, and had few disciples.

Tradition

Theologically, one of the most important developments of the later Middle Ages was a growing tendency to separate Scripture and Tradition, to treat them as two distinct sources of truth. Ockham, in denying that the pope had ultimate authority in matters of dogma, held that the fullness of revelation, much of it handed down by word of mouth, resided in the entire Church, and d'Ailly too denied that all the teachings of the Church were found in Scripture. (On the other side, the English bishop Reginald Pecock [d. ca. 1461] made Scripture superior to the Church and denied the existence of oral tradition.)

Latin Averroism

Latin Averroism—pure Aristotle—still flourished in Italy, especially at the University of Padua, its proponents tending toward a kind of materialism. Its chief representative, Pietro Pomponazzi (d. 1525), taught the Averroist idea that immortality is proper only to God, not to men, although he accepted the immortality of the soul as a doctrine of faith.

Overall, however, the intellectual life of Italy moved in a quite different direction from Averroism. As John of Salisbury had foreseen, the rise of Scholasticism had led to a devaluing of humanistic studies, and the movement later called the Renaissance ("rebirth") was made up of "humanists" seeking to recover ancient classical civilization. It arose first in Italy around 1350, perhaps because Italians were especially conscious of the greatness of ancient Rome and because the Italian universities were independent of church control.

The Renaissance began merely as an interest in "humane letters", including grammar, rhetoric, history, and poetry, which were called the "liberal arts", because they freed the mind. Grammar and rhetoric were taught in the medieval universities but were overshadowed by philosophy, while history and poetry were not part of the curriculum at all and were regarded by philosophers as of a much lower order of truth.

Rhetoric
Whereas for Aristotle man was a "rational animal", humanists regarded the passions as equally important and venerated the imagination as highly as the analytic faculty, jibing at what they considered Scholasticism's arid "logic-chopping", remote from human concerns. Humanists especially emphasized rhetoric—the art of persuasion—which Scholastics held in suspicion because men could be persuaded by things other than logical argument. But for the humanists, this had great religious relevance: whereas the Scholastics engaged in sterile attempts at definition, rhetoric and poetry could move the heart and thereby bring about genuine conversion to a living faith.

Humanists versus Scholastics
Thus there were often bitter quarrels between Scholastics and humanists, especially in vying for influence in the universities and the intellectual world in general. For the most part, these quarrels were not over issues of fundamental truth but over such things as humanist attempts to establish professorships in fields like rhetoric or Greek.

Philology
Humanists were philologists ("lovers of the word"), with specialized knowledge of both the subtleties of language and of ancient manuscripts, and one of their most important works was publishing those old texts, most of them for the first time. Patrons such as the Medici family of Florence kept agents busy acquiring manuscripts wherever they could be found.

Latin remained the language of formal treatises in the West, as well as the language of conversation among educated people. But to the humanists, this had led to Latin's deterioration: it no longer adhered to the stylistic and grammatical standards of the ancients, to which they now sought to return. One of the most popular books of the

The Italian Renaissance

Humanism

Renaissance, the *Christiad* of the Italian humanist Marco Vida (d. 1566), recounted the story of Jesus in the style of the Roman epic poet Virgil (d. 19 B.C.).

The Recovery of Greek

The Greek language had been largely forgotten in the West for centuries, and the earliest humanists could not read it. But they passionately wished to do so, and gradually they learned it—through travel, from Byzantine scholars who immigrated to the West, even from Greek sailors—and by the later fourteenth century it was an essential part of their education. They rediscovered Greek texts in Western libraries and imported other manuscripts from the East, a process stimulated by the fall of Constantinople in 1453.

The humanists paid considerable attention to Scripture, primarily through methods of literary analysis: the precise meaning of words, metaphors, and other poetic qualities. Several humanists made new Latin translations of the New Testament, working from old Greek texts in order to offer an alternative to the Vulgate, and a few of them even learned Hebrew.

The Rediscovery of Plato

In an intellectual culture dominated by Aristotle, the humanists rediscovered Plato, whom they much preferred, because of his poetic mode of philosophizing and his use of the dialogue method, in which truth was not definitively expounded by a master but was discovered through discussion among men of differing opinions.

Patristics

The Scholastics routinely cited the Fathers of the Church, but the humanists published new patristic texts, including those of the Eastern Fathers. Many of the Fathers had been influenced by Plato and could therefore serve as alternatives to Scholasticism, Augustine's intensely personal *Confessions* (the classic expression of Catholic religious experience) having special appeal.

Classical Culture

Most humanists remained believing Catholics, but their attacks on Scholasticism sometimes made them seem unorthodox. As with most intellectual pioneers, they were sometimes carried away with uncritical enthusiasm for new ideas, and a few of them attempted a synthesis between Christianity and classical pagan thought.

Petrarch

Francesco Petrarca (Petrarch, d. 1374), the first important humanist, was an avid lover of the Roman authors Cicero (d. 43 B.C.) and Virgil. With Humanism under suspicion of being pagan, Petrarch attempted to turn the tables on its critics by accusing the Scholastics of being more familiar with the teachings of Aristotle, including his errors, than of Moses and Christ. Aristotle was spiritually deficient, because he could define virtue but his words lacked the power to motivate men to lead virtuous lives, while Plato came closer to the truth, without fully attaining it.

Slyly, Petrarch boasted of his own ignorance, in contrast to the Scholastics' pretense to know things they could not know, and he extolled Christian humility, since the truths of God are known to simple people who lead lives of virtue. He dubbed the Scholastic distinction between faith and reason "insane" because it was impossible for a believer to lay faith aside. In the Augustinian tradition, Petrarch valued will over intellect: it was not possible to know God adequately in this life, but it was possible to love Him, so that virtue was far more important than knowledge.

Salutati
Collucio Salutati (d. 1406) was a humanist influenced by Nominalism's sense of the inscrutable power of God and the consequent inadequacy of natural theology. Following Augustine, he turned inward to discover truth, seeing the human will, conformed to the divine will, as the principal means of discovery.

Humanists adapted the classical idea of Fate or Fortune—the impersonal powers that determined events on earth—to the idea of the all-powerful God. (Some humanists even referred to God the Father by the pagan title "thundering Jupiter".) Thus Salutati urged his fellow Florentines not to flee the plague, because it was God's will, and he stoically accepted the death of two of his sons from the disease.

Valla
Lorenzo Valla (d. 1457) thought free will mysterious, since God foreordained human actions, including the hardening of the heart, in such a way that man could not choose to be virtuous. He wrote a treatise on the Eucharist in which he affirmed the doctrine of the Real Presence but in somewhat naturalistic terms: God was present in many places simultaneously, just as the sun or the human voice, and miracles simply manifested the mysteries of natural existence.

Valla was one of the most uncompromising critics of Scholasticism, because only human experience could be the starting point for the discovery of truth. He denounced the "arrogance" of philosophers (Aristotle, he judged, was damned) and insisted that theology had no need of philosophy.

Historical Consciousness
The humanists' study of the classics gave them a keener sense of history than their predecessors, an understanding of historical context—how things change over time—and a certain skepticism about historical claims, such as the authenticity of relics.

Valla carried that new consciousness to its furthest point, arguing, for example, that the works of Pseudo-Dionysius did not date to apostolic times and writing a commentary on the Greek New Testament that called into question certain passages of the Vulgate. Most important was his demonstration that the *Donation of Constantine* (see Chapter Five above, p. 116) was not written in the time of Constantine but was an eighth-century forgery, a conclusion Valla reached through analysis of the style of the document and the fact that it was not known until the eighth century.

Ficino

Perhaps the most important of the Italian humanists was Marsilio Ficino (d. 1499), the head of the Academy founded at Florence under the patronage of the Medici family, in emulation of Plato's Academy at Athens. Contrary to Valla, Ficino insisted that theology and philosophy needed each other—theology in order to keep philosophy from skepticism, philosophy to save theology from ignorance—and he opposed Nominalism for its separation of faith and reason.

Ficino translated all of Plato, Plotinus, and Pseudo-Dionysius into Latin and wrote a *Platonic Theology*, based on the Augustinian teaching that the image of God could be discovered in the soul, a kind of natural religion that was in principle accessible to everyone. All significant truth was contained in Plato, as a kind of natural revelation of divine reality, but Jesus was the Mediator who led men by stages from the earthly to the spiritual realm for which the exiled soul yearned.

Pico della Mirandola

Giovanni Pico della Mirandola (d. 1494) was a Florentine nobleman who studied Jewish, Muslim, and ancient pagan texts and undertook to show that all systems of belief are ultimately compatible. The Jewish mystical work the *Kabbalah*, for example, was part of revelation, he said, handed down from Moses. (Pico was investigated and briefly imprisoned on suspicion of heresy.)

The Recovery of Hebrew

The French Franciscan Nicholas of Lyra (d. 1349) was rare for his time both in knowing Hebrew and for emphasizing a primarily literal understanding of Scripture, in contrast to the medieval fourfold interpretation. Giannozzo Manetti (d. 1459) was a Florentine diplomat who made a special effort to read Hebrew, translated parts of the Old Testament, and also studied the *Kabbalah*. Eventually, however, he wrote a refutation of Judaism.

Humanist Clerics

Although Humanism was in many ways a lay phenomenon, it was not anticlerical. Of its leading figures, Petrarch was in minor orders and was for a time an official at the papal court at Avignon, Ficino was a priest, and Valla was a layman in the service of Pope Nicholas V, who apparently was not bothered by the discrediting of the *Donation of Constantine*, since the popes no longer cited it as a basis for their authority. One of the greatest Renaissance artists, Fra ("Friar") Angelico (Giovanni da Fiesole, d. 1455), was a Dominican mystic who painted exclusively religious subjects, both in Florence and under papal patronage at Rome.

The "Dark Ages"

The greatest classical writers were pagans, and the humanists' admiration of them logically implied that the coming of Christ had had a negative effect on civilization, a conclusion no humanist reached explicitly.

Petrarch lamented that civilization had lain in darkness for centuries but predicted that it was about to undergo a rebirth. He grieved that Cicero did not know Christ but took comfort in the thought that at least the Roman philosopher had knowledge of the one true God. Like Jerome, Petrarch found Scripture inferior to pagan writings in literary qualities. Salutati contrasted "St. Socrates" with the cowardly St. Peter and thought Socrates would have been the greatest of the martyrs had he been a Christian.

Pagan Heroes

Valla, on the other hand, thought that there were no authentic pagan heroes, since all men were motivated by the selfish desire for pleasure. Poggio Bracciolini (d. 1459), who was for many years a papal bureaucrat, then (like Salutati) chancellor of Florence, disbelieved the legends of Roman history, which he thought constituted a "wretched story". But he praised the courage of a heretic whom he saw burned at the stake, comparing him to Socrates.

Human Nature

The fundamental ambiguity of Humanism was precisely its view of human nature—whether man was by nature good or, left to himself, capable of great evil. The Church continually warned against pride and avarice and urged ascetic renunciation, but this presented a dilemma to the humanists, because the Greeks and Romans did not understand moral failure as the product of sinful human nature but merely as excess, to be constrained by a cultivated sense of moderation and a proper regard for law. Thus without formally denying Original Sin, some humanists in effect seemed to disbelieve in fallen man's inclination to sin. Following classical models, they were trustful of the natural virtues and extolled freedom.

The Paradox of Petrarch

Partly as a counter to Innocent III's treatise on contempt for the world, Petrarch wrote *On Human Dignity*, which he based on the divine image in the soul. Man was lower than the angels in absolute terms but higher by virtue of having been redeemed by Christ, and he had been given lordship over nature, including the power to transform the world. Man's upright posture, unlike that of the animals, pointed to Heaven.

Petrarch later modified this view. His brother was a Carthusian, for whom Petrarch wrote a treatise against worldly vanities. The humanist related how he once climbed to the top of a mountain to admire the beauty of the world but at the summit opened Augustine's *Confessions* at random and was stunned to read there a warning that men admire high mountains but neglect their own souls. He then saw his "aimless wanderings" as an expression of his troubled yearning for salvation and vowed henceforth to concentrate his mind on God.

Valla the Epicurean

Valla held an almost opposite view. There had always been Christian Stoics, but Valla was unique in being a Christian Epicurean, finding virtue in itself to be harsh and unattractive. Thus there could be no such thing as natural virtues; supernatural virtues were the means by which men, who were like animals in everything except their immortal souls, curbed their earthly pleasures in order to live for the eternal pleasure of Heaven.

Love and Lust

A general humanist consensus held that classical poetry offered instruction in the nature and pitfalls of human love and that the pagan poets, having concealed their monotheism behind a fanciful polytheism, offered at least glimpses of the divine.

The traditional teaching about the procreative purposes of marriage was strongly upheld by the Church. The Franciscan preacher St. Bernardino of Siena (d. 1444), for example, accused husbands who practiced contraception of treating their wives as property used for the purpose of satisfying husbandly lust. The humanists, however, while not repudiating the ideal of chastity, were influenced by the writers they admired. Some classical writers, such as Ovid (d. 17), offered a literary model of easy hedonism and frank bawdiness. The courtly love tradition developed literary genres that extolled romantic love and even adultery. Valla denigrated natural virtue to the point where, in the natural order, the prostitute was more enviable than the virgin. For him, there was no inherent value in sexual continence, and a moderate degree of sensuality was desirable.

The humanist Pietro Aretino (d. 1556) wrote outright pornography, and as a young man, the future Pope Pius II also wrote irreverent and scabrous verses, of which he was later ashamed. The *Decameron* (ten tales for each of ten days) of Giovanni Boccaccio (d. 1375) was a compilation of racy stories told in a hedonistic spirit by worldlings who, trying to insulate themselves from the plague, learned a moral lesson—inevitably they all succumbed to the plague.

Pride and Avarice

Classical authors also encouraged pride in the achievement of fame and power, with the accumulation of wealth merely taken for granted. Valla was a realist in politics, seeing the drive for power as dominant and finding no virtue in obeying the law, since in politics *virtue* (from the Latin word for "a male") meant forceful action. Bracciolini held that men were governed by avarice and could be lifted up only by divine grace. Even the monastic life did not bring happiness.

Civic Humanism

Whereas in the North, students not destined for an academic career aspired to church positions, in Italy many became civic officials or bureaucrats, devoting their lives to the interests of their particular cities, a revival of the classical idea of citizenship as the principal avenue of human fulfillment: civic Humanism.

Usury

In the commercial, northern Italian cities, the official prohibition on usury was a serious issue, since banking was one of the principal industries. (Florentine bankers served as papal tax collectors.) St. Antoninus, archbishop of Florence (d. 1459), was both an austere reformer of the clergy and a theologian who cautiously allowed charging interest on loans that were made for investment purposes.

Fame

The culture of Renaissance Italy was under the patronage of ambitious and successful men who commissioned portraits of themselves as a way of displaying their achievements and preserving their memories (the "Fame" of which the Romans had made so much), looking out from their portraits with varying expressions of pride and self-satisfaction.

Funeral monuments became increasingly elaborate, with the body encased in a coffin before burial and the tomb not only asking for prayers but summarizing the deceased's achievements. The tomb of a prince might be surrounded by statues of priests and courtiers weeping and praying on his behalf. For the first time, tombs also bore images that appear to have been realistic likenesses of the deceased, sometimes as though asleep, sometimes with eyes open, awaiting judgment.

Uneasy Consciences

But consciences were not fully at ease. Merchants and bankers who enjoyed wealth and civic prestige often commissioned works of religious art, even built entire churches, as acts of penance for having been too worldly. Sometimes a commissioned painting displayed the mixture of piety and pride that lay behind it: a scene of Christ's Nativity, for example, with the patron and his family kneeling at the crib along with the shepherds.

Cloister and World

The medieval Church's exaltation of the monastic life did not fit readily with Humanism. However, Petrarch, although he was scathing in his criticism of the worldliness of prelates, defended religious life, as did Salutati. But Valla questioned why the term *religious* should be reserved for those who took vows, and he denied that there was a hierarchy of callings in the Church. Some lay people were exposed to greater perils in the world than are monks in the cloister and therefore deserved greater credit, he thought, while many religious acted out of fear. Against the Franciscans, Valla argued that it was not necessary to become a beggar in order to help beggars and it was better to practice spiritual rather than material poverty.

Human and Divine

Some humanists ultimately broke decisively with Aristotle by denying in effect that men had any fixed nature. Ficino thought that men stood outside the fixed order of the cosmos, imitating God in their creative powers and using natural magic as an extension of those powers. As Plato taught, both poets and mystics suffered from a kind of "divine madness".

In their striving to become everything, Ficino announced, men manifested their desire to be like God and their refusal to admit their own limitations. The desire for fame, for example, was really the desire for eternity. Unhappiness therefore stemmed from man's discontent, his peculiar nature that left him unsatisfied. Man created human society because of his unwillingness to face his own loneliness. The reality of this yearning made it unthinkable that men should not be immortal, even divine.

Manetti too argued against Innocent III's exhortation to despise the world and even compared man to the mythical Prometheus, who stole fire from the gods, except that the Christian shaped nature by making use of his God-given powers. Men should not consider themselves lowly, although—because man was reluctant to allow any authority higher than himself—the excellence of human nature was a temptation to sin.

Happiness

Two humanists of Bologna engaged in a print debate over human happiness, with Giovanni Garzoni (d. 1505) emphasizing the Fall of Adam and the human misery stemming from it and Benedetto Morandi (d. 1478) finding each instance of misery to be part of some greater, perhaps unseen, good. The capacity for laughter was a sign of fundamental human happiness, Morandi argued.

Morandi was one of the very few humanists to depart explicitly from Christian orthodoxy, daringly implying that sexual morality was largely a matter of social custom and that suicide was appropriate within the context of pagan ethics. Also unusual for his time, he seems to have believed in the idea of progress: that change makes the world better.

The Summit of Freedom

Pico's *Oration on the Dignity of Man* became perhaps the most famous of all Renaissance texts. Like Ficino, he departed from the traditional idea of a fixed hierarchy of human society and instead celebrated human subjectivity, which gave man the freedom to aspire to the level of the divine but also carried with it the possibility of a great fall.

Traditional Piety

In spite of affluence and Humanism, traditional piety still had a strong influence, even among people who might have seemed to have fallen into a kind of neo-pagan worldliness. Pico was notorious for his sexual escapades, but toward the end of his short life, he considered becoming a monk. Bernardino of Siena, John of Capistrano, and others were immensely popular practitioners of revival preaching, which reached its climax with the Florentine Dominican Girolamo Savonarola (d. 1498).

Savonarola

Florence was the most sophisticated city in Europe, but in 1494, the year of Pico's death, Savonarola, influenced by Joachim of Flora's speculations about the end times, appeared as a prophet of fire and brimstone, warning the Florentines that their worldly ways would lead to eternal damnation. Perhaps surprisingly, many (including Pico) took his message to heart and came forward to throw rich tapestries, clothes, jewels, even books and paintings, onto the "bonfire of the vanities"[11] that Savonarola kindled. The great artist Sandro Boticelli (d. 1510) burned some of his own paintings of pagan subjects.

Savonarola's political involvements caused his undoing. He opposed the ruling Medici family and became an increasingly harsh critic of Pope Alexander VI, who arranged for Savonarola to be burned at the stake on a trumped-up charge of heresy.

Machiavelli

In his famous book *The Prince* (1513), Niccolò Machiavelli (d. 1527) in a sense unwittingly brought humanist optimism to an end, by drawing out the full implications of the natural desire for power— virtue as forceful action—that Valla had identified as the true nature of politics. Machiavelli was the first political thinker to ignore the moral basis of politics and to offer instead a purely realistic analysis, a picture of a world without higher law. (Not insignificantly, he modeled his amoral prince on Cesare Borgia, the son of Pope Alexander VI.)

Although he may have been a believing Catholic, Machiavelli thought the Christian virtues of humility and charity made men weak and vulnerable, and he extolled the ancient pagan religions for fostering virility and boldness. If the prince wished to retain power, Machiavelli advised, he could not be restrained by moral or religious scruples but had to employ terror, deceit, and treachery as necessary. Many people were shocked by Machiavelli's emptying politics of moral content, so that after him an unreservedly optimistic Humanism was no longer possible.

---

[11] The title of a modern novel by Thomas Wolfe, made into a film.

The Visual Arts

The great flowering of art in the Renaissance was in theory a return to the styles of Greece and Rome, but in reality it was one of the greatest bursts of originality in the history of the world.

Architecture

Classical architecture was based on symmetrical harmonies that medieval buildings, with their towers of different heights, flying buttresses, and almost chaotic forests of sculptured figures, often violated. In the 1420s, the Gothic cathedral of Florence was completed by being capped not with a high tower but with a great dome—the largest in the West since Roman times—designed by Filippo Brunelleschi (d. 1446). Thereafter, domes continued to increase in fashion, culminating in St. Peter's in Rome in the later sixteenth century. (Petrarch was the first to dub the medieval cathedrals "Gothic", meaning "barbaric" and "crude", in contrast to classical architecture.) But much of the wealth, effort, and pride that had been invested in cathedrals during the High Middle Ages was now directed into constructing town halls and the urban palaces of the rich.

The Nude

Pictures and statues of nude persons were produced during the Renaissance for the first time since Roman days. While viewers were obviously not insensitive to its erotic content, according to classical theory, the principal purpose of nude art was to celebrate the beauty of the human body, with a perfectly proportioned body reflecting the perfection of the soul.

Religious Themes

Artistic creativity continued to be devoted primarily to religion. A census of Renaissance paintings and sculptures would probably show that three-quarters still portrayed biblical subjects or the lives of the saints, culminating in the great *Pietà* of Michelangelo Buonarroti (d. 1564).

Portraits

But the art of portraiture—likenesses of people that were flattering but also recognizable—was also a humanist rediscovery. During the Middle Ages, the sculptured images of kings and popes, for example, were stereotyped and idealized, not representations of individuals but of the offices they held. Now both sculpture and the revived art of painting on canvas or wood began to show individuals as they really were, even with the crooked noses or bald heads that captured their individuality. Humanist values were also manifest in scenes that captured, for example, the love between husband and wife or parents and children and in a new genre of historical painting representing scenes from classical antiquity or the triumphs of later princes.

Levels of Meaning

The new art could have meaning on several different levels simultaneously. Michelangelo's statue of the biblical *David* was commissioned by the city of Florence and, besides its religious significance,
was meant to celebrate the city's victory over powerful enemies, even
as the boy David had slain the giant Goliath. Michelangelo also
took the opportunity to display a well-proportioned nude body and
demonstrated his genius at making hard marble look like sinews and
flesh.

Later, on the ceiling of the Sistine Chapel in the Vatican (named
for Sixtus IV, who had it built), Michelangelo painted the unfallen
Adam as a perfect human specimen, his muscled body displayed to
fullest advantage as he stretched out his arm to touch the finger of
God, who Himself appeared as an impressive human figure.

Papal Patronage

Even before Savonarola's time, papal support for the new cultural movements was almost complete, not least among some of the more notorious pontiffs of the age, who seemed to imbibe the classical spirit of
easy worldliness.

Beginning with Nicholas V, almost every pope supported Humanism, with the papal court itself becoming a major employer of humanist scholars. Rome had fallen into ruins during the era of the Avignon
Papacy, and Nicholas commissioned some of the greatest artists and
architects to begin an ambitious rebuilding program that lasted two
hundred years. He moved the papal headquarters from the Lateran to
the Vatican and turned the Vatican Library into the greatest collection
of manuscripts in the West. Pius II was himself a noted humanist—his
use of a pagan name (Aeneas Sylvius) being a fashion among humanists—
but he also spent his pontificate in a vain effort to mount yet another
crusade.

Rome

Around 1500, Rome began to supplant Florence as the artistic center,
with more and more artists placing themselves under papal patronage.
Raphael (Sanzio, d. 1520) decorated the papal apartments, and his many
paintings fixed permanently in people's minds the image of the biblical world.

Michelangelo

The strong-willed warrior Pope Julius II was the greatest of the papal
patrons of the arts, commissioning Michelangelo to paint the Sistine
ceiling and to design the original plan for St. Peter's Basilica. He
had strong opinions about these and other works he desired from
Michelangelo and frequently quarreled with the equally strong-
willed artist.

The Northern Renaissance

Burgundy

In the North, the dukes of Burgundy, whose territories included much of the Low Countries as well as parts of France, also patronized art and learning, making Bruges and Ghent centers of a kind of Renaissance. Here, too, much of the art was religious in nature, for example, *The Adoration of the Lamb* by Jan Van Eyck (d. 1441), the first accomplished use of three-dimensional perspective in painting.

Northern Humanism

Northerners were aware of Italian Humanism and often made sojourns in Italy to imbibe it, but some northerners found Italian Humanism too pagan. Some were also scandalized by the worldliness of the papal court. Partly because it interacted with the New Devotion, northern Humanism developed in more consistently Christian ways than in Italy.

Paradoxically, however, this had the consequence that northern humanists were often sharp critics of the Church and even sometimes crossed into heresy, as Italians seldom did. To some extent, there was a spirit of tenacious bluntness in the North that demanded answers to troublesome questions, in contrast to a kind of easygoing sophistication in Italy.

Gansfort

Wessel Gansfort (d. 1489) was a Netherlander educated by the Brethren of the Common Life and personally acquainted with Thomas à Kempis. He remained a layman, learned Greek and Hebrew, and taught at the Sorbonne, where he dismissed even Aquinas as someone whose Latin was faulty and who knew no Greek. For a time, Gansfort was in the service of the scandalous Pope Sixtus IV, who protected him from accusations of heresy. Later he returned to his native Netherlands, where he had considerable influence over younger scholars.

Gansfort epitomized the uncertainties of the age. Under the influence of certain mystical writings, he exalted the power of divine love, which draws everything to itself and renders lesser things unnecessary. Although he insisted that he would believe nothing contrary to the faith, at various times he seemed to teach the primacy of Scripture over the Church, justification by faith, and the priesthood of all believers. He sometimes appeared to deny Transubstantiation, indulgences, Purgatory, and the need for confession.

Rufus

Mutianus Rufus (d. ca. 1526), a priest and yet another product of the Brethren's schools, was influenced by Platonism to the point of almost seeming to become a kind of Manichaean, denying that the carnal side of man had any relationship to God, minimizing Jesus' human nature, and respecting the sacraments only as symbols of divine love. Since the birth of Christ occurred before all the ages, there was truth in all religions, Mutianus claimed, and he frequently cited the Qur'an.

Celtis

Conradus Celtis (d. 1508) was unusual among Northern Humanists in not having been educated by the Brethren and even more unusual in being a kind of pagan in his open embrace of hedonism, his exaltation of human love, and his composition of erotic love poetry. Anti-papal and a fierce German patriot, he urged his fellow Germans to harass the Romans as their barbarian ancestors had done, and he praised the ancient Germanic myths as equal in value to those of the Greeks and Romans. Celtis acquired a vague mystical idea of God from Pseudo-Dionysius and Nicholas of Cusa, but he doubted the immortality of the soul. He ridiculed Transubstantiation and other Catholic doctrines, although he also had a certain semi-superstitious devotion to the Virgin Mary and the saints.

Johannes Reuchlin (d. 1522) learned Hebrew in order to study the Old Testament and the *Kabbalah*, which he learned about from Pico and which he thought contained secret divine revelation handed down from the time of Adam. Because of Reuchlin, the Dominicans of Cologne obtained a ban on the reading of Hebrew books, an act that provoked a fierce quarrel in which humanists satirized the Scholastics as willfully ignorant. But a few years later, Leo X (1513–1522) sponsored the publication of the Talmud in Rome.

Reuchlin

Jacques Lefèvre d'Étaples (Jacobus Faber Stapulensis, d. 1536) was the leading French humanist of the age, influenced both by mysticism and by Neo-Platonism. He made a Latin translation of Paul's Letters that seemed to express the doctrine of justification by faith, and later he produced the first French Bible. With Lefèvre, emphasis on the literal sense became a hallmark of the humanist approach to the Bible.

Lefèvre

The English priest John Colet (d. 1519), although he studied in Italy, thought that the pagan classics had no relevance to Christianity. Deeply influenced by Pseudo-Dionysius (although Valla had denied the alleged identity of that writer), Colet also rejected the Scholastic idea of theology as a science, believing instead that wisdom was attained only through divine illumination. Colet devoted his scholarship to Paul's Letters, paying close attention to the words and to literary style in order to expound their meaning with a fresh eye, largely ignoring centuries of commentaries by theologians.

Colet

Colet combined the love of learning with a reforming zeal that was characteristic of some Christian humanists. He denounced the financial burdens placed on the laity, the abuse of benefices, and legalism, exhorting the clergy to begin to reform the Church by reforming themselves. In a sermon before the court of Henry VIII (1509–1547), he condemned the propensity of Christians to make war on one another.

Colet befriended the Netherlandish humanist Desiderius Erasmus (Erasmus of Rotterdam, d. 1536) and persuaded him to turn his attentions away from purely literary pursuits and to the Bible itself. In time,

Erasmus

Erasmus became the "prince of humanists" and the most influential intellectual of his age.

Erasmus embodied the religious ambiguities of his time. He was of illegitimate birth, his father (he thought) probably a priest. Educated by the Brethren of the Common Life, he imbibed their devotion to simple biblical piety but found their spirit overly rigid and narrow. Aspiring to a life of learning, he entered a branch of the Augustinians but found monastic life also too constricting and left to become secretary to a bishop. Later, when asked to return to the monastery, he protested that he had been too young (seventeen) even to understand what he was doing when he became a monk. His canonical status remained irregular for many years, until he received papal permission to live in effect as a layman.

A Severe Critic

Erasmus was the rare scholar who was also capable of reaching a general audience—those who knew Latin but were not specialists. Throughout his career, he questioned, usually through satire, many aspects of traditional Catholicism: the superstitions of simple people, the hypocrisy of monks and nuns, and academic theology. No one skewered clerical misconduct more effectively than Erasmus, especially in his *Praise of Folly*, which ridiculed both clergy and laity, the high and the low. In the anonymous satire *Julius Excluded* (attributed to Erasmus), the worldly Julius II was denied entry into Heaven because St. Peter did not recognize the bellicose pontiff.

Erasmus wrote a treatise on the education of the Christian prince that was an anticipatory refutation of Machiavelli, emphasizing the need to inculcate Christian virtues in the prince from an early age, so that he would rule entirely for the good of his people, with no thought to his own glory. Like Colet, Eramus thought the prevalence of war among Christians was the greatest betrayal of the Gospel.

A master rhetorician, he was deliberately ambiguous about his real thoughts. Especially from his satires, many people inferred conclusions that Erasmus himself did not state forthrightly, e.g., not only was the monastic life corrupt, it was not an authentic Christian vocation; not only did sacramental ritual foster credulous superstitions, it was an obstacle to faith; and not only was the great edifice of formal dogma remote from the spirit of the Gospel, it was a distortion of Christ's teaching. Some of those who drew these conclusions condemned Erasmus as a heretic, while others welcomed him as a liberator from religious tyranny.

The Greek New Testament

His principal life's work was the recovery of what he considered authentic early Christianity, especially the Fathers of the Church, by making use of the tools of learning. Although he favored vernacular translations of the Bible, his greatest achievement was an edition of the Greek New Testament, based on the best manuscripts he could find and published alongside the Vulgate. His Greek text did not differ from the Vulgate in any crucial way, but it raised two nagging questions: whether for centuries the Bible might have been misunderstood, because no one in the West had access to its original text, and whether scholars like Erasmus could question doctrines and practices on that basis.

Philosophy of Christ
Erasmianism became a reform program with fluid boundaries, aimed at the simplification of the Christian life, made possible by a direct encounter with the Gospel as originally written. He called it the "philosophy of Christ", a deliberately paradoxical phrase, in that Christ was not a philosopher in an academic sense.

St. Thomas More (d. 1535), a friend of both Colet and Erasmus, was an English layman who entered the service of King Henry VIII partly in order to fulfill the humanist hope of marrying wisdom to power. Despite their close friendship, More was unlike Erasmus in his very traditional kind of piety. While studying law, he lived in a Carthusian monastery and was powerfully attracted to the monastic life, eventually abandoning that idea, perhaps because did not feel able to live celibately.

Thomas More

Like Erasmus, More championed humanist learning. His best-known work, *Utopia* ("nowhere"), was an account of a fictional society that, even though lacking Christian revelation, was based on principles of natural justice and shamed Christians who, despite the benefit of the Gospel, had done worse.

The intellectual life of the West changed dramatically in the 1450s with the invention of movable type, which allowed ideas to be spread far more rapidly than was possible through the painstaking copying of manuscripts by hand. Parts of the Bible were naturally among the first products of the new invention; and as the Middle Ages came to an end, a biblically based Christian Humanism stood at the center of the troubled religious life of northern Europe.

Printing

9   Reform and Counter-Reform

The Catholic Reformation

On the eve of the Protestant Reformation, the Catholic Church simultaneously manifested both deep piety and corruption; the religious environment was both rich and confusing.

Lateran V

The Fifth Lateran Council (1512–1517) was the first serious official attempt to reform the Church, although the very circumstances of its meeting revealed the problems. In accord with conciliarist theory, and with royal support in France and Germany, several cardinals summoned a council at Pisa. To counter it, Pope Julius II, who was scarcely a reformer, convened a council at Rome.

True Reform

The most prominent figure at Lateran V was Giles of Viterbo (d. 1532), the general of the Augustinians, who articulated the orthodox Catholic idea that "Religion reforms men; men do not reform religion", meaning that true reform ("to form again") consists simply in bringing one's behavior into accord with truth. Giles recalled the Church of his own day to the purity of the primitive Church and, like Colet and Erasmus, denounced the propensity of Christian kings to make war on one another. He was quite blunt in blaming recent popes for most of the abuses in the Church, but he also professed great hope for Leo X (1513–1521), who had succeeded Julius II.

The Evangelical Spirit

The revival of sacred learning and the discovery of the New World marked the beginning of a great new era, Giles predicted, and—ironically, in view of what would soon happen—so too did the great project to build a new St. Peter's Basilica in Rome. Giles was an "evangelical" insofar as he advocated a closer study of Scripture and the still-controversial use of the Hebrew Old Testament, though he referred to "obstinate Jews", who he believed willfully ignored the meaning of their own prophecies.

Abuses

The bishops at Lateran V were highly critical of the religious orders, because of their semi-independence from episcopal control and their

248

sometimes scandalous behavior. According to one participant, the Council would actually have suppressed the friars had it not been for Leo's personal intervention. Lateran V issued a compendium of condemnations against worldly prelates, bishops neglecting their responsibilities, and cardinals living away from Rome. The Council Fathers castigated the clergy for irregular ways of attaining benefices, nepotism, and unchastity. But the Council was not ready for sweeping reforms, as shown in the fact that it still permitted bishops to hold two benefices.

The Council condemned Averroism, which was still taught in some of the Italian universities, but did not address other questionable schools of thought. Like other councils, Lateran V took notice of apparently small things that it thought had significance, urging, for example, the establishment of pawn shops[1] under Church auspices, to provide affordable loans to the poor.

The sudden and explosive eruption of religious dissent immediately after Lateran V to a great extent destroyed the possibility of moderate, gradual reform. But significant reform movements predated the Council and continued to flourish for decades.

Jiménez

The Spanish church was to some extent reformed around 1500, mainly under the leadership of Cardinal Francisco Jiménez de Cisneros (d. 1517), a Franciscan who also served as the confessor to Queen Isabella of Castile (1479–1504). Personally austere, Jiménez warred on clerical corruption—on one occasion, he even shipped a boatload of uncelibate priests across to Muslim North Africa. He also opposed, as too mercenary, the collection for the new St. Peter's Basilica. In the spirit of the Christian humanist movement, Jiménez founded the new University of Alcalá for the education of the higher clergy and encouraged the scholars there to produce a Bible with the Hebrew and Greek texts alongside the Vulgate.

Reforming Bishops

There were also reforming bishops in Italy and France. Gian Matteo Giberti of Verona (d. 1543) set the pattern for later prelates by his vigorous reform of his clergy, his austere personal life, and his conspicuous concern for the poor. The French bishop Guillaume Briçonnet (d. 1534) briefly made his diocese of Meaux a center of pastoral evangelicalism, harboring both Lefèvre and several people who in time became Protestants.

New Religious Communities

As with every reform in the history of the Church, much of the impetus originated with visionary leaders who battled corruption within the religious orders. Often such efforts resulted in the founding of new religious communities.

---

[1] The pawn shop symbol of three gold balls was originally the symbol of the Medici banking house.

Capuchins

The split within the Franciscan order was resolved in 1517, when the Conventuals were officially separated from Observants, with the two distinguished externally by their respective black and brown habits. But the perennial issue of poverty led Matteo da Bascio (d. 1552) to found a third branch in 1525. Its members were called Capuchins because of the distinctive style of their hoods, and they wore rough, untrimmed beards, in disregard of fashion.[2] The Capuchins espoused radical poverty, and they devoted themselves to works of charity and to preaching in a plain, emotional style popular with common people.

Ursulines

St. Angela Merici (d. 1540) was a lay woman, affiliated with the Franciscans, who brought together a group of consecrated virgins whom she named the Company of St. Ursula, who, according to legend, had been martyred with numerous other virgins by barbarians. The members of the new community continued to live with their families but followed an intense spiritual regimen. Teaching children and ministering to the poor, they might have become the first active community of sisters in the history of the Church, but after Angela's death, the Ursulines were required to become a cloistered order.

Hospitalers

St. John of God (d. 1550) and St. Camillus de Lellis (d. 1614) were soldiers—one Portuguese, the other Italian—who lived worldly lives before conversion. They both founded orders to nurse the sick: respectively, the Brothers Hospitalers and the Ministers of the Sick.

Oratory of Divine Love

The Oratory of Divine Love was founded in Venice—in some ways Europe's most worldly city—by a group of pious priests and laymen who sought to live a genuine Christian life. Three of these men would become major figures in the Catholic Reformation.

Gasparo Contarini (d. 1542) was the scion of a noble Venetian family and served his city as a diplomat. Like many devout people of his time, he was dissatisfied with purely formal piety, and in 1511, he had a religious experience similar to the one Martin Luther would have a few years later, an experience that left him acutely aware of his own sinfulness, the futility of human effort, and his absolute dependence on God's grace. The fact that he remained a layman was indicative of the uncertainties of the age, in that, traditionally, a conversion experience like his would have led to a monastery. Instead, Contarini entered the papal service and was eventually raised to the cardinalate, accepting ordination only when he was named a bishop.

---

[2] Reputedly, the word *cappuccino*—a drink of coffee and whipped cream—comes from the brown of the Capuchin robes and the white of their beards.

Reginald Pole (d. 1558) was an Englishman of royal blood who imbibed the humanist spirit in Italy and befriended Contarini. He returned to England for a time but left in 1530. A third founder of the Oratory, Gian Pietro Carafa, was a bishop and papal diplomat who eventually ascended the papal throne as Paul IV (1555–1559).

Theatines

From the Oratory of Divine Love, there developed a new religious community, founded in 1524 by a bishop, St. Cajetan of Thiene (d. 1547), and dubbed the Theatines after his diocese. Its members, including Carafa, adopted a way of life different from that of both the monks and the friars. They wore no distinct habit and did not chant the Divine Office in common, but devoted themselves to preaching and to works of charity.

The Spirituals

Contarini and Pole were at the center of a loosely unified group that came to be called the "Spirituals", because they identified the principal problem of the Church as the absence of deep inner faith and urged spiritual regeneration as the essence of reform. They were attracted to the Pauline doctrine of justification by faith, because it demanded the inner conversion of the believer. They were wary of the idea of "good works", for fear that it would encourage formalism and reliance on human effort.

The Zealots

Carafa, although linked with Contarini and Pole by a commitment to the reform of the Church, nonetheless looked on the Spirituals with increasing suspicion. He became in effect the head of a rival reform party dubbed the "Zealots" because of their eagerness to use disciplinary means to correct both heresy and moral disorders.

By far the most influential of the new religious communities was the Society (originally Company) of Jesus, whose enemies sarcastically pinned on them a negative epithet that stuck—Jesuits. The order was founded by St. Ignatius Loyola (d. 1556), who was another converted soldier. A minor Spanish nobleman imbued with the spirit of chivalry, Ignatius was a tradition-minded but highly intelligent man with a sense that a changing world required something new, whatever that might be.

Society of Jesus

Knight of Christ

Ignatius' decisive experience of this new world came during a battle in which his leg was shattered by a cannon ball, a new technology that rendered traditional chivalry obsolete.[3] During his long convalescence,

---

[3] Ignatius at this period of his life has sometimes been compared to the fictional character Don Quixote created half a century later, a heroic but somewhat pathetic figure who struggled to live according to ideals of chivalry that were no longer viable.

Ignatius read all the tales of knightly daring he could find, then turned to the lives of the saints. Recognizing the saints as more heroic than the fabled knights, Ignatius was struck with a burning desire to be a knight for Christ.

An Uncertain Calling

Ignatius left his sickbed determined to do God's will but with only a hazy sense of what that might be. At first, he explored traditional channels: visiting monasteries, living for a time as a hermit, imagining a crusade against the Muslims, and actually visiting the Holy Land, where the Franciscans found him rather dangerously rambunctious and advised him to return home.

Ignatius the Student

Sensing the need for an education, whatever use it might have, he practiced humility by sitting with children to learn Latin, then enrolled successively in two Spanish universities. In each, he encountered the spiritual sterility about which reformers complained, which led him to offer guidance to his fellow students, especially concerning sin. This got him into trouble with the Inquisition, under the suspicion that, though a layman, he was in effect assuming the priestly office. But when interrogated, Ignatius was found to be orthodox and was merely warned to cease giving spiritual direction.

The Company Formed

He next went to the University of Paris, then the intellectual center of the Catholic world, and there he attracted a small band of companions, most of them laymen like himself, who sought to live the spiritual life in a serious way. In 1534, they took private vows. Ignatius still hoped to go to the Holy Land to convert the Muslims, so he and his companions went to Venice and waited unsuccessfully for a year to get a ship for the Near East.

Their failure caused Ignatius to conclude that such was not God's will. Instead he and his companions went to Rome to place themselves in the hands of the pope. By now, all of them were priests, and they went about performing basic apostolic tasks—visiting the sick, aiding the poor, instructing children, preaching, hearing confessions, and offering spiritual direction. Although they attracted a following, their unofficial status and the bluntness of some of their preaching also made them enemies, including important members of the hierarchy.

Official Approval

Contarini, however, befriended them, and in 1540, Paul III (1534–1547) recognized them as a new religious order, allegedly exclaiming as he did so, "I see the finger of God here!" The rule that Ignatius presented for papal approval was to some extent similar to that of the Theatines and was in certain ways revolutionary: it departed almost entirely from the patterns of monastic life, even the modified monasticism of the friars. Controversial though it initially was, the Jesuit rule became the model followed by most of the male religious orders founded after their time.

A New Rule

Ordinarily, Jesuits were to live in communities, but Ignatius foresaw that in some cases that might not be possible. They wore no distinctive habit but only the conventional dress of the diocesan clergy. The most controversial feature of their life was that not only did they not gather in the chapel to recite the Divine Office in common, they were actually forbidden to chant it and enjoined to recite it privately.

The point of all this was to orient the Jesuit toward activity in the world, eliminating those things that might impede apostolic zeal. Against the concern that such a regimen might produce worldly men with no spiritual depth, Ignatius prescribed an unusually long period of training and an intense program of personal prayer and meditation, so that, even if a Jesuit found himself away from a community for long years, he might continue to grow in the spiritual life.

A Fourth Vow

All Jesuits took the traditional vows of poverty, chastity, and obedience, and an elite took a fourth vow of special obedience to the pope. Whereas Francis of Assisi had made poverty the keynote of his community, Ignatius emphasized obedience, based on the paradox that free will is most fully exercised by free acts of submission.

Obedience

Unlike the quasi-republican structure of the monastic orders, Ignatius created a highly centralized organization, possibly on a military model, possibly on the model of the absolute monarchies of his day. A Father General was elected by a small number of "delegates" and served for life, with a chain of command emanating downward through regional superiors to individual priests and brothers. Unusual among religious orders in that time, the Society of Jesus had no female branch, and Ignatius forbade Jesuits to give spiritual direction to women.

Holy Pragmatism

Ignatian spirituality could be characterized as a kind of holy pragmatism. In searching for God's will in his own life, Ignatius responded to what he saw as immediate needs, as when he gave spiritual guidance to his fellow students. Also while a student, he often spent long nights in prayer, until he concluded that, if God wanted him to be a student, he needed sufficient time for sleep and study. Asceticism, therefore, was to be practiced by his men only in moderation, so as to maintain the health and strength needed for work.

The Jesuits adopted the motto *Ad majorem Dei gloriam* ("For the greater glory of God"). They discerned God's will with severe detachment, without regard for one's own desires, exclusively in terms of how one might best promote divine glory. Having discerned God's will, it was then necessary to determine the best means of fulfilling it and to pursue those means systematically.

Ignatius instructed his men to judge, in particular situations, the most effective way of winning people to Christ—sometimes boldly and sternly, sometimes softly and by indirection—advising Jesuits to "listen much, say little" until they could discern how best to achieve their purposes. ("Enter by the other man's door; lead him out through yours.") They were to be at ease with both the humble and the exalted, each in the appropriate way, something made possible by their cultivation of "detachment"—having no inner love of worldly things but making use of them insofar as they served the divine purpose.

A Variety of Apostolates

Having been forced to abandon hope of converting the Muslims in the Holy Land, Ignatius directed the early Jesuits toward a variety of roles: theologians and controversialists, advisors to princes, preachers, confessors, pastors, and missionaries. Quite early, Ignatius sent St. Francis Xavier (d. 1555), perhaps his most beloved companion, to the Orient, from which Xavier never returned, and in time, the Jesuits became the largest missionary order in the Church. Because of their missionary zeal, their learning, and perhaps because of their reputation for subtlety, Jesuits were sometimes employed as papal nuncios.

Education

Although the Jesuits eventually came to be thought of primarily as educators, Ignatius was at first reluctant to undertake that work, because it would tie men down to particular institutions, but he was eventually persuaded to acquiesce. Jesuits founded or taught in several universities, and a network of Jesuit secondary schools sprang up all over Catholic Europe in the later sixteenth century. Ignatius was deeply suspicious of Erasmus, but Jesuit education incorporated the study of the classics along with Scholastic philosophy, and it advanced humanist culture by encouraging religious drama.

Rapid Growth

Evidence that Ignatius had indeed discerned the needs of the time was the fact that, except perhaps for the early Franciscans, no religious order in the history of the Church grew more rapidly than the Jesuits in the first few generations of their existence. By 1627, the order had grown to more than sixteen thousand men.

The Protestant Reformation

Luther

As Lateran V drew to a solemn close in 1517, Giles of Viterbo was doubtlessly unaware that, as general of the Augustinians, he was the ultimate superior of a man who, within a few months, would ensure that most of the Council's decrees were forgotten. Although great events are never the work of one man, the life of the German monk Martin

Luther (d. 1546) embodied the late medieval religious crisis in all its dimensions. Christendom was ripe for an explosion, and he lit the match.

The Monk

Luther was in many ways a medieval man, taking for granted that the monastic life was the highest way of living the Christian life and entering a monastery after making an impulsive vow of the kind at which Erasmus would have scoffed. At a time of much corruption in religious life, Luther was a member of a reformed Augustinian house and claimed that on a trip to Rome he was scandalized by the worldliness, even the apparent blasphemous skepticism, of some of the clergy.

Education

Like so many, Luther was educated by the Brethren of the Common Life. Although he had some knowledge of the classics and advocated humanist education as a way of studying the Bible, he was not himself a humanist. When he translated the Bible into German (not the first to do so) he translated from the Vulgate, not from the Hebrew and Greek texts.

Like the humanists, Luther became convinced that Scholastic theology was a distortion of Christian teaching—more Aristotle than Christ. He was trained in nominalist theology and was familiar with Tauler's mystical writings, both of which perhaps gave him his acute sense of God as remote, all-powerful, angry, and condemnatory. Since the will of God was both supreme and inscrutable, men could not ask why they were slaves to sin but simply had to accept the promise of salvation.

Despair

Struggling to be a good monk, and assured by his superiors that he was succeeding, Luther was nonetheless almost paralyzed by the conviction that, despite his best efforts, he was damned, that he was hateful in the sight of God, who saw his every sin and did not forgive him. But at some point, while Lateran V was in session, Luther, rereading Paul's Letter to the Romans, was struck for the first time by what he understood to be the true meaning of the statement: "The just man lives by faith" (see Rom 1:17). Suddenly everything fell into place for him, as he saw his oppressive sense of his own sinfulness not as pathological but as a true understanding of the condition of all men, who were indeed hateful in God's eyes and indeed deserved damnation.

Law and Gospel

Luther then opposed Law to Gospel. The Law was given by God not for man to fulfill, or even to approximate, but in order to show him his utter inability to overcome his sinfulness. The good news of the Gospel was the promise of salvation despite crippling sin—salvation by faith alone, by personal trust in the saving actions of Christ. For Luther, the Church had failed in her most basic task. She could not offer people a sure road to salvation, because she gave them a false sense of their own goodness, based on a concept of natural virtue and on pious practices ("good works").

An Indulgence

Unpredictably, in 1517, Luther's personal spiritual breakthrough exploded into a cataclysmic public conflict, triggered by the papal proclamation of an indulgence to raise funds for the building of St. Peter's Basilica. Some of the money collected in Germany also went to the archbishop of Mainz, to help him pay for the exemptions he had obtained from Rome in connection with his multiple benefices, but this scandalous fact was unknown to Luther and most other people.

Technically, the indulgence was not being sold; recipients had to be truly repentant of their sins, as well as give money, and poor people could gain the indulgence without payment. But even some orthodox theologians considered the practice of granting indulgences overly mechanical and self-centered, and some of the indulgence preachers, notably the Dominican Johann Tetzel (d. 1519), were extremely aggressive and appeared to be engaged in a sordid trade.

On any list of Catholic doctrines, indulgences would not rank near the top in importance, but they proved to be precisely the point where the Church was most vulnerable, because many things came together there in a concrete way: anxiety about sin and salvation, the credibility of official teaching, the significance of external acts, the rapaciousness of some of the clergy, and the apparent sale of a spiritual good.

Ninety-Five Theses

A professor at the University of Wittenberg, Luther formulated his Ninety-Five Theses (which he may or may not have posted on a church door) after encountering people who proudly displayed their indulgence certificates. The Theses were less an act of defiance than an invitation to debate a highly sensitive subject, although not in a spirit of academic detachment, because Luther believed that the salvation of souls was at stake. Without quite saying so, Luther seemed to deny the efficacy of indulgences altogether and even the existence of Purgatory. He implied that there were no temporal punishments due to sins that were forgiven and that good works could not remit those punishments. Such teaching, Luther believed, was a distortion, not actual Catholic doctrine, thus he did not condemn merely the "sale" of indulgences but indulgences themselves.

"Cheap Grace"

Although Luther has come down in history as a champion of human freedom against institutional tyranny, he actually accused the Church of being too easygoing, of falsely assuring people of salvation and thereby short-circuiting their process of repentance. But his anxiety also stemmed from his belief that, in requiring people to confess their sins and to overcome them, the Church was imposing an impossible burden. Christians should instead accept the reality of sin and rely entirely on divine mercy, since, in Luther's view, sin is not so much specific actions as it is man's very nature, his fundamental orientation toward evil.

"A Monkish Quarrel"

The Theses were quickly and widely disseminated, in both accurate and spurious versions, all over Germany and beyond. This widespread distribution, something made possible by the printing press, gave Luther an international influence that Hus, exactly a century before, did not achieve. Leo X initially dismissed the indulgence dispute as a "monkish quarrel" between Augustinians and Dominicans, but he was soon persuaded that the issues were serious and at first tried to use both the carrot and the stick.

"Sola Scriptura"

But Luther remained adamant. His decisive break with the Church occurred in 1519, when he entered into formal debate with the theologian Johann Eck (d. 1543). When Eck demonstrated that the doctrine and practice of indulgences were official Catholic teaching, Luther appealed first from the pope to a general council, then from a council to Scripture, proclaiming that the Bible alone ("*sola scriptura*") was the locus of authority.

Luther published three pamphlets that set forth his basic theology and sharpened his attack on Catholic doctrine. He condemned all "man-made" laws as contrary to the Gospel and charged that such things as indulgences and Purgatory were devised by Church authorities merely to control gullible people and extract money from them.

Condemnation

Leo then formally condemned Luther and excommunicated him in a bull that began, "Arise, O Lord, for a wild boar is loose in the vineyards of the Church." Luther responded with a public burning of the bull and of the Code of Canon Law. The next year he was summoned before Emperor Charles V (1519–1555) and the German princes at the Diet of Worms. (The Diet, from the Latin word for "day", was the parliament of the Empire.) There Luther made a famous speech in which he appealed to conscience and said something like, "Here I stand; I can do no other"—a proclamation that over the centuries gave him the reputation of a modern man upholding the primacy of individual judgment. In reality, however, he believed that conscience had to be subordinated to the authority of Scripture.

A Radical Theology

Luther did not deny Church authority and therefore reject indulgences; rather his conclusion that indulgences were a distortion led him to question Church authority. If the Church was in error on crucial questions—if both indulgences and the monastic life offered false assurances of sanctification—it followed that all other Catholic teachings were also subject to question. In a great rush, Luther then began systematically measuring Church teachings against the Scripture as he understood it, rejecting almost the entire Catholic system: the authority of popes and bishops, seven sacraments (finally affirming only two—baptism and the Eucharist), Purgatory, the invocation of the saints, and many other things.

The Mass
The crucial issue was the sacrificial nature of the Mass. Catholic doctrine, properly understood, held that Christ's sacrifice on the Cross accomplished the redemption of mankind but that in the Mass the fruits of that redemption were made available through time—the continuation of the sacrifice of Calvary. For Luther, this undermined the uniqueness of Christ's sacrifice and made the Eucharist into a "good work" that the congregation offered to the Father. If the Mass was not a sacrifice, it followed that the clergy were "ministers" only, not priests, and all verbal or symbolic implications of sacrifice (priestly vestments, marble altars) were to be suppressed.

An End to Monasticism
After being condemned at Worms, Luther went into hiding and never returned to the monastic life, concluding that the very idea of religious vows was fallacious and that no Christian received a divine call that differed from that of every other Christian. This implied the rejection of celibacy, and after a few years, Luther married one of the many nuns who had left their convents as a result of his exhortations. He and his family lived in what had previously been his monastery.

Reform or Rebellion?
Beginning with Luther himself, the religiously disaffected did not at first think of themselves as breaking with the Catholic Church but rather as attempting to reform her, an expectation that faded as the list of disputed doctrines and practices got longer and longer. As events unfolded, some Evangelicals remained Catholics,[4] while others broke with the Church. For a time, the latter continued to call themselves Evangelicals, not Lutherans, indignantly insisting that they followed Christ, not a man.

The Fate of the Humanists

Erasmus and Lefèvre d'Étaples, whatever their dissatisfactions with the Church, remained Catholics, both dying in 1536. Erasmus made peace and charity the hallmarks of a true Christian and, despite his many criticisms of Catholic doctrine and practice, always made the unity of

---

[4] Evangelicals is a name given to those who developed a theology and a spirituality closely based on the New Testament.

the Church paramount, including a certain deference to papal authority and to Tradition.

Erasmus

At first, Erasmus congratulated Luther, because indulgences were an example of what Erasmus considered superstition. But he was increasingly troubled at what he thought was Luther's heedless divisiveness and dogmatic denial of free will. Erasmus urged mutual tolerance of disputed beliefs—a willingness to think oneself mistaken—but for Luther the meaning of the Gospel could not be left uncertain. Given his positive valuation of human nature, Erasmus also objected to Luther's extreme pessimism, and Luther in turn denounced Erasmus as someone who had let pagan ideas obscure his understanding of the Gospel. Erasmus continued in a deliberately ambiguous position, moving back and forth between Catholic and Protestant cities, finally proclaiming himself a Catholic but spending his last years in the Protestant city of Basle, where he published a late work affirming Catholic teaching.

The Others

The leading humanists of the immediate pre-Reformation generation moved in various directions. After Wessel Gansfort's death, his writings were formally condemned; whatever Gansfort himself might have intended, Luther praised him as a precursor. Reuchlin, although most of his students became Protestants, remained a Catholic, even being ordained a priest shortly before his death. Mutianus Rufus at first befriended Luther but eventually rejected his movement, and the skeptical Conradus Celtis was condemned posthumously by both Catholics and Protestants.

Pirckheimer

Willibald Pirckheimer (d. 1530) was a wealthy German humanist, a friend of both Erasmus and Luther. He wrote to the Pope to defend Luther, but he seemed not to espouse fundamental Lutheran teachings, merely demanding that the Mass be said in the vernacular and that Communion be given to the laity in both kinds. Pirckheimer opposed the introduction of the Reformation in Nuremberg, where he served on the town council and where two of his sisters were abbesses and three of his daughters were also nuns. He defended their way of life as genuinely Christian, although criticizing it as overly formal and tending toward pride. Like Erasmus, he cautioned against breaking with the Church, accusing some of the Reformers of fostering unbridled liberty, calling one former friend "Satan" and saying that he would rather live under papal authority than under that of the Reformers.

If the Protestant Reformation had not been set off by Luther, it would have occurred in a different place around the same time, a classic illustration of the maxim that nothing is so powerful as an idea whose

A Many-Centered Movement

time has come. Other men besides Luther in other countries besides Germany were also demanding changes in the Church.

Zwingli

Huldrych Zwingli (d. 1531) was a parish priest of Zurich, Switzerland. For some time, he urged his flock to adhere more closely to the Scriptures and warned against human innovations in religion, and in 1522, some of his parishioners made the symbolic gesture of eating sausages on Ash Wednesday, thereby defying the laws governing the Lenten fast. The incident created a sensation in the city and provoked a crisis of authority, which was eventually settled by the town government. Zwingli's leadership was officially accepted, so that in effect Zurich left the Catholic Church. Zwingli's teachings were quite similar to Luther's in many ways, albeit he rather defensively denied that his beliefs owed much to the German former monk.

Calvin

What eventually became the most widespread and influential of all Protestant movements did not arise until half a generation after Luther. John Calvin (d. 1564) was a Frenchman who, unusual among Reformation leaders, was a layman, trained as a humanist and a lawyer. As a student at Paris, Calvin was involved with an Evangelical group suspected of heresy, and in 1534, he and others fled the city after a nocturnal incident in which inflammatory religious handbills were nailed up all over the city, including on the bedroom door of King Francis I (1515–1547). Lefèvre d'Étaples fell under suspicion and was among those who fled. Calvin found refuge with Marguerite of Navarre (d. 1549), Francis' sister and queen of the tiny kingdom of Navarre in the Pyrenees.

Eventually, Calvin settled in Geneva, where he was ordained, attempted to set up a model Christian community, and through his *Institutes of the Christian Religion* produced the most comprehensive account of Protestant beliefs. His most famous doctrine was that of predestination: that God decreed from all eternity that some would be saved and others damned, so that no human effort could have any effect. His idea was not substantially different from Luther's, but Calvin imposed a kind of fearful somberness on his followers, based on the awareness of their possible damnation, whereas Luther encouraged people to hope that they were saved.

In a way, the doctrine of predestination was the final culmination of the long-simmering complaint that, both in Thomistic theology and in its piety, the Catholic Church had made God too accessible to man. Luther cried, "Let God be God", and Calvin saw God's sovereign will as all-powerful and beyond questioning by men, so that predestination, including accepting the possibility of one's own damnation, had to be accepted as just.

Ultimately, the Reformation was a battle of ideas, but Catholics were somewhat slow in mounting a defense. Luther did not immediately get the debate he wanted, because at first no one was prepared, a situation that was repeated in Zwingli's Zurich a few years later. Catholic apologists were reluctant to write in the vernacular, lest it seem that doctrine was being submitted to popular judgment, and their formal Scholastic style was not effective against the blunt, even vulgar, rhetoric of Luther and others. Catholics were also slow to make use of the printing press.

Luther's Catholic critics first sought to refute him by showing that his ideas implied things that the Church defined as heresy, an approach that sometimes allowed them to anticipate Luther's ideas even before he articulated them himself. But rather than backing away from those implications, Luther grew increasingly radical.

Bible and Church

The Protestant doctrine of *sola scriptura* struck at the heart of the Church's authority and forced a clarification of Catholic beliefs about which there was not total consensus. At issue was Christ's promise to be with His Church always and the continued presence of the Holy Spirit, from which flowed the authority of doctrines and practices not found explicitly in the Bible but that had unfolded over time. Central to the Catholic position was the fact that the Church herself had determined the canonical text of the Scripture; it was thus impossible to set the Bible over the Church.

Prierias and Cajetan

The Dominican Sylvester Prierias (d. 1523), Leo X's own theologian, actually made the pope superior to Scripture. The Dominican Cajetan (Tommaso de Vio, d. 1534), one of the leading theologians of the day and soon to be a cardinal, was Luther's earliest opponent, sent to Germany by Leo X to persuade Luther to recant. He argued that, while the seeds of all doctrines were found in Scripture, by itself it was inadequate as a guide to revelation. Tradition—something "handed down" and encompassing both the interpretation of Scripture and teachings of Christ not recorded there—also has authority.

Eck

Eck located revelation in the living Church, guided by the Holy Spirit, in contrast to a written Scripture that, if divorced from the believing community, was dead. He and other Catholic apologists often cited the conclusion of the Gospel of John—that Jesus said and did many things that were not written down—and they recalled that He promised to send His Holy Spirit to guide the Church.

Pigge and Ellenborg

The secular priest Albert Pigge (d. 1542) taught that Scripture had authority only because it had been accepted by the Church and that, since Tradition preceded Scripture, it was therefore superior to it. The Benedictine Nicholas Ellenborg (d. 1543) taught that the Holy Spirit supplemented the truths taught by Christ when He was on earth and that the saints were the principal recipients of that inspiration.

Henry VIII

King Henry VIII of England (1509–1547) was a militant Catholic who wrote *The Defense of the Seven Sacraments* to refute Luther, an act for which Clement VII (1523–1534) conferred on him the title "Defender of the Faith", a title the English monarchs still claim. Henry also argued that Scripture was an inadequate guide to truth and defended the seven sacraments on the basis of papal authority.

Thomas More

Thomas More wrote an early *Response to Luther*, making him perhaps the first Erasmian humanist to recognize clearly what was at stake. A few years later, he was commissioned by the English bishops to refute William Tyndale (d. 1536), a priest who had become a Protestant and was sending his books to England from the Low Countries, including the first complete English Bible, which differed from Catholic teaching in some of its translations.

More, who eschewed formal theology and, like Tyndale and Luther himself, often resorted to scatological abuse, asserted that it was not essential that believers read the Bible, so long as the Church interpreted it for them. More had been something of a conciliarist, and he said little about the papal office. Instead, he made what was in a sense a historical, rather than a strictly theological, defense of the Church, extolling Catholicism as an entire way of life, including some things (the veneration of relics) of which he and other humanists had previously been critical. The Church was a great communion embracing all ages and all Christian peoples; her truth was preserved by the general consensus of believers, whereas heretics relied on their own judgments and thereby willfully cut themselves off from the totality of Christendom.

More argued that a vernacular Bible was unnecessary and that direct access to Scripture could be dangerous for untutored people. (Late in the sixteenth century, the seminary set up in France to educate English priests produced the Douai-Rheims Bible, the first Catholic translation into English, which predated the King James Bible but appeared long after Tyndale's translation.)

Sadoleto

Jacopo Sadoleto (d. 1547), an Italian who was a bishop in southern France, wrote an open letter to the Genevans urging their return to Rome, professing loving solicitude for people he said had been misled by crafty seducers who sowed doubt and division. Unlike most Catholic apologists, Sadoleto, who was associated with the

Spirituals, explicitly eschewed "subtle philosophy" in favor of simple obedience to the Word of God as preserved and expounded in the Church.

Baronius
The polemical battle with Protestantism was fought on the basis of history as well as theology. Oratorian Cardinal Caesar Baronius (d. 1607), for example, attempted to show in his *Annals* that the Church had preserved an unbroken tradition over the centuries.

Bellarmine
Ultimately, the most influential Catholic theologian was the Italian Jesuit St. Robert Bellarmine (d. 1621), who presented a systematic case for Tradition and hierarchical authority. (Some of his own writings were briefly put on the *Index*, because they were thought to be insufficiently supportive of papal authority.)

Free Will
Beyond the fundamental question of authority, Catholic apologists affirmed the Thomistic (as opposed to the Ockhamist) position that, while God's will is sovereign, He ordered the universe according to a rational pattern and gave men limited free will.

Deep theological issues probably passed over most people, who understood their faith primarily in terms of piety: Marian devotions, the cults of the saints, prayers for the dead, pilgrimages, the veneration of relics, and indulgences. (Ironically, Frederick the Wise [d. 1525], the elector of Saxony and Luther's protector, had the largest relic collection in Europe, including a feather from the wing of the Holy Spirit and a drop of the Virgin Mary's mother's milk!)

The beliefs and practices that were points at which the Church was vulnerable to the charge of unbiblical superstition were also the anchors of many people's faith. The abolition of indulgences, the closing of shrines and monasteries, the destruction of images and relics, and dramatic changes in the liturgy sometimes aroused popular resistance, as in the 1536 Pilgrimage of Grace, which was an armed uprising in England that came close to succeeding.

The subtle doctrine of the Real Presence was a major issue between Catholics and Protestants, as demonstrated, for example, by people's kneeling, or refusal to kneel, as the Blessed Sacrament passed in procession. But the sharpest conflicts arose when religious changes left people feeling bereft of supernatural help, as happened when prayers to the saints were suppressed. Another blow to the vivid sense of the communion of saints was the denial of Purgatory. This affected people even more deeply, since it seemed to cut them off from their ancestors by forbidding prayers for the dead.

The Crisis of Piety

Mary and the Saints

Devotion to Mary and the saints had long been a source of comfort, but since Protestants insisted that they were no longer to be regarded as intercessors and protectors, their images and shrines were destroyed in those regions controlled by Protestants. The leading Reformers continued to hold that Mary was the Mother of God and a perpetual virgin, but they were so determined to obliterate every trace of what they considered superstition that the figure of Mary almost disappeared from Protestant churches and, eventually, consciousness.

Long-beloved images provoked violent passions, as iconoclasts outraged traditionalists by destroying the "idols" that had long been the embodiment of the sacred. Especially in France and the Netherlands, iconoclasm was often accompanied by gang attacks, including murders, perpetrated by one religious group against another.

Monasticism

Monastic life manifested extremes, from the severe austerity of the Carthusians to houses that had been corrupted by wealth, lax discipline, and the interference of lay patrons—a scandal that sometimes led bishops to suppress religious houses on their own authority. Monasteries served as the destinations of pilgrims, places of hospitality for travelers, and centers of charity for the sick and poor, with considerable variations in their levels of generosity. Their dissolution excised institutions that had been an integral part of the local community for over a thousand years. Their suppression was symbolically revolutionary in seeming to condemn otherworldly asceticism and insisting that the Christian life be lived entirely within the world. A frequent criticism of monks was that they lived unproductive lives and were a drain on economic resources.

The Failure of
Sola Scriptura

The Reformers did not teach the "private interpretation of Scripture" in the sense that each man's personal understanding was to be considered valid for himself. Rather they expected that, shorn of centuries-old Catholic errors, the Bible would speak plainly to everyone and there would be full agreement. But quite early, it became apparent that *sola scriptura* was an inadequate principle, so that almost from the beginning the leading Reformers had to invoke some kind of church authority against the free interpretation of Scripture. (Frustrated that the Bible did not say explicitly what he was convinced it meant, Luther added the word "alone" to Paul's proclamation that "the just man lives by faith", and he considered discarding the Letter of James [which he called "an epistle of straw"] because it exalted good works.)

The Magisterial
Reformation vs.
the Radicals

The Reformers' beliefs required them to hold that the Church had deviated from the authentic Gospel quite early. But Luther, Zwingli, Calvin, and others came to be called the Magisterial Reformers ("teachers" or "masters"), because they upheld the historic creeds against those whose understanding of the Scripture led them in other directions. The Magisterials accepted the authority of the ecumenical councils through the fifth century, by which time the fundamental doctrines of the Trinity (a word that does not appear in Scripture) and the Incarnation had been defined.

Luther and Zwingli

When Luther and Zwingli finally met, they agreed on most things but not on the meaning of Christ's words, "This is My body", with Zwingli insisting that He must have been speaking metaphorically and Luther insisting on the literal meaning, each claiming that the other misunderstood Christ's words. Luther held that, while bread and wine remained, they also became the actual Body and Blood of Christ, a doctrine later called "consubstantiation" ("substances together"), while Zwingli saw the bread and wine as mere symbols of Christ's Body and Blood.

Adiaphora

The question of "externals" also greatly divided some of the Reformers, with Lutherans accepting *adiaphora* ("things indifferent"), so long as the Bible did not explicitly forbid them, while Zwingli and others would only allow those things that the Bible explicitly authorized. Zwingli was the first of what were later called "Puritans", who wanted to "purify" the Church of what they saw as historical accretions that smacked of superstition.

Anabaptists

Luther had to come out of hiding and return to Wittenberg in order to squelch unauthorized innovations by some of his followers, one of whom he expelled from the city for intransigence, even though the man claimed that he was simply implementing Luther's own teachings. Luther also, as did Zwingli, had to confront small groups of "zealots" who, without formal ordination, dared to preach in public and, most seriously, demand that those who had been baptized as infants (practically everyone) be rebaptized as adults, a practice that led to their being called Anabaptists ("to baptize again"). Anabaptists were viewed as politically as well as religiously subversive because, based on their reading of the New Testament, they refused to swear oaths, which were the moral foundation of the legal system; espoused pacifism, even if there should be a Turkish invasion; and in some cases denied the validity of private property.

"Other Spirituals"

Virtually all these "Radicals" proclaimed the Lutheran principle of the freedom of the Christian, who bowed to no authority but God. Those who also got the name "Spirituals" even bypassed Scripture for the direct inspiration of the Holy Spirit. Some of these were Unitarians or "Anti-Trinitarians".

Protestant Scholasticism

The Magisterial leaders denounced the Radicals as false prophets, expelled them from their cities, and often put them to death, while Anabaptists in turn accused those leaders of compromising their own principles. To counteract doctrinal fragmentation, most Protestant groups, including even some Anabaptists, in time adopted formal creeds or "confessions" to which all members were required to adhere. Despite humanist and Protestant hostility to Scholastic theology, some Protestants even began to theologize in the Scholastic mode, as in the Lutheran formula of "consubstantiation", in order to clarify disputed questions.

Church and State

Clergy in Politics

The Church as an institution was deeply involved in politics in the narrow sense, even apart from religious issues. The papacy had its own territorial interests, and prelates were often secular as well as spiritual lords. The Medici popes Leo X and Clement VII (1523–1534) continued to rule Florence through representatives, and cardinals such as Jiménez in Spain, Adrian Florensz (Pope Adrian VI) in the Empire, and Wolsey in England served as ministers of state as well as holding ecclesiastical office. The archbishops of Trier, Mainz, and Cologne were among the seven electors who comprised the inner circle of the German princes. Late in the sixteenth century, a cardinal even served briefly as king of Portugal. (At the other extreme, a Spanish bishop was executed for leading an armed rebellion against Charles I [Charles V of the Empire]).

Political and social prominence did not necessarily mean that a prelate was corrupt. Jiménez and Florensz lived austere lives, and Wolsey, although quite worldly, became increasingly pious toward the end of his life. After his death, he was discovered to be wearing a hair shirt.

Politics and Belief

Ultimately, the success or failure of the Reformation in particular areas was due almost entirely to the policies of its rulers. From the emperor to town councils, responses to the Reformation were determined by a complex interplay of secular interests and religious belief.

The Reformation succeeded mainly in northern Europe, in the territories that had not been part of the Roman Empire. Luther quite deliberately appealed to German resentment of what was considered a Roman sense of superiority, a division that seemed almost to replay the ancient Roman-barbarian conflict. Though Protestantism made some inroads into Eastern Europe, it did not become the dominant cultural influence there.

Charles V

Charles V recognized the emergent Lutheran movement as a threat to imperial unity, but it was only with difficulty that he was able to obtain Luther's condemnation at the Diet of Worms. Although Lutherans stood condemned as heretics, Charles had to keep postponing action against them. (The word *Protestant* was originally applied not to theological dissent but to those who protested Charles V's announced intention of suppressing their movement.)

Failed Compromise

Charles at one point offered the Lutherans clerical marriage and Communion in both kinds, an offer they rejected as too little, even as Pope Clement VII saw it as the emperor's unwarranted assumption of ecclesiastical authority. These were understood by everyone to be disciplinary matters that could be changed (John Fisher said the laity were not given the chalice merely to prevent accidental spills), but knowledgeable people on both sides realized that the issues went much deeper. The Augsburg Confession of 1530 was the first Lutheran statement of faith and was agreed to in part by some Catholics, but it did not achieve complete acceptance and failed to heal the breach.[5]

Church Property

Luther urged the princes to undertake the forcible reform of the Church, if the clergy would not, charging that her great wealth had been stolen from gullible Germans. Like Henry VIII a few years later, princes who accepted Luther's invitation became almost by default the heads of the Church in their domains, justifying their seizure of church property.

Bishops and abbots were among those who accepted Luther's invitation, notably Hermann von Wied (d. 1552), the prince-archbishop of Cologne, and the entire military-religious order of the Teutonic Knights in Prussia, whose last grand master, Albert of Hohenzollern (d. 1568), began the dynasty that would unite Germany in the nineteenth century.

The Free Cities

The Empire also encompassed a number of "free cities", where civic authorities had the last word on such issues as the manner of the celebration of the liturgy. Those authorities tended initially to approach religious conflicts as matters of public order and, after a period of confusion, sought to restore order by favoring one faction over another. In Zurich and Geneva, the town councils responded to religious strife first by sponsoring public debates, then by authorizing the adoption of the Reformers' programs.

The Peasants' War

Lutheranism was almost dealt a fatal blow by the massive Peasants' War of 1524–1525, when thousands of poor farmers rose up against their lords. Although they did not inflict great loss of life, they burned fields and buildings and destroyed the legal documents that defined their servile status. A manifesto issued by the rebels—probably composed by a priest—cited Luther's words about Christian freedom as justification for their actions, and Luther at first responded by condemning the rebellion but also faulting the princes for injustices. But

---

[5] The Confession has been used as the possible basis of agreement between modern Catholics and Lutherans.

when his response was cited by the rebels as further justification or defense of their revolt, he published a pamphlet titled *Against the Robbing and Murdering Horde of Peasants*.

Lutheran Freedom

The rebellion was put down with great brutality, and Luther made it clear that his idea of Christian freedom from Law applied only to spiritual matters, because true freedom was interior. The princes who supported him were reassured by this, and in his subsequent writings Luther exalted political authority virtually without limit.

Münster

Anabaptism was definitively if unfairly discredited when in the period from 1535 to 1536 a group of extreme sectarians seized control of the German city of Münster, which was predominantly Catholic, and acted out a nightmare of antinomianism—putting their opponents to death, proclaiming their own leader to be a divinely ordained king, and not only permitting but requiring promiscuous sexuality and polygamy. The uprising was eventually crushed and, along with the Peasants' Revolt, forced mainstream Protestants to give more authority to law than they had initially been willing to do, especially since Catholics had always warned that the Lutheran idea of freedom would lead to moral anarchy.

The Turkish Threat

Looming always over the German situation was the threat of the Turks, who continually menaced the Empire's eastern borders, causing Charles V to avoid as long as possible the inevitable civil war that would erupt if he attempted to enforce the edict of Worms against the Lutherans. Even the Catholic princes of Germany did not necessarily favor the complete suppression of Protestantism, because such action would strengthen the power of the emperor at the expense of the princes. Charles' move against the Lutherans finally came in 1546, immediately provoking a Protestant rebellion that a dying Luther, because of his view of the sanctity of civil authority, could not bring himself to endorse.

Hapsburgs and Valois

The long-standing Hapsburg-Valois conflict was the central reality of European politics, destroying any possibility of a united Catholic political front. When Charles V was on the verge of defeating the German Lutherans, Henry II of France (1547–1559), even as he struggled to suppress the Calvinists in his own domains, sent an army to help the Lutherans.

Peace of Augsburg

Faced with a stalemate, Charles in 1555 negotiated a settlement—the Peace of Augsburg—that, however limited, was the first official recognition of religious tolerance in European history. He then abdicated in favor of his brother Ferdinand I (1555–1564) and retired to a Spanish monastery, where he lived in austere preparation for death. Ironically, in view of Luther's ringing declarations of spiritual freedom, the Peace of Augsburg was summed up in the maxim *cujus regio ejus religio* ("whose rule, his religion"), which allowed each prince to determine the religion of his subjects and required nonconformists to go into exile, while the free cities were required in theory to tolerate both Catholics and Lutherans. (In some places, those who did not adhere to the official religion could leave the territory on Sunday to worship in a neighboring jurisdiction.)

Ferdinand was relatively tolerant, so that some of the provisions of Augsburg, such as the exclusion of Calvinists and the protection of Catholic property, were not enforced. His successor, Maximilian II (1564–1576), was actually thought to be sympathetic to Lutheranism.

Lutheranism spread rapidly throughout northern Germany and into Scandinavia, where the way was prepared by scholars who had studied abroad. The final decisions, however, were made by the kings of Denmark, Frederick I (1523–1533) and Christian III (1534–1559), who also ruled Norway, and Gustavus I (Vasa), king of Sweden (1523–1560), who also ruled Finland.

Scandinavia

Gallicanism

France

Just as there was an Anglican ("English") church that was founded by Henry VIII in 1534 which split from Rome, there was also a Gallican ("French") church that maintained formal ties to the papacy while seeking to remain as independent as possible. In a concordat ("agreement") that would plague the papacy for three centuries, Pope Leo X officially recognized the French king's right to nominate bishops and many other high church officials, although papal ratification was required.

Huguenots

From Geneva, Calvin sent trained clergy back to France, where they made converts among both the aristocracy and the merchant class. (For unknown reasons, the French Calvinists came to be called Huguenots.) In 1559, the French king, Henry II, was killed in an accident, leaving three young sons—Francis II (1559–1560), Charles IX (1560–1574), and Henry III (1574–1589)—each of whom would rule and each of whom would prove to be weak and ineffective, leaving real power in the hands of their mother, Catherine de Medici (d. 1589), who was influenced by the ideas of Machiavelli.

Civil War

At first Catherine forced Catholics to engage in theological discussion with the Huguenots; however, when an agreement was not forthcoming, both sides began committing acts of violence against each other, especially while their opponents were at worship. The violence escalated into a civil war that lasted for most of the rest of the century. It was essentially a three-way conflict, in which it was impossible to separate religion from dynastic ambitions. Those of the reigning house of Valois were

Catholics, while their cousins the Bourbons (Marguerite of Navarre's family) became the leaders of the Huguenot party. Still another family of cousins, the Guises, accused the Valois of compromising the Catholic faith, put themselves forward as its true champions, and received support from Spain. From time to time, leaders on both sides were assassinated.

The Massacre of St. Bartholomew

In a perilous situation, Catherine, suspicious that both the Guises and the Bourbons wanted to install themselves on the throne, tried to control the kingdom by treading a middle path. She made a series of grants of toleration to the Huguenots, the extent of each one dictated by the political situation at a given moment.

In 1572, the situation was ostensibly resolved when Henry of Bourbon (d. 1610), Marguerite of Navarre's grandson, married Charles IX's sister Marguerite (d. 1615). But the phenomenon of a "mixed marriage" was still unfamiliar. Politics might demand such a union, but Pius V (1566–1572) refused a dispensation, and the ceremony—performed by a Bourbon cardinal—was considered merely a blessing, not a sacramental act.

Six days later, on St. Bartholomew's Day (August 24), Catholics began systematically slaughtering Protestants in Paris and other cities, killing as many as five thousand. The St. Bartholomew Massacre became the most infamous religious atrocity in a century filled with such atrocities. Catherine and Charles may have instigated the massacre, in order once again to pit Guises and Bourbons against one another. (Pope Gregory XIII [1572–1585] ordered a Te Deum sung in Rome in celebration of the event, although he may not have known all the facts.)

Henry IV

The civil war continued. In 1588, the duke of Guise was murdered at Henry III's instigation, and the next year the king himself was assassinated by a Dominican friar, Jacques Clement, probably in retaliation. (Clement was killed on the spot and was venerated by some Catholics as a martyr.)

Henry of Bourbon, who had reverted to Protestantism after St. Bartholomew's Day, now claimed the throne as Henry IV (1589–1610) and made good his claim by taking control of Paris. A few years later, he announced his reconversion to Catholicism, allegedly with the cynical remark, "Paris is worth a Mass", although it was later reported that he had become a sincere Catholic. Pope Clement VIII (1592–1605) recognized Henry as king after his conversion, but the Guises, with Spanish support, continued to make war against Henry, at one point, proclaiming an elderly cardinal as the rightful king.

Edict of Nantes

Henry IV triumphed and in 1598 ended the forty-year-old French religious struggle by issuing the Edict of Nantes, which gave the

Huguenots freedom of worship on the estates of their adherents and in the several hundred towns where they were numerous. Remarkably, they were even allowed to fortify those towns as a defense against any future repeal of the edict. (Clement VIII disapproved of the edict.) Henry IV proved to be a popular king who restored order to the kingdom, but in 1610 he too was assassinated by a Catholic, because of the king's plans for war with Spain.

In England, a rapid series of religious changes were almost entirely acts of state. These began during the reign of Henry VIII and continued for the next forty years.

England

The Royal Marriage

Henry VIII was married to Catherine of Aragon (d. 1536), daughter of Ferdinand and Isabella and Charles V's aunt, a union that gave him only one living offspring, his daughter, Mary (d. 1558). Worried about the survival of the Tudor dynasty and attracted to a younger woman, Anne Boleyn (d. 1536), Henry petitioned Pope Clement VII for an annulment of his marriage, on the grounds that Catherine had previously been married to his older brother. Pope Julius II had granted a dispensation for the marriage, but the king now contended that divine law itself forbade such a union.

Clement VII

Partly in deference to the emperor, Clement followed a policy of delay, probably hoping that Henry's interest in Anne would cool. The basis for the requested annulment was also problematical, since for the pope to acquiesce would be to limit papal authority over marriage, forever thereafter forbidding marriage to a brother's widow as contrary to the law of God. (Another issue was whether Catherine's marriage to Arthur had been consummated, while canon law also forbade Henry to marry Anne because he had previously had sexual relations with her sister.)

The Attack on the Papacy

When the court set up by the Pope to hear the case failed to deliver a verdict, the king's frustration boiled over. Cardinal Thomas Wolsey (d. 1530), who was both Henry's lord chancellor and one of the two papal judges assigned to the case, fell from power. Henry then attempted to pressure Clement by getting Parliament to enact a series of laws designed to curtail papal authority in England—appointments to office, taxes, and appeals to the papal court—and intimidating the bishops by threatening them with prosecution for having accepted Wolsey as papal legate, an appointment Henry himself had arranged.

Excommunication

Apparently wishing to placate Henry as far as possible, Clement quickly confirmed Henry's nomination of the royal chaplain Thomas Cranmer (d. 1556) as archbishop of Canterbury. Cranmer, who had Protestant leanings and was secretly married, immediately declared Henry's marriage to Catherine invalid and officiated at his marriage to Boleyn, whereupon Clement at last reached a decision and excommunicated both Henry and Anne.

"Supreme Head"

Far from being deterred by the papal action, Henry in 1534 had himself declared "Supreme Head of the Church in England", an act without legal equivalent in any other country. Paradoxically, he still considered himself a Catholic and retained almost everything of the old faith, so that people of Lutheran or other heretical inclinations continued to be burned at the stake.

Suppression of the Monasteries

The exception to the king's Catholicism was monasteries (including convents of women) and some other endowed institutions, which he ruthlessly suppressed in order to get possession of their wealth, with their inmates given pensions. But ironically, even after there were no monasteries left in England, to deny the validity of religious vows was still defined as heresy and still carried the death penalty.

King and Bishops

Henry VIII's claim to be head of the Church renewed the old issue between Henry II and Becket—whether the king could be truly supreme in his own kingdom if the Church possessed a higher moral authority. Logically, Henry VIII had Becket's tomb—the shrine of one of the very few Catholic martyrs of the previous half-millennium—destroyed and his remains disposed of.

Most of the English bishops had risen through the royal service, and only one—St. John Fisher (d. 1536)—withstood the king. Henry's position as Supreme Head of the Church meant that loyalty to the pope was now treason, and in a brief period Henry put to death everyone who refused to affirm the new order, including Fisher and Thomas More.

Thomas More

More did not openly oppose the king but instead resigned from public office and retired to private life. But Henry demanded his old friend's overt support; and when More would not give it, he was executed on the basis of perjured testimony. (Erasmus, when he heard of his friend's martyrdom, regretted that More had become involved in matters from which he should have remained aloof.)

Pole

Pole, at first a moderate conciliarist, had written a strong defense of papal authority that earned him the king's undying enmity and led to the brutal judicial murder of Pole's elderly mother, Bl. Margaret Pole (d. 1541). The execution of Margaret Pole was also motivated by the king's fear that the Pole family in some ways had a better claim to the throne than did his Tudor dynasty.

Edward VI

When Henry died, the throne passed to his young son Edward VI (1547–1553), an ardent, theologically precocious Protestant who encouraged Cranmer and others, working through Parliament, to move the Anglican church further toward Continental Protestantism. The liturgy was translated into English and shorn of all implications of sacrifice, clergy were allowed to marry, and Protestant theologians were imported from the Continent to bring England into the mainstream of the Reformation. But in some places, there were popular uprisings against the introduction of the new Book of Common Prayer.

Mary I

When the sickly Edward died at age sixteen, the throne passed to his older half-sister Mary I (1553–1558), Catherine of Aragon's daughter, who repulsed a Protestant effort to deny her the throne and later put down a rebellion that aimed to depose her. Since the survival of a restored Catholicism depended entirely on a Catholic heir, Mary quickly married the future Philip II of Spain (1555–1598). He remained in England for a year but, when no pregnancy resulted and he inherited the Spanish throne, returned home.

The Catholic Restoration

Just as her father and half-brother had used royal authority and a cooperative Parliament to take England out of the Catholic Church, Mary now used the same methods to bring it back, repealing all the ecclesiastical legislation of the previous two decades. In keeping with the new reform spirit, she nominated bishops whose careers had been spent primarily in the Church, not the state, an action whose wisdom was vindicated when all but one of them remained Catholic after her death and had to be deposed by her successor.

Pole returned to England as archbishop of Canterbury and papal legate and in those capacities oversaw the formal return of his native country to the Church. He absolved those who had apostatized and supported the persecution of Protestants but advised Mary not to reclaim the church lands that had been seized by her father. (Instead she founded several new monasteries.)

Carafa remained hostile to his one-time associate and after becoming pope removed Pole as legate and summoned him to Rome, where he would probably have been charged with heresy. Mary, however, withheld the Pope's letter from the cardinal, who continued in his offices until his death, on the same day as Mary's own.

Elizabeth I

The throne then passed to Mary's half-sister Elizabeth I (1558–1603), daughter of Anne Boleyn, who at first gave ambiguous signals as to her personal beliefs but soon committed herself to a Protestant restoration, using royal and parliamentary authority—for the fourth time in twenty-five years—to effect religious change. As "Supreme Governor" of the church (she was not sure that a woman could be "Supreme Head"), she attempted to forge a comprehensive national church that would encompass everyone except "extremists" on both sides.

In the earlier years of her reign, the dominant religious spirit could probably be called conservative. Most people were still attached to old beliefs and practices but were not Catholics in a deliberate, self-conscious way, attending Anglican services while retaining elements of the old faith.

Puritanism

Puritanism—the desire for a Protestantism untainted with Catholic elements like bishops—was strongest in London and the mercantile Southeast, while Catholicism was strongest in the feudal North. In 1569, the last great English feudal uprising occurred, with the rebels gaining control of much of the North and, among other things, restoring the Mass and other elements of the Catholic faith. However, like the Pilgrimage of Grace a generation before and the riots against the Book of Common Prayer under Edward VI, the rebellion was soon crushed.

Excommunication of Elizabeth

Possibly in response to the 1569 rebellion, Pius V the next year excommunicated Elizabeth, dismissing her as a "pretended monarch" and releasing the English people from their allegiance to her. Probably Pius believed that the people were waiting to rise in rebellion if given the right to do so, but the principal effect of the papal bull was to allow the English government to define Catholicism as treason. (Incongruously, a few years later Pope Sixtus V [1585–1590], expressed great admiration for Elizabeth, a woman he thought showed remarkable determination.)

Missionary Priests

Around 1570, missionaries began arriving in England, the best known of whom were Jesuits but most of whom were secular clergy educated at English seminaries in France and Spain. They were missionaries in the sense that ultimately they hoped to convert the entire kingdom, but their immediate task was merely preservative: to provide the sacraments and spiritual guidance to a small minority of recusant Catholics and to persuade those faithful to Rome but willing to accommodate themselves to the Protestant regime that it was wrong to conform to the established church.

Of necessity, Elizabethan Catholicism had a dominantly aristocratic character, since the missionaries could only function by traveling secretly from one great house to another, ministering primarily to landowners, their servants, and their tenants. The numbers they reached were small, but the government had cause for concern at the way in which talented young men from good families, such as the Jesuits St. Edmund Campion (d. 1581) and St. Robert Southwell (d. 1595)—both accomplished scholars and writers—renounced the established church to embrace the old faith.

The story of the English missionaries is one of the most dramatic in the history of the Church, combining a heroic commitment to their cause, including martyrdom, with clandestine cloak-and-dagger activities such as false identities and hiding in secret rooms called "priest holes". Priests, along with those laymen who aided them directly, were treated as traitors if caught—put to death by being hanged, cut down alive, and disemboweled.

Rebellion?
Most Catholics, including most priests, eschewed politics, insisting that their sole concern was the salvation of souls. However, some others, including the influential Jesuit Robert Parsons (d. 1610) and Cardinal William Allen (d. 1594), whom the Holy See treated as the head of the English Catholics, believed that the queen should be overthrown. There was conflict between Jesuits and secular priests on the mission, a conflict that even persisted among those in prison, with the seculars generally taking a less openly resistant stance toward the monarchy.

The Armada
Several half-baked plots against Elizabeth (one of them endorsed by Pius V) were easily thwarted, but after years of preparation, Philip II in 1588 launched his Great Armada against England—thirty thousand men in 130 ships—with the aim of deposing Elizabeth in accord with Pius' bull, although Sixtus V considered the venture foolhardy. Philip aimed to place a Catholic on the English throne, an ambition that perfectly united religious and political interests, since the English had given help to anti-Spanish rebels in the Netherlands and were preying on Spanish treasure ships from the New World. But the Armada was routed by a combination of the English navy and severe storms, and Philip's dream of restoring European Catholicism through military might was thereby crushed. In England, the equation of Protestantism with patriotism was made complete.

Mary Stuart and the Scots
Mary Stuart, Queen of Scots (1542–1567), grandniece of Henry VIII and daughter of a Guise mother, succeeded to the throne of Scotland after having been widowed by Francis II of France. But she found a country that had changed considerably in her absence.

A Scot, John Knox (d. 1572), was perhaps Calvin's most ardent disciple and, having fled the England of Mary Tudor, denounced her cousin. Many of the leading Scottish nobles had become Presbyterians, named after the Calvinist system of church government, and Knox forged in them an iron religious conviction wedded to the traditional feudal determination to be free of royal power. As on the Continent, religious passions were often violent. After the first burning of a Scottish Protestant, a group of men burst in on the archbishop responsible, stabbed him repeatedly, and desecrated his body.

Posthumously, Mary became a Catholic heroine, but she was not a candidate for sainthood. She made no effort to combat Presbyterianism, and her personal life was full of scandal. Her second husband, Henry Darnley (d. 1567), suspected that she was having an affair with her Italian secretary and had the secretary brutally murdered in her presence, partly in the hope of causing her to have a miscarriage. Darnley himself subsequently died in a mysterious explosion, and Mary, in a Protestant ceremony, married James Bothwell, the man suspected of being responsible for the murder.

The marriage occasioned a full-scale rebellion that forced Mary to flee to the protection of her cousin in England. But Elizabeth did not relish Mary's presence and made her a prisoner in a distant castle, where, with or without her own knowledge and cooperation, Mary became the center of various schemes to topple Elizabeth, some of which involved Robert Parsons. After one such plot in 1587, Elizabeth was persuaded to assent to Mary's execution.

James VI and I

But when the never-married Elizabeth died in 1603, the English throne passed to James VI of Scotland (1567–1625), the son whom Mary Stuart had been forced to leave behind as an infant when she fled her own country. Thus he was also James I of England. Though James had been baptized a Catholic, he had been raised as a Protestant.

Ireland

A papal nuncio sent to Ireland in the 1540s stayed only a month and complained that the corruption of the clergy and the fractiousness of the nobles made it impossible to achieve religious reform. But the English government, whose effective power did not extend very far beyond Dublin ("the Pale"), found the Irish equally unreceptive to Protestantism. In many ways, Ireland, so remote from the rest of Europe, remained the only country where pre-Reformation Catholicism survived unchanged, although later in the century, the English seminaries on the Continent also began sending priests to Ireland.

The Netherlands

When Charles V divided his Habsburg domains in 1556, the Netherlands remained under the rule of Spain, even though in geography, language, and religion it would have fit better with the Empire. The contrast between the Netherlands and Spain was almost complete: the former a half-germanic, religiously diverse, predominantly mercantile society; the latter a still largely feudal, Mediterranean society, in which the long struggle against Islam had forged a deep commitment to Catholic orthodoxy.

The people of the Netherlands may not have been tolerant by conviction—there were periodic outbursts of mob violence by one side against the other —but their survival, in a semi-barren land continually threatened by the sea, required hard-working, economically productive people willing to accept almost anyone who met those requirements. The majority were Catholic, with significant Lutheran, Anabaptist, Jewish, and, above all, Calvinist elements.

Philip II

After Charles' abdication, Philip II, as king of Spain and its vast overseas domains, including the Netherlands, was the leading Catholic monarch of Europe, and he took very seriously his divine mandate to defend the Church and suppress heresy. His commitment to the Church fit closely with his idea of absolute royal power, since religious dissent was of its very nature a defiance of the king's authority, but Philip did have a pious streak. His palace of the Escorial was built on a gridiron pattern—because of his devotion to St. Lawrence, the third-century deacon who had reputedly been roasted on such a device—and the royal apartment was like a monk's cell. The popes, however, were wary of Philip, as they had been of his father, because of the Hapsburg claims in Italy. Despite what Philip himself believed, the interests of Spain and the Catholic Church were by no means identical.

Philip could not comprehend the pragmatic economic priorities of his distant Netherlandish subjects, nor could he appreciate their religious diversity, which constituted defiance of his authority. To Philip, toleration of heresy would have been a dereliction of his God-given responsibilities. In 1565, he announced that the Inquisition would be enforced in the Netherlands, an announcement that brought forth immediate protests from almost all sections of society, who both cherished their semi-independence from a distant Madrid and feared the economic consequences of the suppression of Protestantism.

Rebellion

The arrival of a Spanish army under the sometimes brutal duke of Alba (d. 1582), who had earlier invaded the Papal States during the interminable Italian wars, galvanized the Netherlands into massive resistance that was helped by Catholic France in order to strike a blow at Spain. The leadership of the rebellion was put in the hands of William of Orange (William the Silent, d. 1584), a prince who had been both a Lutheran and a Catholic and who now became a Calvinist, largely because the Calvinist bourgeoisie of the province of Holland played the major role in the revolt.

Despite many setbacks, by 1572, the northern Netherlanders had successfully driven out the Spanish troops, leaving Spain in control of the southern provinces that would eventually become the nation of Belgium. The newly independent United Provinces of the north retained a formal policy of religious toleration, but they were increasingly dominated by Calvinists who imposed burdens of various kinds on Catholics. William of Orange was assassinated by a Catholic in 1584, the first political assassination ever perpetrated with a gun.

Poland

In Poland (a much larger country in the sixteenth century than in modern times) Cardinal Stanislaus Hosius (d. 1579) presided over vigorous Counter-Reformation efforts, but there remained a significant Protestant presence. Poland became one of the most tolerant countries in Europe, a place of refuge for sectarians not welcome even in Lutheran and Calvinist lands. The Confederation of Warsaw (1573) included an official guarantee of toleration, although it extended to the princes only.

Hungary

Though it remained mostly Catholic, part of Hungary was under Muslim rule in the sixteenth century. There was a significant Calvinist presence, especially among the nobility.

Persecution and Toleration

Both the ideal and the reality of Christendom as a single international society virtually disappeared in the sixteenth century, but the concept of a unified society based on faith survived and was even strengthened at the national and local levels. Each territorial government believed that it had the duty to uphold true religion, and in the end, the religion of the people was largely determined by their rulers. A few bishops expressed reservations about the use of coercion, on the grounds that it led to insincere conversions.

The Secular Arm

As it was not established in most countries, the Inquisition was not the only body employed in religious persecution. France set up the *Chambre Ardent* ("burning court") to deal with heresy, and in England, heresy was also prosecuted under civil law.

For reasons that remain unclear, the sixteenth and seventeenth centuries were the great age of witchcraft prosecutions in Europe, an activity carried out by Catholics and Protestants with equal zeal.

Martyrdom

In the sixteenth century, for the first time in over twelve hundred years, all serious Christians were potentially faced with the possibility of persecution, as illustrated by the war of words between More and Tyndale, which continued until both were sent to their deaths in 1535— More by his former patron Henry VIII, Tyndale by the Inquisition at Antwerp. The Justinian Code, which was the basis for most European law codes, prescribed the death penalty for heresy because heresy was regarded as a spiritual disease that had to be suppressed lest it kill people's souls.

Erasmus came close to advocating toleration, in his ceaseless urging of forbearance and charity among Christians. But More, while he suffered death for his faith, himself participated in the prosecution of heretics, of which he fully approved,[6] just as Tyndale would probably have approved the burning of Anabaptists by Lutherans and Anglicans, and Calvin burned a Spanish physician, Miguel Serveto (d. 1553), who denied the Trinity. This was not hypocrisy. Men did not demand for themselves a toleration they denied to others but demanded simply that truth be promoted and error punished.

The Radical Reformation

The left wing of the Reformation—those generally if imprecisely called Anabaptists—alone rejected the idea that religious conformity should be enforced by civil authority because they did not think it either possible or desirable to organize the whole society on Christian principles. To the extent they were able, they simply withdrew into little communities where they tried to live according to what they considered Gospel teachings like pacifism and communal property.

Almost alone, the radicals opposed persecution in principle, because they thought most people were damned in any case, and coercion was therefore useless. Those who favored tolerance usually cited Jesus' parable of the wheat and the tares, showing that that there was to be no separation of people until the Last Judgment.

Spain

The long struggle for the *Reconquista* of Spain gradually reached its goal during the fifteenth century. The marriage of Isabella of Castile and Ferdinand II of Aragon (1479–1516) in effect created a united Spain for the first time, although the two kingdoms remained officially distinct. The "Catholic Monarchs", as Pope Alexander VI designated them, mounted a final assault on the Muslim kingdom of Granada, which fell in 1492.

The Conversos

A wave of anti-Jewish violence broke out in Castile around 1400 and soon spread throughout much of the Iberian Peninsula. A century later, at the urging of Jiménez, the crown embarked on a program of forced conversions, creating a new category of people—the *conversos*—who were suspected of secretly practicing their old religion. Theoretically, non-Christians were not supposed to be forced to convert, but having at last vanquished the Muslims, the crown now gave Muslims and Jews a choice between conversion and expulsion. Most chose the former, although a large number also went into exile.

As archbishop of Toledo and Grand Inquisitor, as well as the highest royal official, Jiménez was the most powerful person in Spain after the monarchs themselves, and he organized a kind of crusade in North

---

[6] More's story is widely known in part from the play and film *A Man for All Seasons*, which portrays him heroically but also gives an erroneous impression of his motives. He did not die for the supremacy of the individual conscience but for what he considered obedience to the will of God.

Africa, in which he accompanied the Christian armies in the field and which resulted in the conquest of parts of Tripoli.

Inquisition

Aragon and Castile shared the Inquisition, a special Spanish branch of which was established by papal authority but existed under royal control and was used for political as well as religious purposes, since the presence of large numbers of Muslims and Jews seemed to threaten political stability. The institution became extremely powerful, ranking above the secular courts and even able to prosecute important people. Although many of the accused were found innocent and many of the guilty repented and suffered lesser penalties, approximately five thousand were burned between 1480 and 1530.

The Inquisition was concerned with possible heresy, but its primary interest was in the *conversos*. Probably most of the first generation of converts were in fact of doubtful sincerity. However, later generations produced a disproportionate number of important people who were also exemplary Catholics. The Dominican Tomàs de Torquemada (d. 1498), one of Isabella's confessors and himself the Grand Inquisitor, was of *conversos* stock. Beyond the suspicion that *conversos* were insincere, many Spaniards also became obsessed with the idea of "purity of blood", requiring that people prove that they had no Jewish ancestry before they could be fully accepted into society.

Martyrdom in England

More, Fisher, and a small group of Carthusians and Franciscans executed by Henry VIII were the first Catholic martyrs of the Counter-Reformation. About 130 Catholic priests were killed in the Netherlands during the religious conflicts there, most of them by armies or by mob violence rather than through formal persecution, as also happened in France. By far the largest group of Catholic martyrs was in England. Although almost every ruler executed religious dissenters, persecution under Edward VI was minimal. But Elizabeth I (1558–1603) executed over three hundred—mainly priests, some laymen, mostly men, a few women—who were defined as traitors rather than as heretics.

The number of Catholics martyred during Elizabeth's forty-five-year reign was about the same as the number of Protestants martyred during her half-sister's five-year reign, including Cranmer, after he had twice recanted his heresy, then recanted his recantations. Most of those burned under Mary seem to have been not mainstream Protestants but simple people who belonged to left-wing sects. Protestant propaganda burdened the queen indelibly with the epithet "Bloody Mary", as though she were uniquely intolerant.

Elizabeth I burned an occasional Anabaptist, but during her reign, religious dissenters were usually hanged as traitors. Demanding only external conformity, the Elizabethan government imposed heavy fines on not only Catholics but also native English Protestants who did not attend Anglican services. The severity of the fine varied according to the political situation at the particular moment.

Protestant Martyrs

The first Protestant martyrs of the age were two members of Luther's Augustinian order, burned at Brussels in 1523. An estimated forty-four hundred Protestants were put to death in all countries, many of them by other Protestants, since "Anabaptists" were subject to the death penalty almost everywhere. The largest number of Protestants executed under Catholic auspices were in France and in the Netherlands (including modern Belgium), but in Germany, where the Reformation began, most Protestants were protected by territorial princes sympathetic to their faith.

Roman Inquisition

The Roman Inquisition was given renewed authority in the face of Protestantism, but its effectiveness in the various Italian city-states depended on the cooperation of the local governments, which were influenced by complex political factors. Its activities reached a peak around 1600, when it summoned about four hundred people per decade, many of whom were in effect acquitted and only a small number of whom were put to death, the most common punishments being public penance and relatively short stays in prison.

Bruno
In one of its most famous cases, the Inquisition in 1600 burned Giordano Bruno (d. 1600), a Dominican who was accused of heresy but who was in many ways scarcely a Christian at all—a mysterious figure who combined a precocious interest in science with belief in ancient Egyptian cults, who reportedly called Jesus a conjuror, and who at his execution turned his face away from the crucifix.

Inquisitorial Procedures
The Inquisition operated according to strict rules that were fair by the standards of its time. Most of those summoned were denounced anonymously, but, although not entitled to confront their accusers, they were allowed to submit a list of enemies who might wish to harm them and who were punished if found to be lying. The accused could not be represented by a counsel but could consult one (paid for by the Inquisition, if necessary), and the Inquisitors' handbook included suggestions as to how the accused might answer particular charges.

Recantation
Above all, the Inquisition sought to uncover the truth, not to punish people indiscriminately, since its principal aim was to bring about conversions. Torture was used when a suspect was thought to be lying, but it was used sparingly because the Inquisitors did not want insincere confessions, and such a confession could be recanted within twenty-four hours. The Inquisition often showed greater skepticism

about accusations of witchcraft than did the secular authorities and sometimes even rebuked those authorities for being overly credulous.

Those Investigated

Despite the Inquisition, few Protestants were put to death in Italy and Spain, simply because there were very few and the Inquisition concerned itself with morals, witchcraft, suspicious foreign visitors, and Catholics who had traveled in Protestant lands or had been ransomed from the Muslims and might therefore have been affected by Muslim beliefs. Also investigated were Catholics with questionable beliefs. Under royal authority, the Spanish Inquisition was so powerful that an archbishop of Toledo, Bartolomé Carranza (d. 1576), spent seventeen years under arrest, as the tribunal's complex procedures ground slowly, and was finally released only after retracting certain of his writings that were deemed to be carelessly in error.

Valdés

The works of Erasmus had great appeal to Spanish humanists, but with the advent of Protestantism, the Inquisition began to scrutinize such people. The Erasmian Juan de Valdés (d. 1541) fled to Italy to avoid prosecution, where he enjoyed the patronage of Clement VII and other churchmen, although after his death he was condemned as a Lutheran. (Ochino and Vermigli were close associates of Valdés. See pp. 286–87.)

Questionable Groups

The Spanish Inquisition also concerned itself with the *Alumbrados* ("enlightened ones"), a mystical movement of Franciscan origins that emphasized the direct inspiration of the Holy Spirit and total passivity in the hands of God, a movement with which Loyola was briefly suspected of being in sympathy. The Spanish Inquisition also continued to investigate *conversos*, including those of Portugal, after Spain gained control of that kingdom in 1598. In 1609, the remaining *Moriscos* (Muslims) were expelled from Spain.

Nicodemism

Both Catholic and Protestant authorities warned zealots not to seek martyrdom. Subterfuges—disguises, false names, hiding places, flight—were permitted, but an outright denial of one's faith was not. Nevertheless, recantations in the face of prison or torture were not uncommon. Nicodemism—named after the Pharisee who visited Jesus only in secret—was the name given to those who conformed to the official religion in order to avoid persecution, while continuing to practice another faith in secret. Both Catholic and Protestant leaders denounced this, but there were occasionally notable examples, such as a Swiss bishop who publicly presided at the Catholic liturgy while secretly participating in Calvinist prayer services.

Protestants recalled Old Testament martyrs, while Catholics claimed the innumerable early Christians who had suffered under the Roman Empire. For centuries those saints had been venerated primarily for their patronage (curing illnesses, for example), but now the circumstances of their deaths became once more relevant.

Both Protestants and Catholics kept martyrologies of the recent heroes of their faiths, emphasizing the way in which the martyrs had gone to their deaths joyfully and with unshakable courage but at the same time warning that courage alone was not a guarantee of truth—misguided fanatics might face death as resolutely as true martyrs.

"Sanguis Martyrum"

As in the early centuries, the blood of martyrs was the seed of Christians, as brave deaths on both sides aroused admiration and sometimes conversions. English Catholics dipped cloths in the blood of martyred priests and spirited away parts of their bodies, venerating them as saints long before they were officially canonized.

A Share in the Passion

For Catholics, martyrdom also offered the ultimate way of sharing in the Passion of Jesus, and More meditated on that in prison, passing beyond the theological quarrels with which he had previously been involved. Martyrdom was a meritorious "good work" of the kind that Luther denounced; the martyrs' deaths added to the "treasury of merit" that was available to the faithful through indulgences granted by the Church's authority.

Obedience to the monarch was rendered problematical in the sixteenth century by the fact that many devout believers found themselves living under governments that promoted what the believers considered a false faith. Paradoxically, claims of absolute royal power were sometimes made, as in France, precisely in order to require believers to accept official policies of toleration.

The Right of Rebellion

The right of subjects to rebel, even including the right to assassinate a "tyrant", was asserted by those who opposed such toleration. Calvin himself was skeptical, but some Calvinists asserted that right, as did the Jesuit theologians Bellarmine and Francisco Suàrez (d. 1617), who claimed that the pope alone had authority directly from God and that the authority of the state existed only for the needs of the people. Limits to state authority make rebellion against overreaching authorities permissible. The Jesuit Juan de Mariana (d. 1624) anticipated later theories that government arose from the consent of the governed who create political order to serve human needs.

While neither Catholicism nor Calvinism provided kings with unqualified support, the Calvinist insistence that God alone was holy and everything human was infinitely far from Him was impossible to reconcile with the concept of sacred monarchy. In France, Calvinist iconoclasm even extended to desecrating some of the royal tombs.

Presbyterianism

Whereas Luther, almost by default, created a territorial church controlled by the princes, Calvin in Geneva created a semi-autonomous church that had a somewhat uneasy relationship with the city government but in which law and public policy were supposed to be in close conformity to the Gospel. Calvinism's Presbyterian structure—government by councils of clergy, with strong lay involvement—fit well with the republican government of most of the cities, but Calvinism also appealed to feudal nobles in France, Germany, and Scotland.

Religion and Society

Wealth

Conversely, although Calvinism had a special appeal to the commercial middle class, the Catholic merchants of the Italian city republics did not find it necessary to change their religion. Classical Calvinism did not teach that wealth was a sign of divine favor, nor did Calvinism give birth to capitalism, which had existed for a long time. Both Calvin and some Catholic moralists offered cautious justification for the profit motive and began to distinguish between usury and interest on loans to business ventures, although Luther did not.

But there were differences in economic outlook. In Calvinism, money was to be spent prudently, and thrift was a virtue. While both lay and religious lords lived in palaces and wore brightly colored clothes of rich material, Calvinist businessmen saved money, typically living in more modest houses and wearing the plain black garments shown in their seventeenth-century portraits by the Dutch painter Rembrandt van Rijn (d. 1669).

Morality

There were divisions in the sixteenth century that were as much cultural as religious in nature and that cut across Catholic-Protestant lines. Protestants and Catholics differed very little over practical moral questions, with Protestant leaders continuing to condemn the practice of contraception, for example. But there was some division over public morals. While Catholics, Anglicans, and Lutherans did not condone prostitution, dancing, gambling, or drunkenness, they tended to tolerate those things as perennial and unavoidable sins that could be restrained but not suppressed. Puritans, on the other hand, were those Protestants who attempted to create "godly communities" where public sin was systematically suppressed. Along with Calvinists, they condemned almost all aspects of popular religious culture—art and music, pious practices, and communal celebrations such as fairs and carnivals, some of which Lutherans and Anglicans tolerated.

Perhaps due mainly not to religion but to the development of capitalism, attitudes toward charity were changing. In Protestant countries, the abolition of monasticism implied that poverty no longer had positive value and was to be eliminated by one means or another.

Medieval almsgiving had been somewhat indiscriminate—giving unconditionally to those who begged—something that fulfilled God's will and thereby contributed to one's own salvation. From a worldly perspective, it also showed that the donor was not miserly, that he spent freely on himself and others. But Calvinists demanded greater accountability, so that the campaign to eliminate poverty moved in two directions simultaneously: on the one hand, efforts to lift up the poor through education, and on the other, harsh measures to discourage begging, which was now seen as shameful. Property seized from the Catholic Church, when it did not remain in the hands of those who took it, was to some extent used to endow schools and other philanthropic institutions.

The Poor

The Road to Reform

The Popes

For decades, the popes of the Reformation period were scarcely able to cope with the religious crisis. So fierce were ecclesiastical rivalries that a faction of cardinals once attempted to poison Pope Leo X, who had their leader executed, then packed the Sacred College with thirty-one new appointees. He was succeeded by Adrian VI (1522–1523). A Netherlander who had been the tutor of Emperor Charles V and held high office in the Empire, he would be the last non-Italian pope until 1978. Despite this background, Adrian— yet another student of the Brethren of the Common Life—was a reformer whose austere ways made him unpopular with some of the cardinals. After Adrian's brief pontificate, the cardinals elected Leo's cousin (both were Medicis from Florence) as Clement VII. Like his cousin, Clement was well-meaning but proved unable to deal with the crisis.

The Sack of Rome

Charles V, despite his sincere Catholicism, also remained committed to Hapsburg territorial claims in Italy, which from time to time put him on a collision course with the papacy. In 1527, the imperial troops— mostly mercenaries, many of them Lutherans who had not been paid for a long time—entered Rome and subjected it to a brutal sacking that went on for a week and forced Clement VII to take refuge in the Castel St. Angelo.

The Sack of Rome was one of the low points in the entire history of the city, and Clement interpreted it as divine punishment for his own sins and those of Rome. He was not inspired to embrace a reform program, but he did commission Michelangelo's rendition of the *Last Judgment* in the Sistine Chapel, a terrifying reminder of sin and punishment, in dramatic contrast to the triumphant scenes of the creation the artist had painted in the same place a generation earlier.

Paul III   Papal support for the reforming impulse in the Church began with
Paul III, who had led a scandalous life. He fathered children, and his
ecclesiastical career flourished primarily because of his aristocratic Farnese family connections and the fact that his sister had been one of
Pope Alexander VI's mistresses. By the time of his election, he had
undergone a change of heart, although he still used his office to favor
his children.

The Roman Curia had for a long time been a place of notorious
corruption, and Paul began the mundane but important change—
implemented over decades—of the reform of canon law and papal
finances, especially the abolition of the intricate network of exemptions from rules that had been the cause of so much corruption.

The Commission   Most importantly, Paul named Contarini, Carafa, Pole, and Sadoleto
for Reform   to a Commission for the Reform of the Church, the result of which,
in 1536, was a blunt diagnosis of evils and how they were to be cor-
rected, not sparing the papacy itself. The report contained nothing
new, its importance stemming from the prestige of its authors and the
fact that the Pope accepted it.

Spirituals   Protestantism placed the Spiritual party of Catholic reformers in a difficult position, since the Pauline doctrine of justification was now the
principal basis of dissent from Catholic teaching, forcing men like Pole
and Contarini to struggle to formulate the concept of justification by
faith in such a way as also to affirm that good works did have merit in
the eyes of God.

Regensburg

The viability of their position was tested in 1542, when Contarini
represented the Holy See at a conference at Regensburg (Ratisbon)[7]
in Germany, where an attempt was made to resolve the Catholic-
Lutheran differences. Luther himself did not participate, but his chief
disciple, Philipp Melanchthon (d. 1560), agreed with Contarini on
the nature of justification. However, there proved to be no meeting of
the minds on the ecclesial issues—the priesthood, the Mass, the sacraments, and papal authority. Contarini returned to Rome and died
soon afterward. The failure at Regensburg to some extent ended the
Spiritualist phase of the Catholic Reformation, although it was rumored
that Pole would have been elected pope in 1549 or 1550 had he indicated his willingness to accept the office.

Apostasies

The Spirituals suffered acute embarrassment when Bernardino Ochino
(d. 1564), the third general of the Capuchins and a renowned preacher

---

[7] The site of Benedict XVI's controversial 2007 speech about Islam, possibly chosen
because of its historic ecumenical connection.

of reform, shocked the Catholic world by fleeing from Italy and eventually going to Geneva, where he became a Calvinist. (He moved steadily leftward in his theology and died in Poland, alienated from all recognized religious groups.) Peter Martyr Vermigli (d. 1562), another Italian theologian, also became a Protestant, as did Pietro Paulo Vergerio (d. 1565), at one time the papal nuncio to Germany.

Throughout the history of the Church, great crises have usually been resolved by a general council, and cries for another such meeting began almost as soon as Lateran V ended. But there were formidable issues: whether Lutherans should participate, as they demanded; whether the Council should be fully under papal authority or be semi-independent, in accord with conciliarist theory; and the degree to which secular rulers would exert influence. Not until 1545—more than a quarter of a century after the beginning of Lutheranism—were the obstacles overcome sufficiently to enable Paul III to summon a council at Trent.

Protestants were offered safe conduct to attend (none did), but with the understanding that the assembly would judge them, not engage in dialogue. The Pope remained in Rome but appointed legates directly answerable to himself. Trent, in northern Italy, was technically part of the Empire, which satisfied Charles V, but this led France in effect to boycott the proceedings, thereby leaving the Italian bishops as the large majority of the participants, along with some Spanish and Germans and a smattering of others.

There were recognizable factions at the Council, some along national lines, others doctrinal. As in previous councils, the final decrees were sometimes the result of negotiations that resulted in ambiguous wording. Debates were often acrimonious—on one occasion (reminiscent of St. Nicholas at Nicaea) a Greek bishop angrily yanked out the beard of an Italian prelate.

The first session lasted less than two years, suspended because war broke out in Germany and disease struck the city of Trent. The second session did not meet until 1555, under the aegis of Julius III (1550–1555), who had been one of the original papal legates at the Council. It too soon ended, both because of war and because, following Julius' death and a brief interim pontificate, Carafa was elected pope as Paul IV, and he opposed the Council as a threat to papal authority. The final session of Trent, by far the most productive of the three, met from 1561 to 1563 under the aegis of Pius IV (1559–1565), who officially approved all the conciliar decrees.

Even before the Council, there had been differences between the Spirituals—who gave priority to reform, in the sense of correcting the abuses that Protestants attacked—and the Zealots, who favored an

The Council of Trent

Difficulties

Factions

The Three Sessions

Doctrine and Discipline

all-out offensive against heresy. After much debate, the Council decided to consider disciplinary and doctrinal issues simultaneously, both correcting abuses and clarifying and amplifying doctrine.

The Sins of the Clergy

The Reformation was only peripherally a protest against clerical misconduct. Zwingli, for example, admitted that as a priest he had been unchaste, and Luther jibed at fornicating clergy primarily to urge that they take wives. However, the notorious sins of so many of the clergy, including some of the highest-ranking prelates, made them less than credible as spiritual leaders.

Pluralism

The root of abuses, as had been diagnosed on many previous occasions, was the bishops' neglect of their dioceses, where they were responsible for right order. At the beginning of the Council, there were no fewer than eighty bishops habitually living in Rome and absent from their sees, and one French cardinal simultaneously held three archbishoprics, five bishoprics, and several abbeys. Trent not only required episcopal residence but abolished pluralism and the granting (in effect selling) of exemptions from the residency rule. The Council required that those appointed bishop already be in holy orders, thereby eliminating the abuse whereby laymen (often young boys), or their families, could collect the revenues of their sees without bothering to become priests. The Council also forbade nepotism.

Episcopal Authority

Although those decrees were not controversial in themselves, they provoked debate over whether bishops received their authority from the Holy See or directly from God. Jesuit theologians in particular upheld papal authority, and some bishops expounded an ecclesiology that was almost Eastern Orthodox in its assertions of episcopal autonomy.

Seminaries

While members of religious orders were adequately educated in their monasteries, and elite clergy attended universities, Trent recognized the low state of education of many of the parish clergy, most of whom in effect learned by the apprenticeship system. The Council therefore decreed that each diocese was to establish a seminary ("seed place"), where candidates for ordination could be properly formed intellectually and spiritually and carefully scrutinized as to their worthiness, an institution that came to be adopted by Protestants as well. The phenomenon of the vagabond priest was curtailed by requiring all priests to be directly under a superior and to have a specific assignment. Elaborate procedures were prescribed for dealing with this and other clerical irregularities.

Marriage

The Council forbade "clandestine marriages"—those celebrated without prior public announcement and without the presence of the parish priest and two witnesses—but at the same time it permitted marriage without the consent of the parents, something that some civil governments did not allow. It also issued miscellaneous decrees against dueling and other practices.

To an extent, many Catholics in the earlier sixteenth century were responsive to Protestantism because they found themselves confronted with ideas they had never heard before. (For example, the Eucharist was sacred, but the concept of Transubstantiation meant little.) Thus the Church found herself called upon to clarify teachings that were now seen as imprecise, just as the Protestants had to formulate confessions in order to distinguish true from false understandings of the Gospel. Trent also authorized the first comprehensive catechism of Catholic doctrine.

Clarity of Doctrine

Trent condemned heretical propositions but did not attribute them to anyone by name, a procedure designed to avoid controversies as to whether particular persons actually held the condemned doctrines. Each proposition stated a false belief and declared, of those who held it, "Let them be *anathema*", a Greek word for "condemned".

"Anathema"

The root of all theological issues was the nature and locus of authority. The Council affirmed the authority of the Vulgate, including those books (Tobit, Judith, Wisdom, Sirach or Ecclesiasticus, Baruch, Maccabees 1 and 2) that Protestants had rejected as uncanonical, and it declared that no one could interpret Scripture in ways contrary to the doctrines of the Church. Most significantly, the Council affirmed "unwritten tradition" as a source of truth along with the Bible, the authenticity of that tradition guaranteed by the Holy Spirit.[8]

Scripture

As at Regensburg, the issue of justification was recognized as both the heart of the theological conflict and as the subtlest and most difficult of issues, the opposing errors being on the one hand the Protestant denial of the efficacy of good works and on the other a Pelagian optimism about human nature.[9] All sides appealed to the authority of Augustine, and Jerome Seripando (d. 1563), the general of the Augustinians, played an important role at Trent in ensuring that any condemnation of Protestantism did not catch Augustine himself in its net.

Grace and Free Will

The Tridentine definition of justification was subtle. Men stood condemned because of Original Sin and were saved only by the sacrifice

Justification

---

[8] The modern claim that Tradition merely means the Church's interpretation of Scripture is not borne out by the actual words of Trent, nor does such a theory account for such venerable doctrines as the Assumption of Mary.

[9] As with the early Christological councils, the decrees of Trent on justification and some other issues were forged through a certain amount of compromise and therefore resulted in some deliberate ambiguities, a fact overlooked by those who think the Second Vatican Council was unique in that regard.

of Christ. They had to respond freely to the offer of salvation, but that response was made possible only by "predisposing grace" that was offered to all, without any merit on their part, since God desired that all should be saved. Once accepted, such grace rendered human works meritorious in God's sight, so that, contrary to the Lutherans, justification was not merely "imputed" to men by a merciful God, but men were actually made righteous by Christ's sacrifice.

Men could overcome sin, because concupiscence, although an ineradicable part of human nature, was merely a disposition to sin, not sin itself. As often as men fell, they could be raised up again, especially through the sacrament of penance, because even mortal sin caused the loss only of grace, not of faith.

Although faith was received as a gift, by cooperating with grace and performing good works, believers could grow in hope and charity and be made capable of obeying the Law. But they should also not have "vain confidence" that they could never lose the gift of salvation, as the Protestant doctrine of predestination implied, since, because of their free will, men could either grow in righteousness or lose grace through their own fault.

Indulgences

On the issue that had set off the Reformation, the Council reaffirmed the doctrine and practice of indulgences but decreed that their reception should not (except for the *cruzada* in Spain) be tied to any kind of monetary payment. In response to another frequent complaint, it warned against the abuse of excommunication for trivial purposes, especially those having to do with money.

Ecclesial Issues

The ecclesial issues that had made agreement impossible at Regensburg were defined with relative ease: seven sacraments rather than two; the sacraments as actually conferring grace, not merely symbolizing it; the sacraments as having their effect *ex opere operato*, that is, by objective divine power, not the subjective state of the priest or the recipient; the Mass as the continuation of the sacrifice of Calvary; the Real Presence of Christ in the Eucharist; Transubstantiation; the appropriateness, therefore, of eucharistic adoration; the "power of the keys" whereby priests had the ability to forgive sins in the name of Christ; Purgatory; the invocation of the saints; the veneration of images and relics; prayers for the dead.

On disputed disciplinary issues, priestly celibacy was reaffirmed; celebration of Mass in the vernacular was forbidden; and Christ was declared to be present "whole and entire" under both eucharistic species, thus it was not necessary to receive Communion under both kinds, and laymen were not permitted to do so. As part of the renewed eucharistic piety, Trent also encouraged more frequent Communion, although—surprising to modern Catholics—the Council thought that weekly Communion was sufficient even for those in an advanced stage

of training for the priesthood, and monthly Communion was sufficient for nuns.

Jesuits were among the leading champions of orthodoxy. The Spaniard Diego Laynez (d. 1565), who succeeded Ignatius as General of
the Society, was perhaps the most important theologian at Trent, where
he especially upheld papal authority. The Netherlander St. Peter Can-
isius (d. 1597) guided the Counter-Reformation in Germany, writing
books and pamphlets, preaching widely, and founding schools, all of
which had tangible results in attracting Protestants back to Rome.

Lateran V had urged the censorship of books, and Trent renewed that
demand, leading to the formal establishment of the *Index of Forbidden
Books*, which began with theological works but eventually expanded
to encompass philosophical works considered fallacious and works of
fiction deemed to be immoral. Placing a book on the *Index* did not
necessarily imply its definitive condemnation but merely that it was
deemed imprudent to read it. Even high-ranking prelates might have
their writings banned at least temporarily, and many books were eventually removed from the list.

Trent decreed almost complete uniformity of liturgy throughout the
Church, something that was perhaps made possible for the first time
by the printing press, which allowed the approved Roman Missal (Mass
book) to be used everywhere. The expansion of the Roman Curia
after the Council included a new Congregation of Rites, whose responsibility was to regulate the liturgy, and for the next four hundred years
there would be almost no liturgical change.

Trent was a beginning, not an end, and for the next two centuries,
reform-minded popes and bishops had to struggle against entrenched
political and ecclesiastical interests to implement its decrees. The spirit
of the Catholic Reformation, forged at Trent, was one of strict orthodoxy and morality, deep personal piety, and obedience to Church authority, a revival that was profoundly successful in giving the Church a
character that would endure for four hundred years.

Although sometimes thought of as an attempt to preserve the Middle
Ages, the Catholic Reformation was in fact a new, distinctively modern
chapter in the history of the Church. It was a creative period that
produced new conceptions of religious life (the Jesuits), catechizing and
evangelizing in ways never before attempted, and a daring new style of
religious art—the Baroque.

Pope Paul IV
Paul IV, who as a cardinal had set up the Roman Inquisition and as pope
established the *Index*, enforced clerical good conduct by imprisoning or

exiling those whom he considered corrupt and imposing draconian laws on Rome, where prostitution had been rife. At first, he blatantly favored nephews who showed themselves wholly unworthy, but eventually he turned against them.

Ignatius Loyola had his own mandate of obedience tested when Paul, an old enemy of the Jesuits, after considering suppressing the Society entirely, required the Jesuits to resume the monastic practice of the communal Office, something Ignatius thought undermined their work. (Paul's animosity seems to have stemmed merely from his increasingly rigid suspicion of anything new.) When asked what he would do if the Society were suppressed, Ignatius responded that, after a quarter of an hour in which to collect himself, he would accept it as the divine will. He died during Paul IV's pontificate, without knowing if his order would survive.

Pope Pius IV
Pius IV expelled his predecessor's unworthy relatives, even executing a Carafa cardinal. Pius was himself a nepotist, but some of his relatives proved to be exemplary, notably St. Charles Borromeo (d. 1584), whom Pius made archbishop of Milan, a cardinal, and papal secretary of state when the prelate was only twenty-one years old. Borromeo proved to be the model of a Counter-Reformation bishop.

Pope Pius V
St. Pius V, the last pope to be canonized for three centuries, was an ascetic Dominican who had been head of the Inquisition and who vigorously implemented the decrees of Trent, including publishing the Catechism, Missal, and Breviary (a "short" Divine Office) authorized by the Council.

Pope Gregory XIII
Although Gregory XIII had fathered a child, he was a conscientious pope, particularly in streamlining the papal court to eliminate offices that seemed to be mere excuses to collect fees, thereby reducing some of the taxes that had aroused wide resentment. Gregory's most lasting achievement was promulgating the new calendar that bore his name, which was devised in order to eliminate discrepancies in the existing solar calculations. Among other things, it restored January 1 as the beginning of the new year.

Pope Sixtus V
Highly unusual for the time, Sixtus V, a Franciscan of blunt manners, was of peasant origins. Like Gregory, he had led a less than exemplary life, but once elected he proved to be a draconian moralist like Paul IV, enforcing order in the Papal States, vigorously prosecuting both heresy and civil crime, even imposing the death penalty for adultery. Sixtus also continued the process of restructuring the Roman Curia, limiting membership in the College of Cardinals to seventy and transforming

the cardinals from semi-independent princes into agents of papal government.

Nuncios

In the late sixteenth century, the Holy See formalized its system of papal nuncios ("heralds" or ambassadors), partly because a whole territory could be won back to the Church if the ruler himself were converted. One Jesuit was sent as papal nuncio to the court of Ivan IV the Terrible of Russia (1533–1584), without result. Two others were dispatched to Sweden, where they disguised their identities from everyone but a receptive King John III (1568–1592), who secretly converted but returned to Lutheranism when Gregory XIII refused to authorize priestly marriage, the Mass in the vernacular, or Communion in both kinds for the laity.

The key to reform at the local level was a zealous bishop, of whom there were an increasing number after the midpoint of the century. Borromeo was the model, leading an austere life of prayer and penance, visiting plague victims, and relentlessly striving to reform his clergy. Zealous reformers could expect sometimes fierce resistance—a group of unreformed Franciscans in Milan tried to have Borromeo assassinated as he presided at Vespers in his cathedral, and St. John of the Cross (Juan de Yepes, d. 1591), who was involved in reforming the Carmelites, was at one point abducted by some of his brethren, kept a prisoner, and severely beaten.

Saints

Borromeo

Witness to the success of reform was St. Francis Borgia (d. 1572), a Spanish duke who first brought the Jesuits into his territory, then joined them, becoming Ignatius' second successor as general of the Society. Borgia was the great-grandson of the wicked Pope Alexander VI and the grandson of an archbishop.

Francis Borgia

St. Teresa of Avila (Teresa de Cepeda y Ahumada, d. 1582) joined a Carmelite convent whose nuns were mostly aristocrats who, by traditional Carmelite standards, led somewhat pampered lives. But she underwent a conversion and as mother superior began reforming her convent, requiring the nuns once again to go without shoes ("discalced"); enforcing a strict discipline of prayer, poverty, and self-denial; abolishing the requirement that novices bring dowries with them; and refusing to recognize worldly rank within the convent. Because of this, she was called upon to reform Carmelite houses all over Spain, where she often encountered fierce resistance, and she also founded a number of new convents.

Teresa of Avila

St. Philip Neri (d. 1595) was an eccentric Roman priest who took delight in revelry and jokes and often wore odd clothes. He gathered

Philip Neri

together a group of men to work among the poor, then formed them into a new community, the Oratorians (from the Latin word for "prayer"), who reflected their founder's informal style, eschewing a strict rule and constituting themselves as diocesan priests living in communities. While the Jesuits conducted highly structured retreats, the Oratorians practiced a less formal kind of spirituality, such as small groups that met to pray and discuss spiritual books.

Spiritual Renewal

Penance

Amidst all the upheavals of the century, a great spiritual revival occurred under Catholic auspices. Though in response to the long-standing dissatisfactions with the overly formal, even mechanical, nature of so much traditional piety, the movement was intensified by the Protestant emphasis on faith as an interior state of soul. Trent, in this as in other things, sought for unity between interior and exterior, as in its approach to the sacrament of penance: the formal confession of mortal sins to a priest was required but great stress was also laid on genuine contrition.

Reform of lay morals was part of the general program of renewal, so that in places visited by vigorous preachers there was sometimes a measurable decline in the rate of illegitimate births. Frequent recourse to the sacrament of penance was taken as a hallmark of authentic Catholicism, the primary means through which lay people were disciplined in the practice of their faith. One Jesuit church in Cologne had twenty confessionals to accommodate the large numbers of penitents, and in Spain, vigilant clergy kept track of those who failed to confess, regarding it not only as moral laxity but as a possible sign of heresy.

The Spiritual Exercises

Recalling the spiritual confusion he had encountered among his fellow students in Spain, Ignatius conceived the characteristically bold idea that lay people and secular clergy needed spiritual formation just as vowed religious did. Some late-medieval spiritual directors urged their disciples to undertake "spiritual exercises"—planned and organized regimens of prayer and penance—and Ignatius, who was familiar with much of that literature, composed the "Spiritual Exercises" as a handbook for spiritual directors, laying out for the first time a systematic plan for what came to be called "retreats".

Ignatius had mystical experiences, some of whose authenticity he eventually came to doubt, but Jesuit spirituality was forged primarily for people living in the world. The Exercises were rigorous and systematic, embodying a shrewd understanding of human psychology. Retreatants were to proceed step by step, day by day, beginning with an acute awareness of their own sinfulness and a sincere desire to repent, and with "discernment of spirits"—the ability to recognize when inspirations were from God and when they might originate merely from the individual himself or even from the devil. The retreatants proceeded through a systematic meditation on the Gospels and at a climactic moment were asked to visualize two armies confronting one another across a battlefield—one the army of Christ, the other of Satan—and commanded to make a deliberate choice between them. Having chosen Christ, they were then to embark on a regimen of penance, prayer, and meditation that prepared them to do battle for Him in the world. Frequent confession, preceded by an exacting examination of conscience, was one of the principal means by which the individual maintained his commitment to Christ. At the end, the individual was to assess his concrete situation in terms of how best he could promote the greater glory of God.

Part of the effectiveness of the Spiritual Exercises was that they were adaptable to individual needs and to people at various stages of spiritual development—vocal prayer, which was the recitation of verbal formulae; mental prayer or meditation, which was consciously thinking about holy themes, especially from Scripture; and contemplation, which meant placing oneself in the presence of God and allowing the sense of His presence to suffuse the soul.

Mysticism

The Catholic mystical tradition was carried to new heights during the sixteenth century, especially by the Carmelites in Spain. This greatest flowering of mysticism in the history of the Church, while remaining firmly Catholic, plumbed the interior of the soul more deeply than any Protestant undertook to do.

Teresa of Avila

Besides reforming the Carmelite order, the mystic St. Teresa of Avila wrote a series of books—her autobiography, *The Interior Castle*, and others—that described the movement of the soul toward God more fully than anyone else had ever done. For Teresa, the spiritual life was not the deliberate cultivation of esoteric experiences but simply living and praying as a Christian should. The mystical experience was not to be sought for its own sake, nor was it an exotic psychological state; it was simply the culmination of a life lived entirely for God.

The Practical Life
Although in the mystical experience the soul transcended the mundane world, it did not abandon the world. To the contrary, Teresa, who was herself intensely active all her life, insisted that the spiritual life be lived amidst daily responsibilities, to the point where she even urged superiors to restrict the time for prayer of nuns who neglected their mundane duties.

Orthodoxy
If some earlier schools of mysticism were suspected of heterodoxy, Teresa insisted on complete adherence to the teachings of the Church. Not well-educated herself, she told her readers to submit themselves to the judgment of competent theologians. She was the first woman to be declared a doctor of the Church, because what she lacked in formal theology she more than made up for in spiritual wisdom.

Consolations

For Teresa, as with Ignatius, the individual began with an acute sense of sin and a determination to live a life of virtue, implicitly affirming the efficacy of good works, and proceeding humbly, by means of vocal prayer. (Teresa herself once went for eighteen years unable to pray except from a book.) As the soul entered more deeply into the life of prayer, it received many graces, especially joyful "consolations", sometimes even visions. Such experiences were a sign of progress in the spiritual life but could also prove treacherous if the soul were insufficiently cautious.

Purgation and Illumination

The next stage of development—the "purgative (purifying) way" identified by some previous mystics—occurred when Christ began to strip from the soul everything that was self-centered, depriving it of its comforts. Instead, the soul experienced sufferings, no longer feeling itself to be especially blessed but, to the contrary, having a heightened sense of its own wretchedness. It was thereby emptied, Teresa explained, in order to be filled by a truth that was wholly divine and that enabled the soul to rise above the world and to understand the things of Heaven. This was the "illuminative way" of traditional mysticism. The soul was now blind, in contrast to the many ideas and images it previously had enjoyed, but it was the paradoxical kind of blindness caused by light itself.

Unity

Teresa described the soul's intricate journey into the deepest chamber of itself, where the Bridegroom lived, a journey that could be completed only by a wholly passive surrender to the divine will. In this "unitive way", the soul finally achieved fulfillment of its longing. Teresa described this as an ecstasy, in which her heart was pierced by an arrow and she was set on fire by the Bridegroom's all-consuming love, a pain that she hoped would last forever.

John of the Cross John of the Cross was a younger contemporary of Teresa, and their paths crossed briefly. Since he was a learned theologian, his writings were more systematic than hers, although perhaps less direct and vivid. His major work, *The Dark Night of the Soul*, described the sense of utter abandonment that the soul experienced as it was being led into the high realms of spiritual union.[10]

The Arts One of the major religious divisions of the age was not over doctrine as such but between liturgical and nonliturgical churches—Catholics,

---

[10] After the death of Bl. Teresa of Calcutta, some of her previously unpublished writings revealed that she had undergone that experience for many years. Far from indicating weakness of faith, it was further evidence of her great sanctity.

Lutherans, and Anglicans in the first group, Calvinists and others in the second—a division that profoundly affected the arts.

Thus Zwinglians, and after them Calvinists, smashed statues and stained-glass windows, whitewashed the inside of churches, and allowed no music except the unaccompanied chanting of Psalms. Rembrandt was practically the only Calvinist artist of note, and biblical scenes were practically the only acceptable form of Protestant religious art, although even they were not permitted in churches. In this as in other things, Luther proved to be the most conservative of the Reformers, retaining vestments, candles, altar crosses, paintings, instrumental music, even, for a time, incense and Latin. Swedish Lutherans especially retained a particularly "high" kind of liturgy.

Catholic churches, on the other hand, were huge, lavishly decorated buildings that, along with being places of worship, were in effect museums of painting and sculpture. Trent enjoined an austerity in art and music thought appropriate to the spirit of reform; however, appropriately, the Catholic Reformation inspired great artistic creations (including drama), since one of the most profound differences with Protestantism was the Catholic mediation of the spiritual through the material.

This sacramentalism justified the dazzling new expressions of art and music called the Baroque, a term of uncertain origin. (Because of the Baroque's departures from the ideal symmetries of classical art, it may have derived from a Portuguese word for a twisted pearl.) The Baroque was the preeminent art of the Catholic Reformation, uniting doctrinal orthodoxy with dramatically new stylistic forms. Like the organization of the Jesuits, it was a major example of the highly innovative, in some ways even revolutionary, creativity of the sixteenth-century Church.

The Baroque spread as far as Latin America and Japan, but it flourished best in Europe, its exuberance stemming from religion but made possible by the aristocratic mentality that disdained economic prudence and spent lavishly as a sign of wealth and generosity. It was used also in palaces and public buildings and at one extreme could shade into a mere reveling in sensual splendor.

Both lay and ecclesiastical princes, especially the great papal families of the age—Medici, Farnese, Borghese, Barberini—commissioned artistic works that proclaimed their piety but also their importance. Typically, the façade of St. Peter's in Rome, completed by Gian Lorenzo Bernini (d. 1680), announced not only its patron saint but Paul V Borghese (1605–1621), one of the popes who brought it to completion. Bernini's famous statue *The Ecstasy of St. Teresa* was in a chapel whose patrons, the Coronari family, looked down on her from the box of a theatre, and it embodied the ambiguity of so much Renaissance art: a powerful dramatization

298

of the mystical experience that could also be seen as a celebration of human passion.

Dynamism

Since the universal harmony of Christendom had been shattered, the religious conflicts of the age seemed, at least temporarily, to render the serene spiritual harmonies of the Gothic impossible. Thus the Baroque expressed dynamism rather than settled order and the restless rather than the untroubled spirit. Its palpable stylistic tensions were perfectly suited to express the dramatic struggle to subdue the will, which presupposed the Catholic affirmation of free will and the efficacy of good works. In the Baroque, peace of soul was attainable only through intense and unceasing struggle, as in the Spiritual Exercises and the interior journeys of the mystics. The mystical experience was the highest expression of this striving, making the *Ecstasy of St. Teresa* perhaps the highest achievement of Baroque sculpture—the saint swooning as an angel pierced her heart with a golden arrow.

Rising to the Heavens

The Baroque expressed energies barely held in, the exuberant urge to break through boundaries, restlessness channeled into a longing for infinity, the desire to rise above the mundane world, access to the eternal through the temporal. The path to Heaven was a strenuous one, but glorious rewards were visible to those who dared look up as they struggled. Thus at ground level, Baroque art might portray bewilderingly complex worldly scenes, then lead the eye higher and higher, often culminating in domes painted so as to seem open to the sky, where people visibly escaped into the heavens, where the visible and the invisible, the finite and the infinite, the natural and the supernatural dramatically and gloriously united.

Saints Triumphant

Baroque art tended to be highly celebratory, representing great spiritual triumphs, with creativity lavished on the tombs of both secular and ecclesiastical princes, as in the papal tombs in Rome, which did not invite the viewer to "remember death" but instead represented the popes enthroned and bestowing their blessings. A favorite theme was the entry of a saint into Heaven, as on the tombs of Philip Neri and Ignatius Loyola in their respective Roman churches. Ignatius' tomb showed not only his entry into Heaven but a sculpted representation of damnation—two naked men tumbled into Hell as angels ripped out the pages of heretical books identified on their spines as having been written by Luther and Calvin.

The Piety of Artists

The artists of the age were not merely filling commissions; Michelangelo, Bernini, Palestrina, and most others were devout Catholics who expressed their faith through their creations. Michelangelo agonized over his sins, and in *The Last Judgment* he allegedly painted himself on the skin of St. Bartholomew, which the saint, who was flayed alive, is holding over Hell.

The renewed emphasis on eucharistic piety had effects on architecture. The altar was the focus of the worshipper's attention, often under a magnificent canopy, and the tabernacle was set on the high altar as a visible affirmation of the Real Presence. Churches were built as large open spaces, without rood screens and with as few pillars as possible, in order not to interfere with the worshippers' view of the altar and the monstrance. Since Jesuits did not celebrate the Divine Office in common, their churches also dispensed with the choir stalls that separated the laity from the sanctuary in many medieval churches.

Architecture

As the Baroque style developed, it became the vehicle of Catholic triumph, celebrating an admittedly partial victory over Protestantism and a successful reassertion of the Church's spiritual authority. The theme of the triumph of the soul over the heaviness of earth—its flight to the heavenly realms—blended almost imperceptibly into the celebration of the triumph of the Church over her enemies, both merging into a single event in which the victory of truth over falsehood made possible the soul's triumph over evil.

The Church Triumphant

Sixtus V systematically rebuilt Rome around its most important churches, putting the statues of Peter and Paul on top the columns of the Roman emperors Trajan and Marcus Aurelius and setting up Egyptian obelisks at strategic points around the city, each surmounted by a cross, thereby symbolizing the triumph of Christianity over paganism. The papal project of rebuilding the city provided unparalleled opportunities for architects and artists, and, among others, the Jesuits and the Oratorians commissioned great churches in the new style—Philip Neri the *Chiesa Nuova* ("new church") and the Jesuits the Church of the *Gesù*—although there was some tension between Tridentine austerity and the new style.

Rome Rebuilt

Urban VIII (1623–1644), during whose pontificate the Papal States reached their greatest extent, opened St. Peter's Basilica in 1626 as the greatest structure in Christendom, where almost every detail was a proclamation of a faith that had survived its greatest crisis: the papal throne and the giant statue of St. Peter reaffirming papal authority, the pillars around the high altar serving as huge reliquaries, the wide panoply of saints overlooking St. Peter's Square promising their protection and intercession to the faithful. The opening of St. Peter's marked the successful completion of a project that had begun as a disaster, when the indulgence preached on its behalf triggered events that seemed to threaten the end of the Church. Both the brand-new churches and the rebuilt older ones were monumental testimonies to the revival of the papacy and of the Church herself.

St. Peter's Completed

I0   Reason and Revolution

Religion and Politics

Religion never exerted greater influence in Europe than in the period 1500 to 1660, and perhaps at no time in history was it so closely bound up with politics. But—at first largely unrecognized—it was also being undermined and discredited.

Spain

Spain, which had been in political and economic decline since the death of Philip II, had sunk to the level of a second-rate power, but the Church was perhaps stronger there than anywhere else, due in part to the fact that most bishops were not from the nobility and thus were not secular princes. There were more priests per capita than in any other country, and piety was intense at all social levels. The Inquisition continued, under royal control, but it had relatively little business, since Protestantism was virtually unknown and the influence of skeptical ideas was minimal.

England

In England, Catholics at first hoped for better treatment from the new Stuart dynasty, but when that did not happen a small group hatched the Gunpowder Plot, with the aim of blowing up the houses of Parliament while James I (1603–1625) and the leading men of the kingdom were assembled. Several plotters were executed, including a solider named Guy Fawkes, whose name was thereafter associated with an annual anti-Catholic celebration. A few Jesuits who were not even aware of the plot were also executed.

James and his son Charles I (1625–1649) both had Catholic wives and did not enforce the anti-Catholic laws rigorously. Charles also supported efforts to make the Church of England more "Catholic"— marble altars, altar rails, pictures in church, a heightened emphasis on episcopal authority—which contributed to his overthrow and execution at the hands of the militant Protestants called Puritans. During the Puritan interregnum that followed his death, Catholics were severely persecuted.

Charles II (1660–1685) proposed a blanket policy of limited religious toleration, but Parliament rejected the idea, and he acquiesced passively in the execution of several Catholics in the Popish Plot of 1678—a fraudulent claim that Catholics were conspiring to overthrow Charles in favor of his Catholic brother James.

But Charles, who himself became a Catholic on his deathbed, made a secret agreement with Louis XIV (1643–1715) to restore England to the Catholic Church, and he successfully fended off attempts to deny James the throne.

James II (1685–1688) sincerely desired religious toleration but encountered trouble because he attempted to achieve it by royal edict, without parliamentary agreement, and arrested seven bishops who refused to recognize his decree. When his wife gave birth to a son, thereby ensuring a Catholic succession, many of the leading men of the kingdom invited his Protestant daughter Mary II (1688–1694) and her Netherlander husband, William III (1688–1702) to take the throne, and James fled to France.

After this so-called Glorious Revolution, Catholics continued to be subject to harassment, especially because of Stuart attempts to regain the throne, which reinforced the idea that Catholics were traitors. In 1780, a proposal to grant freedom to Catholics was abandoned when it provoked massive riots in London, in which numerous people were killed.[1] Catholics were officially allowed freedom of worship a few years later, while remaining excluded from public office and subject to various other civil penalties.

Ireland

In Ireland, the blood of martyrs once more proved to be the seed of Christians. A rebellion during Charles I's reign was put down, and a few years later, the Puritan leader Oliver Cromwell (d. 1658) invaded and brutally suppressed all resistance, beginning a policy of seizing the lands of the Catholic nobility and systematically settling English and Scottish Protestants in their place.

But the restoration of the English monarchy did not help the Irish. As archbishop of Armagh, St. Oliver Plunkett (d. 1681) was a reformer according to the prescriptions of Trent, and he braved extreme conditions to minister to his scattered flock. He was captured and executed at London on trumped-up charges of treason, in which Charles II passively concurred.

At the Battle of the Boyne in 1690, William III defeated James II's last bid to regain his throne. It was the decisive "Orange" victory (the name of William's princely house) that marked the beginning of the fierce strife between Catholics and Protestants in northern Ireland that continued even into the twenty-first century.

As priests in Ireland were outlawed, hunted down, and often savagely persecuted by the British crown, Irish seminaries were established in Rome, Spain, France, and the Spanish Netherlands, and priests replaced the aristocracy as the leaders of Irish society, identifying with the people against their English landlords and associating the Church with liberation from English rule.

---

[1] The Gordon Riots, named after the nobleman who incited them, are the subject of Charles Dickens' novel *Barnaby Rudge*.

Near the end of the eighteenth century, Irish Catholics were given legal freedom of worship in exchange for a promise of loyalty to the crown, and the English government not only allowed the opening of the Maynooth Seminary for the training of priests but partly financed it. The Catholic promise of loyalty was kept. Few Irish supported an abortive uprising in expectation of a French invasion, and many poor Irishmen served in the British army.

Netherlands

The Netherlands was a relatively open society, with toleration urged mainly for pragmatic reasons. Catholics were barely tolerated, however, and were not permitted public places of worship.

Thirty Years' War

In 1618, the German Hapsburg prince Ferdinand was elected king of Bohemia and announced his intention of enforcing the minority Catholic faith on a society that included a large number of Husites, as well as Lutherans and Calvinists. But the Bohemian Diet repudiated Ferdinand and elected in his place a German Calvinist prince, Frederick, ruler of the Rhine Palatinate (d. 1632).

Frederick placed restrictions on Catholics, but Ferdinand soon conquered Bohemia, expelled Fredrick from the Palatinate, and also expelled a Protestant prince who had been elected king of Hungary. Ferdinand first assumed both the Bohemian and Hungarian titles himself, then granted them to his son. Ferdinand was subsequently elected Holy Roman Emperor (1619–1637), but the Protestant princes of the Empire rallied in support of Frederick (who did not, however, regain the Palatinate), precipitating the greatest of all religious conflicts—the Thirty Years' War (1618–1648).

Ferdinand II's aims included the strict enforcement of the Peace of Augsburg of 1555, which had excluded Calvinists, although by 1618 only one of the princely electors of the Empire was a Lutheran, while three were Catholic and three Calvinist. Ferdinand also sought the return of all church lands taken since 1555. Other factors complicated the struggle, especially the fact that Ferdinand's cousins, the Spanish Hapsburgs, hoped to regain control of the Netherlands.

Like other "religious wars", the Thirty Years' War was only partly about religion. Religion provided an often murderous passion, and Ferdinand sincerely wanted to promote the Catholic faith, but the Catholic princes were alarmed that he sought to increase imperial power at their expense.

Several times, Ferdinand was close to victory, but each time the Protestant cause was saved by foreign intervention: first by Lutheran Denmark, then by Lutheran Sweden, finally by Catholic France, whose foreign policy was implacably anti-Hapsburg and demonstrated that, when religious and political interests conflicted, the latter always prevailed. The papacy tried to remain aloof from Hapsburg interests, because of the Hapsburgs' continuing designs on Italy. During its final decade, the war was essentially between the two leading Catholic powers—France and Spain—fought on German territory.

In 1648, Emperor Ferdinand III (1637–1657) had to acquiesce in the Peace of Westphalia, which was a victory for the German princes as a whole, who retained the right to determine the religion of their subjects (including Calvinism) and retained church lands seized contrary to the Peace of Augsburg. The northern Netherlands officially gained their independence, while the southern Netherlands (roughly modern Belgium) remained Catholic under Hapsburg rule, first of Spain, then of Austria. Pope Innocent X (1644–1655) condemned the treaty.

The princes' victory in effect reduced the Holy Roman Empire merely to Austria—one German principality among many. Only in his hereditary lands, including Bohemia and other central European territories, did the emperor have the authority to enforce Catholicism as the official faith.

France

The architect of French support for the German Protestants was Cardinal Armand de Richelieu (d. 1642). Of noble birth, at age 22 he was made bishop of a diocese where his family exercised hereditary influence. During almost twenty years as the power behind the French throne, he pursued a foreign policy in which explicit religious considerations had no place, although he invoked the divine authority of the king to silence criticism. The complexity of the situation was reflected in Richelieu's intimate associate, the Capuchin Joseph du Tremblay (the "Gray Eminence", d. 1638), who was, paradoxically, at the same time a kind of mystic, a fervent advocate of a Crusade against the Turks, and an unwaveringly discreet and loyal agent of the crown.

After Richelieu's death, his place at court was taken by another cardinal, Giulio Mazarini (Mazarin, d. 1661), who had been the papal legate before going over to the royal service. One of his achievements was to help bring about the Peace of Westphalia. A layman, he may have been secretly married to the widowed Queen Anne of Austria (d. 1666), mother of Louis XIV.

Poland

In 1772, Poland, one of the largest countries in Europe, was brutally and cynically dismembered by Catholic Austria, Lutheran Prussia, and Orthodox Russia. Although Poland ceased to exist as a separate country, the Polish people retained their own language and culture. Although Pope Clement XIV (1769–1774) remained silent, the Catholic religion came to be the core of their ethnic identity as they resisted both German Protestantism and Russian Orthodoxy.

Absolute Monarchy

Two realities favored the absolute state—control by the monarchies over the churches and the weakening of the feudal nobility, both of which had been effective limits on kingly power in earlier times. The

Church had begun to lose the struggle in the fourteenth century, and by early modern times royal entanglement had compromised her liberty in a number of ways, leaving her semi-impotent before the power of princes.

The Reformation had given the state control of the churches in virtually all Protestant lands, but pious Catholic monarchs also made the Church pay heavily for their support. The absolute monarchies were in effect Erastian, treating the Church as subordinate to the state, an idea already formulated in the Middle Ages but associated with the Swiss physician Thomas Erastus (d. 1583). Some theory of divine-right monarchy prevailed almost everywhere, although countered by theories that emphasized the consent of the governed.

Bellarmine, notably, refuted the theory of divine right expounded by James I of England, primarily in order to affirm papal authority over monarchs but in the process offering cautious justification for the will of the people. The Spanish Jesuit Francisco Suàrez was even more direct in justifying popular sovereignty.

The Papacy

But Catholic theorists of royal absolutism published sweeping attacks on papal authority, even echoing the Protestant claim that it was a medieval usurpation, and secular princes constantly intrigued in the papal conclaves, ensuring that the man elected was often merely the one with the fewest enemies. The Spanish prevented the election of the great historian Baronius in 1605; and during a deadlock in 1740, Cardinal Prospero Lambertini advised the cardinals, "If you want a good fellow, pick me." (He was promptly elected as Benedict XIV [1740–1758].)

Clement XI (1700–1721) was a cardinal of the Roman Curia who was not even ordained a priest until shortly before his election. Elected after a conclave that lasted 241 days, Pius VI (1775–1799) proved to be both an able leader in a great crisis and a nepotist.

As temporal rulers over the Papal States, the popes were participants in international politics; and, while the popes of the era led blameless personal lives, they were notable mainly for whatever diplomatic skills they possessed. Few showed much courage, and most made concessions—surrendering territory or conceding to princes rights over the Church—in order to retain a precarious independence, a strategy that emboldened secular governments to demand still more concessions and left the Church in an increasingly weakened state.

Religious Toleration

The ideal and the practice of religious toleration gradually grew during the seventeenth century, mainly for political reasons.

France

Before 1600, there emerged at the French court a group dubbed the *Politiques*, because they urged that the needs of "policy"—the state—take precedence over the demands of religion, a position that was given urgency by the assassination of Henry III and Henry IV by Catholics. The practice of limited tolerance seemed the only hope for peace.[2]

Richelieu made war on the Huguenots, personally leading the royal armies and destroying the Huguenot fortresses, but mainly because of their semi-independence of royal control. The provisions of the Edict of Nantes granting them toleration remained in effect. But Louis XIV, the longest-reigning monarch in European history, revoked the Edict in 1685, and in some cases, soldiers were billeted in Huguenot houses to force conformity. The revocation sent numerous Huguenots into exile, although many also remained, always in danger of persecution, and even occasionally achieved prominence in national life. In his ceaseless quest to expand his territory, Louis also invaded the Rhine Palatinate and oppressed its Calvinist inhabitants.

The official Assembly of the Clergy condemned the use of force against the Huguenots, and even Jacques-Bènigne Bossuet (d. 1704), the dominant bishop of the age, doubted its wisdom. Pope Bl. Innocent XI (1676–1689), however, congratulated Louis on his action but privately thought it was unwise and ineffective.

Louis acted against the Huguenots mainly because toleration of a nonconforming religion seemed to show that he did not have full control of his kingdom, but he perhaps also had a sense of guilt that he was a less-than-exemplary Catholic. One of his mistresses, Françoise d'Aubigné (Mme. de Maintenon, d. 1719), whom he secretly married, became quite pious and may have encouraged the revocation of the Edict.

After the Glorious Revolution, the principal theorist of toleration was the Englishman John Locke (d. 1704), who urged freedom for all forms of Christianity except Catholicism, which he accused of being politically subversive. Momentously, he also reduced religion to a private matter, allowing people to believe what they wished but requiring them to accept the fact that their faith was merely one among many.

Locke

The Catholic Church herself remained officially opposed to religious toleration, except for Jews. When Jews in Poland were once again accused of having murdered a Christian child and used him in their rituals, a claim dating from the Middle Ages that was used to persecute Jews, the future Pope Clement XIV was sent to investigate and declared the charge to be a libel.

Jews

There was some incipient ecumenism. The unorthodox Dutch Calvinist Hugo Grotius (d. 1645), one of the greatest political thinkers of the age and the author of the concept of international law, carried on

Ecumenism

---

[2] The great question, which remains unanswered after almost four centuries, is whether a "pluralistic" society of multiple creeds eventually fosters an indifference to all creeds.

friendly discussions with Richelieu and hoped for the reunion of the churches under the pope, although he stopped short of actually becoming a Catholic. The German Lutheran philosopher Gottfried Wilhelm Leibniz (d. 1716) had similar ideas and for a time attracted the interest of Bossuet and Innocent XI.

Witchcraft

Inexplicably, even as both the rationalist spirit and the idea of toleration developed, the mid-seventeenth century also marked the height of the systematic witchcraft prosecutions that had been growing in both Protestant and Catholic lands for almost two hundred years. In 1632, a French priest named Urban Grandier was burned at the stake as a sorcerer, accused of having brought about the demonic possession of an entire convent of nuns in the town of Loudun. A Jesuit subsequently conducted a mass public exorcism of the nuns, although his superiors disapproved of his action.

At the same time, there were also an increasing number of skeptics, who either thought that innocent people were being condemned or doubted the reality of witchcraft altogether. Their skepticism was based either on rationalism or on the belief that God's sovereignty could not allow Satan the powers attributed to him. Both the prosecutions and the beliefs behind them declined precipitously in the latter half of the century.

The French Church

In keeping with the *politique* spirit, the decrees of the Council of Trent were not officially accepted in France until after Henry IV's death, and then only by the clergy, not by the monarchy. The Tridentine decrees were thought to violate the freedom of the Gallican church, and the kings wanted as free a hand as possible in dealing with the religious divisions of the kingdom. The long delay meant that French clerical life to a great extent went unreformed, especially because the crown controlled the appointment of bishops. But, once the decrees were accepted, the delay allowed pent-up spiritual forces to explode suddenly in a great flowering in which France replaced Spain and Italy as the center of the Catholic Reformation.

Richelieu

Initially, much of the revival was under the patronage of the Oratorian Cardinal Pierre de Bérulle (d. 1629), who encouraged many of its leaders. Richelieu was genuinely devout, but his support or opposition of reforming movements was largely dependent on how they related to royal policy at a given moment. Royal appointment of bishops tended to produce relatively worldly men of noble birth, but Richelieu to some extent promoted better candidates.

The reformers tended to identify both practical charity and the education of priests as the chief needs of the day, recognizing that often the faith had not penetrated very deeply into the lives of ordinary people and was intermingled with both unthinking worldliness and superstition. Carmelite nuns from Spain, in the branch reformed by Teresa of Avila, were introduced into France under Bérulle's patronage and attracted many members.

The Company of the Blessed Sacrament was founded by devout men at the royal court and eventually expanded to four thousand members in sixty towns. Secretive in its activities, it performed works of charity, financed reform movements, and attempted to influence royal policy, as in opposing the toleration of Huguenots. Richelieu tried to dampen its zeal, and Mazarin suppressed it, although it continued to exist unofficially.

St. Francis de Sales (d. 1622) was officially bishop of Calvinist Geneva, which he was never allowed to visit, but in France he succeeded in winning back thousands of Huguenots to the Church. Rare for a bishop, he personally catechized children. His classic *Introduction to the Devout Life* had a profound effect especially on lay spirituality, teaching that holiness need not be dramatic but consisted in the sanctification of daily life in all its details, including marital love.

Francis de Sales

Although he had been part of Bérulle's circle, de Sales moved in a different direction. Influenced by Loyola, he espoused a kind of Christian Humanism that encouraged a cheerful attitude, advising that vices be rooted out by cultivating their corresponding virtues, including natural virtues.

The Community of the Visitation was gathered together by the aristocratic widow St. Jane Frances de Chantal (d. 1641), under de Sales' guidance. Like the Ursulines in the previous century, the Visitadines were originally a group of pious ladies devoted to education and works of charity, but they too were required to become an officially chartered, cloistered order, after which they spread throughout France and French North America, working primarily as educators of girls.

As a young priest, St. Vincent de Paul (d. 1660) was captured by Muslims and taken to North Africa, where he became the slave of a former Franciscan with three wives, whom he persuaded to repent and with whom he returned to France. Partly because of his unique experiences, Vincent moved in high circles, serving as chaplain to a princess and becoming nominal abbot of a Cistercian monastery, at a time when such benefices were still granted to men who did not discharge their official duties.

Vincent de Paul

Vincent experienced a calling to revitalize the faith in France and serve the poor while serving briefly as pastor of a rural parish where the church was in ruins and the sacraments neglected. He repaired the building with his own hands and effected a spiritual revival. At Bérulle's request, he then became a pastor in Paris, where he continued to move in aristocratic circles but worked especially among the poor and sick. He became a friend of de Sales, at whose canonization proceedings he testified, and at de Sales' death gave up all his benefices. Vincent attended the dying Louis XIII (1610–1643) and was the spiritual advisor of his widow, Anne of Austria, although Mazarin resisted his influence and ridiculed him.

The members of the Congregation of Priests of the Mission (Congregatio Missionis), which Vincent founded in 1625, were commonly called either Vincentians or Lazarists, after their headquarters in the former monastery of St. Lazare in Paris. With Richelieu's support, Vincent drew up a plan for the evangelization of France. Called "The Mission", the program aimed primarily at rural France, where Vincent and others had discovered the superficial character of much of the faith, bordering on paganism and including such things as riotous drunkenness on major feast days. The Lazarist mission extended even to criminals serving as galley slaves.

Vincent identified the low state of the parish clergy as the chief problem, and he established minimal criteria for ordination, along with regular exercises for priests and seminarians that emphasized practical pastoral training. "Missions", which became extremely popular, were week-long visits to parishes by passionate preachers who sought to touch the hearts of their hearers and bring about moral and spiritual conversion. Supported by Richelieu, the Lazarists conducted missions even in Paris, including the royal court; and Lazarists, Jesuits, and others exported the practice to other Catholic countries.

Female Orders

Vincent was deeply moved by the plight of the poor and recruited groups of women—the Ladies of Charity—under the direction of an aristocratic widow, St. Louisa de Marillac (d. 1660), to work among them, especially to look after abandoned children. In 1646, an affiliated group, the Daughters of Charity, was officially approved as a religious community, the first community of women in the history of the Church who were not strictly cloistered.

Seventeen teaching orders of women were founded in the century following. However, an English woman, Mary Ward (d. 1645), was actually imprisoned by the Inquisition and the community she founded, the Institute of Mary, suppressed, because they did not live in cloisters. (Her cause for canonization has been introduced.)

Male Orders

Like Vincent, St. John Eudes (d. 1680) preached in rural areas and became convinced of the need for better priests. He left the Oratorians and with Richelieu's support founded both the Society of Jesus and Mary to run seminaries and a group of women to work with reformed prostitutes.

Jean-Jacques Olier (d. 1657) was a worldly priest who underwent conversion under Vincent's influence and founded a seminary in Paris that took its name from Olier's parish—St. Sulpice. The Society of

St. Sulpice (Sulpicians) became the leading educators of the diocesan clergy, with special concern for their inner spiritual formation.

Armand-Jean de Rancé (d. 1700) was a secular priest and an absentee abbot. The death of his mistress brought him to conversion, and he assumed the active direction of the Cistercian abbey of La Trappe, which was said to have only six monks, who supported themselves by thievery and poaching. De Rancé attracted new recruits and soon transformed La Trappe into a legendary center of monastic austerity—with severe fasts, perpetual silence, and other penances—so that the Order of the Cistercians of the Strict Observance became known as Trappists. (Many of the monks, including de Rancé himself, became seriously ill because of the austerities.) The irascible de Rancé provoked a public quarrel with some Benedictines by his claim that authentic monasticism required hard manual labor, from which study and scholarship were deviations.

St. Louis-Mary Grignion de Montfort (d.1716), who nursed the sick and for a time lived as a ragged beggar, founded two religious communities: the Missionaries of Mary and the Brothers of the Holy Spirit, who pursued Vincent's goal of evangelizing the rural areas.

St. John Baptist de la Salle (d. 1719) founded a school for boys in the parish of St. Sulpice and, in order to ensure that it would serve only the poor, forbade the teaching of Latin, which was considered essential for gentlemen. La Salle's school taught practical subjects like bookkeeping and arithmetic and required manual labor by its students. In time, his Brothers of the Christian Schools (*Fratres Scolarum Christianarum*) became a major educational influence all over Europe.

Private devotions multiplied: retreats for lay people; frequent Communion; exposition of the Blessed Sacrament; and Forty Hours' Devotion, which was originally a watch from Holy Thursday until Holy Saturday but now held at various times of the year. The Divine Praises ("Blessed be God") were composed to counter the blasphemies of the growing number of skeptics.

Eudes promoted the medieval devotion to the Sacred Heart, but it spread especially because of the Visitation nun St. Margaret Mary Alacoque (d. 1690) and her Jesuit spiritual director St. Claud La Colombière (d. 1682). While urging humble self-abasement, Margaret Mary went quite far in her ecstatic celebration of the soul's intimate union with God. The new cult[3] was held in great suspicion by some and for a time was denied official approval.[4]

Devotions

---

[3] The term *cult* is officially used for private devotions and does not necessarily have pejorative connotations.

[4] There are many instances in the history of the Church of individuals who were held in suspicion, and even sometimes condemned, but were later canonized, based on the assumption that what is from God would eventually prove itself.

Jesus' display of His bleeding but compassionate Heart was an invitation to repentance, one of the numerous contemporary antidotes to Jansenist pessimism (below). In time, it became one of the most popular of all devotions, with the image of the Sacred Heart commonly on display in churches and private homes and many Catholics making a novena of nine first Fridays in reparation for sin. The custom of the "holy hour" also originated with Margaret Mary.

Baroque   The Baroque style was the last great manifestation of predominantly religious art in the history of Western civilization: its visual expressions mainly inspired by the Catholic Reformation, its music having both Catholic and Protestant form.

Baroque architecture came relatively late to the German lands, but there it had its last, and in some ways most spectacular, flowering, for example in Salzburg and the great abbey churches of Bavaria and Austria.

Baroque music was often religious, as in the work of William Byrd (d. 1623), a Catholic who wrote music for the Anglican liturgy; the Italian-French Jean Baptiste Lully (d. 1687); and the Italian priest Antonio Vivaldi (d. 1741). The Baroque in music culminated in the Austrian Catholics Franz Josef Hayden (d. 1809) and Wolfgang Amadeus Mozart (d. 1791) and in the Lutherans Johann Sebastian Bach (d. 1750) and George Frideric Handel (d. 1759), who occasionally wrote music for Catholic patrons.

At its height, Baroque exuberance sometimes crossed a line into a theatricality that threatened to compromise its spiritual purpose, with the worshippers as spectators, some distance from the sanctuary. Some liturgies were compared to the new secular genre of opera, combining the elements of text, music, "scenery", "costumes", and dramatic reenactments. Some incorporated the court ceremonial of the monarchy, such as bishops in procession wearing fifty-foot trains held up by servants. (De Sales resolved to pray the rosary during such liturgies, so as to make profitable use of the time.) The Holy See forbade translations of the Mass into the vernacular even for the private use of worshippers, a ban that was not consistently enforced but was in effect for two centuries.

For reasons that are not clear, while the tradition of religious music continued strong, religious painting declined in the later seventeenth century. The Fleming Peter Paul Rubens (d. 1640) continued the Baroque paradox of sacred themes executed in exuberant, even worldly, ways, and the Spaniard Bartolomé Esteban Murillo (d. 1682), an austere and devout man, was the last major religious painter in an unbroken tradition that extended back to the Middle Ages. A century later—uncharacteristic of his age—Giovanni Battista Tiepolo (d. 1770) was the last major artist to paint religious subjects.

Baroque Spanish statues were often painted in gaudy colors, with the sufferings of Christ and the martyrs carried to the furthest point of graphic detail. In Bavaria and Austria, statues of saints were surrounded by plaster clouds, and on Ascension Day in Italy, an image of Jesus was taken up to the ceiling of the church on a wire, while an image of a dove descended on the same wire on Pentecost.

Some great writers remained devout believers, like the Spaniard Lope de Vega (d. 1635), who wrote plays on religious subjects, and the French playwrights Pierre Corneille (d. 1684), who translated the *Imitation of Christ*, and Jean Racine (d. 1699), who was close to the ultra-devout Jansenists. The Jesuits continued to use drama as a means of instruction and inspiration in their schools.

The English poet John Dryden (d. 1700) was raised a Puritan, converted successively to Anglicanism and Catholicism, and defended the necessity of an infallible Church to guard against false understandings of Scripture. The poet Alexander Pope (d. 1744) was also a Catholic, although perhaps a merely nominal one.

Unforeseen at its peak, the glorious French Catholic revival evolved into one of the greatest crises in the history of the Church, contributing in no small measure to the eventual wreck of both church and state in France. The crisis began because of the divergences between Augustine and Aquinas on the fundamental but extremely subtle issue of the relationship between grace and free will, which was not entirely resolved at Trent. In the century following, it became the most contested Catholic doctrine—the central issue in seventeenth-century French Catholicism.

Augustinianism

The Flemish theologian Michael Baius (d. 1589) was condemned for holding what seemed like an extreme Augustinian view that bordered on Calvinist predestination. Toward the end of the sixteenth century, Jesuit theologians charged that Dominicans slighted free will, while the Dominicans countered that the Jesuits did not fully recognize the need for grace. Pope Paul V ordered an end to the dispute, decreeing that both positions were within the bounds of Catholic orthodoxy.

The Spanish Jesuits Suàrez and Luis de Molina (d. 1600)—the former perhaps the most influential theologian of the seventeenth century—taught that God foresaw free human choice and gave graces to individuals to aid their salvation but they could freely reject those graces. But Bérulle and many of his disciples were Augustinians in seeing the human will as severely impaired by sin and holding a version of the doctrine of predestination.

The Flemish bishop Cornelius Jansen (d 1638), in his book *Augustine*, emphasized that God was remote and inscrutable, an understanding that had been particularly strong since the time of Ockham and that was taken to its furthest point by Calvin. For two centuries, Jansenism continued to be the single most influential and tenacious modern Catholic heresy.

Jansenism

Jansen attempted to win over Protestants by showing that authentic Catholicism also recognized that men were incapable of keeping the Commandments; that God's will was absolutely sovereign; and that grace was wholly unmerited, freely given, and incapable of being resisted. Human nature was so corrupt that it was possible to sin without willing to do so.

Port-Royal

Jansen's priest-friend Jean-Ambrose de Hauranne, abbé[5] de St. Cyran (d. 1643), who knew Richelieu, Bérulle, de Sales, and de Paul, spread Jansen's ideas in France, especially through the convent of Port-Royal, a fashionable community of Cistercian nuns near Paris. There the way of life had been lax under a superior from a prominent family, Angélique Arnauld (d. 1661), who became abbess at the age of eleven but later underwent a conversion that motivated her to transform the convent into a model of austere piety.

Like Angélique, some of the leading figures of the French Catholic revival were worldly people who underwent conversion and developed a strong sense of sin. When Port-Royal moved into Paris from the countryside, it began attracting people seeking spiritual guidance under St. Cyran's direction. Members of the Arnauld family were conspicuous converts to Jansenist doctrines and practices, which helped give the movement notoriety, but as controversy developed, Richelieu came to regard St. Cyran as dangerous and had him imprisoned, after which Angélique's priest-brother, Antoine Arnauld (d. 1694), became the movement's leader.

Condemnations

Jansen's work was condemned by the Sorbonne, by the king, and by several popes. As shown by his revocation of the Edict of Nantes, Louis XIV took seriously his coronation oath to oppose heresy, and as many as two thousand Jansenists were imprisoned during his reign. After Jansenism's initial condemnation in 1654, many of its institutions were closed by royal authority. Angélique was forced to retract her expressions of anguish over the huge number of souls she believed were condemned to Hell and her claim that it was not appropriate for men to inquire into God's justice. Antoine Arnauld fled to Flanders, and in the Netherlands, Jansenists formed a schismatic church.

The nuns of Port-Royal resisted, despite efforts by Bossuet and others to persuade them, leading the archbishop of Paris to characterize them, famously, as "pure as angels and proud as devils". The monastery was suppressed, even its cemetery was dug up, and its nuns were scattered to other convents, although they later regrouped at the old Port-Royal in the countryside near Paris.

---

[5] *Abbé* means literally "abbot", hence "father", and in France was used for priests in general.

The Jansenist response to official condemnations was to accept them in principle, protest that in fact they did not hold the condemned propositions, and reformulate their teachings in such a way as to try to escape the condemnations. But this strategy led merely to further condemnations, culminating in a 1713 decree by Clement XI that some bishops refused to accept.

Jansenist Spirituality

The heart of Jansenist spirituality was its sense of the immense gulf that separated man from God, a sense of sin that required continuous penance. Because they thought many people were predestined to damnation, Jansenists denied that Christ died for all men and symbolized this by crucifixes on which His arms were stretched vertically over His head, thereby showing that He did not embrace the whole world and that the entry to Heaven was very narrow.

Jansenist criticism of popular piety at times seemed to veer close to Protestantism. They were cool to a Marian piety that regarded Mary as a kindly and forgiving Mother; in their view, she was almost as high above mankind, and as inaccessible, as her Son.

Jansenists discouraged frequent Communion, because men were wholly unworthy to approach the holy table, a teaching that seemed to deny the power of the sacraments to transform those who received them and reserve them instead for those already saved. By contrast, de Sales advocated weekly Communion, and Vincent, who was at first friendly with St. Cyran, broke with him over the same issue. (St. Cyran jibed that Vincent was "ignorant", and Vincent replied, "I am even more ignorant than you think.")

The term *Jansenist* referred to those who held, or appeared to hold, the condemned propositions concerning nature and grace, but it was used much more loosely to designate anyone who held to very strict moral principles.

The Jansenists themselves were conspicuous for their austere lives and—repelled by easy worldliness—held even ordinary pleasures, such as the enjoyment of food or the appreciation of the beauties of nature, in suspicion.[6] As a result, those influenced by the movement avoided attending purely social gatherings. (De Sales was suspect to Jansenists because he had cautiously permitted worldly pleasures like dancing and the theatre.)

Jesuit Moral Theology

The Jesuits, because of their emphasis on free will and a kind of "humanism" that saw God's presence in ordinary things, were Jansenism's greatest antagonists. Following Ignatius, Jesuits sought to influence every area of culture and make it Christian, while Jansenists, fearing that

---

[6] In modern times, the term *Jansenist* has sometimes been misused to denigrate any strict sense of moral and religious obligation, including things that are in no way deviant or heretical.

Christians themselves would thereby be corrupted, advocated withdrawal from the world. One of the disputes of the Renaissance was revived, as Jesuits praised, and Jansenists condemned, works of art and literature on classical pagan themes—the Jesuits finding a fundamental human wisdom and goodness even among pagans.

Devotion to the Sacred Heart, which was especially promoted by the Jesuits, emphasized the love of Jesus and His accessibility to those who sought Him, and Jesuits, following Aquinas, taught the existence of natural human virtues that made restraint possible. Mistrusting display and exuberant joyfulness, the Jansenists also mistrusted much of Baroque religiosity, including devotion to the Sacred Heart. By contrast, the Jansenists had a strong sense of God's remoteness, man's helpless proneness to sin, and the soul's predestination to Heaven or Hell.

The Jansenists castigated the Jesuits for holding that it was possible to do good without conscious thought of God and that there was no guilt except in a deliberately sinful act. In response, the Jesuits warned against scrupulosity—a compulsive and exaggerated sense of one's own sinfulness that plagued a disordered soul.

Jesuit moralists developed the theology of casuistry ("cases"), in which general moral principles were illustrated by hypothetical examples, in order to give confessors practical guidance—a system that was criticized for being excessively legalistic and encouraging the search for moral loopholes. The Jansenists accused Jesuits of catering to the lax consciences of the aristocracy by, for example, allowing a lady to attend a ball on a day when she had received Communion or allowing the reception of Communion by a married couple on a day when they had had intercourse.

Whereas Jansenists taught that the actual emotion of sorrow was necessary for the forgiveness of sins, the Jesuits taught that fear of Hell was sufficient. The Jesuits also taught that, of several reputable opinions on a moral question, Catholics were free to choose any one that seemed credible (Probabilism). When that theory was officially condemned, the Jesuit alternative was Probabiliorism, which held that the individual had to follow the most probable opinion. Rigorists—mostly Jansenists—held that in each case the strictest opinion must be followed.

Pascal

The layman Blaise Pascal (d. 1662), the most important Catholic thinker between the sixteenth and nineteenth centuries, had a close relationship with the Jansenist movement. For a time, he lived a rather worldly life, but he underwent conversion and often visited Port-Royal, where his sister was a nun. Pascal's Jansenist spirituality was manifest in the fact that, chronically ill and in pain, he said he did not wish to be cured, because illness was the natural state of man. Also, he persuaded a close friend to break off his engagement in order to live a life of sanctity. (A relative of the jilted woman tried to have Pascal killed.)

After the condemnation of Jansenists, Pascal supported their claim that they did not teach the condemned propositions. When his niece, who was also a nun of Port-Royal, underwent what he regarded as a miraculous cure, he thought that it proved that Jansenists could not be heretics. Pascal was the Jesuits' most formidable antagonist, satirizing them as sophistical promoters of fallacious moral teachings.

Mysticism

Jansenists generally eschewed mysticism, because it seemed to narrow the gulf between man and God, but among others, there was a continued strong interest in the inner spiritual life, which was analyzed with great subtlety by numerous authors. A dominant theme was "the practice of the presence of God"—a habitual sense of being in His presence even when not consciously praying or meditating.

Most spiritual writers, on the other hand, emphasized the passivity of the mystical experience—the individual could not seek it, and it was not granted to everyone—and it was from this sense of passivity that the other principal heresy of the age was derived.

Quietism

Quietism originated with the Spanish priest Miguel de Molinos (d. 1696) and may have been influenced by the *Alumbrados* heresy. It took its name from the fact that in its extreme form it advocated a completely passive surrender to the will of God, the abandonment of all human effort toward salvation, even the effort to resist temptation. ("I desire to desire nothing, but I do not even desire that.") Quietists appeared to have no need of the sacraments or any other religious "externals".

Molinos taught at Rome and at one point attracted the support of the future Pope Innocent XI, but he was later accused of immoral relations with women and imprisoned by Innocent. His fate posed an intriguing question about Quietist spirituality—did Molinos actually commit fornication, because he did not resist temptation, or was he innocent but made no effort to defend himself?

Quietist beliefs were espoused in France by a rather unstable widow, Jeanne-Marie de Guyon (d. 1717), who claimed mystical experiences, traveled with a friar with whom she achieved "complete fusion of souls", was tormented by the Great Beast of the Apocalypse, and wondered if she bore the Baby Jesus within her. She taught that one should be indifferent to one's own salvation, that sin was involuntary, and that to commit a sin that one abhorred was the greatest sacrifice an individual could offer to God. The soul was completely in thrall to the devil and could only await divine deliverance, not hoping or praying for it, lest it not be God's will.

Archbishop François Fénelon (d. 1715), one of the great prelates of the age, was eager to promote heartfelt piety as an antidote to religious formalism, and he saw in Quietism the potential for the soul to expand until it reached the divine. But Fénelon compromised himself by encouraging Mme. Guyon while attempting to moderate her teachings. Bossuet, who thought she was mad, moved against her with the support of Louis XIV, and she was imprisoned until Mme. de Maintenon, who was something of her disciple, interceded.

Although the Molinos and Guyon episodes were eccentric, Quietism was not a peripheral movement, in that many devout people shared its sense that one should place oneself entirely in the hands of God. But as a heresy, it provoked an anti-mystical reaction, so that throughout much of the eighteenth century spiritual writers were closely scrutinized for Quietist tendencies and several, including even a cardinal, were forced to retract.

Skepticism   Much of the intellectual and spiritual dissatisfaction of the period from 1300 to 1600 came from the belief that reason had been valued too much by Scholastic theology. There was no philosopher of the first rank during the sixteenth century, which was dominated instead by theological disputes about the meaning of the Bible, but there were stirrings of skepticism about religion.

In the middle of the Reformation, the popular French satirist François Rabelais (d. 1553), a physician and sometime monk, mocked what he considered the extreme credulity and fanaticism of religion, although the extent of his own skepticism is uncertain. He was condemned by some Church authorities but protected by others.

Tomasso Campanella (d. 1639) was an Italian Dominican who was imprisoned and tortured by the Inquisition, primarily for his interest in magic and his semi-mystical speculations about a future City of the Sun that would replace existing kingdoms. For a time, his speculations were taken seriously by both the papacy and various civil governments.

Michel de Montaigne (d. 1592) was a believing Catholic, a civic official connected to the *Politiques*, who professed a highly personal, common-sense kind of skepticism that raised questions but did not attempt to resolve them. Montaigne, who thought that uncertainty was endemic to human nature, marveled that anyone could be so sure of his beliefs as to kill and be killed for them.

Pyrrhonists—named for an ancient Roman philosopher—cast doubt on all certainties. While some doubted religion, many were religious believers who used skeptical arguments against their theological opponents in order to show the need for some kind of authority—the Bible for Protestants, the Church for Catholics.

In the seventeenth century, the claims of reason once again came into their own, although in ways very different from the Middle Ages. The two centuries after 1600 came to be called the Age of Reason, when reason came to deny divine revelation.

Although he lived long after the age of skepticism had begun, Bossuet was in a sense the last great exponent of an untroubled confidence in the existing cosmic order, someone who might have well have said,

"God's in His heaven and all's right with the world." In his *Discourse on Universal History*, he ranged serenely over the past to show the hand of Providence clearly discernible in every age.

The Scientific Revolution

Copernicus

The earliest and most dramatic incidence of potential conflict between faith and reason came from the new astronomy. For some time, astronomers had been entertaining speculations of the sun, not the earth, as the center of the universe, and in 1543, the Polish astronomer Nicolaus Copernicus (d. 1543), a cleric in minor orders, published a treatise proposing that idea. His hypothesis was not based on empirical observation but on the attempt to overcome certain mathematical anomalies in the geocentric model of the universe.

Galileo

For decades, the new theory was confined largely to scientific circles, but by using a telescope, the Italian physicist Galileo Galilei (d. 1642) saw that the surface of the moon was irregular, like that of the earth, and that the planet Jupiter had four moons—facts that contradicted the Aristotelian claim that the heavens were unchanging and were made of a different substance from the earth. Emboldened by these discoveries, Galileo in 1615 presented the Copernican hypothesis to the general educated public. It provoked strong reactions pro and con, and he was summoned before the Inquisition and examined by Bellarmine.

Since earliest times, the Catholic tradition had insisted that faith and reason must ultimately harmonize, so that in principle the Galileo dispute was not over whether science or religious authority was supreme but over facts—whether Copernicanism was true. (There were in fact errors in the new theory, although it was a decided improvement on the geocentric model. Copernicanism was not conclusively proven until much later.)

The Jesuit Response

Jesuits, notably Christoph Clavius (d. 1612), who had devised the Gregorian calendar, were among the leading astronomers of the day, and the German Jesuit Athanasius Kircher (d. 1680), who was possibly the most learned of Galileo's contemporaries, proposed important theories concerning volcanoes, acoustics, and other natural phenomena. Some Jesuits were better empirical astronomers than Galileo and pointed out that the Copernican theory remained unproven. Most Jesuits held the theory of the Danish astronomer Tycho Brahe (d. 1601): that the planets revolve around the sun, but the sun in turn revolves around the earth.

Bellarmine objected that the heliocentric picture of the universe contradicted certain passages of Scripture where the sun was said to move. Beyond this, the thesis contradicted Aristotle's claim that the heaviest matter, which was assumed to be the earth, was naturally at the center of the universe, just as common-sense experience seemed to show that the earth was stationary while the sun moved. Aristotle's philosophy was the intellectual foundation of Scholasticism, so that Bellarmine and others feared that to discredit Aristotle's astronomy might discredit much of Catholic theology as well. Galileo responded that the Bible did not intend to impart scientific knowledge but merely made use of the world view common at the time it was written.

Bellarmine did not demand that the Copernican theory be denied even if it were proven true but commanded that, since it was not proven, Galileo could only teach it as a theory useful for the study of astronomy and should not upset people's faith by insisting on its truth. Galileo agreed, but in 1632, he published a second book setting forth the heliocentric theory even more boldly than before and refuting objections.

Galileo was again summoned before the Inquisition, where the issue in part revolved around exactly what Bellarmine, who was now dead, had told Galileo in 1616. Galileo was forced to retract under pain of prosecution for heresy and spent the remainder of his life under a kind of house arrest, although still engaged in scientific investigation. (In 1992, Bl. John Paul II formally stated that the Church had erred in condemning Galileo, and later Pope Benedict XVI praised Galileo as someone whose work helped men to "contemplate with gratitude God's works".)

Scientific Progress

Almost all areas of science developed very rapidly in the seventeenth century. Some research practices encountered resistance from the Church, such as the dissection of human bodies for the study of anatomy, while some findings prompted new and difficult questions. Early discoveries in geology, for example, were beginning to raise questions about the age of the world as set forth in Genesis.

However, the successes of the new physical speculations were dazzling, and they pushed the study of nature into the center of the culture. The word *science*, which had traditionally meant simply "knowledge", was increasingly limited to the empirical study of the physical world, which was viewed as alone providing true knowledge.

Descartes

The French philosopher René Descartes (d. 1650) emerged from his Jesuit education dissatisfied that the philosophers of the past had been unable to agree on the nature of truth, just as different peoples and nations differed in their laws and customs. Bérulle, among others, encouraged Descartes in his quest to overcome that failure.

Partly to refute Pyrrhonism, Descartes began the search for truth by undertaking to doubt everything that could be doubted, so that whatever remained would be certain. As it turned out, he could doubt absolutely everything, including the existence of God, and while the world outside his mind might be a figment of his imagination, he could not doubt his own existence as a thinking being.

But, he reasoned, the idea of God—of an infinite Being—could not be the product of a finite mind and therefore had to be true. God was a necessary Being whose existence guaranteed the existence of the external world, since the all-good God would not allow men to be systematically deceived.

Descartes seemed to have created a new synthesis between faith and reason, and his philosophy was accepted by Antoine Arnauld and Bossuet, among others, while his principal disciple was the Oratorian Nicolas de Malebranche (d. 1715). Some Catholics were attracted to Cartesianism as an antidote to materialism, since he made a sharp separation between mind and body. Augustinians approved of the fact that, unlike Aristotle and Aquinas, knowledge for Descartes did not come through the senses but was innate in the mind. (Malebranche explained the interaction of mind and body by God's action of planting in the mind an idea each time the body experienced a sense impression.)

Bacon

Francis Bacon (d. 1626) was an English lawyer who was so impressed by the new science that he urged that almost all the learning of the past be discarded and the search for truth begin again, based on empirical investigation.

Descartes and Bacon were each impressed by different aspects of the new science—Descartes by mathematics, Bacon by the painstaking sifting of empirical facts. Because of the revolutionary ideas of the new science, each saw the past as a burden on the present.

Bacon was an Anglican, and both he and Descartes attempted to protect religious belief from doubt. Descartes said, as he embarked on the journey of doubt, that he would continue to live according to the teachings of the Church and the laws of the state, and Bacon said that religion, since it was based on divine revelation, was beyond empirical proof or disproof. Both were sincere. However, they protected religious belief by in a sense making it irrelevant, which allowed later generations to conclude that there could be no rational basis for faith.

Newton

Isaac Newton (d. 1727) completed the scientific revolution by formulating a few simply stated laws that explained the movement of all bodies, from the planets to the smallest grains of sand. He was a serious Anglican, albeit with an eccentric theology, who believed that he had placed religious belief on firmer ground than ever before, by showing that the universe had to have been planned and governed by a superior intellect.

Jesuit physicists generally opposed Newtonianism, seeking to preserve Aristotelian physics as mediated by Aquinas. But others, especially some Oratorians, saw Newton's model of the mechanical universe as discrediting magical beliefs, thereby allowing miracles to be understood as occurring only through the power of God, who temporarily suspended the laws of nature.

Pascal   Pascal was almost alone in seeing fully what was involved in the scientific revolution, attempting to overcome skeptical rationalism several generations before that skepticism had fully emerged. He was himself a great mathematician, one of the inventors of calculus and of a kind of mechanical calculator.

Despite his Jansenist strictures against worldliness, he associated with gamblers in order to study mathematical odds, from which he formulated a science of probabilities. In the gambling rooms, he noticed that the threat to the Catholic faith came not from philosophical skepticism but mainly from a casual worldliness that he called "Libertinism". To counter this, he formulated his famous "wager" to convince the Libertines to embrace the faith—if God existed they gained everything, whereas if He did not exist they lost nothing.

The wager, however, gives a misleading picture of Pascal, who was deeply devout and not in the least self-interested and calculating. Sewn into the lining of his coat was a cryptic reminder of a mystical experience he once had. Beyond the idea of the wager, he strove to formulate a highly original defense of Christianity that by the time of his early death had only reached the stage of aphoristic notes that are usually called simply *Pensées* (Thoughts).

While the new science seemed to reveal a serenely ordered universe under God's presiding intelligence, Pascal pronounced, with regard to Descartes, "The god of the geometers is not the God of Abraham, Isaac, and Jacob", meaning that Descartes had merely proven the logical necessity of a Supreme Being, not the existence of the living God.

Lurking beneath some of the resistance to the new science was the sense, often only half-conscious, that man was being dethroned from the center of the universe, which was now revealed to be a vast, cold place that took no notice of his existence. Pascal above all fully sensed this profound disorientation and confessed, "Those infinite spaces frighten me." But, reflecting on the irony that man, however great he thinks himself to be, can be killed by a drop of water, Pascal confronted that reality with characteristic boldness: in nature man was indeed a fragile reed, but he was a thinking reed, whose consciousness allowed him to encompass the vast impersonality of the universe, even if that universe knew him not.

While he did not reject arguments for the existence of God based on the order of the universe, he saw that in some ways the very objectivity of the scientific world, of the impersonality of the universe, had thrown man back on his own resources, and it was in that experience that Pascal sought a new basis for faith. Insofar as his theology can be discerned, Pascal was an Augustinian and in a sense a forerunner of modern Existentialism, his starting point being man's profound sense of unease and anxiety in the world, the root of which was the fact that by nature man yearned for infinity yet was himself finite, his longings and aspirations destined to be thwarted. Many of the *Pensées* were sharp observations on the paradoxes of human existence, a perception consonant with Jansenist pessimism. For Pascal, the only solution to the human dilemma was faith in that Being who was fully human but who elevated humanity to the level of eternity—Jesus Christ.

Building on the work of Renaissance humanists like Valla, the new spirit of critical inquiry expanded beyond the physical world into the study of history, hence to a reassessment of the Church's past.

The French Benedictine Jean Mabillon (d. 1707), whom de Rancé accused of not living as a true monk, evaluated the sources for the history of the early Church, and the Bollandists, a group of mainly Flemish Jesuits (named after their founder), did the same for the lives of the saints. Historical studies sometimes posed troublesome problems, as when the Bollandists disproved the Carmelite tradition that their order had been founded on Mount Carmel by the prophet Elijah, doubt was cast on whether the so-called Athanasian Creed had actually been composed by St. Athanasius, and certain venerable documents were proven to be forgeries.

But the greatest controversy was caused by the French Oratorian Richard Simon (d. 1712), who was expelled from his order after publishing a book denying that Moses was the author of the Pentateuch and anticipating modern biblical criticism in other ways as well. Simon was not a religious skeptic and thought of himself as in some ways refuting the Protestant appeal to the Bible, by showing that the authority of the Church was necessary to overcome scriptural uncertainties.

Despite Pascal's reservations, the new science seemed to require a kind of natural theology, as Descartes insisted. God was seen as the ultimate principle of intelligibility in the universe, so that even most of the Church's enemies considered atheism irrational. The impetus for "natural religion" also came from the growing reaction against the bitter religious conflicts of the previous century. There began a search for a religion that transcended theological differences and was accessible to everyone.

The term *Deism*, from the Latin word for God, is now conventionally used for this rational religion, while *Theism*, from the Greek equivalent, is used to designate belief in a personal God. But the terms were often used interchangeably in the eighteenth century, and "natural religion" was a more common term than either.

Deism was an abstraction in which God was the divine engineer, architect, or clock-maker who designed and built a complex mechanism but then left it to move according to its own laws. The moral law—natural law—was part of that same order and could be known entirely through reason.

Deism existed in both mild and strong versions. Some orthodox Christians, seeing Deism as a way of persuading skeptics of the existence of God, merely deemphasized the distinctiveness of Christianity, while others, even some clergy, restricted belief to what they thought could be proved.

As Pascal foresaw, "natural religion" was by no means necessarily Christian and often coexisted with doubts about revealed religion. It was often espoused by a new intelligentsia who tended toward free thought and lax morals—precisely Pascal's "Libertines". There was a growing skepticism about Christianity, which after Louis XIV's death burst into the open.

The Persistence of Faith

But although Deism created a gulf between the religious culture of much of the educated classes and the beliefs of most other people, traditional religion remained vital. Thus Jansenist claims about miracles were widely believed, and Louis XV of France (1715–1774) was thought to have offended God by his adulteries and was blamed for no longer "touching for the king's evil" (curing scrofula by his royal touch), a ceremony he felt unworthy to perform.

Catholic Europe appeared to be stable and serene, under the rule of princes who supported the Church and with ubiquitous public manifestations of religion—large and beautiful churches, elaborate liturgies, frequent public processions, and many other things. The Church's spiritual strength lay in her deep appeal to the imagination and the emotions, ranging from the highly personal apologetics of Pascal to popular beliefs that bordered on superstition. Popular preachers validated Pascal's famous claim that "the heart has its reasons of which reason knows nothing". In both Catholicism and Protestantism, the "religion of the heart" was extolled as an antidote to what was considered a desiccated rationalism.

Parish missions were still effective, and retreat houses were established for lay people to make the Spiritual Exercises. Confraternities of pious laymen remained strong, especially the sodalities ("companionships") that were composed mainly of alumni of Jesuit schools and included people of high rank, including bishops.

Many kinds of devotion flourished, especially that of the Sacred Heart, the newly established stations of the cross, and Marian piety of various kinds. The first reported private Marian apparition in the history of Europe was to a French shepherdess, Benoite Rencurel (d. 1718), in 1664. The incident was the forerunner of numerous later such events: the girl claimed repeated visions in which Mary commanded her to warn people about their sins, the site attracted numerous pilgrims, and miraculous cures were reported, with Church authorities making no official judgment.

Saints

As in every age, there was sanctity in the Age of Reason, even in high places. Venerable Louise of France (d. 1787), daughter of the promiscuous Louis XV, joined a strict Carmelite convent.

One of the favorite saints of the age was sixteen hundred years old: St. Joseph, the foster-father of Jesus, who for reasons that are unclear was not popular until early modern times. The growth of his cult in the seventeenth century was probably related to the renewed devotion to the loving Jesus, as in Sacred Heart and Marian devotions.

St. Benedict Joseph Labre (d. 1783) was one of the strangest saints in the history of the Church. A Frenchman, he was rejected by various religious orders and became a kind of tramp, affronting in his person almost every social convention of the age. He lived by begging in various places but finally in Rome, where he slept in the Coliseum in order to associate himself with the martyrs.

St. Paul of the Cross Danei (d. 1775) was an Italian who founded the Passionists (*Congregatio Passionis*—Congregation of the Passion), primarily to preach missions centered on Christ's Passion and especially in reparation for the irreligion of the age. Paul was so effective a mission preacher that his hearers were often reduced to tears as he dramatically recounted the Passion story.

Liguori

St. Alphonsus-Mary Liguori (d. 1787), also an Italian, was a lawyer from an aristocratic family who founded the Redemptorists (*Congregatio Sanctissimi Redemptoris*—Congregation of the Most Holy Redeemer), especially for the evangelization of the common people, and also served as a diocesan bishop. Like the Passionists, the Redemptorists included female branches of cloistered contemplatives.

Liguori was a major influence on spirituality, emphasizing Christ's love and that of Mary, whom he venerated as "Mediatrix of all Graces", a belief that, while it came to be believed by many, has not been officially accepted by the Church. Once again in contrast to the Jansenists, he taught that fervent prayer, freely embraced, brought salvation, and he urged the cultivation of emotions like love and fear.

Liguori was also the only significant theologian of the eighteenth century, the leading moral theologian of the age, and a doctor of the Church. He revived a modified kind of Probabilism and wrote books that for the next century were standard guides for confessors. He followed the milder Jesuit moral theology rather than Jansenist rigor, insisting that "God is not a tyrant" and advising confessors against being overly inquisitive. Significant in terms of later controversies, he held that, if a penitent did not realize that contraception was a sin, the confessor should leave the conscience undisturbed. (After about 1650, upper-class families in Western Europe were having fewer children.)

Social custom was moving slowly toward the idea of "companionate marriage" based on mutual attraction, and the future Pope Benedict XIV even justified elopement, on the grounds that the power of the sacrament rendered such a marriage holy. In a sense, the traditional idea of marriage and the romantic idea of courtly love were being harmonized.

Royal Court Culture   But it was in France, which had assumed the spiritual leadership of the Catholic Reformation, that the greatest trials of the Church occurred in early modern times, as the revival cooled and weaknesses were exposed.

Tellingly, the French were reserved in their response to the Baroque. There were few French buildings as unrestrainedly exuberant as some in Italy and elsewhere, because French culture was to a great extent controlled by the monarchy and under Louis XIV the Baroque was replaced by a classical spirit that emphasized order, regularity, good taste, reason, and clear ideas, as embodied in the royal palaces of the Louvre and Versailles.

Bossuet justified divine-right monarchy, arguing that a stable society had to be based on divinely ordained obedience to authority. He departed from the doctrine of Bellarmine and Suàrez, according to which subjects had rights, including the right of resistance to unjust government. Bossuet was sincerely pious, performed his episcopal duties conscientiously, and took great interest in the various schools of spirituality, but he was also a classic court bishop, for whom the authority of the monarchy was seamlessly interwoven with the faith. (In the chapel at Versailles, the king looked down on the altar from a balcony, while the congregation faced not the altar but the king, on whom it was forbidden to turn one's back.)

Gallicanism   The Gallican movement severely undercut papal authority in France, where the kings had obtained from the pope control over the appointment of bishops and most bishops submitted to royal power. Louis XIV consistently nominated bishops for political reasons, many of whom were absentees from their dioceses, and he fell into a protracted conflict with Pope Innocent XI over the king's claim to collect the revenues of all vacant dioceses.

During that dispute, the Assembly of the French Clergy issued the *Gallican Articles*, according to which the king was not subject to any higher authority "in temporal things" and could not be deposed. The pope was supreme in "spiritual matters" but subject to correction by a general council and in France limited by the laws of the kingdom.

Innocent XI condemned the *Articles* and refused to confirm the king's nominees for a number of vacant dioceses, but Innocent XII (1691–1700) acquiesced. The *Articles* were then officially withdrawn, although they continued to be widely held.

Louis XIV was in fact devout and had a bad conscience about his adulteries, enduring chastisement from the pulpit, briefly banishing one of his mistresses from court after a priest refused her absolution, and undergoing personal reform at the hands of Madame de Maintenon. For a time, he endured blunt sermons by the courageous Fénelon, but Fénelon had a monumental dispute with Bossuet, his former teacher—essentially over Quietism—and was banished from court. Louis then pressured Innocent XII to condemn Fénelon, who received the news as he was entering the pulpit and who proceeded to preach a sermon on obedience. Later, however, he became an open critic of royal absolutism.

The Church continued to be involved in politics. The practice of royal government through a cardinal continued with André-Hercule de Fleury (d. 1743), regent and first minister for Louis XV. When Bishop Étienne-Charles de Loménie de Brienne (d. 1794) was proposed as archbishop of Paris, Louis XVI (1774–1793) refused with the words, "No. The archbishop of Paris ought at least to believe in God." But if Loménie was not fit to be archbishop of Paris, he was qualified to serve briefly as Louis' first minister, after which he was made a cardinal.

State of the Church

The condition of the institutional Church—authentic piety in the midst of worldliness—was similar throughout Europe.

Patronage and family connections meant a great deal in obtaining promotion, and there was an almost impassible gulf between higher and lower clergy. Bishops were seldom parish priests but were drawn from the ranks of cathedral canons and professors. Except in Spain, there were a disproportionate number of aristocratic bishops, especially younger sons of noble houses, whose quality was uneven. Despite the decrees of Trent, there were still some pluralists, some of whom were quite worldly and primarily political in their outlook, alongside others who were very dedicated. Most were conscientious.

The financial gulf between bishops and cathedral clergy on the one hand and village priests on the other was enormous, and many of the lower clergy—some of them impoverished village pastors—resented the huge disparity of income between themselves and their superiors. Dating from the Dark Ages, many parishes were still under the control of a patron—a cathedral chapter, a monastery, a wealthy layman— who had the right to appoint the curé (the priest who had the "care" of the parishioners) and who doled out a stipend to him. Despite reforms, the system also survived in some monasteries, where the abbot was an absentee—not even a monk—who was entitled to the revenues.

The Church was extremely wealthy (owning about 10 percent of all the land in France, more than half in Bavaria), and high-ranking clergy lived in luxury, as was thought befitting their offices. But much episcopal wealth was used for charity and education, since the Church was the only institution that took responsibility for those needs—one Spanish archbishop, for instance, fed thirteen hundred people a day during a famine.

The quality of the priesthood was uneven. Most village priests seem to have been respected men devoted to their flocks, even if in many cases they were poorly educated. Large urban parishes, however, housed numerous sinecures—corps of priests who enjoyed endowed benefices but of whom only a few had pastoral responsibilities (Chartres cathedral had eighty canons), an abuse that stemmed in part from a superfluity of priests, although vocations declined during the eighteenth century.

About half the clergy belonged to religious orders. Although most of those were vowed to poverty, there was nonetheless a popular image of monasteries as full of idlers, in contrast to the hard-working parish curés. As a privileged class, clergy of all ranks had long been vulnerable to attack, with occasional scandals fueling popular anticlericalism, which was often motivated not by skepticism but by Jansenist rigor and contempt for such misconduct. In the Affair of the Diamond Necklace,[7] for example, Cardinal Louis-René Rohan of Strasbourg (d. 1803) was at the center of a sordid sexual intrigue that may have involved Queen Marie Antoinette (d. 1793). The aristocratic bishop Maurice de Talleyrand-Périgord (d. 1838), who claimed to have been forced into the priesthood by his family, kept a mistress even while a seminarian.

Intellectual Defects

The Church's greatest failure was intellectual. Theologically, it was a rather barren age, and for two centuries after Pascal, there was no major Catholic thinker, while an indeterminate part of the educated classes, including clergy, lost the faith or compromised it.

Most of the defenders of orthodoxy, especially the Jesuits, remained Thomists. Others, however, were self-consciously modern in outlook, and the Oratorians especially espoused a Cartesianism that turned out to be a philosophical blind alley. Over time, Descartes' system seemed less and less persuasive to many people and what eventually remained was only his insistence on the obligation of universal doubt—modern man was to be skeptical of all received ideas.

While some Catholics sought to bring their faith as close to enlightened Deism as possible, others did the opposite, readily admitting that many beliefs (the Trinity, Transubstantiation) were mysteries but arguing that this showed that they emanated from the infinite God, whom man could not comprehend.

Catholic apologists appealed to experience against abstract critical reason, demonstrating the truth of the faith by citing all the miracles that had occurred from biblical times to their own day. This argument, however, begged the question, since the skeptics also doubted the reality of miracles. (The argument posed a particular problem for Jesuits, in that the Jansenists claimed a number of miracles as proving the truth of their own beliefs.)

The Philosophes

The self-styled Enlightenment—so-called because its adherents claimed to have emerged from the darkness and superstition that had long prevailed and for which the Church was primarily responsible—began in

---

[7] The subject of a film by that name.

France and spread from there all over the Western world. Its apostles were called *philosophes*, meaning not "philosophers" in the formal sense but something like the modern term "intellectuals".

New secret societies like the *Rosecrucians* (their symbol being the "rosy cross") and the *Illuminati* ("enlightened") falsely claimed an ancient lineage, exalted science, and harbored outright antagonism to Christianity. The Freemasons, whose historical origins are obscure (they claimed descent from the medieval stonemasons' guilds), were mainly composed of men dissatisfied with organized religion who sought to transcend it through a Deistic creed. Despite their Deism, the emotional need for religion survived in those societies, which incorporated ritualistic, semi-mystical elements into their rationalist creeds. Such groups had some success in undermining Christianity, although their exact role is uncertain because of their secrecy. Freemasonry was condemned by a succession of popes, but the movement had influence even within the Church, including priests among its members. Philip, duke of Orléans (d. 1793), the cousin of Louis XVI, was the chief of the French Masons.

Mankind, the *philosophes* announced, had been freed by the new science. They readily admitted that from a purely scientific standpoint their age was less profound than the previous century ("We stand on the shoulders of giants"), but they ignored the fact that most of those giants had been believing Christians.

The critical spirit manifested itself in the demand that every belief and every institution justify itself rationally, precisely the thing Descartes had said he would not do. It was a demand that logically applied to the entire Old Regime (the society of the period roughly from 1500 to 1800), which to a great extent justified its existence by the authority of tradition. The *philosophes* openly questioned the legitimacy of most institutions but questioned the monarchy only obliquely, partly out of fear of royal power, partly because some of them hoped that "enlightened despots" would use their authority to change society.

The *philosophes* made use of books, pamphlets, plays, caricatures, and every other kind of propaganda, with their great *Encyclopedia*—an attempt to present all available knowledge in a properly rationalistic way—especially effective. Mere fashion played a part in the acceptance of new ideas that seemed daring and exciting, as in the institution of the *salon* ("room"), a kind of party presided over by fashionable hostesses, where witty *philosophes* dazzled and amused many of the aristocracy and the clergy. (An index of the way in which fashion had invaded the Church was the bishops, including conscientious ones, who wore their miters perched on top of powdered wigs.)

Although the new ideas turned out to be subversive, at first the institutions of French life appeared so solid and secure that it seemed possible to throw verbal rocks at them without doing serious damage. Princes, including ecclesiastical princes, even used Enlightenment ideas of rationality and efficiency to justify imposing uniformity and order on their often quite diverse jurisdictions.

Enemies of Faith

The dominant intellectual figure of the age was François-Marie Arouet (d. 1778), who wrote under the name Voltaire. Like Descartes, he was educated by the Jesuits, but he soon abandoned Catholicism and came to see the Church as the chief enemy of mankind ("crush the infamous thing"), because in his opinion she exercised power through ignorance and superstition.

Religion was the creation of the "first knave and the first fool", in the words of Marie-Jean Condorcet (d. 1794), a *philosophe* of noble birth, and its influence over society, especially in education, had to be destroyed. The Church's influence included not only her authority over institutions of formal learning but, prior to the age of mass literacy and the popular press, the Sunday sermon, which was the chief means by which most people were exposed to ideas.

Since the *philosophes* placed their faith in reason, it followed that only the educated—the enlightened—could be trusted. Thus it was thought necessary that, while the process of enlightenment was going forward, the common people still had to undergo the discipline of supernatural religion. Voltaire even built a chapel for the peasants on his estate.

The *philosophes* encountered relatively little official repression, largely because the censorship machinery of the Church and the government was somewhat lax and inefficient. The official royal censor was actually sympathetic to new ideas, and much depended on a writer's political and social connections. Voltaire went into exile several times and was several times thrown into prison, but when he died, in what turned out to be one the last years of the Old Regime, he was hailed as a great hero and buried in Paris in a triumphant kind of secular liturgy.

Although Voltaire recognized the force of both Pascal and Bossuet's ideas, on the whole the *philosophes*, sensing that they were in the ascendancy, did not attempt to refute their opponents fairly. The aim of the Enlightenment was not toleration but the replacement of one kind of orthodoxy by another, demanding liberation from political and religious authority but by no means espousing complete freedom of expression. The *philosophes* themselves were quite willing to use repression, including appeals to the official censors, to silence their opponents.

Enlightened Catholics

Whereas the *philosophes* were driven by passionate conviction and an urgent sense of mission, for a time most Catholic intellectuals seem to have been complacent about the threat, and many, including clergy, were eager to prove that they too were enlightened. A group of

Benedictines at the abbey of St. Germain in Paris complained of their monastic discipline and said they wanted to be known as scholars, not monks; students at the great Paris seminary of St. Sulpice rioted because they were not allowed to wear powdered wigs and attend the theatre. A seminarian tried to stab their rector, Jacques-André Emery (d. 1811), in his bed.

Even Benedict XIV at first praised some of Voltaire's work, although he later condemned it. Voltaire dedicated his book on Muhammad to the Pope, who at first did not comprehend that Voltaire's ridicule of Muslim beliefs as absurd was a way of insinuating the same thing about Christianity.

Although the *philosophes* savagely attacked the Jesuits as ignorant bigots, in general the Jesuits were better educated and more rigorous in their thinking than their opponents. At first, the Jesuits even greeted the *Encyclopedia* with qualified approval (some of it was in fact plagiarized from Jesuit writers), but then began compiling their own *Dictionary*, with the similar aim of making all knowledge available to the educated public.

Neo-Paganism

The Enlightenment sought to answer definitively the unanswered question of Renaissance Humanism that had been interrupted by the Reformation—whether ancient pagan culture had been superior to Christianity. The Old Testament was considered to be the chronicle of an uncivilized people, and attitudes toward Jesus ranged from seeing Him as a moral teacher whose doctrines had been distorted by His followers to seeing Him as a fraud or as self-deluded.

Edward Gibbon (d. 1794) was an Anglican who briefly became a Catholic, then a skeptic. His *Decline and Fall of the Roman Empire* endeavored to prove in massive detail that the triumph of the Church had been the triumph of ignorance and barbarism. (He partly built on the research of Catholic scholars like Mabillon, while ignoring their belief in a divine purpose in history.)

The Enlightened view of history was the story of the gradual emergence of mankind from barbarism, requiring that the old order be repeatedly destroyed in order to make room for "progress"—change that brought continuous improvement. Such progress, measured in worldly terms, was the highest good, replacing the salvation of souls, which was now condemned as a kind of deluded fanaticism. (Some *philosophes* did believe in personal immortality, but only in terms similar to those of ancient paganism.)

Deism

Most *philosophes* were Deists. Voltaire denounced atheism, because it would both make the universe unintelligible and encourage anarchy, and extolled "natural religion" or the "religion of reason". Its principal difference with Christianity was its denial that there could be such a thing as divine revelation. "Worship" simply meant respecting the order of the universe, and men obeyed the divine will merely by adhering to that order.

Both Catholics and *philosophes* believed in natural law—that moral truth could be understood by reason. But Catholics saw immorality as inherent in fallen human nature, while the *philosophes* believed that it was merely the product of ignorance and tyranny. The *philosophes* made human happiness—understood in a worldly sense and restrained only by respect for the rights of others—the highest moral good.

A New Morality

There was a kind of Enlightenment "sexual revolution", in which common violations of the Sixth Commandment were justified—pornography, for instance, for the first time became a thriving industry. But just as Machiavelli's blunt extolling of naked power in a sense showed the limits of Renaissance Humanism, so the limits of the Enlightenment's "natural man" were perhaps demonstrated by the infamous Marquis Donatien-Alphonse de Sade (d. 1814), who perpetrated rape and torture on servant girls and tried to elevate his vices into a philosophy of life ("sadism"). (He died in an asylum.)

"Natural Man"

The fundamental debate over human nature was complicated by the Jesuit-Jansenist split, in that the Jesuits agreed with the *philosophes* that there are natural human virtues. Orthodox Catholics could accept the idea of progress in a limited way, while insisting that a perfect society could never be achieved, while for Jansenists there could be no such thing as progress, since men were slaves to sin and all human effort was ultimately futile.

The Jansenists were almost the only people of the time who denied natural religion, and they charged that the Jesuits, by entertaining such an idea, made Christianity merely an option.

Certain political theorists, notably Hobbes and Locke, posited a "state of nature" that existed before there was organized human society, and some Enlightenment thinkers saw it as a perfect time, prior to later corruptions. The idea was carried to its furthest point by Jean-Jacques Rousseau (d. 1778), born a Calvinist in Switzerland and briefly a Catholic, who repudiated the whole idea of sin and blamed society for all moral evil. He extolled the most primitive kind of existence as the most virtuous and authentic, a teaching he claimed to have found in Jesus' warnings against worldliness. Thus, in addition to skeptical rationalism, Christianity was assailed by a kind of new religion that retained the religious instinct while repudiating Christianity.

Catholic Divisions

By the middle of the eighteenth century, the Enlightenment had mounted a systematic and passionate attack on the Church and on the Old Regime in general. But in many ways, internal Catholic disputes were equally important.

In the seventeenth century, the Sorbonne professor Edmond Richer (d. 1631) asserted that parish priests, as the direct successors of Jesus' seventy-two disciples, had authority independent of their bishops, an idea that carried Conciliarism one step further. Most German bishops were territorial princes who pursued their own interests above that of the Church and were anti-papal, including the prince-bishops of Trier, Mainz, and Cologne, who were electors of the Empire.

The German bishop Johann Nikolaus von Hontheim (d. 1790), writing under the name of Justinus Febronius, revived conciliar theories, making the pope merely a kind of presiding officer in the Church and holding that diocesan bishops receive their authority directly from Christ. (He recanted after his work was condemned by Clement XIII [1758–1769].)

Febronius did not attribute religious authority to the state, but his ideas were readily adapted for that purpose. Like Gallicanism, Febronianism was a logical corollary of the idea of the absolute state: the prince has responsibility for the spiritual as well as material welfare of his people and therefore needs to have authority over the Church.

Enlightened Despotism

The Enlightenment's contempt for traditions of all kinds appealed to self-consciously enlightened rulers who wanted to reorganize their realms in order to centralize their power and make it more efficient, a goal to which the Church, and especially the papacy, was at least a passive obstacle. Though not hostile to religion as such, these "enlightened despots" redrew diocesan and parochial boundaries to conform to the units of civil government, seized what they considered the Church's excessive wealth in order to use it for other purposes, claimed authority over seminaries to ensure that priests would be properly "enlightened", suppressed "superstitious" practices, and abolished holy days that interfered with productive labor.

In accord with the Enlightenment idea that the purpose of religion is the improvement of society, the monastic orders were a special target, because the contemplative life seemed idle and unproductive. (The nursing orders of nuns, on the other hand, were respected.)

As late as 1731, the prince-bishop of Salzburg in Austria expelled all Protestants from his domain, something he was entitled to do under the Peace of Westphalia. But Enlightenment reform programs usually included some degree of religious freedom, something that the Catholic clergy generally opposed.

In 1768, the diocesan Synod of Pistoia, Italy, meeting under the authority of the grand duke Leopold of Tuscany (1765–1792), officially espoused Jansenist doctrines about salvation, decreed the use of the vernacular in the liturgy, and proclaimed its essential independence from the papacy. After being condemned by Pius VI, Pistoia's decrees were revoked, and the bishop, Scipione de'Ricci (d. 1810), was forced to resign.

Josephinism   Emperor Joseph II (1765–1790), Leopold's brother, thought of himself as an enlightened despot and adopted Febronian principles so sweeping that Leopold dubbed him "the sacristan", because he even went so far as to decree the number of candles on the altar at Mass.

Joseph closed seven hundred monasteries of contemplative religious, pruned the liturgical calendar, redrew diocesan boundaries, forbade the publication of papal bulls, and undertook supervision of the Catholic schools, including seminaries, a policy of state control of the Church that came to be called Josephinism. Although Joseph met with the increasing disapproval of his mother, Empress Maria Teresa (1740–1765; d. 1780), and although Pius VI traveled to Vienna in an unsuccessful attempt to dissuade him from his policies, he usually had the cooperation of the bishops.

Because they went against deeply ingrained habits of piety, the religious programs of the enlightened despots were usually unpopular. The Synod of Pistoia was rejected by the people of the diocese, who drove De'Ricci out because of his attempt to suppress Marian and Sacred Heart devotions, and Austrian peasants later welcomed invading French armies, because the overthrow of their emperor permitted a return to traditional piety.

Assault on the   Although as far as possible they followed Ignatius' injunction to remain
Jesuits   in the favor of princes (some served as confessors to kings), and although they educated the sons of the elite, the Jesuits were the target of increasingly aggressive hostility on the part of Catholic monarchs, because they were directly subject to the pope. The Jesuits were dubbed "Ultramontanists" because their loyalty was "across the mountains" (Alps) and therefore a threat to the supremacy of the state.

Combining Enlightenment ideas with brutal ruthlessness, Portugal during the ministry of Sebastião de Carvalho e Mello, Marques de Pombal (d. 1782), in a sense foreshadowed the French Revolution, taking the lead in attacking the Jesuits. When an attempt was made on the king's life in 1758, Pombal blamed the Jesuits and effected their wholesale expulsion or imprisonment. (One was even strangled and burned as a would-be regicide.)

Jansenism   In France, both king and pope condemned Jansenism, which gradually lost most of its aristocratic following but continued strong, with a few sympathetic bishops and a good deal of clerical support, especially in Paris. Sometimes violent divisions arose from the policy of some bishops, especially in Paris, of withholding the sacraments from anyone who would not affirm the papal condemnation of the movement. Jansenists appealed to the Parlement, which espoused the Jansenist cause as a way both of affirming Gallicanism and of putting a limit on royal power, making use of Jansenist grievances without sharing Jansenist beliefs.

Like most religious groups at the time, Jansenists did not espouse religious freedom for everyone but only for "the truth", of which they were the sole possessors. Anti-Jansenist priests were arrested on the grounds that the denial of the sacraments was a violation of civil rights and a slander on those affected.

The Jansenists were closely watched by the police, but they managed to build a quasi-underground network, including an effective clandestine press that waged a propaganda war against both civil and ecclesiastical authority, contributing in no small measure to the undermining of authority that made the French Revolution possible. They allied themselves with the Parlement in attempting to check royal authority, with Gallicanism in rejecting much of papal authority, and with Richerism in undermining episcopal authority.

Jansenists claimed that God approved their movement by miraculous cures, and one such incident in Paris created such popular excitement that the government tried unsuccessfully to suppress its manifestations, which included apocalyptic prophecies and frenzied outbursts by people allegedly inspired by the Holy Spirit. Processions, either by Jansenists or their opponents, were a major way of publicly witnessing to controversial beliefs.

Partly because they were repeatedly condemned by Church authority, Jansenists emphasized a "spiritual" Church in which hierarchy was relatively unimportant. They relied heavily on lay leadership, encouraging lay people to read the Bible in the vernacular and use vernacular missals at Mass, practices that aroused further suspicion that they were crypto-Protestants. By their unremitting, and ultimately successful, hostility to the Jesuits, the Jansenists unwittingly aided the triumph of unbelief in France, since the Jesuits were by far the most effective defenders of orthodoxy.

The Suppression of the Jesuits

In 1761, the Parlement of Paris, the highest law court in France, forbade the Jesuits to accept new members and closed their schools, of which there were well over a hundred, far more than those of any other order. A few years later, Jesuit involvement in the Caribbean trade led to their being sued by various creditors, which gave the Parlement an opportunity to urge their expulsion from France as enemies of the crown. Virtually all the French bishops opposed the expulsion, but Louis XV reluctantly agreed, because he needed the Parlement's help in his chronic financial troubles.

One by one, Catholic states began expelling the Society. Clement XIII vigorously defended the Jesuits, but the Catholic powers continually increased their pressure, at one point temporarily seizing the papal territory of Avignon and hinting at the possibility of schism. Clement XIV was elected after a three-month conclave on which the princely enemies of the Jesuits brought strong pressure, and in 1773, he acquiesced in the Society's suppression, something that went completely against the papacy's own interests and once again demonstrated its impotence.

There were twenty-three thousand Jesuits at the time of the suppression. Many were imprisoned for years under harsh conditions, some herded onto ships and deposited on the shores of the Papal States, others receiving grudging sanctuary from various other governments. Ironically, the Society remained officially in existence only in Protestant Prussia and Orthodox Russia, whose rulers did not recognize the papal decree and who valued the Jesuits' educational work.

The French Revolution

Before the Storm

Through all this, the monarchy was losing much of its spiritual charism, especially because Louis XV's notorious adulteries, for which his Jesuit confessors, despite their reputation for laxity, refused him absolution. Louis was a sincere believer who accepted that he was unworthy, and his conspicuous failure to receive Communion raised fears that he and the kingdom no longer enjoyed divine favor.

Like his predecessors for many centuries, Louis XVI was crowned in ceremonies that symbolized the divine character of the monarchy. In contrast to his grandfather-predecessor, he led an exemplary life and at first won popular respect by, among other things, once again touching for the king's evil. But the crown's chronic financial crisis and worsening poverty among the common people, caused by a series of bad harvests, eroded that popularity.

Besides the complexities of the Jansenist controversy, the secular ideas of the Enlightenment had also been long discrediting established institutions and beliefs, although by 1789 most of the *philosophes* were dead and those who were not soon perished on the scaffold. Voltaire, relying on the power of persuasion and education, would probably not have approved of the hysterical passions that fed the Revolution. But, whatever Rousseau would have thought, his exaltation of spontaneous human emotion provided some justification for fanatical violence.

The Failure of Reform

While ideas served as its ultimate rationale, the Revolution would not have occurred when and how it did except for a specific concrete events that served as its trigger. Louis XVI was cautiously open to reform. The Old Regime was only fitfully repressive—its critics on the whole survived and even thrived, the hated Bastille had long since ceased to be a political prison, and in 1787, the government decreed religious toleration, something that most bishops opposed.

Because of his chronic financial deficits, in 1789, the king was reluctantly persuaded to summon the Estates General, France's principal representative assembly, which had not been called since 1614. The meeting began with a solemn Mass of the Holy Spirit, and for a time, religious observances continued to be part of its proceedings. No one at the time foresaw the savage attack on the Church that would soon follow.

Of the three estates, the Third—commoners, mostly of the upper middle class—was reform-minded and sought to alleviate the financial crisis by depriving the nobility of their privileged exemption from taxes. Although the clergy were in principle also not taxed—instead they offered the king a periodic "free gift"—a substantial number of clergy in the First Estate also favored reform, as did some of the nobles in the Second.

The bad harvests of the 1780s caused serious want and much popular discontent. While the privileged members of the Estates General debated reform, riots broke out both in Paris (the destruction of the Bastille) and in the countryside, alarming the Estates and giving them a sense of urgency about change. Partly under the leadership of Talleyrand and two priests—Emmanuel Sieyès (d. 1836) and Henri Grégoire (d. 1830)—the Estates quickly abolished all feudal privileges and created a "constitutional monarchy". An elected National Assembly, with Talleyrand as president, was given legislative power, and the king's authority was limited—reforms whose enactment was celebrated with a solemn Te Deum. But there were unresolved issues: the practical one of the continuing financial crisis and the ideological one of the authority of the Church.

The two issues were "resolved" by the same action—the seizure of the wealth of the Church, an action proposed by Talleyrand. As during the Reformation, the sale of church property, much of which was bought by devout Catholics, created a class of people who had a vested interest in the legitimacy of the new government. The Assembly also abolished tithes, which for many centuries had been the support of most of the clergy. With those gone, they were to be paid salaries by the government, a plan some of the lower clergy favored, hoping it might correct the imbalance of income between themselves and their superiors.

The Attack on the Church

Here the opponents of the Church saw their opportunity: the clergy were in effect to become employees of the state. The Civil Constitution of the Clergy, which Louis XVI reluctantly signed but which Pius VI eventually condemned, required all priests to take an oath of loyalty to the government and to swear that they no had no higher loyalty, a provision specifically aimed at papal authority.

Grégoire, who had Jansenist sympathies, successfully proposed the abolition of all papal taxes in France, the same action that had begun Henry VIII's break with Rome 250 years before. Bishops and priests were to be elected by laymen, including non-Catholics, and were subject to governmental supervision, while parish and diocesan maps were redrawn and a large number of dioceses suppressed.

Monasteries were virtually abolished, including those—Cluny, Citeaux, Clairvaux, all of them in a decayed state—that had played so formative a role in the history of the Church. Nuns were not required to take the oath, but their convents were officially disbanded. Some nuns were reduced to begging, but many communities existed as best they could, serving as clandestine centers of Catholic life. There was a concerted attack on clerical celibacy, partly on the grounds that priests had an obligation to produce children for France, partly because celibacy was recognized as a major source of the priestly charism. Many clergy soon married.

Education was secularized to the point where in time even former priests and religious were barred from teaching, so there would be no danger of inculcating "counterrevolutionary" ideas in the young. The Sorbonne—most of whose faculty having refused the oath—was closed.

The government also extended religious toleration, making non-Catholics fully equal to Catholics. Marriage was defined as a civil contract regulated by the government, and divorce was allowed for the first time.

The Civil Constitution, which Talleyrand later admitted was a mistake, split the nation, forcing people to choose between the rapidly evolving Revolution and their religious loyalties. Half the clergy—Trappists, Carthusians, and Capuchins in particular as well as 153 of the 160 bishops—refused to take the oath and were deprived of their offices. Thirty thousand of them, including most bishops, fled the country.

The other half took the oath, including Loménie de Brienne, Talleyrand, and Grégoire, who succeeded Talleyrand as president of the Assembly. A new group of "constitutional bishops" were named, including Grégoire, with Talleyrand presiding at their consecrations in order to provide apostolic succession. But in many places, the "constitutional clergy" were treated as intruders by their parishioners and even met with violence. Where acceptable priests were not available, lay people without access to the sacraments kept their faith alive through organized pious devotions.

Emery remained at his post after St. Sulpice was closed. He attempted to provide moral guidance to the clergy as to what might or might not be acceptable under the oath, advice that offended royalists by treating the revolutionary government as entitled to obedience from its subjects.

The Vendée   In the Vendée region in the west, massive armed rebellion against the new revolutionary government broke out, plunging the area into a decade of civil war and terrorism in which 250,000 people perished. The uprising was initially provoked by the new policy of compulsory conscription of men into the army, but it also had deep religious roots. Although at first the clergy did not support the rebellion, they were soon among its leaders, as the rebellious armies marched into battle under banners of the Sacred Heart, singing hymns, sometimes with chaplains carrying the Blessed Sacrament. The Vendée rebels themselves sometimes committed brutal atrocities, but, in the first modern act of what could be called deliberate genocide, the revolutionary government set out virtually to exterminate the people of the Vendée, including mass drownings when individual executions proved too slow.

The attack on the monarchy and the attack on the Church were intimately linked, since the king's authority was said to be divinely conferred. At Rheims, revolutionaries destroyed the vial of holy oil—claimed to have originally been sent from Heaven—that for centuries had been used to anoint each new king.

Attack on the Monarchy

In 1792, fearing that a conforming priest would not respect the seal of the confessional, the king demanded to go to confession to a priest who had not taken the oath. When this was refused, he and the royal family attempted to flee the kingdom, only to be caught, brought back to Paris, and imprisoned.

The aristocrats and clergy who had fled the kingdom raised the alarm in various European courts, especially Austria, the home of the French queen, Marie Antoinette. Louis' unsuccessful flight, along with the approach of foreign armies determined to restore him to power, allowed the more radical revolutionaries, under the dominance of the lawyer Maximilien Robespierre (d. 1794), to demand absolute loyalty and to turn all disagreement into treason.

Especially in Paris, popular radicalism was both spontaneous and organized, some of it financed by the duke of Orléans, who hoped to destabilize the monarchy so that he could become king. This radicalism was centered in the Jacobin Clubs—named for an abandoned monastery where they met—which roused the "little people" to action in the streets and enforced revolutionary orthodoxy. The club included priests, one of whom, the "red priest" Jacques Roux (d. 1794), led demands for economic equality.

The Radical Revolution

In the Reign of Terror, innumerable suspicious persons, including any priest who had not taken the oath, were systematically rounded up, some immediately killed by mobs, others subjected to speedy trials at the hands of revolutionary tribunals and carted off to the guillotine, which was the new, "efficient" instrument of mass execution.

The Terror

Loyal Catholics were accused merely of the crime of "fanaticism". Approximately five thousand priests were imprisoned at one time or another, many of whom never emerged alive. In contrast to the concern for efficiency symbolized by the guillotine, many died of disease while crammed into rotting ships. Nuns who continued to live in communities were subjected to mob violence and sometimes arrested, with sixteen Carmelites guillotined one by one as they chanted the

Veni Creator ("Come, Creator Spirit").[8] Lay people who were conspicuously devout or who harbored priests were also sometimes sentenced to death.

The king and queen were publicly executed, as was their daughter Elizabeth, who had once aspired to be a nun, while the Dauphin (crown prince) probably died in prison. A majority of the clerical members of the Assembly, all of whom had taken the oath, voted for the death of the royal family. But Talleyrand, whose uncanny ability to anticipate the course of events made him the most famous survivor in history, fled the country, and soon the Terror began to entrap revolutionaries who were considered deviant in some way.

"Dechristianization"   Even clergy who had taken the oath were now forbidden to exercise their ministries, and all churches were closed or converted to secular uses like stables. Most had their images defaced, and a few (notably the great abbey of Cluny) were razed completely. The tolerance granted Protestants and Jews was short-lived, as the revolutionary government soon forbade all religious practices except those cults created by the state itself.

Some ex-clergy, often claiming that they had been seduced into the priesthood while too young to understand, themselves became ruthless agents of repression. Eight "constitutional bishops" perished on the scaffold, and Loménie de Brienne committed suicide in prison. But Grégoire boldly continued to wear his episcopal robes and spoke out against the persecution of religion.

Refugee clergy and religious found themselves rebuffed or only grudgingly received in Catholic countries that feared the growing military power of France. In Italy, some Jansenist bishops were even sympathetic to the Revolution, and Francis II of Austria (1792–1835) thought the Civil Constitution compatible with Josephinism. Spain, where exiled French clergy set up a seminary, was more hospitable and, ironically, many refugees found a kindly welcome in England, where Catholics had only very recently been granted minimal official toleration. During the 1790s, there were seven thousand exiled priests in England, as compared to only three hundred natives.

Although there was an inevitable surge of atheism, Robespierre himself opposed irreligion and tried to purge atheists, because he considered Deism essential to forging a completely new moral order, even a new species of man. The Revolution attempted to establish an entirely new religion, making use of words like *catechism, martyr, gospel,* and *missionary* in ways connected with political orthodoxy. There was a new calendar, beginning with the year One, according to which Sundays were forbidden to be observed in any special way and fish could

---

[8] The subjects of the novella *The Song at the Scaffold* by Gertrud von le Fort and the modern opera *The Dialogues of the Carmelites* by Francois Poulenc.

not be sold on Friday. New feasts and rituals were decreed, such as that of the Supreme Being.

The Cathedral of Notre Dame in Paris became the Temple of Reason, with an actress enthroned on the altar as a goddess, and the church of the Madeleine (Magdalen) was given the pagan name the Pantheon ("all the gods") and made a burial place for national heroes. Saints' names for children were abolished, especially in favor of classical pagan names like Brutus.

Compulsory optimism was at the heart of the new creed, with the doctrine of Original Sin considered one of Christianity's major errors. The Revolution promised the achievement of a perfect society and a perfect mankind.

"Liberty, Equality, Fraternity"

Where the Gospel was not rejected altogether, it was said to teach the social equality of all men, something the Revolution was at last achieving. The revolutionary slogan "Liberty Equality, Fraternity" set in motion a fanatical drive to destroy all social ranks and was itself a major cause of the suppression of liberty. (Paradoxically, religious orders had to be forcibly suppressed because their vow of obedience was considered an intolerable infringement on liberty.)

As some revolutionaries saw that even they were not safe from Robespierre's ruthlessness, he himself became the target of a coup and perished on the guillotine in 1794. The Terror then subsided under a new government called the Directory. At first, limited religious toleration was restored, including the right to conduct schools, and the constitutional church, which satisfied few people, was left to fend for itself, without official status. But after a few years there was renewed repression, and when a French general was killed in Rome by a papal soldier, the French army took Pius VI prisoner and brought him to France, where he soon died.

The Directory

By now, no one in France could command real authority, and civic order was precarious. The Directory was weak, and a successful military commander, Napoleon Bonaparte (d. 1821), organized yet another government—the Consulate—which he dominated. In this, he was aided by Sieyès, who had been repelled by the Terror, and by Talleyrand, who returned from exile after the fall of Robespierre. Napoleon was essentially a Deist and an enthusiastic supporter of the Revolution, but he was also a realist who sought power above all and who tried to avoid the mistakes of the Directory, including its unpopular repression of religion.

The Age of Napoleon

Pope Pius VII (1800–1823) was elected at Venice, because Napoleon's troops occupied Rome. Extraordinary for the time, the new pope had once stated that democracy could bring benefits to mankind. In 1801,

An Uneasy Truce

the master papal diplomat Cardinal Ercole Consalvi (d. 1824) succeeded in negotiating a concordat ("agreement") with Napoleon, a pragmatic settlement that sought to protect the interests of the Church as far as possible, without necessarily conceding legitimacy to the regime. (Originating in the Middle Ages, the concordat was a strategy that the Holy See would increasingly employ over the next century and a half.)

Both those Catholics who refused to recognize the legitimacy of the Revolution and those hard-core revolutionaries who wanted to crush the Church felt betrayed by the 1801 agreement. But the Pope and the First Counsel each saw advantages—for Napoleon, the end of religious strife in France and papal recognition of his legitimacy; for Pius, limited toleration for the Church and the defeat of both Gallicanism and the powerful prince-bishops of Germany, since by the terms of the Concordat the papacy alone represented the Church.

The constitutional church thus came to an end, with more than half its bishops submitting to the Pope and the rest either resigning or being deposed. But the Pope also had to agree to the resignation of those few remaining bishops who had originally rejected the Civil Constitution. The government would nominate new bishops, subject to papal ratification, and bishops would appoint lower clergy approved by the government. The diocesan boundaries drawn up under the constitution remained, and all bishops were to take an oath of loyalty to the state in which they swore to refrain from participating in any action "harmful to the public peace".

Renewed Persecution

But, as has often been the case over the centuries, in the end papal diplomacy failed to save the Church from a determined secular power. In 1804, Napoleon proclaimed himself Emperor of the French (1804–1815). Pius VII came to Paris to preside at the coronation, but Napoleon, not wishing to appear to receive his authority from the Church, placed the crown on his own head. (The legend that at the last moment he snatched the crown from the Pope's hands appears to be untrue.)

Soon the emperor began to interpret the Concordat in increasingly restrictive ways and to press the papacy into an alliance against France's enemies. When Pius continued to act independently, Napoleon seized the Papal States and brought the Pope forcibly to France, where he was bullied into making concessions that he soon repudiated. Pius then began rejecting imperial nominees for bishoprics.

Napoleon proclaimed his son King of Rome and made it clear that he intended to control the papacy as an arm of imperial policy. Along the way, Talleyrand once again fled France, and, bravely, the aged Emery was virtually alone in confronting the emperor to his face.

Wherever French armies were successful, Napoleon, who redrew the entire map of Europe, placed his relatives or close associates in power and imposed the principles of the Revolution, including restrictions on the Church and the seizure of church lands. He abolished the

Holy Roman Empire, which became merely "Austria", and unintentionally helped restore the integrity of the German hierarchy by abolishing the prince-bishoprics, thereby allowing the bishops to exercise better their primary duties as spiritual leaders.

During the Napoleonic occupation, the Spanish cortes, the chief legislative body of the kingdom, abolished the Inquisition and introduced other religious reforms, even though clergy made up a significant minority of the delegates. But on the whole, the Spanish, who now gave a name to the ancient tactic of "guerilla" fighting ("little warfare"), resisted Napoleon most fiercely, partly motivated by their Catholicism and often led by their priests, a large number of whom were arrested, killed, or deported.

When Napoleon was defeated by the combined European powers in 1814, the Pope was able to return to Rome, only to be seized again when Napoleon regained his throne the following year. The aged Pope was released for the last time after Napoleon's final defeat at Waterloo in 1815. But, alone among the European heads of state, Pius was willing to receive Napoleon's mother and other relatives as refugees, and he interceded to try to make the conditions of Napoleon's exile less severe.

The Fall of Napoleon

I I   Modernity

Beginning before 1800 and extending over two centuries, there occurred, simultaneously, the greatest revolutions in the history of the world—political, social, economic, intellectual, and scientific.

The Restoration   The attack on religion by the French Revolution had led to the downfall of the entire Old Regime and to decades of near chaos, so that even people of skeptical mentality now came to believe that religion was necessary. (The aged Talleyrand, repenting on his deathbed, turned his hands over to remind the attending priest that, as a bishop, he had already been anointed on his palms.)

De Maistre   To Joseph de Maistre (d. 1821), a diplomat in the service of the principality of Savoy, the Revolution had been a cleansing fire that restored Christendom—a whirlpool in which God had destroyed and made new, with the revolutionaries, against their own will, serving as His agents. The destruction of the Old Regime and the Gallican church had been necessary for the revival of Christendom, thought de Maistre, and the Revolution had also revealed the anarchic character of popular sovereignty, showing that fear of punishment and obedience to authority—that of the pope above all—alone could suppress the disorders wrought by human sinfulness.

Congress of Vienna   Following Napoleon's defeat, the great powers assembled in the Congress of Vienna in order to restore Europe as much as possible to the conditions of 1789. Based on the principle of "legitimacy", dynastic rights as they existed prior to the Revolution were renewed for several royal families.

Cardinal Consalvi, the papal secretary of state, was recognized as the most able diplomat at the conference, obtaining the return of almost all the Papal States that had been lost. But, despite his achievements, the relationship of church and state in the nineteenth century was a tangled skein almost everywhere. Catholic Austria led the way in restoring the prerevolutionary regimes, but Josephinism survived, as did Febronianism among some German and Italian bishops. In France, the close alliance with the restored Bourbon monarchy also restored a kind of Gallicanism.

New Ideologies

The history of the West after 1815 was to a great extent the history of continuing conflict among competing ideologies: Conservatism, Liberalism, Socialism, Nationalism, and others. Antagonisms of race, nationality, class, and religion, all of which were perennial in human affairs, were now the proverbial genies that could not be put back into the bottle. It was during this period that the familiar division of politics into liberal and conservative ("left" and "right", from the seating arrangements in the French National Assembly in 1790) came into common use.

Conservatism

Conservatism was a defense of monarchy and social privilege, resting on the force of tradition; it assumed that the old ways, having survived for so long, were presumably the best ways. Society was seen as an organism in which each person functioned as part of a hierarchy. Following the Congress of Vienna, an ecumenical Holy Alliance was forged among Protestant Prussia, Catholic Austria, and Orthodox Russia—all pledged to suppress rebellion wherever it reared up. Whatever their personal beliefs, such conservatives always recognized the social importance of religion.

Liberalism

Liberalism was in a sense the unfinished agenda of the Revolution— relativizing the traditional authorities of church and state, free elections, governments answerable to their citizens, basic civil liberties— and it was embraced by much of the growing middle class. Liberalism did not necessarily require the end of monarchy, which was still regarded by many people as the natural form of government. But the monarch had to accept a limited role defined by a constitution, an arrangement that, through much conflict, was eventually worked out in most European monarchies.

Vatican Response

Consalvi, the consummate diplomat, believed that the Holy See should avoid rigid positions, so as to be able to survive in the changing world. Thus, under Pius VII, the Holy See remained aloof from the Holy Alliance when rebellions broke out against the Austrians in Italy, and it officially recognized Latin American countries that threw over the rule of Spain. When Charles X of France (1824–1830), brother of the guillotined Louis XVI, was overthrown in a second revolution, Pope Pius VIII (1829–1830) reluctantly recognized the new regime of the liberal monarch Louis Philippe (1830–1848). The Holy See responded to these situations mainly by diplomatic means, concluding a series of concordats with various states that achieved (usually only temporarily) the restoration of some lost rights. But under Pope Gregory XVI (1831– 1846), the papacy essentially made a strategic alliance with Conservatism, and that brought its own problems.

The Liberal Order

Church leaders were resistant to Liberalism because of the belief that the social and political orders were based on divine law and could not be altered merely by human will and that rebellion was wicked because of the inherent sinfulness of human nature. The idea of popular sovereignty was therefore seen as a kind of idolatry of the popular will. Even many liberals admitted that their political program was necessarily based on a relativistic philosophy that denied the possibility of absolute truth.

Anti-Religion

The antagonism between the Church and Liberalism was thus a vicious circle—the Church condemned Liberalism as a subversion of order, while liberals opposed the Church as a remnant of the Old Regime and an enemy of progress. Wherever it triumphed in Catholic lands (France, Spain, Belgium, various Italian states, the newly independent countries of Latin America), Liberalism tended to curtail the Church's rights; while in dominantly Protestant lands (Prussia, the Netherlands, Switzerland), it allied itself with the Reformation churches. The Masonic Order was now a champion of Liberalism and sometimes openly atheistic. In many countries, it was an implacable foe of the Church.

Liberal Coercion

In countries without a tradition of religious toleration, Liberalism was often violent, provoking fierce Catholic opposition in turn. Mob violence against churches or priests often went unpunished, and protesting bishops were sometimes imprisoned or exiled. Liberal governments often violated their own professed principles, but the Church could not readily claim the protection of those principles, because most of the hierarchy rejected them, instead claiming toleration for Catholicism on the grounds that the true faith could not be suppressed. The hierarchy opposed the extension of religious liberty to Protestants by Catholic governments because "Error has no rights" and freedom of religion would undermine the divine authority of the state.

The Limits of Toleration

In practice, most countries adopted limited toleration in order to avoid civil strife. There was minimal freedom of worship, so that non-established churches were often not allowed to call attention to themselves by building steeples, for example. In the British Isles, only Anglican places of worship could officially be called churches, all others being mere "chapels".

A disputed issue in every country with an official religion was the legal standing of marriages performed by clergy of other churches. Only gradually did governments recognize such unions, in the face of opposition by the clergy of the established churches. In Protestant lands, governments sometimes forbade Catholic priests to require the partners in a mixed marriage to promise to raise their children as Catholics. In some ways, the most important part of the liberal program was universal, state-sponsored education, which to a great extent was intended to bring about the secularization of society, an issue that continued to fester well into the twenty-first century.

Besides attempting to control education, states unfriendly to Catholicism interfered with the appointment of bishops and restricted or suppressed religious orders. The restored Jesuits were expelled from Switzerland and Russia and for a time were again suppressed in France, although they were allowed to function there under a different name. (They were not permitted back into Switzerland until 1973.)

In England, Liberalism came closest to living up to its professed beliefs. In 1829, despite the opposition of George IV (1820–1830) and fierce popular anti-Catholicism, the government, under the hero of Waterloo, the duke of Wellington (d. 1852), granted Catholics most civil rights.

The Papal States

The papacy was most directly confronted with the forces of Liberalism in the Papal States themselves. After their restoration in 1815, all the reforms introduced under French rule were repealed, against Consalvi's better judgment, so that, for example, clergy once again held most government posts and Jews were returned to the ghettoes, where on Sundays they were required to listen to sermons haranguing them for their stubborn resistance to the Gospel. The Papal States were among the last European countries to allow torture in regular criminal proceedings.

Intense agitation for change followed the 1815 restoration, including acts of terrorism and armed rebellions, many of them organized by an anticlerical secret society called the Carbonari ("charcoal-burners", because they originally met in the forests), which had Masonic links. The rebellions were put down by force, including numerous executions. Some of the rebels wanted to abolish papal rule altogether, while others demanded a modernized administration, a degree of self-government, and a guarantee of personal liberties. The popes, however, introduced only minor reforms. These disorders exposed a dilemma that the papacy had long had to face: the Catholic powers, especially Austria, often interfered in Italian affairs in ways that constricted the autonomy of the Papal States, but Austrian armies were sometimes needed to suppress Italian rebellions.

Lamennais

While many Catholics could see no alternative to the traditional alliance of throne and altar, a bold new vision—simultaneously both conservative and radical—was proposed by the French priest Hughes-Félicité de Lamennais (d. 1854). He proposed nothing less than that the Church should put herself at the head of the new liberal movements, with the clergy taking control of what he considered to be an inevitable new revolution, in order to establish a society infused by Christianity and guaranteeing liberal freedoms.

Lamennais began as a royalist, a traditionalist, and an Ultramontane. But his opposition to Gallicanism eventually forced him to abandon his royalism and to seek ways of christianizing the new social and political movements, basing political liberty on the teachings of the Church concerning human free will. Lamennais proclaimed that divine providence was bringing a new order into being and urged the practice of apostolic poverty as the antidote to social injustice. He had a profound sense of the Church as a spiritual society, without which kingdoms would collapse, and he opposed union of church and state as the reduction of the Church to a mere political institution.

Lamennais was radically democratic, not primarily in a political way but with a mystical faith in "the People", whom he considered the recipients of divine inspiration, guided by the Church. His movement provoked mistrust because his separation of religion from politics seemed dangerously radical to conservatives and highly reactionary to liberals.

Lamennais appealed to the pope to lead a new Christendom, and for a time, Leo XII (1823–1829) seemed sympathetic. But Lamennais was censured by the archbishop of Paris and, appealing to Gregory XVI (1831–1846), found himself condemned by that pope as well. Increasingly bitter, he abandoned Christianity altogether and appealed directly to the people, refusing the last sacraments and dying outside the Church.

Liberal Catholicism

Some of Lamennais' disciples, such was the noted apologist Charles de Montalembert (d. 1870), submitted to Church authority and became the leaders of what was sometimes called liberal Catholicism, which meant a vague conviction that the Church should come to terms with what was good in modern civilization without compromising her soul. While most liberal Catholics remained clearly on the side of orthodoxy, a few did not, notably the German historian and theologian Johann Ignaz von Döllinger (d. 1890), originally an adherent of Lamennais' blend of radical politics with Ultramontanisn. Döllinger became increasingly anti-papal in both politics and theology.

Nationalism

The medieval concept of Christendom was of a single society of diverse peoples united by a common faith, and it thus had no room for the modern idea of nationality. While elements of Nationalism existed in earlier times, it only came into its own with the French Revolution, when loyalty to the nation replaced loyalty to the king, requiring from the citizen not only obedience but inner adherence and emotional fervor. The state itself became a kind of church, based on faith, its power derived from orchestrated passion.

During the nineteenth century, the spirit of Nationalism was kindled all over the world. While it could be supportive of Catholicism, it triumphed most completely in Protestant Prussia and anticlerical Italy. Since it represented the forces of change, it was held in deep suspicion by Church authorities. Beginning with the French Revolution, universal military conscription was enacted by nationalist regimes, not only in order to provide the state with armies but as a way of inculcating patriotic conformity in the people, an educational function that was, once again, in competition with the Church.

Nationalism thrust in two opposite directions: seeking to dismember states in which disparate peoples were yoked together under a single government and seeking to unite people of the same ethnic identity who lived scattered under different governments. The Catholic Austrian Empire represented the first pattern, with the Catholic Hungarians chief among those who sought independence. After 1815, Catholics in various countries subject to non-Catholic governments began asserting themselves. Catholics in what had been the Austrian (southern) Netherlands chafed under the rule of the Protestant (northern) Netherlands; Catholics in Poland resisted the periodic persecution at the hands of their Russian rulers; and Catholics in Ireland demanded more rights from England.

Catholic Nationalists

Polish Nationalism took on a deeply Catholic character. Some of its proponents, such as the mystical poet Adam Mickiewicz (d. 1855), compared the sufferings of the Polish people to those of Jesus Himself and proclaimed Poland as the "Christ among nations".

Poland

Poland, Ireland, and the southern Netherlands showed how the newer political movements might serve Catholic interests, with clergy, including bishops, among the leaders agitating for political independence. In all cases, however, Pope Gregory XVI admonished his flock to remain obedient to their lawful rulers, even going so far as to characterize the Russian czar as a loving father to his Polish subjects. Belatedly, the Pope recognized his naïveté and was able to obtain some concessions for the Poles.

Gregory XVI

In the revolutions of 1830, the southern Netherlands gained their independence from the North under the name of Belgium. It enacted a liberal constitution that formally separated church and state while protecting the rights of the Church.

Belgium

In the southern three-fourths of Ireland, the small Protestant minority, who were mostly of English descent, owned almost all the land, with the Catholic majority living merely as tenant farmers subject to arbitrary eviction and having to pay tithes to the church of Ireland.

Daniel O'Connell—"the Liberator" (d. 1847)—made use of religious and ethnic loyalties to forge an alliance of Catholicism, Liberalism, and Nationalism that involved clergy, laity, and even some Protestants. He opposed overt rebellion and demanded not complete independence from England but full political and religious rights, most

Ireland

of which were eventually granted. He neither sought nor received papal approval, although he died en route to meet the Pope. In general, the clergy, including most of the bishops, at least tacitly supported his movement, although the terrorist Fenian movement was condemned by both the bishops and the Pope.

In the years just prior to O'Connell's death, Ireland was devastated by the Potato Famine, when the crop that was the staple of most Irishmen's diet succumbed to blight. Over seven hundred thousand Irish died of starvation or disease, and millions more emigrated in the greatest natural catastrophe to strike a Western country since the Black Death.

Germany and Italy

Germany (a collection of essentially independent principalities) and Italy (mainly divided between the Papal States and various territories ruled by foreign powers) were the chief battlegrounds of the kind of Nationalism that sought to amalgamate separate states into one.

In the struggle over who would dominate a united Germany, Protestant Prussia defeated Catholic Austria and also successfully laid claim to territories in the Catholic Rhineland, where it harassed Catholics believed to be a threat to national unity. Prussia represented a conservative kind of Nationalism, effected not by the popular will but by the actions of an authoritarian government.

Bl. Pope Pius IX (1846–1878) was a one-time papal diplomat who at his election was a popular diocesan bishop viewed by some as a kind of liberal. While making it clear that he condemned Liberalism as a philosophy, he granted amnesty to those imprisoned in past rebellions, authorized railways and independent newspapers in his domain, and issued a constitution for the Papal States. Giuseppe Mazzini (d. 1872), the leader of the Nationalist *Risorgimento* ("coming to life") movement in Italy, hailed Pius at his election and even proposed that the papacy might serve as leader of a united Italy, while the archconservative Austrian prime minister Klemens von Metternich (d. 1859) was dismayed at the tenor of the new pontificate.

1848

But events moved with great speed. In 1848, revolution suddenly broke out all over Europe, with people on both sides of the barricades swept along by intense passion. Both Louis Philippe and Metternich were forced to flee, and the king of Prussia had to grant a constitution. In Paris, Archbishop Denis Affre, attempting to bring peace to the streets, was shot dead, perhaps accidentally.

Full-scale rebellion broke out in the Papal States, partly because the Pope refused to embrace Italian Nationalism by supporting a revolt against Austria. One of the Pope's closest advisors was assassinated, his funeral disrupted, and his body thrown into the Tiber. Pius fled from Rome, and by the time of his return, he had come to view the new movements of the age with unrestrained loathing. For the remainder of his pontificate, he pursued very conservative policies, closely advised by his secretary of state, Cardinal Giacomo Antonelli (d. 1876), probably the last cardinal who was a deacon only, not a priest.

France was one of the few places where the 1848 revolution was successful. Despite Affre's death, some Catholics hailed the Second Republic as a new beginning that was not hostile to the Church. Louis Napoleon Bonaparte, nephew of the great emperor, served as president of the Republic, then had himself proclaimed emperor (1852–1871) as Napoleon III (the title "Napoleon II" was claimed by Napoleon Bonaparte's son [d. 1832], who never ruled). An adventurer, Louis Napoleon had participated in an unsuccessful Carbonari revolt in Italy, after which the future Pius IX had helped him to escape. The emperor's policies toward the Church in France vacillated according to the degree that he needed Catholic support, but he supplied troops to guarantee the continued independence of the Papal States and to protect the foreign missions.

The extent to which Pius IX was at odds with modern sensibilities was dramatically illustrated when a Jewish boy living in the Papal States, Edgar Mortara (d. 1940), was taken from his parents to be raised as a ward of the Pope, because he had been secretly baptized by a Catholic maid. (Mortara came to idolize the Pope and eventually became a priest.) Pius could not comprehend the outrage that the incident provoked even among some Catholics.

Papal Authority and Power

The Mortara Case

In 1864, Pius IX issued the famous *Syllabus of Errors*, attached to the encyclical *Quanta Cura* (With Great Care), condemning numerous modern ideas, above all the idea that the state was the ultimate authority in human affairs. The *Syllabus* declared the Church's independence from the state, including the Catholic state, in all areas of religious and moral life and proclaimed the "fullness of papal authority" even in areas which did not concern faith and morals.

Syllabus of Errors

The most controversial passages in the document condemned the propositions that the Catholic religion should not be "the only religion of the state" and that there should be freedom of worship and speech, things that tended to produce "corruption of morals and religious indifferentism", according to the Pope. The ultimate problem, as Pius saw it, was the liberal idea of a "neutral" state without an official religious foundation, which was a denial that society needed to be subordinated to divine law. The Pope affirmed the divine origin of all legitimate authority and condemned the claim that ultimate sovereignty rested with the people.

Religious Freedom

Summing up, Pius proclaimed, "If anyone thinks that the Roman Pontiff can and should reconcile himself and come to terms with progress, with Liberalism, and with modern civilization, let him be anathema."[1]

Liberalism Condemned

---

[1] Pius IX, *Syllabus of Errors*, 80, www.papalencyclicals.net/pius09/p9syll.htm.

Pius' condemnation of Liberalism obviously owed a great deal to his traumatic experiences early in his pontificate, which made Liberalism appear to be a sham that promised freedom while imposing restrictions, sometimes even outright persecution, on the Church.

Quanta Cura and the *Syllabus* aroused fierce reactions. In some places, the document was publicly burned, and in France, bishops were warned that they would be arrested if they had it read from the pulpit. No prominent Catholic rejected the document outright, but it seemed to preclude even the possibility of liberal Catholicism. For a century afterward, some people attempted to interpret it in the narrowest possible way, even as others read into it more than the Pope perhaps intended. His intentions were in some ways uncertain, in that, for example, to deny that the pope must reconcile himself to modern society did not necessarily mean that he might not choose to do so, and to deny that democracy was the only legitimate form of government was not to say that it was illegitimate.

Pius' proclamation of Church authority directly challenged the state and allowed him to see the validity of at least some rebellions. He was, for example, virtually the only European ruler who denounced yet another savage Russian suppression of a Polish uprising, a complete reversal of his predecessor's habitual defense of political authority.

Risorgimento

The Italian *Risorgimento* had liberal political goals based on an appeal to a past Italian cultural greatness that was now being revived. Most Italian nationalists, many of whom were Masons, saw the papacy as an obstacle both to greater freedom and to Italian unification and were candid about their eventual goal of abolishing the Papal States, which bisected the peninsula. Mazzini and others wanted a republic, but the kingdom of Sardinia, a liberal monarchy that ruled much of northern Italy and had curtailed the rights of the Church, took the lead in unification. Victor Emmanuel II of Sardinia was also proclaimed the first king of Italy (1861–1878).

Fall of the Papal States

The Papal States began falling to the Sardinians a piece at a time, and nationalists demanded that Rome be made the Italian capital. Pius was both offered bribes and threatened in order to get him to surrender, but he refused both, saying that the Papal States had been given to him by God in stewardship and he had no right to relinquish them. But when France went to war with Prussia in 1870, Napoleon III had to withdraw his forces from Rome. For a time, the city was defended by the small papal army and by volunteers from all over the Catholic world, but, as Victor Emmanuel's army besieged the city, Pius ordered his troops not to shed unnecessary blood and hoisted the white flag of surrender.

A plebiscite appeared to show an overwhelming majority of the people of the Papal States favoring union with the kingdom of Italy, and Victor Emmanuel was installed in the Quirinal Palace that had been the principal papal residence. Pius IX withdrew across the Tiber to become the self-imposed "prisoner of the Vatican", a living protest against what he deemed to be a crime against God. Although the kingdom of Italy offered the Pope certain concessions, including monetary indemnities, Pius refused them in principle. Italian Catholics were told not to vote or otherwise participate in the civic life of what was declared to be an illegitimate state.

The question of the papacy's "temporal power" remained an issue in Catholic circles for many years. The argument in its favor was both theoretical—the Papal States were bestowed by God—and practical: How could the Pope be secure in the exercise of his spiritual authority unless he ruled an autonomous principality free of the secular powers? But on balance, the loss of the Papal States proved to be beneficial to the Church. They were only a fragile protection for papal autonomy, and fifteen hundred years of fighting for territory often had a deeply corrupting effect on the papacy.

Church Reforms

After 1870, the spiritual authority of the papacy increased. Pius devoted himself to Church reforms that increased the ecclesiastical importance of his office: broadening membership in the College of Cardinals and basing it primarily on merit; expanding the Roman Curia and giving it major responsibilities; establishing colleges in Rome for seminarians from all over the world; appointing bishops with less regard for the opinion of secular governments; establishing the custom of *ad limina* ("to the threshold") visits of bishops to Rome; using papal nuncios ("heralds") as representatives to the various national hierarchies, not just to governments; and establishing many new dioceses, especially in mission lands.

Spirituality

After the defeat of Napoleon, there occurred one of the great revivals in the history of the Church, although some regions, having been deprived of their priests, never fully recovered. The peasantry had remained loyal to the Church throughout the eighteenth century, and now many of the secularized bourgeoisie also returned to religion, although many of the intelligentsia continued to adhere to Enlightenment skepticism. The spiritual revival was especially measured in a great increase in religious vocations and the founding of new religious orders.

The Restored Jesuits

Pius VII restored the Society of Jesus in Italy in 1804 and restored it to the universal Church a decade later, calling it a "powerful new oar on Peter's bark". Jesuits once again lived their special vow of obedience to the pope and, consequently, were once again the targets of agitation, especially because of their involvement in education.

New Communities

France, having led the way in the destruction of the Church, also led the way in her revival through new orders: among many others, the

Society of Mary (Marianists, founded by Bl. William-Joseph Chaminade [d. 1850]), the Society ("Madames") of the Sacred Heart (St. Madeleine Sophie Barat [d. 1865]), the Oblates of Mary Immaculate (St. Eugene de Mazenod [d. 1861]), and the Congregation of Holy Cross (Bl. Basil Anthony Moreau [d. 1873]).

Monastic Revival

Monasticism had been all but wiped out in France, but it underwent a dramatic revival in the Benedictine house of Solesmes, under the abbot Prosper Guéranger (d. 1875). Meanwhile, Jean-Baptiste Lacordaire (d. 1861) almost single-handedly revived the Dominican order in France, becoming the most celebrated preacher of the age. (Both men had been disciples of Lamennais.)

The Curé of Ars

St. John Vianney (d. 1859) was the best-known and most revered French saint of the nineteenth century, a man who dramatically demonstrated the continuing power of the faith in people's lives. At first thought to lack the intelligence necessary for the priesthood, he spent almost four decades as *curé* of the obscure village of Ars, where his reputation for works of charity, heroic self-denial, and simple but heartfelt preaching attracted thousands of people.

He had a powerful sense of the sinfulness of mankind and longed to become a Trappist and devote himself to penance, but instead he spent as many as eighteen hours a day in the confessional. (When offered a ribbon of honor by the French government, he declined, because it had no resale value and thus would be of no use to his work with the poor.)

The Irish Revival

Ireland underwent a remarkably rapid spiritual recovery after the Potato Famine. Under the leadership especially of Cardinal Paul Cullen (d. 1878) of Dublin, who had been rector of the Irish College in Rome, the reforms of Trent were belatedly introduced into a church that had finally emerged into the light after centuries of quasi-underground existence. In every measurable way (church attendance, reception of the sacraments, popular devotions, educational and charitable work), Ireland came to be seen as perhaps the most intensely Catholic society in the world. (At one time, religious vocations were so plentiful that half of all Irish priests served abroad.) Some bishops were outspoken champions of independence, but Cullen concentrated on religious matters, of which the major issue was the National (public) schools, which had a Protestant bias.

John Bosco

St. John Bosco[2] (d. 1888) was perhaps even more famous than the Curé of Ars. An Italian of scholarly interests and attainments, he founded the Oratory of St. Francis de Sales especially to work with abandoned

---

[2] Known as "Don Bosco"; *Don* ("lord") was a priestly title in Italy.

or abused boys. He invoked de Sales' name because he ministered to his young charges with mildness and a spirit of trust.

St. Thérèse of Lisieux (Thérèse of the Child Jesus; the Little Flower, d. 1897) was a French girl who at age fifteen was allowed to enter a Carmelite convent. She died when only twenty-four, but her post-humously published writings, describing her imperfections, anxieties, sufferings, and mortifications, laid out a "little way" to sanctity, the significance of which was eventually recognized when she was made a doctor of the Church in 1997. Thérèse became one of the most popular saints of the twentieth century. Unable to fulfill her desire of going to the missions, she became instead the patroness of the missions.[3]

In the history of the Church, innumerable people have reported private visions of Christ or His saints, but in the nineteenth century such experiences became the focus of a number of popular movements, and since that time there have been more than two hundred alleged visitations by Mary in various parts of the world.

Anna Katherina Emmerich (d. 1824) was a German nun who, after her convent was closed under Napoleon, retired to a private house and apparently experienced the stigmata. She claimed to have received special revelations of things not revealed in Scripture: the hidden life of Jesus at Nazareth, Mary's life after Jesus' death, and other things. Her claims attracted both fervent credulity and much skepticism.

A unique and bizarre heresy called the Maravites ("followers of Mary") arose in deeply Catholic Poland in the early nineteenth century, when a nun not only claimed visions but said she had been mystically united to the second Person of the Trinity. The sect, which used the vernacular in the liturgy and ordained women to the priesthood, attracted hundreds of thousands of followers at its peak.

In 1830, St. Catherine Labouré (d. 1875), a Daughter of Charity in a Paris convent, felt herself drawn to the chapel in the middle of the night, where the Virgin Mary gave her the design for the Miraculous Medal that became a popular Marian devotion.

In 1849, three children in the French village of La Salette also had a vision of Mary that attracted numerous pilgrims. Other visions followed, as at Knock in Ireland.

Lourdes

The most influential of these nineteenth-century visions was at Lourdes, France, in 1858, where a peasant girl, St. Bernadette Soubirous (d. 1879), had a series of visions of a lady who said of herself, "I am

---

[3] Her blood sister, who was a nun in the same convent, was an avid photographer, so that Thérèse is the first saint of whom numerous pictures exist, some of them unposed informal scenes.

the Immaculate Conception", a dogma only recently officially proclaimed and which the uneducated Bernadette probably did not fully understand. Lourdes captured the imagination of the world, its story eventually told even in a popular Hollywood film (*The Song of Bernadette*) and it became one of the world's greatest pilgrimage places, the scene of countless reported miracles of healing.

Fatima

Marian piety culminated at Fatima in Portugal in 1917, when three peasant children saw visions of Mary, who preached a message of repentance, warned of coming catastrophes, and gave the children three "secrets" to convey to Church authorities. The Fatima devotion became immensely popular.

Pope Pius XII (1939–1958) was especially devoted, perhaps because the Virgin's first reported apparition occurred on the day of his consecration as a bishop. Heeding one of the Fatima admonitions, he consecrated the world to the Immaculate Heart of Mary during World War II, and immediately after the war over seven hundred thousand people—one-tenth of the entire population of Portugal—came to Fatima on the anniversary of the apparitions. Pius XII also gave strong impetus to Marian devotion by his proclamation of the dogma of the Assumption in 1950.

Official Caution

In each case, the authorities' initial reaction to alleged visions was almost always negative, even hostile. But if the visionaries persisted even in the face of threats and obloquy, their claims were often examined sympathetically. Mainly because of Lourdes, the Church developed a formalized procedure for dealing with apparitions. Such revelations are classified as "private", meaning that they do not have to be believed and can add nothing substantial to the original deposit of faith. But they might be declared free of error and "worthy of credence by the faithful". At Lourdes, a special medical bureau was set up to investigate alleged cures.

Eucharistic Congresses

Beginning in the early twentieth century, "eucharistic congresses" were periodically held all over the world—massive gatherings of Catholics to pay homage to Christ in the Blessed Sacrament and to hear sermons from leading prelates encouraging them in their faith. Besides their devotional purpose, the congresses served as dramatic public evidence of the vibrant life of the Church.

The Social Apostolate

Humanitarianism

Humanitarianism—organized efforts to alleviate the sufferings of the poor, the sick, the insane, the imprisoned, children, and animals—flourished in the nineteenth century. It sprang from Christian roots but was virtually the only movement of the age that transcended religious and political differences. For some people, it was an alternative to formal religion, and it diverged philosophically from orthodox Christianity to the degree that it considered earthly paradise an attainable goal.

Nineteenth-century people were not necessarily more compassionate than their forebears, but they were less fatalistic. Technological innovations in agriculture, sanitation, medicine, and other areas for the first time in history made it possible to eliminate many kinds of suffering that had been considered unavoidable. But belief in progress was called into question by the fact that those same technological changes were creating their own kinds of suffering. In particular, the nature of poverty was changing because of the industrial revolution, which transformed rural peasants into urban laborers crowded into slums and dependent on the insecurity of wages.

Laymen in the nineteenth century—some of them emerging from Lamennais' circle—had an importance unprecedented in the previous history of the Church in their attempt to transform society according to Christian principles.

Frédéric Ozanam (d. 1853) was a French historian who supported the Revolution of 1848 but was also powerfully drawn to the Middle Ages, which he extolled as a time of social and cultural wholeness infused by faith. He and his associates attempted to rediscover the roots of that culture in order to bring them to bear on contemporary society. Like most Catholic reformers throughout history, they saw practical charity as essential.

Ozanam and the St. Vincent de Paul Society

Ozanam and his friends took direction from the Daughters of Charity, who were among the few people working with the poorest of the poor (like the destitute described in Victor Hugo's 1862 novel, *Les Misérables*), visiting them in their hovels and doing whatever was possible to alleviate their sufferings. Ozanam and his friends established the Society of St. Vincent de Paul, which rapidly spread beyond France. The organization was the most important practical development in Catholic charity in the nineteenth century.

Among the various "liberties" that Liberalism demanded was the "free market" (labeled *laissez-faire* ["let it act"]), in which unfettered competition and the law of supply and demand would set prices and wages. Liberalism aimed to abolish most economic regulations, so as to allow the market to flourish unhindered, a radical departure from the centuries-old system in which economic activities were closely regulated by law for the sake of justice.

Laissez-Faire

The various movements called Socialism were mainly a response to liberal economic philosophy, positing a society based on harmony and cooperation rather than competition. The "Utopian Socialists", such as Claude de Saint-Simon (d. 1825), were heirs to Rousseau and dreamed of an ideal society based on innate human goodness.

Utopian Socialism

Marx Karl Marx (d. 1883), who insisted that his own theories were scientific, despised the Utopians for not realizing that coercion was necessary to achieve their goals. He was an atheist and a materialist who insisted that revolutionary violence be directed at religion (the "opiate of the people") as well as at those with political power and economic wealth. When "Communards" briefly got control of Paris in 1871, they executed a number of "enemies of the people", including the progressive-minded Archbishop Georges Darboy (d. 1871). (After the Commune's failure, twenty thousand Communards were themselves executed.)

Industrialism The Church had relatively little experience with urbanized industry; and, while there was much concern with poverty, including sometimes heroic programs of charity, few Catholics of the time thought deeply about industrialization itself. (Famously, Pope Gregory XVI was so opposed to technological change that he forbade railways from being extended into the Papal States and would not install gas lights in Rome.) Catholic leaders tended to take for granted the traditional, closely knit agricultural society and saw the new industrialism as subversive of traditional values, destroying the rural communities where the Church had been an integral part of the social fabric for fifteen hundred years. *Laissez-faire* economic philosophy was seen as giving free rein to acquisitiveness and allowing industrialists to grow rich at the expense of their underpaid workers, yet another instance of the liberal abuse of freedom.

Von Ketteler The German bishop Wilhelm von Ketteler (d. 1877) and the French layman Philippe Buchez (d. 1865) were among those who responded to industrialism creatively. Both advocated "workers' associations" partly modeled on the medieval guilds and similar in some ways to labor unions but taking responsibility for the entire lives of their members. Ketteler and Buchez were radical for their time in asserting that the workers had God-given rights, such as a just wage, that should be secured through organized action.

Kolping The Catholic social program was implemented best in Germany, where a priest, Bl. Adolf Kolping (d. 1865), helped put Ketteler's ideas into practice. He established workers' groups that had their own religious devotions, clubhouses, newspapers, credit unions, and insurance programs and that at their height numbered more than one hundred thousand members.

Rerum Novarum Catholic social thought received its greatest impetus from the 1891 encyclical *Rerum Novarum* (*On Capital and Labor*; literally "new things", hence "revolution") of Pope Leo XIII (1878–1903), which drew on the ideas of Ozanam, von Ketteler, and others and was widely hailed for its statesmanship, even by non-Catholics. Leo bluntly condemned the heartlessness of the unrestrained free market and affirmed the dignity of labor and the laborer's right to a just wage. But he also affirmed the right of private property and condemned Socialism and Communism for denying that right and subordinating everything to the state. The Pope affirmed the Catholic ideal of a cooperative social order based on justice, an almost unique perspective at a time when the harsh doctrine of "Social Darwinism" (the "survival of the fittest") clashed with the equally harsh Marxist doctrine of inevitable class conflict and the necessary use of force.

Catholic Principles

Out of the German school and *Rerum Novarum*, a basic set of Catholic social principles evolved: the spiritual welfare of mankind as the highest purpose of society, the primacy of the family, natural rights, a spirit of cooperation rather than conflict, private property as modified by the demands of justice, and "subsidiarity"—the principle that every social issue should be resolved at the most immediate level possible, first the family, then local government, and the central government only as a last resort.

Distributive Justice
According to Catholic theory, the accumulation and concentration of private wealth and the vagaries of the "free market" need to be balanced by the requirement of "distributive justice": the distribution of material goods in such a way that no one is denied a fair share, a principle that permits government intervention in the economy through taxes, labor laws, welfare programs, and even the redistribution of wealth.

Corporatism
As it developed, one major strain of Catholic social thought was called Corporatism, an ideal according to which society was to be organized around natural social groups or "corporations"—churches, families, and trades. Inspired by the medieval guilds, Corporatism conceived of society as a unified entity based on a spirit of cooperation among all classes that facilitated consensus rather than a clash of interests or majority rule. In Corporatism, strikes and other kinds of conflict were to be avoided by free discussion among all parties, then by submitting disputes to binding arbitration enforced by the government. (Because of this idea, priests sometimes served as mediators in labor disputes.) Employers were to take a fatherly interest in their workers rather than treat them merely as instruments of production.

Harmel
These ideas were put into practice in the textile factories of the French industrialist Leon Harmel (d. 1915), who sought to establish ideal Catholic communities for his workers and even led groups of as many as ten thousand on pilgrimages to Rome. But such paternalism was criticized

for making workers dependent on the good will of their employers rather than empowering them to claim their rights.

Labor Unions   Although the idea of labor unions did not fit well with Corporatism, some Catholics endorsed them, leading to disagreements as to whether Catholics should be part of the general labor movement or should form their own unions. The English Cardinal Henry Edward Manning (d. 1892) strongly supported the aspirations of the working class, even to the point of personally mediating strikes. Von Ketteler supported unions in Germany, and the hierarchy of the United States persuaded the Holy See to rescind its condemnation of such groups as "secret societies".

The Welfare State   Paradoxically, the first movement toward the modern "welfare state" was under the conservative premier Otto von Bismarck (d. 1898) of Germany, something that was possible because the philosophy of *laissez-faire* was identified with his political opponents, the liberals. The Catholic Center Party supported such things as old-age pensions and payments to injured workers, seeing them as natural applications of Catholic social principles.

Secularization   After the initial revival, there was a gradual falling off in church attendance in most countries in the nineteenth century. Many of the aristocracy treated it primarily as a social duty, while it was still relatively high among the middle classes, very high among the peasants, and sharply declining among the urban working class. Secularization was also reflected in such things as the growing practice of civil marriages, Sunday as primarily a day for leisure and recreation, and the practice of cremation.

Contraception   Even though the sale of contraceptives remained illegal everywhere, the practice of birth control increased. The Holy See, while recalling Liguori's advice not to disturb the consciences of the ignorant, nonetheless held that the official teaching should be disseminated. It was assumed that it was usually husbands who insisted on practicing contraception and that wives were innocent if they cooperated reluctantly in *coitus interruptus* but not if they allowed their husbands to use condoms.

Catholic Marriage   Leo XIII reiterated the Catholic doctrine of marriage, once again affirming its indissolubility, condemning divorce as one of the greatest of modern evils, and identifying the family as the foundation of society. He definitively affirmed that marriage, even more than it was a contract, was a free union based on mutual love, an understanding that had previously been considered a theological opinion. Gradually, the idea was accepted that the husband and wife are the actual ministers of the sacrament of matrimony, with the priest serving as the principal witness.

Except in the Anglo-Saxon countries (for reasons that are unclear), urbanization led to secularization, in that peasants tended to lose their ties to religion as they moved to towns and cities, partly because the Church was unable to keep up with urban growth. In the later part of the century, some parishes in Paris were said to have as many as 120,000 nominal parishioners.

Urbanization

More nebulously, secularization may have been promoted by the severing of ties to the land. No longer did the peasant contend with unpredictable cycles of nature dependent on the divine will; increasingly, he was part of an industrial process that was all too obviously under human control. There was a new idea of progress based on dramatic scientific and technological advancements—the Eiffel Tower in Paris, for example, was intended to be a man-made structure that soared over every church.

The Cult of Progress

Intellectually, the nineteenth century continued to be a troubled time for religion. While the *Syllabus of Errors* attracted the greatest attention because of its position on politics, it also condemned a series of philosophical errors: rationalism, by which reason alone could know truth; pantheism, in which the universe itself was divine; naturalism, which denied the reality of the supernatural; indifferentism, which held that all beliefs were mere opinions; and utilitarianism, which made practical results the sole guide to moral action.

The Syllabus of Errors

In a sense, the Enlightenment ended with the skeptical Scottish philosopher David Hume (d. 1776), who sought to undermine the "natural religion" of Deism, and the pious German Protestant Immanuel Kant (d. 1804), who held that the mind cannot know reality in itself but only in terms of its own categories, such as causality, time, and space. Like Hume, Kant thought the existence of God could not be demonstrated by reason, but he postulated it as necessary in order to support the moral law.

The End of the Enlightenment

Deriving partly from Rousseau, the cultural movement called Romanticism (ultimately named after the city of Rome) created a new intellectual climate that, like the Enlightenment, became a permanent influence in Western civilization. In part, a reaction against Rationalism, Romanticism deepened the sense of reality beyond what could be explained rationally, requiring that religious belief once more be taken seriously.

Romanticism

Three examples of the new attitudes are de Maistre, Novalis, and Chateaubriand. Anticipating later psychological theories, de Maistre rediscovered the darker side of life that the Enlightenment had denied. He saw human culture as an underground stream flowing from subterranean sources and only partially understood by reason, a world of rich symbolism that could not be explained. Novalis (Friedrich von Hardenberg, d. 1801), a German Lutheran who exalted the Middle Ages, condemned the Reformation for having fragmented Christianity and the Enlightenment for its rational skepticism. François de Chateaubriand (d. 1848), a French aristocrat who first supported the Revolution but then fled the Terror, published *The Genius of Christianity*, which argued for the truths of Catholicism on the grounds of their aesthetic and imaginative appeal to the depths of the human soul.

Mystery

The key to Romanticism was "mystery". To the Romantics, reality was so profound and impenetrable that the only appropriate attitude was one of humble submission. Religious dogmas, precisely because they were inexplicable by reason, embodied the deepest truths, and religious rituals, far from being meaningless formalism, expressed those truths in symbolic ways (an insight later developed by the discipline of anthropology).

Medievalism

The term *Romantic* came to imply a dreamy, entirely subjective sense of reality. Even when Romanticism was overtly Christian, it could involve a superficial love of ritual and a desire to recapture the color and drama of the Middle Ages. The latter was marked by a fascination with the secrets (both holy and devilish) hidden in monasteries and convents—dark cloisters, picturesque robes, gaunt monks, and mysterious rites. These images even had an effect on Guéranger and other monastic reformers of the age.

Romantic Challenges to Christianity

But Romanticism was dangerous to religion in that its ultimate tendency was a kind of pantheism—the deification of nature itself. It provided a seductive, powerful alternative to Christianity, a new way of disbelieving that accused Christianity of having captured the sense of mystery for its own purposes.[4]

The philosopher G. F. W. Hegel (d. 1831), also a German Protestant, was a kind of Romantic who saw "Spirit" as incarnate in history, with religion as its symbolic expression. Spirit continually disclosed itself, revealing higher and higher levels of meaning in each age, with Jesus merely one of Spirit's highest manifestations. In the same tradition, the German composer Richard Wagner (d. 1883) wrote operas on medieval subjects like the quest for the Holy Grail but turned them into celebrations of pagan mysticism.

Perhaps the ultimate Romantic hero was the English poet George Gordon, Lord Byron (d. 1824), who cast himself in the role of a superman who had risen above all laws and systematically flouted traditional morality.

---

[4] The modern New Age movement is simply the latest manifestation of this kind of Romanticism.

Some nineteenth-century scientists were outright materialists for whom the physical world alone was real or positivists who saw the scientific method alone as a valid approach to truth. But others were devout Catholics—notably the Austrian Augustinian abbot Gregor Mendel (d. 1884), who laid the foundations of the science of genetics, and the French layman Louis Pasteur (d. 1895), who pioneered the germ theory of disease. A perhaps unexpected result of the new science was a strengthening of the traditional condemnation of abortion, as scientists discovered that life began at conception.

Catholics and Science

The theory of evolution, developed by Charles Darwin (d. 1882), was completely materialistic. Man was no longer above nature but was subject to blind laws. Herbert Spencer's (d. 1903) application of evolution to social life—"the survival of the fittest"—claimed that nature rewarded amoral self-interest. Ideas about evolution set off a conflict with religion that still rages, although from the beginning there were Catholics who thought it possible to reconcile the two, by positing that God at some point intervened in the natural process to create the human soul.

Evolution

Especially in Germany, Romanticism sometimes had the effect of making it seem that religion was not to be understood literally. Along with the scientific spirit, this culminated—mainly in Protestantism—in an almost compulsively skeptical view of the Bible. Attempting to be scientific, the "Higher Criticism" called into doubt the fundamental historicity of the Scriptures, thereby depriving Christianity of any solid claim to intellectual credibility and essentially reducing it to a vague kind of moralism. Ernest Renan (d. 1892), a former seminarian at St. Sulpice, especially encouraged such skepticism.

Biblical Criticism

Historical scholarship, including Catholic historical scholarship, came to a legitimate maturity in the nineteenth century, especially through the publication of sources, such as the 383 volumes of the writings of the Fathers of the Church published by the French priest Jacques Migne (d. 1875). But the close study of sources by the French priest-archaeologist Louis Duchesne (d. 1922) called into question some of the legends of the saints, especially those concerning St. Denis, the apostle of France. Other beliefs about the early history of the Church were also doubted. (Duchesne once lost a teaching post because he questioned the legend that St. Mary Magdalen had migrated to Gaul after the Resurrection.)

Historical Scholarship

In premodern cultures, tradition tended to be venerated and change treated with suspicion. In modernity, however, that outlook was reversed, as the "modern" was automatically assumed to be superior to the old and change promised wisdom and freedom. The new

Modernism

cultural phenomenon of Modernism insisted that men were obligated to adapt themselves to change in all its forms, so that in all areas of cultural life—philosophy, theology, the arts—modernists began an experimental quest for what was new and daring. This was especially manifest in intellectual relativism—the contention that there were no truths as such, merely ideas which seemed true at particular times or places, a philosophy that over time caused society to abandon many of its earlier moral principles.

Atheism

Thus the Western mind in the nineteenth century ranged from mysticism to Materialism, from deep religious faith to atheism, with some people taking the rejection of Christianity even further than the Enlightenment had done. Atheism, while still not fully respectable, was more respectable than it had been. The German philosopher Friedrich Nietzsche (d. 1900), with his famous proclamation of the "death of God", took doubt to its furthest possible point, in an act of ferocious rebellion against the very idea of God.

Theology

In this environment, attempts to synthesize Catholic theology with compatible aspects of secular philosophy were difficult and were sometimes condemned by the Vatican. Even attempts to find new ways to defend Catholic belief against the assaults of modernity were sometimes looked at with suspicion.

The Tübingen School

The German theologians Johann Adam Möhler (d. 1838) and Matthias Scheeben (d. 1888), while not abandoning the Scholastic method, returned to patristic sources and developed Catholic doctrine in terms of its mysteries. Scheeben was to a great extent responsible for the recovery of the Pauline doctrine of the Mystical Body of Christ that would have great influence in the twentieth century.

Rosmini

Bl. Antonio Rosmini (d. 1855), founder of the Institute of Charity (Rosminian Fathers) and the Sisters of Providence, was a revered priest who lamented the Church's "five wounds": lack of lay participation in the liturgy, the inferior education of priests, political interference in the appointment of bishops, and clerical attachment to wealth. He favored the papacy's giving up its temporal power and thought that, properly understood, democracy is a legitimate form of government.

Rosmini was an original theologian whose works were at one time placed on the *Index*, under the suspicion that he taught that men had a direct natural intuition of God, prior to their reception of grace. But Pope John XXIII (1958–1963) and Pope John Paul I (1978) were influenced by his writings. As head of the Congregation for the Doctrine of the Faith, Cardinal Joseph Ratzinger exonerated Rosmini, and as Pope Benedict XVI (2005–) he beatified him.

While Aquinas' thought enjoyed preeminence in the Church, it was by no means universally followed. Pope Leo XIII initiated the "Thomistic Revival", affirming that Catholics should embrace truth wherever it is found but extolling Aquinas as the primary philosopher, the source of a unified view of reality that all Catholics should achieve.

The Thomistic Revival

What was in some ways the most important Catholic intellectual development of the nineteenth century emerged in an unlikely place—Protestant England. The Oxford Movement of the 1830s and 1840s brought many Anglicans into the Catholic Church and left a deep and lasting Catholic imprint on Anglicanism itself. The leading lights of this movement were called "Tractarians" by their contemporaries because of the "tracts for the times" they published.

The Oxford Movement

The greatest of these was Bl. John Henry Newman (d. 1890), an Anglican clergyman who became a Roman Catholic. The most original Catholic thinker since Pascal, Newman joined the Oratorians and was eventually made a cardinal. (Although ritual was recognized as having been integral to the early Church, love of ritual was not part of the original Oxford Movement and played no role in Newman's conversion.)

Newman

Religious Liberalism

The real conflict was not between Catholics and Protestants as such, Newman thought. Rather the enemy of both was religious Liberalism, whose essence was the denial of dogma and the exaltation of private judgment in matters of belief. Against this, Protestantism, because of its reliance on Scripture alone, provided no defense.

The Development of Doctrine

Newman recognized that historical consciousness—the awareness that everything changes over time—posed a greater challenge to religious belief than did science (he accepted the theory of evolution), in that the historical bases of even fundamental Christian beliefs were being called into question. Part of his achievement was to reconcile historical consciousness with faith.

Searching the writings of the Fathers, Newman found what he considered to be the essentials of Catholicism, and his theory of the "development of doctrine"—formulated just before he entered the Catholic Church—was aimed primarily at Protestants who accused the Church of having added to the revelation found in Scripture. According to Newman's theory, everything essential to the faith was present embryonically in the Gospel, but many elements, even the fundamental doctrine of the Trinity, emerged only gradually. All such development had to be an organic growth from the original seed, harmonizing with previous expressions of the faith.

The Immaculate Conception

A contemporary example was Pius IX's 1854 proclamation of the dogma of the Immaculate Conception, which had been commonly believed for centuries, although it had been doubted by some leading theologians, notably Aquinas himself. The doctrine was thought to be implicit in the angel Gabriel's salutation to Mary as "full of grace", hence as free from sin, something necessary in order for her to be worthy to bear the Redeemer.

The Grammar of Assent

Newman recognized that the skepticism of the Enlightenment had made it impossible to insulate religious belief from doubt, but he affirmed, famously, that "a thousand difficulties do not make a doubt." The foundation of religious certitude was for him the ultimate question. Strict rationalism, he argued, was appropriate to subjects like mathematics, but it was not the way by which men knew what was of ultimate significance. Reason as such led only to "notional assent", which was the acceptance of an idea in a purely abstract way. In contrast, he outlined what he called the "illative sense"—numerous particular insights that eventually coalesced, not into iron certitude but into a high degree of probability. (By contrast, the Scholastics, notably Aquinas, precisely claimed to have achieved certitude rather than probability.) By such a process, rather than by formal argument, the individual came to sense the divine order of the universe and the fundamental rightness of Christian teaching and could offer "real assent" to them, an act that involved the entire person.

Although Newman was steeped in the Church Fathers and some medieval writers, he had not been educated as a Catholic and had rather slight familiarity with the Catholic theology of his day. This, along with his theory of the development of dogma and his theory of knowledge, made his orthodoxy suspect to some people. His proposal to establish a Catholic house at Oxford was vetoed by the English hierarchy, who thought it dangerous for Catholics to attend a Protestant institution, and his attempt to found a Catholic university in Dublin failed. He would later be made a cardinal and recognized as one of the greatest Catholic theologians.

The Arts

The Gothic Revival

From about 1750, for the first time since the early centuries, the Church inspired no original architectural style of her own. But the Gothic, which since the Renaissance had been disdained by cultivated artistic tastes, was among those aspects of medieval civilization that came back into favor because of Romanticism. Eugène Viollet-le-Duc (d. 1879) "restored" the cathedral of Notre Dame in Paris, with special attention to dramatic elements like gargoyles, and Augustus Welby Pugin (d. 1852), a convert from Anglicanism, established the Gothic Revival as the preferred style of public architecture for the next century, employed even in Protestant churches and in civic buildings like the English Houses of Parliament.

Painting

During the Romantic period, a few leading artists—Jacques-Louis David (d. 1825) and Eugène Delacroix (d. 1863)—occasionally painted religious subjects, but for the most part, the visual arts separated themselves from religion. The best religious art was competent but unoriginal, and very few leading artists were religious believers.

Music

But for reasons that are by no means clear, the same was not true of music. Ludwig von Beethoven (d. 1827) burst out of the formalism of the Baroque style as a man of two worlds: at the same time a promethean rebel and a devout Catholic. Besides the pantheism of the "Ode to Joy" in his *Ninth Symphony*, or his paean to the superman in his *Third Symphony*, he composed numerous Masses and other religious pieces. The Austrian Franz Schubert (d. 1828), the Pole Frédéric Chopin (d. 1849), and the Frenchmen Hector Berlioz (d. 1869) and Charles Gounod (d. 1893) were major composers who continued to write Masses and other religious compositions. After a very irregular life, the Hungarian Franz Liszt (d. 1886) joined a Franciscan order and for a time lived in a monastery and studied for the priesthood while creating religiously inspired works.

Sentimentality

The nineteenth century saw the beginning of mass-produced culture of pictures, statues, books, and newspapers. In earlier times, high art differed from popular art only in terms of the artist's skill. Now, however, there was a popular market that consciously diverged from high style. Popular religious art made an immediate appeal to emotional piety, especially the Infant Jesus or His Mother, who were represented with a fetching sadness or sweetness. Images of the Sacred Heart made that devotion sentimental as well, something that was far from its original spirit. Paralleling the popular taste in religious statues and pictures, and alongside the complex liturgical compositions of serious composers, there was a continually expanding popular repertoire of sentimental hymns, especially those devoted to Mary.

The First Vatican Council

Pius IX's summoning of the Vatican Council in 1869 was intended to bring to a climax his two decades of struggle against modern errors, and for that purpose, he considered the solemn proclamation of the dogma of papal infallibility to be essential. The Council, the first since Trent three centuries before, was perhaps the best attended in the history of the Church: 754 bishops, more than twice the number at Trent. For the first time, secular governments were not officially represented, which led to some official protests, including that of Napoleon III, whose troops were protecting Rome from the Italian armies. The Eastern Orthodox responded contemptuously to what they considered a condescending invitation to send observers.

Papal Infallibility   The idea of papal infallibility was already widely accepted, and Pius did not ask the Council to approve it, lest it appear that he received his authority from the Council. He merely waited until the Council voted to proclaim it. Pius' courage in the face of adversity was compromised to some degree by his increasingly irascible self-will. Thus, while ostensibly remaining aloof while the Council Fathers debated infallibility, he exerted strong pressure on wavering bishops. To a bishop who invoked the authority of Tradition as distinct from that of the pope, Pius was reported to have announced, "I am Tradition."

Resistance   Some bishops were troubled by the doctrine of infallibility because they thought it implied that they received their authority solely from the pope, rather than being direct successors of the Apostles. The issue had been raised at Trent, but it would not be definitively settled at Vatican I.

A substantial minority of the Council Fathers, including most of the Germans, were "inopportunists" who thought the definition was likely to be misunderstood and to provoke unnecessary hostility. Newman too was an inopportunist, although he quickly submitted, and there was tension between him and Cardinal Manning, who was also a convert Anglican clergyman but very Ultramontane. Archbishop Darboy of Paris, who would be executed by revolutionaries the next year, was a Gallican so opposed to the definition of papal infallibility that he tried to persuade Napoleon III to intervene to prevent it. The liberal English lay historian John Dalberg, Lord Acton (d. 1902), also wanted the secular powers to intervene. Döllinger, Acton's former teacher, vehemently rejected the doctrine in principle, just as he had publicly opposed the dogma of the Immaculate Conception.

A preliminary vote showed 451 in favor of the dogma, 62 in favor "conditionally", and 88 opposed. On the eve of its solemn ratification, the opposition leaders agreed that, rather than vote "*non placet*" ("it does not please me"), they would absent themselves. But two bishops, including Edward Fitzgerald of Little Rock (d. 1908), apparently failed to get the message and were the only ones to vote against the solemn proclamation. (Fitzgerald then reportedly told the Pope, "The Little Rock humbly submits to the Big Rock [Peter].")

But in Germany a schism called the Old Catholics developed under Döllinger's leadership, making common cause with the schismatic Jansenists in the Netherlands, although Döllinger himself later broke with the Old Catholics when they rejected priestly celibacy, confession, indulgences, prayers to the saints, and other Catholic practices.

"Ex Cathedra"   Infallibility was understood as encompassing only matters of faith and morals that were solemnly proclaimed by the pope *ex cathedra* ("from the throne"), a limitation necessary in order to exclude the doctrinal

errors of some popes, such as John XXII's espousal of "soul sleep". The pope could not create new dogmas but merely authoritatively define what were already the Church's beliefs.

Besides papal infallibility, the major doctrinal action of the Council was its proclamation that faith and reason were harmonious and that reason was capable of knowing the existence of God. (The alleged error of Rosmini was his claim that men had a natural intuition of God's divine nature, not just of His existence.)

Faith and Reason

Unprotected from the advancing Italian armies, the Council adjourned hastily and indefinitely. It was not formally ended until 1962.

An Abrupt End

When Pius IX died, after the longest pontificate in the history of the Church, he was succeeded by Leo XIII, an elderly curial official who had long been a diocesan bishop. Leo would preside over the Church for twenty-five vigorous years and would depart notably from some of his predecessor's policies, although he too was firmly opposed to most of the things condemned in the *Syllabus*.

The Democratic Era

For many years, Newman considered himself to be "under a cloud", but it was lifted when Leo made him a cardinal in his first consistory, thereby seeming to encourage theological speculation. Leo also encouraged biblical scholarship and historical research, especially by opening the Vatican Archives to scholars and enjoining historians always to tell the truth, no matter how uncomfortable it might be.

Liberal Policies

The separation of the Church from monarchical politics—inconceivable when Lamennais advocated it in 1831—was achieved under Leo, guided by his secretary of state, Cardinal Mariano Rampolla (d. 1913).

    The perils of an alliance with Conservatism were revealed in the fact that some of the champions of traditional order were among those imposing restrictions on the Church. Catholic Austria continued the policies of Josephinism to some extent, and for a time, the Church's chief antagonist was the German premier Bismarck, a devout Lutheran who was the epitome of political Conservatism.

The Perils of Conservatism

Kulturkampf

In his *Kulturkampf* ("culture war") against the Church, which was also imposed in the German-ruled parts of Poland, Bismarck excluded Catholics from government offices, abolished Catholic schools, expelled all religious except some nursing nuns, closed seminaries, made candidates for the priesthood attend state universities, required government approval of all clerical appointments, and made civil marriage mandatory for everyone. A dozen bishops and eighteen hundred priests who resisted were jailed and subjected to ruinous fines.

The Center Party

Many Catholics, especially in the Rhineland, emigrated. But others took advantage of the democratic process to mount a highly effective resistance, and in the end, the Church was actually strengthened. The Center Party, which was primarily Catholic, achieved great electoral success, so that after a short time, Bismarck had to back down, and the Vatican was able to negotiate a concordat. Three of the bolder bishops, however, had to resign, and the appointment of theology professors was made subject to the approval of the government. The leaders of the Center Party were ignored by the Vatican, which was mistrustful of an independent lay group.

Belgium

In Belgium, liberals turned against the Church only to be met, as in Germany, with a highly effective Catholic electoral organization that came to dominate Belgian politics for the next generation. Belgium was one of the few countries where the Church retained responsibility for higher education, so that the University of Louvain (Leuven) became a leading center of Catholic intellectual life.

Switzerland

Liberal Switzerland, where Catholics were in a minority, mounted its own *Kulturkampf*, officially recognizing the schismatic Old Catholics, expelling priests, and imprisoning a bishop. For a time, there was actual civil war between Catholic and Protestant cantons, but eventually the government pulled back from its hostile stance.

France

In France, the Third Republic was at first conservative and supportive of the Church, but the perennial issue of education soon brought conflict. The anticlericals sought to control the system, especially the universities, precisely in order to impede handing on the faith to new generations, and the Catholic intellectual presence was largely excluded. Many Catholics were uncompromising monarchists who recalled that the Republic had been launched with the blood of martyrs—the great Basilica of Sacré Cœur (Sacred Heart) was built to tower above Paris in memory of those executed by the Commune of 1871.

Many French Catholics did voluntarily what Pius IX commanded Catholics in Italy to do—refrain from all participation in civic life under what was deemed to be an illegitimate government. But Leo counseled patience and, when no French bishop appeared willing to do so, persuaded Cardinal Charles-Martial Lavigerie (d. 1892) of Tunisia, a French colony, to make an open gesture of acceptance of the Republic. Many Catholics were appalled, but Leo encouraged others in their *Ralliement* ("rallying") to the Republic.

Leo was far from being a liberal, but he recognized a question of crucial importance for the Church: Was it possible to be a Catholic in a modern state, or were Catholics in effect obligated to work toward the increasingly impossible goal of restoring the monarchies of the

Old Regime? He warned against the excesses of democracy but accepted it on a pragmatic basis.

As with the Mortara case in Italy, the Dreyfus Affair in France in the 1890s hardened divisions and demonstrated how far removed some Catholics were from even the positive aspects of Liberalism. Alfred Dreyfus (d. 1935) was a Jewish army officer convicted of treason on the basis of falsified evidence and sent to the brutal penal colony of Devil's Island. His case became a *cause célèbre* in which Leo privately expressed doubts about his guilt but monarchist Catholics rallied against him, mainly out of anti-Jewish[5] prejudice. (Dreyfus was eventually exonerated and won the highest medal of valor in World War I.)

The Dreyfus Case

In the end, the *Ralliement* did not accomplish what Leo hoped for, as the Third Republic became increasingly anticlerical, partly in response to the Dreyfus Affair. The Assumptionists, who had waged a particularly bitter anti-Dreyfus campaign, were expelled and, in an effort to save other religious orders, the Pope acquiesced in yet another expulsion of the Jesuits, but to no avail. In 1905, two years after Leo's death, the other religious orders were also suppressed, their houses closed by the police, and two thousand religious schools shut down.

A Hostile Government

All church property was in effect seized by the state and public subsidies of the clergy ended, plunging many priests into severe poverty. Unofficial private associations were formed to take control of church buildings that the Church herself could no longer officially own. A positive result of the new anticlericalism was that the government decreed complete separation of church and state, which meant that it could no longer demand a voice in the appointment of bishops.

The Church eventually recovered a good deal of influence in France because of the First World War of 1914 to 1918. The Vatican acquiesced in a law requiring priests to serve in the military, and over forty-six hundred died in the service of their country, while the victorious French armies were led by the devout Catholic Marshal Ferdinand Foch (d. 1929). The Church regained her schools, although in law her property still belonged to the state. The canonization of Joan of Arc in 1920 was intended to recognize the new harmony.

Recovery

St. Pius X (1903–1914) was a patriarch of Venice who, unlike most of his predecessors, came from the peasant class and had never been a papal official. He was elected after Rampolla's candidacy had been vetoed in the name of the Austro-Hungarian emperor Franz Josef (1848–1916), a traditional privilege that Pius X immediately abolished. (Pius

Pius X

---

[5] The term *anti-Semitism* is inaccurate, in that many Semites in the Near East are not Jews and are even antagonistic to Jews.

was canonized in 1954, the first pope so recognized since Pius V in 1712.)

The Curia Reformed

Pius X thoroughly reorganized the Roman Curia, which was now made up of thirteen "congregations" dealing with particular subjects, along with certain specialized "commissions" and various ecclesiastical courts and tribunals. The leading congregations were the Holy Office, the guardian of orthodoxy; the Consistorial, which advised the pope on the appointment of bishops; Propaganda Fidei, for the missions; and Rites, for the regulation of the liturgy.

Vatican Policy

In public affairs, Pius X for the most part eschewed diplomacy in favor of strong public protests against injustices, including the continued Russian and German oppression of Catholics in Poland and the anticlerical government that came to power in Portugal in 1910. He expressed sympathy for the desire of the Irish to be free of British rule.

Italy

Italy remained the one country where Leo XIII had not followed a policy of accommodation, insisting that, because of its seizure of the Papal States, it was founded on a fundamental injustice. Devout Italian Catholics refrained from voting, which allowed secular liberals to dominate national life. Instead, Catholics organized the *Opere dei Congressi* ("works of the congresses"), a union of specialized groups of Catholic laborers, journalists, teachers, and other occupations, who had a significant influence in public life. Pius X officially suppressed the group when it began to move toward independence from Church guidance, but he finally authorized Catholics to vote in elections.

While he took strong stands on matters of principle, Pius was opposed to an overly politicized Catholicism, which was one of the reasons he condemned the Opere. He also condemned the aggressively democratic *Le Sillon* ("the furrow") movement in France and expressed his disapproval of the Center Party in Germany, which he thought had become overly nationalistic.

Action Française

Near the end of Pius' pontificate, some of the works of the influential French journalist Charles Maurras (d. 1952) were placed on the *Index*, but, mindful of Maurras' support of the Church against the anticlericals, the condemnation was not announced. Maurras was an atheist and founder of the *Action Française* movement that valued Catholicism as integral to French identity. He called for a renewed union of throne and altar and regarded Jews as inherently inimical to French identity. His movement had considerable Catholic support, including many clergy, but Pius XI (1922–1939) condemned it and, in a highly unusual action, required the Jesuit theologian Louis Billot (d. 1931) to resign from the College of Cardinals because of his espousal of the condemned movement.

Modernism

Pius X was a vigorous champion of orthodoxy who warned that criticism of the Scholastic method was itself a sign of potential heterodoxy and once again proclaimed Thomism to be the preeminent Catholic system of thought, directing that it serve as the basis of all theology. In two encyclicals in 1907—*Pascendi Dominici Gregis* (Feeding the Lord's Flock) and *Lamentabili Sane Exitu* (With Truly Lamentable Effect)—Pius condemned a theological movement he called Modernism. Although he considered it to be "the synthesis of all heresies", Modernism was in some ways original, in that it was the first heresy in the history of the Church that openly invoked the "spirit of the age" as the ultimate criterion of truth.

Historicism

In a sense, Modernism was Hegelian, in that the unfolding of history was said to demand the adaptation of Christian doctrine to changing times, whether or not this was done consciously. It also owed much to Darwinian evolution, and above all, it developed in the shadow of liberal Protestantism, which had moved along the same road decades before and to which Newman, in his theory of the development of doctrine, attempted to provide an orthodox response.

Modernists tended to a radical historicism, believing that it was impossible to transcend the limits of one's own age and that attempts to do so were illusory. The historic creeds could not remain permanently valid, since they expressed merely the times in which they were formulated. Modernists were especially hostile to Thomism, which they regarded as a desiccated relic of the Middle Ages.

Loisy

The first and most important of the modernists was the French secular priest Alfred Loisy (d. 1940), who studied modern biblical criticism in order to refute Renan but instead became himself a skeptic. Loisy renounced the priesthood even prior to Pius' condemnation of Modernism and years later admitted that at the time of the condemnation he believed nothing in the Nicene Creed except that Jesus had suffered under Pontius Pilate.

Convinced by Renan that the quest for the "historical Jesus" was futile, Loisy saw the Catholic emphasis on Tradition as the alternative, making it unnecessary to ground faith in an infallible Scripture. The Holy Spirit was always guiding and directing the Church, which could therefore express spiritual truths in the language of each new age. But for Loisy, the Holy Spirit did not mean the third Person of the Trinity but something closer to the "spirit of the age", while Tradition was merely the Church's way of accommodating to historical change.

Tyrrell   George Tyrrell (d. 1909) was an Irish Protestant convert who, after several warnings, was expelled from the Jesuits. He was one of the few intellectual converts of the age who found doctrinal orthodoxy a burden rather than a blessing. Even before the condemnation of 1907, he had come to hate the papacy.

Von Hugel   Friedrich von Hugel (d. 1925) was an Austrian nobleman living in England. Although not a strong proponent of evolution, he shared with other modernists the belief that science had raised new questions for religious faith and that believers could not rely on dogmatic authority. Von Hugel too was deeply influenced by modern biblical criticism, for which he sought to compensate by appealing to a sense of "transcendence" inherent in the human soul, meaning a realization that there are higher, deeper, more mysterious realities beyond the empirical. Access to these realities was made possible by religious mysticism.

Von Hugel was a man of seeming paradoxes. Like other modernists, he was unfavorable to Scholasticism, but unlike some, he was not strident nor did he allow himself to express doubt concerning any official doctrine. Most paradoxically, he considered himself an Ultramontane, although he was devastated by the papal condemnation of Modernism. Personally, he was deeply devout, spending hours in front of the Blessed Sacrament and regularly praying the rosary, practices consistent with his sense of the faith as essentially an inner spiritual reality.

Von Hugel functioned as a kind of broker for the modernists, familiarizing them with each other's work and offering strong moral support to those censured by ecclesiastical authority. (Probably because he was a layman, he received no personal censure in the modernist condemnation.)[6]

Blondel   The French lay philosopher Maurice Blondel (d. 1949) also regarded Scholastic philosophy as overly abstract and proposed instead that the assent to truth involved the entire human person, including will, imagination, and emotion, a position somewhat like Newman's idea of assent. Like von Hugel, Blondel aimed to show that the human quest for truth stemmed from an inherent sense of a higher reality, an awareness of something beyond human experience. Evidence of transcendence lies everywhere in the universe, waiting to be apprehended.

The most controversial of Blondel's ideas was his claim that, since such evidences were indeed found everywhere in the world, "the supernatural" was really natural. Like Rosmini, his work was held in suspicion because of the fear that he denied the necessity of divine grace

---

[6] Over time, the Church has rarely condemned lay people for heresy, regarding false teaching as especially pernicious when espoused by priests, who have a duty to instruct the faithful in sound doctrine.

and reduced belief to a natural phenomenon. After considerable anguish, Blondel announced his acceptance of the papal condemnation, on the grounds that he did not hold any of the condemned propositions.

Henri Bremond (d. 1933) was a French Jesuit and historian of spirituality, which he saw as a way of evading the demands of Scholastic orthodoxy without explicitly denying them, since he believed the real Tradition of the Church was found not in dogmas but in the lives of saints. Often in tension with his superiors, Bremond too left the Society of Jesus and became a secular priest and, disregarding the fact that Tyrrell had been excommunicated, officiated at his fellow ex-Jesuit's funeral.

Bremond

After Modernism was condemned, all candidates for the priesthood had to swear a special oath against it. Encouraged by Pius X's secretary of state, the aristocratic Spanish-English Cardinal Rafael Merry del Val (d. 1930), a secret organization called the Sodality of St. Pius V gathered material on suspected modernists, especially seminary professors, and submitted it to the Holy See, which sometimes took action against the accused. The Sodality tended to cast its net very wide, often on the basis of hearsay, and ensnared some people who were in fact orthodox. (The future popes Benedict XV and John XXIII were on its lists of suspects.)

The Anti-Modernist Oath

Pope Benedict XV (1914–1922) was elected partly because he was not associated with what were regarded as the rigidities of Pius X's pontificate, and he immediately replaced Merry del Val. Benedict's election brought an end to the systematic hunting of modernists, because, while he strongly reaffirmed the anti-modernist condemnations, he insisted that they be implemented responsibly.

Benedict XV

Benedict's pontificate was dominated by the First World War (1914–1918), where in each country the majority of Catholics patriotically supported the war effort. The German and French bishops both issued statements proclaiming the justice of their respective causes. Far more legitimately, Cardinal Désiré Mercier (d. 1926) of Malines (Mechelen) fearlessly denounced German atrocities against the Belgian people.

The "Great War"

Benedict worked indefatigably for a negotiated settlement and sponsored humanitarian efforts to alleviate the sufferings of both prisoners of war and civilians, efforts that prompted the secular-minded Turkish government to erect a statue in his honor after the war. Besides the end to hostilities, the Pope had more specific aims: keeping Italy out of the war, lest a victory strengthen its anticlerical government against the Church; preserving the Muslim Ottoman Empire, in order to keep Russia from promoting an aggressive Orthodoxy in the Near East;

The Papal Program

and preserving the Austro-Hungarian Empire as the last great Catholic state in Europe. He denounced anti-Jewish outbursts in Poland and was friendly to the idea of a Jewish state in Palestine, although he was anxious to insure Christian access to the Holy Places.

Rejection

Most of Benedict's goals failed, as Italy entered the war on the winning side and the Austro-Hungarian and Ottoman Empires were defeated and dismembered, although the Bolshevik Revolution marked the end of Russian Orthodox expansion. Benedict was disheartened by his failure to end the conflict, as most of the great powers ignored his peace proposals. Others coldly rejected them, and the Holy See was excluded from participation in the Versailles Peace Conference.

The Peace Settlement

In most ways, the Versailles settlement was a failure, as demonstrated by the outbreak of World War II only two decades later. In principle, the popes strongly approved the idea of international cooperation, but the Holy See was excluded from the League of Nations, an organization the popes considered inadequate in any case, and the Vatican continued to pursue its goals mainly through a series of concordats.

Between the Wars

Pius XI (1922–1939) was a professional librarian who served as a papal diplomat, then as archbishop of Milan for only a few months before his election as pope. He ruled the Church during what has been called the Age of the Dictators, and he showed both diplomatic skill and great boldness in dealing with political conditions for which there were no real precedents. The period between the two world wars was a time of widespread and severe religious persecution.

The Soviet Union

The new Union of Soviet Socialist Republics (USSR) attempted to exterminate all religion, including various Catholic minorities. Under the leadership of Joseph Stalin, the Soviet Union was a police state based on terror. The Orthodox church continued to exist subject to the most severe restrictions, with its clergy often functioning as government agents.

Benedict sent aid to the USSR during a famine, although, except in Ukraine, Catholics were a small minority. As the government moved to destroy the Catholic Church, Pius XI appealed for freedom and, when this went unheeded, made a clandestine attempt to reestablish the hierarchy, an effort that was discovered and thwarted. A large number of Soviet Catholics were put to death in the mid-1920s, and in the early 1930s, the Soviet government deliberately starved millions of Ukrainian peasants to death, as part of its attempt to socialize agriculture.

New States

In dismembering the Austro-Hungarian Empire, the Versailles conference created the new states of Czechoslovakia and Yugoslavia, both of which were ethnically and religiously divided, containing large

Catholic populations side by side with various kinds of Protestants and secularists in Czechoslovakia and Serbian Orthodox and Muslims in Yugoslavia. In both countries, the Church encountered considerable harassment. The new state of Turkey began systematically oppressing, even to the point of genocide, various Near Eastern peoples, some of whom (Lebanese, Syrians, Armenians) were Catholic.

Following a revolution in 1910, Mexico became one of the fiercest anti-religious regimes in the world, virtually outlawing the practice of the faith. Priests who continued to minister to their people were systematically hunted down and killed,[7] notably the Jesuit martyr Bl. Miguel-Agostino Pro, who was shot by a firing squad in 1927, his arms outstretched in the form of a cross. In the late 1920s, desperate Catholics mounted an armed *Cristeros* rebellion against the government, until urged to cease by the Holy See. The government violated its promise not to engage in reprisals, but the persecution gradually ceased in the later 1930s.

Mexico

Portugal experienced rather chaotic conditions after World War I, and for a time, the government was unfriendly to the Church. This changed in 1932 with the ascent to power of the economist Antonio Salazar (d. 1970), a devout Catholic who appealed to the social teachings of the Church as the basis of his policies. But his suppression of free elections and of many basic civil liberties, as well as his ardent commitment to colonialism, made him unpopular with many Portuguese.

Portugal

The Germany of the 1920s—called the Weimar Republic after its capital city—was an unstable structure plagued by severe economic problems and strong opposition from both sides of the political spectrum. Officially secular, it respected religious freedom, even allowing religious instruction in the state schools.

Weimar Republic

One benefit of the peace settlement was that Catholic Poland at last gained its independence, and thus its religious freedom, from Germany. In the period between the wars, Poland was a dominantly Catholic country, as reflected in its laws and its charitable and educational systems.

Poland

The Catholic hierarchy in Ireland cautiously supported the abortive Easter Uprising against Great Britain in 1916 and criticized the conscription of Irishmen into the British Army. After the war, the bishops supported a second rebellion that led to the establishment of the

Ireland

---

[7] See the Graham Greene novel *The Power and the Glory* and the movie, *For Greater Glory* (June 2012).

new Irish Free State (Éire), which did not include the predominantly Protestant six northern counties known as Ulster or Northern Ireland.

The Irish Republican Army (IRA), which was influenced by Marxism, denounced the settlement and embarked on terrorist tactics—employed in tandem with Protestant violence in Ulster—that continued into the twenty-first century, often condemned by the bishops. A broader Republican movement, led by Brooklyn-born, half-Spanish Eamon De Valera (d. 1975), also opposed the settlement. But after being imprisoned for a time, he accepted the situation and for decades was the dominant figure in Irish political life.

The Irish Free State adopted a constitution that guaranteed religious liberty for all but gave the Catholic Church a "special place" in Irish life, notably the primary responsibility for operating educational and charitable institutions. Éire sought to base its laws on Catholic moral principles, such as not permitting divorce, and by 2010 was the only Western European country that did not permit abortion.

Social Doctrine

In 1931, Pius XI issued the encyclical *Quadragesimo Anno* (In the Fortieth Year), commemorating *Rerum Novarum*. It restated Catholic social teaching on the rights of labor and even more strongly endorsed Corporatism (sometimes called Syndicalism).

Inspired by the two great social encyclicals, "social Catholicism" in practice meant strong support of labor unions and of the welfare state. But the integrity of the family was considered paramount, so that "social Catholicism" diverged from most labor unions in advocating a "family wage"—paying men on the basis of how many dependents they supported, thereby making large families possible and making it unnecessary for mothers to enter the work force.

Distributism

In England, a movement that included the writers G. K. Chesterton (d. 1936) and Hilaire Belloc (d. 1953) promoted Distributism as an alternative to both Socialism and free-market capitalism. Distributists urged that ownership of property be shared as widely as possible, thereby making each family secure and independent and encouraging smaller scale economic activities.

In practical terms, Catholic social movements often tried to organize cooperatives for buying and selling goods almost at cost and credit unions whereby people pooled their savings and offered loans to their members at low rates of interest. Some of these efforts resulted in worker-owned businesses. Some socially minded Catholics strongly advocated a return to the land, judging modern urban life to be inherently corrupting of both religion and morals, and from time to time, experimental agricultural communities were founded, although all eventually failed.

Catholic Action

Catholic Action (a term not often used in the United States) grew out of the varying efforts of Catholics to deal with the modern secular state. As endorsed by the popes beginning with Pius X, it was alternatively called the "lay apostolate", meaning lay Catholics in the world attempting to reshape society according to moral and spiritual principles, guided by the hierarchy. How this was to be done depended on the circumstances of particular countries, so that Catholic Action at different times might be considered either "right wing" or "left wing".

As in France, the relationship between the Church and the state improved in postwar Italy. Luigi Sturzo (d. 1959), a priest of Catholic Action who had been active on behalf of peasants and miners, founded the Popular Party with Pius XI's permission, whereby Catholics ended their long abstention from national politics and began to have a major impact on Italian life.

The Age of Dictators

Italy

Mussolini

But Italian politics in the years between the wars proved extraordinarily complex and treacherous, because of the rise of Benito Mussolini (d. 1945), a one-time left-wing socialist who had become an extreme Italian nationalist. He came to power in 1922, at the head of a fascist movement that took its name from the *fascis*, an ancient Roman symbol of authority. Sturzo, because he headed a movement that was an effective counter-force to the fascists, was forced into exile.

The Lateran Treaty

Although personally contemptuous of religion, Mussolini recognized the spiritual power of the Church and therefore moved away from the anticlerical policies of the previous Italian governments, to the point where, in the Lateran Treaty of 1929, the six-decade stalemate between Italy and the Holy See was at last resolved. Pius XI came to the papal throne already prepared to effect such a resolution, as shown in the fact that at his coronation he gave his blessing *urbe et orbe* ("to the city and to the world") publicly, from the balcony of the Vatican Palace, something that his three immediate predecessors had refused to do. The Lateran Treaty in effect settled the fifteen-hundred-year-old question of the temporal power of the papacy, which the popes now implicitly recognized as neither necessary nor appropriate to their office.

Vatican City

The treaty financially compensated the Holy See for its loss of property and recognized the independent state of Vatican City—356 acres surrounding St. Peter's Basilica and assorted other properties in Rome—an arrangement that gave the popes official security and independence, as they were no longer reliant merely on the good will of the Italian government. The treaty also gave the Church a special place in Italian life, providing for religious instruction in the schools and official observance of holy days and not permitting divorce.

Fascism

But Mussolini's initial friendliness to the Church masked sinister forces that would soon reveal themselves. He came to power partly through the actions of his Black Shirts—bands of uniformed men who provoked street brawls and intimidated their opponents by force and who continued to operate even after Mussolini had become the official head of state. Fascist Italy was not under a complete reign of terror, but critics of the regime were often imprisoned or sent into exile.

Italian Fascism, along with Soviet Communism, was among the first manifestations of Totalitarianism, a system of government that seeks to unify all of life under the power of the state, while denying that there is any independent sphere of human activity. Inevitably, Totalitarianism takes on the character of a religion, demanding ultimate loyalty from its people and inspiring a religious attitude toward the state, which is often marked by a charismatic leader preaching passionate sermons to adoring crowds, massive processions, sacred symbols like the *fascis* and the German *swastika*, patriotic music and art, and huge new temples dedicated to the cult of the state. Fascism and Communism differed more in theory than in practice. The former was intensely nationalistic, the latter officially committed to an international classless society, though the USSR in practice pursued its own national interests single-mindedly. Communism abolished private property while Fascism retained it only under close state control and in the state's interests. Fascism glorified war and conquest as the highest human endeavors, as the USSR also became highly militarized. Communism was officially atheistic and sought to destroy religion, while fascist governments allowed limited religious liberty only so long as it did not hamper the state's aims.

Christ the King

In establishing the feast of Christ the King (December 1925), Pius XI proclaimed that no earthly power could claim superiority to religion and that the Church, in the name of Christ, was the ultimate custodian of moral and spiritual truth. The Pope insisted that states and peoples were subject to natural law, which transcends both the authority of the ruler and the will of the people, because it is rooted in the nature of the universe itself and ultimately in the will of God. Natural law was not religious dogma but the concrete application of truths that were known by reason.

Fascism Condemned

The Pope condemned the theory and practice of Fascism in 1931, not only for its atheism but because of its demand for ultimate loyalty, its glorification of military force, its extreme nationalism, and its denial of basic human rights and dignity. For a time, Mussolini's government backed away from a confrontation with the Church. When Italy invaded Ethiopia in 1935, Pius XI protested privately. Bl. Ildefonso Schuster (d. 1954), cardinal archbishop of Milan, supported the invasion of Ethiopia but later denounced Mussolini's racist ideas.

But Catholic Action was inherently a rival to Fascism, because it diverted loyalty away from the state, and the Black Shirts sometimes broke up Catholic meetings and suppressed Catholic publications. Tellingly, the government forbade Catholic Action to sponsor athletic activities, lest sports bind young people more closely to the Church than to the state.

Corporatism

Even in democratic countries, some Catholics who were not sympathetic to Fascism in other ways thought they saw the Catholic idea of Corporatism in the fascist economic system, which organized society into "syndics" made up of representatives of various industries, under the authority of a government that coordinated their activities for the good of the state. Distinctively Catholic labor unions were outlawed, however, and the "common good" was defined as the interests of the all-powerful state.

Above all, Spain was the cauldron of religious strife during the 1930s. *Spain* With no tradition of democracy, all parties tended to seek complete domination of national life and the annihilation of their rivals if possible. Leftist groups—ranging from relatively moderate socialists, through communists, to self-proclaimed anarchists seeking to destroy all government—agreed in seeing the Church as their great enemy, because her influence penetrated so deeply into Spanish life.

Civil War

When the monarchy was abolished in 1931, a leftist coalition announced that Spain was no longer a Catholic country, and mob attacks on clergy and churches, sanctioned by the government, soon followed. In 1936, General Francisco Franco (d. 1975) initiated a rebellion that turned into bitter civil war in which the Republican (Loyalist) government in power received aid from the Soviet Union and Franco's Nationalists got aid from Nazi Germany and fascist Italy. The war was brutal. About sixty-five hundred priests and religious were killed, many savagely butchered, especially by Anarchists, while the Nationalists sometimes dealt equally ruthlessly with their enemies, including priests who supported the Republicans out of a desire for Basque independence.

International attitudes to the war tended to follow religious lines, with most journalists publicizing atrocities by the Nationalists while ignoring or minimizing those on the other side. Catholic opinion everywhere tended to see Franco's struggle as a kind of crusade, although some leading Catholics considered the war too morally ambiguous for ready partisanship.

Franco

Franco won a complete military victory in 1939 and became the virtual dictator of Spain, executing thirty thousand former enemies and imprisoning four hundred thousand more. But he lost the propaganda war, so that for decades Spain was treated as a kind of pariah among Western nations, not least because of the prominent role of the Church in national life and its official denial of religious freedom.

Although Franco's Spain was often characterized as fascist, Franco successfully did a balancing act during World War II. He rebuffed invitations to join Germany and Italy, while allowing their planes to fly over Spanish territory. However, he extended safety to thousands of Jews fleeing Germany and France.

Germany

The Rise of Hitler

Although the National Socialist Party (Nazis) in Germany did not ordinarily call themselves fascists, it was there that Fascism achieved its greatest power. After World War I, the Austrian ex-soldier Adolf Hitler (d. 1945) started a movement similar to Mussolini's Black Shirts and attempted to seize power by force, an effort that landed him in prison. Afterward, he entered politics, playing on German resentment of the Versailles settlement, and soon the Nazi Party was a substantial minority in the Reichstag (parliament). Nazism began in predominantly Catholic Bavaria, but as tensions developed between the Nazis and the Church, that territory gave the Nazis less support than other areas, and the German bishops condemned Nazi racism and ultra-nationalism.

Anti-Christian

Hitler was born a Catholic but renounced his faith early, partly because his worship of naked power could not be reconciled with Christian morality. (Because of its teachings about love, forgiveness, and humility, Nietzsche had called Christianity a "slave religion".) Just as Mussolini sought to associate his regime with the pagan Romans, the Nazis invoked the old Norse gods as appropriate deities for a warlike people.

The Concordat

In 1933, Hitler was asked to form a coalition government, an invitation supported by the Catholic Center Party, and the bishops withdrew their condemnation of the Nazis. But once in power, Hitler discarded those who thought they could control him and outlawed all other political parties, including the Center Party. He despised all religions and intended to eliminate them once he had conquered Europe but in the meantime dealt with the Catholic Church pragmatically, applying pressure but stopping short of alienating the large number of German Catholics. The Holy See signed a concordat with the new government, in order to protect the rights of the Church as far as possible, and as far as possible the majority of the German hierarchy tried to work within the framework of that agreement, sending notes of protest to the government over various issues but refraining from public condemnation.

Popular Support

Many Catholics, including clergy, remained loyal to the Nazi regime, although it soon became apparent that its ideology was incompatible with Christianity. Many believed in that ideology, many more willingly supported Hitler because of Germany's economic recovery, and an undetermined number remained passively supportive of Hitler out of fear, as the government increasingly made use of police-state tactics.

Hitler embarked on policies that made him immensely popular, especially public-works projects to alleviate the unemployment of the Great Depression. Above all, he appealed to the wounded pride of Germans smarting from their defeat in World War I, rearming Germany in defiance of the Versailles treaty and stirring up often hysterical nationalistic feelings, expressed above all in aggression toward other nations. Even more than Italy, the German state demanded absolute loyalty from its citizens.

Austria

In Hitler's native Austria, a Social Christian Party, with elements of anti-Judaism, emerged after World War I, and a priest, Ignaz Seipel (d. 1932), even served briefly as head of state. Under the devout Catholic chancellor Engelbert Dollfuss (d. 1934), Austria abolished parliamentary democracy and moved toward the kind of corporate state that *Quadragesimo Anno* seemed to enjoin. After Dollfuss was assassinated by Nazi agents, his policies were continued by the equally devout Kurt von Schuschnigg (d. 1977). In 1938, Germany both invaded Czechoslovakia and annexed Austria, where the Germans were welcomed by many, notably Cardinal Theodor Innitzer of Vienna (d. 1955). But Pius XI rebuked Innitzer, who recanted and later came to the defense of the Jews. Schuschnigg was sent to a concentration camp.[8]

Racial Purity

Nazism's fanatical anti-Jewish campaign was based on a theory of racial purity partly derived from the Darwinian idea of the "survival of the fittest"—the strongest people, who were presumed to be those of northern Europe, were destined to rule their inferiors and had to protect themselves from contamination by lesser races. Hitler identified the large Jewish population as an alien element that weakened the German nation, even though many Jews were well assimilated into German life, and he made

---

[8] After the war, he became a professor at the Jesuit St. Louis University in the United States.

Jews scapegoats for Germany's defeat in World War I. The Nazis intensified their campaign against the Jews in the later 1930s, culminating in the death camps where about six million people perished.

Faulhaber

Cardinal Michael von Faulhaber of Munich (d. 1952), a political conservative who had been critical of the Weimar government, was one of the few people who dared speak forcefully against the regime. From the beginning, he denounced Nazi racial ideas and reminded Germans of the Jewish origins of the Christian faith, something that, despite Nazi threats, he continued to do as attacks on the Jews intensified throughout the 1930s. Cardinal George W. Mundelein of Chicago (d. 1939), who was of German extraction, was also among the first to condemn Hitler, dismissing him contemptuously as a mere "paperhanger". (Insofar as he had an occupation, Hitler was actually a failed artist.)

Eugenics

The idea of *eugenics* ("well born"), which advocated "selective breeding" in order to strengthen the racial stock and to eliminate "inferior" people, had for some time been propagated even in democratic countries like the United States. Germany now became the first country to introduce compulsory sterilization for the physically handicapped, the mentally defective, and others. Individuals with these infirmities residing in hospitals and other institutions were euthanized, with over eighty thousand being gassed and cremated, a program that was strongly denounced by Bl. Clemens von Galen (d. 1946), bishop (later cardinal) of Münster.

Pius XI

Pius XI pointedly absented himself from Rome when Hitler made a state visit, at a time when, under Hitler's prodding, Italian Fascism was becoming officially anti-Jewish, and the Pope once famously proclaimed, "Spiritually, we are all Semites." With Faulhaber's help, Pius issued a stinging rebuke to the Nazis in his 1937 letter *Mit Brennender Sorge* (With Burning Anxiety), a document that the Pope arranged to have smuggled into Germany and read from the pulpits. He followed this the next year by an encyclical that was a kind of syllabus of errors of fascist ideology. Early in 1939, Pius was preparing to issue an even more uncompromising denunciation of Nazism, especially its racism, in an encyclical partly written by the American Jesuit John LaFarge (d. 1965), but the Pope died before the document could be issued, and its existence remained unknown for decades.

Persecution

Papal condemnations provoked an immediate Nazi reaction, but instead of making martyrs, Hitler at first tried to discredit priests as moral leaders. A number were arrested, a favorite tactic being to prosecute them for alleged crimes such as smuggling foreign currency, which showed that they were in league with Germany's enemies, and sexual misconduct, especially with young people.[9] Officially sanctioned mob vandalism of churches and a prohibition on religious orders receiving new members followed, and in 1940, the government began to close religious houses and schools.

Pius XII

In an unusually short meeting, the conclave of March 1939 elected Cardinal Eugenio Pacelli, the first secretary of state to ascend the papal throne in almost three centuries, his speedy election undoubtedly due to the fact that he was by far the prelate best qualified to confront the darkening international situation. The new Pope was from a noble Roman family and had spent his entire career in the papal diplomatic service, including the crucial post of nuncio to Germany just after World War I. As Pius XII (1939–1958), it would be his duty to govern the Church during one of the most difficult times in human history.

The Dilemma

Pius was acutely aware of the dilemma of two regimes pitted against one another, both of which were savagely hostile to religion—Nazi Germany and the Soviet Union. (As nuncio to Germany after World War I, he had both faced down a threatening communist mob and witnessed the beginnings of Nazism.)

The Soviet police state was even more terrifying than that of Germany, and it oppressed religion more fiercely; as a result, some people—possibly the Pope himself—judged that either Germany could be a bulwark against Communism or that Germany and the USSR might destroy each other. But as it turned out, Germany was the greater immediate threat, because of its naked assaults on other countries.

War

World War II began when Germany invaded Poland on September 1, 1939, an act that provoked England and France (the Allies) to declare war against the German juggernaut. Mussolini supported his German ally, and the two of them formed the Axis bloc. Most Germans, including most Catholics, probably supported Hitler's war effort, at least until it became obvious that defeat was inevitable, but there was some German resistance, for example, the White Rose, a group of Catholic and Protestant university students who produced anti-Nazi and anti-war tracts.

Martyrs

In German-conquered lands, priests sometimes joined resistance groups trying to sabotage the conquerors—eventually three thousand priests

---

[9] It is difficult to judge how many were in fact guilty, although the prosecutions were designed primarily for propaganda purposes. The fact that allegations of this kind were used against the Church by hostile regimes perhaps caused the Vatican to discount more credible claims later.

perished at the hands of the Nazis. Those who resisted openly were martyred, including Bl. Bernhard Lichtenberg (d. 1943), provost of the cathedral in Berlin; the German Jesuit Alfred Delp (d. 1945); the Netherlandish Carmelite Bl. Titus Brandsma (d. 1942); and the Austrian layman Bl. Franz Jäggerstätter (d. 1943).

Attack on the Jews

In every country conquered by the Germans, the systematic elimination of the Jews followed, along with that of other groups, including two million Catholic Poles. The Nazis defined Judaism in terms of ancestry instead of religion, so that, along with many other Jewish converts to Catholicism, the German Carmelite nun and philosopher St. Edith Stein (Sr. Teresa Benedicta of the Cross) was deported in 1942 from the German-occupied Netherlands to the Auschwitz death camp in Poland, where she was killed. The timing of the deportations seemed designed to punish the Dutch Catholic bishops who had issued a public statement condemning the Nazi persecution of the Jews.

Kolbe

Over 160 priests perished in Auschwitz alone. The Polish Franciscan St. Maximilian Kolbe (d. 1941) sheltered Jews until he was himself sent to Auschwitz, where he volunteered to undergo death by starvation in place of the father of a family.

Puppet States

As the German armies marched across Europe, they set up puppet governments in the conquered territories. That of Slovakia was headed by a priest, Josef Tiso, who was hanged by the Soviets in 1947. In France, some Catholics supported the invaders, many from expediency, some because they thought France had been defeated because of its own spiritual and moral degeneracy. The devout Marshal Philippe Pétain (d. 1951), a hero of the First World War who believed armed resistance was impossible, became head of a puppet government set up at Vichy.

Papal Policy

Pius XII deplored the German invasion of the Netherlands, Belgium, and France in 1940, and he gave sanctuary in the Vatican to the diplomats of the Allied powers who were trapped in Rome when the war began. As in the previous war, the Vatican continually tried to provide food, medicine, and other humanitarian services to prisoners of war and refugees on both sides. But, as in the previous war, the Holy See remained officially neutral, and Pius refrained from condemning any of the participants by name. He repeatedly called for a peace conference but found, like Benedict XV, that his voice was seldom heard, partly because both sides sought "unconditional surrender".

Help for the Jews

Without mentioning the Nazis or the Germans by name, Pius condemned racism in his Christmas speech of 1942, and in private audiences he denounced anti-Jewish policies. If he was not as outspoken as he might have been, he may have been motivated by the fact that, when bishops did speak out boldly—in the Netherlands and other places—the Nazis retaliated with even more ferocious acts. Pius encouraged both Vatican diplomats and the various national hierarchies to save as many Jews as possible, and those diplomats helped smuggle Jews to safety from German-occupied countries, many of them to Franco's Spain. Catholic agencies and individual Catholics hid Jews or shielded them with false certificates of baptism.

Under German orders, Mussolini's government eventually began deporting Jews to death camps, but thousands were hidden in religious houses in Rome, some in the Vatican itself and in the papal summer residence at Castel Gandolfo. In the end, 85 percent of Italian Jews were saved. Late in the war, when the existence of the death camps was confirmed, the Holy See and its various nuncios lodged strong protests against the systematic internment of Jews and others, and direct Vatican intervention persuaded the Nazi puppet government of Hungary to stop deporting Jews to Germany. The Church served as a major agency of international relief after the war, especially through Catholic Relief Services in the United States and the organization *Misereor* ("have mercy") in West Germany.

A Perilous Position

Despite the Lateran concordat, the Vatican was completely at the mercy of the Italian state and remained in that perilous situation throughout most of the war. The Germans themselves occupied Rome in 1943, and Hitler's government is known to have regarded Pius as an enemy and to have developed a secret contingency plan to seize him and take him to Germany. Without knowing of the plan, the Pope himself gave serious consideration to moving the seat of the papacy elsewhere, even of abdicating.

Postwar Reckonings

At the end of the war, Pétain was imprisoned, and the French government, under the equally devout Catholic Charles de Gaulle (d. 1970), demanded that the Vatican remove twenty-three bishops thought to have collaborated too closely with the Vichy government. It was a major diplomatic achievement of the papal nuncio, Angelo Roncalli, the future Pope John XXIII, to reduce that number to two. Also after the war, some priests and religious, presumably because of fascist sympathies, helped suspected war criminals escape to South America.

Soviet Conquest and Persecution

As a result of the war, the Soviet Union gained control of large sections of Germany and Austria; all of predominantly Catholic Poland, Hungary, Czechoslovakia, and Lithuania; and a religiously divided Yugoslavia. The communists began a severe persecution of the Church that would last for forty years.

Bl. Aloysius Stepinac, archbishop of Zagreb (d. 1960), was subjected to a show trial and sentenced to prison for alleged collaboration with the Nazi puppet government of Croatia, although in fact he had often denounced the Nazis, helped Jews, and opposed the government's program of forcing Serbian Orthodox to become Catholics. He was made a cardinal while in prison and was eventually released under house arrest.

The Hungarian bishop Bl. Zoltàn Meszlényi (d.1951) froze to death in prison after having preached against the regime, and the Hungarian Cardinal Josef Mindszenty (d. 1975) became a worldwide symbol of the victims of communist tyranny when he was imprisoned for seven years, after undergoing a show trial similar to Stepinac's. After his release, he took sanctuary in the American embassy in Budapest and eventually, with reluctance, went to live in Rome.

Cardinal Stefan Wyszyński (d. 1981) of Warsaw, who had also worked against the Germans during the war, was also imprisoned for a time by the communists, and Cardinal Josef Beran (d. 1969) of Prague was exiled.

The Postwar World

The United Nations

The Holy See in principle supported the formation of the United Nations at the end of the war, and the U.N.'s Universal Declaration of Human Rights owed much to the French Catholic philosopher Jacques Maritain (d. 1973) and the Lebanese Greek Orthodox diplomat Charles Malik (d. 1987).

Catholic Statesmen

In the period immediately after the war, serious Catholics held the highest offices in France (de Gaulle, Robert Schuman [d. 1963]), West Germany (Konrad Adenauer [d. 1967]), and Italy (Alcide de Gasperi [d. 1954] and Amintore Fanfani [d. 1999]). To varying degrees, they pursued agenda based on religious principles.

Adenauer, who had been a major figure in the Center Party and was twice imprisoned by the Nazis, helped found the Christian Democratic Union, a coalition of Catholics and Protestants that enacted a unique system by which tax money was apportioned to religious groups according to the number of their members, a system that allowed groups like *Misereor* to be exceptionally generous in supporting charitable causes around the world.

De Gasperi, who during the war had to take refuge from Mussolini in the Vatican, was one of the founders of the Italian Christian Democratic Party, which grew partly out of Catholic Action. The Christian Democrats were especially a bulwark against Communism. In 1948, Pius XII warned the Italian people not to vote for the communists, as they appeared ready to do, thereby thwarting what might have been the only communist victory achieved anywhere through democratic means.

The Church's Influence

Through both the dark years (1920 to 1945) and the brighter years (1945 to 1965) the social and cultural influence of the Church was greater than it had been for a long time. Pius XI and Pius XII were respected as moral leaders, and Catholic intellectuals attracted the attention of the secular culture.

Although defenders of the modernists charged that their condemnation in effect put an end to genuine Catholic intellectual life, the six decades after 1907 saw a cultural flowering in the Church unequaled since the seventeenth century, principally led by intellectual converts who were attracted precisely because of Catholic dogmas, not in spite of them.

Early Leaders

Among the earliest representatives of the Catholic intellectual revival were the convert English Jesuit Gerard Manley Hopkins (d. 1889), a pioneer of modern poetry; the English apologists Chesterton (also a convert) and Belloc; and the Frenchmen Charles Péguy (d. 1914) and Léon Bloy (d. 1917).

Through both journalism and more ambitious works, Chesterton and Belloc entered into direct battle with the modern world, boldly asserting the eternal validity of Catholic doctrine and looking to the Middle Ages as the high point of human history.

Péguy, who was killed in battle, became disillusioned with Socialism at almost the very moment of the papal condemnation of Modernism and soon rediscovered his Catholic faith. He was a leading figure in French intellectual life, and he too appealed to the values of the Middle Ages in order to unmask the spiritual emptiness of modern civilization. Also at the moment Modernism was being condemned, Maritain, a nominally Protestant French layman who was sunk in despair to the point of suicide, converted to the Catholic faith, finding a lifeline in precisely the Thomistic philosophy that the modernists scorned.

Philosophy

The revival of Thomistic thought was at the heart of the intellectual revival, but this "Neo-Thomism" marked something of a break with what was commonly taught in seminaries. The French historian Étienne Gilson (d. 1978), by immersing himself in the original sources, rediscovered a Thomism that he thought had been ignored or distorted not only by various modern philosophies but by other Catholic philosophies as well, and he began a project to recover authentic Thomism. As against Kantianism in particular, the key point for Gilson was Thomistic "realism"—the ability of the mind to perceive the actual existence of the objects it contemplated, unmediated by the categories present in the mind itself. The intellect intuited the real existence of beings, not merely its own ideas.

Jacques Maritain, who held various academic appointments and was for a time French ambassador to the Holy See, endeavored to show that medieval philosophy, far from being outdated, remained perennially valid, applicable in areas ranging from poetry to politics. He traced all the disorders of the modern world—moral and cultural as well as political—to the abandonment of "right reason", of which Thomism was the highest achievement.

For several decades after World War II, French thought was dominated by a philosophy dubbed *Existentialism*, which resisted definition but could be described as the sense of the world as an arbitrary place with no inherent meaning, a condition that gives men a radical freedom to define themselves and determine the meaning of their lives.

Existentialism in the full sense was by definition incompatible with Christianity, but the French convert Gabriel Marcel (d. 1973) insisted that, as a man, the believer too experiences existential despair, which he transcends by encountering God in the midst of that despair. For Marcel, the act of faith itself was an exercise of existential freedom, and he therefore rejected all philosophical systemization, including "proofs" for the existence of God, which he thought would in effect rob people of their freedom by leaving them no choice but to believe.

History and Science

The convert English historian Christopher Dawson (d. 1970) ranged over all of history, explicating better than anyone had ever done the crucial importance of religion at the heart of every civilization.

Catholics also contributed to scientific thought. A Belgian secular priest, Georges Lemaitre (d. 1966), was one of the greatest physicists of modern times, anticipating the Big Bang theory, which posits that the universe began in a great explosion from a single atom.

The Arts

The Catholic revival was especially strong in literature, with the Frenchmen François Mauriac (d. 1970) and Georges Bernanos (d. 1948), the Englishmen converts Graham Greene (d. 1991) and Evelyn Waugh (d. 1966), the Norwegian convert Sigrid Undset (d. 1949), and the American Flannery O'Connor (d. 1964). At the heart of most of their "Catholic" novels was the dramatic reality of sin and the crisis it causes in a person's life.

Catholic music flourished with the Frenchmen Maurice Duruflé (d. 1986) and Olivier Messiaen [d. 1992]) but, for whatever reason, the Frenchman Georges Rouault (d. 1958) was virtually the only important Catholic painter. After World War II, numerous churches were designed in self-consciously modern styles, but no distinctive style of church architecture developed except that of the eccentric Spaniard Antoni Gaudi i Cornet(d. 1926), who designed structures of an inimitable (and unimitated) quasi-baroque strangeness.

A Time of Strength

Having recovered from two world wars and a severe depression, the Western world experienced a time of renewed productivity and hope for the future. When Pius XII died in 1958, the Church appeared to be, despite severe persecution in some countries, stronger than she had been for a long time.

12   To the Ends of the Earth

The West had largely been converted to Christianity by the year 1000, while the rest of the world was, for various reasons, inaccessible to Europe. Thus, with the failure of the Crusades, Christian missionary activity all but ceased for half a millennium, except for the Nestorians of Persia and Mesopotamia, who spread their faith across Asia. The Nestorians reputedly founded monasteries in China in the eighth century, encouraged by emperors who accepted Christianity as one kind of wisdom among several, and there were still Nestorians in China four hundred years later.

The End of the First Missionary Era

The Mughals (Mongols) of the early thirteenth century were the last of the great marauding peoples, sweeping across the globe under the legendary Genghis Khan (d. 1227) and others, conquering territory that stretched from China, where Nestorians also became established at the Mughal court, to Hungary.

The Mughals

In 1245, Innocent IV sent a delegation under an Italian Franciscan archbishop, Giovanni da Pian del Carpini (d. 1252), to acquaint the Great Khan Kuyuk (d. 1248) with the Catholic faith and ask him to cease the wholesale slaughter of conquered peoples. Members of the mission described the Mughals as a moral and religious people who were nonetheless given to extreme cruelty. Kuyuk expressed puzzlement at the Christian message and countered it by claiming that the Mughal victories demonstrated that the gods did not favor the Christians. Louis IX of France also sent emissaries to the Khan, one of whom, the Flemish Dominican William of Rubrouck (d. 1293), participated in a formal debate in which the monotheistic Christians and Muslims vanquished the polytheistic Buddhists.

Kublai Khan (d. 1294) asked the Venetian merchant Marco Polo (d. 1324) to have the Pope send a hundred Christian scholars to his court, in order to establish the truth of conflicting religious claims. The scholars were not sent, but a second papal delegation went to China under another Italian Franciscan, John of Montecorvino (d. 1328). John made a favorable impression on the Great Khan Timur (Timur the Lame—Tamerlane, d. 1405) and made some converts. John was made an archbishop at Beijing (Peking), with jurisdiction over several suffragan sees, a mission that lasted until the Mughals were themselves conquered by the Ming Chinese in 1370.

A New Age of Discovery

The humanist spirit of the Renaissance stimulated a general curiosity about the world, a curiosity that could be satisfied for the first time because of the remarkable technological achievements of the Middle Ages in sailing and navigation.

Interest in the wider world was also fed by religious currents. The Portuguese Prince Henry the Navigator (d. 1460) was a pious ascetic who dreamed of discovering new worlds to replace those lost to the Muslims. The Italian sailor Christopher Columbus (d. 1506), who was influenced by some of the messianic expectations of Joachim of Flora, believed that the conversion of distant pagan peoples would usher in the last days.

Henry encouraged exploration that bore fruit as Portuguese voyagers began to open large parts of the world to the Europeans, for the first time confronting vast areas of the globe of whose existence they were barely aware, whole societies of people who had never heard of Christ. Under the leadership especially of the religious orders—first Franciscans and Dominicans, later Jesuits—the Church began her greatest period of missionary activity in terms of extent and complexity.

God, Gold, and Glory

The Europeans may have traveled mainly for love of adventure, but they were soon followed by merchants willing to risk large sums in perilous voyages and by government officials and soldiers claiming the rights of the crown over new territories. Explorers were invariably accompanied by priests, and on landing in each new territory, Mass was celebrated, the cross raised, and the flag planted, thereby claiming the territory for a European monarch.

The motives for expansion have been summarized as "God, gold, and glory"—the first the priority of priests, the second of merchants, the third of government officials and soldiers—and from the beginning, European expansion embodied a tension between religious and worldly motives. Learning languages that had no relation to any European tongue was the most immediate, and often most difficult, challenge the Europeans faced. Soldiers led the way, learning what was necessary to obtain basic information from the natives, such as the location of major settlements.

Missions and Colonialism

Missionaries had to depend on worldly men merely in order to reach distant lands, and over time, few missions succeeded unless they were connected with permanent outposts of European civilization. As a result, missionary activity was unavoidably implicated in what came to be called colonialism or imperialism—European countries conquering or otherwise dominating other areas of the world. Thus from the beginning, the modern missionary movement was closely tied to the various European powers, which gave missionaries access to new lands and financial support by governments but also brought them endless political interference.

America

Columbus

Contrary to stereotype, Columbus' belief that the world was round was not ridiculed; most educated people of the time thought so. Bishop Alejandro Geraldini (d. 1525) supported Columbus at the Spanish court, pointing out that many earlier writers, including saints, had been in error about geography. By sailing west from Spain, Columbus hoped to find a shorter route to India, and when he landed on the Caribbean island he named San Salvador ("holy Savior"), he thought he had succeeded. (Geraldini became the first bishop of San Salvador [renamed Santo Domingo—"Holy Lord"] and wrote one of the earliest accounts of the geography of the new land.)

Spain and Portugal

In the fifteenth century, a series of papal bulls gave Portugal the authority to explore and claim new lands. But in 1493, because of Columbus' voyages, the Spanish Pope Alexander VI drew a line that divided the entire world between Spain and Portugal in such a way that Spain was able to claim most of the territory of the New World, although Portugal got the huge territory that became known as Brazil.

"Indians"

The first "Indians" whom Columbus encountered seemed peaceful and gentle, although several of his men were later killed. Columbus' treatment of the Indians vacillated between kindly and harsh. He brought six of them back to Spain as slaves, where they became Catholics. Ferdinand and Isabella served as their godparents and immediately forbade further enslavement. Columbus was soon shunted aside by the more ruthless and rapacious *conquistadors* ("conquerors").

Aztecs

The various natives of Mexico lived in terror of the brutal Aztecs, whose great empire was said to be rich in gold and silver. In 1518, the *conquistador* Hernando Cortés (d. 1547) invaded Mexico, defeated Aztec armies much larger than his own, and received from Emperor Montezuma II (d. 1520) an acknowledgment of Spanish rule. The Spanish were greatly helped by the Indian nations who saw their arrival as an opportunity to throw off the yoke of the Aztecs, as well as by their own possession of firearms and horses, neither of which the Aztecs had. But the circumstances of the conquest were also closely involved with religion.

Montezuma may have deferred to the Spanish because of an Aztec legend that white gods had once visited Mexico and would one day return; and, paradoxically, Cortés' often brutal tactics probably increased his religious authority. During his advance toward Tenochtitlàn (Mexico City), he systematically destroyed "mosques" (as he called the Aztec temples) and smashed their idols. But rather than causing the Aztecs to resist more forcefully, this may have confirmed their suspicion that the invaders possessed a divine power greater than their own. The Spanish capture of Montezuma had the same effect, since it demonstrated the emperor's impotence; in fact, it soon provoked a rebellion of some of his own people, who assassinated him.

As warriors, there was perhaps little difference, morally, between the Spanish and the Aztecs. But the Spanish were deeply shocked by the Aztec practice of human sacrifice, in which, over the years, thousands of people, especially enemies taken in battle, had been led to the top of a great pyramid and ritually slaughtered in order to placate the gods of war.

The Rights of the Natives

The most basic question, which the Spanish attempted to address to some degree, was their right to be in the New World at all. While some theologians justified the conquest, the Dominican Francisco de Vitoria (d. 1546) boldly proposed that each local community, although subject to some kind of international law, was autonomous and self-governing, including those of the Indians. Their paganism, therefore, even including human sacrifice, did not deprive them of their rights. The Dominican theologian Cajetan, perhaps the leading Catholic theologian of the day, held a similar view, and Pope Paul III also insisted that pagan Indians had rights.

Most of the laymen attracted to the New World seem to have been driven by a hardhearted lust for wealth and power, so that neither the temporal nor the spiritual welfare of the Indians meant much to them. Mexico turned out not to be rich in gold, which was not discovered in abundance until the Inca kingdom of Peru was conquered several decades later, but Indians were forced to work in wretched mines or on *encomiendas*—large estates set up to produce various profitable commodities.

The popes forbade the slave trade early in the fifteenth century, when it had begun to revive in the expanding Portuguese empire, and the prohibition was reenacted periodically. But the prohibition was essentially ignored, and in the drive to make the new lands profitable, Indians were often treated as slaves, a practice that Columbus himself favored. Ferdinand and Isabella issued decrees to mitigate the Indians' condition, but the crown itself claimed most of the profits from the colonies, and it was difficult to control the men actually on the scene. (One viceroy was assassinated in Peru when he tried to enforce the royal decrees.)

Churchmen tended to be sympathetic to the Indians—when settlers complained to a bishop that the Indians gave off a foul odor, he replied, "It is you who stink to me!" The Indians' greatest champion was Bartolomé de Las Casas (d. 1566), a Spaniard who originally came to Mexico to take possession of an *encomienda*. He was ordained a diocesan priest and, after a Dominican denied him absolution in confession because of his treatment of the Indians, underwent a conversion and returned to Spain to plead the Indian cause, later returning to Mexico as a bishop.

Besides being opposed by laymen with vested interests, Las Casas was also opposed by some Franciscans who justified the bad treatment of the Indians. After a time, he returned to Spain to plead the Indian cause passionately once again and, in a formal debate at the royal court, vanquished a theological opponent who relied heavily on the justification of slavery made by Aristotle. Las Casas went so far as to explain, if not to justify, the practice of human sacrifice, on the grounds that all men knew they were creatures and owed their existence to their Creator. Thus, without the benefit of divine revelation, the Aztecs might naturally think that God demanded from them the sacrifice of human lives.

Las Casas wrote several books recounting in sickening detail the mistreatment of the Indians—books that, ironically, became a principal source for the English Protestant "Black Legend" about Spanish Catholic cruelty, a legend that seldom acknowledged that it was a Spanish bishop who was the source of the story.

The Decimation of the Natives

While many Indians were worked to death in mines and on *encomiendas*, and many were killed outright by cruel masters, by far the greatest damage was unintentional: the Spanish carried germs and viruses to which the Indians had no previous exposure, hence no resistance. During the course of the sixteenth century, millions died of diseases, especially smallpox, all over Latin America.

Mestizos

The Spanish attitude to the Indians was complex. Unlike the English, who tried to keep the Indians at a distance, the Spanish rather freely intermingled with them, even taking Indian wives and concubines, so that ultimately the predominant strain in Latin American society became the *mestizos* ("mixed race").

Originally, there was some debate among the Spanish as to whether the Indians were men of the same race as their conquerors. A few clergy thought that the apparent innocence of some tribes showed that they had not shared in the Fall of Adam and thus had no need of redemption, while the savagery of the Aztecs led others to judge that they were subhuman. But Church authorities quickly decreed that the Indians were human and therefore ought to be evangelized.

The Imperative of Evangelization

Dominicans in particular insisted forcefully that all Christians, not only the missionaries, had an obligation to convert the heathen and that churches must be built and every effort made to lead the Indians to the faith. Ferdinand and Isabella forbade the use of force to convert them, but that decree too was often ignored. The Spanish effort to convert the Indians was unmatched by Protestants, possibly because of their belief in predestination, which implied that those who had not heard the Gospel were not intended by God to hear it. (The New England Puritans tended to dismiss the Indians as merely children of the devil.)

Thomistic theology held that God had planted in human hearts both a yearning for Himself and a knowledge of right and wrong, so that, following those instincts, good pagans would in time realize the falsity of their religion and embrace Christianity when it was preached to them. (Left unclear was whether those who had never heard the Gospel could be saved.)

Some Europeans thought that the natives, although most were polytheists, already grasped certain basic elements of the Christian faith, such as the creation of the universe by an all-good God and the rudiments of the moral law. Some explorers thought they recognized images of the Virgin Mary in pagan temples and concluded that Mary had graciously appeared to native peoples who did not realize who she was.

Obstacles

But from the beginning, conversion efforts were plagued by problems that would never be entirely resolved: a chronic shortage of priests, despite which Indians were excluded from ordination; a semi-feudal social system in which the poor (mostly Indians) were often treated abominably; and a popular piety that was intense but also semi-pagan.

The Problem of Inculturation

On the other hand, anticipating the insights of modern anthropology, a few missionaries recognized that the native world was a seamless web of beliefs, rituals, social structures, and nature itself, all so closely interwoven that an entire world would have to be changed if the natives were to be truly converted. As in Europe during the Dark Ages, the Church thus confronted the issue of how the Gospel could be incarnated in a culture very different from that of the missionaries themselves.

Indians were not educated in the Western sense, so that issues of doctrine, so passionately debated in Europe, meant little to them. They learned the catechism by rote, and when the Spanish crown set up the Inquisition in the New World, it did not inquire into possible heresy among the Indians, who were deemed too simple to embrace false doctrine, but attempted instead to root out witchcraft. (Two *conquistadors*, however, were burned as heretics in 1528.)

Mestizos' culture thus created its own kind of Catholicism, with the missionaries incorporating elements of the native cultures, sometimes deliberately, sometimes because the people simply continued in many of their old ways. Most perhaps continued living in two worlds, invoking both pagan and Christian powers, sometimes in the same rituals.

Many transferred the cults of their old gods to Catholic saints, with Catholic rituals and the priests who performed them thought to have magical powers. Indians responded strongly to vivid descriptions of the rewards and punishment of the afterlife.

Thus, as in the Dark Ages, conversion was less a matter of accepting new beliefs than of submitting to a new power that was recognized as superior to the old—Jesus and His saints could conquer demons, including the old gods, and save men from every kind of evil. Because of the pagan worship of the sun, monstrances were often crafted with a circle of gold rays around the center, showing that Christ was the true sun, the source of all light. (In a reversal of influence, this radial type of monstrance was introduced into Europe from the New World.)

As in late Roman times, churches were often erected on the foundations of pagan temples, with the idols buried beneath them and basins that had been used to collect the blood of sacrificial victims turned into baptismal fonts, demonstrating that Christ had triumphed over the old gods and that one good God had created everything, so that even objects devoted to evil could be turned to good. Particularly significant was the fact that, since Christ shed His blood for everyone, the old bloody sacrifices were not needed to appease an angry god.

Guadalupe

Conversions were slow in coming, but a crucial change occurred in 1531, when St. Juan Diego (d. 1548), an Indian convert who was somewhat elderly by the standards of his society, heard singing while on his way to Mass and saw a vision of a beautiful lady who addressed him affectionately in his native tongue. She identified herself as the Mother of God and told Juan Diego that she wanted a church built on the site of her appearance, establishing a link between the New World and the Old by identifying herself with Guadalupe, a Marian shrine in Spain.

At first, the bishop was skeptical, but he was convinced when, at the lady's bidding, Juan Diego brought roses blooming in the cold of winter. As the roses tumbled out of his cloak, an image of the lady appeared on the cloth: dark-complexioned and wearing a kind of belt used by pregnant Indian women. A church was then built to enthrone the image, which now rests in a modern structure on the same site.

This Marian apparition seemed to affirm dramatically the suitability of Indian culture to receive the Christian message and the inherent worth and dignity of the Indian people themselves. This dramatic expression of the Catholic faith soon brought nine million native converts into the Church—the greatest mass conversion in history—and Our Lady of Guadalupe became the focal point of Mexican Catholicism and eventually the patroness of the Americas.

Effects of Conversions

The Church in Latin America continued to grow, with almost all its inhabitants becoming at least nominal Catholics, and for many, the faith went very deep. Much from the church of Europe was replicated

in the New World, including a system of education eventually including seventeen universities throughout Latin America, the oldest—at
Lima and Mexico City—predating Harvard by more than a century.
A number of great baroque churches were built all over Latin America, and the visual arts flourished. A cloistered Hieronymite nun from
this period, Juana de la Cruz (d. 1695), is considered a major poet of
the Spanish language.

Latin America also produced saints, including the Spaniard Turibius
of Lima (d. 1606), a reforming archbishop who tried to protect the
Indians; Rose of Lima (d. 1617), a native Peruvian who lived the mystical life in emulation of Catherine of Siena; Martin de Porres (d. 1639),
born at Lima of a Spanish father and a black mother, who as a Dominican lay brother cared for the poor and destitute; and Peter Claver
(d. 1654), a Spanish Jesuit who devoted his life to the slaves of the
Caribbean. (Rose was canonized in 1671, the first saint of the Americas.)

But although a few were ordained, Indians were considered unsuited
to the priesthood. Men of pure Spanish blood were preferred, with
mestizos, Indians, *mulattos* (those of mixed black and white lineage),
and blacks in descending order of preference.

The Paraguay
Reducciónes

In many ways, the most remarkable chapter in the history of the Latin
American missions, and one of the most remarkable anywhere at any
time, were the *reducciónes* established by the Jesuits in Paraguay in the
seventeenth century. By 1700, these communities embraced one hundred thousand Indians, perhaps the most successful social experiment
ever attempted.

The missions took their name from the attempt—later tried in
California—to "reduce" the Indians, that is, to settle them in com-
pact, highly organized communities, since nomadic peoples or those
living in scattered villages often lost the faith. Each *reducción* was a
large square, surrounded on three sides by the homes of the Indians
and on the fourth side by a church, workshops, and other communal
structures. Each *reducción* was entirely self-sustaining, with the Indians
taught agriculture, herding, and basic crafts. White men, especially
merchants, were barred, and the Indians were even permitted by the
Spanish crown to form armies for their own protection.

The *reducciónes* were undone in the 1750s in the most brutal manner
possible, as part of Pombal's fanatical attack on the Church, after he managed to obtain Paraguay from Spain, perhaps precisely in order to suppress the *reducciónes*, a manifestation of the spirit of Josephinism and
Gallicanism. The Jesuits were ordered to announce to the Indians that
they must leave the *reducciónes*, with no provision of any kind, and when
the missionaries protested, the Portuguese government sent a cooperative Jesuit to threaten them with excommunication. The local bishop
was an appointee of the crown, and the timid Jesuit leadership in Rome
also ordered the Paraguay Jesuits to obey. The Indians, however, kept up

an armed rebellion for five years, until they were finally crushed and the *reducciónes* obliterated.[1]

The conquest of Spain and Portugal by Napoleon a generation later allowed a series of rebellions to erupt in Latin America, as a result of which most of the colonies gained their independence within a few years.

Clergy were on both sides of the struggle for independence. Some believed that their oath of fidelity to the Spanish monarch was morally binding, while others propagated radical Enlightenment ideas. Two Mexican priests—Miguel Hidalgo y Costilla (d. 1811) and José Maria Moreles (d. 1815)—helped to raise rebel troops, commanded them in battle, and were eventually captured and shot.

The Holy See vacillated, supporting the restoration of Spain's colonies after the defeat of Napoleon but a few years later appointing bishops without reference to the Spanish king, which in effect recognized Latin American independence. (The future Pius IX was the first pope to visit the New World, as a member of a papal delegation in 1823.)

Endemic Troubles
After independence, the history of Latin American Catholicism was to a great extent the story of complex and troubled relationships between the Church, the governments in power, and various forces for political and economic change. Latin American Catholics had a deep piety and were loyal to the Church. But, in addition to the chronic shortage of priests, both clerical and lay concubinage was common (both Hidalgo y Costilla and Moreles fathered children), especially in rural villages. Religion was often experienced primarily as adherence to traditional rituals—some of them dubiously Christian—rather than as a force for moral and spiritual transformation.

Anticlericalism
At first, some of the newly independent states confirmed the special status of the Church. But, as with European Liberalism, the spirit of independence often came to be directed against the Church as part of the oppressive Old Regime. Anticlerical Freemasonry was a powerful influence among liberal leaders, and the Church was stripped of her extensive lands while her influence over education was curtailed. Ecuador, briefly, was an unusual exception under Garcia Moreno (d. 1875), who declared it to be an officially Catholic country dedicated to the Sacred Heart, where both the Masonic Order and all condemned books were banned, an experiment that came to an end when Moreno was assassinated.

---

[1] The episode is highly fictionalized in the film *The Mission*.

India

The Portuguese

Pope Alexander VI's division of the world applied to the Far East as well as to the New World and thereby gave the Portuguese a claim to India. As Columbus was discovering the West while searching for the East, Portuguese were traveling to the East around the southern tip of Africa. The Portuguese were quick to establish trading posts on the southern coast of the Indian subcontinent, primarily in order to exploit the vastly profitable spice trade.

An Ancient Culture

The Europeans' attitude toward Asia was entirely different from their attitude toward America, since Asia was not wholly unfamiliar territory and its various kingdoms were very ancient, rich, and sophisticated, therefore not to be dismissed as almost subhuman. Strategically, the Europeans could not simply conquer but had to bargain with local princes for concessions.

St. Thomas Christians

The Europeans also found that Christianity was not entirely strange to Asia. The St. Thomas Christians (see Chapter Seven above, p. 211) were centered around the island city of Goa, which the Portuguese conquered and turned into a trading center. Goa was soon made a diocese, and from that base Franciscan missionaries were able to extend their activities into neighboring territories.

Xavier

Missionary activity of all kinds received a new impetus and new directions from the arrival in India in 1541 of St. Francis Xavier (d. 1552). Xavier had been one of Ignatius Loyola's earliest companions, and Ignatius, who thirsted for the conversion of the world, sent him to the East only a year after the Society of Jesus was officially approved. Xavier's mission was the first application of the new Jesuit system of formation and organization. Unlike the Franciscans and missionaries of other orders, he went to his new assignment entirely alone, knowing that he would probably never return. (Homesick for his brethren, he cut their signatures out of the letters he received and kept them in a locket.)

A Holy Man

Xavier's asceticism fit well with the Indian image of the holy man. He wore sandals and a dirty tattered cassock, slept on the beach when necessary, observed stringent fasts, and tried to avoid the company of women. Begging, he found, far from being a cause of shame, was often respected as the sign of a holy man who had renounced all worldly goods. He was outspoken in his denunciation of the Europeans in India, not excluding some missionaries—men who lived scandalous lives, mistreated the natives, and were themselves the greatest obstacles to conversions.

The Devil's Work

For Xavier, the realities were quite simple—innumerable souls were being lost because of a false religion that was probably of the devil.

Just as human sacrifice proved to the Spanish that the Aztec religion was evil, so *suttee* in India—the custom by which a widow threw herself on her husband's funeral pyre—proved the evil of Hinduism. *Suttee* was an obligation from which Christian converts were freed, and it was suppressed even among the Hindus in the lands the Europeans controlled. As in Mexico, some explorers found what they thought were images of the Virgin Mary in native temples, but Xavier demanded that all idols be destroyed. And he pressed men into giving up their concubines.

Mass Conversions

In journeys outside the security of Goa itself, Xavier quickly made large numbers of converts, whom he baptized as soon as possible, on the basis of minimal catechetics. He administered so many baptisms at one time that he sometimes had to have his arm supported as he poured the water. (His best-known relic, kept at Goa, is his right forearm.) He spent many hours hearing confessions and urged Ignatius to send men who were not necessarily learned but who were physically strong.

Castes

Indian society was divided into *castes*, social groups determined by birth and rigidly defined, from which there could be no escape except, they believed, through reincarnation. The highest caste were the Brahmins, men who were supposed to be both learned and deeply spiritual and who, if they did not actually rule Indian society, at least set its tone. At the other extreme was the caste of those who were literally "Untouchable", people whose conduct in a previous life had supposedly merited their being reborn as hewers of wood and drawers of water.

Xavier's rapid evangelization of India brought with it the question of whether the faith could be inculturated in the caste system. The Europeans also took for granted that mankind was arranged in a social hierarchy and that those in the lower orders had to show deference to those above, but Christianity taught that all social groups were equal in the sight of God, while in India the castes were rigid manifestations of the inflexible divine will.

Most of Xavier's converts seem to have been from the Untouchables, which meant that the Church might attract large numbers of people but could never hope to convert Indian society as a whole. By converting to Christianity, Untouchables overcame their shameful and exploited status, but few Brahmins became Christians, if only because to do so would be to lose all social status, by associating with Untouchables.

Indonesia

Praying at the tomb of St. Thomas, Xavier felt inspired to go to the Molucca Islands (modern Indonesia), where the Portuguese had an outpost and there were already a few Christians. He spent two years there, with more limited success than in India. Feeling strongly the devil's presence, he performed a number of exorcisms after spending the night in prayer. Islam was a strong presence in the Moluccas, and Xavier found what other Christians had discovered before him— Muslims were especially resistant to conversion, due perhaps to their strict monotheism, which caused them immediately to rebuff all talk of a trinitarian God; the fact that the Qur'an contained its own account of Jesus; and the fact that apostasy from Islam was punishable by death.

"Rice Christians"

Returning to India as the superior of the Jesuit mission (he summarily dismissed from the Society a Jesuit who had failed to go on a dangerous assignment), Xavier found that some converts continued to worship idols secretly and some were even drawn back completely into paganism. Other missionaries questioned whether Xavier's converts had been properly instructed and raised the issue of what would later be called "rice Christians"—those who accepted baptism because of the material benefits it offered. The phenomenon posed a serious dilemma for missionaries, in that they had obligations in charity to help poor pagans but such charity might seem like enticement.

Inculturation

St. Paul's College, heavily supported, like other missionary projects in India, by the king of Portugal, was set up at Goa to train native priests, teaching them Latin so that they could study theology and celebrate the liturgy. Xavier, however, wanted less emphasis on philosophy and theology and more on practical experience. (In one of his few conscious efforts at inculturation, he urged that the penitential season of Lent be transferred to the summer, since otherwise there would be no fish available.)

Problems

Despite the bad example of some Europeans, the missions continued to attract a large number of converts, mainly from the lower castes, and native Indians entered the Jesuit order in such numbers that the Indian province of the Society, encompassing all of East Asia, was soon larger than all the others combined. But in the 1570s, an official Jesuit visitor, the Italian Alessandro Valignano (d. 1606), arrived for an inspection and found conditions deplorable: poverty, injustice, lawlessness, and waning zeal on the part of the missionaries. Some Indian Jesuit houses had slaves, since certain kinds of labor were thought to be degrading for free men, although the slaves were supposed to be eventually freed.

De Nobili

More than half a century after Xavier's death, the Italian Jesuit Roberto de Nobili (d. 1656), also working in India, raised ideas about inculturation that differed radically from Xavier's own. De Nobili feared that, so long as most converts came from the lower caste, Catholicism would never be fully accepted in India and that in order to convert the whole society it was necessary to convert the Brahmins.

Natural Theology

De Nobili knew more about Hinduism than any of his contemporaries, because he made the arduous effort to learn the Sanskrit and Tamil languages in which the Hindu sacred books were written. Like all Jesuits of his era, he was a Thomist, and the Thomistic emphasis on natural theology—the truths knowable by the mind even before it receives divine revelation—underlay his efforts. De Nobili attempted to bring his audience as far as possible toward Christianity by reasoning, in the Thomistic manner, from visible effects to their causes (the Creator), proving the attributes necessary to such a Creator (all-knowing, all-powerful, eternal), and establishing that ultimately the truths of God, because they are infinite, are beyond human understanding and requires divine revelation.

But there were serious differences between Catholics and Hindus that could not be compromised: monotheism, Christ as the only Son of God and Savior, the practice of *suttee*, and belief in reincarnation. De Nobili argued that those unacceptable beliefs were the irrational degeneration of truths that had once been known but had been lost. The term *Veda*, referring to Hindu sacred texts, derived, he thought, from this original revelation given to the Indians by God. Indian laws, of which the Brahmins were in a sense the custodians and interpreters, were often wise and just, based on the knowledge of good and evil that God had implanted in the human heart. Thus no radical change in the laws was necessary.

De Nobili's Approach

Tacitly rejecting Xavier's methods, de Nobili urged the missionaries to dispel pagan darkness gradually and not to make frontal assaults on Indian beliefs and practices. Certain things, such as habits of dress and diet, seemed cultural only, and he repeatedly cited the ways in which the early Christians had adapted the Gospel to Greco-Roman culture.

Most important was the missionaries' acceptance of the caste system, particularly their respect for the Brahmins. De Nobili urged that the missionaries themselves live as Brahmins, adopting the customs and attitudes appropriate to their learning or their high birth. To be despised as a follower of Christ was one thing, he argued, but to be despised as a person of low social class was another. Implicitly, he seemed to consign the apostolate of the Untouchables to the lower-class Franciscans.

The core of de Nobili's argument was that the Brahmins were not a religious group at all but merely a highly respected class of learned men, so that they could be baptized yet retain all the habits of their class. In great detail, he analyzed their dress, diet, and other things in order to demonstrate that these had social significance only, not religious. In addition, he argued, their significance would change if the Brahmins converted.

Condemnation

De Nobili received the endorsement of some of the Catholic hierarchy in India and of Robert Bellarmine. But his work was condemned by Pope Urban VIII in a decision that was soon reversed. Overall, de Nobili seems to have made few intellectual converts, and he complained that often those with whom he debated seemed merely confused. He was a pioneer in the theology of inculturation, but he seems to have underestimated the difficulty of separating the religious and social threads of an ancient and tightly woven culture.

Indian Mughals

The Christian presence in India was almost entirely confined to the South. Much of northern India was ruled by the Mughals, several of whose *khans* were only nominally Muslim and not only allowed Jesuits into their territories but permitted them to challenge Muslim and Hindu sages in public debates. Some even privately expressed interest in the Catholic faith. But the last of these, Shāh Jahān (d. 1666), famous as the builder of the Taj Mahal, finally committed himself to Islam and outlawed Christianity.

Japan

Xavier was tantalized by stories told by travelers from distant Japan—that the Japanese were a curious people who yearned to know the truth and even had their own monasteries. In 1549, he achieved his dream of going there, arriving on a merchant ship and for the first time leaving the security of a transplanted European settlement, venturing, with little support, into largely unknown territory.

The Daimyos

Despite many efforts, Xavier was unable to obtain an audience with the almost mythical emperor, whose power—perhaps unknown to Xavier—was actually quite weak and who was dominated by officials called *shoguns*. But some *daimyos* (feudal lords) were friendly to the stranger, in part because they wanted to open trade relations with the Spanish and Portuguese.

Xavier discovered that in Japan begging was shameful and his shabby and humble appearance, which had made him credible to the Indians, had the opposite effect on the Japanese, who thought there could be little wisdom in someone who was so obviously a failure. Following the Ignatian principle of detachment—making use of worldly things without desiring them—he obtained good clothes from a European ship and found that he was now listened to more respectfully. From European merchants, Xavier also obtained such things as clocks, eyeglasses, telescopes, and muskets, gifts that impressed the *daimyos* and helped gain him a reputation for wisdom.

From the beginning, the *bonzes* (Buddhist monks) were Xavier's chief enemy. These spiritual leaders of Japanese society quite correctly saw him as a formidable rival and intrigued against him at the courts of the *daimyos*, without whose at least passive tolerance the missionaries could make no headway. Despite his normal asceticism, Xavier ate meat and fish as a sign that it was permitted, since the *bonzes* abstained.

Feudal Politics

Xavier made heroic journeys on foot to visit as much of the island as he could. At first, conversions were very few, although in time, there were opportunities for mass baptisms of the simplest people, so long as they abandoned their idols. As in India, he ordered the destruction of pagan temples wherever the *daimyos* permitted. There was often political rivalry between *daimyos* and local Buddhist monasteries, which were deeply involved in the feudal politics of Japan, so that the *daimyos*, especially those who valued trade with the Europeans, did not automatically side with the monks.

Xavier encountered Buddhism and to a lesser extent Shintoism—an ancient Japanese religion centered around the veneration of ancestors—without having a name for them. Both religions were complex and in their highest expressions very sophisticated. He sometimes engaged in formal debates with *bonzes* and, whereas in India he had valued missionaries' physical stamina over their intellectual achievements, he now urged his superiors in Rome to send learned men.

Theological Debates

He confirmed that some Japanese were indeed curious, requiring answers to difficult questions—how was the universe created, was there a difference between men and animals, was there personal immortality? When asked why God had waited so long to send the Gospel to Japan, thereby condemning earlier generations to Hell, Xavier replied evasively, pointing out that the pagans had at least a rudimentary knowledge of the moral law but not stating explicitly whether their ancestors were damned.

He developed a simple catechism, translated into Japanese and organized around the story of salvation, beginning with Adam and Eve and culminating with Christ. In accord with Ignatian principles, Xavier sought to use whatever in Japanese culture might help to promote the Gospel, making use of some pagan terms, such as those for angels and demons. With virtually no knowledge of the Japanese language, Xavier at first relied on an Indian interpreter who had previously visited Japan. But when some of his hearers either laughed or walked away in confusion, Xavier discovered that the word the interpreter was mistakenly using for God actually meant "the big lie".

Catechesis

This raised the question to what extent Catholic doctrine, formulated in Hebrew and Greek terms, could be transplanted to other cultures. To avoid confusion, Xavier henceforth simply used the Latin word *Deus* and stopped using the Buddhist term for "the Highest Power" lest it merely confirm the pagans in what they already believed. As in the early centuries of the Church, the crucifix, the proudest symbol of Christianity, was a stumbling block to the Japanese, who— encouraged by the *bonzes*—saw it as merely a shameful punishment imposed on criminals.

Sexual Morality

Xavier claimed that Japanese parents were naïve in sending their sons to be educated by the *bonzes*, who had great prestige but were pedophiles. In debate, the *bonzes* denied that there was any moral fault involved, and Xavier replied that the distinction between male and female was fundamental to creation.

Developments in the Japanese Missions

India served as the training ground for Jesuits sent to Japan, where there were about thirty thousand Catholics in 1570 and 150,000 a decade later. The interests of the missionaries and the European merchants coincided, as the possibility of trade was held out to the various *daimyos* in order to obtain permission to proselytize. The *daimyo* Oda Nobunaga of Osaka (d. 1582) was particularly friendly, actually persecuting Buddhists and saying that he would convert to Catholicism if he were allowed to keep his many mistresses.

Native Japanese were at first admitted to the Society of Jesus, but the policy was soon reversed, as the superior of the Japanese mission, the Portuguese Francisco Cabral (d. 1609), came to regard the natives as treacherous, perhaps due mainly to the fact that the missions were at the mercy of shifting political winds. To Cabral, the Japanese were an inferior people who would have to remain semi-permanently under European spiritual tutelage and would have to adapt European ways in order to live as Catholics.

The official visitor Valignano arrived in 1579, and he and Cabral soon came to embody opposing philosophies of mission. Based on his reports to Rome, Valignano's philosophy was eventually accepted, and he became perhaps the first modern man to formulate clearly the policy that would, at least in principle, govern all subsequent Catholic missionary activity: that native cultures were to be respected insofar as they did not impede the faith. (Pope Gregory the Great had enunciated a similar principle, which went as far back as St. Paul's treatment of Gentile converts.)

Inculturation

Valignano wrote a kind of guide to inculturation, following the Ignatian exercise of weighing the factors both in favor and against continuing the Japanese mission. The negatives, which were admittedly serious, were the facts that conversions were slow and dependent on unpredictable political and economic factors and that converts were often tepid and easily slid back into paganism. On the other side were the facts that the mission was the only access the people of Japan had to the Gospel and that dubious converts of one generation might produce fervent souls in the next. Valignano was highly conscious that resources—both in men and in money—were being stretched thin, but he urged that the missionaries continue to seek converts instead of concentrating on the care of the flock they already had.

Native vocations were slow in coming, partly because of the difficulty of learning Latin. As in India, most of the Jesuit vocations were from the higher classes. Valignano mitigated the practice of having converts destroy pagan temples, and he allowed the observance of traditional Japanese feasts, provided they were stripped of their religious rituals.

Some converts had already proved their faith by enduring persecution, while those who lapsed did so under pressure from their lords and often because they rarely saw a priest and those they did see did not know the Japanese language. As the Apostles had done, it was sufficient for the time being to get the pagans merely to abstain from idols and from fornication, Valignano thought.

Respect for the Japanese
He saw that the mission was impeded by the perceived arrogance of some Europeans (Cabral inflicted "blows and harsh words" on the converts) and insisted that European missionaries learn Japanese. Contrary to Cabral, he expressed admiration for the natives' stoical endurance of hardship and their courtesy, although admitting they could also be inscrutable and cruel. (Valignano had some contempt for Indians and blacks, but he called the Japanese "white people".) Perhaps, he predicted somewhat daringly, there might in time even be a Japanese bishop.

Liturgy
The Japanese loved show and ceremony, Valignano found, so that as soon as possible it was desirable to build substantial churches, not, however, in the Japanese style, because that would constitute emulation of the pagans. Although Ignatius had enjoined his men to celebrate the liturgy simply, Valignano thought that in Japan it should be celebrated with as much solemnity as possible.

Japanese Customs
On the practical level, Jesuit seminarians were to be allowed their native diet (they found some European eating habits disgusting) and their accustomed posture (half-crouching, half-sitting) when eating or studying. Table utensils were not be used, since they were not the Japanese custom and, contrary to Xavier's practice, meat was not to be eaten where it offended the Japanese. Jesuits could wear sandals, and their cassocks might resemble kimonos.

Valignano compiled a kind of etiquette book for Jesuits who might miss the subtleties of Japanese culture. A man of social standing should not carry his own umbrella, should not travel alone, and might ride a horse or walk but could not ride a lowly kind of animal like a donkey.

Complex procedures governed hospitality and relations with persons of various social classes, and appropriate gifts were to be given. Men could wear their hats in church, since, in contrast to European custom, not to do so was considered a sign of disrespect.

Pagan Morality

Respecting customs was one thing, but differences in morality were more problematic. Childhood marriages were common in Japan, and therefore divorces were as well, and Valignano wondered if such marriages were valid in the eyes of the Church. Also problematic was the practice of suicide, which was not only permissible in Japanese culture but virtually obligatory, in order to escape dishonor. (Valignano wondered how to reconcile this pervasive concept of honor with Christian humility.) Slavery was to be tolerated, but Jesuits should make efforts to help runaways.

Canon law forbade ordaining a man who had committed a homicide, but impulsive killings were common among the Japanese, whom Valignano said resorted to the sword more quickly than to harsh words or blows. He thus recommended that the rule should be invoked only against those who committed the deed after conversion.

Franciscans

At first, the pope had given the Japanese mission entirely to the Jesuits, but Franciscans began arriving in increasing numbers, and the mission was weakened by differences between the two orders that erupted into quarrels. Jesuits were said to eat better food and to wear better clothes than the Franciscans, something that was not a matter of personal preference but a pragmatic judgment as to what the Japanese expected. The Franciscans continued to beg, which in Japan led to loss of social status. Jesuits nursed the sick, but touching lepers and the very poor was hateful to many of the very cleanly Japanese, so that the care of such people was mostly left to the Franciscans, an ironic application of an Ignatian principle, in that most Jesuits probably felt an obligation to help the poor but were required to make a pragmatic judgment as to whether that would aid their mission.

The Silk Trade

The Far East missions were heavily subsidized by the Spanish and Portuguese governments, and the missionaries sometimes chafed under the restrictions that could impose. In order to liberate themselves at least in part, the Jesuits became directly involved in the lucrative silk trade that flourished all over the East, serving as middlemen for international transactions. Although the pope at one point ordered the Jesuits to cease their involvement in the trade, it continued, drawing the Jesuits into political intrigues and making them vulnerable to the charge of being agents of foreign governments. Valignano thought this involvement was imprudent, just as he was suspicious of the missionaries' close dependence on friendly *daimyos*.

After 1600, English and Netherlandish merchants also began to visit Japanese ports, and some tried to undermine the Jesuits in order to undermine the Spanish and Portuguese traders. The situation varied greatly from one province to another, but in all cases, the Jesuits were dependent on the unpredictable attitudes of the *daimyos*.

Competition

The *daimyo* Toyotomi Hideyoshi (d. 1598), who succeeded Nobunaga, almost immediately turned against the Christians. The largest concentration was in the port city of Nagasaki, and in 1597, in a preview of things soon to come, he ordered the crucifixion of twenty-six Christians, including six Franciscans, accused of being foreign spies. After Hideyoshi's death, the persecution temporarily abated. However, in 1614 the *shogun* Tokugawa Ieyasu (d. 1616) ordered the expulsion of all the missionaries. Many left, although some continued to minister in secret.

Persecution

The persecution continued after Ieyasu's death and spread throughout Japan. An organized propaganda war accused the Christians of undermining the imperial state and the authority of the *daimyos*; their monotheism was said to be insulting to the many gods. Eventually, there were five thousand Catholic martyrs, of whom only seventy were Europeans. They were subjected to inhuman tortures, the worst of which was to be hung upside down over pits of excrement, slowly dying of asphyxiation. Many apostatized, including one Spanish Jesuit who was rumored to have himself become a persecutor, although his full story is unknown.[2]

Unfortunately, martyrdom did not seem to have the same effect in Japan as elsewhere. Christianity was founded on the idea of the holiness of martyrdom, but Japanese culture found martyrdom almost incomprehensible. Christians were supposed to follow the law of God, which might conflict with that of the state, and hence regarded martyrdom as the seal of their faith. Japanese culture, however, recognized no transcendent moral law. The civil law embodied the highest moral principles, including obedience, and those who were put to death were seen as mere criminals.

The Tokugawa dynasty, founded by Ieyasu, ordered the expulsion of all foreigners from the empire, including Spanish and Portuguese merchants. A trade pact was then made with the Protestant Netherlanders, who were not allowed on the mainland of Japan and could neither proselytize nor practice their religion—even Bibles were banned. In an episode almost unparalleled in history, Japan made the radical decision to obliterate all the foreign influences it had absorbed over the previous fifty years and to return to its ancestral ways. The door was shut to all foreigners and would remain so for over two centuries.

Foreigners Expelled

---

[2] The persecution is the subject of the searing novel *The Silence* by the Japanese Christian Paul Endo.

China

The Lure

After three years in Japan, Xavier, now the superior of all the Jesuit missions in the East, returned to Goa, not with the intention of staying but in the hope of being able to venture into the vast, mysterious empire of China, possibly to find the court of the legendary Prester John (see Chapter Seven above, p. 202). Except for the island of Macao, the Chinese Empire had long been so rigidly closed to outsiders that shipwrecked Portuguese sailors had been imprisoned and tortured after taking refuge there.

Although Xavier managed to obtain the official title of papal nuncio to China, the Portuguese government at Goa would not permit him to travel there. Characteristically, he took matters into his own hands, arranging in 1552 for a ship to put him ashore on an island off the Chinese coast, from whence a smuggler would take him to the mainland. While waiting for the smuggler, this greatest missionary in the history of Christianity after St. Paul, took sick and died, alone.

Missionaries Admitted

Missionaries were not allowed into China until a generation after Xavier's death, once again mainly because of the lure of trade with the West. After the suppression of Christianity in Japan, many young Jesuits in Europe asked to be assigned to China, partly in the hope of martyrdom. Those who were sent were highly trained in theology, philosophy, and the sciences and undertook a new kind of mission strategy, the kind that de Nobili would advocate later—approaching the Chinese at the highest intellectual level, converting the whole culture by first converting its head. The Italian Michele Ruggieri (d. 1607), who arrived around 1580, made serious efforts to learn the Chinese language and compiled a catechism but found that the Chinese balked at the idea that God could have become man and especially at the idea that He had died on the Cross.

Ricci

The key figure in the Chinese apostolate was the Italian Matteo Ricci (d. 1610), who had been a novice in Italy under Valignano and who arrived in China in 1583. He eventually settled in the imperial city of Beijing, although, as in Japan, he never gained access to the semi-mythical emperor. Like Xavier, Ricci exemplified Ignatius' realization that a Jesuit might have to live for many years away from any community.

Anti-Buddhism

Ricci wished to be seen by the Chinese as a wise man and, like his predecessors in Japan, brought them clocks, maps, and other intriguing Western inventions. At first, he wore the robes of a Buddhist monk, but as he came to understand the cultural scene, he changed into the robes of a Confucian scholar and became a severe critic of Buddhism. (De Nobili was also very anti-Buddhist, accepting the Hindu charge that Buddhists were atheists.)

Ricci realized that for the most part Buddhism was not respected by the class called the *mandarins* (a word actually coined by the Portuguese)—educated men who held important offices and who set the direction of Chinese culture—who saw it as a popular religion filled with superstitions. Ricci seems not to have understood that some Buddhist ideas had been adopted into Confucianism, and in particular he failed to grasp the Buddhist concept of "nothingness"—the obliteration of all particular identities in one great unity.

Confucianism

Most mandarins were Confucians, followers of the semi-legendary sage who had been more a philosopher than a theologian and whose emphasis on respect for one's ancestors, tradition, law, social and political order, self-discipline, and personal integrity suited the needs of the great empire that the mandarins helped to govern.

Ricci probably attributed to Confucianism a greater coherence than it actually possessed, seeing it as a system remarkably congruent with Christianity and with the Greco-Roman Stoicism that had strongly influenced the Christian tradition. He therefore set out to convince the mandarins that they need not abandon the age-old wisdom of Confucius but instead could deepen that wisdom by embracing the wisdom of Christianity. Christianity could supply what Confucianism lacked—a comprehensive and coherent account of the entire universe, its origins, and ultimate goal.

Pure Confucianism, Ricci asserted, was a survivor from the remote ancient time which the Chinese regarded as a golden age, the equivalent of Paradise in the Jewish and Christian account. In time, however, corruption set in. Chinese ambassadors who heard of the wisdom of Christianity traveled west to find it but ended their journey in India, Ricci speculated, where they adopted Hinduism by mistake. Buddhism, an offshoot of Hinduism, contained numerous false myths and rituals and was the enemy of true wisdom.

Apologetics

Ricci published a comprehensive summary of his ideas just a few years before his death, in the form of a dialogue between a Christian and a Confucian in which the Christian answered all the pagan's questions and converted him. Ricci set out to bring Confucianism and Christianity as close together as possible, but he followed the Ignatian principle of tailoring the message to the capacity of the hearers, probably judging that certain "hard sayings" would require years of preparation.

Ricci began with the creation of the universe, the necessity that one Lord should rule over everything, and the necessity that such a Being must be a person—an understanding beyond such vague Chinese phrases as "the Ultimate Being". In particular, he explained the true meaning of the Confucian phrase the "Lord of Heaven", which he said the Confucians had conceived because of the natural knowledge of Himself that God placed in all people but which needed to be clarified and deepened by the revealed wisdom of Christianity. (Later Jesuits, fearful that this Confucian term would merely encourage the Chinese to continue worshipping their ancestral deities, debated over the proper word, without fully resolving it.)

Refuting the idea of reincarnation, Ricci spent considerable effort proving the immortality of the soul and the reality of Heaven and Hell, without which goodness would not be rewarded and evil punished and which were therefore strong factors in human motivation. Confucians taught that human nature was essentially good and needed merely to be cultivated, whereas Ricci argued that the will could be perverted and needed guidance from on high.

Only toward the end of his treatise, did Ricci treat of Christianity, and specifically of Catholicism, in the concrete. He did not acknowledge the religious divisions of the West and made only brief reference to the papal office, but he expounded at length on the meaning and utility of celibacy, which he found to be a stumbling block to the Chinese. Nor did he speak of other difficult Catholic doctrines, such as the Real Presence. The idea of the Mass as a sacrifice would have seemed almost subversive to the Chinese, because the emperor alone was qualified to offer sacrifice. Almost Ricci's only concession to Catholic practice was the injunction that to enter the kingdom of the Lord of Heaven it was necessary to undergo cleansing with water, which wiped away all past wrongs.

Initially, he referred to Jesus only to explain the meaning of the title "Jesuit". But toward the end of the treatise, he revealed that at one point in history the world had fallen into such evil ways that, out of compassion, the Lord of Heaven had chosen a chaste woman to bear a son who taught the people before returning to Heaven. In keeping with the character of Christianity as a historical religion, Ricci dated the Incarnation quite precisely, from the reign of a particular Chinese emperor.

Perhaps not wishing to perplex his readers with the doctrine of the Trinity, Ricci did not distinguish Father and Son but explained that Jesus was Himself the Lord of Heaven, His divinity proven especially by His many miracles and by the fact that He was venerated as a holy man. Because of the earlier rejection of Ruggieri's catechism by the Chinese, Ricci never recounted the narrative of the Passion, death, and Resurrection of Jesus, although at the time of his own death he was in the process of translating the Bible into Chinese.

Converts

Ricci was naturally opposed by Buddhist scholars and also by some Confucians who thought he was distorting the pure teaching. He did not aim at mass conversions and made only a few converts among the mandarins, converts to whom, presumably, he imparted the fullness of Catholic teaching and some of whom proved to be able and influential apologists for the Catholic faith. Paul Xu Guangqi (d. 1623) and Michael Xang Tingyen (d. 1627) were important imperial bureaucrats who were attracted to Christianity partly because of the antidotes, such as the daily examination of conscience, it provided to the corruption of the imperial court. No Jesuit achieved the dream of being allowed to evangelize the emperor, in part because a phalanx of eunuchs guarded access. However, even a few eunuchs were converted, as were some ladies of the court.

Ricci Honored

Although Ricci was sometimes harassed and threatened by hostile mobs, he was honored at his death by being allowed to be buried in the imperial city of Beijing, a privilege usually denied to foreigners. A few years after his death an archaeological discovery showed that Christianity (probably Nestorian) had existed in China many centuries before, something that gave the faith renewed prestige.

By 1600, there were other Jesuits in China and about twenty-five hundred converts. As in Japan, the emperor was weak (a fact perhaps not apparent to the missionaries), so that toleration of Christians depended primarily on local authorities, some of whom initiated persecutions from time to time. After Ricci's death, the Jesuits expanded their activities beyond elite circles, and by the end of the seventeenth century there were two hundred thousand Christians in China, almost a hundred times the number at the beginning.

Growth

Franciscans and Dominicans began coming to China in the generation after Ricci's death, as did the Paris Foreign Mission Society, which had been founded under the aegis of the Company of the Blessed Sacrament. As happened in India and Japan, a division once again developed between two different approaches to mission activity.

In Ricci's plan, the stakes were very high, in that the conversion of the mandarins would have led to the conversion of the entire Chinese empire. But the plan essentially failed. The Franciscans had much greater success than the Jesuits with direct appeals to the common people, using a strategy similar to that used to convert the barbarians of the Dark Ages: the promise of release from the power of demons and the prospect of eternal life, combined with concrete things like statues, rosaries, and public processions manifesting divine power. Some of the missionaries were regarded as miracle workers.

Franciscan Methods

While the early Jesuits learned the language of the mandarins, other missionaries had to cope with innumerable local dialects; despite the best efforts, verbal communication between priests and people was

Native Vocations

often poor. A request to the Holy See to allow the liturgy to be translated into Chinese was never answered. But the Latin language was a major barrier to a native priesthood, and the Holy See ruled that Chinese priests could recite the liturgy without understanding the specific words, so long as they understood their general meaning.

With few natives being ordained, expansion of the Church into rural areas often left converts with inadequate pastoral guidance. Trained catechists often served as the leaders of local communities, with occasional visits by a priest to administer the sacraments.

The canonical category of "consecrated virgin" was the means by which women shared in this lay leadership, performing works of charity, instructing the faithful, and administering baptism in those frequent situations where newborn infants were in imminent danger of death. (It was a delicate situation, in that suspicious pagans sometimes claimed that baptism actually killed babies.) Candida Xu (d. 1680) was a Catholic who converted her pagan husband, and after his death, she followed the ancient calling of the holy widow who devoted her life to works of charity and support of the Church. Another ancient pattern that reappeared was that of young women rejecting the husbands chosen for them by their families, in order to live a life of religious dedication. Since the authority of the family was very strong in China, this was sometimes a major point of conflict with the culture.

In 1659, the Holy See established three vicariates in China, each governed by a European bishop but with the intention that they develop a native clergy. Gregory Luo Wenzao (d. 1691), a Franciscan, was the first native Chinese priest and bishop, although his promotion was opposed by some European missionaries.

Schall   Some Jesuits remained active among the mandarins and even got access to the imperial court. In particular, the German Adam Schall (d. 1666), one of the "wise men from the West", gained enormous prestige by accurately predicting an eclipse. He was put in charge of the imperial astronomical office, which was important because the stability of the emperor's reign was thought to depend on a perfect harmony between the earth and the cosmos. Schall made a number of converts. Other Jesuits also served as court astronomers, and the German Jesuit Athanasius Kircher (d.1680), although he did not visit China, compiled the first Chinese dictionary and a Coptic dictionary as well.

When the Manchu Dynasty conquered China in 1644, Schall and other Jesuits were for a time imprisoned. Schall managed to establish good relations with the new rulers, who reprieved him after he had had been sentenced to death on false charges of being a spy and restored him to his position as director of imperial astronomy. (He was denounced even by some of his fellow Jesuits for being too involved with the new regime.)

Throughout the later seventeenth century, the Church in China was divided by what came to be called the "Chinese rites controversy", a disagreement that brought into high relief the ambiguities of inculturation. The principal dispute centered on whether Catholics might participate in certain traditional rituals, some having to do with their own ancestors, others with the figure of Confucius.

"The Chinese Rites"

The Jesuits tolerated the rituals, on the grounds that they were merely a way of honoring people who deserved honor, while the Franciscans and Dominicans insisted that both the ancestors and Confucius were being treated as gods. (Confucius was called by the Chinese word that the missionaries used for "saint", thus making the precise meaning of that word crucial.) The issue involved basic elements of Chinese culture: funeral rites in a society in which honoring one's ancestors was a fundamental obligation, public ceremonies expressing submission to the emperor, and appropriate honor to the philosopher who was considered the wisest of men.

The issue was several times appealed to Rome, with varying results. In 1704, the Holy Office ruled against the Jesuits, a decision that was debated by theologians in Europe and that continued in effect despite occasional minor concessions.

The emperor K'ang-hsi (1661–1722) wrote to the Pope that the disputed rituals were civic in nature, not religious, and he was incensed at what he considered an act of contempt for Chinese customs, while the Jesuits complained that their ministry was severely compromised. A bishop who undertook to enforce the decree was subjected by K'ang-hsi to an inquisition that showed his ignorance of Confucian thought, after which he was expelled. A papal legate sent to uphold the decree died under house arrest by the Portuguese at Macao, acting at the instigation of the Chinese government.

The episode was a major watershed in the history of Chinese Christianity, and in retrospect it appears that both sides in the dispute were in a sense correct. Sophisticated Chinese, such as those ministered to by the Jesuits, might have seen the disputed rituals as largely symbolic, whereas for simple people both their own ancestors and Confucius himself were gods.

Half the missionaries left China after 1704, but, subject to intermittent persecution, the Church survived. A final papal decree in 1742 required that all missionaries take an oath not to tolerate the disputed rituals.

Missionaries had entered Tibet in the sixteenth century, but without lasting effect. Later, the Italian Jesuit Ippolito Desideri (d. 1733) penetrated the almost inaccessible mountain land, where he immersed himself in the culture and tried unsuccessfully for six years to convert the Buddhists. (He denounced the Dalai Lama as a "monstrous idol".)

Tibet

Philippines   The Spanish brought Catholicism to the Philippine Islands—named for the Spanish king—in the mid-sixteenth century. The Church flourished there from the beginning, with Manila serving in a sense as the ecclesiastical center of the entire Far East, the base from which missionaries often set out for other lands.

But the church of the Philippines resembled the church of Latin America more than that of the Far East, since Spain ruled the islands outright rather than depending on trading concessions. Something like the feudal system of landholding was set up, and an intense native piety developed that, as in Latin America, incorporated many pagan elements.

Missionary Expansion

Developments in Missions

Propaganda Fidei

The Holy See regarded missionary activity as of the highest importance, and the office of *Propaganda Fidei* ("spreading the faith")[3] was established in 1622 to oversee missionary activity all over the world. The European powers claimed control over the Church in the colonial lands, so that the king of Portugal, for example, insisted on the right of approving bishops in India. To counteract this, *Propaganda* created the new office of "vicar apostolic"—a bishop who had jurisdiction over a mission territory directly under the Holy See but did not hold title to a diocese.

The Nineteenth Century

Toward the end of the eighteenth century, the missions suffered a severe decline everywhere, because of the suppression of the Jesuits in 1773 and the disruptions of the French Revolution and Napoleonic period. A dramatic missionary revival was part of the general religious revival after 1815. In the first half of the nineteenth century, almost fifty new missionary communities were founded in Europe.

Native Clergy

Gregory XVI, although he had been a cloistered Camaldolese monk, had also been prefect of *Propaganda*, and he had a strong interest in the missions, as did all the popes who followed him. In the twentieth century, Benedict XV strongly reiterated the policies the Holy See had favored almost since the beginning of modern missionary activity: the recruitment of native clergy and urging the missionaries to identify with the native people more than with their own countries. Pius XI appointed a lower-caste Indian bishop, personally consecrated the first native Chinese bishops, and appointed the first native Japanese bishop. In order to coordinate missionary activity, he centralized the apostolate, including the dispersal of funds, under the *Propaganda*.

---

[3] The word *propaganda* only later came to have its negative connotation of partisan falsehood. Literally, it meant merely the dissemination or encouragement of certain ideas.

Monasteries

The missionary presence was not only on the level of the active apostolate. Contemplative monasteries and convents were founded in a number of mission countries, their purpose not to make converts directly but to pray for conversions and to serve as examples of the spiritual power of the faith.

Finances

Whereas earlier missions had been supported either by religious orders or by European governments, in the new missionary era the entire Church was made conscious of her responsibility. The French laywoman Ven. Pauline Jaricot (d. 1862) founded the Society for the Propagation of the Faith to collect small amounts of money from a large number of people on a regular basis; other groups also began collecting funds.

The Whole World

The great missionary revival left almost no part of the globe untouched as, for the first time in history, missionaries were realistically able to obey Christ's command to preach the Gospel to all nations. By 1875, there were six thousand missionaries throughout the world, a disproportionate number of whom were from France. In 1820, there were only 275 native priests in Asia and Africa, but by 1900 there were seven thousand, although there were still no native vicars apostolic or bishops.

Colonialism

Missionaries were considered part of their mother country's "civilizing" process and to some extent necessarily depended on the protection of their governments, but the link between missionary activity and colonialism was tenuous. French missionaries, for example, did not wish to carry out the policies of anticlerical governments at home, and they sometimes clashed with colonial officials. For the first time, Catholic missionaries also found themselves in competition with Protestants, who had belatedly embraced the idea of the conversion of the world.

India

Except for the region around Goa, the Church's presence in India was extremely weak at the beginning of the nineteenth century but then began to revive. The Portuguese government continued to exercise control over the hierarchy, leading the Holy See to set up several vicariates independent of the archbishopric of Goa. Strenuous efforts were made to recruit a native clergy, and catechisms and other necessary books were translated into the Tamil language. Native religious communities were established, and when one such order of sisters refused to teach girls of lower castes, a second community was founded expressly for that purpose. By 1870, there were a million Catholics in India, although the Church remained weak in the north.

On the whole, India has perhaps the most religious culture in the world, in which both Hinduism and Islam continue to exert significant influence. Christians are officially tolerated but are often harassed and subject to mob violence. There are abundant religious vocations.

Japan

After Western gunboats—unbidden—entered Japanese ports in the 1850s, some Japanese recognized that Western technological superiority was the key to power, even to survival, and in a dramatic reversal of the draconian policies of the previous 250 years, Japan suddenly opened itself to the outside world. In the next decade, a conspiracy of younger men effected the Meiji Restoration—named after an imperial title—by making use of the emperor's semi-divine authority to begin adopting the material civilization of the West, even including its clothes and architecture.

Openness to the West, the new rulers reluctantly recognized, required freedom for Christian missionaries, who soon began entering Japan in significant numbers, although conversions remained rather sparse. A vicariate was created in 1876.

The Hidden Church
In one of the most remarkable episodes in the entire history of the Church, French missionaries discovered a small number of secret Catholics living around Nagasaki, a people who had been preserving their faith without priests for over two hundred years. The Meiji government first arrested these survivors but released them after appeals from the European powers. These secret Christians recognized the missionaries on the basis of oral traditions concerning the Virgin Mary and the birth of Jesus and the fact that Jesus lived for thirty-three years and died on the Cross. They had been baptizing their own children and knew the teaching that an act of perfect contrition would remove all sins without priestly absolution.

Education
Although the religion of only a very small minority, Catholicism played some role in Japanese life. In the early twentieth century, German Jesuits opened Sophia University in Tokyo, which became one of the most respected educational institutions in the country, although it did not engage in active proselytization.

Shintoism
In the twentieth century, the government opposed Buddhism and promoted patriotic Shintoism. As Japanese nationalism and militarism grew more intense in the period between the world wars, some Catholics had qualms of conscience about participating in ceremonies to honor the war dead, fearing that this involved a pagan religion. After investigation, *Propaganda* in 1939 allowed such participation,

thereby, in effect, rescinding the decrees against the "Chinese rites" that had been issued in the eighteenth century.

World War II

On the eve of World War II, the hundred thousand Japanese Catholics were shepherded by native bishops. But all foreign missionaries were ordered to leave the country (not all complied).

The city of Nagasaki, the historic center of Japanese Catholicism, was one of the targets of the American atomic bomb. Takashi Nagai, a convert to Catholicism and a survivor of the blast, lived in the rubble of the ruined city, dying of radiation poisoning and advocating the healing of his people through the renunciation of militarism and reconciliation with the Allies. He came to be respected by both Catholic and non-Christian Japanese as a national hero.

A Secular Culture

After the war, Japan, perhaps because of American pressure, allowed greater religious freedom than any other non-Western country, and there was a wave of conversions to Catholicism. But Japan also took on the characteristics of a modern secular culture, pragmatic and materialistic in its outlook and seemingly uninterested in religion, so that the number of Catholics never went above half a million.

China

In China, the elite gradually lost interest in Western science, and hence in Western missionaries. There were intermittent persecutions, although missionaries continued to arrive. As they would soon do to Japan, the European powers after 1840 forced the imperial government of China to grant substantial concessions in return for trade, including "treaty ports" and other territories semi-independent of Chinese rule, where missionaries could work freely, under the armed protection of the European powers. By 1870, there were four hundred thousand Chinese Catholics.

The End of the Empire

By the end of the century, the old Empire was tottering, while the authority of Confucianism was weakened by the European incursions. Unlike in Japan, the movement for change owed much to missionary influence. But Christianity in China was thereby identified with the most blatant kind of European imperialism, and Christians were the inevitable targets of anti-foreign movements.

Hostility

Even works of charity could be grounds for hostility. Because of the ancient custom of leaving unwanted babies (mostly girls) to die of exposure, nuns took abandoned infants into their orphanages, but they were then sometimes accused of using the babies for body parts. The nuns also drew hostility for opposing the custom of painfully binding girls' feet to achieve the smallness that was considered attractive.

Martyrs

There were a number of Christian martyrs, and on several occasions, British and French troops invaded the country to put down rebellions and to enforce freedom for missionary activity. With the support of the imperial government, over thirty thousand Catholics were killed in the Boxer Rebellion of 1900 (so-called because its organizers practiced the martial arts). The failure of the rebellion soon led to revolution and to the deposition of the last emperor in 1912, by which time Western secularism had made inroads among Chinese intellectuals.

Growth

In 1926, Pius XI consecrated six native Chinese bishops in Rome, the next year a Catholic university was opened in Beijing, and monasticism flourished. On the eve of World War II, there were over three million Catholics in China, including a number of native priests and religious. A remarkable story was that of the Chinese foreign minister Lu Tse-tiang (d. 1949), who married a Belgian lady, converted to Catholicism, became a Benedictine monk after his wife's death, and was eventually elected abbot of a monastery in Belgium.

World War II

Catholic religious were conducting over nine thousand Chinese elementary schools at the beginning of World War II, but during the 1920s, civil wars erupted in China among various regional warlords. An organized nationalist movement under Chiang Kai-Shek (d. 1975) for the most part supported Christianity, and an organized insurgent communist movement under Mao Zedong (d. 1976) was antireligious. The Japanese conquests of China during the 1930s brought great hardships, in which some Catholics played heroic resistance roles.

Communism

After the war, the Church quickly revived. Half the clergy were Chinese, more missionaries began to arrive, and in 1946, Archbishop Thomas Tien of Peking (Beijing, d. 1967), a Divine Word father, became the first East Asian cardinal. But with the triumph of Mao's communists in 1949, severe persecution began. Within a few years, some missionaries, such as the American Maryknoll Bishop James A. Walsh (d. 1981), were sent to prison for long terms, and all others were expelled. Many Catholics were killed; many more were imprisoned; and Tien and others went into exile.

While the practice of Christianity was never officially outlawed, the government sought to break its back. A favored tactic was to gather a village together and accuse its priest of numerous crimes, encouraging his parishioners to heap yet further condemnations on him. In the end, he was usually killed, along with those parishioners who failed to cooperate in his "trial".

The "Patriotic Church"

In 1957, the communist government established a "Patriotic Church" made up of Catholics who professed loyalty to the state and allowed the state to approve their bishops, while members of the "Underground Church" refused such cooperation and remained subject to persecution. Several bishops cooperated in the establishment of the "Patriotic Church", perhaps thinking that it would be a means of continuing to provide sacraments for the people. However, when those bishops began consecrating other bishops, who were appointed by the government without papal approval, schism resulted.

During the worst period of Mao's terror, even the Patriotic Church was persecuted, although conditions began to improve after his death. By 2010, the government was to some extent cooperating with the Vatican in the appointment of bishops, although there were still serious tensions.

Korea

Catholicism came to Korea in a unique way, when in 1789 a Korean diplomat, Yi Sunghun, was converted by Catholic priests in China. He returned home and quickly made other converts who, based on their slight knowledge of the early Church, elected a bishop and several priests who began celebrating Mass even though they were not ordained.

When they discovered their error, they imported a Chinese priest, Bl. James Zhou Wenmu, to be their pastor. He was sheltered by a wealthy widow, Bl. Columba Kang Wen-suk (Kim), until she, Zhou Wen-mo, and Yi Sunghun were discovered and executed in 1801. Missionaries were sent from France, but persecution was severe, with eight thousand Catholics put to death in a single episode. A modest recovery occurred in the later nineteenth century, when France undertook to protect the Catholic missions in what eventually became a predominantly Protestant country. North Korea fell under brutal communist oppression after World War II, and persecution there was often savage. On a visit to Korea in 1984, Pope John Paul II canonized 103 out of an estimated ten thousand Korean martyrs, the first such ceremony ever held outside the Vatican.

Vietnam

The Indochina (the peninsula on which Vietnam, among other countries, is found) missions were in a relatively healthy state at the beginning of the nineteenth century, demonstrated by the fact that Catholics there remained faithful in the face of a ferocious persecution that lasted for fifty years after 1820. The French subsequently established hegemony in the region, and Catholics, although a small minority, played an important role in the society.

After the Second World War, having been freed from the Japanese, French Indochina erupted in rebellion against the mother country. When the French finally withdrew, the United States undertook to defeat the insurgents, many of whom were communists. At the time, there were almost three million Vietnamese Catholics, mainly in the South, ruled by the president Ngo Dinh Diem (d. 1963), a Catholic whom the rebels accused of being a Western puppet. The United States first connived at Diem's murder, then abandoned the war altogether, which led to the inevitable triumph of the communist North and the severe persecution of Catholics, which continued intermittently into the next century.

The Philippines   The Philippines were lost to Spain in the Spanish–American War of 1898 and became an American protectorate. That in turn provoked a full-scale native rebellion, part of which involved the schismatic Philippine Independent church. There was a good deal of resentment toward the Franciscans because they owned great estates, and the American government acquiesced in the seizure and redistribution of those lands. For a time, the church in the Philippines was governed by bishops from the United States, but gradually a native hierarchy was established.

After World War II, the United States belatedly kept its promise of restoring Philippine independence and, as in Latin America, the Church often played a crucial role in politics. Cardinal Jaime Sin of Manila (d. 2005) rallied hundreds of thousands of people for prayers and peaceful demonstrations against the tyrranical regime of Ferdinand Marcos (1965–1986). Massive outpourings of people caused Marcos to flee the country and brought the pious Corazon Aquino to power (1986–1992). The Philippines, 80 percent of whose people are Catholics, remains by far the largest Catholic country in Asia, with a relatively high rate of church attendance (over half) and an abundance of religious vocations.

The Near East   While the majority of Catholics in the Near East were members of Uniate Rites, official protection by the French government allowed Latin-Rite missionaries to become active in the nineteenth century. (Napoleon III once intervened militarily in Lebanon after a massacre of Christians by Muslims.) Because the Muslims had shown themselves extremely resistant to conversion, missionaries in the Near East settled on the strategy of making their presence known through works of charity and education, so that over time the Christian spirit might penetrate the culture. Numerous hospitals and orphanages were established, and the Jesuits in particular founded several colleges. World War I brought an end to French protection, and after that, there was intermittent persecution of the Church, especially by Turkey.

North Africa   North Africa had been one of the great centers of the early Church, but the Christian presence, except in the northeast corner of the continent, was wiped out by the successive barbarian and Muslim invasions of the Dark Ages. Jesuits went to North Africa in the late sixteenth century and succeeded in converting a king of Abyssinia, but his successors repudiated his action, and the missionaries were all martyred. Beginning also in the sixteenth century, there was some Catholic presence in sub-Saharan Africa, because of trading posts, set up mainly by the Portuguese. But these were swept away during the chaotic period of 1773 to 1815.

Missionaries began to return to Africa with the colonial conquests of the nineteenth century. France conquered Algeria in 1830, but the anticlericalism of the liberal monarchies imposed restrictions on missionary activity in the colony. For diplomatic reasons, the government encouraged Islam even as it discouraged Catholicism.

Lavigerie

But then Archbishop Lavigerie of Algiers (see Chapter Eleven above, p. 368) defied Napoleon III and embarked on a vigorous program of practical charity and evangelization. Seeing Algeria as the gateway to the African interior, Lavigerie founded the White Sisters and the White Fathers, who first worked among the North Africans, speaking Arabic and wearing white robes and red African-style hats. They had minimal success, although the Church remained an important presence through her charitable and educational institutions. The Holy Ghost Fathers were founded by Jakob Liebermann (d. 1852), a convert from Judaism, specifically to minister to oppressed blacks in Africa and the Caribbean. To further this ministry, they encouraged native vocations.

Foucauld

St. Charles de Foucauld (d. 1916) was a French soldier who lived a dissolute life but underwent conversion and entered the Trappists in North Africa. Recognizing the missionaries' lack of success, he attempted to bear witness to the Gospel by living as a hermit on the edge of the desert and ministering to the poor. He was regarded by the Muslim Berber tribesmen as a holy man but made no converts. Later, he moved his hermitage even farther into the interior of the continent. However, with the First World War raging in Europe, he was murdered by tribesmen who accused him of being a French spy. The Little Brothers and Sisters of the Sacred Heart were founded later in accord with a rule he had drawn up in expectation of attracting companions.

Missionaries gradually ventured southward into African regions previously little known to Europeans, to some extent dependent on the authority of the Portuguese, French, and Belgians who laid claim to those territories. Africa presented its own obstacles and opportunities for evangelization. Traditional African culture was deeply religious, in that the reality of the supernatural was taken very seriously but often in the form of belief in sorcerers and devils, who were thought to be very powerful and in need of placating.

Africa

Obstacles

The practice of polygamy was common in many places, and there was no tradition of celibacy. In addition to native cults, Islam also was strong in the African interior, where the White Fathers fought against both polygamy and the still-flourishing slave trade. A number of the earliest missionaries were massacred, even when protected by companies of papal guards whom Lavigerie recruited. In 1885–1887, the king of Buganda (modern Uganda) ordered the brutal execution of eighty Catholics, including some of his own young pages who refused to submit to sodomy. St. Charles Lwanga and his companions were dismembered and burned, the first martyrs of sub-Saharan Africa.

Growth

The faith in Africa spread with some rapidity, and the missionaries adopted a method previously used in the Chinese missions—training lay catechists to work in remote rural villages between visits by priests. The first native bishop was appointed in 1939, and the first cardinal, Laurean Rugambwa (d. 1997) of Bukeba (Tanzania), in 1961.

The End of Colonialism

The end of colonialism in Africa after World War II led in some places to a rejection of Christianity as an imperialist imposition, even though the Church generally opposed such practices as *apartheid* (segregation) in South Africa. The persecution of the Church by some of the new governments, as in the Congo, often had the effect of stimulating a revival of Catholicism. The most severe persecution has been in the Sudan, where for decades the Muslim government has in effect tried to exterminate Christianity.

Some of the newer African nations (Rwanda, Burundi) were split by bitter, even genocidal, civil wars between different tribal groups. Catholics, including clergy and religious, were inevitably drawn into those conflicts, often as victims or as ministers to the victims but sometimes as perpetrators of atrocities.

Oceania

In some ways the starkest challenge to mission activity in the nineteenth century was in the islands of Oceania, which were hitherto almost unknown to Europeans and which manifested a wide variety of cultures. A number of missionaries were summarily slaughtered, some eaten by cannibals, upon landing on an unfamiliar island.

Hawaii

When the first French missionaries landed in the Sandwich Islands (kingdom of Hawaii) they were forcibly expelled by men who were functioning both as traders and as Protestant missionaries. When the queen obtained the help of the French to allow the priests to return, there was an international incident which involved armed conflict between Catholics and Protestants.

Damien of Molokai

Few saints in the history of the Church have received, both in his own lifetime and later, the fame and admiration of St. Damien (Joseph) de Veuster (d. 1889). The Flemish priest of the order of the Sacred Hearts of Jesus and Mary volunteered to work among society's ultimate outcasts, the lepers confined to the Hawaiian island of Molokai, knowing he would never be allowed to leave the island and would most likely die of the disease.

In the face of the vile smells and hideous bodily deformations caused by Hansen's Disease, Damien was practically the only person of his time willing actually to touch lepers, whom he nursed in their squalid huts and eventually prepared for burial, even digging their graves. He farmed and with his own hands built chapels, hospitals, and houses. Through preaching, confession, the Mass, and eucharistic adoration, he attempted to instill courage and hope in people who were sunk in despair and who often compensated by orgies. Confined to the island, he made his own confession by shouting his sins to a priest on board a ship in the harbor.

His superiors considered Damien impetuous and foolhardy and were suspicious of the worldwide publicity he inspired. They were not the only ones: a Protestant minister in Hawaii wrote a defaming letter about Damien, which was subsequently published in a Sydney Presbyterian newspaper and then famously rebutted by the non-Catholic author Robert Louis Stevenson.

Mariane Cope

Eventually, reliable helpers began to arrive on Molokai, and after Damien's death, one of these, the German-American nun St. Marianne Cope (d. 1918), helped turn the mission into a flourishing center of both physical and spiritual ministration.

Latin America

The great irony of Latin America is the fact that, while in theory it is the most thoroughly Catholic region of the globe, it has always been mission territory, due to the chronic shortage of native priests. During the 1950s, some dioceses in the United States began to send their priests there, because of the dearth of native clergy.

Economic Problems

Perhaps the root of a troubled history was the survival of a system that was in many ways still feudal, with great wealth in the hands of a relatively few large landowners and the majority of the people poor peasants. Economic modernization did not necessarily lead to improvement, as peasants who moved to the cities as laborers were forced to accept low wages and faced often chronic unemployment.

Historically, the Church in Latin America tended to support conservative governments that were tolerant of religion and allowed the Church influence in critical areas of society such as education. This policy, however, required virtually ignoring the social doctrines of the Church, until after Word War II, the bishops began cautiously to endorse economic and social change and found it increasingly necessary to criticize governments. Land reform became a fundamental issue, although seldom resolved.

Dictators

But there was only a weak tradition of liberal reform in Latin America, so that the path of change was seldom orderly and peaceful and often erupted into open violence between the forces of order and the forces of change. Typically, as with the quasi-fascist dictator Juan Perón of Argentina (d. 1974), a strong ruler came to power with the support of the military, only to be later deposed by the same military, with all democratic rights suspended.

Cuba

Cuba was one of the least religious of Latin American countries. The bishops attempted to remain neutral as pressure for change built up, and they were at first cautiously receptive to the movement of Fidel Castro, which took power in the revolution of 1959. Castro, however, soon proclaimed Cuba a communist state and began imposing severe restrictions on the Church that still remained in place half a century later.

Frei

In a unique episode in Latin American history, during the 1960s, the Christian Democratic Party in Chile, under Eduardo Frei (d. 1982), was able to effect social and economic change based to some extent on Catholic social principles, although the basic problem of land reform was not solved. But Frei's demonstration that change was possible led to demands for still swifter and more radical change, and after he left office, a Marxist dictatorship took power, only to be overthrown by a right-wing dictatorship supported by the military.

Martyrs

The entrenched forces in Latin America were often ruthless, as were the unofficial "death squads" in Argentina that during the 1980s murdered hundreds of people suspected of opposing the government. In El Salvador, at different times, Archbishop Oscar Romero (d. 1980), six Jesuit teachers, and four nuns from the United States were murdered because of their opposition to the regime. On the other side, leftist guerillas espousing Marxist ideas also employed assassination and other terrorist methods.

Costa Rica

Costa Rica remained one of the most prosperous and stable Latin American countries and also one of a handful of countries in the world that continued to recognize Catholicism as its official religion.

Protestant Missions

After World War II, various Protestant groups began to make Latin America a center of missionary activity, on the grounds that the prevalent Catholicism did not represent the true Gospel. Over the ensuing decades, Protestants had modest success, because of the priest shortage and because popular Catholic piety was vulnerable to the charge of superstition.

Altogether the number of Catholics in Asia grew from 12.5 million to 121 million between 1900 and 2010 and from 6.5 million to 128 million in Africa during the same period. Around 1965, the great modern era of missionary activity came to an abrupt end, partly because of the crisis that followed the Second Vatican Council, partly because some of the mission churches had become self-sustaining. Africa, the Philippines, and India in particular now began sending priests to Western countries, almost as reverse missionaries.

Mission Growth

I3   The New Nations

Commonalities

The religious histories of Canada, the United States, and Australia belong together. All three were at one time part of the British Empire, English became their national language, and in many ways the British heritage was their dominant cultural influence. Each was officially mission territory until the twentieth century, but each depended on foreign clergy, especially Irish, not primarily to convert non-Christian natives but to care for the huge numbers of Catholic immigrants. With some regional exceptions, bishops of Irish descent were dominant in the three countries until at least the middle of the twentieth century.

Modernity

They were the New Nations because—politically, economically, and socially—they were the first truly modern societies. It was there that the Church first came to terms with a kind of modernity different from that of Europe, learning by trial and error how to exist in a democratic society.

The British Enlightenment

To a great extent, the New Nations were different from Europe because the British Enlightenment coexisted with organized religion. Unlike in Europe and Latin America, there was never any attempt to use the power of the state to suppress Christianity. Anticlericalism, which is mainly a phenomenon of dominantly Catholic countries, was mild.

Toleration

In time, the influence of the British Enlightenment achieved what European Liberalism promised only hypocritically—full religious toleration. Any attempt to suppress religion would have been fatal to the secularist cause, since each of the New Nations was dominated by a strong Protestantism whose hegemony survived until the middle of the twentieth century in Canada and Australia and even beyond that in the United States. Planted in the New Nations were evangelical Anglicanism, Methodism, the Oxford Movement, and Scottish Calvinism. Additionally, in the United States were various indigenous religions and the Puritanism that evolved into Evangelicalism and Fundamentalism.

Religious prejudice merged with chauvinism, so that Catholics were often accused of disloyalty to their adopted countries, but to some extent Catholics' sheer numbers protected them from the antagonisms of that culture. Catholics in the New Nations endured a great deal of hostility, but no one was ever executed for his faith, very few were killed by mob violence, and few were even imprisoned.

Anti-Catholicism

Anti-Catholic antagonism, as by the Masonic Order, was Protestant in character, not militantly secular or anticlerical. The Protestant ascendancy created a paradoxical situation for Catholics, in that they were often a harassed minority but at the same time the religiosity of the culture meant that Christian belief of some kind was almost a social imperative.

Christianity Assumed

While Catholics were on the defensive toward Protestants, unbelievers were on the defensive toward Protestant Christians, so that Catholics were mostly spared the acids of anti-religious modernity. Christianity was simply taken for granted as the foundation of society, and skeptics were kept on the margins. Unlike in Europe, the governments of the New Nations deputized religious ministers to witness marriage vows that were held binding in civil society and witness the signing of civil marriage licenses. There was seldom any threat to the existence of church schools, rather the major conflicts—sometimes very sharp—were over whether the government should fund such schools. Religious education flourished at all levels, often encouraged by the state.

The Faith of the Immigrant

Unlike other parts of the world, in both the New Nations and the British Isles themselves, immigration—both from abroad and from country to city—did not lead to massive loss of faith, a fact that was especially remarkable in the case of the Irish, most of whom had no experience of urban life prior to migrating. Instead, those urban cultures proved to be supportive of belief, and pastoral methods were successful, so that for the most part it was only in the British Isles and its former colonies that the industrial working class remained practicing Christians.

Canada

The Vikings

The first Europeans to reach North America were a party under the Viking chief Leif Erikson, which reached Newfoundland around the year 1000. After the initial voyages, which led briefly to a settlement, there was no further European contact until 1500, and even then, the European powers were slow to exploit North America, because it did not seem likely to yield great profits.

Quebec

The French founded the trading post of Quebec in 1608, but for a long time, New France was sparsely populated. Its chief economic resource was furs, requiring many of the males to be gone from the settlements for long periods of time living in the wild, and the colony had a reputation for moral and spiritual laxness. Near the mid-century, a group of French Jesuits—among the most heroic saints in the entire history of the Church—came to New France for the purpose of converting the Indians and had some success among the Hurons.

Jogues and Other Martyrs

St. Isaac Jogues (d. 1646) was captured by the ferocious Iroquois (lethal enemies of the Huron) had his fingers chewed off, and was saved from death by being ransomed, in what became New York State, by a Netherlandish Protestant trader. Jogues returned briefly to France where, scrupulous in observing the rubrics, he would not celebrate Mass until he had received a papal dispensation from the requirements concerning the holding of the sacred elements at Mass. He returned to New France and was soon martyred by the Iroquois.

This was followed three years later by the death of five other Jesuits, including St. John de Brébeuf (d. 1649), who had worked among the Hurons for over thirty years. In each case, martyrdom was by a slow process of dismembering and burning, followed by cannibalism.[1] Brébeuf was greatly admired for his strength and dedication, and the Indians ate his heart in order to assimilate his courage. But the mission was completely destroyed.

Kateri Tekakwitha

St. Catherine (Kateri) Tekakwitha (d. 1680) was the orphaned daughter of a pagan Iroquois father and a Catholic mother. She lived among the French Canadians and was venerated for her piety and works of charity.

The Missions

Missionary activity among the Canadian Indians was hampered by the fact that they were a semi-nomadic people, which forced the early Jesuits often to follow them on their hunting journeys, sleeping on the ground, and eating their food. Some missionaries attempted, with limited success, to gather the Indians into villages where they could live the sedentary lives of farmers, since experience showed that the converts would abandon the faith if they drifted away from the mission centers.

Jesuit Relations

The missionaries made strenuous efforts to learn the native languages, compiling dictionaries and other written records of those unwritten tongues. Their *Relations*—detailed reports to their superiors in Europe on the state of the missions—paid close attention to native cultures.

A New Power

As in the Dark Ages of Europe, the missionaries' credibility rested to some extent on the belief that they possessed powers superior to those of the Indian *shamans*. The missionaries helped the Indians by their rudimentary medical knowledge, but this was a two-edged sword: when

---

[1] The novel and film *Black Robe* is a fictionalized account of the story.

diseases broke out, the missionaries were sometimes blamed for causing them, which they may sometimes have done inadvertently.

Native Religion

The Indians had their own religious beliefs, which the Jesuits tried to
use as a basis for proselytization. As always, the problems of inculturation were subtle. The Indians believed in the Great Spirit, but the
missionaries were reluctant to apply that term to God, lest potential
converts see it as confirmation of their old beliefs. Because some of
the Indians practiced cannibalism, the missionaries also did not emphasize the doctrine of the Real Presence of Christ in the Eucharist. As
in many other cultures, polygamy was a major barrier to real conversion.

Catholic Leaders

New France was at first under the bishop of Rouen (France), but
Quebec was made a diocese in 1674, its first bishop Bl. François Laval
(d. 1708). The colony produced some religious vocations. Laval started
a seminary; French-born St. Marguerite Bourgeoys (d. 1700) founded
the Sisters of Notre Dame of Montreal; and St. Marguerite d'Youville
(d. 1771) started the Sisters of Charity of Quebec (the Gray Nuns).
The French Ursuline Marie of the Incarnation (d. 1672) migrated to
Quebec and taught children while also living the life of a mystic.

Religion in the Colony

The British Conquest

After the British conquest of Quebec in 1763, the new government
sponsored an influx of Protestant settlers for the express purpose of
ensuring a Protestant ascendancy, and it forcibly deported many of the
French (Acadians) living in the eastern maritime districts.[2] The government also tried to restrict the liberty of Catholics, but when Catholics engaged in passive resistance, then rebuffed an appeal to support
the American rebellion in 1776, the crown granted them limited toleration. The relatively few native clergy were for a while supplemented by French priests fleeing the Revolution.

Catholic Loyalty

During the War of 1812, Canadian Catholics once again proved their
loyalty to the crown, which therefore removed the remaining restrictions on their freedom. Joseph-Octave Plessis of Quebec (d. 1822),
the first Canadian archbishop, greatly expanded the Church's network
of schools and began the policy of urging the peasantry to remain on
the land in order preserve their culture.

Religious Division

Canada was officially divided, Protestants predominating in Upper Canada (Ontario) and Catholics in the eastern part of the country, especially Lower Canada (Quebec). But an anti-British uprising by the

[2] The subject of the poem *Evangeline*, by Henry Wadsworth Longfellow.

Québecois in the 1830s, which the bishops opposed, led to reprisals, and in 1840, the two colonies were reunited, which gave Protestants a substantial majority. However, the Catholic minority proved to be politically skillful and managed to retain their full rights, including public funding for their schools.

Growth of the Church in Canada

Canada received its first cardinal, Elzéar-Alexandre Taschereau of Quebec (d. 1898), in 1886, and in 1908, the country was officially declared to be no longer a mission territory. Outside Quebec province, there was still considerable anti-Catholicism, often a legacy of the Orangemen of the seventeenth century and often centered in Masonic lodges, but after the united Dominion of Canada was established in 1867, the Church, under mostly Irish bishops, grew and flourished in other provinces besides Quebec, especially because of Irish and eastern European immigration. Catholics became prominent in Ontario, where Toronto eventually became Canada's major see.

In the more remote western and prairie provinces, Catholics were especially ministered to by the Oblates of Mary Immaculate, who had gone to these remote regions earlier in the century to convert the Indians. In the latter part of the century, missionaries from both Canada and the United States began to evangelize the natives of the far North, often loosely called Eskimos. In Alaska, the Jesuits were in the unusual position of being in competition with a group which did not ordinarily proselytize—the Russian Orthodox, who had made a number of native converts while the territory was under Russian rule.

The Culture of Quebec

The culture of Quebec, where Catholics virtually controlled the school system, was of the kind that the Enlightenment had undermined in Europe. Nowhere did Catholicism permeate every aspect of life as it did there: intense piety; a large number of religious vocations; the clergy as the natural community leaders; an unusually high birth rate, with divorce not permitted; and a tenacious attachment to the French language. The Québecois were sometimes dissenters from national policy, opposing massive immigration for fear that it would dilute French identity and rebuffing the call for volunteers in World War I.

The shrine of St. Anne de Beaupré at Quebec became a major pilgrimage place, as did St. Joseph's Oratory in Montreal, which attracted pilgrims because of St. André Bessette (d. 1937), a Holy Cross brother whose ill health and lack of education led to his being assigned the most menial tasks but who gained a reputation for holiness and miraculous cures.

Duplessis

Quebec's status as the most Catholic society in the world climaxed during the premiership of Maurice Duplessis (d. 1959), when its clergy functioned as political and social leaders and its largely rural economy, customs, language, and political loyalties were all intimately tied to religion. Duplessis' *Union Nationale* was often corrupt, and it systematically ignored Catholic social teaching, but it protected both French identity and the privileged place of the Church. For a time, the *Union Nationale* had the tacit support of the Holy See, to the point where Pius XII even removed from office an archbishop who opposed Duplessis.

Liberal Catholics

Effective opposition to the *Union Nationale* was launched in the early 1960s by a group of Catholic intellectuals who planned the long-term modernization of Quebec society. The group included the future Canadian Prime Minister Pierre Elliot Trudeau (d. 2000) and was supported at first by Cardinal Paul-Émile Léger of Montreal (d. 1991).

Part of its program was the repeal of laws against divorce, contraception, and pornography, a repeal that, coinciding with the worldwide upheaval dubbed "the Sixties", produced a powerful hedonistic reaction. Trudeau was the symbol of a new kind of Catholicism that had little regard for doctrinal orthodoxy or traditional morality but understood itself almost entirely in terms of liberal social programs.

Religious Decline

In the years following the Second Vatican Council (1962–1965), the key signs of religious vitality in Quebec—church attendance, religious vocations, marital stability, and birth rate—declined dramatically, and there was a strong reaction against clerical authority of any kind, as popular culture zestfully embraced hedonistic ways. By 2010, Canada had the lowest birth rate in the Americas and one of the lowest rates of church attendance.

Education

Catholics entered into a distinctive arrangement with the state-sponsored university system, founding their own residential colleges. Laval University at Quebec City and St. Michael's of Toronto, under the Basilian Fathers, eventually became two of the leading centers of Thomistic philosophy in the world.

Unlike in the United States, Canadian Catholics were successful in getting state support for their schools in most provinces. However, by the twenty-first century, some provincial governments were mandating curricular changes that went against Catholic teaching, especially on sexual morality.

The United States

Ethnic Zones

What would eventually become the United States of America was in colonial times divided roughly into three zones: the Spanish Southwest; the Protestant, chiefly English, East Coast; and the French Mississippi Valley. Each had a quite distinct religious history.

The Spanish　　Francisco de Coronado (d. 1554) led an expedition, which included a priest, through the Southwest in 1540, shortly after the Spanish had claimed Florida.

Santa Fe

Santa Fe ("holy faith") was founded in 1610. Franciscans came to New Mexico late in the sixteenth century, setting up *reducciónes* (gatherings) for the Indians, whose settled way of life in *pueblas* (villages) enabled the missionaries to enjoy some success. But here as elsewhere, they had to mount opposition to native customs, especially polygamy, and they found the Spanish soldiers as much a hindrance as a help. Unlike the more scholarly Jesuits of New France, the Franciscans seldom learned the Indian languages and instead required their converts to memorize the Latin or Spanish words for the doctrines of the Church.

In 1680, a major Indian rebellion killed twenty-one Franciscans and many others, temporarily wiping out the Spanish settlements, which were later reestablished. The *Penitentes*—a confraternity of men who wore hoods and cloaks, carried the cross in procession, and engaged in public acts of penance like scourging—began early in the Southwest and flourished long after the mission era ended.

California Missions

The Italian Jesuit Eusebio Kino (d. 1711) came to the Southwest shortly after the 1680 rebellion, and the bishop of Durango (Mexico) made him "vicar of California", which then included Arizona. It was Kino who established the first of the California missions.

After the Jesuits were suppressed in the Spanish domains in 1767, Franciscans from Mexico were sent to California to continue missions. Eventually, there was a chain of twenty-one, stretching from San Diego to San Francisco and including at their peak perhaps twenty thousand Indians.

The greatest of the California missionaries was the Spanish Franciscan Bl. Junipero Serra (d. 1784), who founded nine missions, traveling up and down the Pacific coast mainly on foot. Serra was regarded as a saint in his lifetime and practiced penances that may have contributed to his death (for instance, when preaching he expressed repentance for his own sins by repeatedly striking himself hard on the chest with a stone).

The Mission System

The missions were communities from which the Indians, most of whom had been forest-dwellers, were allowed only an occasional "vacation". They lived communally—married couples together, unmarried men and women in separate houses that were locked at night—all engaged in common agricultural and craft labor.

There were to be no forced conversions, but those Indians who did convert thereby came under the authority of the missionaries. The regime was paternalistic, based frankly on the belief that the Indians were childlike and therefore required both love and a firm hand. (Some Spaniards dubbed themselves "reasonable people" in contrast to the Indians, a designation Serra rejected.)

The missionaries sought to make their communities self-sufficient in every way and to that end implemented a strict daily schedule of prayer, work, and rest. Runaways were forcibly returned, and, as in Europe itself, corporal punishment was inflicted on those who violated the laws. European clothes were worn, churches were built with adobe mud but in the baroque style, and Spanish was the common language, since there were over fifty Indian dialects in California and many Indians could not understand each other.

Liturgy
The Indians were found to love music and imagery, so the friars made use of both for purposes of evangelization, encouraging native artists to compose sacred songs, paint religious scenes, and act out dramas illustrating the life of Christ. The missionaries often preached about the terrors of Hell that awaited the unrepentant.

Pagan Survivals
As had occurred after the conversion of Rome, the missionaries sought to christianize the Indians' calendar through the observance of holy days in place of pagan feasts. As with every other enterprise of mass conversion in the history of the Church, the Indian converts retained many of their old customs and beliefs, on the border between what was merely social and what was religious. The liturgy on feast days spilled over into *fiestas*—celebrations that retained pagan elements— and many Indians probably lived in a dual religious world in which the old deities and powers were still real.

The missionaries, who often spoke of their loneliness, scrupulously observed all Church laws. Long before California was a wine- producing area, for example, the failure of wine to arrive from Mexico might prevent the celebration of Mass for long periods.

The End of the Missions
The era of the California missions was relatively brief. Enlightenment influences had caused the Jesuits to be suppressed in Spain, and by the 1770s, the same influences had reached California, causing the government to reorganize the Indians into self-governing *pueblas* independent of mission control. Serra opposed the experiment, which soon failed.

Around 1800, the Indian population began to decline sharply, because of disease. When Mexico won its independence from Spain, California passed to Mexican rule. In 1833, when only a minority of the missions still had resident priests, the Mexican government decreed their complete secularization and appropriated their lands.

Texas

Missions were established in Texas also in the early eighteenth century, but many were later abandoned. Mission San Antonio became a fort (the famous Alamo).

Florida

On the East Coast, the first permanent settlement in what would become the United States was St. Augustine, in what would later be Florida (1565). Founded by the Spanish, it was eventually taken by the English and lost its Hispanic character.

The English   *Maryland*

In 1634, Charles I of England appointed a Catholic convert, Cecil Calvert, Lord Baltimore (d. 1675), to be proprietor of the new territory of Maryland, which was officially named for Queen Henrietta Maria (d. 1669), although Calvert probably intended to honor the Virgin Mary. (The first settlement was called St. Mary's.)

Maryland was not a Catholic colony, merely a place where Catholics could worship freely. The ships Ark and Dove—the "Catholic Mayflowers"—brought the first settlers, including two Jesuits, although a majority of the settlers were Protestants. Soon an attack by Protestant Virginians burned St. Mary's and forced the governor and the two Jesuits to flee briefly. Catholic estates were plundered and four Catholics were hanged.

Toleration

Subsequently, the Maryland Toleration Act forbade harassment or persecution of anyone who believed in Jesus Christ, making Maryland the only colony, other than predominantly Baptist Rhode Island, to allow this freedom. Despite the fact that the Calverts were in effect the owners of the colony, events there depended heavily on the English government. The Toleration Act was passed a few months after Charles I was beheaded in a rebellion led by Puritans. Protestants soon seized the government of Maryland and repealed the Act; however, it was reenacted at the Restoration of the monarchy in 1660.

After the Glorious Revolution overthrew the Catholic James II in 1688, Maryland was made a royal colony, the English penal laws against Catholics were declared to be in force, and conformity to the Church of England was required. The laws were enforced somewhat irregularly, but they could be quite stringent, even to the point of requiring Catholic widows to be deprived of their children. Similar laws existed in the other English colonies, although there was some Catholic presence in Quaker Pennsylvania.

Catholic Life

Catholic life in Maryland mirrored Catholic life in England itself, in that it was centered on the estates of the gentry and dependent on the sufferance of the government. Some Catholics remained influential, but there were apostasies, including members of the Calvert family.

The Jesuits

The Jesuits supported themselves by farms of their own which, like those of the gentry, were often worked by slaves. Some effort was made to convert the Indians. The few priests traveled constantly on horseback to visit small communities where Mass was usually celebrated and baptisms, confessions, marriages, and funerals conducted in private homes.

The Carrolls

Charles Carroll of Carrollton (d. 1832) was one of the most important men in Maryland—a signer of the Declaration of Independence and a strong supporter of the American Revolution. His cousin John Carroll (d. 1815) studied in Europe, as was common for upper-class Maryland Catholics, and became a Jesuit. After the suppression of the Society, John returned to Maryland and ministered to the flock who lived around his mother's estate. At the outbreak of the Revolution, he was part of a delegation (including Benjamin Franklin [d. 1790]) sent to Canada to seek Canadian neutrality, a mission that failed because England had recently granted religious toleration to the Quebec Catholics.

The First Bishop

John Carroll, like Charles, was an ardent patriot, proclaiming Catholic support for the Revolution and the new government. After the war, he was the leader of a group of priests who told the Holy See that it was inappropriate that they should continue under the authority of the vicar apostolic of London. Carroll himself was first made prefect apostolic over the United States, then in 1789, the first American bishop, in effect elected by his fellow priests and confirmed by Rome. There were then about twenty-five thousand Catholics in the thirteen new states—about 1 percent of the population. In 1808, dioceses were established at Boston, New York, Philadelphia, and Bardstown (Kentucky), and Baltimore became an archdiocese.

Religious Liberty

Before appointing Carroll, the Holy See queried the fledgling American government as to whether the appointment was acceptable and received the surprising answer that it was of no concern to the government. At that time, and for a long time afterward, the United States was the only country in the world where it was possible for the Church to erect dioceses and parishes, establish charitable and educational institutions, and appoint clergy without at least the formal approval of the government. Most important, in theory, this religious liberty was not conferred by the state but was a natural right enjoyed by all, so that the Church did not have to depend on concessions wrung from unfriendly governments through fragile concordats.

Democratic Ideas

In general, Carroll opposed bringing foreign priests to America, and in keeping with the spirit of the new nation, he at first proposed to the Holy See that bishops in America be elected by the senior clergy, that the United States be free of the authority of the Congregation of Propaganda, and that Mass be celebrated in the vernacular, accommodations that he thought would make the Church appear less foreign and more democratic. But as he began to exercise episcopal authority, he apparently changed his mind about those matters.

Sulpicians

Paradoxically, in order to train clergy for a new country that had been spawned by a revolution, he found it necessary to welcome French Sulpicians fleeing the revolution in their own country. For two generations, the Sulpicians were perhaps the most important religious community in America, with a number of them, including two of Carroll's successors, serving as bishops. They started St. Mary's Seminary in Baltimore, which Carroll hoped would be the seedbed of native vocations, although for a long time most students were foreign. The first priest ordained in the United States (1793) was the French Sulpician Stephen Badin (d. 1853).

Religious Women

Native vocations among women were more plentiful—a half dozen new congregations were established around 1800, notably the Sisters of Charity, founded in Maryland by the aristocratic convert St. Elizabeth Anne Seton (d. 1821). Remarkably, the first woman to become a nun from what would eventually be the United States was not a Marylander but Lydia Longley (d. 1758), a Puritan girl from Connecticut who was kidnapped by Indians and taken to Canada, where she was eventually ransomed and entered a convent.

A Free Church

In his famous work *Democracy in America*, the French Catholic nobleman Alexis de Tocqueville (d. 1859) informed Europeans that the fact that there was no official church in the United States did not indicate irreligion but quite the opposite—nowhere was religion the subject of such interest, and the churches were stimulated to great efforts in order to win free adherents.

Religious Indifference?

But the radical newness of this arrangement raised questions that would take a long time to resolve. Catholic teaching held that the state had an obligation to promote religion and morality. While, in practical terms, it was an immense benefit for Catholics to live in a neutral state, that very neutrality seemed to show that the American state did not accept its responsibility. This was a problem for many Protestants as well. No one proposed an official national church, but until the

1830s, some individual states still retained official churches, and some people were troubled by the absence of any mention of God in the Constitution.

Common Morality

For a century and a half after the Constitution was ratified, the prevailing view was that all religions fostered a common morality that was the necessary basis of a good society. People of all religions were presumed to be able to live harmoniously together under a state that was neutral toward specific religions but not toward religion as such.

The Second Great Awakening

Practically all the Founding Fathers were influenced by the British Enlightenment, and some were Deists. But the views of this elite soon ceased to be the governing spirit of the new nation, as the shift from republicanism to some kind of equalitarian democracy gave greater weight to the beliefs of people who were largely unaffected by the Enlightenment. To the dismay of President Thomas Jefferson (1801–1809) and others, there occurred a great resurgence of Evangelical faith—the Second Great Awakening that stamped on the country a deeply Christian character that survives into the twenty-first century.

Religious Rights

Despite the prevailing anti-Catholicism, Catholics found that their rights were generally protected by the Supreme Court, which at various times confirmed the legal independence of private religious colleges; upheld the right of churches to import foreign clergy (because "we are a Christian nation"); recognized Catholic marriage as satisfying civil requirements; allowed the Church to receive bequests; permitted tax exemptions to religious bodies; held that charitable institutions under religious auspices were not "sectarian" and could receive public money; and found that a monk's vow of poverty did not violate the constitutional guarantee of personal liberty. A crucial feature of the American legal system was the principle that internal church disputes, if brought before the secular courts, were to be decided according to the church's own laws, in order to minimize the possibility of governmental interference in internal church affairs.

Education

The environment was so favorable to religious education that in 1844 the Supreme Court seriously considered the claim that prohibiting the teaching of religion in a privately endowed school constituted blasphemy. The court allowed the innovation only because the donor had no malicious intent toward religion.

For a long time, private religious colleges far outnumbered state institutions in the United States, and Catholics took full advantage of the opportunity, eventually founding almost three hundred institutions of higher learning, not including seminaries—vastly more than in any other country. The first, Georgetown, was established by Carroll in 1789, and the Jesuits alone eventually founded twenty-eight such institutions. Over time, colleges were also opened by the Dominicans, the Holy Cross Fathers, and other male orders, while colleges for women were opened and operated by religious sisters.

Lay Trusteeism

The democratic American spirit threatened the integrity of the Church in one important respect—lay trusteeism. Although it had European roots and some of its most ardent supporters were immigrants, lay trusteeism seemed to harmonize with the Puritan ecclesiastical system called congregationalism.

In some cases, parishioners claimed title to the parish property and the right to hire and fire their pastors, even to elect their bishops. But it was not primarily a lay-clerical rivalry. In almost every case, the dispute centered around two rival pastors—one appointed by the bishop, the other by the trustees—occasionally involving public brawls between rival factions. The disputes raged on and off for decades, especially on the East Coast. The Holy See condemned lay trusteeism as a violation of canon law, and bishops sometimes excommunicated dissidents. Some bishops allowed lay trustees in an advisory capacity, so long as the bishop retained title to the parish property and the authority to appoint and remove pastors.

Finances

The democratic character of the church in the United States was also reflected in the fact that it was heavily dependent on the free-will offerings of the faithful. Despite poverty, Catholics built often imposing churches and funded charitable institutions of all kinds, which, since most Catholics were poor, required a large number of small contributions. A common method of parochial support was pew rental (sometimes pew auction), which allowed the better-off people to sit in the most desirable locations for Sunday Mass and left the majority to find whatever places they could.

The French

De Soto

In the second of the three ethnic-religious zones that became the United States, a Spanish expedition under Hernando de Soto (d. 1541) got beyond the Mississippi. A Franciscan member of that party, Juan de Padilla, remained to convert the Indians in what is now northeast Kansas, soon becoming the first North American martyr (1542).

Marquette and Joliet

In the later seventeenth century, Jesuits from Canada began doing missionary work throughout the Great Lakes region. Based on Indian stories about a great river, the Jesuit Jacques Marquette (d. 1675) and the layman Louis Joliet (d. 1700) rediscovered the Mississippi and traveled much of its length. They originally named it the Immaculate

Conception, but the name did not stick. The French eventually reached the Gulf of Mexico and claimed the entire Mississippi Valley.

Indian Missions

The Jesuits penetrated south from the Great Lakes, establishing a series of Indian missions throughout the upper part of the Mississippi Valley and also ministering to the few French settlers attracted to the area by the lure of furs. (The parish of Cahokia [Illinois], opposite St. Louis, claims to be the oldest continuous parish in the United States, having been founded as an Indian mission in 1699.) There were some missionary martyrs.

The Plains Indians were nomadic hunters, which hampered the missionary efforts, and polygamy was once again a great obstacle to conversion. It was common among the Indians, and the French trappers often took Indian concubines, an arrangement that was considered objectively sinful but that also often served as the missionaries' entry into Indian society. In the eighteenth century, the Franciscans and the Society of the Foreign Missions of the Seminary of Quebec also began sending priests into the territory. Lead and other minerals were discovered on the west side of the Mississippi, bringing an influx of settlers into what would later become Missouri.

New Orleans

New Orleans was founded in 1718, and from there, French settlements were established to the north along the Mississippi, so that in time there was a continuous, albeit sparse, chain extending from the Gulf of Mexico to the Great Lakes. The first academy for Catholic girls in what would become the United States was established by the Ursulines at New Orleans in 1727.

The Upper Mississippi

Following the Seven Years' War (1756–1763), France had to cede the "Illinois Country" to England and transfer the west side of the Mississippi to Spain, although the majority of the white inhabitants of the valley were still French in origin. The territory ceded to Spain was placed officially under the diocese of Havana, but in practice it remained under Quebec, which, since England now ruled Canada, also had jurisdiction over the Illinois Country. The transfer of the territory to Spain led almost immediately to the expulsion of the Jesuits and therefore to an acute shortage of priests.

"The Americans"

During the American Revolution (1775–1782), rebel forces advanced into the Illinois Country, and Pierre Gibault (d. 1804), who was virtually the only priest left in the territory, persuaded his mostly French parishioners to welcome the Americans. After being returned to France under Napoleon, the Louisiana Territory was sold to the United States in 1803, giving the new nation unlimited access to the rest of the vast continent. After the Louisiana Purchase, the territory was quickly settled by "Americans"—easterners of mainly British Protestant stock—and its French character was diluted.

Louisiana

The diocese of Louisiana was established in 1815, but the Creole clergy in the state of Louisiana were said to be Gallicans who resisted the reform programs of their bishops. The first bishop, the Sulpician Louis DuBourg (d. 1833), a native of Santo Domingo, was essentially driven out of New Orleans by the clergy and moved his seat to St. Louis, which became a diocese in 1826. Despite its heavily Catholic character, Louisiana never exerted proportionate leadership in the Church nationally.

The Upper Mississippi

Bishop Benedict J. Flaget of Bardstown (d. 1850), a French Sulpician, found the Catholics of the upper Mississippi Valley, who had been without priestly guidance for years at a time, to be also extremely lax, but around 1820, an influx of missionaries began a revival. Flemish Jesuits, French Sacred Heart Sisters, and a multinational group of Vincentians arrived in Missouri almost simultaneously, originally committed to evangelizing the Indians but increasingly devoted to the pastoral needs of white people.

St. Rose-Philippine Duchesne (d. 1852), superior of the Sacred Heart Sisters, established schools for girls throughout the Louisiana Territory. The Vincentians and the Jesuits both established seminaries barely a hundred miles apart, and the Jesuits took charge of a school that eventually became St. Louis University, the first university west of the Mississippi.

Badin was an intrepid missionary in Kentucky and territories farther west, as was the Flemish Sulpician Charles Nerinckx (d. 1824), who founded the Sisters of Loreto at the Foot of the Cross to establish schools on the frontier. In the new state of Michigan, the French Sulpician Gabriel Richard (d. 1833) was a major figure in civic life: a founder of the state university and Michigan's first Congressman. (Ironically, he was in jail for debt when he was elected.)

Eclipse of the French

The Irish Bishop (later Archbishop) Peter Richard Kenrick of St. Louis (d. 1896) discouraged French priests from serving in his see when he first arrived in 1841. A few years later, the first bishop of Little Rock, the Irishman Andrew Byrne (d. 1862), arrived with a contingent of Irish priests, whereupon all the French priests departed.

The Indians

The relentless westward push of white settlers led to the repeated seizure of Indian lands, the forcible relocation of their occupants, and the frequent breaking of treaties by the federal government. During the 1830s, the Jesuits from Missouri began extensive evangelization of the Indians, following the Missouri River all the way to Montana and establishing a chain of missions across the northwestern tier of the country. Missionaries were almost the only white people involved with the Indians whose motives were not mercenary, and the famous Flemish Jesuit Pierre de Smet (d. 1873) attempted, with limited success, to represent the Indians' interests.

Mission Rivalries

Another obstacle to Catholic missionary activity was aggressive competition with Protestants. As the Indians came under the authority of the federal government, the various tribes were assigned to different churches, usually favoring the Protestants, the only instance in American history when the Church's pastoral activity was restricted by law. For educational purposes, the government provided financial support for the missions and tended to overlook the fact that a major part of that education was religion.

Westward Movement

After 1840, the new nation began to advance westward into the Hispanic areas of the continent, beginning with the "Anglo" Texans' rebellion against Mexico, which led to the Mexican War that brought Texas into the Union. The gold rush of the 1840s brought many people to California, including many Catholics, and fostered the popular image of California as the "promised land". Temporarily leaping over most of the territory between the eastern Rocky Mountains and the western Sierras, the United States accepted California into the Union in 1850. The Holy See established a vicariate for Texas and dioceses in Los Angeles and Santa Fe and solidified the ecclesiastical organization of the vast country by making Oregon City (later Portland) and St. Louis into archdioceses.

Eclipse of the Spanish

As it had done in the Mississippi Valley, the westward movement diluted the older ethnic character of California Catholicism, so that in time Hispanics found themselves outnumbered by the Irish and under the authority of mainly Irish bishops. The survival of Hispanic culture was strongest in New Mexico, but the celebrated Archbishop Jean-Baptiste Lamy of Santa Fe (d. 1888)[3] was a Frenchman who considered the conduct of his Hispanic priests and the folk piety of his flock less than satisfactory. He ignored the classic Spanish mission style of architecture and built a cathedral in Romanesque style, in order to emphasize the European heritage.

---

[3] His life is fictionalized in the classic novel *Death Comes for the Archbishop*, by Willa Cather.

From the beginning of the new nation, there was continuous immigration, much of it by Catholic Irish. But the great age of immigration began shortly after 1840, coinciding exactly with the beginnings of the great westward push. The Irish were by far the largest Catholic immigrant group, with over four million in the period 1820 to 1920. Germans were the largest immigrant group overall—five and a half million—but only a fifth of them were Catholics.

Thus the religious and ethnic character of both the East and the Midwest (as the region between the Alleghenies and the Rocky Mountains came to be known) altered substantially. People of British ancestry gradually ceased to constitute a majority in the East, while, paradoxically, Catholics in the former Louisiana Territory now constituted a much smaller percentage of the population but grew hugely in terms of total numbers.

"Americans"

The fact that Carroll came from a distinguished aristocratic family had much to do with public acceptance of his faith and conversions to the Catholic Church from the upper echelons of society. Since the Holy See sought to appoint native bishops when possible, throughout the nineteenth century, a disproportionate number of bishops—two of them Carroll's successors at Baltimore—were drawn from the ranks of converts, usually former Episcopalians.

There was some dissatisfaction with the French clergy, especially bishops, who were considered autocratic and were accused of not bothering to learn English, although the first bishop of Boston, Jean de Cheverus (d. 1836), was respected even by Protestants. (He was in a sense the first American cardinal, achieving that honor as archbishop of Bordeaux.)

The Ethnicity of Bishops

Most bishops were Irish, if for no other reason than that they spoke the dominant language. But most of the earliest Irish bishops were not even working in the United States when appointed and were sent from abroad specifically to assume the office. (The first two bishops of New York were Irish Dominicans stationed in Rome, the first of whom got no closer to New York than Naples.)

French bishops were sometimes suspected of Gallicanism, while the Irish bishops were strongly Ultramontane. A rare Czech appointee, St. John Nepomucene Neumann (d. 1860), the Redemptorist bishop of Philadelphia, became the only canonized member of the American hierarchy.

John England

Paradoxically, Carroll's "Americanist" ideas were especially kept alive by one of the immigrant Irish bishops, John England of Charleston (d. 1842), who had been a strong supporter of the independence of his native land and who extolled the American idea of liberty as the hope of the world. England promulgated a "constitution" for his diocese, including an elected body of laymen to advise the bishop, although all matters pertaining to the faith remained under the authority of the clergy.

Architecture

Carroll's idea of Americanization was reflected in the dominant early style of church architecture. His cathedral in Baltimore was designed by Benjamin Latrobe (d. 1820), who also designed the new Capitol in Washington, D.C., as well as the cathedrals in Bardstown and Cincinnati. Like his civil buildings, all of Latrobe's churches were built in the Federal, or Greek revival, style favored at the time, though it was not distinctively religious. But by the time of the Civil War, American Catholics' increasing links to Europe were reflected in the revival of Romanesque, Gothic, and Baroque styles, which predominated in church architecture until World War I.

Growth

By 1870, the number of Catholics had increased to 4.5 million—12 percent of the total population. Until 1914, the United States allowed almost unlimited immigration, a policy that especially favored Catholics from southern and eastern Europe: Italians, Poles, Hungarians, Slovaks, and others. With this increase in the Catholic population in 1875, came the appointment of the first American named a cardinal while holding an American see—Archbishop John F. McCloskey of New York (d. 1885). After that, the country was never without a representative in the Sacred College: two in 1910, four in 1924, five in 1946.

Anti-Catholicism

Both the elite and the masses in the Mississippi Valley were mostly Catholic at the time of the Louisiana Purchase, and Catholics there were never treated as outsiders, even as "Americans" poured into the territory. But in the East, especially New England, the Anglo-Saxon elite openly regarded Catholics as interlopers who had to be kept in their place, while in the West and Southwest the native Hispanic population was often treated as a conquered people. (During the Mexican War of the 1840s, American troops sometimes desecrated Catholic churches, which provoked some of the Irish in their ranks to desert to the Mexicans, who named them the San Patricio Brigade.)

"Know-Nothings"

Prior to the Civil War, when massive immigration was still new, anti-Catholic violence—collectively dubbed the Know-Nothing Riots after a loosely organized secret society—erupted in several cities of the United States. A convent school was burned to the ground near Boston, a papal nuncio was mobbed in Cincinnati, and a stone sent by Pius IX for the new Washington Monument was dumped into the Potomac. The fraudulent memoir of a supposed nun—*I Leaped over the Wall*—spread the most lurid tales of convent life. While some of this anti-Catholic hostility was "nativism"—hatred of foreigners—at its core it was religiously motivated. Some immigrants, especially Germans, were "freethinkers" who fomented anti-Catholic prejudice against the Church as the principal enemy of civilization.

Elite Prejudice

The crudity and violence of popular anti-Catholicism was sometimes condemned by the Protestant elites, but those elites harbored their own kind of prejudice, which was a combination of the classic Protestant view of Catholicism as a distortion of Christianity and the Enlightenment claim that it was repressive superstition. Elite opinion deplored the *Syllabus of Errors* and the definition of papal infallibility and favored both Italy's seizure of the Papal States and Germany's *Kulturkampf*. For a time, Harvard Law School would not admit graduates of Jesuit colleges, on the grounds that their education did not qualify them.

Ethnic Parishes

Irish bishops in the United States, in contrast to the efforts of the Quebec hierarchy to preserve French culture, found the immigrant culture of their non-English-speaking flocks troublesome. Ethnic parishes were ubiquitous but were often sources of tension.

Germans

There were few German bishops except in the state of Wisconsin, where St. Francis de Sales Seminary at Milwaukee was the principal training ground for German American priests, and after 1880, there were practically no bishops except Irish and German. German Catholics lived in all parts of the country but especially in the German Triangle stretching between Cincinnati, St. Louis, and Milwaukee. During the 1880s, the movement called Cahenslyism—named after a German layman who was head of a society to fund the American missions—complained to the Holy See that German Americans were treated as second-class citizens and asked that they be given more German bishops, a plea that was rebuffed.

Schism

Other ethnic groups considered themselves to have even less influence. The only schism in the history of the United States, the Polish National Church, was founded in Scranton, Pennsylvania, in 1896 by Poles unhappy with their Irish bishop. It remained small and marginal.

The Language Issue

Strictly speaking, there were no Irish parishes as such, merely parishes where English was the language of confessions and sermons, and ethnic parishes were regarded as concessions. (In St. Louis, for example, large and imposing churches built by German Catholics were officially considered mere "chapels of ease" of English-speaking parishes.)

Ethnic parishes were sometimes considered obstacles to the assimilation of immigrants into American culture, but the reality was more complex. They allowed immigrants to ease into the culture over time and minimized culture shock, preserving the old languages and customs even as the second generation became "Americanized". Germans in particular were devoted to parish schools, as places where their language and customs could be passed on along with their religion.

The Fidelity of the Immigrants

Some bishops in the United States thought it was urgent that the immigrants settle in rural communities, and a few, such as the otherwise modern-minded John Ireland of St. Paul, even sponsored projects for reestablishing the European pattern of farming communities, with the Catholic faith at their center. But ironically, it was precisely certain rural areas that turned out to be dangerous to the faith, as the sheer size of the country made it difficult to provide priests for much of the South and West, and many immigrants became Protestants. By contrast, the Church was highly successful in providing for the pastoral needs of her mushrooming urban flock. While there were many thriving Catholic agricultural communities, especially in the Midwest, American Catholics became a predominantly urban people. Overall, the immigrants kept their faith, and the system of ethnic parishes had much to do with that fact.

Parochial Schools

Education

The "common schools", which began to spread after 1850, were objectionable to Catholics because they were essentially Protestant, requiring prayers and readings from the Protestant Bible, often led by ministers, and punishing Catholic children for not participating. Catholics began establishing their own schools in large numbers around the time of the Civil War, and the Third Plenary Council of Baltimore (Baltimore III, 1884) mandated that all parishes sponsor them. A decade later there were four thousand throughout the country, enrolling seven hundred and fifty thousand children. Baltimore III also authorized what came to be called the *Baltimore Catechism*, which was used in Catholic schools for the next eighty years.

The bishops were not in total agreement about educational strategy. Some agitated to make the public schools religiously neutral, but that effort succeeded only in Cincinnati, where it was promoted primarily by "freethinkers", with Catholic and Jewish support, and was criticized by some Catholics for making public education secular. Archbishop John Ireland of St. Paul (d. 1918) for a time promoted a cooperative arrangement between Catholic and public schools, a proposal that some other bishops opposed and that public-school officials also eventually rejected. In 1925, the Supreme Court, pronouncing,

"The child is not the mere creature of the state", overturned an anti-Catholic Oregon law requiring all children to attend public schools. But the Church was rarely successful in getting tax support for her schools.

The Catholic Schools

Partly because of the perceived Catholic sympathy for slavery, the Republican Party after the Civil War increasingly exploited anti-Catholic and anti-immigrant feeling. President Ulysses S. Grant (1869–1877) seemed to give in to such prejudice in urging that no public funds be given to Catholic schools, and a Republican effort in Congress to initiate a constitutional amendment to that effect failed in a purely partisan vote.

Politics

Brownson

Virtually the only Catholic intellectual of substance in nineteenth-century America was Orestes Brownson (d. 1876), a spiritual seeker who passed through Calvinism, liberal Protestantism, Unitarianism, agnosticism, and the utopian Brook Farm experiment before becoming a Catholic. Brownson thought the time had come for the United States to lead the world spiritually, but it could do so only if it abandoned a weak and compromised Protestantism for an unwavering Catholicism.

Sternly orthodox, Brownson was nonetheless suspect because for a time he also made common cause with liberal Catholics in Europe, such as Montalembert and Acton. He extolled American democracy and opposed the establishment of Catholic schools, proposing instead that Catholics serve as leaven in the public schools. His great critic, and perhaps the most influential American Catholic journalist of the nineteenth century, was also a convert—James A. McMaster (d. 1886) of the *New York Freeman's Journal*, who strongly opposed every liberalizing tendency in the Church.

Eventually, Brownson came to mistrust pure democracy, as tending toward a kind of philosophical relativism, and he supported a theory—held especially by many Southerners—whereby the individual states could nullify an act of the federal government. But unlike many other advocates of states' rights, Brownson was also vehemently anti-slavery (McMaster was equally anti-abolitionist) and supported the Union in Civil War.

"Rum, Romanism, and Rebellion"

Due to the Republican opposition to funding Catholic schools and other reasons, Catholics, especially the Irish, flocked to the Democrats, demonstrating their power in 1884, when a Protestant minister's sneer that the Democrats were the party of "rum, Romanism, and rebellion" cost the Republicans New York City and thereby the presidential election. In the northern cities, Catholics partly coped with discrimination by mastering the arts of democratic politics (with both a small and a large "D"), taking advantage of their constantly growing numbers to elect their own people to office. The Irish were especially skillful at urban politics, putting together the "machines" that survived into the 1960s and beyond.[4]

Labor Unions

Catholics' adherence to the Democratic Party also owed much to their status as mostly laborers, since the Republicans, in both image and reality, were the party of business owners. Catholics became leaders in the emergent labor movement. The Holy See condemned the Knights of Labor, an early union headed by the Catholic Terence V. Powderly (d. 1924), calling it a "secret society" akin to the Masons, because it kept its membership secret and required its members to take an oath, but Cardinal James Gibbons of Baltimore (d. 1921) persuaded the Vatican to lift the ban.

The Sisters

The Church's mission was heavily dependent on the labor of sisters, who greatly outnumbered priests and who, besides teaching, were the chief ministers of charity in hospitals and orphanages and in the personal care of invalids and the destitute. They worked heroically during the frequent epidemics, lived among the very poor in the cities, endured the most extreme hardships and dangers on the frontier, and often died young.

Many foreign orders came to the United States, notably the Sisters of Mercy from Ireland, the Daughters of Charity from France, and the School Sisters of Notre Dame from Germany. The Italian immigrant St. Frances Xavier Cabrini (d. 1918), who founded the Missionary Sisters of the Sacred Heart to work in hospitals and other institutions, in 1946 became the first American citizen to be canonized. Congregations also continued to be established in America. Rose Hawthorne Lathrop (d. 1926), the convert daughter of American author Nathaniel Hawthorne (d. 1864), founded a community of sisters primarily to care for indigent cancer patients.

Lay Organizations

Possibly because of the democratic, "voluntaristic" character of American society, religious organizations of all kinds flourished: the Holy Name Society for men, the Altar and Rosary Society for women, the St. Vincent de Paul Society to help the poor, and ethnic organizations of all kinds. An Irish priest in Connecticut, Michael McGivney (d. 1890), founded what became the largest and most important of these—the Knights of Columbus, its name chosen to recall the Catholic origins of the nation. Each of these groups had a

Catholic Life in America

---

[4] The novel and film *The Last Hurrah*, by Edwin O'Connor, dramatizes the complexity of the historical reality, including the ambivalence of the Catholic hierarchy.

predominantly religious purpose, but they also served as social organizations and provided life insurance and aid to members in need. Along with the church and the school, they constituted a complete Catholic world.

Piety

As in Europe, devotions of all kinds—the rosary, novenas and shrines to various saints, the Forty Hours' Devotion—were extremely popular, as was the parish mission in which visiting priests, especially Passionists or Redemptorists, preached every night for a week. These missions were the Catholic equivalent of the Protestant revival, aiming at personal conversion, with exhortations to greater piety and severe warnings against common sins like drunkenness. American Catholics were very faithful in going to confession, with long lines on Saturdays and before great feasts.

Slavery   Few Catholics were involved in the anti-slavery movement, and many regarded the movement as a malign effort by extremists to undermine the social order with a concept of "liberty" that had proven to be destructive in Europe. (Daniel O'Connell lost influence among some American Catholics because of his denunciations of slavery.) On the other side, some abolitionists, such as the Presbyterian minister Elijah P. Lovejoy (d. 1837), who was murdered by a mob in Illinois, were as much anti-Catholic as they were anti-slavery.

Papal Condemnations

Since the fifteenth century, the popes had condemned the slave trade, and one of the ways in which a self-consciously "American" Catholicism diverged from Rome in the nineteenth century was precisely on the slavery issue. Bishop England was pro-slavery, and most of the Catholic elite of Maryland and the lower Mississippi Valley, Bishop Carroll among them, owned slaves, with little apparent crisis of conscience. Some religious communities owned slaves, and one Maryland superior was removed by the Jesuit general for having allowed slave families to be broken up through sales.

Pro-Slavery Catholics

The Supreme Court's Dred Scott decision, holding that slaves had no rights, was written by Chief Justice Roger Brooke Taney (d. 1864), a Marylander who achieved the highest office held by any American Catholic prior to 1961. Several Maryland Catholics were implicated in the plot to assassinate Abraham Lincoln, although the extent of their involvement is unclear.

Despite the repeated papal condemnations of slavery, few clergy called for emancipation, a rare exception being Archbishop John B. Purcell of Cincinnati (d. 1883). The only American textbook of moral theology, by the Irish Archbishop Francis P. Kenrick of Baltimore (d. 1863), justified the institution and, citing St. Paul's Letter to Philemon (see verses 8–22), even defended the highly controversial Fugitive Slave Law, which required that runaway slaves be forcibly returned to their masters.

The Civil War

Catholics fought on both sides in the Civil War, although Louisiana was the only Confederate state that had a large Catholic population. There was an impression at the time that most Irish tended to be pro-Confederate and most Germans pro-Union, and Irish Catholics were among the chief perpetrators of the Anti-Draft Riots in New York City, during which more than a hundred people, mostly blacks, were killed on the streets.

Bishop Patrick N. Lynch of Charleston (d. 1882) was sent as a Confederate emissary to Pius IX to persuade the Pope to recognize the Confederacy officially. The Pope's response is uncertain. It was rumored that he was open to recognizing the Confederacy if slavery were abolished. Meanwhile, Bishop Michael Domenec of Pittsburgh (d. 1878), a Spanish Vincentian, attempted to promote the Union cause in Europe.

Reconstruction

Southern Catholics resisted Reconstruction, and Bishop William H. Elder of Natchez (d. 1904), who later succeeded Purcell in Cincinnati, was briefly jailed for disobeying the orders of the occupying Union army. By a narrow margin, the Supreme Court overturned the conviction of a Missouri priest who, under orders from Archbishop Peter Kenrick (Francis' brother and a former slave owner), refused to take an oath of loyalty to the Union.

"Wage Slavery"

Some Catholics, such as Archbishop John J. Hughes of New York (d. 1864), criticized the North in the same way that some Southerners did, arguing that the plight of the industrial laborer was, if anything, even worse than that of the slave—who was often cared for throughout his entire life by his master—because the factory worker was trapped in an entirely heartless and impersonal system that, caring only for profit, often paid him less than he needed to live.

Black Catholics

Despite widespread racial prejudice among American Catholics, Augustine Tolton (d. 1897), who was born a slave in Missouri, became the first black priest in the United States. Rebuffed by various American seminaries, he completed his studies at the College of the Propaganda in Rome and worked in black parishes in Illinois. James A. Healy (d. 1900) of Portland, Maine, the son of a white father and a slave mother, was the first black bishop in the United States and until the 1960s the only one.

Religious Orders

The Josephites, an offshoot of the English missionary Mill Hill Fathers, were a male community founded primarily to work among blacks. Elizabeth Lange (d. 1882), a Cuban immigrant of Haitian ancestry, and a New Orleans black woman, Ven. Henriette DeLille (d. 1862), both founded communities of black sisters: the Oblates of Providence and the Sisters of the Holy Family, respectively. St. Katharine-Mary Drexel (d. 1955), daughter of an aristocratic Philadelphia family, used her fortune to establish the Sisters of the Blessed Sacrament, who worked among black and Indian women and welcomed their membership. She also founded the nation's only black Catholic university, Xavier of New Orleans.

"Americanism"

Bishop Domenec, although he was Spanish, gave offense at the First Vatican Council by predicting that Catholics in the United States would not only soon outnumber those in Italy, but they would also be better Catholics. It was a speech that foreshadowed the greatest crisis in the history of the Church in the United States—"Americanism".

The exact nature of "Americanism" was vague. A few people advocated a vernacular liturgy, the abandonment of distinctive habits for nuns, and a respectful ecumenical dialogue with Protestants, but on the whole, the movement was merely a rather uncritical enthusiasm for American society. The leaders were often impulsive and given to battle cries such as "Church and Age Unite!"; sometimes they demanded that the American political system be followed everywhere.

John Ireland

Archbishop Ireland, who was dubbed "the consecrated cyclone", was the leader of the Americanist bishops. He dismissed the contemplative monastic life as unsuited to American culture and was an almost frenetic champion of the greatness of the nation, seeing himself as engaged in a great battle for the direction of the American church. Despite his enthusiastic belief in the principle of separation of church and state, he often meddled in politics to promote his ecclesiastical agenda.

Assimilating the Immigrants

Although Ireland championed labor unions, he got on well with some of the leading businessmen of the "Gilded Age" and was unusual among Catholics in being an ardent Republican, seeing Catholic loyalty to the Democratic Party as a further sign of their failure to enter fully into American society. The American church of his day was all too obviously a community of immigrants, and on one occasion Ireland exclaimed in exasperation that he would welcome a return to the conditions of John Carroll's day, when the flock was much smaller but was also truly American.

Temperance

Ireland was also embarrassed that the Irish immigrants had a reputation for drunkenness and criminality, and he urged "temperance" (total abstinence from alcohol) on his people. (An Irish Franciscan, Theobald Mathew [d. 1856], promoted the temperance movement with evangelical fervor, considerable episcopal support, and some success.)

Gibbons

Gibbons served as the Americanists' protective patron, no one doing more than he to establish the image of the Church as completely at home in American society. A bishop for over half a century, Gibbons appeared to the public as a simple, kindly, humorously self-deprecating man imbued with the democratic spirit. He was routinely called upon to offer public prayers on patriotic occasions and, although the Church did not allow official ecumenical activities, regularly appeared alongside non-Catholic clergy, with whom he seemed to enjoy cordial relations. Although the war of 1898 was fought against Catholic Spain, and although many Catholics for various reasons opposed American entry into World War I, Gibbons epitomized the patriotic spirit, giving proof that a Catholic could be a loyal American.

Catholic University

The Catholic University of America was founded in 1888 directly under the hierarchy and intended to be mainly a graduate institution for clergy. Some of its founders—Bishop John Lancaster Spalding of Peoria (d. 1916) and its first rector, Bishop John J. Keane (d. 1918)—were Americanists who also intended it to be a more "modern" institution than the Jesuit schools they considered reactionary. Keane insisted that little emphasis be placed on the study of the Middle Ages.

Apostolic Delegation

The Apostolic Delegation was established in the United States in 1893, mainly because of complaints to Rome by American priests that they were being mistreated by their bishops.

The most famous case was that of Fr. Edward McGlynn (d. 1900) of New York City, who was excommunicated by Archbishop Michael A. Corrigan (d. 1902)—the leader of the anti-Americanist bishops—for espousing radical social ideas like the "single-tax movement" and for denouncing Corrigan as a tool of wealth. (Ironically, most of the "Americanist" bishops had been born in Ireland, whereas Corrigan was a native of New Jersey.) The first apostolic delegate, Archbishop Francesco Satolli (d. 1910), reinstated McGlynn and was for a time friendly to the Americanists. Later he seemed to ally himself with the conservative wing of the hierarchy led by Corrigan.

Vatican Involvement

Although it had been building up for decades, the Americanist crisis erupted primarily because of the first religious community for men founded in the United States—the Paulists (Congregation of St. Paul). The community was started just before the Civil War by Isaac Hecker (d. 1888), a convert from Methodism who, like Brownson, was briefly associated with the utopian Brook Farm experiment. Hecker became a Redemptorist but was dismissed from that community after a dispute with his superiors. Also like Brownson, Hecker believed that the United States, as a land of innovation and hope, was ripe for conversion to Catholicism, because the Church affirmed human freedom and the possibility of natural virtue. He emphasized the presence in each person of the Holy Spirit, inspiring and guiding good actions. In contrasting Catholicism with the theological pessimism of classical Calvinism and Lutheranism, he appeared not to notice the growth of a liberal Protestantism that was even more optimistic than Catholicism.

Without his saying so explicitly, Hecker's hope seems to have been that the United States could be converted through its social elite, who had first to be shown that Catholicism was not a foreign entity but something that resonated with American culture at the deepest level. A number of the early Paulists were converts, some from prominent families, one an astronomer at Harvard.

The crisis came to a head at the end of the century in a roundabout way—through a French translation of a biography of Hecker written by one of his priests. Based on the book, liberal French Catholics claimed to discern certain distinctive progressive features of American Catholicism, a claim that, along with reports to Rome from the United States itself, prompted a Vatican investigation.

Pope Leo XIII sent two letters to the American bishops—*Longinqua Oceani* (Wide Expanse of the Ocean) and *Testem Benevolentiae* (Witness of Good Will)—arguing that, while separation of church and state was tolerable, it need not be adopted everywhere and that the state should give positive support to religion. The Pope's diplomatic rebuke urged American Catholics not to exalt their own culture at the expense of the universal Church or value the natural over the supernatural virtues and the active over the contemplative life.

The "Phantom Heresy"

Americanism has been called "the phantom heresy" because it was in no sense a real heresy (Leo did not say that it was), merely a set of attitudes that, carried far enough, might have become heresy. The Americanists submitted to the papal warning, with Gibbons saying that he knew of no one who actually held any of the censured opinions. Because of Americanism, Keane was replaced as rector of the Catholic University.

Modernism in the United States

Pius X's condemnation of Modernism a decade later raised the question of whether Americanism was a species of the same thing. But the connections were tenuous. Although Ireland once offered Alfred Loisy a professorship in the St. Paul seminary, the Americanist leadership seemed to have little understanding of the doctrinal issues at stake with Modernism. When Ireland and Spalding visited France, Loisy was disappointed that they did not seem interested in the questions that exercised him.

Insofar as Modernism was an issue in the United States, it was in the still-gray area of modern biblical criticism. The Paulist William Sullivan (d. 1944) was deeply affected by that criticism, concluding that the true meaning of the Gospel lay in its moral teachings and excoriating the Church because of her dogmatic tradition, which, he charged, was completely out of step with American democracy. He left the Church and became a Unitarian minister.

Five other Paulists resigned from the priesthood because of the condemnation of Modernism, as did the Jesuit theologian William Fanning (d. 1920) and John R. Slattery (d. 1926), the general of the Josephites. John Zahm (d. 1921), a Holy Cross father, was censured by the Holy See for cautiously espousing the theory of evolution. The *New York Review*, published at the New York archdiocesan seminary, was suppressed after it published articles on biblical criticism and summaries of modernist theology. Henry Poels (d. 1948), a Netherlander who was professor of Scripture at Catholic University, was forced to resign and, although the Americanist bishops sometimes presented the issue as one of academic freedom, they in turn forced the resignation of a German priest-professor whom they regarded as their enemy.

Growth

Just as Catholic intellectual life in Europe was by no means thwarted by the condemnation of Modernism, so the Catholic Church in the United States flourished in the sixty years following the warning against Americanism. Over the next sixty years, American Catholics came to be considered exceptionally loyal to the Holy See. Even after immigration was severely restricted, the American church continued to grow exponentially—from ten million members in 1914 to forty-five million fifty years later. Its various institutions multiplied, religious vocations were plentiful, and there was a high level of Mass attendance.

Foreign Missions

The United States ceased officially to be a mission country in 1907; and, while it would continue to receive priests from abroad, it would increasingly send its own sons and daughters to the most distant parts of the world. In 1911, two Boston priests founded the Foreign Mission Society of the United States, commonly called Maryknoll, which became one of the most important missionary groups in the Church, especially for its services in China.

The American Church Matures

Monasticism

Another sign of the maturing of American Catholicism was the slow development of contemplative monasticism. In the 1840s, Trappist houses were established in Kentucky and Iowa. For many decades, most of the monks were from Europe, but in the twentieth century, Americans too began to join.

The Church and Social Issues

The Social Apostolate

Rerum Novarum was well received in the United States, even by some secular liberals, and there was a strong sense of "social Catholicism" fostered in particular by German Americans influenced by the work of von Ketteler and others. The *Zentral Katholik Verein* (Central Catholic Bureau) functioned as both a fraternal organization and a movement to propagate the German school of Catholic social thought.

Labor Unions

It was not obvious, however, how European corporatism fit in America, and in practice, Catholic social thinkers settled for the more pragmatic stance of supporting labor unions and condemning both unrestrained capitalism and Socialism, which for a time had a large following in the United States. A Minnesota priest, John A. Ryan (d. 1945), was the leading exponent of this "social Catholicism", integrating all aspects of Catholic social thought by emphasizing the crucial importance of the family and society's obligation to support its integrity.

The Restoration of Society

Immediately after World War I, the bishops, advised by Ryan, issued a proposal for the "restoration" of society that resembled in many ways the programs of the secular Progressives of that era, albeit arrived at by an entirely different philosophical route. The proposal called for public works projects to stimulate employment, freedom for trade unions, minimum-wage laws, compensation for the unemployed and the disabled, and heavy taxes on great wealth.

The Catholic valuation of community was contrasted with modern "individualism". Faced with the growing claim that poverty required some families to practice birth control, Ryan insisted that the solution was the "just wage" and various kinds of public support. The bishops exhorted women to withdraw from the work force, in order to devote themselves to their families, and some bishops opposed child-labor laws, on the grounds that they constituted undue interference with the autonomy of the family.

The New Deal

Based on the bishops' 1919 statement, the New Deal of President Franklin Roosevelt (1933–1945) seemed to Ryan and others to be the fulfillment of Catholic social teaching. Bishop Francis Haas of Grand Rapids (d. 1953) served on several government commissions, and

Roosevelt's policies were also strongly supported by Cardinal Mundelein and a few other prelates. Because of this seeming episcopal endorsement, and because of their own working-class status, American Catholics were among the strongest supporters of the liberal "welfare state".

Coughlin

During the New Deal, neither Ryan nor Mundelein was the most audible Catholic voice on social questions. A Canadian priest living in Detroit, Charles Coughlin (d. 1979), for a few years had a national radio program and published a magazine, both of which attracted a wide following by no means exclusively Catholic. Coughlin offered highly provocative judgments about a range of issues. Starting from an orthodox Catholic base, his criticisms of the free market soon led to passionate condemnations of capitalism itself, which he claimed was essentially a conspiracy whereby a few plutocrats controlled the world by manipulating governments. At the same time, he rejected Socialism. He offered, however, no clear alternative to the systems he condemned.

At first, Coughlin strongly supported the New Deal and saw Roosevelt as a kind of savior. But he soon condemned Roosevelt as himself a servant of wealth, and he increasingly identified Jews as the principal malefactors in international affairs. His attacks on Roosevelt and his anti-Jewishness led to strong criticism in Catholic circles, and at the beginning of World War II, he was forced to give up his public career, at the instigation of the Vatican.

Dorothy Day and the Catholic Worker

A very different kind of Catholic social witness was that of Dorothy Day (d. 1980) and her Catholic Worker movement. Although the movement never attracted more than a small handful of people, it was widely known through its newspaper ("a penny a copy"), which pricked the consciences of many middle-class Catholics and attracted considerable secular notice as well.

Day was a convert from Communism in the fevered world of the New York radicalism of the Great Depression. She started the Catholic Worker in 1933, at the beginning of the New Deal, in order to witness to the Gospel by living a life of voluntary renunciation and dedication to the poor, an idea she considered far more radical than Marxism or other materialist doctrines.

The Worker movement, which defined itself as nonviolently "anarchist", considered capitalism an inherently unjust and exploitative system, but Socialism too as materialistic and giving too much power to the state. The Worker solution to social problems was a fundamental conversion of heart by which people would overcome greed and selfishness and live simply, according to the Sermon on the Mount.

The movement eventually included thirty "houses of hospitality" throughout the country, places where all who appeared at the door were fed, and sometimes housed, without question. The permanent residents of those houses—many of them of middle-class origins—intended to exemplify the authentic Christian way of life, living very simply, sharing everything in common, and serving the poor. Day thought that communal, self-sufficient farms were the most authentic expression of the Gospel, and several were established, although without great success.

The roots of the Worker philosophy lay in French Catholic thought of the earlier twentieth century as explicated by Charles Péguy, Léon Bloy, and Jacques Maritain. Day herself was unquestionably Catholic, saying that she would close her movement if ordered by her bishop to do so. (In fact, she had at least passive support from otherwise conservative prelates.) Over a period of fifty years, the Worker movement attracted a good deal of praise and some obloquy but little emulation, precisely because of its disarmingly simple radicality. (Day was a pacifist, and some of her early disciples broke with her at the beginning of the Second World War.)

The Church in the Modern World

Anti-Catholicism

Perhaps because the Church's growth seemed to threaten an eventual Catholic dominance, anti-Catholicism remained strong. The Know-Nothings were succeeded by the American Protective Association and the Ku Klux Klan, the latter starting as an anti-black vigilante group after the Civil War that revived after the First World War with anti-Catholicism and anti-Jewishness on its agenda as well. In 1928, the Catholic governor of New York, Alfred E. Smith (d. 1944), was decisively defeated as the Democratic candidate for president, a defeat in which overt anti-Catholicism played a major role.

In his public statements, Smith minimized his religion as much as possible, and Americanist Catholics sometimes seemed to underestimate the degree of this anti-Catholicism, thinking that it could be defused by demonstrations of good will and moderation. Gibbons had discouraged the formation of an organization to defend the Church, although after the First World War, the bishops set up the National Catholic Welfare Council (NCWC) to represent Catholic interests in public life and began to hold annual meetings.

Popular Culture

Despite this hostility, American Catholicism began to blend into popular culture, a process of inculturation to American mores that took place half-instinctively, without much conscious reflection. There were, however, sources of tension between Catholicism and the forces of secularization.

Alarmed over mounting complaints about morality in entertainment, the film industry chose a Jesuit, Daniel A. Lord (d. 1955), to write a code that would govern Hollywood productions for almost forty years, a code whereby sexual subjects were to be handled with restraint and good would always triumph over evil. During the 1940s, priests were highly sympathetic characters in a series of popular films— *Boys' Town, Fighting Father Dunne, Going My Way, The Bells of St. Mary's*, and *The Miracle of the Bells*. The first two films were about actual priests, one of whom—Edward Flanagan (d. 1948) of Boys' Town in Omaha— attained a legendary status for his pioneering efforts to reclaim delinquent boys through trust and love rather than through severe discipline.[5] (On a visit to his native Ireland, Flanagan openly criticized the treatment of troubled boys by Catholic institutions, condemning the kind of brutality that would become a public scandal fifty years later.) Ironically, however, this popular adulation of the priest in one way did little to make Catholicism more comprehensible to non-Catholics, since his sacramental role was treated merely as a kind of ceremonial adjunct to his real work of helping those in need. Taken at face value, such films denied the reality of sin ("There is no such thing as a bad boy") by portraying apparent evil as merely the result of misunderstanding or neglect.

Beginning in 1920, the football team of the University of Notre Dame—hitherto a relatively obscure Midwestern school—was perennially among the best in the nation, attracting a huge following among Catholics who had never attended college and even many non-Catholics. The close link between religion and football—players said they were honored to play for "Our Lady's School" and received Communion before every game—made Catholic piety seem normal and manly to people who might have otherwise thought of it as strange and superstitious.[6]

Catholics in the Wars
Nativists accused Catholics of being disloyal to their adopted country, but in both world wars, heavy Catholic participation, and stories of heroic chaplains, refuted the charge. Catholics' patriotism was further demonstrated by their fervent anti-Communism during the Cold War of the 1950s, which was motivated by the atheism and religious persecution perpetrated by communist regimes in Eastern European countries to which many American Catholics traced their ancestries. Encouraged by their spiritual leaders, American Catholics prayed for the conversion of Russia at the conclusion of every Mass and saw history as climaxing in a titanic struggle against godlessness, in which America's chief enemy was also the chief enemy of the faith.

[5] The film *Fighting Father Dunne* was about Peter Dunne (d. 1939) of St. Louis, who employed similar methods on a smaller scale.
[6] The film *Knute Rockne of Notre Dame*—about the legendary coach who was a late convert from Lutheranism—captures that spirit.

Sheen

Catholic radio programs of various kinds began to multiply during the 1930s, and, unpredictably, during the 1950s, one of the most popular figures in the new medium of television was a bishop who was a veteran of Catholic radio. Fulton J. Sheen (d. 1979), the national director of the Society for the Propagation of the Faith, produced weekly telecasts that actually drew audiences away from variety shows and situation comedies.

Sheen was famous for bringing well-known converts into the Church (the author and ambassador Clare Booth Luce [d. 1987], for example), and his lectures and books effectively expressed the spirit of the 1950s in their philosophical critique of secular culture, their anti-Communism, and their insistence that faith in God was the only answer to both personal and social problems. Sheen was a kind of ecumenist, in that he refrained from criticizing Protestantism, and he attracted many non-Catholics. To Catholics, he spoke warmly of such things as Marian devotions and the pope, but to more general audiences he offered a message that the God of Catholics, Protestants, and Jews would bring peace of soul and comfort from the trials of modern life.

A Flourishing Church

The two decades following the Second World War were, in measurable terms, the peak of American Catholic history, with a high rate of church attendance, abundant religious vocations, and a strong sense of loyalty to the Holy See. The United States was generous in sending both people and money to the foreign missions, and the maturing of its religious life was proven by the growing attraction of the contemplative life for which Archbishop Ireland had seen little value—the Trappists could scarcely build monasteries fast enough to accommodate the influx of vocations.

Suburbia

With almost total success, the Church also faced a new material challenge—the massive movement of people from cities to suburbs, requiring the sudden establishment of many new parishes, or the expansion of old ones, in the same way that massive immigration from Europe had been accommodated in the previous century. In an era of large families, the typical new suburban parish built its school first and held services in the gymnasium until it was possible to build a church that, when finished, was often so utilitarian that it was indistinguishable from many other buildings.

The move from city to suburb was also successful from a spiritual standpoint, in that the communal life of the new parish, in a new suburb lacking traditional institutions, was if anything more intense than in the city. The parish school was the key, the place where parishioners came to know one another, cooperated on fundraising projects, and participated in sports (the usual variety for the children, bowling for their fathers). Adolescents gathered in the gymnasium to pray the rosary in front of a statue of Mary, followed by a chaperoned dance, while the Ladies' Sodality and the Holy Name Society sponsored both social and religious functions for adults.

Priests seldom left the parish grounds except in black suits and Roman collars, but on the grounds, they commonly wore sport shirts and at parish picnics drank beer and joined in the games (including games of chance), successfully blending an easy approachability with a sacerdotal character of which the laity remained highly respectful.

Episcopal Leadership

The American hierarchy had long been governed by what were sometimes called the "brick-and-mortar bishops", men whose chief skill was in administration and fundraising, a skill on which the postwar suburbanization placed a premium. In a different way from Sheen, Cardinal Francis J. Spellman of New York (d. 1967) epitomized the American church of the era—a consummate brick-and-mortar bishop who wielded considerable political influence and was taken very seriously when he spoke on public issues.

Liberal Anti-Catholicism

But while the identification of the Catholic Church with anti-Communism and sound moral values did much to overcome animosity at the popular level, anti-Catholicism among the intellectuals if anything increased, as Catholics' undoubted patriotism was now taken as proof that they had blind loyalties and did not appreciate real freedom. Film censorship and laws prohibiting the dissemination of contraceptives (although most such laws had been enacted by Protestant legislators) were cited as proof that Catholicism was a repressive and dangerous religion. For most American liberals, the Spanish Civil War was a holy crusade in the opposite way it was for many Catholics.

John Dewey (d. 1952), the most influential of all American philosophers, thought that education should inculcate a "religion of democracy" as a deliberate substitute for traditional faiths, and liberal intellectuals in general disapproved of Catholic schools as engaged merely in indoctrination. During the 1950s, the writings of the professional anti-Catholic Paul Blanshard (d. 1980) attracted a good deal of attention, including the endorsement of leading Protestants such as the theologian Reinhold Niebuhr (d. 1971). Logically, the claim that Catholicism was a religion of authoritarian superstition applied to much of traditional Protestantism and Judaism as well, but Catholics were the largest and most influential religious group and therefore bore the brunt of the attack.

Religious Liberty

Most Catholics were as much bewildered as offended by the charge that they did not accept democracy, but there was a theological problem of which most were also unaware—officially the Church had never accepted the idea of religious liberty as it was understood in the modern West. The standard teaching remained that, while it would be imprudent to establish Catholicism as the official religion of a country where many people were not Catholic, it was appropriate, perhaps even obligatory, to do so where Catholics were a large majority. The ideal state could not be religiously neutral or indifferent.

After World War II, that doctrine was reexamined by the Jesuit John Courtney Murray (d. 1967), who justified religious liberty not on the basis of indifference to truth but out of respect for the dignity and freedom of the individual, something that made coercion improper. Murray believed that the Founding Fathers of the United States accepted the idea of natural law, so that the state had to follow correct moral principles, independent of particular religious teachings. (Abortion, he thought, could never be justified, given the fundamental right to life asserted by the Declaration of Independence.) But prevailing theological opinion was against Murray, and for a time, he was forbidden to write or teach on the subject.

Racial Justice

As distinct from the attitudes of Catholics in general, official Catholic support for racial equality had been clear for a long time. During World War II, the Jesuit John LaFarge (see Chapter Eleven above, p. 382), an aristocratic convert, founded the Catholic Interracial Council, the first organized effort to bring black and white Catholics together. After the war, some bishops took strong stands in favor of racial integration: Bishop Vincent Waters of Raleigh (d. 1974); Archbishop Joseph F. Rummel of New Orleans (d. 1964), who excommunicated white Catholics for defying his authority; and Archbishop (later Cardinal) Joseph E. Ritter of St. Louis (d. 1967), who faced down resistance by threatening to do the same.

The Civil Rights Movement

But the civil rights movement of the 1960s brought new complications. Priests and nuns were in the front ranks of those who poured into Southern towns to march for racial equality, and the hierarchy made the Church's official position clear. But when the same marchers appeared in heavily Catholic neighborhoods in Northern cities, they were sometimes pelted with rocks by "ethnic" Catholics who thought they were being pressured to surrender their old neighborhoods. "White flight" greatly accelerated the Catholic move to the suburbs, and many old city parishes were either closed or became in effect mission centers for work among inner-city blacks, few of whom were Catholic.

Hispanic Immigration

While European immigration practically ended before World War II, after the war there was a substantial influx of Mexicans into California and the Southwest, and of Puerto Ricans into New York City. These Catholics required new pastoral strategies, beginning with priests learning Spanish. As with earlier immigrant groups, the Church was often the vehicle for the preservation of Hispanic cultures, and some bishops, notably Archbishop Robert Lucey of San Antonio (d. 1977), were champions of Hispanic rights. There was considerable clerical support for the United Farm Workers, which was composed mainly of Hispanic immigrants.

Kennedy
In 1960, John F. Kennedy became the first Catholic to be elected president (1961–1963), although he encountered religious prejudice almost as strong as Smith had faced in 1928. Kennedy sought to overcome that prejudice by denying that his religion could or should have significant influence on public policy, and many Catholics, ecstatic at finally having one of their own in the White House, accepted that claim.

The Catholic Left
But in one of the great ironies of history, within five years of Kennedy's death, after many attempts over many decades to show that Catholics could be good Americans, the Church suddenly came under criticism from the opposite direction. Kennedy authorized American military intervention in the Vietnam War, an involvement that rapidly expanded after his death. Before long, that war, along with the civil rights movement and the amorphous but potent "counter-culture", fused into the greatest upsurge of radical agitation in American history.

The moral legitimacy of the Second World War had been questioned by very few Catholics—some bishops even claimed that Catholics could not be conscientious objectors. But the Jesuit moralist John Ford (d. 1988), who later proved to be the most staunchly orthodox of theologians, thought that the bombing of cities by the Allies, especially the atomic bombs dropped on Hiroshima and Nagasaki, was immoral. Most Catholics paid little attention to Ford, and Murray thought he was mistaken.

But in the new American "mainstream", the patriotism and concern for personal morality that had made Catholics acceptable were now embarrassments, and the Catholic New Left, almost invisible up to that time, was suddenly thrust into the center of national attention. It was led by the Berrigan brothers—the Josephite Philip (d. 2002), who soon left the priesthood, and his Jesuit brother Daniel. They accused the government of perpetrating an immoral war and accused bishops like Cardinal Spellman, who made regular visits to military bases, of abetting that injustice. The Catholic New Left's distinctive tactic was to engage in symbolic, almost liturgical, acts—pouring blood on draft records and denting the nose cones of rockets—differing from the secular left in its religious roots and its professed philosophy of nonviolence.

But in the fevered atmosphere of the time, "nonviolence" was an elastic concept. The Berrigans served as character witnesses for a terrorist who set off a bomb that killed a young father, and the Berrigans and several of their associates served prison terms for a botched plot to kidnap government officials. In St. Louis, a Carmelite friar—praised by his confreres as a man of deep spirituality—went to prison for a failed attempt to get money for radical causes by robbing a Catholic rectory at gunpoint.

The counter-culture, which was an integral part of the New Left, posed a severe problem for Catholics, as issues of personal morality came to outweigh politics. Some of the Catholic Worker communities, for example, were fractured by violations of Dorothy Day's rule that drugs and extramarital sex were not be permitted on the premises. Ford, despite his judgment about the immorality of bombing, was effectively ostracized by his fellow Jesuits because of his continued stand against contraception. The leftist *National Catholic Reporter* supported radical politics and the sexual revolution in about equal measures.

Catholic Republicans

But as some American Catholics moved sharply left, many others took the equally unusual step of moving away from the Democratic Party. To some extent, this was because, as they grew more prosperous, they became more Republican in their economic philosophy, but the move also resulted from the Democratic Party's shifting left and repudiating, among other things, the socially conservative, strongly anti-communist stance of many Catholics. Blue-collar workers deserted the party, and Catholic labor leaders in the traditional mold, like George Meany (d. 1980) of the American Federation of Labor–Congress of Industrial Organizations (AFL-CIO), were excluded from its inner circles. The Democrats came to embrace a secular agenda in which abortion was defined as a fundamental "right", thereby making it a defining issue even for liberal Catholic politicians.

Bernardin

After the Second Vatican Council, the NCWC was reestablished as the National Conference of Catholic Bishops (NCCB), which functioned, among other things, as a lobbying organization. The key figure was Bishop Joseph L. Bernardin (d. 1996), general secretary of the organization and later cardinal archbishop of Chicago. Under his leadership, the NCCB continued, as it had long done, to favor liberal economic programs. Bernardin urged a "consistent ethic of life", which meant embracing support for programs that help the poor while opposing abortion and the death penalty. But few politicians accepted his invitation, and liberal economic programs often subsidized contraception and abortion for the poor.

(The NCCB was renamed the United States Conference of Catholic Bishops [USCCB] in 2001.)

Abortion

More and more Catholics in public office supported legal abortion. John Kennedy's younger brother Edward (d. 2010) served in the Senate for decades and, advised by Jesuit theologians, was a staunch supporter of legal abortion. The Jesuit Robert Drinan (d. 2007) served for ten years as a passionately pro-abortion Congressman, until finally required by the Holy See to relinquish his seat. Kennedy, Drinan, and other Catholics acquiesced in the secularist claim that abortion was a purely "sectarian" issue and promised that they would not "impose" their religion on others.

Anti-abortion Catholics invoked Murray's claim that the practice was forbidden by natural law, which did not rest on religious authority. The pro-life movement demonstrated its potency by enacting whatever limits on abortion were still legally possible after the Supreme Court in 1973 found it to be a constitutional "right": a ban on federal funding; electing pro-life politicians to public office at all levels; and simply keeping the issue alive, to the point where after almost four decades, a majority of Americans favor limiting the practice.

American Catholics in the Twenty-First Century

The administrations of Presidents George W. Bush (2001–2009) and Barack Obama (2009–) divided Catholics sharply. Liberals condemned the American invasion of Iraq and Bush's economic policies and denied that his position on abortion and other issues justified Catholic support. The division deepened because of Obama's successful enactment of a national health-care program that the bishops opposed and that required Catholic institutions to provide insurance for their employees that included contraception (including abortifacients) and sterilization.

One result of the Catholic shift to the Republicans was that in 2010 six of the nine justices of the Supreme Court were Catholics (one appointed by Obama). Three were Jewish and none Protestant, something that would have been unthinkable even twenty years before.

While "mainline" American churches were declining numerically in the early twenty-first century, the Catholic Church experienced a slight increase, attributable mainly to the immigration of Hispanics, who by now constituted a third of American Catholics. Many of the immigrants entered the country illegally; and, while a large majority of Americans favored enforcement of the immigration laws, the bishops urged that all immigrants be made welcome.

In 2010, the United States had the fourth largest Catholic population in the world—almost seventy million. Estimates of regular church attendance varied between a third and a half of self-identified Catholics.

Australia

Penal Origins

The continent that would become Australia was discovered by the Portuguese in the sixteenth century but was not settled by Europeans until 1788 when, unique among the nations of the world, it was established by Great Britain primarily as a penal colony on what would become New South Wales on the mainland and an island called Van Diemen's Land (later Tasmania).

A quarter of the convicts were Irish, both from Ireland itself and from England, including a few convict priests. A minority of the prisoners had been convicted of political offenses, but most were common criminals whom the chaplains found to be virtually incorrigible—given to drink, sexual license, and violence and seldom open to religious influence.

The English Benedictine William Ullathorne (d. 1889), who came to Australia in 1833, reported that conditions of convict life were so intolerable that those who were sentenced to death rejoiced and those who were reprieved wept. He lamented that the few priests were morally not much better than those they served.

Catholicism

The first Mass ever celebrated in Australia was at Sydney in 1803, the celebrant being a convict Irish priest. But after an insurrection a year later, the government disallowed further priestly ministrations and required all convicts to attend Anglican services. According to legend, the reserved Blessed Sacrament was left behind when the last priest was deported from Sydney, and for several years it was the center of devotion for the handful of free Catholics living there.

Catholic chaplains were restored in New South Wales in 1820, their salaries paid by a British government that weighed the hope that religion would reform the prisoners against the fear that priests might stir up further resistance. Catholic services were not allowed in Van Dieman's Land until the 1840s. Official policy vacillated with each governor. For a time, for example, all orphan children were placed in Anglican institutions, to be raised in that faith, and priests were not allowed to visit Catholic soldiers in military hospitals. But eventually these and other restrictions were lifted.

The End of Transportation

Convicts who had served their sentences were ordinarily freed and could seek to enter the mainstream of society. Transportation of convicts to New South Wales ceased in 1840 and to Tasmania in 1854. Free settlers began immigrating from Europe—a great many from Ireland—but they tended to be very poor, a fact that, combined with the convict legacy, made the overall tone of Australian society, as many of the clergy saw it, uncivilized and irreligious.

Polding

The church in Australia was first under the vicar apostolic of London, then under the vicar apostolic of the French colony of Mauritius. In

1834, the diocese of Sydney was established, its first bishop being the Benedictine John Bede Polding (d. 1877), who had been Ullathorne's teacher in England. Ullathorne became Polding's vicar general, handling administrative matters for the bishop (who was constantly traveling) and serving as the target for numerous attacks by disgruntled priests and laity. Before long, Ullathorne returned to England, where he became a prominent bishop.

The Monastic Dream

For some years, Polding's apostolate was governed by a unique dream—that the church in Australia would be organized on the basis of Benedictine monasticism, which, as in the Dark Ages, would serve as the spiritual center radiating outward. But the dream was not well suited to the actual conditions of the continent, and even Ullathorne came to think it was impractical. The monastery Polding founded in Sydney had its own troubles, leading some of the monks to leave the community, and the diocesan clergy strongly resisted the monastic idea, which was eventually abandoned. During the 1840s, several new dioceses were established, and Polding was made an archbishop.

A Scattered Flock

Polding himself tacitly admitted its impracticality by his own heroic, almost ceaseless, pastoral work—traveling vast distances on horseback, visiting remote settlements that had not seen a priest in years, living away from his monastic community for long periods. Most of his flock were Irish and increasingly, against his better judgment, he began importing priests from Ireland, a policy that soon produced another kind of tension.

The practice of the faith was also hindered by the number of people who left the coastal cities for "the Bush", where the shortage of priests made it difficult, even impossible in some cases, to provide adequate pastoral care. Priests who did serve in those remote areas, away from episcopal oversight, might themselves fall prey to alcohol or lax sexual mores. Some managed to get control of substantial tracts of land, including land that was supposed to belong to the Church, forcing bishops to battle both lay trusteeism and pastors who claimed personal ownership of their parish property.

Aborigines

Pius IX reminded the Australian bishops of their responsibility for the Aboriginal ("from the beginning") natives, and Polding considered their treatment a disgrace, an instance of "civilized" Europeans perpetrating barbarism. The Spanish Bishop José Serra (d. 1886) of Western Australia succeeded in obtaining legislation to protect a people who in some cases were victims of what amounted to genocide. For the most part, however, the laws remained unenforced, and mission efforts among a largely nomadic people had only limited effect.

The Irish

Also during the 1840s, large numbers of Irish began arriving in flight from the Potato Famine, and a gold rush in Victoria in the 1850s brought many more. The condition of the immigrants was often miserable. Polding undertook to meet each arriving ship, in order to aid in a transition to a new life, and a widow, Caroline Chisholm (d. 1877), did heroic work among the immigrant children. (Attacked by Protestants as an agent of the pope, and distrusted by some Catholics for being English, she eventually returned home, where she died in poverty.)

The Irish were unshakable in their ethnic identity, of which religion was a crucial part, but bishops judged that for some ethnicity was by far the more important part of their identity, such that Irish who were fiercely loyal to their religion might also be extremely lax in its practice. One estimate placed the rate of regular church attendance at less than a quarter, and many parents did not bother to ensure that their children received religious instruction.

Irish Clergy

As time went on, most of the men appointed bishops in Australia were Irish, many of them sent out directly from their homeland; a large majority of the lower clergy were also from Ireland. The first native Australian priest was ordained in 1867, but vocations remained relatively few. Irish bishops sought to reproduce in Australia the ecclesiastical patterns that prevailed in their homeland, where the clergy were the natural leaders of an oppressed people. In Ireland, Catholics almost always married Catholics, for example, so that in Australia the hierarchy officially forbade "mixed marriages", a rule that was often evaded or ignored.

Polding believed that part of the Church's mission was to civilize what he considered a semi-barbarous people, and he found many of the Irish priests to be an obstacle to that goal because they were crude, poorly educated, and of dubious morality. He particularly denigrated the alumni of All Hallows College in Dublin, whom he thought the Irish bishops were eager to get rid of. Perhaps because of the popular conviction that all prisoners brought to Australia had been victims of English injustice, opposition to authority was strong, often directed at the hierarchy by both laity and clergy, and accompanied by abusive rhetoric.

Many of the Irish priests disliked Polding simply because he was English, and for others, his monastic ideal and his cultured personality seemed, despite his undeniable pastoral zeal, snobbish and out of touch with the needs of the flock. On the other hand, Irish bishops and priests complained that Englishmen in general, and Archbishop Polding in particular, were unsuited to lead what should be an Irish church, a position that was effectively represented in Rome by Paul Cullen (see Chapter Eleven above, p. 352).

Irish bishops were known for their authoritarian ways, an extreme example being John Brady (d. 1871) of Perth, who summarily expelled a community of Spanish Benedictines from his diocese (among them the future Bishop Serra), forcing them to embark on a three-day journey on foot during Holy Week, carrying the cross as they went. Brady was removed by the Holy See in 1850 but refused to recognize the decree and, supported by a mob, at one point scuffled with his appointed successor in the sanctuary of a church. Excommunicated, he returned to Ireland still considering himself bishop of Perth.

Vaughan and Moran

When Polding died, he was succeeded by another English Benedictine, Roger Vaughan, bishop of Hobart, Tasmania (d. 1883), whose appointment was strongly opposed by the Irish bishops. When Vaughan died on a visit to England, his successor was Patrick Moran (d. 1911), a bishop in Ireland who was Cullen's nephew and had served as his secretary. Such were the prevailing ethnic feelings that Moran coldly informed Vaughan's brother, the future Cardinal Herbert Vaughan (d. 1903) of Westminster, that there was no interest in Australia in returning Roger's body for burial in his cathedral, something that did not happen until 1946.

Barely a year after his appointment, Moran was made the first Australian cardinal, an honor that was rumored to be compensation for his having been passed over for the archbishopric of Dublin, a surmise given credibility by the fact that after Moran's death no other Australian prelate received the red hat for thirty-five years.

Sectarian Strife

Sectarian strife was intense well into the twentieth century, with both Protestants and Catholics engaging in extreme polemics. Protestant immigrants from Northern Ireland were numerous and were especially bitter in denouncing the Church and demanding that Australia be a Protestant society. Catholics were characterized as drunkards and gamblers, ignorant slaves of a false religion, while Catholics condemned Protestantism as itself a false religion that glorified private judgment and thereby led to the moral breakdown of society. Religious and ethnic loyalties were often the basis of bitterly fought election campaigns, and as early as 1830, a few Catholics managed to attain public office in the new colony of Victoria, which was not a penal colony.

Education

Next to basic pastoral work, education was seen by the bishops as the key to sustaining the faith in a hostile environment. For a time, the colonial government provided subsidies for all church schools, of whatever denomination, but these were gradually withdrawn. Despite losing this support, the Catholic schools remained under the official scrutiny of government with respect to their level of educational quality. Poor Catholics had a great deal of difficulty supporting their own system, and for almost a century, the bishops campaigned for the return of school subsidies, in the conviction that state schools, which tended to have a Protestant character, were a danger to the faith.

An official Australian "Penny Catechism" was issued in the 1880s, almost simultaneously with the *Baltimore Catechism* in the United States. Also like the *Baltimore Catechism*, it remained in use until the 1960s.

Schools Run by Religious

St. Mary McKillop (d. 1909), Australia's first canonized saint, founded one of the numerous female communities called the Sisters of St. Joseph. Her sisters followed poor laborers into the Bush especially in order to educate their children, an act of independence for which she was briefly excommunicated by the bishop of Adelaide. The Jesuits opened a few secondary schools, but their classical system of education was less popular with the laity than the more practical instruction provided by the schools of the Irish Christian Brothers (distinct from the followers of de la Salle) and the French Marist Brothers.

Higher Education

For a long time, relatively few Catholics attended universities, but Catholic colleges were nonetheless founded at the universities of Sydney and Melbourne, as places where Catholic students could live among their own, under supervision, taking general courses in the secular university but receiving instruction in their colleges in sensitive subjects like philosophy. By the year 2000, there were three independent Catholic institutions of higher learning.

Protestantism The Catholic hierarchy successfully opposed making the Anglican church the official religion of Australia, urging instead that all religions remain on an equal footing. In 1901, Moran, after having strongly supported Australia's entry into the British Commonwealth, refused to attend the official ceremony because the Anglican archbishop of Sydney was given precedence over him.

Australian Protestantism was in measurable decline by 1900, something that Catholic leaders often pointed out in predicting that Catholicism was the religion of the future. Perhaps partly because of this Protestant decline, religious antagonisms did not abate. The newly formed Australian Protestant Defense Association was countered first by the Australian Catholic Truth Society, then by the Catholic Federation. Moran, however, hoped that Catholics would gain full acceptance in Australian society, and on the whole, he did not pursue aggressive policies. But he did speak of Australia as part of "the Irish spiritual empire", and Irish identity remained strong, despite increasing immigration from other countries. In 1870, half of all Australian Catholics were from Ireland, but by 1908, Irish were only a fifth.

Because most Catholics were of the working class, and because the more conservative parties were seen as dominated by Protestants, by 1900, the Labor Party was attracting most of the Catholic vote, a trend that Moran encouraged. Inspired by *Rerum Novarum*, he publicly supported strikes and, even though the bishops were at pains to insist that the Labor Party was not socialist, once urged that the coal industry be nationalized. But as a minority, most Catholic Labor politicians were reluctant to champion the bishops' demand for the restoration of subsidies for Catholic schools, and some Laborites of a radical bent were even hostile to the Catholic presence in the party.

The Labor Party

Moran was succeeded by Michael Kelly (d. 1940), rector of the Irish College in Rome, but the leadership of the Australian church actually passed to Daniel Mannix, archbishop of Melbourne from 1917 to his death—at almost 100—in 1963. Mannix, who was president of the Maynooth Seminary in Ireland at the time of his appointment, was perhaps the single most important figure in Australian Catholic history and one of the most remarkable prelates anywhere in the modern Church. He was unequaled in his boldness and possessed great rhetorical skills, especially a sharp wit, traits that kept him in the public eye continuously for fifty years.

Mannix

World War I

Especially because of their Irish tradition, Australian Catholics tended to have only conditional loyalty to the British Empire. Many favored the Netherlanders of South Africa against the British in the Boer War of the late 1890s, and World War I, which was regarded in Ireland as merely a defense of British imperialism, was equally unpopular with Catholic Australians.

Mannix, who through half the war years was still only a coadjutor bishop, stopped just short of urging Catholics not to enlist in the military, and other bishops endorsed such service only with the reminder that Catholics were fighting for an Australian government that unjustly denied them their right to school aid. Mannix vigorously opposed military conscription, which was twice defeated in popular referenda in which he played a role. (The labor unions were also opposed.) Catholic passions were aroused when a German-born priest who made inflammatory remarks was first imprisoned, then deported from Australia.

Mannix was increasingly critical of the war itself, to the point of provoking Protestant demands that he too be deported. But after the war, in a characteristically bold gesture, he confounded charges of disloyalty by riding in a St. Patrick's Day parade in an open car, accompanied by fourteen Catholic recipients of the Victoria Cross, Britain's highest award for bravery in battle.

Irish Ties

Australian bishops with close ties to Ireland took a great interest in the mother country and openly favored Irish independence. They condemned the abortive Easter Uprising of 1916 and the atrocities that accompanied the rebellion after the war, but they held the British government primarily responsible for poisoning the atmosphere.

Mannix was completely dedicated to the cause of Irish independence, and in 1920, he embarked on an extended journey in its support. After making a triumphant tour of the United States, he set sail for Ireland itself, where his mother was still alive. But the British government announced that he would not be allowed to land, intercepted his ship, and took him to England, apparently under arrest. In London, he was allowed considerable freedom by an increasingly embarrassed government, and he used that freedom to make speeches, give interviews to the press, and administer the last rites to an Irish nationalist dying in jail in a hunger strike. (Mannix blamed the government's callousness for the man's death.)

Mannix supported the Republican movement under De Valera, which rejected the Anglo-Irish Treaty of 1922. As a result, Mannix was denied an official welcome by the archbishop of Dublin while leading a pilgrimage to Ireland a few years later, because he declined to promise that he would not speak about politics. (Mannix later successfully counseled De Valera to swallow his misgivings and enter politics.)

Coming of Age

The Vatican established an Apostolic Delegation in Australia just before the First World War, perhaps primarily because of complaints that Irish bishops disregarded canon law and ruled in arbitrary ways. But Australia did not cease officially to be a mission territory until 1976, the year after the first Aboriginal priest was ordained.

Australian Catholicism showed itself vigorous in many ways. The Holy Name Society flourished, as did popular devotions. The Sydney archdiocese started its own radio station, and Leslie Rumble (d. 1975), a Missionary of the Sacred Heart, gave radio talks that sold seven million copies when published. Catholic young men's groups were conspicuous participants in the national passion for football.

Native Clergy

By the 1920s, four-fifths of Catholics in Australia had been born there, and the Irish influence was waning. An organized group of clerical alumni of the Sydney archdiocesan seminary—St. Patrick's at Manly—openly urged that ties with Ireland be loosened, an idea accepted by the Vatican in accord with its general policy of encouraging native vocations. Kelly's first coadjutor bishop was an Irish priest from Rome, but when the old archbishop finally died in 1940 he was succeeded by a native Australian, Norman Gilroy, who later became Australia's second cardinal. (Mannix was perhaps too controversial to be given the red hat.)

Catholics in Social and Political Spheres

In the post–World War I period, Australian Catholics were to some extent divided along class lines. The growing middle class and the few wealthy sought integration into society, while the large working class saw that society as essentially hostile. The first group sometimes found Mannix an embarrassment, and some openly criticized him. Sectarian conflict flared up again as a result of wartime experiences. In New South Wales, there was a proposal in effect to shut down Catholic schools and to punish priests who upheld the ban on mixed marriages. The Knights of the Southern Cross, modeled after the Knights of Columbus in the United States, were founded to defend Catholic rights.

Catholics were coming of age politically. The first Catholic prime ministers of Australia were the Laborite James Scullin (1929–1931) and the Liberal Joseph Lyons (1931–1939), neither of whom, however, moved on the perennial Catholic issue of public aid to private schools.

Intellectual Stirrings

In the 1930s, Australian Catholicism experienced its first significant intellectual stirrings, in a culture that was sometimes thought of as philistine.

Frank Sheed (d. 1984) was one of the most important Catholic laymen in the world during the first half of the twentieth century. Trained as a soap-box orator by the Catholic Evidence Guild in England, he undertook the same apostolate in his native Australia, and became a popular author. He and his wife, Maisie Ward (d. 1975), who was also an author, founded Sheed and Ward, which for decades was the most important Catholic publishing house in the English-speaking world, with offices in London and New York.

In Melbourne, a handful of laymen formed the Campion Society— named for the Elizabethan Jesuit martyr—for the purpose of studying Catholic literature, especially the English Catholic intellectual revival then in full flower. Although small, the group had considerable long-term influence.

B. A. Santamaria

Melbourne Catholicism in the 1930s also gave birth to a unique phenomenon that eventually had an impact on Australian society of a kind without parallel in any other modern country. Shortly after Dorothy Day founded the Catholic Worker movement in New York, a miscellaneous group of laymen from the Campion Club started a Catholic Worker group in Melbourne as well, publishing their own *Catholic Worker* newspaper, edited by a young law student named B. A. Santamaria (d. 1998). The paper's circulation eventually reached a remarkable seventy thousand.

Soon, however, Santamaria left the Catholic Worker, which in time became his severe critic. With the full support of Mannix, he and several others undertook to establish a formal program and a national office for Catholic Action suited to the Australian situation. There was difficulty from the beginning, in that some bishops thought Catholic Action should be under direct episcopal control, while Mannix wanted its lay leaders to be essentially independent.

Mannix was a strong critic of capitalism, and in that spirit, Santamaria and his colleagues sought to transform Australian society in fundamental ways—establishing a pervasive Christian spirit of morality and using politics for the purpose of implementing Catholic social teachings, such as Distributism, subsidiarity, and the family wage. At first, they worked within the Labor Party, but many in the party looked on them suspiciously, as ideologues enamored of utopian ideas rather than pragmatic political goals.

"The Movement"

During World War II, communists managed to gain a significant foothold in some Australian labor unions, and thereby in the Labor Party itself, and after the war, again with Mannix' full blessing, Santamaria embarked on an organized campaign to expel the communist influence, employing the same tactics of secret organization and infiltration that the communists themselves used. There were five thousand members of this Catholic Social Study Movement, which came to be called simply "The Movement". In 1945, the archdiocese of Sydney suspended its support for the official Catholic Action body of which Santamaria was an official, and The Movement, now calling itself the National Civic Council, went its own way, without official approval.

In 1954, a prominent Labor Party leader denounced The Movement in the strongest terms, implying a Catholic plot to take over the party, as a result of which many Catholics withdrew from the party and others were expelled. The Movement then proved capable of influencing so many voters that for almost two decades the Labor Party was kept out of office at the national level. This split in the Labor Party accelerated a trend whereby Catholics, as they entered the ranks of the middle class, moved away from Labor and toward the Liberal Party, which had long been thought of as a Protestant bastion. Only a few months before Mannix' death, it was the Liberals who enacted what the Australian bishops had so long sought, and what Labor had so long failed to deliver—public aid to private schools.

The Movement's influence was primarily in Victoria, since from the beginning Archbishop Kelly, and later Cardinal Gilroy, considered the Melbourne version of Catholic Action far too independent and both The Movement and Mannix himself far too confrontational. Gilroy presented his case in Rome, and the Vatican ruled that Catholic Action groups should not engage in politics, a ruling that was allowed to stand despite Mannix' personal appeal to Pius XII. Thus events of the postwar period opened a split between Melbourne and Sydney Catholicism that persisted for decades.

Growth

In 1935, only 17 percent of Australians were estimated to be Catholics— half of them regular churchgoers—a decline from earlier times that was due partly to a drift away from the Church. But substantial Catholic immigration occurred after World War II, raising Catholics' proportion of the population to 27 percent.

Although weaker than it had been fifty years before, Catholicism in the United States in the third Christian millennium was in many ways healthier than anywhere else in the Western world. Ironically, this may have been due mainly to the continued vitality of conservative Protestantism, which helped sustain an overall social climate favorable to religion. By contrast, neither Canada nor Australia had a significant movement that could be called Evangelical or Fundamentalist and, as those countries became less Protestant, in a sense they also became less Catholic.

The Church everywhere in the West faced the question of what, if any, presence she could have in a pluralistic society. The history of the New Nations, which had wrestled with that question from their beginnings, provided perhaps the best guidance.

The Future of the New Nations

I4   Joy and Hope, Grief and Anguish

John XXIII   The papal conclave of 1958 elected Cardinal Angelo Roncalli, the former nuncio to France, who had been serving as patriarch of Venice. John XXIII (1958–1963) was unusually old (seventy-seven) when elected, and conventional wisdom assumed that he had been chosen as a brief transitional pontiff. But to the contrary, his pontificate would turn out to be one of the most momentous in the entire history of the Church.

Style   In a sense, the "style" of the new Pope was more important than his specific policies. Apart from anything he decreed or authorized, John immediately effected a revolution in the public image of the papal office, an abrupt transition from the concept of the pope as ruler to the pope as kindly pastor. Whereas Pius XII was tall, thin, aloof, austere, and aristocratic, John was short, rotund, and informal, given to making jokes at his own expense, and he deliberately departed from papal protocol by the kinds of guests he received (the Anglican archbishop of Canterbury, the atheist son-in-law of the Soviet premier Nikita Khrushchev [d. 1971]). John signaled that he would no longer be the "prisoner of the Vatican" when he left Rome to visit the Marian shrine of Loreto and other places in Italy. His first trip outside the Vatican was to a prison, an act meant to exemplify the ancient papal title of "servant of the servants of God".

Myths   Because of John's style, few popes have had so many myths woven about them. Thus he was often called the "peasant pope", although in fact his family might be called lower middle class. Dubbed "pastoral", he spent part of his career in administration and the rest as a Vatican diplomat, culminating in only five years as head of a diocese. Far from being simple, he was intellectually and politically sophisticated. John's spiritual diary, *The Journal of a Soul*, revealed a man of deep traditional piety, and his "liberalism" was qualified by such acts as mandating the teaching of Latin in all seminaries, at a time when it was being phased out in many places, and mandating the inclusion of St. Joseph in the Canon of the Mass after the Fathers of the Second Vatican Council had shown no interest in the matter.

John's pontificate was one of the most momentous in the history of **A Council** the Church mainly because of the Council, which, to the surprise of everyone, he summoned less than a year after his election, at a time when most Catholics had probably never even heard of such a thing. (An "ecumenical council" is a gathering of the entire Church and does not refer to the ecumenical movement to which Vatican II would give its support.) Although Pius XII had considered the possibility, there had been no such gathering since the Vatican Council of 1870 (now called Vatican I), which had never been officially dissolved. Some of John's advisors urged caution, but he brushed aside all misgivings.

"A New Pentecost"

Precisely why the Council was summoned remains somewhat uncertain. John announced its goals as "the renewal of the spirit of the Gospel in the hearts of people everywhere and the adjustment of Christian discipline to modern-day living".[1] He spoke of a "new Pentecost" and stated serenely that, since the teachings of the Church were firm and not in doubt, the Council would not concern itself with doctrine but would be primarily a "pastoral" council.

A Healthy Church

For the most part, the Church at the time seemed quite healthy. The rate of church attendance in many countries was remarkably high (over three quarters of Catholics attended Sunday Mass in the United States), religious vocations were abundant, and Catholics seemed very serious about their faith, although they were sometimes criticized as neglectful of social justice and overly formalistic or mechanical in their piety. Clerical scandals were rare, the level of priestly education and zeal was high, and not since the patristic period had the laity been so well instructed in their faith. Since World War I, the importance of the Holy See in international affairs had been recognized in the number of countries with which the Vatican had official diplomatic relations: up from only fifteen at the beginning of the century to seventy-eight by 1968.

Evangelization

It is likely that John thought that the "new Pentecost" would build on this foundation to bring Christ to the nations. He hoped for nothing less than the conversion of the world, something that required Catholics to put aside the defensiveness that had characterized the Church since the Counter-Reformation.

A "Pastoral" Gathering

In his opening address in 1962, John called on the Council to take account of the "errors, requirements, and opportunities" of the age and regretted that some people ("prophets of gloom") seemed unable

---

[1] Walter B. Abbot, S.J. (ed.), *The Documents of Vatican II* (New York: Guild Press, 1966), 704–5.

to see any good in the modern world. At the same time, he affirmed the infallibility of the Church and said that her dogmas were settled and "known to all", so that the conciliar task was merely one of presenting those dogmas in new ways.

But the papal proclamation was ambiguous, in ways that would turn out to characterize the Council and its results even more. What was authentic renewal and how was it to be achieved? How should essential discipline be adjusted to modern culture? Even a "pastoral" council had to be clear about its beliefs. Contrary to what John apparently intended, Vatican II ended up giving much of its attention to the internal life of the Church, a scrutiny that resulted in a crisis of Catholic identity without historical parallel. John died after the first session of the Council and was succeeded by Cardinal Giovanni Battista Montini of Milan, who ruled as Paul VI (1963–1978).

Vatican II

Public Interest

Vatican II met in a glare of publicity greater even than Vatican I, including the press all over the world and the relatively new electronic media. The intense interest that even many non-Catholics took in the proceedings was an acknowledgment of the Church's importance, albeit in some ways an ambiguous compliment. It was the best-attended council in history: composed of 2,500 bishops and 150 superiors of male religious orders, from all over the world, plus innumerable official "observers" and *periti* (specialists) who advised the voting delegates on matters of theology and canon law.

The Agenda

There was a crisis from the beginning, when many of the Council Fathers objected to the work of the various preparatory commissions—mainly members of the Roman Curia—that had been set up to formulate the schema (agenda) of the Council. The tension arose from the desire of many of the Fathers to open discussions as widely as possible, without restriction. John acquiesced in the demands for new schema, which were then formulated mainly by committees of the Council Fathers themselves.

Blocs

The Fathers were by no means of one mind—there were various blocs working to achieve diverse goals, often in opposition to one another—but the procedural squabble was in many ways the decisive event of the Council, representing a crucial victory for what was now being called the "liberal" party.

"Progressives"
The leadership of that party, and in many ways of the Council itself, came mainly from five Western European countries, the most influential prelates being Cardinals Bernard Alfrink (d. 1987) of the Netherlands; Leo Jozef Suenens (d. 1996) of Belgium; Achille Lienart (d. 1973) of France; Julius Doepfner (d. 1976) and Joseph Frings (d. 1978) of Germany; and

Franz Koenig (d. 2004) of Austria. The majority of the Council Fathers tended to defer to the opinions of those prelates and a few others, such as Cardinal Giacamo Lercaro (d. 1976) of Bologna.

Theologians

Over the previous century, those five countries had nourished the most vigorous and sophisticated Catholic intellectual life, and as theological questions arose, bishops were influenced by the men recognized as the most accomplished theologians of the age: the Jesuits Henri de Lubac (d. 1991) and Jean Danielou (d. 1974), the Oratorian Louis Bouyer (d. 2004), and the Dominican Yves Congar (d. 1995) in France; the Dominican Edward Schillebeeckx (d. 2009) in the Netherlands; the Jesuit Karl Rahner (d. 1984), the Redemptorist Bernard Haering (d. 1998), and the diocesan priest Joseph Ratzinger in Germany. These *periti* were influential both in shaping the thought of the prelates whom they advised and in working behind the scenes with other bishops and *periti*. The influence of this northern European group was due partly to their well-organized efforts to shape the discussions.

But despite its intellectual brilliance, in some ways the Church in Western Europe appeared less than vigorous, in terms such as church attendance and religious vocations. Some countries, France in particular, seemed top-heavy—rich in intellectual life but with an eroding popular base—so that their vigorous intellectuality was partly motivated by a certain sense of crisis, the urgent need to make the faith more credible to "modern man". By contrast, the Church in the British Isles, southern Europe, Australia, Canada, and the United States, to say nothing of the Third World, lacked great intellectual achievements but appeared to be in a relatively healthy pastoral state. Most of the bishops from those countries seemed to see little urgency in many of the questions that came before them, and some expressed bewilderment as to why change was necessary at all.

"Conservatives"

Open resistance to the prevailing conciliar spirit came from some diocesan bishops, notably Cardinal Giuseppi Siri (d. 1989) of Genoa, but especially from certain members of the Roman Curia, such as Cardinal Alfredo Ottaviani (d. 1979), prefect of the Holy Office, whose primary responsibility was to safeguard doctrinal orthodoxy. In the end, most of the conciliar decrees were consciously balanced, often by a very careful choice of words. This balance would later allow both "liberals" and "conservatives" to claim conciliar authority for their interpretations.[2]

Ironically, in view of the later claim that the Council democratized the Church, deference to authority was a major factor in determining

Authority

---

[2] Such ambiguity has been characteristic of many councils. Nicaea by no means settled the question of Christ's divinity, and Trent left unresolved the relationship of grace and free will.

the outcome. Papal leadership, and an unquestioned faith in the Church's inerrancy, led most of the Fathers to support the final decrees that emerged from the debates. No decree received more than a small number of dissenting votes.

Theological Currents Preceding the Council

Although many of the actions of the Council took the world by surprise, all of them grew out of ideas that, perhaps little known to most Catholics, had been coming to fruition for a long time. Modernism, as condemned in 1907, had been only a marginal influence in the Church, and it did not survive in an organized way. However, the modernists raised questions to which later thinkers sometimes returned, usually without being conscious modernists. Those questions were fundamental: whether beliefs transcended the historical era in which they were formulated; whether it was necessary to adapt those beliefs to the spirit of each age; to what extent belief was the product of a human religious sense rather than of supernatural revelation; whether modern scholarship, especially biblical studies, had discredited certain beliefs; and whether the Catholic faith had to be understood only in terms of Thomistic theology and philosophy.

Ressourcement

The situation was complex. While most theologians were Thomists, some, especially in France and Germany, were moving in other directions. Their principal approach came to be called *ressourcement* ("recovery of the sources"). A return to the Church's scriptural and patristic roots during the millennium before the advent of Scholasticism was being advocated by de Lubac, Danielou, Bouyer, Congar, Ratzinger, and the Swiss priest-theologian Hans Urs von Balthasar (d. 1988).

There was often a strong Thomistic reaction against this theology based on *ressourcement*, and the dispute between the different approaches to faith resembled that between Scholastics and humanists at the time of the Renaissance. To proponents of the "New Theology", Scholasticism, while true, was abstract and remote, whereas Thomists thought that the "New Theology" was dangerously imprecise, providing no objective basis for faith.

De Lubac

Following Augustine, de Lubac argued that the distinction between reason and faith did not take sufficient account of the inherent human yearning for God and thereby unwittingly helped prepare the way for secularization. This theory had aroused suspicion against both Rosmini and Blondel, on the grounds that it did not recognize the necessity of divine grace in order to know God, and de Lubac was accused of softening the distinction between the natural and the supernatural to the point of obliteration, making faith seem to be almost a natural human phenomenon.

Pius XII's 1950 encyclical *Humani Generis* (The Human Race) was a check on the New Theology, seeming to criticize de Lubac without naming him, explicitly warning against assuming the theory of evolution to be true, and insisting that the doctrine of Original Sin required that the human race be descended from a single set of parents. Partly because of this papal warning, until the time of Vatican II, the New Theology was taught primarily in a few Jesuit and Dominican theologates in Europe, with Thomism continuing to dominate most seminaries and universities. But by the time of the Council, de Lubac's orthodoxy was no longer in question, and the influence of *ressourcement* was obvious in all the conciliar decrees, especially their strong scriptural foundations.

Aggiornamento

A second new theological approach, which was later called *aggiornamento* ("updating"), moved in the direction of modernism[3] by making the demands of contemporary culture its chief concern. *Aggiornamento* owed much to the Canadian Jesuit philosopher Bernard Lonergan (d. 1984), who distinguished the "classical" from the "historical" mentality, arguing that the former—a belief in a stable and unchanging mental universe—was now discredited and that theology had to operate within the historical mode. This question of changing mentality Newman had tried to resolve by his theory of the development of doctrine.

Transcendental Thomism

Transcendental Thomism was an alternative to the mainstream Thomism of Gilson and Maritain. It originated at Louvain University and sought to take account of Kant's claim that the mind cannot know things in themselves but only "phenomena" that present themselves through the mind's own categories (time, space, causality, and other things). Transcendental Thomism was so called because it posited a fundamental affinity for God within the human soul that allowed men to transcend ordinary knowledge.

Rahner was a Transcendental Thomist and emphasized this inherent human ability to know God, even speaking of the "anonymous Christian" who in effect possessed the faith without being aware of it—a theory that went much further than de Lubac and marked a clear departure from the theology of *ressourcement*. Although Rahner shared some of the interests of *ressourcement*, he became the intellectual leader of *aggiornamento*. The related "incarnational theology"—so called because it claimed to take seriously the fact that God entered human history in Jesus—made "human experience" rather than classical dogma the center of theological speculation.

Moral Theology

Although most theologians of *ressourcement* were only secondarily interested in moral theology, Catholic moral teaching also underwent development prior to the Council, although more at the hands of philosophers than of theologians.

---

[3] At first, proponents of *aggiornamento* denied any connection with Modernism, but in time, some acknowledged it candidly.

Phenomenology

The Jewish Edmund Husserl (d. 1938) was the founder of phenomenology, a philosophy that sought to understand reality as it was actually experienced by men. On the border between objectivity and subjectivity, it proved especially insightful into human relationships. Phenomenology appealed to some Catholics (Edith Stein was Husserl's student) as a corrective to scientific materialism, in that even physical objects retained a spiritual significance that science could not understand—a house was not merely a material structure but had special meaning for those who inhabited it.

This philosophy had special relevance to marriage, beginning with the German layman Dietrich von Hildebrand (d. 1977), who was also a student of Husserl and who immigrated to the United States to escape the Nazis. Hildebrand spoke of marriage's dual purpose—the procreation of children that was its objective reality and the spiritual unity of the spouses that was the experience at its heart. Sex without love, even between married persons, was therefore a moral disorder, and the union of the spouses was the highest good of marriage, reaching its ultimate fulfillment in the begetting of children.

Personalism

Influenced by Blondel in particular, the French layman Emmanuel Mounier (d. 1950) articulated what he called Personalism, a philosophy in which truth was known not abstractly but by an intuition into the inexhaustible mystery and inner freedom of the person. Personalism's practical significance was uncertain, in that at different times Mounier was sympathetic to both Fascism and Communism. He became increasingly critical of the Catholic Church. Personalist moral theologians rejected traditional casuistry (see Chapter Ten above, p. 314) as a minimalist approach to morality, since God called His people to perfect love, not merely to the avoidance of sin.

On birth control and other issues, there were stirrings of dissatisfaction in Western Europe especially. There was a growing sense that the Church needed to try new ideas in order to stem the religious decline.

The Conciliar Decrees

Revelation

Biblical Studies

Although scholarly biblical studies had sometimes generated skepticism, Leo XIII affirmed in principle the legitimacy of archaeology, history, and linguistics, provided they were undertaken in the spirit of faith. He authorized the establishment of the Dominican École Biblique ("school of the Bible") in Jerusalem, under Marie-Joseph Lagrange (d. 1938), and set up the Pontifical Biblical Commission to encourage and oversee such studies. Under Pius X, the Pontifical Biblical Institute was established in Rome under Jesuit auspices. Pius XII also gave qualified approval to biblical scholarship, reminding Catholics that, while the Bible was divinely inspired, it was written through human agencies, making scholarship crucial in such things as archaeological discoveries, the precise meaning of words, and the historical context in which biblical events occurred.

During the 1950s, scholars at the École Biblique produced the Jerusalem Bible, a rendering of the Scripture in modern French that was soon translated into English and began to supplant the Douai-Rheims edition that had been in use for 350 years. Over the next several decades, there was a proliferation of new biblical translations in many languages, and Catholics even began using Protestant versions.

Vatican II strongly urged Catholics to make Scripture the center of their spiritual lives, reminding them that the truths of Scripture were salvific—those things God had revealed to man for the sake of his salvation. The Scriptures were both divine and human in their authorship, and human error could enter in on matters that were not salvific.

Tradition

There was, however, sharp debate over the nature of revelation, with some Fathers fearful that an emphasis on Scripture alone would undercut certain Catholic beliefs (the Assumption, for example) that had come down through Tradition. In the end, the Council reaffirmed the authority of Tradition, which had been a major point of contention between Catholics and Protestants since the Reformation, but returned to the patristic understanding of Tradition not as a source of authority separate from Scripture but precisely as the Church's own understanding of Scripture: the Bible as received not by individuals but by the ecclesial community guided by the Holy Spirit.

The Mystical Body

The Church

The theology of the Church was a basic concern of the Council, the foundation on which everything else would be built. The recovery of the concept of the Mystical Body of Christ, expounded by St. Paul, was one of the achievements of nineteenth-century theology, confirmed by Pius XII in 1943. It moved beyond thinking of the Church primarily in juridical or institutional terms—as a formal organization with members and rules—and sought to recover a sense of her as a spiritual entity that transcended her institutional structure. Properly understood, this required a deeper kind of spirituality: not merely living piously and morally in order to receive grace but entering into mystical union with Christ Himself, in which a person embraces dying and rising with Christ in order to be completely transformed by Him.

Other Models

In its decree on the Church *Lumen Gentium* (Light of the Nations), the Council invoked other images besides that of the Mystical Body: the Church as the People of God ("*Laius*"); the New Israel of Christ's followers bound together by faith; and the "Pilgrim Church", those pursuing their journey toward the heavenly Jerusalem, a reminder that men had no earthly dwelling.

Hierarchy

Hierarchy was integral to the doctrine of the Mystical Body, since, as St. Paul said, no part of a body could claim to act independent of the others and the whole body was governed by its head. But the relationship between hierarchical authority and shared authority ("collegiality") was reopened at Vatican II, because Vatican I had defined only the authority of the papal office, not that of the bishops.

Collegiality

Lumen Gentium defined episcopal collegiality to mean that bishops were not simply agents of the Holy See but had apostolic authority in their own right. Historically, they had often acted in consort, especially in the ecumenical councils. But some Council Fathers were fearful that this might be understood as a revival of late-medieval Conciliarism. Paul VI personally intervened to ensure that in *Lumen Gentium* episcopal authority was limited by the dogma of papal infallibility, forthrightly asserting that, while it was appropriate that the Holy Father consult the bishops in the exercise of his Petrine office, his authority was valid without episcopal affirmation. (In fact, no pope has ever made a solemn doctrinal declaration without consulting the bishops; most such declarations have been made by councils.) Scarcely touched by the Council was the question of how the idea of collegiality applied at other levels of the Church.

Morality

Contraception

Organized promotion of birth control grew throughout the twentieth century, and in 1930, Pius XI issued the encyclical *Casti Connubii* (Chaste Marriage), the most complete exposition to date of the Catholic theology of marriage. The encyclical reaffirmed the Catholic teaching on contraception only a few months after the Church of England became the first Christian body to justify the practice officially, although the Anglican bishops warned that it could be used only for "grave reasons".

"Rhythm"

Catholic Personalists were far from justifying contraception. However, their philosophy seemed to imply that, although procreation could never be deliberately thwarted—something that would constitute a violent disruption of the marital union—not every sex act had to be potentially procreative. (The marriage of sterile couples, or of couples too old to beget children, was always permitted by the Church.) Some traditional Catholic moralists questioned the legitimacy of what was then called the "rhythm method"—temporarily limiting sexual relations to the infertile periods that occur naturally in a woman's menstrual cycle—but Pius XII in 1951 declared it to be licit if used for good reasons, including poverty or ill health.

"The Pill"

By the time of the Council, there was considerable agitation for the Church to accept at least some kinds of artificial birth control, especially the newly developed "Pill", which produced in the woman an artificial infertility. In Belgium and the Netherlands, the Pill was even endorsed by several bishops. Paul VI intervened to take the issue off the floor of the Council, appointing a special commission to study it. In its decree *Gaudium et Spes* (Joy and Hope), the Council explicitly recognized the dual purpose of marriage as both procreation and the loving union of spouses.

Worker Priests

During the Second World War, a number of priests were sent to concentration camps, where they ministered to other prisoners under extreme conditions, outside the normal structure of priestly life. In France, some priests were forced to work in factories during the war and, with direct experience of the falling away of so many industrial workers from the Church, voluntarily returned to such jobs after the war, living together in small communities and hoping to evangelize the workers.

This "worker-priest" experiment was cautiously approved by the hierarchy, but in a way it turned out to be symptomatic of the fallacy of much postwar liberal Catholicism—bold and imaginative but pastorally ineffective. Few workers were attracted back to the Church, some priests abandoned their vocations, and others embraced the Marxism that was deeply imbedded in the French working class. The Holy See first imposed restrictions and eventually suppressed the experiment. (Significant in terms of his liberal image, it was John XXIII who did so.)

Celibacy

Most priests of the time seem to have been living faithfully and zealously, and the Council's decree on the priesthood affirmed traditional discipline. A few Council Fathers raised the issue of celibacy, but Paul VI forbade its discussion.

Religious Life

Noting the decline in European religious vocations after the war, Pius XII urged the "modernization" of religious life, albeit in accord with its traditional purposes. The Council prescribed both *ressourcement* and *aggiornamento* for the renewal of religious life, enjoining religious communities to return to the original vision of their founders but also to make prudent adjustments to modern life.

Call to Holiness

The Council's principal message to both the clergy and the laity was the "universal call to holiness" in whatever one's state of life. The Council recalled Paul's teaching about the priesthood of the laity—that they joined with the priest in offering the holy sacrifice, an idea that had been almost forgotten as a result of the Protestant insistence on the "priesthood of all believers".

Lay Apostolate

Through Catholic Action and other movements, lay activity had been continually growing during the twentieth century. The Legion of Mary, founded by the layman Frank Duff (d. 1980) in Dublin in 1921, was a major apostolate in many parts of the world, its members working especially among the poor, with prostitutes, and with those who had lapsed from the faith. In England, two primarily lay groups—the Catholic Evidence Guild and the Catholic Truth Society—aggressively championed the Church in a somewhat hostile environment, with the former group witnessing to the faith while standing on actual soapboxes, taking on all comers. There were few lay theologians before the Council— Frank Sheed, an able popularizer, being one of the very few—but laymen were active in every other area of Catholic intellectual life.

Apostolic Mandate

In defining the role of the laity, Vatican II for the most part adapted the Catholic Action concept, focusing entirely on the apostolic mandate of the laity, who were enabled by their baptism to engage in evangelization, to renew the temporal world. It said nothing about the participation of the laity in the governance of the Church.

Liturgy

Of all the changes wrought by the Council, none were more dramatic and far-reaching than those in the liturgy.

Emperor Joseph II and other "reformers" of the Enlightenment period wanted to simplify the sacred rites, to make them in a sense more "efficient", and they even discussed the use of the vernacular. But their program ended with the French Revolution and had no influence on what was later called the liturgical movement.

The Liturgical Movement

That movement began with Prosper Guéranger in the monastery of Solesmes in the nineteenth century. In attempting as far as possible to re-create monastic life as it was lived in the Middle Ages, he placed the liturgy once more at the center of Catholic life, his multivolume work *The Liturgical Year* being the first modern attempt to encourage a piety centered on the liturgy.

The liturgical movement continued to develop principally in Benedictine monasteries in Germany and Belgium and was brought to the United States mainly through St. John's Abbey in Collegeville, Minnesota. The movement was primarily monastic, because the celebration of the Mass and the Divine Office had always been the monks' principal task, and they possessed both the education and the time to celebrate the liturgy in all its fullness.

Gregorian Chant

Part of Guéranger's program was the revival of Gregorian chant, which had all but disappeared from Catholic worship. The music of the "High Mass" was often written by contemporary composers and performed by professional orchestras and choruses, while in ordinary parishes, the music consisted mainly of pious hymns.

Pius X

Pius X came to be considered the patron of the liturgical movement, because he both strongly endorsed the revival of chant and strongly encouraged frequent Communion. He allowed children to make their First Communions at an early age and thereby went against Jansenist prejudices that prevailed even among many people who were not Jansenists.

The Sacred Mysteries

Guéranger's idea of authentic liturgy was a Romantic kind of medievalism, but later scholars sought to recover the worship of the early Church, concluding that over the centuries numerous accretions had developed that obscured its original meaning. The Italian-German priest Romano Guardini (d. 1968) was the most important theologian of the liturgical movement, relating liturgy to the most basic mysteries of the faith and showing it as the center of Catholic life. Based on the theology of the Mystical Body, the German Benedictine Odo Casel (d. 1940) explained the liturgy as not only the continuation of the sacrifice of Calvary, through which the faithful receive grace, but as a divine mystery into which the faithful fully enter, in order to die and rise with Christ.

The Liturgical Calender

To achieve this, liturgists emphasized the "seasonal cycle"—Christmas, Epiphany, Holy Week, Pentecost—over the "sanctoral cycle" that commemorated the saints, and they also sought to limit the frequency of Masses for the dead, which in many parishes made up most of the weekday liturgies. In each case, the proper celebration of the liturgy was in tension with popular devotion.

Pius XII seemed to give his blessing to the liturgical movement when in 1951 he authorized the restoration of the Easter Vigil to its proper place on Holy Saturday evening or early Easter morning, replacing the anomalous custom of celebrating it on Saturday morning. It was an especially significant reform that was intended to make the Paschal mystery the heart of the Christian life.

The Social Dimension

The liturgical movement also had a strong social dimension, teaching that in the liturgy both individuals and the community are transformed, so that they in turn can transform the world at the most profound level, elevating people to a higher level of being and meeting the most desperate of all human needs—salvation from the powers of darkness. In the United States, especially through the Benedictine Virgil Michel of Collegeville (d. 1938), interest in the liturgy was often linked with racial justice and other social issues.

"Active Participation"

Worshippers had always believed that something of eternal significance was taking place on the altar—that Christ Himself was present—and most people assisted at Mass in a spirit of deep reverence, even if they did not fully comprehend it. But the achievement of what Pius X called "active participation" in the liturgy by the laity was the chief purpose of the liturgical movement, with *participation* understood as being present in a prayerful spirit, attending closely to the rites, and understanding their meaning, although not necessarily singing and praying along with the priest.

Slowly, the liturgical movement moved beyond the monasteries, awakening in some priests and laity a new appreciation of the liturgy, at a time when many people probably found popular devotions more meaningful. Overall, however, the movement had only modest impact. A small minority of lay people used bilingual daily missals that enabled them to pray the Mass with the priest; a very few began to pray the daily Divine Office; and in advanced circles, the "dialogue Mass" allowed the congregation to make the Latin responses that were ordinarily rendered only by the acolytes. Some liturgists favored use of the vernacular, but it was not a central issue.

The Vernacular

The conciliar decree on liturgy embodied the rich theology that lay behind all this, speaking of liturgy in a mystical way, as a foretaste of the New Jerusalem, a glimpse of Heaven itself. Of all the things for which Vatican II is known, the movement from Latin to the vernacular is perhaps most famous, but in fact the Council did not mandate that move but merely conceded that under some circumstances the vernacular might be appropriate in some parts of the liturgy. Gueranger gave "pride of place" to Gregorian chant, which had been neglected, but newer styles of music were also encouraged.

Mary

Marian piety flourished in the twentieth century, and some bishops wanted the Council to issue a special decree on Mary, even to proclaim her as "Co-redemptrix" with Jesus. Instead, the Council included a statement about Mary in *Lumen Gentium*, defining her role within the total economy of salvation, in order to overcome any belief that Mary offered a way alternative to Christ's own redemptive sacrifice.

Ecumenism

Next to liturgy, ecumenism was perhaps the Council's most dramatic legacy. The ecumenical movement was a Protestant, and to a much lesser extent Eastern Orthodox, development of the early twentieth century. By the end of the century, however, the movement was being led by the Catholic Church.

The Ecumenical Movement

Pius IX had bluntly told the Protestants that Vatican I was yet another opportunity for them to repent their errors, and both Benedict XV and Pius XI warned against the danger of seeming to make religious belief the subject of negotiations. As a result of the Oxford Movement, there was some ecumenical rapprochement between Catholics and "High Church" Anglicans, although Leo XIII, after study, pronounced Anglican orders "absolutely null and utterly void".[4] During the 1920s, there were unofficial Catholic-Anglican discussions ("the Malines conversations"), tolerated by the Holy See, under the patronage of Cardinal Mercier.

Unofficial Encounters

During World War II, some informal ecumenism developed between Protestants and Catholics engaged in the struggle against the Nazis in Germany, the Netherlands, and France, and in England there was a formal ecumenical organization—the Sword of the Spirit—that for a time enjoyed hierarchical approval. After the war, both Catholic and Protestant scholars began writing accounts of the Reformation that sought understanding rather than mere polemics. Bouyer, a convert from the very small French Lutheran church, was especially influential on the Catholic side. In 1949, a Boston priest, Leonard Feeney (d. 1978), was first expelled from the Jesuit order, then excommunicated, for persisting in his teaching that no one who is not a Catholic can be saved, starting a schismatic movement that was only reconciled to the Church decades later.

John XXIII

John XXIII began the Catholic ecumenical initiative even before the Council, largely by his personal openness to non-Catholics, whom he addressed as brothers. The Holy See had declined to join the World Council of Churches when it was formed in 1948, but in 1961, it began sending observers to its meetings. John established the Secretariat for Promoting Christian Unity under the German Jesuit Cardinal Agostino Bea (d. 1981), Pius XII's former confessor. Protestants and Eastern Orthodox were invited to send observers to the Council,[5] their presence making Vatican II unique among councils.

---

[4] The validity of Anglican orders is complicated by the fact that many Anglican clergy can trace their orders back to Eastern Orthodox bishops, the validity of whose orders the Catholic Church recognizes.

[5] The claim that the Protestant observers helped shape the conciliar decrees, such as that on the liturgy, is untrue.

Religious Truths

The Council itself identified religious truth as present in what was in effect a series of overlapping circles, with all Christian faiths possessing some degree of truth but "the fullness of Christ's truth" present only in the Catholic Church.

The new ecumenism appeared revolutionary to many, a complete reversal of what had previously been taught. It was, however, merely a change of perspective, in that the Catholic Church had always recognized the core of orthodoxy in Protestantism (the Trinity, the divinity of Christ) but had previously emphasized its errors. Now she chose to recognize its truths, as the basis of imperfect brotherly unity.

Eastern Orthodoxy

Ecumenical priority was inevitably given to the Eastern Orthodox, who were recognized as sharing most of the Catholic faith. Separation from the Orthodox was viewed by the Council Fathers as a lamentable historical misfortune, and the mutual excommunications of 1054 were formally rescinded after the Council.

Protestants

The Council warned against a false ecumenism based on an indifference to, or a misinterpretation of, doctrine. However, under Bea's direction, official dialogues were initiated, especially with Lutherans and Anglicans. In practical terms, the immediate effect of ecumenism was to alter Catholics' and Protestants' attitudes toward one another, as for the first time they were allowed, even encouraged, to pray together both formally and informally, although they could not share the Eucharist.

The Jews

The conciliar decree on the Jews reaffirmed that the death of Jesus was the fault of the entire, sinful human race, not of the Jews specifically, and recalled the Jews' status as God's chosen people and the role of their faith in the economy of salvation. (Some Near Eastern bishops spoke against the decree because it would offend their people.) Pope John personally ordered the expunging of the term "perfidious Jews" from the liturgy of Good Friday.

Non-Christians

The Church's approach to non-Christian religions required, not ecumenism, which applies only to Christians, but some kind of interreligious dialogue based on natural theology, which posits the ability of men to know the existence of their Creator. Thus Hinduism, Buddhism, and other religions were said to possess a core of truth, although they remained in need of the Gospel.

Church and World

Sympathy

Gaudium et Spes—usually called "The Church in the Modern World"—was often identified as the heart of the Council's message, the charter

of *aggiornamento*. Its tone differed from many earlier Church documents in that it did not primarily warn or condemn but instead expressed
sympathy and understanding for a world that possessed an unfulfilled
longing for truth and justice.

Characteristic of this optimistic tone, *Gaudium et Spes* made only
oblique reference to the fact that the twentieth century had already
seen a persecution of Christians more severe than any in the entire
history of the Church. Despite vigorous efforts by some Fathers, the
Council did not condemn Communism by name.

A Loving Mother

In announcing Christ as the "Light of the Nations", *Lumen Gentium*
claimed for His Church a position superior to that of every other
institution, and *Gaudium et Spes*, far from uncritically embracing the
world, also boldly asserted the Church's superiority over secular culture. The burden of the conciliar message was that, so long as men
relied merely on their own resources to achieve good, they would
always be disappointed, that only the saving Gospel of Christ could
provide fulfillment. The Church was like a loving mother—sympathetic
but always providing the world with firm guidance.

The Signs of the Times

The title of the decree *Gaudium et Spes*—taken from the first three
Latin words of the text—was in a sense misleading, in that after "joy
and hope" the very next words were "grief and anguish" (*luctus et
angor*), the juxtaposition of the two phrases accurately expressing the
balanced stance which the Council took toward the world. The Church,
according to *Gaudium et Spes*, undertook to "read the signs of the
times", discerning in the movement of history how the world needed
guidance, searching for what was positive in secular culture in order
to build upon it. The Council even dispassionately analyzed various
kinds of atheism, in order to understand their appeal.

A Wide Agenda

By far the longest of the conciliar decrees, *Gaudium et Spes* attempted
to deal with all aspects of the modern world: the human sense of
alienation, the economy, war and peace, the family, and many other
things. It mandated economically developed nations to help poorer
ones, condemned the arms race and all wars against civilians, made
blunt reference to "the plague of divorce" and the "abominable crime"
of abortion, judged deliberately childless marriages to be a tragedy,
and reminded the faithful of the Church's condemnation of artificial
birth control.

Opposition

One of the actions of the Council that attracted the most notice was
its decree on religious liberty, *Dignitatis Humanae* (Human Dignity),
which was also one of the most controversial within the Church

Religious Liberty

herself, drawing the largest number of negative votes of any conciliar document, albeit still only a small minority. The disapprobation of some Council Fathers reflected a long-standing Catholic view that religious liberty could only be justified for pragmatic reasons, in those cases where it was not expedient to prohibit the practice of other faiths.

Murray and Maritain

This outlook seemed to place an unbridgeable gulf between the Church and almost all modern Western societies, and it had been questioned especially by John Courtney Murray. After being under a cloud, Murray was brought to the Council through the efforts of Cardinal Spellman, and he was the only American theologian to have any significant influence there. Maritain perhaps had even more influence on *Dignitatis Humanae* than did Murray, since Maritain, after having for a time been politically reactionary (he supported *Action Française*), became an enthusiastic supporter of democracy as the best of all political systems, given the other possible choices.

Human Dignity

Properly understood, *Dignitatis Humanae* reaffirmed that "error has no rights" but also affirmed that men who may be in error do have rights. The decree's title summed up its teaching: that the basis of toleration was not indifference to truth but respect even for those who might be in error. The Church foreswore coercion in matters of faith as a violation of the spirit of the Gospel, as most of the early Fathers had done.

Social Doctrine Since *Quadragesimo Anno*, the popes had not addressed social and economic questions very directly. But beginning with John XXIII, there were a series of encyclicals identifying such questions as a crucial concern, applying Catholic principles to changing times.

John XXIII

The social message of *Gaudium et Spes* had been anticipated by John XXIII. His *Mater et Magistra* (Mother and Teacher, 1961) was a strong restatement of the principles of distributive justice, and *Pacem in Terris* (Peace on Earth, 1963) called on the world to achieve lasting peace by transcending national and ideological differences. Both encyclicals were bids by the Church to play a formative role in resolving social problems, and they attracted a great deal of favorable response. John offered Catholic principles as the basis for a just society everywhere, because those principles were not merely Church doctrine but were based on natural law.

Papal Journeys

This claim to transcendent teaching authority was also symbolically manifest in the pope's new role as a public figure. John XXIII had broken with custom by leaving Rome. Now, beginning with the

Holy Land, Paul VI made nine world journeys, giving the papacy a new level of public recognition.

Modernization

In the conciliar environment, certain concrete changes had lasting significance. The papacy and the papal administration were given an updated look that was more accommodating to modern sensibilities.

Beginning with John's easygoing informality, the monarchical trappings of the papacy, such as the triple tiara and the coronation ceremony, were phased out. Later, the pope would no longer be carried on his throne but would walk in processions or be transported by a "popemobile" (Pope John Paul II's innovation).

The Curia

The Roman Curia was reorganized, and permanent secretariats (Pontifical Councils) were established for the Laity, the Family, Christian Unity, Non-Christians, and Dialogue with Unbelievers, among other things. There had been demands for the internationalization of the Italian-dominated Curia, and Paul VI quickly moved to achieve that. Partly in order to accommodate an increasing number of cardinals from outside Europe, the College of Cardinals was increased to 120 from the traditional number of 70.

Freedom

The Council seemed to encourage freer theological speculation. The *Index* was abolished, the Holy Office was renamed the Congregation for the Doctrine of the Faith (Ottaviani soon retired), and those accused of unorthodox teaching were guaranteed a formal hearing.

Paul VI greatly admired Maritain, was sympathetic to the New Theology, and thus seemed uniquely qualified to preside over the implementation of the Council. But tragically, his pontificate would prove to be in many ways a long series of crises at every level.

Even though John XXIII had said that the Council would not issue new dogmatic decrees, the fact that practically every aspect of Catholic belief had come under discussion inevitably raised both expectations and fears. Before the Council had even ended, there was widening disagreement as to its meaning.

The first phrase of *Gaudium et Spes*—"joy and hope"—seemed to validate optimism, proclaiming the Church's openness to the world, while its second phrase—"grief and anguish"—was largely ignored. But reading the signs of the times proved to be far more difficult than *Gaudium et Spes* foresaw in its measured judgments.

"The Sixties"

Wholly unforeseen, just as the Council ended, the worldwide cultural revolution called "the Sixties" began. It was nothing less than a frontal assault on all forms of authority, and had the Council been held a

In the Wake of the Council

A Time of Crisis

decade earlier, during the more stable 1950s, it is likely that the post-conciliar upheaval would have been far less severe.

"Liberation"

Unrecognized at first, it soon became clear that attempting to counter secularism by moving closer to the secular culture produced largely negative results. "Modernization", rather than satisfying the discontented, merely whetted the appetite for more of the same. As had been happening to liberal Protestantism for some time, rates of church attendance and religious vocations among Catholics began to fall, almost exactly in proportion to how "progressive" the Church became. For many Catholics, the meaning of their faith now consisted mainly in continuous efforts to free themselves from the past.

Dialogue

Along with every crisis came the newly popular idea of "dialogue". While in principle engaging in dialogue did not require the participants to surrender their own beliefs but merely allowed them an opportunity to try to understand those of others, in practice it often had the effect of leaving all questions permanently open, as opposed to the exercise of teaching authority. Especially during the first twenty years after the Council, a variety of formal dialogues were undertaken—with various religions, with Marxists—but with relatively meager lasting results.

Traditionalists

The first crisis occurred shortly after the Council's end, when a number of small groups calling themselves Traditionalists questioned the Council's authority, especially its decrees on liturgy, ecumenism, and religious liberty. The most important of these was the Society of St. Pius X (SSPX), founded by the French Archbishop Marcel Lefebvre (d. 1991), who had been a papal nuncio in Africa, general of the Holy Ghost Fathers, and a participant in the Council, where he signed his name to all its decrees. The movement proved to be of some importance in France but was marginal in most other places. To some extent, it had ties with those who advocated monarchy as the only legitimate form of government, and one of its bishops, an English convert, was fiercely anti-Jewish. The SSPX started a seminary in Switzerland, and Lefebvre was first suspended from the episcopal office for ordaining priests and sending them to set up schismatic parishes in various parts of the world, then excommunicated for consecrating bishops, both without canonical authority. Although these "traditionalists" went into schism, a graver crisis was caused by some who claimed to accept the authority of the Council.

The Media

Given the immense media interest in the Council's proceedings, it was perhaps less important what the Council actually did than what people thought it did. Thus certain bishops and *periti* entered into a working alliance with certain journalists, with both becoming in effect "participant-observers" reporting the events and at the same time seeking to influence them, fixing in the popular mind a lasting impression of what the Council was doing.

The gist of such reporting was that at long last the Church was admitting her many errors and coming to terms with modern culture. The Council Fathers were divided into heroes and villains, "liberals" and "conservatives", and the conciliar deliberations were presented as morality plays in which open-minded progressives repeatedly thwarted the plots of Machiavellian reactionaries. Consequently, people who understood almost nothing of the theological issues believed that the Council's "real" purpose was simply that of repealing rules that had become burdensome.

Euphoria

Measuring the Council's effects is difficult, because many of those effects were matters of mood or tone rather than of concrete actions. The conciliar process itself proved to be a transforming experience for many people who may have given little previous thought to the questions there discussed. A major psychological factor was the heady experience of swift and unexpected change. In 1960, almost no one predicted the virtual abandonment of the Latin liturgy, for example; but, when the Council Fathers seemed to support such a change, it became an irresistible temptation for some to continue pushing further and faster, as what had been thought of as stone walls of resistance turned out to be papier-mâché.

For many, the postconciliar period therefore proved to be a time of rudderless experimentation, with change itself apparently now the only new certitude. In that environment, the distinction between essentials and nonessentials was for many people no longer clear. If Catholics could now eat meat on Fridays, why could they not get divorced, especially if the purpose of the Council, and of "Good Pope John", was to make the faith less burdensome?

But in another sense, at first not fully understood, the attention paid to "externals" was not disproportionate, because in a sacramental religion material things are doorways to the spirit. Thus an aversion to Friday abstinence or to nuns' habits sometimes revealed something much deeper.

Uncertain Trumpets

Many of the Council Fathers, after they returned to their dioceses, seemed themselves uncertain as to what had been intended. Bishop Fulton Sheen, for example, while briefly serving as bishop of Rochester, supported the most liberal of his priests and stated on television that the Church might now permit contraception. Caught in the postconciliar crossfire, he soon resigned his see. On the whole, the bishops themselves made little systematic effort to catechize the faithful (including priests and religious) on the Council's meaning and relied instead on certified "experts" in every area of Church life. As at the

Council itself, the traditional concept of obedience was used to persuade reluctant Catholics to conform to the new ways.

Collegiality

Although *Lumen Gentium* clearly stated that episcopal authority could not be exercised except in union with the Holy See, collegiality was often problematic in the postconciliar era. The chief way of exercising that collegiality was the newly established international synod of bishops held in Rome every three years to address particular questions, with some of its members elected by their fellow bishops in each country, others appointed by the Pope. These synods themselves sometimes became the occasion for bishops to challenge papal authority, as Archbishop John R. Quinn of San Francisco did on one occasion.

Episcopal Conferences

The concept of collegiality also led the hierarchy in the various countries to form themselves into national or regional conferences, and some national conferences appeared not to support certain official teachings, such as that on birth control. The National Conference of Catholic Bishops (later, the "United States Conference of Catholic Bishops") issued numerous public statements—on national defense, on economic justice, on the pastoral care of homosexuals—that were presented as the collective opinions of the hierarchy but that some bishops found seriously deficient.

A Crisis of Faith

Theological Divisions

The theologies of *ressourcement* and *aggiornamento* began to move in opposite directions very soon after the Council, opening an increasingly unbridgeable chasm. Along with Schillebeeckx, Haering, and to a lesser extent Rahner, the German-Swiss priest-theologian Hans Küng was the increasingly bold and abrasive chief spokesman for *aggiornamento*, demanding that the Church accommodate herself to a changing culture, while de Lubac, Danielou, Maritain, Balthasar, Bouyer, Ratzinger, and others protested what they considered distortions of the Council.

The Conciliar "Spirit" and the Theology of Aggiornamento

Where the conciliar decrees did not explicitly support their agenda, some advocates of *aggiornamento* began to appeal to the Council's "spirit", which was said to transcend its actual decrees and in some cases might even contradict them. Thus, ironically, the authority of the Council was itself relativized.

The ultimate question, which was reaffirmed virtually without discussion by the Council itself, was whether the Church teaches with divine authority or whether her doctrines merely represent human striving for some kind of transcendence. Some now understood the Council in Hegelian and modernist terms, as merely an episode in the history of the Church's unfolding self-understanding, its function not to make authoritative pronouncements but merely to facilitate the movement of the Church into the next stage of historical development.

The existence of an authoritative Magisterium that decides matters of doctrine was increasingly denied, either openly or implicitly, a denial that was especially aimed at papal authority. Theologians of *aggiornamento* sometimes spoke of a "second magisterium" of theologians themselves, parallel to that of the hierarchy and ultimately having more authority than the hierarchy, on the grounds that theologians alone fully understood the faith.

A "Second Magisterium"

In many ways, the ultimate source of the crisis lay in biblical studies. While successive popes had encouraged such studies, Pius XII warned of the danger of an approach to the Bible entirely dependent on scholarly opinion and requiring the reader to prescind from the divine character of the Scriptures. Prior to the Council, Catholic scholars had done their work in accord with such papal injunctions, but afterward, some of them speedily adopted precisely the methods against which Pius had warned.

Biblical Studies

Largely as a result of the Council, Catholics were encouraged to study the Bible as never before but, ironically, they were also often told that it was not an altogether reliable guide to knowledge of Jesus. Liberal Protestant exegetes had long been wedded to the historical-critical method, and in the decades following the Council, numerous new Catholic commentaries were published that employed that method.

The Historical-Critical Method
In principle, the method itself could lead the reader to see the Old Testament not as prophetic—foreshadowing and preparing for the New—but to understand it solely as a collection of documents about the Jews. The Gospels were said to have been composed long after Jesus' death, by various local communities seeking to validate their own distinctive beliefs by claiming particular Evangelists as the authors of their sacred books and emphasizing certain stories about Jesus at the expense of certain others.

At first, it was suggested that only the "infancy narratives" might not be historical, whereas belief in Jesus' bodily Resurrection was essential to the faith. Soon, however, it became increasingly difficult to draw such lines, and the Resurrection itself was redefined in symbolic or psychological terms, such as the Apostles' witnessing to the deep and lasting impression Jesus had made on them.

The Gnostic Gospels
By the end of the twentieth century, liberal scholars had ceased to treat the New Testament even as a uniquely authoritative book for Christians, as the rediscovered texts of the ancient Gnostic "gospels" of Thomas, Philip, Judas, and others were given equal authority.

This "demythologizing" especially occurred with respect to distinctively Catholic teachings, such as the claim that Jesus founded the Church and gave Peter primacy over her or that "This is My Body" was to be understood literally. Logically, given their assumption of the Bible's errancy, some theologians of *aggiornamento* claimed that classic Catholic dogmas, as found in the creeds and in the decrees of Nicaea and Chalcedon, had ceased to be meaningful.

The Theology of Aggiornamento

Christology from Below

Schillebeeckx expounded a "Christology from below" that, while not explicitly denying the ancient creeds, prescinded from them in order to focus on modern people's "experience" of Jesus—"who Jesus is for me". Schillebeeckx' approach would not allow for a clear affirmation of Jesus' divinity and in practice led to a new kind of Arianism that spoke of Him in terms like "someone in whom God was present in a special way".

The "Anonymous Christian"

Rahner was committed to *aggiornamento* in that his principal concern was to reconcile the faith with modern German philosophy. His precise meaning was often unclear, but he was increasingly unwilling to affirm classical Catholic doctrine and increasingly hostile to the exercise of magisterial authority. His idea of the "anonymous Christian", who embraced Gospel values without perhaps realizing it, made the need for the Church seem problematic. Some theologians now distinguished the Kingdom from the Church, claiming that Christ's intention had been to establish not the latter but the former—the reign of truth and justice on earth.

Teilhard

Although he was not a theologian, the French Jesuit paleontologist Pierre Teilhard de Chardin (d.1955) became for a time the most influential figure of *aggiornamento*, formulating a theology based on what he considered to be the ultimate truth of modern science, a cosmic theology derived not only from human history but from the evolution of the entire universe. Teilhard, who died seven years before the Council began, had been ordered by his superiors not to publish his theories. After his death, his books began to appear, but they had no direct influence on the Council's deliberations.

In man, according to Teilhard, the universe had evolved to a new level and now moved toward an "omega point" at which all differences would converge, a "Christogenesis" ("birth of Christ") that was the ultimate fulfillment of creation. Teilhard's theories bore some resemblance to the patristic doctrine of cosmic redemption, but he seemed to understand this transformation as a wholly natural process in which sin, and therefore the need for redemption, was transcended and the universe underwent a kind of pantheistic divinization.

Although his influence gradually waned, Teilhard enjoyed a significant vogue in the two decades following the Council, not least because he seemed to provide both a scientific and a theological foundation for the spirit of optimistic euphoria. He was rhapsodic over the atomic bomb as a dramatic manifestation of the new powers being unleashed, and he subscribed to theories of racial superiority. In private, he was scathing in his condemnation of much of the Catholic theological tradition.

The theology of *aggiornamento* had its greatest impact in morals, where the spirit of dissent took hold because of its immediate practical implications, especially for sexuality. The old casuistry was a system of rules and laws that provided people with concrete direction; and, once those rules had been deemphasized, many people became morally confused.

Morality

Self-Fulfillment
Reversing traditional spirituality, emphasis was now placed on the idea of "self-fulfillment" as a necessary condition for psychological health, in effect a revival of Pelagianism, with its wholly optimistic view of human nature. In many places, the practice of confession all but disappeared.

Conscience
Haering, the American priest-theologian Charles Curran, and others now began to cite people's "lived experience" to justify behavior (primarily sexual) that had previously been considered sinful. The individual conscience was turned into an absolute, and the traditional teaching that conscience must be formed in accord with objective morality was largely ignored.

Moral Relativism
"Situation ethics", as developed by liberal Protestants and adopted by some Catholics, denied absolute moral laws and evaluated the morality of acts primarily on the basis of circumstances: the motives of the people involved, their particular problems, even such things as their gender and social class. "Consequentialism"—essentially the principle that "the end justifies the means"—judged the morality of actions primarily on the basis of their likely results.

Contraception
Birth control was the crucial issue that required Catholics to decide whether they recognized the Church as an authoritative moral teacher. The fact that Paul VI set up a special commission to study the question led many people to assume that Church authorities themselves were uncertain and that the teaching was therefore about to change. Although their work was supposed to be confidential, in 1966, some members of the commission revealed to the media that a majority

recommended acceptance of contraception, thereby heightening the expectation of change.

At first, some Catholics thought that, if the Church acknowledged error in her teaching about birth control, her credibility on other moral issues would be preserved, or that contraception could be permitted only to married couples and then only to postpone pregnancy, not to prevent it altogether. These positions soon proved to be untenable, however, as the "sexual revolution" burst on the Western world as nothing less than a denial of traditional sexual morality in all its aspects. The "contraceptive culture", for the first time in history, completely severed the connection between sex and procreation and defined sex as existing primarily for the sake of pleasure.

Catholics as a whole had begun to engage in sexual behavior not measurably different from that of nonbelievers. The Catholic divorce rate rose to the level of the general population, and the number of ecclesiastical annulments increased geometrically.

When Paul finally issued *Humanae Vitae* in 1968, reaffirming the traditional teaching, there was an explosive rebellion, orchestrated in the United States by prominent theologians led by Curran.

Education   Based on new theological currents, religious education at all levels underwent a postconciliar revolution. The Thomistic establishment swiftly collapsed, and many Catholic institutions of higher education became centers of eclectic philosophy and dissenting theology. Shortly after the Council, a group of Catholic university presidents in the United States declared their independence from Church authority. Some Catholic institutions went out of existence, and some became officially secular, while most continued to claim a Catholic identity that was vague and undefined. Seminaries were not unaffected, and a generation of priests was trained in an environment in which theological dissent enjoyed as much authority as official teaching.

Catechetics   The nature of catechetics had been under revision for some time, especially promoted by the *Lumen Vitae* ("light of life") Center in Brussels. Instead of the traditional approach, in which students learned doctrines, the new catechetics promised to inculcate in them a lively personal faith, through Bible study, liturgy, and many other things, paying close attention to the psychology of the students and the pedagogical methods appropriate to their ages.

On the assumption that all education has to resonate with the student's own experience, the new catechetics tended to minimize distinctive Catholic beliefs, even to the point of treating formal doctrine as an obstacle to living faith. The result was several generations of young Catholics who had never been taught the essentials of their faith and tended to understand it primarily as a vague kind of humanitarianism.

Nowhere was the postconciliar tension between *aggiornamento* and *ressourcement* more pronounced than with regard to the liturgy. The liturgical movement had struggled for decades to make Catholics appreciate the Eucharist as the center of their lives, but, once liturgical "reform" had been enacted, participation in the Eucharist fell off sharply almost everywhere.

Responsibility for implementing liturgical reform was given to the *Concilium*, a committee whose work received at least the passive acquiescence of the Holy See. The key figure was the Italian Vincentian archbishop Annibale Bugnini (d. 1982).

The Demise of Latin

The normative text of the *Novus Ordo* ("new order") Mass was in Latin, and it was celebrated in Latin at papal ceremonies, but most Catholics were unaware that a Latin liturgy of any kind was still permitted. Both Latin and Gregorian chant all but disappeared. The "new Mass" constituted the most sweeping liturgical changes ever implemented in so brief a time.

Versus Populum

Next to the vernacular, perhaps the most significant innovation was Mass celebrated *versus populum* ("facing the people"), something which, like the vernacular, was not mandated by the Council but soon became all but universal. To make this possible, permanent altars were often removed from churches and replaced by freestanding wooden tables.

Dramatic Changes

Other dramatic changes to the Mass included placing the sacred vessels on a side table at the beginning of Mass rather than having them veiled on the altar, allowing laymen to handle those vessels, offering the chalice to the laity in Communion, the abolition of the prayers at the foot of the altar at the beginning of Mass and of the Last Gospel at the end, the Liturgy of the Word no longer conducted by the priest at the altar, and the abolition of the "solemn High Mass" in which the celebrant was assisted by deacon, subdeacon, and other ministers. (The Council restored the office of permanent deacon but abolished the subdiaconate.)

Pruning

The Concilium suppressed large parts of the "Tridentine Rite"; "purified" the Mass of what were deemed excessive genuflections, signs of the cross, and repetitive prayers; and authorized vernacular translations that were not literally faithful to the official Latin texts but sought instead for "dynamic equivalency". Old churches were often ruthlessly stripped of their side altars, statues, stations of the cross, and other things, in order to minimize their Romanesque, Gothic, or Baroque styles that were deemed no longer to speak to "modern man".

"Active Participation"

"Active participation" was now taken to mean that the congregation must join vocally in all prayers not exclusive to the priest and most hymns. Liturgists emphasized the communal nature of the Mass to the point of strongly discouraging, if not actually forbidding, priests from celebrating Mass in private, and concelebration by more than one priest was restored for the first time since the early centuries. The Divine Office was also translated into the vernacular and substantially revised, including a wider variety of readings, some of them from modern sources.

The discouragement of private Masses raised questions about the meaning of the Mass itself. Traditionally, it was a communal act in the sense that it was celebrated for the benefit of people who were not physically present, especially for the dead. Now, however, it seemed to be the celebration only of those who were actually present.

Funerals

The *Requiem* Mass was suppressed in favor of the funeral liturgy as the joyful celebration of resurrection. There were, however, theological difficulties: exclusive emphasis on resurrection seemed to imply that the deceased was already in Paradise, so that the funeral homily often functioned as a eulogy of the deceased and the practice of praying for the dead seemed unnecessary.

Devotions

Liturgists judged that for most Catholics the heart of the faith lay in pious devotions rather than the Mass, and the Council warned against an overemphasis on such devotions, while also calling for their preservation. But, as with Latin and chant, many of those devotions disappeared completely, their suppression creating a subjective spiritual hunger that the liturgy itself did not entirely satisfy.

A Modern Style

Changes were initially justified as a return to the practices of the early Church, thus to a presumably more authentic manner of celebration. Soon, however, liturgists began the systematic introduction of modern modes of celebration—in language, music, symbolism, and other things—seeking to make liturgy "relevant" by deemphasizing its mystical elements and assimilating it to contemporary culture. "Active participation" came to be measured by the subjective effects the liturgy had on its participants through the use of contemporary language, new ritual practices like balloons and dancing, and "folk" music in commercially popular styles.

"Creativity"

Primary emphasis was now placed on the Eucharist as a community meal, so that for some people the greeting of peace, which had not been part of the Tridentine Mass, became the high point of the celebration. The inevitable logic of the drive to make liturgy "relevant" was the idea that each congregation should create its own liturgy. Although the Council expressly forbade priests to make changes in the rites, Bugnini himself urged toleration of unauthorized experimentation. Thus some congregations composed their own prayers, chose their own readings, and dispensed with vestments and other signs of the sacred.

Religious Life

In some ways, the severest crisis in the postconciliar period was in priestly and religious life, a crisis that went to the very identity of those states, as in the practice of referring to the celebrant of the Mass as the "presider", thereby minimizing his sacerdotal status and making him primarily a representative of the community. The vocation of priests and religious was now defined primarily as that of "service", which made renunciation for the sake of the Kingdom—celibacy especially—seem merely burdensome.

The Decline of Discipline

Priests and religious gave up their vocations in large numbers, and even many of those who remained were troubled. Religious discipline, which had been at a high level on the eve of the Council, declined sharply, as heterosexual relationships were not uncommon and homosexuality among priests came to be a serious problem. Bishops showed a certain reluctance to deal with it, even when the Holy See ordered that known homosexuals not be admitted to seminaries, and several bishops were themselves implicated.

Sisters

Before the Council, women religious were probably more devout, and lived more austerely, than priests. But on the whole, they also had less education, so that at first they depended heavily on male leadership to guide them through postconciliar change. Cardinal Suenens wrote an influential book urging sisters to come out of their cloisters.

Renewal
"Renewalists" at first promised a phenomenal revitalization of religious orders, including dramatic numerical growth, if sisters modified or discarded their traditional habits, liberalized their strict discipline, and ventured into new apostolates. The Council's injunction to religious to rediscover their original charisms was largely disregarded, a prime example of *aggiornamento* overcoming *ressourcement*. Communities of women who for centuries had run schools and hospitals now abandoned those ministries, thereby causing a major crisis in Catholic education and health care.

Democracy
The idea of "self-fulfillment" as a necessary condition for psychological health was a novelty in religious life and rendered the very concept of obedience unacceptable, so that some religious communities

no longer spoke of "superiors" but of "presidents" or "leaders". The modification, then the abandonment, of traditional religious habits marked the beginning of the end of religious life as it had existed for centuries. Instead of growth, the number of sisters in the United States declined by over 65 percent in the period from 1965 to 2010, with comparable declines in all other Western countries. In many communities, vocations all but ceased.

A Noted Failure
The most celebrated "renewal" story in the United States was that of the Immaculate Heart Sisters of Los Angeles, whose program of *aggiornamento* was guided by the prestigious psychologist Carl Rogers (d. 1987), a one-time student for the Protestant ministry who had developed a negative attitude toward religion. The Immaculate Heart "renewal" was a paradigm for many others that followed: favorable publicity, optimistic expectations, the use of fashionable techniques of "behavior modification", and a personified villain (Cardinal James F. McIntyre [d. 1979]). The community soon fell apart. Many sisters left; those who remained split into opposing factions; there were few new members; and most apostolates were abandoned. In time, the community virtually ceased to exist.

A Vacuum
Many religious, having abandoned both traditional spiritualities and traditional ministries, created vacuums waiting to be filled by new absolutes—left-wing politics, environmentalism, and above all feminism. Catholic feminism included lay women, but its most aggressive leadership came from women religious. The new feminist faith required sisters to see themselves as having been exploited laborers in their traditional apostolates and to pursue new careers, often living outside any community structure. At the farthest point, Catholic feminists invoked mythical goddesses and other female spirits and practiced neo-pagan rituals.

Male Communities

The crisis of religious life deeply affected most male communities as well, although they tended to be less openly rebellious than female groups and less likely to abandon community life and traditional apostolates like education.

For example, at the end of the Council, the Society of Jesus, the largest male community in the Church, had thirty-six thousand members throughout the world, but by 2010 that number had fallen well below twenty thousand. The leadership of the Society announced that a "fundamental option for the poor" was the very reason for its existence, a priority that had not been previously recognized and that made it difficult to justify much of the Society's traditional educational and pastoral work.

For forty years after the Council, various ecumenical commissions (Catholic-Anglican, Catholic-Lutheran) periodically announced agreements among their members, which did not, however, officially bind the participating churches. But, despite promising beginnings, ecumenical dialogue with "mainline" Protestant groups faltered over time, because the major thrust of liberal Protestantism was precisely against authoritative creedal statements, so that the search for official agreement on doctrine proved to be of decreasing relevance. Even the most daring Catholic theology came to seem timid in the postconciliar environment, when leading Protestant theologians began to speak of "religionless Christianity" and even of "the death of God". In addition, liberal mainline groups eventually ordained women as clergy and tended to accept the sexual revolution, including abortion and homosexuality.

Ecumenism

By the time of the Council, most people understood that Catholicism could no longer be treated solely as a Western religion, but European prelates still made up 39 percent of the Council, almost three times the number of any other regional group. Yet missionary activity was then at its highest point in the history of the Church, and "Third World" bishops were also numerous at the Council, although their participation was relatively slight.

The Missions

Integral to the revolution of "the Sixties", however, was cultural relativism: the claim that every belief was merely an expression of the culture that gave rise to it and none could lay claim to transcendent truth. Thus Christianity, which from its very foundation was an aggressively missionary religion, was dismissed by many as merely a form of Western "cultural imperialism". In this context, the theological emphasis on "lived experience", Rahner's "anonymous Christian", and the Council's favorable view of non-Christian religions combined to provoke a severe crisis of missionary identity.

Cultural Relativism

There were demands for yet further inculturation, such as accepting polygamy in Africa, but even heavily "inculturated" forms of Christianity were now seen as unwarranted intrusions on cultures that had their own religions. Thus missionaries, like every other category of priests and religious, began to give up their vocations in large numbers. Of those who remained, many pulled back from the very idea of making converts, even to the point of defining their task in terms such as "helping people to be better Hindus".

Some missionaries turned to political action as their justification—helping to overthrow the vestiges of colonialism and creating a better world in economic and social terms. The Kingdom itself was seen as the earthly reign of justice, achievable by human effort, from which thoughts of eternity were a distraction. The Church was merely a means by which the Kingdom could be achieved, and the "anonymous Christian" worked for social change, possibly without interest in religion at all.

Liberation Theology

Some Catholics in Latin America were attracted to Liberation Theology, an entirely new development of Catholic social doctrine that began in Germany but whose principal proponents included the Jesuits Jon Sobrino and Juan Luis Segundo (d. 1996) in Chile, the Brazilian Franciscan Leonardo Boff, and the Peruvian secular priest Gustavo Gutiérrez. (Boff left the Franciscans after being ordered to moderate his commitment to Liberationism.) At Medellin (Colombia) in 1968, the Latin American bishops' conference endorsed the "preferential option for the poor" and gave cautious encouragement to Liberationism, of which some bishops, notably Archbishop Helder Câmara of Recife, Brazil (d. 1999), were enthusiastic supporters.

"Ortho-Praxis"

For Liberation Theology a certain concept of social justice was the core meaning of the Gospel, requiring from Christians an unqualified commitment to the transformation of society—"ortho-praxis" ("right action") rather than orthodoxy. While not explicitly denying classical doctrines concerning sin, redemption, and eternal life, Liberation Theology deemphasized them almost to the vanishing point, lest they divert people from the social struggle. A religion that preached such doctrines was dismissed as a "bourgeois" distortion of the Gospel, motivated by the desire to protect social privilege.

Marxism

Liberation theologians were Marxists in seeing society as fundamentally a conflict between rich and poor and demanding commitment to the social struggle as an act of faith, without reserve. Some priests and religious actively participated in would-be revolutionary movements, in order to demonstrate "solidarity with the oppressed", and leftist Catholics everywhere enthusiastically praised such movements as the only hope for the future.

Ostpolitik

In some communist countries, notably Hungary and Czechoslovakia, Catholics were encouraged by their bishops to cooperate with the regimes as much as possible, a policy (*Ostpolitik*—"Eastern policy") that was also followed by a Vatican that apparently assumed that Communism could not be defeated. A group of Jesuits teaching in Rome even identified the Chinese communist dictator Mao Zedong as the hope of the world, the most authentic contemporary representative of the Gospel.

Base Communities

As an alternative to the "institutional Church", Liberation Theology extolled "base communities" that supposedly arose from the people's own awakening sense of injustice, their spontaneous discovery of the principles of liberation. But most such communities seem to have depended on an elite educated leadership, who were always few in number and had short life spans.

Meanwhile, however, many Hispanics, including many who immigrated to the United States, converted to Evangelical Protestantism, partly because of what amounted almost to the evacuation of their traditional faith after the Council. Told that their ancient pious practices were superstitious, and urged to adopt a this-worldly theology instead, many concluded that true Christianity had been kept from them by the Church.

Protestant Gains

Every disputed issue in the postconciliar Church unavoidably involved the concept of the Church herself. The term "Pilgrim Church" changed from that of a humble and devout traveler following a marked path toward the heavenly Kingdom to that of a spiritual explorer following his own lights. For some, the concept of the "People of God" gave rise to the expectation that the Church would now be governed democratically.

A Democratic Church

In connection with the Bicentennial of the United States in 1976, Cardinal John F. Dearden of Detroit (d. 1988) presided over the Call to Action Conference in his see city. Although made up primarily of clergy, religious, and lay employees of the Church, the conference aggressively advocated, among other things, an end to mandatory priestly celibacy, the ordination of women to the priesthood, and changes in Catholic sexual morality. The failure of the Church to embrace that agenda left a legacy of resentment that still festered decades later.

Call to Action

Feminists, many of them male, were usually the angriest. After initial hesitation, Church authorities admitted women to the ranks of lectors (readers), ministers of Communion, and acolytes (servers) at Mass, which gave rise to the expectation that they would soon be ordained to the priesthood as well. Church authorities pointed out that, except among the early Gnostics, there was no precedent for this in the entire history of the Church, but the feminist demand for ordination became increasingly strident, denouncing the hierarchy as "patriarchal". In a few cases, women were "ordained" as priests or bishops in ceremonies the Church did not recognize as valid. There was a partially successful demand for "inclusive language" in Scripture and liturgy, primarily on the grounds that words like *man* and *mankind* excluded women and should not be used. Some feminists went so far as to refuse to speak of God as "He" or as "Father".

Feminism

The influence of religion in the West, which seemed to be substantial for two decades after World War II, declined very sharply in the decades after the Council, making the region that had guided the Council the

Secularization

most secular in the world. The gravest crises occurred in precisely those countries that had previously been thought of as mostly Catholic.

Netherlands   Catholics in the Netherlands were a very large minority who, because of centuries of treatment as second-class citizens, had become highly conscious of their identity, to the point of developing their own sub-culture of labor unions, communication networks, and educational institutions. (They were also, proportionate to their population, the greatest Catholic missionary country.)

For a period during and after the Council, the Netherlands made a bid to provide the universal Church with a model of renewal. An official national synod boldly called for change in almost every area of Church life, and priests and people, often cautiously encouraged by their bishops, undertook almost unlimited experimentation. For a brief time, the new "Dutch Catechism" for adults was extolled as the purest expression of the Council, but soon Netherlanders themselves were dismissing it as too conservative.

The Catholic subculture quickly collapsed, and Netherlandish Catholicism became the most liberal in the world, even as the Netherlands overall became one of the most secular and morally permissive nations in the world. Forty years after the Council, the quality of religious belief and practice was such that one of its bishops declared sadly that the country had become mission territory.

Spain   After World War II, Francisco Franco pursued a successful program of economic modernization in Spain, but, inevitably, this new found economic prosperity led to social and cultural unrest. Although Franco sometimes clashed with the Catholic hierarchy over his refusal to extend political freedoms, his authoritarian regime was closely identified with the Church and with traditional morality, so that after his death in 1975 there was a popular reaction against religion and toward an easy hedonism.

Ireland   Until the 1990s, Ireland was still regarded as a very Catholic society, but there also sudden prosperity led to a hedonistic reaction against the Church, fueled by revelations of clerical pedophilia that the bishops had ignored. Ireland, however, remained one of the very few Western nations that did not permit abortion.

Italy   In Italy, a substantial majority of citizens, in defiance of their hierarchy, voted to legalize divorce, and in time, the Italian birth rate dropped, becoming the lowest in Europe.

Malta   The tiny island republic of Malta could be considered the most Catholic European country, officially proclaimed as such in its constitution and forbidding divorce and abortion. However, even there, weekly Mass attendance fell from 82 percent in 1967 to barely half by 2010.

In Poland, freedom from Communism proved to be a mixed blessing, as a hedonistic "consumer society" spread from the West, and by 2010, the rate of Mass attendance had fallen to 60 percent. *Poland*

If the experience of liberal Protestantism exposed the essential fallacy of an uncritical accommodation with secularity, the experience of the Netherlands, Spain, Ireland, Quebec (see Chapter Thirteen above, pp. 431–32), and some other places also exposed the essential fallacy of Integralism, the demand that political, social, and economic life be intimately bound up with religion, an ideal of medieval Christendom that was shattered by the Reformation and the French Revolution. *Integralism*

The essential fallacy of Integralism was that, in such a closed system, change of any kind, even beneficial change, necessarily caused instability and thereby undermined religion. The conditions of modern life are such that no society can remain permanently protected from the forces of the modern world, and people who have been inoculated against those forces can often withstand them better than those who have been protected. In the terms of *Dignitatis Humanae*, the authentic Christian life must be lived in freedom.

Cardinal Montini participated in the first session of the Council and, although he said relatively little from the floor, was considered preeminently a man of the Council. His election as pope was completely expected—many had thought him worthy of the office already in 1958—and he was given the responsibility of bringing the Council to a conclusion and overseeing its implementation. **A Troubled Pope**

Prior to his nine-year episcopacy, the future Paul VI had spent his entire career in the service of the Holy See and, although not even a bishop, was recognized as one of the most important men in the Vatican under Pius XII. He also did pastoral work, especially as chaplain to university students in Milan. He was strongly anti-fascist, and his students were sometimes physically assaulted by Black Shirt gangs. *Career*

But by neglecting to make him a cardinal, Pius effectively excluded Montini from achieving the papal office in 1958, a neglect that John XXIII immediately remedied. (The reasons for Pius' sending Montini away from Rome, then failing to make him a cardinal, are uncertain, but in some sense Pius probably considered him too liberal.)

It was Paul VI's cross to preside over the Church during this great crisis. A disciple of Maritain, he saw the growing split between *aggiornamento* and *ressourcement* and, although he was inclined by nature to be open to new ideas, his sympathies ultimately lay with the *ressourcement* school, who were now deemed "conservative". He conferred the cardinalate on de Lubac, Danielou, and Congar and offered it to Maritain, who declined. Ressourcement

Social Teaching

Paul continued the modern papal tradition of addressing the social issues in an authoritative way, directed to the entire world. *Populorum Progressio* (The Progress of Peoples, 1967) seemed to accept the modern economic theory that poverty is best overcome not by redistributing wealth but by the economic development of the entire society, which improves the lot of everyone. But the Pope identified the poverty of the "Third World" as to a great extent the fault of the developed nations and called for an equitable sharing of resources, including technology to facilitate development, not as charity but as an obligation of justice.

Firm Action

Prior to *Humanae Vitae*, Paul showed himself as capable of action. He intervened to ensure that *Lumen Gentium* would adequately respect papal infallibility, declared on his own authority that Mary is the Mother of the Church, instructed the Council Fathers not to discuss clerical celibacy, vetoed an attempt by the Jesuits to weaken their vow of special obedience to the pope, and suddenly replaced Bugnini as the overseer of liturgical change.

Indecision

Paul sometimes anguished publicly over the many crises of the Church, even lamenting that "the smoke of Satan has entered the Church", but he often seemed indecisive. Although he made a special effort to encourage the use of Latin in the liturgy, he did nothing to alter the direction of liturgical change and took no decisive action against the rising tide of often militant theological dissent. Having touched off a firestorm with *Humanae Vitae*, the Pope seemed reluctant to mandate its acceptance. Several national bishops' conferences appeared to dissociate themselves from the encyclical, and when Cardinal Patrick A. O'Boyle (d. 1987) of Washington suspended a number of priests who had rejected it, he was required by the Holy See to reinstate them.

The exodus of men from the priesthood became a flood in part because under Paul it was the policy of the Holy See to release priests from their obligations almost for the asking. The laxity seemed to correspond with the number of annulments granted to married couples, which as already noted, also increased geometrically.

Ultimately, it was left to Paul's successors to begin the process of authentic renewal. Although in a sense the Council had seemed to modify papal authority through collegiality, a strong papacy proved to be the only means of maintaining the unity of the Church in the face of the centrifugal forces unleashed by the Council.

John Paul II

An Exceptional Pope

Paul's immediate successor, John Paul I, survived for barely a month, and the next conclave had a wholly unanticipated and electrifying effect, when it chose as pope the intellectual leader of Polish Catholicism, Cardinal Karol Wojtyła of Kraków. Authentic renewal occurred during the pontificate of Paul VI, but it was often obscured by more negative events. Under John Paul II (1978–2005), the fruits of renewal began to be seen.

John Paul II was the only Polish pope in history and the first non-Italian in 455 years. He studied for the priesthood during the Nazi occupation of Poland, for a time hiding in the basement of the archbishop's palace, and for the rest of his life remembered with anguish that the notorious Nazi death camp of Auschwitz was located in his native country. After the fall of Nazism, he spent his entire priestly career amidst the communist government's unceasing attempts to undermine the Church.

Progressively Conservative

Like some of the major figures of the Counter-Reformation, he was innovative in the service of orthodoxy. A philosopher, poet, and playwright, he was perhaps the most intellectually formidable man ever to ascend the papal throne, and perhaps no one was better qualified to integrate *ressourcement* with whatever was valid in *aggiornamento*. The maturation of the seminal ideas of the Council, after fifteen years of confusion, was to a great extent due to the work of the Pope himself.

A Council Father

As a former participant, he fully understood the Council, and during his pontificate—the third longest in history after St. Peter and St. Pius IX—the Council's purposes at last began to be fulfilled, perhaps more often than not in ways—both good and bad—the Council Fathers did not fully foresee. One by one the issues began to be addressed.

World Traveler

World journeys were the distinguishing mark of John Paul's pontificate, as he traveled almost continuously, visiting every inhabited continent—many places more than once—to be greeted everywhere by huge crowds jubilantly shouting their devotion. People who did not necessarily accept his teachings, nor even understand them, nonetheless often had a strong personal admiration for him.

An International Curia

Because of their experience at the Council, many liberals considered the Italians to be an obstructive conservative bloc and urged that membership in the Roman Curia be broadened. But this internationalization, which began under Paul VI, proved to be one of the more ironic outcomes of the Council. Under a non-Italian pope, the Curia was indeed internationalized, but some of the Italians now turned out to be liberals, while some non-Italians were among the leading conservatives. For example, Cardinals Jorge Medina Estévez of Colombia and Francis Arinze of Nigeria—successive heads of the Congregation for Divine Worship—acted to correct liturgical abuse.

The Synods

Almost immediately upon taking office, John Paul acted to stem the flood of departures from the priesthood, only rarely granting requests for laicization. He used the triennial episcopal synods to resolve the uncertainties of collegiality, allowing free discussion, then himself synthesizing the various opinions into a final document that embodied the consensus of the Magisterium.

Küng

John Paul manifested his concern for orthodoxy almost immediately upon his election, when he declared officially that Hans Küng, who had become the most conspicuous spokesman for dissent and was by now in effect a liberal Protestant, was no longer to be considered a Catholic theologian.

Social Teaching

John Paul continued to expound Catholic social teachings to the world.

The Family

Familiaris Consortio (On the Christian Family, 1981) once again affirmed the family as the indispensable basis of the social order, identifying its nature as the primacy of self-giving love, modeled on the internal love of the three Persons of the Trinity.

Labor

In *Laborem Exercens (On Human Work*, 1981), the Pope reiterated the traditional Catholic respect for the dignity of labor, affirming the workers' right to employment and urging the developed countries to be generous in receiving immigrants.

Globalization

In *Sollicitudo Rei Socialis (The Church and Social Order*, 1987), John Paul II raised moral questions about "globalization"—the international free market in which poorer nations continued to fall behind richer ones—which he characterized as a kind of neo-colonialism. He urged both the developed nations and international organizations to reduce or cancel the debts of the developing countries that helped keep those countries in poverty.

The Market

Centesimus Annus (Hundredth Year, 1991), which commemorated the issuance of *Rerum Novarum*, cautiously endorsed the free market as the most efficient means of organizing the economy, while again warning against unfettered economic competition. *Centesimus Annus* was the first social encyclical following the fall of Communism, and John Paul praised the West's respect for freedom and human dignity while warning against "consumerism"—the perversion of freedom into the pursuit of superficial material goals, a kind of practical atheism.

Personalism

Perhaps John Paul's most important achievement was his theology of human sexuality, which was made possible by his assimilation of both classical and modern philosophies. He was strongly influenced by personalism and by the phenomenology of the German Max Scheler (d. 1928), who had twice been converted to Catholicism and twice apostatized. The future pope's doctoral dissertation on the mystical theology of St. John of the Cross integrated the latter's Thomism with his phenomenological descriptions of the mystical state.

The Mystery of Sexuality

As cardinal, John Paul had influenced Paul VI in the writing of *Humanae Vitae*, which, despite its being largely regarded as merely a reaffirmation of traditional prohibitions, in reality set forth a positive theology of human sexuality in which sexual disorders were shown to dishonor the true dignity of sexuality. As pope, John Paul developed that positive vision into the "theology of the body", the most profound and comprehensive theory of human sexuality ever conceived, affirming in almost mystical terms the flesh as part of God's good creation. In the act of love, husband and wife give themselves unreservedly to one another, culminating in the act of procreation in which they share in God's own creative act, genuine love freeing *eros* from mere lust. John Paul reaffirmed celibacy, not as a denial of sexuality but as the willingness to give oneself to everyone in love, as a witness to the Kingdom where, as Jesus said, men neither marry nor are given in marriage.

The Culture of Death

The Pope identified "the culture of death"—epitomized by abortion, euthanasia, and other direct assaults on human life—as in opposition to this affirmation of the body. He also included capital punishment, which, in contrast to earlier popes, he came close to condemning as inherently immoral. At its root, according to the Pope, the culture of death was nothing less than a refusal to accept the divine invitation to participate in the work of creation. At the heart of modern secular culture was a kind of nihilism, a rebellious rejection of every ultimate truth.

The New Feminism

In the face of often angry demands for the ordination of women to the priesthood and the feminist claim that motherhood restricts women's freedom, John Paul expounded what was sometimes called "the new feminism", in which woman's highest dignity lies precisely in her free response to the divine invitation to participate in creation, her openness to the divine call in imitation of Mary. Moving beyond the mere invocation of tradition as the justification of the male priesthood, John Paul based it on St. Paul's comparison of marriage to the union of Christ and His Church, with the priest representing Christ and the Church His Bride.

Ecumenism

Eastern Orthodoxy

John Paul II made relations with the Eastern Orthodox a high priority of his pontificate but, while ancient doctrinal and liturgical issues to some extent faded into the background, the Orthodox in general were resistant, partly because of historic grievances like the Fourth Crusade. Ironically, the fall of Communism complicated the matter, as some Russian Orthodox leaders opposed the presence of other Christian groups in the former Soviet Union, and many Orthodox regarded the Uniate (Eastern-Rite Catholic) churches as a kind of provocation.

Evangelicalism

During John Paul's pontificate, ecumenism took an unexpected turn in the United States, in the encounter between Catholics and the kind of Protestants variously called Evangelical or Fundamentalist, who tended historically to be anti-Catholic. Scarcely noticed at first, Evangelicals had replaced liberals as the dominant element within American Protestantism, and some Catholics were surprised to discover that they had more in common with Evangelicals than with liberal fellow Catholics.

The new ecumenism usually began with cooperation on practical moral issues like abortion but soon led to the realization that those moral principles were themselves based on traditional Christian beliefs, including the divine authority of the Scripture and the unchanging truth of the faith. Ecumenical prayer and Bible-study groups followed.

Protestants of this kind were almost invisible in Europe, so that the Holy See had not engaged in formal dialogue with them. But in America, there began to be significant ecumenical activity at the "grass roots" level, without anticipating formal reunion. As with the Eastern Orthodox, such activity revealed the paradox that, to the degree that people held strongly to their own beliefs and were unwilling to compromise, they might also respect others who held equally strong beliefs.

Christ Alone

The Congregation for the Doctrine of the Faith (CDF)—now under Joseph Ratzinger—was praised by Evangelicals and severely criticized by liberals for issuing *Dominus Jesus* (Lord Jesus). This document is a restatement of the classic Christian teaching that the world is saved solely through Christ and reproves theologians who hold that Jesus was perhaps only one of a number of equally authentic revelations of God to mankind.

"New Age"

Ironically, the relationship between Christianity and pagan beliefs became an issue even in nominally Christian lands, including the United States, because of the neo-pagan renaissance broadly called the New Age, a kind of neo-Romanticism that criticized Catholicism not as superstitious but as overly rational. The movement was essentially a search for personal spiritual "fulfillment". "Spirituality" was distinguished from "religion" and orthodox Christianity condemned for confining spirituality within doctrinal boundaries.

The New Age movement, which attracted many feminists, including religious sisters, proved to be even more inimical to genuine religion than was rational skepticism, because it set itself up as the true religion that transcended all others, exploiting the natural human religious sense in order to undermine Christianity. The movement revived belief in ancient pagan deities, reincarnation, magic, astrology, the occult, and even witchcraft. Supposedly outmoded ritual elements like candles, incense, vestments, and chanting were resuscitated.

Perhaps the most significant event of John Paul's pontificate was the sudden collapse of Communism in the later 1980s, something that Paul VI's *Ostpolitik* had assumed was not possible but that John Paul played a major role in bringing about.

The Collapse of Communism

The Church in Poland

Only in Poland, under the bold leadership of Cardinal Stefan Wyszyński (d. 1981), did the Church as an institution offer significant resistance to the communist regime. The Church in Poland had long been the soul of resistance to the regime, the Catholic faith so deeply ingrained in the people that the government, while making occasional martyrs, could not suppress it. (An outspoken priest, Bl. Jerzy Popieluszko [d. 1984], was brutally murdered and, although several government officials were later convicted of his killing, none were ever punished.)

Solidarity

The Solidarity movement combined religion, nationalism, and labor militancy to organize strikes, massive rallies, and other acts of anti-government resistance so effectively that only military intervention by the Soviet Union could have crushed it. John Paul clearly stood behind Solidarity, to the point where it was thought that he would actually go to Poland in the event of a Soviet invasion. In the end, the Soviets allowed the regime to collapse, thereby beginning of the process by which the other communist dominoes, including the Soviet Union itself, fell one by one. (In 1981, John Paul was shot and seriously wounded by a mentally disturbed Turk who may have been acting for the Soviet government.)

Liberationism

John Paul faced Liberationism directly in Nicaragua, where the hierarchy at first opposed a right-wing dictatorship, then became equally critical of the new Marxist "Sandinista" government (named after an early Nicaraguan radical). Cardinal Miguel Obando served as the leader and symbol of the many Nicaraguans who opposed the Sandinistas' curtailment of liberties, including their harassment of the Church. But the government included four left-wing priests, who defied the Holy See when told to relinquish their government posts and whom, during an official visit, John Paul publicly rebuked. (The Sandinistas eventually fell from power but later returned.)

Marxism

John Paul's confrontation with the Sandinistas was partly due to his experiences in Poland, where Marxism had shown itself to be an instrument of tyranny rather than of liberation. Marxism held that violent revolution alone would bring about the "classless society", and the Catholic left in Latin America was often ambivalent about the violent tactics of guerilla groups. Meeting with John Paul at Puebla, Mexico, in 1979, the Latin American bishops in effect rescinded their endorsement of Liberationism at Medellin.

The Fruits of the Council

Dogma

Ratzinger

Ultimately, no one contributed more to the process of postconciliar renewal than Ratzinger, who was by far the most important of the non-Italians named to the Curia. First as a professor, then briefly as archbishop of Munich, finally as prefect of the CDF, he did more than any other single person to clarify and deepen the meaning of the Council, bringing the theology of *ressourcement* to fruition in ways that were rooted in the New Testament and the early Church Fathers but also spoke to modernity.

Balthasar

Both John Paul and Ratzinger were strongly influenced by Balthasar, who came to be recognized as the most important Catholic theologian of the twentieth century. (John Paul named him a cardinal, but Balthasar died before he could be invested.) Balthasar was a man of immense learning who incorporated much of the Western cultural tradition—philosophical, literary, artistic—into his theology. But unlike the proponents of *aggiornamento*, he looked primarily inward, to the deepest mysteries of the faith.

His theology was an extended meditation on those mysteries, culminating during the climactic days of Holy Week, when the redemption of mankind was accomplished. To Balthasar, theology was a "theo-dramatic": a story of overwhelming power and beauty that summoned mankind to respond in awe and reverence to God's communication of Himself to His people.

Condemnations

Under Ratzinger, the CDF began to act vigorously to correct questionable teachings, issuing official warnings against several theologians and in some cases ordering them to cease teaching and publishing.

Although theologians sometimes complained that they were condemned without being understood, they were in fact being judged by a man whose intelligence and theological attainments were superior to their own.

Continuity

Ratzinger insisted on the essential continuity between the "preconciliar" and "postconciliar" Church. There was no "spirit of Vatican II", in the sense of a meaning that was dependent on changing human culture, because the Council derived its very authority from God. Somewhat daringly, he suggested that *Gaudium et Spes* had been excessively optimistic about the state of the world.

Scripture

In Scripture, Ratzinger acknowledged the achievements of the historical-critical method but proposed that it had reached the limits of its usefulness, to the point where it now actually obscured the full meaning of Scripture, which was accessible only through faith. Christians could not approach the Bible as outsiders studying a historical book. Based on Vatican II's understanding of Tradition, Ratzinger insisted that Scripture disclosed its full meaning only within the community of the Church, in the act of worship, since the biblical canon was defined by the Church as precisely those works appropriate to be read in the liturgy. Ratzinger advocated a recovery of the exegesis of the Fathers, who read both the Old and New Testaments as the revelation of the mystery of Christ.

Liturgy

Although he had strongly supported the liturgical movement, Ratzinger after the Council became one of the most trenchant critics of liturgical change, arguing that the process ignored the way in which the ritual life of the Church was deeply rooted in the mystical community and therefore could not be changed by sudden fiat, which made the liturgy seem merely a human project rather than divinely ordained. Instead of attempting to harmonize the "old" and "new" liturgies, he lamented, bureaucrats maximized their disjunction, so that there now needed to be a "reform of the reform".

Ad Orientem

Even prior to the Council, the principal historian of the liturgy, the German Jesuit Josef Jungmann (d. 1975), argued that the *versus populum* position was inappropriate if the Mass was "an immolation and homage to God". Now Ratzinger and others pointed out that, contrary to some liturgists' claim, *versus populum* was not the original practice. In the early Church, the celebrant usually faced eastward (*ad orientem*), at the head of the congregation, looking in the direction from which Christ will come again.

Episcopal Conferences

Ratzinger contended that national episcopal conferences illegitimately restricted the authority of individual bishops, who in their individual dioceses possessed an apostolic authority not given to them collectively except in general councils in communion with the pope.

Liberationism

Liberation theology was severely criticized by the CDF under Ratzinger. Both he and John Paul defined the Christian meaning of liberation as including the reform of social structures but above all as liberation from the bondage of sin, which was rooted in human nature and was therefore the ultimate cause of social injustice. Social change would always fail, and even result in greater injustices, if the necessary spiritual reform did not occur. The distinction between Kingdom and Church was invalid, Ratzinger insisted, because the Kingdom that Christ promised was in fact Himself, sacramentally present in the Church.

The Catechism

A major instrument for clarifying doctrinal confusion is the *Catechism of the Catholic Church*, which was promulgated by John Paul II. Developed under Ratzinger's overall supervision, the new universal *Catechism*, the first since the Council of Trent, made authentic Catholic teaching, on every subject, readily accessible to non-theologians.

Ex Corde Ecclesiae

In 1990, John Paul wrote *Ex Corde Ecclesiae* (From the Heart of the Church), summoning Catholic universities to recover their religious identity, reminding them that the university itself was a creation of the medieval Church. But in the United States, where most such universities were located, only a few institutions responded to that call.

Religious Life

Despite the overall decline of vocations, some dioceses and religious orders continued to attract a significant number. Following an investigation by the Holy See, the quality of some diocesan seminaries in the United States improved notably by 2000, and seminarians almost everywhere were described as more traditional than clergy of an older generation.

The Jesuits

When John Paul asked the Society of Jesus to combat atheism, the leadership replied that this could be done best by promoting social change, not by confronting atheism on the intellectual level. The Pope later made an effort toward the reform of religious life by taking the extraordinary step of appointing a Jesuit to be his "personal delegate" in governing the Society, an action that caused bitterness on the part of some Jesuits, because it was seen as a papal repudiation of the leadership of their general, Pedro Arrupe (d. 1991). After a time, the Society's self-government was restored, and it appeared that little had changed.

New Communities

Repeating a pattern that has recurred throughout the history of the Church, as older religious orders declined, new ones flourished, although some smaller communities, especially of female contemplatives, remained largely unaffected by the postconciliar confusion.

Missionaries of Charity

The most notable new female community was the Missionaries of Charity, originally founded by an Albanian nun, Bl. Teresa of Calcutta (d. 1997), to work especially with the poorest of the poor in India—the abandoned and homeless taken off the streets to be cared for in their last hours. Partly because of the fame of Teresa herself, the new community grew rapidly and soon extended its apostolate to many parts of the world, including the United States. The Missionaries serve as a living example of the continued "relevance" of traditional religious life, in that they have responded to the most desperate needs of the age but nonetheless live in convents, wear religious habits, and have adoration of the Blessed Sacrament as the heart of their spirituality.

Mother Angelica

Contemplative religious life took a wholly unexpected turn in the story of a Poor Clare abbess, Mother Angelica Rizzo, head of a monastery in the heavily Evangelical Protestant state of Alabama, who managed to put together by far the most successful Catholic communications network in history, making her one of the best known and most influential Catholics in the United States. Her Eternal Word Television Network (EWTN) produced television programs that were beamed all over the world and for many people served as the pole star of Catholic piety and belief during a time of confusion. Among other things, it was a means of rekindling both Marian and eucharistic piety.

Legionaries of Christ

Ostensibly the most successful of the new male religious communities were the Legionaries of Christ, founded in Mexico in 1940 by a diocesan priest, Marcial Maciel (d. 2008), but not well known until the 1980s, when it was noticed that they were experiencing phenomenal growth.

The Laity

After the Council, lay people began to play important roles in almost every aspect of church life, including the liturgy, the social apostolate, and the intellectual life. Through diocesan and parish councils of various kinds, they exercised new responsibilities. But although some liberals saw the new "age of laity" primarily as emancipation from hierarchical authority, the lay apostolate developed quite differently from what they expected.

"The Movements"
John Paul strongly encouraged what he called "the movements". These predominantly lay organizations that in a sense existed parallel to the hierarchical structure of the Church, developed from below and promised spiritual and apostolic renewal.

Opus Dei
Opus Dei ("the work of God") was founded in Spain in 1928 by a diocesan priest, St. Josemaría Escrivà (d. 1975). Although directed by priests, it was in some ways the most significant lay movement of modern times, embracing over eighty thousand members worldwide, a majority of whom were married but lived under the spiritual direction of priests and under the disciplinary authority of their own bishop.

Part of Opus Dei's original significance was the fact that, whereas traditional European Catholicism had always been cool, even hostile, to industrialization, Opus Dei enthusiastically embraced technological modernity and successfully combined it with traditional piety. (Franco modernized Spain partly by using the skills of "technocrats" affiliated with the movement.) *Opus Dei* members were especially active in journalism, business, technology, and education, including a major new Catholic university at Navarre in Spain. In some countries (but not the United States), they were also active in politics.

Other Groups
In the postconciliar period, other important new lay groups included the Cursillo ("little course") of intense spiritual exercises undertaken within a very brief period of time; Focolari ("hearth"), founded by the laywoman Chiara Lubich (d. 2008); Communione e Liberazione ("Communion and Liberation"); Regnum Christi, also founded by Maciel; the Neocatechumenate; and the Community of St. Egidio, the latter two being lay groups devoted to prayer and works of charity.

The Charismatic Movement
The most influential expression of popular piety in the postconciliar period—once again wholly unanticipated—was the charismatic movement, which began at Duquesne University in Pittsburgh and spread rapidly, first throughout the United States, then to other countries.

Recalling that all baptized Christians receive the Spirit, the movement sought to respond to the inspiration of the Holy Spirit, including the recovery of the *charisms* described in Acts: discernment, spontaneous prayer (including speaking in tongues), prophesying, and physical and spiritual healing.

At first, it was a wholly unauthorized lay movement, and it remained predominantly lay even after it gained ecclesiastical approval. Since being a charismatic was largely a matter of personal inspiration, the movement had no universally recognized central authority, hence it harbored considerable variety. In a sense, it existed alongside the hierarchical Church, sometimes with the support of bishops and parish priests, never in overt opposition to them. At its peak, around 1990, the movement affected millions of people in virtually every place where Catholics were found, some living in tightly knit communities, others participating in mass rallies or small prayer groups.

Communities
The desire to replicate the pattern of the early Christians led many charismatics to live in communities governed by strict discipline and adhering closely to traditional moral teachings at a time when many Catholics were rejecting them. Although the movement had multiple centers, the most important was the Word of God Community in Ann Arbor, Michigan, composed of several thousand members who provided spiritual and intellectual guidance to charismatics all over the world.

Decline
Many people testified that charismatic piety rekindled their dying faith, and it provided many with a way of leading a Christian life during a troubled time, perhaps often filling the void left by the near disappearance of traditional devotions. But the reliance on personal inspiration meant that fervor inevitably cooled over time, and splits developed within communities. By the end of the twentieth century, the organized charismatic movement was a shadow of its former self, but its influence was lasting, a wholly unanticipated fruit of Vatican II.

Marian Piety
Marian piety underwent a major revival beginning in the 1970s, partly through reports of Marian apparitions in various parts of the world. By far the most influential of these was at Medjugorje in Yugoslavia (later Bosnia-Herzegovina), where three young people reported numerous visions of Mary over a period of several years. For the next three decades, millions of pilgrims came to the town, and many people reported miraculous occurrences and a lasting revival of their personal faith and piety.

The cult of Medjugorje was promoted primarily by Croatian Franciscans, but almost from the beginning the local bishops officially expressed reservations about its authenticity, in time condemned it, and even publicly criticized a cardinal for endorsing it as a "place of prayer and repentance". The Medjugorje cult differed from the classical Marian pattern in that some of the "seers" continued to report apparitions years after the original event, even in distant places far away from Medjugorje itself.

Conservative Laity
One of the great ironies of postconciliar Catholicism is the fact that, despite the "emancipation of the laity", priests and religious were always the backbone of liberal movements, whereas conservative lay people

not only often lacked clerical support, they might even find themselves in direct opposition to their priests and bishops.

After the Council, especially in the United States, conservative lay people organized aggressively, publishing polemical books and journals and founding schools at every level, all independent of ecclesiastical control, a kind of lay activism that would have been impossible before the Council. (Mother Angelica's apostolate—a cloistered nun at the head of a huge communications network—would also have been impossible before the Council.)

Education

The Council's affirmation that the parents were the primary educators of their children became the basis for considerable lay resistance to the new catechetics and also to the growing practice of "home schooling"—parents teaching their own children rather than enrolling them in schools.

Lay people also founded high schools and colleges independent of hierarchical control, with minimal clerical presence. Unlike the Society of St. Pius X, which was a priestly organization, most lay conservatives did not question the Council itself but its interpretation. They affirmed their loyalty to the pope, to whose authority they appealed, if necessary, against that of the bishops.

The Pro-Life Movement

In the United States, no postconciliar event so galvanized Catholic energy as the transformation of abortion into a constitutional right by the Supreme Court in 1973. The pro-life movement emerged as the single most effective lay apostolate of the post–Vatican II period, working with the bishops but independent of their authority, officially ecumenical and even nonsectarian.

The New Millennium

Benedict XVI

Ratzinger's election as Benedict XVI in 2005 was a surprise to many, in that, as the official guardian of orthodoxy, he was often the target of liberal attack as a "divisive" figure. His quick election was therefore an unambiguous decision by the cardinals to continue the path of renewal laid out by John Paul II.

Ratzinger had been an adolescent in Germany in the waning years of World War II and, like other German young men of the time, was forced to join the Hitler Youth and the German Army, from which he deserted at his first opportunity. A diocesan priest, he became one of the leaders of the New Theology, although he was a generation younger than most of its noted practitioners.

As a *peritus* at Vatican II, Ratzinger was considered a liberal, but as the paths of *ressourcement* and *aggiornamento* diverged after the Council, he decisively followed the former, partly because the cultural revolution of the later 1960s, which was strongly felt in Germany, underlay so many of the demands for change.

As pope it fell to Benedict to preside over the Church at a time of great scandal. The gravest stain on the Church during John Paul II's pontificate was the revelation of sexual abuse—primarily of boys and male adolescents—perpetrated by priests, a devastating scandal not because a tiny percentage of priests perverted their calling, but because in many cases bishops knew of the abuses and took no decisive action. Incalculable damage was done to the Church's credibility, and the blot on her reputation is likely to survive for many years.

U.S. and Ireland
At first, the abuses seemed to be largely a problem in the United States, where the Church had to pay many millions of dollars in damages to an ever-lengthening list of victims. Eventually, however, the revelation of even worse cases erupted in Ireland. Benedict publicly rebuked the Irish hierarchy and appointed a commission of investigation, and several bishops resigned, including John Magee of Cloyne, who had been secretary to three popes. By 2010, new allegations of sexual abuse were coming to light in other places and the harm to the reputation of the Church seemed likely to get worse. Benedict repeatedly expressed sorrow and anguish over the sufferings of the innocent victims, some of whom he met personally.

Legionaries of Christ
The story of the Legionaries of Christ proved to be an especially severe scandal. The Legion was for years criticized for excessive rigidity and for fostering a cult of personality around Maciel, whom some former Legionaries accused of serious sexual misconduct. The charges were categorically denied by Legion officials, and during John Paul's pontificate attempts by Ratzinger to initiate an investigation were blocked by others in the Papal Curia. But after Ratzinger became pope, the Holy See finally verified the charges of sexual abuse of seminarians, bigamy, and systematic financial irregularities. Maciel was stripped of all authority and soon died, and an official investigation of the Legion left its future in doubt.

As the greatest theologian ever to serve as pope, following the greatest philosopher ever to do so, Benedict has devoted much of his pontificate to teaching, continuing the work of *ressourcement* in public talks—later published—on the New Testament and the Fathers of the Church. He has traveled widely, although less so than John Paul, with a series of "world youth days", inspiring intensely enthusiastic responses by huge crowds.

Benedict's first encyclical was *Deus Caritas Est* (*God Is Love*), which, after decades of papal emphasis on justice, reminded the world of the primacy of charity, not in a paternalistic or condescending way

The Sexual Abuse Scandal

Papal Theology

Social Teaching

but as something that goes beyond what is strictly due. In the same encyclical, as a kind of corollary to John Paul's theology of the body, Benedict in a sense reclaimed for Christianity the concept of love as *eros*, something natural to the human person, to be sanctified by *agape*. Like his predecessors, Benedict lamented the specter of war that hung over the world and urged that resources used for military purposes be devoted instead to peace.

Reform of the Reform

It was perhaps in liturgy that Benedict hoped to have his greatest effect, a "reform of the reform" to recover the sense of liturgy as a divine action in which men are privileged to participate. Elements of this reform included greater use of Latin as a vehicle of tradition and a unifying liturgical language; translations that were both more beautiful and more faithful to the original; communicants kneeling to receive Communion on the tongue; and the renewed use of sacred gestures like genuflections and striking the breast. The Pope gave blanket permission for all priests to celebrate the Tridentine rite, a permission that seemed to be utilized disproportionately by younger priests. Significantly, he expressed belief that the priest at Mass should face *ad orientem*, as head of the congregation facing East toward God, rather than *versus populum* (toward the people). The *ad orientem* position, he believed, was more appropriate to the Mass as primarily an act of worship rather than a community celebration. Though he continued to celebrate most public Masses *versus populum*, a crucifix is placed on the altar in front of him, the celebrant, providing the "Eastward" focus.

Traditionalists

Benedict once characterized groups like the Society of St. Pius X as infected by an un-Catholic "sectarian zealotry", but he lifted the excommunication of their bishops, although they were still forbidden to exercise their offices. The Pope initiated discussions aimed at reconciliation, but the Society's official spokesmen insisted that such reconciliation could not take place unless the Church explicitly repudiated the "errors" of Vatican II.

Devotions

Popular devotions, especially eucharistic adoration and the rosary, revived under John Paul and Benedict, and for several decades there was immense interest in the Holy Shroud, a cloth kept at Turin, Italy, that bears the image of a man with wounds like those of the crucified Jesus and that many believe was His burial cloth.

Ecumenism

Benedict continued to seek better relations with the Eastern Orthodox, with more apparent success than John Paul had experienced. The patriarch of the Russian Orthodox church, which had been cool to ecumenical overtures, proposed to cooperate with the Catholic Church in opposing militant secularism in Europe.

Anglican Conversions

But although official dialogue with Anglicans continued, in time it became obvious that it was unlikely to bear significant fruit, as Anglicanism moved in an increasingly liberal direction.

Prior to the Council an occasional married convert clergyman had been allowed to become a Catholic priest, and afterward such permissions were given fairly freely, primarily to clergy from the Anglican Communion (under the 1980 Pastoral Provision of Pope John Paul II). During Benedict's pontificate, the Holy See announced, in response to formal requests, that it was willing to receive into the Church entire organized groups of Anglicans from various countries. These groups had broken with the Anglican Communion primarily because of women clergy and the acceptance of homosexuality. The Anglican groups would be under the authority of their own "ordinaries" (who might be priests or bishops) and could retain elements of their liturgy. Married clergy could be ordained as priests but, as with the Eastern Orthodox, only celibates could be bishops. Both liberal Catholics and some Anglicans denounced the conversions as a violation of ecumenism.

The Jews

Relations with the Jews after 2000 were severely marred by a sudden and fierce campaign of slander against Pius XII, who was condemned as a Nazi sympathizer complicit in the Holocaust. But by no means was all the slander by Jews, and some Jews defended the Pope.

A Resurgent Islam

Until almost the year 2000, Islam, despite its huge numbers, was regarded as almost a marginal influence in the world. Then it suddenly underwent a dramatic resurgence, politically as well as religiously, in conscious rivalry to the West and to Christianity, a rival potentially as formidable as Communism had once been. (A major and undeveloped theological issue was Vatican II's statement that Muslims, like Christians and Jews, "adore the one merciful God".)

Besides government persecution in various officially Muslim countries, especially the Sudan, Christians were subjected to frequent mob violence in Pakistan and other Muslim states where they were legally tolerated. Turkey, an officially secular country, classified Christian missionaries with Muslim terrorists, and an Italian archbishop serving in that country was murdered by his Muslim driver, who shouted, "I have killed the Great Satan!"

But Islam's greatest challenge to the West was massive Muslim immigration to Europe, where, combined with a very low birth rate among nominal Christians, it seemed likely in time to become the majority religion in what was once called Christendom.

Just as it had supported the United Nations, the Holy See supported the formation of the European Union (E.U.) in the early twenty-first

Europe

century. But in its constitution, the Union refused to acknowledge Christianity as even a historical influence in Western civilization. Benedict, who perhaps chose his papal name in homage to the founder of Western monasticism, who is also the patron saint of Europe, was especially concerned to remind his fellow Europeans of the religious basis of their civilization. (Among European states in 2010, Catholicism was the official religion only in Lichtenstein, Malta, Monaco, and Vatican City.)

The Worldwide Church

Growth and Decline

Benedict presided over a Church that had doubled in size since the Council. By 2010, there were well over a billion Catholics in the world—about 17 percent of the total population—the second largest religion after Islam. Brazil was the largest Catholic country in the world, followed by Mexico. Europe still accounted for a quarter of all Catholics, but the growth of the Church there fell well short of the overall population growth, while in Latin America it barely kept pace.

Latin America

By the beginning of the twenty-first century, the governments of most Latin American countries, despite the fact that their people were overwhelmingly Catholic, were pursuing a secular agenda like that of Western Europe, as the Church struggled, often unsuccessfully, against legalized abortion, homosexual "marriage", and other issues. The bishops of Venezuela repeatedly clashed with the socialist President Hugo Chavez, whom they accused of attempting to establish a dictatorship.

Asia and Africa

The Church was growing fastest, and appeared to have more spiritual vitality, in parts of Asia and Africa than in the West, especially as measured by religious vocations. While Catholics were only 17 percent of the population of Africa, their number had multiplied fifteen times since Vatican II, and, while they were only 3 percent of the population of Asia, their number there had tripled during the same time. At the same time, Africa, along with the Middle East, was the site of greatest aggression by radical Muslims against Christians.

India

Although India by no means had the largest Catholic population in the world—Catholics were barely 1 percent of its huge population—it had the largest number of seminarians and female religious in the world. India had far more Catholic schools and hospitals than all of North America put together; there were many converts, and the rate of religious observance was high. Despite the popular image of Hinduism as virtually a pacifist religion, Christians were subjected to violence, including murder, in various parts of the country, often with the connivance of the local government. Catholic leaders protested but also reminded their flocks that the blood of martyrs was the seed of Christians.

The gravest threat to the Church was secularization. Various U.N. and E.U. agencies defined abortion as a fundamental "right", to be protected by all governments, and, claiming authority over the internal affairs of its member countries, the E.U. ruled that crucifixes in Italian schools were a violation of religious freedom. Reflecting the dechristianization of Europe, Italy's ultimately successful appeal of the ruling was not supported by a single major Western country, although—also reflecting the changing cultural and political scene—it was supported by formerly communist Bulgaria, Romania, and the Russian Federation, and by Muslim Morocco. The existence of the International Criminal Court and similar agencies seemed to threaten the Church's freedom, in that atheists and some others demanded that Church leaders, including the pope, be prosecuted for the "crime" of condemning abortion and homosexual activity.

The threats, however empty, showed how the meaning of religious liberty in a pluralistic society had changed in the decades since *Dignitatis Humanae*, as some liberals now argued that the Church's stand on such moral issues constituted unwarranted "interference" in what should be an entirely secular society, that religious believers as such had no legitimate voice in pubic affairs. In some democratic countries (for example, France and Canada), Protestant clergy were convicted of the "crime" of speaking against homosexuality from the pulpit, while in the United States, some Catholic agencies ceased placing children for adoption after various state governments ruled that the agencies had to facilitate adoption by homosexual couples. The epidemic of "AIDS" (Acquired Immune Deficiency Syndrome), often spread through homosexual sexual activity, stimulated new attacks on the Church for not endorsing contraception as a means to thwart the spread of sexually transmitted diseases.

But Benedict strongly reaffirmed the principles of *Dignitatis Humanae*, even citing the American Revolution as marking a new stage in the development of religious liberty—a government that favored no religion but was not hostile to any. Ironically, *Dignitatis Humanae*, which was originally seen as a belated effort by the Church to accept the principle of liberal tolerance, by 2010 placed the Church in the forefront of the defenders of freedom.

The protection of nature—"environmentalism"—was by 2010 perhaps the principal social and political issue facing the world. Extreme environmentalists tended to be overtly anti-Christian, not least because they identified men as the chief threat to nature and therefore favored draconian measures to control population and condemned the Church for her position on contraception and abortion. Some environmentalists, including some Catholics, went so far as to deify nature as a living being—*Gaia*—and practiced nature worship.

The Crisis of Civilization

Dechristianization

Religious Freedom

Environmentalism

Benedict urged the protection of the environment on the basis of a theology of creation, a divine act from which the goodness and dignity of the world derived. Nature evolved not by blind chance but according to the divine plan, and it was precisely man's divinely given stewardship that required nature, including human life at all its stages, to be conserved and cherished.

Christian Humanism

In 2010, the frontiers of morality stood at a point that had been mere science fiction at the time of Vatican II. Besides abortion, euthanasia, and suicide, the issues included surgically induced sex changes, artificial insemination, cloning, and the "creation" of life in laboratories, often to be destroyed for embryonic stem-cell research.

The crisis was metaphysical even more than moral, in that the very identity of humanity was being called into question by a seemingly irresistible, all-devouring technology and by men determined to deny both higher moral truth and any concept of inherent human significance.

Since the Enlightenment, secularists had accused the Church of being anti-humanist, because she subordinated man to God. But by the beginning of the twenty-first century, it had become apparent that without God the dignity of man could no longer be affirmed, that many secularists had come to reject humanism precisely because it placed man at the summit of nature. Thus, ironically, the Catholic Church, as she had since the time of her birth, claimed to be both the representative of God and the chief witness to true Humanism.

Conclusion

Faith allows believers to approach the past with a certain serenity, as shocked and appalled as any nonbeliever at "man's inhumanity to man" but nonetheless ultimately hopeful. History is indeed the war of good against evil, but the progress of that war is hidden from human eyes.

The fundamental barrier to any full understanding of history is the simple fact of human fallibility. Genuine understanding would require omniscience—the pattern of history could be fully seen only by someone above history. But the search for such a supra-historical vantage point is obviously futile. The end of history is beyond history, and history cannot reveal its own inner meaning.

A related fallacy stems from man's limited temporal horizons. If, as some early Christians believed, the Roman Empire came into being in order to prepare the way for the birth of the Savior, this was not at all evident to pious Jews longing for the Messiah. They experienced the Roman incursion as merely another of those periodic mysterious catastrophes that fell upon them. But hindsight also does not suffice. An argument can be made for the providential role of the Empire in preparing the way for Christ, but in other respects the Empire was a formidable obstacle to the spread of the Gospel. Providence was indeed at work, but it is presumptuous to think that men know exactly how.

If Christianity is by far the most historical of all religions, from another point of view it is problematic why Christians should respect history at all, since the Gospel foretells its termination. "All this will pass away" (see Mt 24:35). All will be gathered into eternity.

Thus, for Christians, there can be no final understanding of history in this life. No one knows when history will reach its end, and the believer is enjoined by Christ to refrain from all such speculation. If mankind survives another million years, its view of history will change profoundly, as all the carefully delineated eras that are now part of the historical record will recede into a very remote past, to be disposed of by future historians in the twinkling of an eye.

Suggestions for Further Reading

General

Aries, Philippe. *The Hour of Our Death*. New York: Oxford University Press, 1981.

Benedict XVI. *Holy Men and Women*. San Francisco: Ignatius Press, 2012.

Bouyer, Louis, C. Orat. *Women in the Church*. San Francisco: Ignatius Press, 1979.

Brusher, Joseph S., S.J. *Popes through the Ages*. Princeton, N.J.: Van Nostrand, 1964.

Butler, Alban. *Lives of the Saints*. 4 vols. New York: P.J. Kenedy and Sons, 1956.

Connery, John R., S.J. *Abortion: the Development of the Roman Catholic Doctrine*. Chicago: Loyola University Press, 1977.

Graef, Hilda. *Mary, a History of Doctrine and Devotion*. 2 vols. New York: Sheed and Ward, 1963–1965.

Hughes, Philip. *The Church in Crisis: A History of the General Councils*. Garden City, N.Y.: Doubleday, 1960.

Jaki, Stanley. *The Road of Science and the Way to God*. Chicago: University of Chicago Press, 1978.

Jedin, Hubert. *Ecumenical Councils of the Catholic Church*. Freiburg: Herder, 1960.

Jungmann, Joseph A., S.J. *The Mass of the Roman Rite*. 2 vols. New York: Benziger, 1950.

Knowles, David, O.S.B. *Christian Monasticism*. New York: McGraw-Hill, 1969.

McNeill, John T. *A History of the Cure of Souls*. New York: Harper, 1951.

Norris, Herbert. *Church Vestments*. Mineola, N.Y.: Dover Books, 2002.

Olsen, Glenn W., ed. *Christian Marriage*. New York: Crossroad, 2001.

Pastor, Ludwig von. *History of the Popes.* 40 vols. St. Louis: B. Herder and Co., 1895–1935.

Pourrat, Pierre, S.S. *Christian Spirituality.* 4 vols. Westminster, Md.: Newman Press, 1953.

Watkins, Basil, O.S.B., ed. *The Book of Saints.* New York: Continuum, 2002.

Chapters One to Four

Benedict XVI. *Jesus of Nazareth.* 2 vols. San Francisco: Ignatius Press, 2007, 2011.

———. *Jesus, the Apostles, and the Early Church.* San Francisco: Ignatius Press, 2007.

———. *Church Fathers: from Clement of Rome to Augustine.* San Francisco: Ignatius Press, 2008.

Bouyer, Louis, C. Orat. *The Spirituality of the New Testament and the Fathers.* New York: Desclee, 1963.

Carroll, Warren H. *The Founding of Christendom.* Front Royal, Va.: Christendom College Press, 1985.

———. *The Building of Christendom.* Front Royal, Va.: Christendom College Press, 1987.

Chadwick, Henry. *The Early Church.* Baltimore: Penguin, 1967.

Daniel-Rops, Henri. *The Church of the Apostles and Martyrs.* 2 vols. Garden City, N.Y.: Doubleday, 1962.

Gorg, Peter H. *The Desert Fathers.* San Francisco: Ignatius Press, 2011.

Grant, Robert M. *Early Christianity and Society.* San Francisco: Harper and Row, 1977.

Guarducci, Margherita. *The Primacy of the Church of Rome.* San Francisco: Ignatius Press, 2003.

Lienhard, Joseph T., S.J. *The Bible, the Church, and Authority.* Collegeville, Minn.: The Liturgical Press, 1995.

Page, Christopher. *The Christian West and Its Singers.* New Haven, Conn.: Yale University Press, 2012.

Pelikan, Jaroslav. *The Emergence of the Catholic Tradition.* Chicago: University of Chicago Press, 1971.

Ratzinger, Joseph (Benedict XVI). *The Spirit of the Liturgy.* San Francisco: Ignatius Press, 2000.

Sommer, Carl J. *We Look for a Kingdom.* San Francisco: Ignatius Press, 2007.

Chapters Five and Six

Benedict XVI. *Church Fathers: from St. Leo the Great to Peter Lombard.* San Francisco: Ignatius Press, 2010.

Bouyer, Louis, C. Orat., Jean Leclercq, O.S.B., and Françoise Vandenbroucke. *The Spirituality of the Middle Ages.* London: Burns & Oates, 1968.

Brooke, Christopher. *The Twelfth-Century Renaissance.* London: Thames and Hudson, 1969.

Carroll, Warren H. *The Building of Christendom.* Front Royal, Va.: Christendom College Press, 1987.

———. *The Glory of Christendom.* Front Royal, Va.: Christendom College Press, 1987.

Clark, Kenneth. *Civilization.* New York: Harper and Row, 1969.

Daniel-Rops, Henri. *Cathedral and Crusade.* Garden City, N.Y.: Doubleday, 1963.

Dawson, Christopher. *The Making of Europe.* New York: Sheed and Ward, 1932.

———. *Religion and the Rise of Western Culture.* London: Sheed and Ward, 1950.

Deanesly, Margaret. *A History of the Medieval Church.* London: Methuen, 1965.

Gilson, Etienne. *The History of Christian Philosophy in the Middle Ages.* New York: Random House, 1955.

Knowles, David, O.S.B. *The Evolution of Medieval Thought.* New York: Vintage, 1962.

Lawrence, C.H. *Medieval Monasticism.* New York: Longmans, 1984.

———. *The Friars.* New York: Longmans, 1994.

Leclercq, Jean, O.S.B. *The Love of Learning and the Desire for God.* New York: Fordham University Press, 1961.

Leff, Gordon. *Medieval Thought.* Harmondsworth, England: Penguin Books, 1958.

Male, Emile. *The Gothic Image.* New York: Harper and Row, 1958.

McGinn, Bernard, and Patricia Ferris McGinn. *Early Christian Mystics.* New York: Crossroad, 2003.

Morris, Colin. *The Discovery of the Individual.* New York: Harper and Row, 1972.

Page, Christopher. *The Christian West and Its Singers.* New Haven, Conn.: Yale University Press, 2012.

Panofsky, Erwin. *Studies in Iconology.* Oxford: Oxford University Press, 1939.

Pelikan, Jaroslav. *The Growth of Medieval Theology*. Chicago: University of Chicago Press, 1978.

Schutz, Bernhard. *Great Cathedrals*. New York: Harry N. Abrams, 2002.

Southern, R. W. *The Making of the Middle Ages*. New Haven, Conn.: Yale University Press, 1961.

————. *Western Society and the Church in the Middle Ages*. Harmondsworth, England: Penguin Books, 1970.

Von Simson, Otto. *The Gothic Cathedral*. New York: Pantheon, 1956.

Weinstein, Donald, and Rudolph M. Bell. *Saints and Society*. Chicago: University of Chicago Press, 1982.

Zarnecki, George. *The Monastic Achievement*. New York: McGraw-Hill, 1972.

Chapter Seven

Attwater, Donald. *The Christian Churches of the East*. 2 vols. Milwaukee: Bruce Publishing Co., 1947.

Carroll, Warren G. *The Glory of Christendom*. Front Royal, Va.: Christendom College Press, 1993.

Chadwick, Henry. *East and West*. Oxford: Oxford University Press, 2003.

Hussey, J. M. *The Orthodox Church in the Byzantine Empire*. Oxford: Oxford University Press, 1986.

Madden, Thomas F. *The New Concise History of the Crusades*. Lanham, Md.: Rowman and Littlefield, 2005.

Nichols, Aidan, O.P. *Rome and the Eastern Churches*. San Francisco: Ignatius Press, 2010.

Pelikan, Jaroslav. *The Spirit of Eastern Christendom*. Chicago: University of Chicago Press, 1974.

Rice, David Talbot. *Byzantine Art*. Harmondsworth, England: Penguin Books, 1962.

Riley-Smith, Jonathan. *The Crusades*. New Haven, Conn.: Yale University Press, 2005.

Robertson, R. G., C.S.P. *The Eastern Christian Churches*. Rome: Institutum Studiorum Orientalium, 1999.

Roscasalvo, Joan L. *The Eastern Catholic Churches*. Collegeville, Minn.: Liturgical Press, 1992.

Chapter Eight

Bouyer, Louis, C. Orat., Jean Leclercq, O.S.B., and Françoise Vandenbroucke. *The Spirituality of the Middle Ages*. London: Burns & Oates, 1968.

Carroll, Warren G. *The Glory of Christendom*. Front Royal, Va.: Christendom College Press, 1993.

Clark, Kenneth. *Civilization*. New York: Harper and Row, 1969.

Deanesly, Margaret. *A History of the Medieval Church*. London: Methuen, 1965.

Duffy, Eamon. *The Stripping of the Altars*. New Haven, Conn.: Yale University Press, 1992.

Dawson, Christopher. *Religion and the Rise of Western Culture*. London: Sheed and Ward, 1950.

Gilson, Etienne. *The History of Christian Philosophy in the Middle Ages*. New York: Random House, 1955.

Knowles, David, O.S.B. *The Evolution of Medieval Thought*. New York: Vintage, 1962.

Leff, Gordon. *Medieval Thought*. Harmondsworth, England: Penguin Books, 1958.

Mollat, Guy. *The Popes at Avignon*. New York: T. Nelson, 1963.

Panofsky, Erwin. *Studies in Iconology*. Oxford: Oxford University Press, 1939.

Schutz, Bernhard. *Great Cathedrals*. New York: Harry N. Abrams, 2002.

Spitz, Lewis W. *The Religious Renaissance of the German Humanists*. Cambridge, Mass.: Harvard University Press, 1963.

Trinkaus, Charles. *In Our Image and Likeness*. 2 vols. Chicago: University of Chicago Press, 1970.

Weinstein, Donald, and Rudolph M. Bell. *Saints and Society*. Chicago: University of Chicago Press, 1982.

Chapter Nine

Bedouelle, Guy, O.P. *The Reform of Catholicism*. Toronto: University of Toronto Press, 2008.

Bireley, Robert, S.J. *The Refashioning of Catholicism*. Washington: Catholic University of America Press, 1999.

Bourke, J. *Baroque Churches of Central Europe*. London: Faber and Faber, 1958.

Bukofzer, Manfred. *Music in the Baroque Era*. New York: W. W. Norton, 1947.

Carroll, Warren H. *The Cleaving of Christendom*. Front Royal, Va.: Christendom College Press, 2000.

Clark, Kenneth. *Civilization*. New York: Harper and Row, 1969.

Dawson, Christopher. *The Dividing of Christendom*. New York: Sheed and Ward, 1958.

Dicken, E. W. Trueman. *The Crucible of Love*. [Spanish mysticism.] New York: Sheed and Ward, 1963.

Dickens, A. G. *The Counter-Reformation*. New York: Harcourt, Brace, and World, 1969.

Duffy, Eamon. *The Stripping of the Altars*. New Haven, Conn.: Yale University Press, 1992.

Evennett, H. Outram. *The Spirit of the Counter-Reformation*. Notre Dame, Ind.: University of Notre Dame Press, 1978.

Hsia, Ronnie Po-Chia. *The World of Catholic Renewal*. New York: Cambridge University Press, 1998.

Kamen, Henry. *The Rise of Toleration*. New York: McGraw-Hill, 1967.

Mullett, Michael. *The Catholic Reformation*. London: Routledge, 1999.

O'Connell, Marvin R. *The Counter-Reformation*. New York: Harper and Row, 1974.

Pelikan, Jaroslav. *Reformation of Church and Dogma*. Chicago: University of Chicago Press, 1984.

Pope-Hennessy, John. *Introduction to Italian Sculpture*. New York: Phaedon, 1963.

Weinstein, Donald, and Rudolph M. Bell. *Saints and Society*. Chicago: University of Chicago Press, 1982.

Wittkower, Rudolph, and Irma B. Jaffe. *Baroque Art, the Jesuit Contribution*. New York: Fordham University Press, 1972.

Chapter Ten

Bireley, Robert, S.J. *The Refashioning of Catholicism*. Washington: Catholic University of America Press, 1999.

Burleigh, Michael. *Earthly Powers: the Clash of Religion and Politics*. New York: HarperCollins, 2005.

Carroll, Warren H. *The Cleaving of Christendom*. Front Royal, Va.: Christendom College Press, 2000.

Chatellier, Louis. *Europe of the Devout*. New York: Cambridge University Press, 1989.

Daniel-Rops, Henri. *The Church in the Seventeenth Century*. 2 vols. Garden City, N.Y.: Doubleday, 1962.

————. *The Church in the Eighteenth Century*. New York: Doubleday, 1964.

————. *The Church in an Age of Revolution*. New York: Doubleday, 1965.

Hsia, Ronnie Po-Chia. *The World of Catholic Renewal*. New York: Cambridge University Press, 1998.

Kamen, Henry. *The Rise of Toleration*. New York: McGraw-Hill, 1967.

McManners, John. *The French Revolution and the Church*. New York: Harper and Row, 1969.

Weinstein, Donald, and Rudolph M. Bell. *Saints and Society*. Chicago: University of Chicago Press, 1982.

Chapter Eleven

Burleigh, Michael. *Earthly Powers: the Clash of Religion and Politics*. New York, 2005.

Carroll, Warren H. *The Cleaving of Christendom*. Front Royal, Va.: Christendom College Press, 2000.

Daniel-Rops, Henri. *The Church in an Age of Revolution*. New York: Doubleday, 1965.

————. *A Fight for God*. New York: Doubleday, 1965.

Hales, E. E. Y. *The Catholic Church in the Modern World*. Garden City, N.Y.: Doubleday, 1960.

Jedin, Hubert, ed. *The Church in the Modern Age*. New York: Crossroad, 1981.

McCool, Gerald, S.J. *Catholic Theology in the Nineteenth Century*. New York: Seabury, 1977.

Nichols, Aidan, O.P. *From Hermes to Benedict XVI*. Mundelein, Ill.: Hildenbrand Books, 2009.

Royal, Robert. *Catholic Martyrs of the Twentieth Century*. New York: Crossroad, 2002.

Rychlak, Ronald. *Hitler, the War, and the Pope*. Huntington, Ind.: Our Sunday Visitor Press, 2000.

Chapter Twelve

Alden, Dauril. *The Making of an Enterprise*. [Jesuit missions.] Stanford, Calif.: Stanford University Press, 1996.

Bailey, Gauvin. *Art on the Jesuit Missions*. Toronto: Toronto University Press, 1999.

Boxer, Charles. *The Christian Century in Japan, 1549–1650*. Berkeley, Calif.: University of California Press, 1967.

Brockey, Liam. *Journey to the East: the Jesuit Mission in China.* Cambridge, Mass.: Harvard University Press, 2007.

Caraman, Philip, S.J. *The Lost Paradise: the Jesuit Republic in South America.* New York: Seabury, 1976.

Carroll, Warren H. *The Cleaving of Christendom.* Front Royal, Va.: Christendom College Press, 2000.

Charbonnier, Jean-Pierre, M.E.P. *Christians in China, A.D. 600 to 2000.* San Francisco: Ignatius Press, 2007.

Dunne, George H., S.J. *Generation of Giants.* [China.] Notre Dame, Ind.: University of Notre Dame Press, 1962.

Elison, George. *Deus Destroyed.* [Japan.] Cambridge, Mass.: Harvard University Press, 1991.

Faupel, J. F. *African Holocaust.* New York: P.J. Kenedy, 1962.

MacCormack, Sabine. *Religion in the Andes.* Princeton, N.J.: Princeton University Press, 1991.

Miramaki, George, S.J. *The Chinese Rites Controversy.* Chicago: Loyola University Press, 1985.

O'Malley, Vincent J., C.M. *Saints of Asia.* Huntington, Ind.: Our Sunday Visitor Press, 2007.

Pike, Frederick. *Conflict between Church and State in Latin America.* New York: Knopf, 1964.

Ricard, Robert. *The Spiritual Conquest of Mexico.* Berkeley, Calif.: University of California Press, 1966.

Spence, Jonathan. *The Memory Palace of Matteo Ricci.* New York: Viking-Penguin, 1984.

Zupanov, Ines. *Disputed Mission.* [India.] Oxford: Oxford University Press, 1999.

———. *Missionary Tropics.* [India.] Ann Arbor, Mich.: University of Michigan Press, 2005.

Chapter Thirteen

Barry, Colman J., O.S.B. *The Catholic Church and the German Americans.* Milwaukee: Bruce Publishing Co., 1953.

Birt, Henry N., O.S.B. *Benedictine Pioneers in Australia.* 2 vols. London: Herbert and Daniell, 1911.

Cross, Robert D. *The Emergence of Liberal Catholicism in America.* Cambridge, Mass.: Harvard University Press, 1958.

Ellis, John Tracy. *Catholics in Colonial America.* Baltimore: Helicon, 1965.

Fogarty, Gerald P. *The Vatican and the American Catholic Hierarchy, 1870–1965.* Collegeville, Minn.: Liturgical Press, 1985.

Fogarty, Ronald. *Catholic Education in Australia, 1806–1950.* 2 vols. Melbourne: Melbourne University Press, 1959.

Gauvreau, Michael. *The Catholic Origins of Quebec's Quiet Revolution.* Montreal: McGill-Queens University Press, 2005.

Gleason, J. Philip, *Contending with Modernity.* [Higher Education.] New York: Oxford University Press, 1995.

McAvoy, Thomas T., C.S.C. *The Great Crisis in American Catholic History.* Chicago: Regnery, 1957.

McGreevy, John T. *Catholicism and American Freedom.* New York: W. W. Norton, 2003.

Moran, Patrick. *History of the Catholic Church in Australasia.* Sydney: Oceanic Publishing, n.d. [1896.]

Murphy, Terence, and Oswald Stortz, eds. *Creed and Culture.* [Canada.] Montreal: McGill-Queens University Press, 1963.

O'Brien, Eris M. *The Dawn of Catholicism in Australia.* 2 vols. Sydney: Angus and Robertson, 1928.

O'Farrell, Patrick. *The Catholic Church and Community in Australia.* London: Longmans, 1977.

O'Toole, James M. *The Faithful, a History of Catholics in America.* Cambridge, Mass.: Harvard University Press, 2008.

Parkman, Francis. *The Jesuits in North America.* Modern Edition, Boston: Little Brown, 1963.

Santamaria, B. A. *Daniel Mannix.* Melbourne: Melbourne University Press, 1984.

Walsh, H. H. *The Church in the French Era.* [Canada.] Toronto: Ryerson, 1966.

Chapter Fourteen

Allen, John L. *Future Church.* New York: Doubleday, 2010.

Benestad, J. Brian. *Church, State, and Society.* Washington: Catholic University of America Press, 2010.

Capovilla, Loris. *The Heart and Mind of John XXIII.* New York: Hawthorn Books, 1964.

Guardini, Romano. *The Spirit of the Liturgy.* New York: Benziger, 1930.

Hitchcock, James. *Catholicism and Modernity.* New York: Continuum, 1978.

———. *The Recovery of the Sacred.* New York: Seabury, 1974.

Lamb, Matthew L., and Matthew Levering, eds. *Vatican II.* New York: Oxford University Press, 2008.

Nichols, Aidan, O.P. *From Hermes to Benedict XVI*. Mundelein, Ill.: Hildenbrand Books, 2009.

———. *The Idea of Doctrinal Development*. Edinburgh: T. and T. Clark, 1990.

Ratzinger, Joseph (Benedict XVI). *The Spirit of the Liturgy*. San Francisco: Ignatius Press, 2000.

Trower, Philip. *The Catholic Church and the Counter-Faith*. Oxford: Family Publications, 2006.

———. *Turmoil and Truth*. San Francisco: Ignatius Press, 2003.

Wiltgen, Ralph M., S.V.D. *The Rhine Flows into the Tiber*. New York: Hawthorn Books, 1967.

INDEX